M000315086

CLAUDIAN

*Poetry and Propaganda at
the Court of Honorius*

Eucherius, Serena, Stilico (? and head of Maria inset between Eucherius' shoulder and Serena's elbow) on a diptych (now in the cathedral treasure at Monza) issued in 396 in commemoration of Eucherius' promotion to tribune and notary. From R. Delbrück, *Die Consulardiptychen*, Vol. II (Walter de Gruyten, Berlin)

CLAUDIAN

Poetry and Propaganda at the Court of Honorius

ALAN CAMERON

OXFORD
AT THE CLARENDON PRESS

OXFORD
UNIVERSITY PRESS

Great Clarendon Street, Oxford OX2 6DP

Oxford University Press is a department of the University of Oxford.
It furthers the University's objective of excellence in research, scholarship,
and education by publishing worldwide in

Oxford New York

Auckland Bangkok Buenos Aires Cape Town Chennai
Dar es Salaam Delhi Hong Kong Istanbul Karachi Kolkata
Kuala Lumpur Madrid Melbourne Mexico City Mumbai Nairobi
São Paulo Shanghai Singapore Taipei Tokyo Toronto

and an associated company in Berlin

Oxford is a registered trade mark of Oxford University Press
in the UK and in certain other countries

Published in the United States
by Oxford University Press Inc., New York

© Oxford University Press 1970

British Library Cataloguing in Publication Data

Data available

ISBN 0-19-814351-6

1 3 5 7 9 10 8 6 4 2

Printed in Great Britain
on acid-free paper by
Biddles Ltd.,
Guildford and King's Lynn

PREFACE

A LARGE book on a poet little read even in universities might seem to require justification, if not apology. I offer neither.

Merely as a unique historical source for a crucial period of Roman history Claudian's works have an outstanding value and interest. This has (of course) long been realized by historians, though no one has yet submitted them to the searching scrutiny they deserve and require. For a critical assessment of so tendentious a writer is an essential preliminary to the writing of a proper history of Stilico's regency. It is because their authors did not write this book first that even such acute and important studies of the period as S. Mazzarino's *Stilicone* (1942) and É. Demougeot's *De l'unité à la division de l'empire romain* (1951) go astray on a number of major points.

My own interpretations of these points—which have led me to a more balanced verdict on the aims and achievements of Stilico—flow in general from a principle of supreme simplicity: Claudian's poems must be read in chronological order. When a propagandist writing against a fast-changing political background says things later which he did not say at the time—or indeed changes his story altogether after a year or so—we are surely justified in regarding at least one and probably both accounts with some suspicion.

Earlier studies have suffered from two sorts of error in particular. They have combined details from different versions (e.g. the two accounts of the Gildonic war, separated by nearly three years) into one composite picture without inquiring why they differ in the first place. And they have shown a curious reluctance to query even the most flagrant of Claudian's misrepresentations. No one, they argue, writing for contemporaries on contemporary events, would have dared to tell a lie. Perhaps we know better nowadays. The events of August 1968, for example, gave a startling relevance to Claudian's (preposterous, but widely accepted) claim that the East 'invited' Stilico to intervene in its affairs in mid 399. In any case, Claudian seldom stoops to anything so crude as an outright lie: he twists, omits, glosses over, skirts around. In short, a master propagandist.

But Claudian is much more than a propagandist. He is also more than the 'last of the Roman poets', the formula in which he is duly evoked in postscripts to literary histories.

There is, of course, some validity in this approach. For the decade between 395 and 404 Latin poetry became once more in the hands of Claudian what it had been in the Flavian age. It was never to be the same again, and it is arguable that Claudian not only revived but killed it as well.

There is another approach, however, without which Claudian cannot be seen in true perspective. Not merely was he by birth a Greek; he had already composed poetry in Greek before changing his language with his domicile and becoming court poet to Honorius. Indeed, while he stands alone among Latin poets of his age, he is but one among many in the Greek literary scene.

Attention has often been called to the coincidence that the annals of Latin literature close, as they open, with a Greek—or rather two Greeks, Claudian and Ammianus Marcellinus. There is more to it than coincidence. With characteristic insight the incomparable Wilamowitz once included Ammian in a history of *Greek* literature—much to the indignation of most subsequent students, who never cease to stress the Roman characteristics and outlook of Ammian's history. And rightly so. Certainly Ammian *is* the last of the Roman historians. But distant (and worthy) heir of Tacitus though he is, the only living historiographical tradition in Ammian's day was Greek. He is also the first surviving representative of the great early Byzantine school of contemporary historiography that culminates in Procopius.

Claudian is a similar Janus-figure. His Latin poems are our fullest source for the thriving school of Greek professional poets of which he is a representative member.

Claudian's debt to his Latin predecessors is so deep and so

obvious that it has obscured the fact that his contemporary poems are nevertheless basically Greek in form, the first Latin versions of a genre with Hellenistic roots but developed to a professional skill by the rhetoricians and poets of the late Empire.

We must not, of course, fall into Wilamowitz's exaggeration, and underestimate the transformation which the Greek contemporary poem underwent in its fusion with the idiom and techniques of Silver Latin epic. The result is something strikingly Roman in spirit and style—but not something that can be understood in terms of the Roman tradition alone. This is why I have laid more emphasis on the contemporary Greek than the more remote Latin background (important, but more obvious and already adequately documented). In fact, I have tried throughout to view Claudian against the background of his times, not just as a distant epigonos of the poets of the Silver Age, but as a writer worthy of study for his own sake. Coleridge saw this better than many moderns when he commended Claudian and left Silius unread.

It was not till the rest of the book was already in the hands of the Press that I realized the interest and even importance of pursuing the story of Claudian's influence on Medieval and English literature. Add to this the fact that (apart from Manitius on the Medieval side) there are no *collectanea* or *Vorarbeiten* such as exist on the *Fortleben* of other Latin poets to act as guides through unfamiliar terrain, and it will be appreciated that my concluding chapter is only intended as the merest illustrative sketch.

Parts of the book have been delivered as lectures at various institutions in this country, the United States, and Canada; parts have been awarded the Baynes and Conington Prizes at London and Oxford respectively.

My acknowledgements to published works are fully recorded in the annotation—often, alas, by way of rebuttal. I could wish that this had not been necessary, but where my views differed widely from those generally held, it would have been misleading to state them without full justification.

Several chapters have benefited from the advice and encouragement of a number of learned friends: Peter Brown, John Matthews, Arnaldo Momigliano, Oswyn Murray, Otto Skutsch, and Martin West. I am particularly grateful to Oswyn Murray for starting me off on the track that led to the last chapter, and to John Matthews and Timothy Barnes for their painstaking assistance with the proofs.

But the most penetrating of all my critics in the five years odd of the book's gestation has been my wife Averil: at a first reading (snatched from her own duties, academic, domestic, and maternal) she would at once put her finger on every weakness and inconsistency in successive batches of pages heavy with alterations and sellotape. It is to her that I dedicate this book.

A. C.

Bedford College, London
31 July 1969

CONTENTS

Eucherius, Serena, Stilico *Frontispiece*

Abbreviations xi

Stemma of the House of Theodosius xiv

Chronologia Claudianea xv

I. THE POET FROM EGYPT 1

II. FROM PANEGYRIST TO PROPAGANDIST 30

III. TECHNIQUES OF THE PROPAGANDIST 46

IV. RUFINUS 63

V. GILDO 93

VI. EUTROPIUS 124

VII. ALARIC 156

VIII. THE PAGAN AT A CHRISTIAN COURT 189

IX. CLAUDIAN'S AUDIENCE 228

X. TECHNIQUES OF THE POET 253

XI. *DOCTUS POETA* 305

XII. CLAUDIAN AND ROME 349

XIII. LAST DAYS 390

XIV. CONCLUSION 419

APPENDIXES

A. The date of the *De Raptu Proserpinae* 452

B. The date of the Latin *Gigantomachia*: Claudian and Prudentius 467

C. Zosimus, John of Antioch, and Eunapius on Stilico's
two expeditions to the Balkans   474

D. Triphiodorus and Nonnus   478

Bibliography   483

Addenda   490

Index   495

ABBREVIATIONS

The following works are cited by author's name and page number only:

Birt   T. Birt, preface to his edition of Claudian (*Mon. Germ. Hist.*, *Auct. Ant.* x, 1892).

Demougeot É. Demougeot, *De l'unité à la division de l'Empire romain 395–410: essai sur le pouvoir impérial* (Paris, 1951).

Fargues   P. Fargues, *Claudien: études sur sa poésie et son temps* (Paris, 1933).

Heitsch   E. Heitsch, *Die griechischen Dichterfragmente der römischen Kaiserzeit* (*Abh. d. Akad. d. Wiss. Göttingen*, Phil.-Hist. Klasse, 3. 49), i^2 (Göttingen, 1963), ii (Göttingen, 1964).

Mazzarino S. Mazzarino, *Stilicone: la crisi imperiale dopo Teodosio* (*Studi pubblicati dal R. Istituto italiano per la storia antica* iii), Rome, 1942.

Page   D. L. Page, *Greek Literary Papyri* i: *Poetry* (Loeb series), London, 1942.

Romano   D. Romano, *Claudiano* (Palermo, 1958).

My own publications are generally referred to without the author's name.

Other abbreviations are either self-explanatory or in accordance with the usual conventions (following those listed at pp. ix–xix of the *Oxford Classical Dictionary* more closely than the occasionally mystifying initials of *L'Année philologique*). Note however *PLRE*, for the *Prosopography of the Later Roman Empire*, edited by A. H. M. Jones, J. R. Martindale, and J. Morris, to be published by the Cambridge University Press in 1970. Some works (especially those with long and cumbersome titles) are cited in abbreviated form in the notes, and, to save space again, I have generally omitted the titles of periodical articles in the notes: fuller details will be found in the bibliography.

I have used the following abbreviations in citing Claudian's poems (they are listed here in the order in which they appear in the standard modern editions, which, confusingly enough, is neither chronological nor in accordance with the traditional numbering of the poems: these numbers I have added in brackets, since references to Claudian are often given by poem number instead of title):

Prob.   *Panegyricus dictus Probino et Olybrio consulibus* (1).
pr. Ruf. i, ii *In Rufinum, praefatio* to Books i, ii (2, 4).
Ruf. i, ii   *In Rufinum* i, ii (3, 5).

Gild.	*De Bello Gildonico* i (15).
Eutr. i, ii	*In Eutropium* i, ii (18, 20).
pr. *Eutr.* ii	*In Eutropium, praefatio* to Book ii (19).
Fesc. i–iv	*Fescennina de Nuptiis Honorii Augusti* i–iv (11–14).
Nupt.	*Epithalamium de Nuptiis Honorii Augusti* (10).
pr. *Nupt.*	Id., *praefatio* (9).
III Cons.	*Panegyricus de tertio consulatu Honorii Augusti* (7).
pr. *III Cons.*	Id., *praefatio* (6).
IV Cons.	*Panegyricus de quarto consulatu Honorii Augusti* (8).
Theod.	*Panegyricus dictus Manlio Theodoro consuli* (17).
pr. *Theod.*	Id., *praefatio* (16).
Stil. i, ii, iii	*De consulatu Stiliconis* (or *laus* or *laudes Stiliconis*), Books i, ii, iii (21, 22, 24).
pr. *Stil.* iii	Id., *praefatio* to Book iii (23).
VI Cons.	*Panegyricus de sexto consulatu Honorii Augusti* (28).
pr. *VI Cons.*	Id., *praefatio* (27).
Get.	*De Bello Getico* (less correctly, *Gothico* or *Pollentino*: cf. Fargues, p. 28, n. 3) (26).
pr. *Get.*	Id., *praefatio* (25).
c.m. i–liv	*carmina minora* i–liv (Birt's numeration).
Rapt. i, ii, iii	*De Raptu Proserpinae*, Books i–iii (33, 35, 36).
pr. *Rapt.* i, ii	Id., *praefatio* to Books i, ii (32, 34).

In general I have used Birt's text (1892) throughout, but have not hesitated to print alternative readings where necessary, usually with suitable justification. Koch (1893) and the erratic Jeep (1876–9) render occasional service. The only full commentary still worth consulting is that of Gesner (i–ii, 1758); the only volume (of two) published by G. Koenig (1808) is also useful. Otherwise there is a batch of dissertations, of varying merit and utility: *Ruf.*, by H. L. Levy (New York, 1935); *Eutr.*, by both P. Fargues (Paris, 1933) and A. C. Andrews (Philadelphia, 1931); *Get.*, by H. Schroff (*Klass.-phil. Studien* viii, 1927); *VI Cons.*, by K. A. Müller (Berlin, 1938); *IV Cons.*, by Fargues (Aix-en-Provence, 1936); for *Rapt.* there is J. B. Hall's edition (Cambridge, 1969), not available at the time of writing (the information quoted on p. 425 was supplied to me in advance by the kindness of the author). In the absence of a full commentary, M. Platnauer's Loeb edition of 1928 (though not free of errors) is often helpful (V. Crépin's French translation of 1933 much less so). When quoting in translation I have several times made use of Platnauer's version, sometimes with slight modifications, always (I hope) with due acknowledgement.

Note: Stilico or Stilicho? The 'correct' form is certainly Stilico (cf. Demougeot, p. 129, n. 64), but Greek writers wrote Στελίχων, and MSS. of Claudian, Symmachus, the Codes (for what this is worth in such a matter) usually Stilicho. Both forms are found in official Latin inscriptions (cf. Birt, p. ccx). It may well be that Claudian (and perhaps Stilico too) preferred the more literary and Roman looking (if incorrect) aspirated form, but for reasons which I can no longer recall and would not care to justify, I have always omitted the aspirate, and that is the way the name appears throughout this book, for consistency's sake in quotations from Claudian no less than in my own text.

STEMMA OF THE HOUSE OF THEODOSIUS

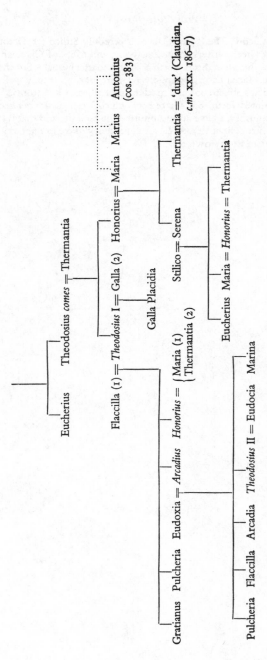

For continuation down into the sixth century, see the stemma in J. B. Bury, *Later Roman Empire* i² (1923), xvii. The earlier details are after J. R. Martindale, *Historia* xvi (1967), 256.

CHRONOLOGIA CLAUDIANEA

394	6 September	Battle of the river Frigidus.
395	early January	Recitation of *Prob.* at Rome.
	17 January	Death of Theodosius at Milan.
	27 April	Marriage of Arcadius and Eudoxia.
	September	Stilico's expedition to Thessaly.
	?	*c.m.* xl, xli (*Epp. ad Probinum, Olybrium*).
	18 November	Murder of Rufinus in Constantinople.
396	early January	Recitation of *III Cons.* at Milan.
?396/7		*Rapt.* i.
397	early in the year	*c.m.* xxi (*De Theodoro et Hadriano*).
	„ „	*c.m.* xxii (*Deprecatio ad Hadrianum*).
	„ „	*Ruf.* i, pr. *Ruf.* i, recited at Milan.
	summer	Stilico's expedition to the Peloponnese.
	„	Stilico declared *hostis publicus*.
	late summer	*Ruf.* ii, pr. *Ruf.* ii, recited at Milan.
	autumn	Gildo cuts off corn supply to Rome.
	? November	Mascezel's expedition sails for Africa.
398	early January	*IV Cons.* recited at Milan.
	? February	Marriage of Honorius and Maria. *Fesc.* I–IV, *Nupt.*, recited at Milan.
	March	Defeat of Gildo.
	April	Recitation of *Gild.* at Milan.
	summer	Death of Mascezel.
399	early January	Recitation of *Theod.* at Milan.
	spring	Recitation of *Eutr.* i at Milan.
	summer	Revolt of Tribigild.
	August	Fall of Eutropius.
	September	*Eutr.* ii, pr. *Eutr.* ii, recited at Milan.
400	early January	*Stil.* i–ii recited at Milan.
	February	*Stil.* iii recited at Rome.
	? March	*Coup d'état* of Gainas in Constantinople.
	?	Bronze statue of Claudian erected in the Forum of Trajan in Rome.
400/1		*c.m.* xxxi (*Ep. ad Serenam*).
		Claudian's marriage and honeymoon to Libya.

401/2		*c.m.* l (*In Iacobum*).
402	Easter Day	Battle of Pollentia.
	May/June	*Get.* recited at Rome.
	July/August	Battle of Verona.
? 400–2		*Rapt.* ii–iii.
404	early January	*VI Cons.* recited at Rome.
? 404		*c.m.* xxx (*Laus Serenae*) begun.
		Latin *Gigantomachia* begun.
		Death of Claudian.
405		Stilico's second consulate.
406		Battle of Faesulae.
408	23 August	Execution of Stilico.

I

THE POET FROM EGYPT

VERY little is known about the life of Claudius Claudianus. The only contemporaries to mention him are St. Augustine and Orosius,[1] who tell us merely that he was a poet and a pagan. A statue erected in his honour in the forum of Trajan adds the information that he rose to the post of tribune and notary in the Imperial service.[2]

A detailed history of the period embracing Claudian's poetical activity was written by a rhetorician from Sardis called Eunapius, and continued by Olympiodorus, a poet and diplomat from Egyptian Thebes. Since Claudian won considerable fame in his lifetime, both as a poet and as propagandist of the all-powerful Stilico, it is possible that one or other of these works might have told us something about him. Unfortunately both have perished, and we possess only the scrappy and careless epitome compiled c. 501 by the ex-lawyer Zosimus,[3] which does not even mention Claudian.

Indeed, the most important source by far for the period as a whole is Claudian himself. His panegyrics, invectives, and epics are beyond price for the historian who would reconstruct the

---

[1] See p. 191.   [2] *CIL* vi. 1710 (*ILS* 2949): see pp. 390, 490.

[3] Zosimus will be mentioned often in the pages that follow. For bibliography to 1958, see G. Moravcsik, *Byzantinoturcica* i². 577–8, and there is a wordy but helpful chapter in W. E. Kaegi, *Byzantium and the Decline of Rome* (1968), 99–145. For his dates, see *Philol.* cxiii (1969), 106 f. In his narrative Zosimus seems to have followed his sources very closely (a fact apparently unknown to Kaegi, and somewhat damaging to many of his assumptions), so closely, indeed, that when he changes from Eunapius to Olympiodorus between 404 and 407 his attitude to Stilico switches instantly from hostility to benevolence. For Zosimus and Eunapius, see *CQ* N.S. xiii (1963), 232 f.; *Harvard Studies* lxxiii (1968), 247–80; and Appendix C below. On Eunapius, most recently, I. Opelt, *RAC*, s.v.; on Olympiodorus, E. A. Thompson, *CQ* xxxviii (1944), 33 f., with my remarks in *Historia* xiv (1965), 476.

troubled years that follow the death of Theodosius the Great: not
so much for the facts they record (which are fewer than is sometimes imagined) as for the insight they offer into the inner work-
ings of the politics and intrigues of the day (which is deeper than
generally supposed). Unfortunately, in the best epic tradition,
they tell us very little about their author. Rather more is to be
gleaned from his epigrams, though little in the way of personal
details.[1]

His date of birth is unknown, but he appears still to have been a
young man when he arrived in Rome in 394.[2] In a poem written
in 397 he could still blame an error of judgement on his 'lubrica
aetas' (*c.m.* xxii. 6). He calls himself the *sodalis* of Olybrius, the
youthful consul of 395, and compares their friendship to that between Pylades and Orestes. This suggests that Claudian was at
any rate not much older than Olybrius, who was barely 20 at the
time. 370 would probably not be far out for his birth.

Despite his Latin names,[3] Claudian was an Egyptian, as he
makes perfectly clear in two epigrams. One he wrote to a certain
Gennadius, who was, Claudian claimed,

> Graiorum populis et *nostro* cognite *Nilo* (*c.m.* xix. 3).

In another he appeals to a high official called Hadrian as a fellow
Egyptian:

> Audiat haec *commune solum*, longeque carinis
> nota Pharos . . . Nilus . . . (*c.m.* xxii. 56 f.).

[1] See pp. 393 f. on those that relate to his later career.

[2] It is possible (though hardly more) that he is related to the sophist Claudian,
brother of Maximus of Ephesus, who taught at Alexandria (Eunapius, *Vit. Soph.*
vii. 1. 4, p. 473). But if so, surely grandson rather than son (as sometimes assumed).

[3] It has often been alleged (e.g. by Platnauer, Loeb edn. i (1928), xii, n. 1, and
most recently by M. Hadas, *Hist. of Latin Literature* (1952), 390) that Claudian's
father was also called Claudius Claudianus. This is based on a simple mistrans-
lation of *CIL* vi. 1710, '[Cl.] Claudiani, v.c. | [Cla]udio Claudiano, v.c. . . .' as
'to Cl. Claudianus, *son of* Cl. Claudianus'. In fact (of course) the occurrence of the
name in the genitive is not a reference to Claudian's father (in this case the dative
would have preceded the genitive), but merely an example of the common contemporary practice of placing the *honorand*'s name (or *signum*, if he had one) in the
genitive in large letters at the top of such dedicatory inscriptions. For parallel
contemporary examples from Rome, cf. *CIL* vi. 1725, 1735, 1749, etc.

Earlier in the same poem he styles Alexander the Great 'conditor hic *patriae*'. This must mean, precisely, Alexandria. And that Claudian was indeed an Alexandrian is explicitly stated by Suidas (or 'Suda', according to taste), in an entry taken over from the sixth-century biographical dictionary of Hesychius of Miletus.

But there are two other texts which respectable scholars have sometimes preferred to this clear testimony. Sidonius Apollinaris refers to Claudian allusively as 'Pelusiaco satus Canopo'.[1] But anyone familiar with Sidonius' style will realize at once that this is only his usual precious way of saying just 'Egypt'—a trick he had picked up from Lucan's 'Nilusne . . . et Pelusiaci tam mollis turba Canopi'.[2]

Second, John the Lydian,[3] who refers to Claudian as οὗτος ὁ Παφλαγὼν ὁ ποιητής.[4] But he is using the word παφλαγών (as Birt realized)[5] in the sense 'blusterer' or 'windbag' that it regularly bears in Aristophanes' uncomplimentary references to Cleon. From the earliest times Παφλαγών had become a byword for the windbag, just as Φρύξ was for the coward. That the word was still used in this sense in John's day is proved by an exactly parallel example in Procopius,[6] which was explained in this way by J. Haury[7] quite independently of Birt's discussion and apparently without knowledge either of the parallel from John or of another from Palladas.[8] The reason why John should have been moved to call Claudian a windbag will become apparent in a later chapter.[9] It is sufficient for the moment to conclude that there is no reason to doubt the testimony of Hesychius, confirmed as it is by Claudian's own explicit statement, that he was born in Alexandria.

---

[1] *Carm.* ix. 274. [2] *Phars.* viii. 542–3.

[3] Cf. J. Turcevič, *Byz. Zeit.* xxxiv (1934), 1 f.; Romano, p. 10, n. 3; both following F. Bücheler, *Rhein. Mus.* xxxix (1884), 282 f.

[4] *De Mag.* i. 47: the (mainly Italian) practice of referring to John as 'Laurentius Lydus' is based on a misapprehension; Λαυρεντίου (*sic*) in Photius, *Cod.* 180, *init.*, p. 125*a* Bekker is the name of John's father, in the genitive (cf. E. Stein, *Bas-Empire* ii (1949), 730, n. 1).

[5] pp. iv–v. [6] *Anecd.* xvi. 7.

[7] *Byz. Zeit.* ix (1900), 674. [8] *Anth. Pal.* xi. 340.

[9] Below, p. 245.

The point is worth emphasizing. H. J. Rose, for example, claims that Claudian 'writes in Egypt (and therefore, since he was a man of letters, in Alexandria)'.[1] But though it may have been true in Callimachus' day that an Egyptian man of letters would inevitably have been an Alexandrian, it was certainly no longer true in Claudian's. By the fourth century Egypt had become the most prolific source of poets in the whole Empire. Indeed, it is hardly possible to name a single prominent Greek poet of the fourth and fifth centuries who was not either an Egyptian or at any rate educated in Egypt. As Eunapius wrote in *c.* 400: 'The Egyptians are mad about poetry.'[2] Yet, of all this host of Egyptian poets, only Claudian and Palladas[3] are attested as Alexandrians. Almost all the others were from the Thebaid. The most fertile breeding ground of poets at this period was without doubt Panopolis, a city which, Herodotus had noticed, was already in his day receptive of Greek culture. It can boast Nonnus, Triphiodorus, Cyrus, Pamprepius, and Horapollon among its alumni.[4] Of the many other Egyptian poets of the fourth, fifth, and early sixth centuries, a surprisingly large number are expressly recorded as hailing from other cities in the Egyptian hinterland, almost all from Upper Egypt. In roughly chronological order we have Soterichus from Oasis,[5] Helladius[6] and Cyrus[7] from Antinou-polis, Andronicus from Hermupolis,[8] Eudaemon from Pelu-sium, Heracleides from Memphis,[9] Olympiodorus from Thebes,[10] Colluthus from Lycopolis,[11] Christodorus from Coptus,[12]

---

[1] *Handbook of Latin Literature*[3] (1954), 529, n. 193.

[2] ἐπὶ ποιητικῇ σφόδρα μαίνονται (*Vit. Soph.* x. 7. 12, p. 493).

[3] Except for the obscure Pancratius, addressed in two letters of Procopius of Gaza (*Epp.* 31, 133). Ammonius and Helladius taught in Alexandria (Socrates, *Hist. Eccl.* v. 16).

[4] Cf. *Historia* xiv (1965), 472.

[5] Suid., s.v., and cf. *PLRE*, s.v.   [6] Photius, *Cod.* 279.

[7] Photius, *Cod.* 279 *ad fin.* (date uncertain, but probably of the fourth century).

[8] Photius, loc. cit.; cf. *Historia* xiv (1965), 487–9; and *PLRE*, s.v.

[9] Libanius, *Epp.* 228, 229, 291, 292, 839. For Eudaemon, *PLRE*, s.v.

[10] Photius, *Cod.* 80 and 314 *init.*; cf. *Historia* xiv (1965), 476, n. 37; and E. A. Thompson, *CQ* xxxviii (1944), 43 f.

[11] Suid., s.v. and cf. *OCD*[2], s.v.

[12] Suid., s.v.; *Anth. Pal.* ii; and cf. *OCD*[2], s.v.

another Christodorus from Thebes,[1] and last (and certainly least) Dioscorus from Aphroditopolis.[2] Cleobulus,[3] Harpocration,[4] Serenus,[5] and the unnamed poet mentioned by Themistius in 377[6] are described as 'Egyptian' without further detail, and Musaeus, author of *Hero and Leander,* is perhaps to be added to their number.[7] In addition, we have now quite a corpus of anonymous fragments from the work of lesser Egyptian poets of the age, some in the autograph copies of the poets themselves, with their own manuscript corrections. For example, part of a poem on the Persian war of Diocletian and Galerius in 297–8 (probably not, as once supposed, the work of Soterichus),[8] part of another on an Egyptian campaign by Heraclius, a general of the Emperor Zeno,[9] and another on a campaign of an otherwise unknown general called Germanus against the Blemmyes.[10] One piece of especial interest is a fragment of a cosmological poem on the foundation of Hermupolis.[11] The most recent such find (published 1967) is a fragment from Antinoupolis of a panegyric on a governor called Archelas.[12]

No doubt many of these poets studied for a while in the lecture rooms and libraries of Alexandria, but clearly Alexandria was no longer the only city in Egypt with either the schools or the literary traditions to turn out a poet. There was nothing any more for an Egyptian to be ashamed of in not being born in Alexandria. Nonnus proudly proclaimed: Νόννος ἐγώ, Πανὸς μὲν ἐμὴ πόλις,[13]

[1] Suid., s.v.
[2] Heitsch XLII, for fragments and bibliography.
[3] Libanius, *Ep.* 361. 2.   [4] Libanius, *Ep.* 368.
[5] Photius, *Cod.* 279 *ad fin.*
[6] *Or.* xxix. 347a (probably Horapollon, cf. *Historia* xiv (1965), 488).
[7] Cf. now T. Gelzer, *Mus. Helv.* xxiv (1967), 129 f., and P. Orsini's Budé edition of 1968.
[8] Heitsch XXII (Page 135); cf. Keydell, *Hermes* lxxi (1936), 465–7.
[9] Heitsch XXXIV (Page 144).   [10] Ibid. XXXII (Page 142).
[11] Ibid. XXIV; cf. Keydell, loc. cit.
[12] *Pap. Antin.* iii. 15 (not, however, as its editor Barns supposes, from an iambic panegyric: the fragment probably comes from the preface to a hexameter panegyric, as I have argued (with numerous parallels) in *CQ* N.S. xx (1970).
[13] *Anth. Pal.* ix. 198, with A. Wifstrand, *Von Kallimachos zu Nonnos* (Lund, 1933), 166–8.

and Olympiodorus boasted that Homer himself had been born in Egyptian Thebes.[1] So Claudian would not have needed to claim Alexandria for his native city unless it had been the simple truth.

Moses Hadas has argued that, since Claudian does not mention his Alexandrian origin in his major Latin poems, he must have become ashamed of it when living in Rome and Milan.[2] But Alexandria was the third city of the Empire. Compare the proud epitaph of an earlier Alexandrian at Rome:[3]

Θρέψε μ' Ἀλεξάνδρεια, μέτοικον ἔθ[αψε δὲ Ῥώμη,]
αἱ κόσμου καὶ γῆς, ὦ ξένε, μη[τροπόλεις].

Naturally there was no call for Claudian to touch on personal details in formal epics and panegyrics. But in the epigrams quoted above he admits it quite openly. Nor would anyone who wanted to keep his Egyptian origin dark have written a long discourse on the sources of the Nile (*c.m.* xxviii)—or an epigram on the crocodile![4] Nothing can safely be built on the contemptuous allusion at *Eutr.* i. 313 to the 'Aegyptia somnia' of John, a hermit who lived in the Thebaid desert. For it was not so much John's prophecy (concerning Theodosius' victory over Eugenius) that Claudian was ridiculing, as the personal capital Eutropius had been making out of the fact that it was he who had obtained the prophecy from John. And it may be not over fanciful to detect here a trace of the traditional hostility of the Alexandrian to the native Egyptian, the despised Copt.[5]

As an Alexandrian, Claudian's native speech will naturally have been Greek, and we learn from an epigram he wrote,

[1] *Hist.*, frag. 33 (*FHG* iv. 65*a*). Greek poets of the Empire in general were proud of their native cities. The Oppians refer with pride to their home provinces of Syria and Cilicia respectively (*Cyn.* ii. 125 f., 156 f.; *Hal.* iii. 7 f., 205 f.), and Quintus is known as Quintus of Smyrna solely because he himself chose to impart this information (xii. 308 f.).

[2] *H. of Lat. Lit.* (1952), 389; cf. Levy, *TAPhA* lxxxix (1958), 91, for a similar, though more sophisticated view.

[3] Peek, *Gr. Versinschr.* 1017: the punctuation is not quite certain (cf. L. Robert, *Hellenica* ii (1946), 105, n. 2).

[4] *c.m. app.* ix (quite possibly genuine—though by no means necessarily written in Egypt, as Romano, *Appendix Claudianea*, p. 46, supposes).

[5] Cf. *Byz. Zeit.* lvii (1964), 284–5, for possible traces of this attitude in Palladas.

probably in 395, to Anicius Probinus, the other of the two consuls of that year, that up till then his literary output had been exclusively in Greek:[1]

> Romanos bibimus *primum* te consule fontes,
> et Latiae cessit Graia Thalia togae (*c.m.* xli. 13–14).

One of these Greek poems will have been the *Gigantomachia*, of which two fragments survive. The first, the preface to the poem, makes it clear that it was recited in Alexandria. Seven epigrams preserved in the *Greek Anthology* are ascribed to a Claudian, but which, if any, of these are from the hand of our Claudian is still uncertain.[2] That two or three of them are *not* by him seems certain. Unlike the Greek *Gigantomachia*, their metrical technique bears clear traces of the baleful influence of Nonnus, who wrote something like fifty years after Claudian's death.[3] They must presumably, therefore, be by another, later, Claudian.

The existence of such another Claudian is usually inferred from a passage in Evagrius' *Ecclesiastical History* (i. 19). Evagrius, writing in 593, says that in the reign of Theodosius II (408–50), φασὶ καὶ Κλαυδιανὸν καὶ Κῦρον τοὺς ποιητὰς ἀναδειχθῆναι. Cyrus rose to fame probably in the 430s, and was consul in 441. But not one of our Claudian's poems can be dated as late as the reign of Theodosius II. Indeed, it is almost certain that by 408 he was dead.[4] Evagrius' Claudian, then, would seem to be a good candidate for this later Claudian. And there is another piece of evidence. The lemma to *Anth. Pal.* i. 19, one of the epigrams ascribed to Claudian, states: 'This is the Claudian who wrote on the origins (Πάτρια) of Tarsus, Anazarbus, Berytus, and Nicaea.' Now it so happens that this epigram is one of those that cannot possibly have been written by the author of the *Gigantomachia*. It is

---

[1] Appendix A, p. 458.

[2] A. Lesky is the most recent scholar to accept (without discussion) the authenticity of all seven (*H. of Greek Literature* (Engl. trans. 1966), 814).

[3] See Keydell, *Bursians Jahresbericht* 230 (1931), 121, and, for a useful summary of the divergent views, L. R. Lind, *Class. Phil.* xxix (1934), 69 f. Cataudella's attempt to date the *Dion.* before 381 (*Stud. Ital.* xi (1934), 15 f.) is refuted by Keydell, *Gnomon* xxxviii (1966), 27, n. 5.

[4] See p. 418.

hardly more than a cento of phrases from Nonnus, and cannot therefore have been written before at least *c.* 450. On the face of it, then, a neat picture can be built up of a Claudian who wrote these four Πάτρια and a number of epigrams in the reign of Theodosius II.[1]

Unfortunately, things may not be quite so straightforward. In the first place, Evagrius, writing as he was almost two centuries later, may simply have put our Claudian in the next reign by mistake (the vague φασί suggests that he was not altogether certain of his chronology). The way he links Claudian with the great Cyrus without further explanation suggests that he was writing of a famous poet. Now our Claudian was without question the most talented and distinguished poet of his generation, court poet for almost a decade. He exercised a hypnotic effect on his Latin successors, like Sidonius Apollinaris, and may be presumed to have made a similar mark in the Greek world. Thus Evagrius' bare allusion to 'Claudian the poet' fits our Claudian much better than this shadowy later Claudian, author of feeble Nonnian centos.

Secondly, the lemmata to the *Anthology* are notoriously untrustworthy. All that it would be safe to deduce from the lemma in question is that the lemmatist knew of *a* Claudian who wrote these Πάτρια. It is suggestive that he attached this piece of information to the very first occurrence in the *Anthology* of a poem ascribed to a Claudian (i. 19). Homonymous poets are frequently confused in the ascriptions and lemmata of the *Anthology*,[2] and it is unlikely that a tenth-century lemmatist had any valid grounds for distinguishing between the author of *Anth. Pal.* i. 19 and the author of the *Gigantomachia*. It would be unwise to rule out the possibility that he was simply mistaken in identifying the author of the Πάτρια with the author of *Anth. Pal.* i. 19. It may perfectly well be that the author of the Πάτρια is none other than our Claudian.

A plausible case can be made out for supposing that this is

---

[1] So W. Schmid, *RAC* iii (1957), 168–9.

[2] See in general, A. S. F. Gow, *The Greek Anthology: Sources and Ascriptions* (Hell. Soc. Suppl. Paper ix, 1958).

indeed so. The writing of Πάτρια, foundation-legends of the ancient cities of Greece and Asia Minor, was much in vogue in the fourth and fifth centuries. Christodorus of Coptus is credited with six such Πάτρια, including one on Thessalonica in twenty-three books. Many of these foundation-legends are alluded to, either at length or in passing, by Nonnus in his gigantic *Dionysiaca*, obviously drawing on this sort of literature.[1] Now, interestingly enough, two of the longest Πάτρια that he works into his poem are those of Berytus and Nicaea—two of the four attested by the Palatine lemma. Book xli includes in fact two quite different accounts of the founding of Berytus (51–154, 155–427), and it is suggestive that the second opens with the words: 'but there is a more *recent* version' (ἀλλά τις ὁπλοτέρα πέλεται φάτις). Nonnus must have got his material from somewhere, and what more suitable or likely source than the only attested Πάτρια Βηρύτου?[2]

As for the long account in *Dion.* xv–xvi of the founding of Nicaea (by Dionysus in memory of a nymph he had driven to suicide), from the scale and character of Nonnus' treatment, R. Keydell long ago suggested that he was drawing on a full-scale Πάτρια Νικαίας.[3] The most recent study of the episode, by G. D'Ippolito,[4] contests this conclusion on the ground (reasonable if true) that no such work is attested. Neither scholar, it seems, was aware of the Πάτρια Νικαίας recorded by the Palatine lemma.

There is no similar section in the *Dionysiaca* on the founding of Tarsus and Anazarbus, presumably because neither had any connection with the saga of Dionysus. All the same, there are two very suggestive allusions to Tarsus in the course of the section on

---

[1] See the brilliant section in L. Robert's *Villes d'Asie Mineure*[2] (1962), 297–317 (promising a monograph on the theme at p. 317, n. 4), and also R. Dostálová, 'Alte Vorderasiatische Lokaltraditionen in Nonnos Dionysiaka', *Klio* xlix (1967), 39 f.

[2] As suggested by R. Reitzenstein, *Das iranische Erlösungsmysterium* (1921), 182 f. Reitzenstein, however, accepted that *Anth. Pal.* i. 19 was by the famous Claudian, and for this and other reasons his case as formulated is untenable: cf. Keydell, *Bursian* 230 (1931), 111–12, and in *Hermes* (1936), 465. For a commentary on the Berytus section, see R. Dostálová-Jeništová, *List. Fil.* v (1957), 36 f.

[3] *Hermes* lxii (1927), 400 (cf. *PW* xvii. 1. 907).

[4] *Studi nonniani* (1964), 90.

Berytus. At *Dion*. xli. 85 Nonnus states categorically that Berytus was founded before Tarsus, and at xli. 335 f. he alludes to a dispute (which he again settles in favour of Berytus) as to whether Berytus, Arcadia (in Crete), Argos, Sardis, or Tarsus was the first city ever. Plainly, then, Nonnus was familiar with the story of the founding of Tarsus. Of course, it may be that he just took over the references to Tarsus from his source for Berytus; but this possibility, too, has attractive implications. For if the Πάτρια Βηρύτου on which Nonnus drew was written by a man who had also written a Πάτρια Ταρσοῦ, then one might have expected the legend of Tarsus to be used therein as a yardstick.

It is surely very striking that Nonnus should have been familiar with the subject-matter of three out of the four Πάτρια attested by the Palatine lemma. By contrast, of the six Πάτρια written by Christodorus, on Constantinople, Thessalonica, Nacle, Miletus, Tralles, and Aphrodisias, Nonnus does not allude to a single one.[1] It may be just that Dionysus had never had anything to do with any of these cities—or it may be that, when Nonnus wrote, the appropriate legends had not yet been sifted and written up into regular Πάτρια. For Christodorus wrote a full half century after Nonnus.

The obvious inference is that the Claudian who wrote the Πάτρια of Berytus, Nicaea, and Tarsus wrote before Nonnus and was used by him. It would be much less plausible to suppose that he was inspired to write his Πάτρια by a reading of Nonnus, for, considerations of general probability aside, we should still be left with the problem of Nonnus' sources, and have to postulate a second series of Πάτρια on the same cities written before Nonnus.

If, then, the Claudian who wrote the Πάτρια of Berytus, Nicaea, and Tarsus wrote before Nonnus, plainly he cannot be the later Claudian, the servile disciple of Nonnus. And if he is not this later Claudian, then who can he be but the famous Claudian?—unless we are prepared to postulate the existence of yet another poet called Claudian who wrote in the fourth or early fifth

---

[1] He does just mention the eponymous heroes Miletus and Byzas in passing.

century. For Πάτρια do not seem to have been written before the fourth century, and the legend of Berytus was designed to lead up to its later fame as the leading law school of the Empire (cf. Nonnus xli. 391 f.), a position it did not attain before the fourth century.

That Nonnus should have read the Greek works of his fellow countryman Claudian is likely enough on general *a priori* grounds. In addition, Keydell and Braune have plausibly argued that Nonnus was familiar with some of Claudian's Latin work. Particularly striking, as Reitzenstein pointed out,[1] is the parallelism between the joint role of Physis and Aion at the founding of Berytus (first version) in Nonnus, and their joint appearance in Claudian's remarkable section on the cave of Aion in *Stil.* ii. 424 f. —a passage which again bears a strong resemblance to Harmonia's visit to Astraios in *Dion.* vi (and for Aion, see too *Dion.* vii. 23 f.). Another close parallel is between the cosmic maps which Proserpina and Harmonia weave into their robes at *Rapt.* i. 246 f. and *Dion.* xli. 277 f. respectively: in both cases a map of the earth, sea, and heaven, with Ocean flowing round the whole—and in both cases, too, the weaving was done in a closely guarded palace.

Obviously, if Nonnus had read Claudian's Latin work, then he is very likely to have read his Greek poetry—in particular, given Nonnus' own interests, his Πάτρια and mythological poetry. The gigantomachy theme bulks large in Nonnus (*Dion.* i–ii, xlviii), and it will be argued below that he was directly influenced by Claudian's Greek *Gigantomachia*.

If, then, the later Claudian loses the Πάτρια attested by the lemma to *Anth. Pal.* i. 19, this only leaves him with two or three very feeble epigrams, and further reduces the likelihood that it is he whom Evagrius mentions in the same breath as Cyrus of Panopolis. A further point to be mentioned in this connection is that Evagrius places his Claudian under Theodosius II (408–50). On the now generally accepted chronology, Nonnus wrote *c.* 450, or possibly even a little later. None of the many disciples

---

[1] *Iran. Erlösungsmyst.* 183–5, and cf. Keydell, *Gedenkschrift G. Rohde* (1961), 112–13. On Nonnus and Latin, see below, p. 20.

he bewitched can be dated before *c.* 470.[1] So this later Claudian should probably be placed with them, in the late fifth or early sixth century, perhaps a century later than the famous Claudian. So unless, again, we are prepared to accept the possibility of another famous Claudian, writing between our Claudian and the later Claudian, we should probably do best to conclude that Evagrius is a little out in his chronology, and does indeed mean to refer to our Claudian.

Of the seven epigrams ascribed to Claudian, *Anth. Pal.* i. 19 and ix. 139 may confidently be ascribed to the later Claudian as being post-Nonnian, and with them i. 20 on metrical grounds. Of the rest (v. 86, ix. 140, 753, 754) none shows any clear trace of Nonnian influence (though with such short poems no firm conclusions are possible), and all could perfectly well be by our Claudian. For example, v. 86,

Ἵλαθί μοι, φίλε Φοῖβε· σὺ γὰρ θοὰ τόξα τιταίνων
ἐβλήθης ὑπ' Ἔρωτος ὑπωκυτέροισιν ὀϊστοῖς,

is not an epigram proper at all,[2] and may well be a fragment from a longer poem, probably from a speech in an epic (there are many speeches which begin like this in Nonnus).[3]

That ix. 753-4 are by our Claudian may be regarded as certain. Both epigrams (one in hexameters, the other in elegiacs, a favourite trick of the day)[4] describe a toy or curiosity, a hollow crystal ball with water inside. No fewer than eight of the Latin epigrams indubitably by our Claudian are devoted to precisely the same subject. The chances of two different poets called Claudian independently deciding to write a series of epigrams on

[1] See P. Friedlaender's important article in *Hermes* xlvii (1912), 43 f. (unaffected by the criticisms of A. Ludwich, *Musaeus*[2] (1929), 3-5). Friedlaender's terminus was the reign of Anastasius, but the discovery of the Pamprepius papyrus (Heitsch XXXV—I accept the ascription) has lowered it to the reign of Zeno, and Heitsch XXXIV perhaps to *c.* 470 if Keydell's restoration and identification for line 37 are accepted (*Byz. neugr. Jahrb.* xii (1936), 8 f.).

[2] Cf. Keydell, *Byz. Zeit.* lii (1959), 361.

[3] Cf. several such epic fragments in *Anth. Pal.*: e.g. ix. 125 (see p. 314), ix. 128-9 (by Nestor of Laranda). The two lines x. 120 (ἄδηλον in *Anth. Pal.*) are in fact Nonnus (*Dion.* xlii. 209-10).

[4] Cf. *Athenaeum* xlv (1967), 144 f.

a hollow crystal ball with water inside must be remote.[1] Furthermore, one of the Latin epigrams can help to establish the text of one of the Greek ones.[2] In all editions, ix. 754 is punctuated as follows:

Εἴπ' ἄγε μοι, κρύσταλλε, λίθῳ πεπυκασμένον ὕδωρ
τίς πῆξεν;—Βορέης. Ἢ τίς ἔλυσε;—Νότος.

Compare now c.m. xxxiv. 1–6:

Lymphae, quae tegitis cognato carcere lymphas,
    et quae nunc estis quaeque fuistis, aquae,

(The 'cognatus carcer' is the crystal ball, which Claudian takes to be ice, and therefore made of the same substance as the water it encloses. What puzzles Claudian, in this as in all the other seven epigrams, is that the centre could remain liquid while the exterior was 'frozen'.)

quod vos ingenium iunxit? *qua frigoris arte*
    torpuit et maduit prodigiosa silex?
quis tepor inclusus securas vindicat undas?
    interior glacies *quo liquefacta Noto*?

Now surely what Claudian wrote at *Anth. Pal.* ix. 754. 2 is:

τίς πῆξεν Βορέης, ἢ τίς ἔλυσε Νότος;

'qua frigoris arte torpuit' exactly represents τίς πῆξεν Βορέης and 'quo liquefacta Noto', τίς ἔλυσε Νότος. The traditional punctuation, while undoubtedly elegant from the purely stylistic point of view, has little relevance to the problem of the water inside the crystal.

There is a further close parallel between the other of the Greek

---

[1] Fargues (p. 8, n. 4) suggests that *Anth. Pal.* v. 50 (anonymous) is by Claudian on the ground of its similarity to Claudian c.m. xv and xvi (all three on the poet in love). But the similarity is not nearly so striking here, and it may well be that Claudian is simply translating the Greek epigram. Translation, more or less literal, of Greek epigrams was very fashionable in the circles in which Claudian moved (cf. F. Munari's excellent paper in *Philologus* cii (1958), 127 f.). *App. Barb. Vat.* attributes the poem to Rufinus (cf. L. Sternbach, *Anth. Plan.*, *App. Barb. Vat.* (1890), 92–3). There is little to be said for Stadtmueller's attribution of v. 77 to Claudian (Rufinus in *Anth. Pal.*: cf. Wifstrand, *Von Kall. zu Nonnos*, 158).

[2] Cf. Birt, p. lxxiii.

epigrams on the crystal ball and another of Claudian's Latin epigrams. At ix. 753. 2 Claudian says that the crystal

δεῖξεν ἀκηρασίοιο παναίολον εἰκόνα κόσμου.

Compare *c.m.* li. 1:

Iuppiter in parvo cum cerneret aethera vitro.

It seems hard to credit that such very close parallels between the Latin and Greek epigrams on this very uncommon subject are due to mere coincidence. It would seem that the phenomenon of the water in the crystal so intrigued Claudian (perhaps he owned one) that he treated the same theme in Greek and Latin, just as he later wrote (or started) a *Gigantomachia* in Latin as well as in Greek.

The Greek *Gigantomachia*, if no worse, is certainly no better than most of the other mythological poetry being produced in such abundance in fourth- and fifth-century Egypt. Claudian can have been barely 20, still at home in his native Alexandria, when he wrote it. But it is not enough to blame the short-comings of the poem on the 'immaturity' of the author. For the Latin *Gigantomachia*, perhaps the last of Claudian's poems and still unfinished at his death, is no more successful—and for the same reasons. The battle of the giants, while potentially such a promising theme for a really sublime epic, nothing less than the struggle for the mastery of the very universe, is in fact almost impossible to handle satisfactorily. It is all too likely to degenerate into a catalogue of bizarre battles, with mountains and constellations being tossed from side to side with ridiculous abandon (the gigantomachy in the first two books of the *Dionysiaca* is a grotesque example).

Romano[1] compares Claudian with Hesiod, and finds the *Gigantomachia* lacking the religious inspiration of the *Theogony*. It is inappropriate enough even to make the comparison: still more so to judge Claudian by Hesiod. Whatever religious purpose the myth had had in the eighth century before Christ could hardly have been expected to survive unchanged into the very different world of the fourth century after. Neoplatonists like Macrobius

[1] p. 17.

and Proclus might continue, through allegory, to find a moral purpose in the myth,[1] but for the poets of the Empire without exception, it offered no more than a splendid opportunity to describe hideous monsters in their death-throes, the uprooting of whole mountains and rivers, and sundry other congenial suspensions of the laws of nature. To take the example of Nonnus again, no one could feel that his Zeus had any moral right to the victory he wins over Typhoeus (Typhoeus did at least fight fairly, if fantastically, which is more than could be said for Nonnus' Zeus). It would be surprising indeed if the young Claudian had chosen the theme for any higher motives than these.

Romano's discussion does little more than collect all the Homeric echoes in the *Gigantomachia*, and emphasize the influence of Homer on Claudian. But what Greek poet of any period was not influenced by Homer? Indeed, there is much that is Homeric even in the work of Nonnus, in other respects so un-Homeric a poet. Far more interesting (and important) to consider the un-Homeric features in Claudian's Greek epic style. It is certainly less Homeric than, for example, Quintus of Smyrna. And the moment we reflect on the rhetoric and extravagant hyperbole that characterize Claudian's Latin epic style, it will be appreciated that his Greek style might have been expected to have more in common with Nonnus than Quintus.

One of the most noticeable differences between early and late epic is in the treatment of epithets.[2] First, there are many more of them in the later poets: as against something like 40 per 100 lines in Apollonius, there are usually well over 100 per 100 lines in Nonnus. The two fragments of Claudian's *Gigantomachia* are too short to permit any really significant statistics, but with almost 50 in 75 lines, he is well on the road from Apollonius to Nonnus,

---

[1] Cf. F. Vian, 'La guerre des géants devant les penseurs de l'antiquité', *REG* lxv (1952), 1 f., at pp. 27 f. Cf. also, on a different sort of allegory (physical rather than moral) in Nonnus (and Claudian), Keydell, *Gedenkschrift G. Rohde* (1961), 105 f.

[2] On the whole subject, see Wifstrand, *Von Kall. zu Nonnos*, chapter ii, *passim*, whence I draw all my figures (except for Claudian, whom Wifstrand did not consider).

though still far short of the exuberance of his fellow countryman. Nor is there much trace of Nonnus' riotous use of pregnant and predicative epithets. But at *Gigantomachia* 69 we do find, as often in Nonnus, two epithets to one word, and at line 44 a very characteristic Nonnism, a noun used as epithet. Aphrodite is described as θεμένη . . . ἐπ᾽ ὄμμασιν ἄγγελον αὐγήν. ἄγγελος αὐγή is the beam of light which acts as a messenger, the reflection, that is, from her mirror.[1] Another feature of later epic is the increasing tendency to place attributive epithets before rather than after the noun. In a sample 500 lines of Apollonius there are rather more than 50 after, just under 100 before. But in a sample 200 lines of Nonnus, 160 before and just over 30 after—a striking difference of proportion. We must remember again that the sample is small, but with 29 out of 35 before, and only 6 after, the proportion in Claudian is the same as in Nonnus, 5 : 1.

Another small but readily measurable development of later epic is the growing avoidance of the definite article. It is a tendency that can be traced back to Apollonius, but culminates (as usual) in Nonnus, who uses the article very sparingly, and in distinctly unhomeric situations. Colluthus and Musaeus duly follow suit, with Triphiodorus here as elsewhere revealing that he is not of their number by his closer adherence to Homeric practice.[2] Claudian has only one example, τῇ Κύπριδος ὄλλυτο μορφῇ (line 54), where Koechly (violently, but not perhaps absurdly) proposed τάχα or τότε for τῇ.

One last point. It is notorious that later Greek epic became progressively more dactylic. Of the 32 possible combinations of dactyl and spondee in the hexameter, Nonnus uses only the 9 most dactylic; his disciple Paul the Silentiary only 6.[3] Triphiodorus is betrayed again by his 17 varieties: Quintus and the Oppians have more still. Claudian has only 12. Once more, of course, the sample is really too small, but it is surely more than a coincidence

---

[1] B. Lavagnini, *Aegyptus* (1952), 459, feebly emends to ἄγγελον αὐγῆς, 'messagero di luce' (i.e. mirror).

[2] A. Svensson, *Der Gebrauch des bestimmten Artikels in der nachklassischen griechischen Epik* (Lund, 1937), and cf. Appendix D, p. 479.

[3] A. Ludwich, *Beiträge zur Kritik des Nonnos* (1873), 45 f.

that Claudian's favourite 10 combinations include all Nonnus' favourite 9.[1] So Claudian's style is not unaffected by the slight but significant developments of his age. There is no trace yet of the more minute metrical refinements of Nonnus, of his restrictions on the use of elision, of his monotonous regulating of the accent at caesura and line-end. But for all this there are unmistakable foreshadowings of Nonnian style in the description of Aphrodite preparing herself for battle. She used no conventional weapons, writes Claudian gaily:

Κύπρις δ' οὔτε βέλος φέρεν οὔθ' ὅπλον, ἀλλ' ἐκόμιζεν
ἀγλαΐην.

She tidied her hair in front of the mirror (44–6), added (unheroic detail!) a touch of eye-shadow (47), and disarmed the giants with her come-hither look:

εἰ δέ τις αὐτῇ
ὄμμα βάλοι, δέδμητο.

But the most interesting passage is 50–1:

εἶχε γὰρ αὐτὴ
πλέγμα κόρυν, δόρυ μαζόν, ὀφρῦν βέλος, ἀσπίδα κάλλος,
ὅπλα μέλη . . .

There are many such passages in Nonnus.[2] For example, *Dion.* xiii. 483:

ἔγχος ἔχων στόμα θοῦρον, ἔπος ξίφος, ἀσπίδα φωνήν

and vii. 21:

νεύματα μῦθον ἔχων, παλάμην στόμα, δάκτυλα φωνήν.

And more particularly, as in Claudian, of Aphrodite:

ἔγχος ἐμὸν πέλε κάλλος, ἐμὸν ξίφος ἔπλετο μορφή,
καὶ βλεφάρων ἀκτῖνες ἐμοὶ γεγάασιν ὀϊστοί·
μαζὸς ἀκοντίζει πλέον ἔγχεος . . .
οὐ τόσον αἰχμάζεις ὅσον ὀφρύες . . .   (xxxv. 171 f.).

[1] A. Ludwich, *Rhein. Mus.* xxxvi (1881), 304–5. N. Martinelli's assertion to the contrary (*Misc. Galbiati* ii (1951), 68 f.) is based on inadequate knowledge of Nonnian metric (ignoring the Nonnian scholarship of a century and ridiculing Ludwich, he relies on his own analysis of the first 100 lines of the *Dionysiaca*: his criteria are loose enough to prove anything).
[2] Friedlaender, *Hermes* xlvii (1912), 53 f.

Compare also xxxv. 42 f.:

> στῆθος ἔχεις ἅτε τόξον, ἐπεὶ σέο μᾶλλον ὀϊστῶν
> μαӡοὶ ἀριστεύουσι . . .

And xlii. 235 f.:

> ἔγχεα κούρης
> ὀφθαλμοὶ γεγάασιν ἀκοντιστῆρες ἐρώτων,
> παρθενικῆς δὲ βέλεμνα ῥοδώπιδές εἰσι παρειαί.

It is interesting too to note in Claudian's δόρυ μαӡόν and in ἄνθεα μαӡῶν at line 49 a foreshadowing of Nonnus' obsession with the female breast in erotic descriptions. We have seen grounds already for supposing that Nonnus had read lost poems by Claudian. This, the only opportunity we have of comparing the two poets directly, strongly suggests that Nonnus had read and been influenced by even this youthful work of Claudian.

For us, deprived as we are of the bulk of pre-Nonnian Imperial epic, Nonnus appears as a great innovator, a new stage in Greek epic. But an unexpected papyrus find[1] has now revealed what might really perhaps have been suspected all along, that Nonnus should be regarded rather as the most striking surviving representative of a development in Greek epic which had long been maturing.[2] Triphiodorus has always hitherto been taken on stylistic grounds to be a follower and imitator of Nonnus. He uses a number of words and turns of phrase hitherto supposed to have been, if not actually coined, at least given general currency by Nonnus (though in other respects, especially metrical, it has long been recognized that he is curiously irregular in his allegiance to the master). The new papyrus shows that Triphiodorus wrote perhaps a century *before* Nonnus. Now Claudian's Latin works exercised a profound influence on later Latin epic. It may be that his Greek poetry, further from Nonnus than Triphiodorus in some respects, but closer in others, marked a similar stage in the development of Greek epic.

---

[1] I owe my knowledge of this third- to fourth-century papyrus of Triphiodorus (unpublished) to the kindness of Dr. John Rea. On the un-Nonnian features in his metric and style which render the new date less astonishing, see Appendix D.

[2] Cf. (briefly) M. L. West, *CR* N.S. xiv (1964), 214.

We need not doubt Claudian's explicit statement that he had not published any poems in Latin till 395—so long as this is understood as meaning formal poems formally recited. For it is inconceivable that he had never written anything at all in Latin before then. His very first Latin poems reveal a knowledge of Latin literature, a grasp of the niceties of the Latin language, and a mastery of the techniques of Latin epic equal if not superior to those of any of his contemporaries, whose native language it was. Evidently he had long been composing in Latin quite as fluently as in Greek.

It had always been extremely rare for Greeks to take the trouble to learn what most of them had never ceased to regard as a barbarian tongue. In the later Empire, Latin was at more of a premium, but only at a strictly practical level, for those with designs on one of the careers where at least a smattering of Latin was still essential; the law, the army, or the civil service. It would not be easy to refute Gibbon's observation that there is not one allusion to Vergil or Horace in the whole of Greek literature from Dionysius of Halicarnassus to Libanius. Libanius, indeed, affected complete and ostentatious ignorance of the language, requiring an interpreter even to make out a letter written in Latin. The Emperor Julian was able to make himself understood in Latin ('Latine . . . disserendi sufficiens sermo' as Ammian[1] patronizingly remarked), but (in T. R. Glover's phrase) 'seems guiltless of the most rudimentary acquaintance with Latin literature'.[2]

In contrast to this conventional attitude, no doubt as a result of the increased emphasis laid on Latin in Egypt after Diocletian, there is clear evidence that the language was studied there in the fourth and fifth centuries. Papyri have revealed that many Egyptians began in the fourth century not merely to acquire the smattering of legal jargon in Latin that was required for the bar, but to read a modest range of classical authors, and this not only in the traditional centres of learning (most papyri come from small towns like Oxyrhynchus). With a word-for-word crib pupils

[1] xvi. 5. 7.
[2] *Life and Letters in the Fourth Century* (1901), 33, n. 1 (and cf. p. 358 below).

battled their way through Cicero's *Catilinarians*, as well as Sallust and other prose works. In verse, predictably enough, Vergil dominated. There are more papyri of Vergil than of any other Latin writer.[1] In recent years several juxtalinear texts of the *Aeneid* have come to light (none earlier than the fourth or later than the sixth century), some marked with accents and symbols denoting quantity. But the 'silver' poets were read too: even so hard a poet as Juvenal was being studied with an elaborate commentary in fifth-century Antinoupolis.[2] And if this is true of the cities of Upper Egypt, there are likely to have been much better facilities in Alexandria. Early in the fifth century Proclus came from Lycia and, towards its end, Severus, future patriarch of Antioch, from Sozopolis to study with the Latin rhetors of Alexandria.[3]

In view of these considerations, it is not really so surprising as is usually thought that several Egyptian poets of the age reveal some knowledge of Latin poetry. Christodorus, for example, alludes, in his only extant poem, to the *Aeneid*,[4] and it is arguable that Triphiodorus, too, had read Vergil.[5] Olympiodorus could certainly read Latin (he even quotes some Latin words in one of the surviving fragments of his *History*), and if (as has been argued) he studied the *History* of Ammian before embarking on his own, it is a fair assumption that, being a poet by profession, he had read some Latin poetry too.[6] Nonnus seems to have read and imitated Ovid, and in all probability some of the Latin (as well as Greek) poems of Claudian.[7]

---

[1] Cf. P. Collart, *Rev. de Phil.* xv³ (1941), 112 f.; R. Cavenaile, *Corp. Pap. Lat.* (1958), 7–117; G. Zalateo, *Aegyptus* xl (1961), 196 f.

[2] R. Rémondon, *J. Jur. Pap.* iv (1950), 244 f.; C. H. Roberts, *JEA* xxi (1935), 199 f., *Aegyptus* xv (1935), 297 f.

[3] Zacharias, *Life of Severus* (trans. Kugener, *Patr. Orient.* ii (1907)), p. 11, and Marinus, *Life of Proclus*, 8.

[4] *Anth. Pal.* ii. 414 (cf. R. G. Austin, *Aeneid* ii (1964), p. 289).

[5] Funaioli, *Rhein. Mus.* lxxxviii (1939), 1 f.; Keydell, *Bursian* 230 (1931), 130 f.; 272 (1941), 46, *Gnomon* xxxiii (1961), 282, n. 2.

[6] Thompson, *CQ* xxxviii (1944), 52.

[7] J. Braune, *Nonnus und Ovid* (1935), and in *Maia* i (1948), 176 f.; Keydell, *Bursian* 272 (1941), 39; D'Ippolito, *Riv. di Fil.* xc (1962), 300 and *Studi nonniani* (1964), *passim*, with Keydell in *Gnomon* xxxviii (1966), 26–7. On Quintus and

Of course, it is unlikely that more than a fairly small number of especially keen students attained to any real familiarity with Latin literature, and very unlikely that more than a handful could write Latin poetry themselves with any degree of fluency. But in view of the attitude of such as Libanius, it is significant enough that there were any. And on the evidence of papyri we may certainly assume that Claudian was not alone in being able to compose in Latin. One particularly interesting find has given us a school exercise representing a pupil's attempt to rewrite in his own words a passage from *Aeneid* i, a task which he accomplished in tolerable, if uninspiring, hexameters.[1] The gap between Claudian's Latin poems and the scribblings of such puny poetasters is, of course, immense. But we all have to learn some time. What matters is to have established the background which made Claudian possible. For even such a genius as Claudian's does not flourish in a vacuum. It remains astonishing, but no longer inexplicable and unparalleled, that 'in the decline of arts and Empire a native of Egypt, who had received the education of a Greek, assumed, in a mature age, the familiar use and absolute command of the Latin language, soared above the heads of his feeble contemporaries, and placed himself, after an interval of three hundred years, among the poets of ancient Rome'.[2]

The extent and character of Claudian's cultural attainments will be discussed in Chapter XI. They would have been regarded as fairly considerable by his contemporaries. From this we may safely deduce that he came of a reasonably well-to-do family. An education such as he must have received was normally beyond the pocket of any but the comfortably-off. St. Augustine's father had to save up for some time before he could afford to send his son to the rhetor at Madauros, and Augustine would not have been able to complete his studies at Carthage at all, when his father died, but for the timely financial assistance of

Latin poetry, see most recently (criticizing Vian) Keydell, *Gnomon* xxxiii (1961), 278–83.

[1] C. H. Moore, *Class. Phil.* xix (1924), 322, and R. Cavenaile, *Les ét. class.* xviii (1950), 285 f.

[2] Gibbon, Chapter xxx, *ad fin.*

a family friend.[1] Those who were really determined to have the
best education money could buy would study rhetoric for anything from four to nine years. It was common to spend several
years in Antioch or Alexandria and then a few more in Athens
or Constantinople, and study under several different professors.
St. Basil, for example, after completing his studies at Caesarea
went on to Constantinople and then to Athens. Those with
parents prepared and able to subsidize it, reckoned to study under
all the most celebrated teachers of the day, wherever they
taught.[2]

Claudian will doubtless have spent a few years studying in
Alexandria. Astronomy, mathematics, and medicine were speciali-
ties of Alexandria, over and above its long-established reputation
in the more traditional subjects, rhetoric and philosophy. It may
well be to lectures attended in Alexandria that Claudian owes
his lively interest in these subjects. And it will have been the
numerous talented *grammatici* who taught in late fourth-century
Alexandria—Palladas, Horapollon, Ammonius, Helladius, often
accomplished poets themselves, and staunch pagans to a man—
who encouraged him in his study of the poets.[3] But it is quite
possible that he studied in Athens, Antioch, or Constantinople as
well.

But Claudian did not acquire this education simply with a view
to becoming a 'gentleman of parts'. His career cannot be understood aright unless it is realized that he was a professional poet. It so
happens that he is the only member of a flourishing Egyptian school
of professional poets whose works have survived.[4] These poets
studied with care all the techniques of the various poetical genres in
which they might be called upon to compose. The panegyric, the invective, the epithalamium, the epitaphium—all had their rules and
secrets. Claudian's panegyrics reveal intimate (though intelligent)

---

[1] Jones, *LRE* ii. 1001, though cf. too *Historia* xiv (1965), 472, n. 15 and *Cahiers
d'histoire mondiale* x (1967), 653 f.

[2] Cf. A. Müller, *Philologus* lxix (1910), 292 f. on student life and travels in the
fourth century.

[3] See pp. 192 f.

[4] Cf. my paper in *Historia* xiv (1965), *passim*.

familiarity with the patterns and precepts laid down by third-
and fourth-century rhetoricians like Menander and Aphthonius.[1]

Such a poet would usually start his career by writing a panegyric
on some local dignitary. A generation before Claudian, Andronicus of Hermupolis embarked on a career which led him
all over the East and perhaps to Rome as well, by reciting
a panegyric on his fellow townsman, the *comes* Phoibammon.
Cyrus of Antinoupolis started by lauding a local *dux* called Maurice.[2]
They would, of course, be recompensed for their services, either
in cash or with a post in the civil service carrying immunity from
the oppressive taxes and curial duties. Libanius advises his friend
Heraclianus to have his praises sung by the poet Diphilus—but
warns him that it will not be ἀμισθί.[3] And the wretched scribblings of Dioscorus of Aphrodito actually end with a request for
money.[4]

The more able poets would soon leave Egypt and wander
from city to city in search of rich patrons. Two striking
examples are Cyrus and Pamprepius, both from Panopolis. Cyrus
was a great success in Constantinople, where he wrote panegyrics
on the Emperor and Empress and, before long, rose to be city and
praetorian prefect concurrently—an unprecedented honour—and
eventually consul. Pamprepius travelled widely before striking
lucky in Athens, where his poetical talents won him a chair and
a rich wife. But he was later obliged to leave Athens in a hurry,
and made for Constantinople, where a panegyric on Zeno's
powerful minister Illus gained him a position of great influence
as Illus' right-hand man, much the sort of relationship in which
Claudian was to stand to Stilico. Olympiodorus, Andronicus,
and Christodorus were all much-travelled men as well. The same
is true of lesser figures, such as Diphilus and Eudaemon: and even
those for whom wider travels are not attested would normally
spend a while in Constantinople (e.g. Ammonius, Harpocration,

---

[1] See below, p. 253.
[2] Photius, *Cod.* 279, *ad fin.*
[3] *Ep.* 969.
[4] Heitsch XLII, 5. 62 (= 9. 20, cf. 16. 6), τῷ σῷ ὄρεξον οἰκέτη ὄλβου χεῖρα. For
other examples, *Historia* xiv (1965), 477–8.

Helladius, Horapollon—all Egyptians),[1] a clear sign of the changing times. In late Republican and early Imperial days it was to Rome that Greek poets had flocked from all directions—Philodemus from Gadara, Crinagoras from Mytilene, Philip and Antipater from Thessalonica, and many others, down to that well-connected globe-trotter Nestor of Laranda, early in the third century.[2]

Romano expresses surprise that Claudian should ever have decided to leave his native Egypt. But if we view him against this background, it would be far stranger if he had been content to stay all his life in Alexandria.

Romano has also argued that Claudian's poetical activity passed through two phases: the first when he drew his inspiration from mythological subjects, the second from contemporary themes. Such a view is anachronistic and misconceived. The two sorts of poetry he wrote are merely proof of Claudian's versatility. The poet of the later Empire did not normally write by inspiration. And he was initiated into the secrets of poesy, whatever he might say himself, not by the Muses on Mount Helicon, but by the *grammaticus* in the schoolroom.[3] His school exercises will naturally have included mythological as well as historical and contemporary themes. This is certainly true of the prose declamations of Libanius and the fifth-century sophists of Gaza. Of course the poets principally studied and imitated in the schools will have been the

[1] *Historia* xiv (1965), 485 f., 497 f. for the evidence. In addition, Christodorus' presence at Epidamnus some time in the 480s is attested by *Anth. Pal.* vii. 697–8 (see my forthcoming *Early Byzantine Epigrams in the Greek Anthology*).

[2] C. Cichorius, *Römische Studien* (1922), 294–373, and for Nestor's travels and patrons see the inscriptions (missed by Keydell in *PW* s.v. Nestor 11) collected by J. and L. Robert, *REG* lvii (1944), 239–41, no. 205, and ib. lxviii (1955), 293–4, no. 298. For the poets of Philip's *Garland*, see now the commentary by Gow and Page (2 vols., Cambridge, 1968), with *GRBS* ix (1968), 331 f.

[3] It is no coincidence that so many poets of the age were *grammatici* themselves. To name only Egyptians, no fewer than twelve of those mentioned already in this chapter are attested as *grammatici*—a striking proportion when it is reflected how little we know about most of them (Ammonius, Eudaemon, Harpocration, both the Helladii, Horapollon, Musaeus, Palladas, Pamprepius, Serenus, Triphiodorus: for the evidence and its wider implications, see *Historia* (1965), 491 f., and add Lib. *Ep.* 361. 2 for Cleobulus).

mythological poets *par excellence*, Homer and the Alexandrians. Here again Egypt saw a revival of the mythological epic in the late Empire: witness the gigantic *Dionysiaca* of Nonnus, the diminutive Trojan epics of Triphiodorus and Colluthus, and Musaeus' *Hero and Leander*. But it is probably fair to assume that most poets of the day could write both mythological and contemporary poetry with equal ease. At any rate Claudian was certainly not unique in this respect. Soterichus of Oasis wrote (under Diocletian) mythological and historical epics as well as panegyrics, and Colluthus wrote panegyrics and an epic on the Persian war of Anastasius as well as his mythological poems. There is no need, therefore, to assume that all Claudian's mythological poems, Latin as well as Greek, were written before 395,[1] or that he wrote only mythological poems before then. Like Soterichus, Colluthus, Christodorus, and probably many others, he doubtless wrote contemporary and mythological poetry indifferently at all periods of his life as the mood, or the wishes of his patron at the time, found him.

Is it necessary, moreover, or even legitimate, to make such a sharp distinction between mythological and contemporary poetry? Claudian's contemporary poetry contains a not inconsiderable amount of mythological matter, in the form of numerous similes and *exempla*. His epithalamia consist of little else. And the Πάτρια so popular among poets of the day, tracing (in the fashion of the Hellenistic κτίσεις)[2] the history of a city from its foundation far back in the mythological past, must presumably, like Callimachus' *Aetia* or Ovid's *Fasti*, have been a mixture of history and myth.

All that is known of Claudian's career before he arrived in Rome is that he recited his Greek *Gigantomachia* in Alexandria.[3] In an elaborate nautical metaphor he likens his audience to the

---

[1] In fact it will be argued in Appendix A that Bk. i of *Rapt.* was written *c.* 396/7, and that Bks. ii–iii were among his last works.

[2] Cf. R. Pfeiffer, *History of Classical Scholarship* (1968), 144.

[3] This follows from the lack of either evidence or probability that Claudian ever returned to Alexandria after his arrival in Italy (see below, p. 416). For the fallacy of its 'immaturity', p. 14.

waves of the sea dashing around him while, placing his trust in the bark of Helicon, he hurries on to the prize with his cargo of song. The reference to a prize (ἄεθλα) may indicate that the poem was recited at a contest.[1] He styles himself δεινὸς ἀοιδός, a title which certainly implies that this was not his first public recitation,[2] and in the preface to only the second poem he recited in Italy he refers to himself as being 'Pieriis temptatum *saepius* antris', (*pr. III Cons.* 15). It would not be unreasonable to conjecture that some of these earlier poems were panegyrics, or possibly an epic on the campaign of some general who had scored a success against a troublesome frontier tribe like the Blemmyes. Fragments of several such epics of about the right date have turned up upon papyri, but it would be hazardous to claim them for Claudian.[3]

If he is indeed the Claudian who wrote the Πάτρια on Berytus, Tarsus, Anazarbus, and Nicaea, then he will presumably have visited all the cities in question and been paid by the local councils for his services.[4] More than one critic has drawn attention to the very large number of allusions to the sea and sailing in Claudian's works (already in the preface to his Greek *Gigantomachia*) and it may not be over-fanciful to see confirmation here that he was, like most of his fellow poets of the day, a widely travelled man.[5] It is interesting to note that Berytus, Anazarbus, Tarsus, and Nicaea are all nicely placed on a leisurely route from Alexandria to Constantinople. As, too, is Smyrna (*c.m.* ii). And an epigram devoted to a description of the harbour at Smyrna would certainly seem

[1] I was perhaps unnecessarily sceptical about this point in *Historia* xiv (1965), 487, n. 98. For such contests, less frequent by Claudian's day than in earlier times, see ib. 485.

[2] I am at a loss to see how N. Martinelli, *Misc. Galbiati* ii (1951), 48, can draw the opposite inference.

[3] E. Griset, *Contributi a Claudiano Alessandrino poeta greco* (Pinerolo, 1930) attributes Heitsch XXXIII (p. 142) to Claudian, but on wholly insufficient grounds (cf. Keydell, *Bursian* 272 (1941), 13).

[4] See p. 391, n. 2.

[5] e.g. C. Günther, *De Claud. Comparationibus* (1894), 37; J. C. Rolfe, *TAPhA* l (1919), 146. Nautical imagery is similarly prominent in the writings of the much travelled Jerome (cf. A. S. Pease, *Harvard Studies* xxv (1914), 85).

to license the conjecture that he had visited that city.[1] The *In Eutropium* in particular shows that Claudian knew much about the geography and antiquities of Asia Minor (a fact that was even used by one scholar to support the notion that Claudian was a Paphlagonian).

That he had been to Constantinople is likely enough on *a priori* grounds, and *Ruf.* ii. 348 f. and *Eutr.* ii. 335 f. suggest that his knowledge of the city was based on first-hand acquaintance. Most of the other Egyptian poets of the day had been there (pp. 23-4), and the necessary evidence that Claudian went too is perhaps provided by one of his Greek epigrams. We learn from it that while Claudian was reciting a poem 'in the forecourt of Helicon' (ἐν προθύροις Ἑλικῶνος) a servant stood by holding a stool for him, but that when Claudian grew tired and wanted to sit down, for some reason the servant failed or refused to give it to him.[2] The library of Constantinople is described in another epigram in the *Anthology*[3] as οἶκος Ἑλικῶνος, and since the forecourt of a library would be a very suitable place to give a recitation, it seems reasonable to conclude that it was here that Claudian recited his poem.

Birt suggested that the inscription to the great Egyptian obelisk, erected in the Hippodrome of Constantinople by Theodosius in 390, was written by Claudian, and he has recently been followed by Romano. From this it would follow that he

---

[1] Birt (p. lxii) disputes this, arguing that 'fuit Smyrna in deliciis apud epigrammatographos descriptivi generis'. It is certainly true that there are a number of fourth- to sixth-century epigrams on Smyrna in the *Anthology* (add to Birt's examples, ix. 615-16, 631, 642, 662, xvi. 34, 42, 43), but all of them celebrate specific buildings there, and most were plainly inscribed on those buildings. Obviously therefore they were written by people who *had* visited Smyrna. Moreover, the fact that so many such epigrams found their way into *Anth. Pal.* does not prove that Smyrna was a specially popular theme for epigrams in general: only that someone went round Smyrna collecting epigrams off public buildings, and that this collection was used for the anthology of Cephalas.

[2] *Anth. Pal.* ix. 140. The ascription to our Claudian cannot be regarded as certain. ix. 139 is by the later Claudian, but the juxtaposition need prove no more than that Cephalas (perhaps mistakenly) thought they were both by the same Claudian. It is not obviously post-Nonnian.

[3] *Anth. Pal.* xvi (= *Anth. Plan.*) 70: cf. *Athenaeum* xliv (1966), 38 f.

was writing in Constantinople five years before we first pick
up his story in Rome. It has further been deduced therefrom that
he was a protégé of Theodosius, and accompanied him on his
expedition to put down the western usurper Eugenius in 394.
This would neatly explain his arrival in Italy in the latter half of
394. However the 'verbal parallels' between Claudian's writings
and the inscription adduced by Birt and Romano are confined
to commonplace tags from the stock of Latin poetry, tags which
are indeed found in other inscriptional poems as well. And it is
hard to see how the ascription of such a clumsy, not to say un-
metrical, piece to such a polished writer as Claudian was ever
seriously entertained.[1] The obelisk of Theodosius may safely be
eliminated from the scanty evidence for the early life of Claudian,
and with it all the hypotheses erected thereon.

One further reason for denying any connection between
Claudian and Theodosius is that, if Theodosius had appreciated
Claudian's poetic skill, Claudian would not have confined his
demonstration of it to a five-line inscription. Inevitably he would
have composed a full-scale panegyric on Theodosius. And if he
had really been in Theodosius' suite in 394, then he would hardly
have thrown up the golden opportunity of writing an epic on
the Emperor's victorious campaign. Yet not only is there no
trace of any poem by Claudian on Theodosius: he specifically
states in the preface to his first panegyric on Honorius in January
396 that it was the very first time he had performed before an
emperor ('*iam* dominas aures, *iam* regia tecta meremur').[2]

How long before 394 Claudian left Alexandria is unknown: if
he voyaged up Asia Minor to the capital, writing Πάτρια as he
went, probably two or three years before then. Since he was a
pagan, indeed a 'paganus pervicacissimus' according to Orosius,
it would be attractive to date his departure to 391. For in that
year Theophilus, the patriarch of Alexandria, mobilized bands of
fanatical monks to destroy all the pagan temples and statues of

---

[1] For full discussion, cf. *Athenaeum* xliv (1966), 32 f. For the obelisk, see G.
Bruns, *Istanbuler Forsch.* vii (1935), and p. 47 below.
[2] *Pr. III Cons.* 17, and cf. p. 35.

Alexandria. There were bloody riots and much loss of life on both sides, but victory rested with Theophilus, and many unrepentant pagans were obliged to leave in some haste. Among them were the two Alexandrian poet–grammarians, Helladius and Ammonius, and the philosopher, Olympius. Palladas was apparently prevented from teaching.[1] If Claudian had not already left Alexandria by then, he will have been too prudent to stay much longer.

Be this as it may, some time probably in 394, he decided that the time had come to put his Latin Muse to the test, and set sail for Rome.

[1] Socrates, *HE* v. 16: cf. *JRS* lv (1965), 21 f., especially 27 f.

II

FROM PANEGYRIST TO PROPAGANDIST

ROME in the late fourth century was not a city which welcomed foreigners. Ammianus Marcellinus, a Greek ex-soldier from Antioch, has left us a vivid record of the reception he met with when he retired to Rome. The parasitic urban *plebs* resented the extra mouths that ate their bread, and were always clamouring for foreigners to be expelled from the city, especially in times of scarcity. And the highly exclusive aristocrats only condescended to speak to foreigners when it suited them. They would be all over you one day, grumbles Ammian, and cut you dead the next. And if they did invite a foreigner to dinner, it would certainly not be a literary man, but someone they could talk chariot-racing to, or dice with. They thought of nothing but fine clothes and extravagant food, and kept their libraries locked up like the family vault.[1]

With all due allowance made for Ammian's embittered exaggerations,[2] it would not seem on the face of it that Claudian was going to find it easy to establish himself in Rome. Yet within only months of his arrival he had won the favour of the most illustrious of all the senatorial families, the Anicii. And though one might perhaps have expected Claudian, a pagan,[3] to have approached one of the old pagan families, the Symmachi or Albini, he tried his fortune instead with the leading Christian house in Rome. The very first poem he recited in Italy—indeed his very first published work in Latin[4]—was a panegyric in

[1] Amm. Marc. xiv. 6 and xxviii. 4. For a full account of Roman society at this period, see F. Homes Dudden, *Life and Times of St. Ambrose* i (1935), 28 f., who, however, takes too seriously the tendentious and idealized portrayal in Macrobius' *Saturnalia* (cf. *JRS* lvi (1966), 36).

[2] On Ammian and the aristocracy, see *JRS* liv (1964), 15 f. and the similar approach of F. Paschoud, *Roma Aeterna* (1967), 60 f.; cf. too now R. Syme, *Ammianus and the Historia Augusta* (1968), 142 f.

[3] On this see Ch. VIII.   [4] Cf. Appendix A, p. 458.

honour of two members of that house, the brothers Olybrius and Probinus. They were to be consuls together for 395—an unheard-of honour: and the more so since both were still only in their teens. A very distinguished commission for this young Egyptian poet, newly arrived in Rome, and known so far only for his work in Greek. It is hardly likely that one so qualified would have landed such a prize purely on his own merits, and it is reasonable to conjecture that he had brought with him to Rome a letter of introduction from some patron, acquired in Alexandria or elsewhere, who had connections among the Anicii. Similarly, when we find an aristocrat like Symmachus corresponding with another Egyptian poet, Andronicus from Hermupolis, we may be sure that Andronicus was introduced to Symmachus by their mutual friend Libanius. We actually possess the letters in which Libanius commends Andronicus and yet another Egyptian poet, a certain Harpocration, to Themistius, so that both should get off to a good start in Constantinople.[1] However this may be, it does not look as if Claudian was subjected to the humiliations and frustrations that Ammian met with in his attempts to break into society.

There was a tradition going back to late Republican times of Greek poets seeking the patronage of Roman aristocrats, from Piso and Philodemus in Cicero's day to the stream of inscriptions attesting Nestor's Roman connections under the Severi.[2] The *Greek Anthology* is full of courtly verses on their Roman patrons by Crinagoras, Antipater, and their circle. Claudian is the last of a long line.

It was no trifling event, as is often stated or implied, which first exercised Claudian's Latin Muse. The investiture of the *consules ordinarii* in Rome was accompanied by extravagant pomp and lavish display. Invitations were sent out to all who counted for anything in high society, in the form of delicately carved

---

[1] The material is collected in *Historia* xiv (1965), 487–8.
[2] Cf. G. W. Bowersock, *Augustus and the Greek World* (1965), ch. x, and p. 24, n. 2, above for Nestor (on his date, see G. Barbieri, *Athenaeum* xxxi (1953), 168–9).

ivory diptychs, and to refuse such an invitation without the most
pressing of excuses was considered the height of bad form. And
for the benefit of the *plebs* elaborate games were given, and for-
tunes spent in procuring the rarest beasts and the finest gladiators
for the arena. True, the consulate was not what it had been in the
good old days: indeed perhaps the most important actual duty
the consul performed was to preside at his games, after which he
was left 'to the undisturbed contemplation of his own magnificence'. Nevertheless it is a serious error to dismiss the consulate
of the late Empire as an empty show, devoid of significance and
purely decorative.[1] It still remained the crown of any man's
career.[2] It was moreover the supreme mark of the Emperor's
favour, and vouchsafed to very few. While there were several
prefectures and military commands, there could only be two
consuls in a year,[3] and since the Emperor or Emperors often held
the office themselves, there were extremely few vacancies left
for commoners. And the choice of the two Anicii as consuls for
395 had a further significance.[4] It was symbolic, a gesture to the
many pagans still left among the aristocracy of Rome even after
the collapse of the pagan cause with Eugenius at the battle of the
river Frigidus in September 394, that there was still a place in the
Empire for the Roman aristocracy—if, like the Anicii,[5] they were
Christians.

    Claudian's poem is simple and unpretentious enough in con-
ception. An introductory section praises the illustrious forebears
of the young men, as required by the rules of the genre:[6]

---

[1] As (after many others) does A. Marsili, *Antiquitas* i (1946), 52.

[2] A. Chastagnol, *Rev. hist.* ccxix (1958), 231.

[3] Suffect consuls still continued (longer, indeed, than Jones, *LRE* ii. 532,
supposed: cf. E. Stein, *Bas-Empire* ii. 68), but by the early fourth century the
honour had lost all its earlier importance, being omitted even from a man's
cursus honorum on inscriptions. Ordinary consuls held office for the whole year
(Chastagnol, *Rev. hist.* ccxix (1958), 236).

[4] A. Alföldi, *Conflict of Ideas in the Late Roman Empire* (1952), 36, naïvely
remarks that Probinus and Olybrius could only have obtained their consulates
through bribery.

[5] On the Anicii in the fourth century, cf. O. Seeck, *Symmachus* (1883), xc–cvi.

[6] On these 'rules', see below, p. 253.

> quemcumque require
> hac de stirpe virum; certum est de consule nasci.
> per fasces numerantur avi (*Prob.* 13 f.).

There follows a long eulogy of their father, S. Petronius Probus, whose distinguished career had taken in a consulate and no fewer than four praetorian prefectures. Vergil, improving on Homer, had found a hundred tongues insufficient to sing of all the crime and punishment in Tartarus: Claudian found the same number inadequate to tell of the deeds of Probus. But even Probus was outdone by his sons:

> sed nati vicere patrem, solique merentur
> victores audire Probi. non contigit illi
> talis honor, prima cum parte viresceret aevi;
> non consul cum fratre fuit (61 f.).

He dilates at length on Probus' extraordinary generosity: a virtue attested also by Ammian. But Ammian's praises are tempered by his doubts concerning the source of the wealth Probus gave away so freely ('iuste an secus, non iudicioli est nostri', xxvii. ii. 1).

The scene changes to the battlefield by the river Frigidus three months before. Theodosius, looking (of course) like Mars himself, is still perspiring with exhaustion after his victory. The goddess Roma appears, vividly described as she arrives in her flying chariot, her hair flowing in the breeze, with threatening helmet and blazoned shield. She tells the Emperor of two outstanding youths she has been nurturing with especial care, the match of the Decii and Metelli, the Scipiones and Camilli of old. And who should they turn out to be but—'pignora cara Probi'.

> Pieriis pollent studiis multoque redundant
> eloquio; nec desidiis dapibusve paratis
> indulgere iuvat . . . (150 f.).

These might not seem very impressive qualifications for the consulate, especially when set against those of the Decii and Scipiones. But neither having yet reached his twentieth year, there was simply nothing better to record in the section allotted to πράξεις.

Theodosius agrees at once to Roma's request that he should designate them consuls for the following year out of respect for their late father (by no means the whole reason, as we have seen), and

> extemplo strepuere chori, collesque canoris
> plausibus impulsi septena voce resultant (175–6).

The scene changes again. This time we see Probus' widow Proba, the dowager of Roman society,[1] decking out her sons for the great day—

> credas ex aethere lapsam | stare Pudicitiam . . . (194 f.);

she excelled all wives just as Probus had excelled all husbands: it was as if the two sexes had competed to produce their best! Then Father Tiber appears, proudly rejoicing in this unprecedented honour paid to two of his citizens, and crowing over his less fortunate colleague, the Eurotas:

> respice, si tales iactas aluisse fluentis,
> Eurota Spartane, tuis (236 f.).

The poem closes with a charming epilogue addressed to the year, 'bene signatum fraterno nomine tempus'.

All these themes Claudian develops with great skill, in perfect command of both his material and his medium. It would have been hard to make a better job of such an unpromising subject as the sons of Probus. 'Coepistis quo finis erat', Claudian had told them. Time was to show that this premature consulate was the end as well as the beginning of their respective careers. Neither was a true son of his father. In his first recital in Rome Claudian had revealed himself a master of the popular and profitable art of panegyric.[2] Most remarkable of all, here was an Egyptian writing better Latin than any native-born Roman of the day. It is not

---

[1] Still alive in 410 to open the gates of Rome to Alaric (Procopius, *Bell. Vand.* i. 2. 27); cf. Oost, *Galla Placidia* (1968), 96, n. 32.

[2] Romano, p. 54, says that with *Prob.* Claudian entered on to 'terreno nuovo per lui, che aveva trattato prima soltanto temi mitologici'. There is no evidence that this is so, and it certainly seems most unlikely. Claudian must have written many panegyrics before 395 (in Greek) like every poet of the day.

without reason that, under the year 395, later chroniclers state after their usual bald manner: 'hoc tempore Claudianus poeta innotuit.'[1]

The poem is precisely what it purports to be—a panegyric on the consuls of 395 and their illustrious line. Though the Emperor Theodosius was still alive at the time and holding court not far away in Milan, very little is said about him. His great victory over Eugenius is only mentioned to provide a suitable context for Roma's request. With the victory only three months old at the recitation and perhaps only weeks old in the early stages of composition, it would have been understandable if Claudian had devoted the greater part of his panegyric to it, and perhaps only introduced the honour paid to the Anicii as one manifestation of Theodosius' generosity. Yet in fact it is hardly an exaggeration to say that Theodosius is only introduced to enhance the glory of Probus, by placing his praises in the mouth of the Emperor himself. There is not a word in the whole poem of Stilico, or of the young Honorius, so recently created Augustus of the West. Clearly, as yet Claudian had no ambitions at court.

Nor does he glorify the Roman senate as a whole, as is often claimed. It is the Anicii alone on whom he heaps his praises. He declares emphatically that no other family in Rome is their equal:

> nec quisquam procerum temptat, licet aere vetusto
> floreat et claro cingatur Roma senatu,
> se iactare parem (18 f.).

This of itself would hardly please the lesser (and especially pagan) senatorial families, who resented the way the Anicii curried favour with the Christian Emperor. Moreover he goes on to damn those defeated at the Frigidus as 'Furiae rebelles' (138), although a number of the most important senators of the day had supported Eugenius—not least the Nicomachi Flaviani.[2] Claudian's brief was to praise the Anicii, and this, no more and no less, is exactly what he did.

---

[1] For references see Fargues, p. 12.

[2] On the last pagan stand, cf. H. Bloch, *Harv. Theol. Rev.* xxxviii (1945), 199 f., *Paganism and Christianity in the Fourth Century*, ed. A. Momigliano (1963), 193 f.

Apart from the more material rewards he no doubt received for his services, Claudian also won the personal friendship of both consuls. We possess some elegant verse epistles addressed by him to both of them while he was absent from Rome, presumably at Milan. He describes himself as Olybrius' *sodalis*, and uses the words *amor* and *ignis* of their relationship. He reproaches both for their delay in writing to him: a purely conventional theme, as may be seen from its monotonously frequent appearance in the dreary epistles of Symmachus, but suggesting, nevertheless, that he was on terms of some intimacy with them. He compares his relationship with Olybrius to that between Vergil and Augustus. It was quite something for a young Egyptian adventurer newly arrived in Italy to be able to count two Roman consuls among his friends.

After such a spectacular start and with such patrons, it cannot have come as a great surprise to Claudian when later in the year he was invited to deliver a panegyric on the consul for the following year, who was to be the Emperor Honorius himself. Theodosius had died at Milan on 17 January 395, and Honorius was now sole Emperor of the West. It may be that Claudian received an unsolicited invitation from the court, but it seems more likely that it was procured for him by the influence of one of his Roman patrons. In the preface to the poem he recited there, he merely says: 'me . . . audet magna suo mittere *Roma* deo' (the 'deo' being of course Honorius). But in his letter to Probinus he had written:

> incipiensque tuis e fascibus omina cepi
> fataque debebo posteriora tibi (*c.m.* xli. 15–16),

which suggests that he was then pinning his hopes of advancement on Probinus.

Imperial panegyrics have been the subject of some controversy. What precisely was their purpose? They used to be dismissed merely as gross flattery, the result of desire for gain or an obsequious nature on the part of the panegyrist; or of an inflated sense of self-importance on the part of the recipient. One more sophisticated view is that the panegyrist was depicting the perfect prince, in the hope that the Emperor addressed would take the hint and model himself on this pattern.[1] Others have thought of the panegyrist as a sort of public relations officer, and the panegyric as designed to represent the Emperor as he himself wanted his subjects to think of him.[2] All three of these motives will often have been present in varying degrees, but it may be that the primary role of the panegyric was simply to serve as part of the all important ceremonial of such occasions,[3] like the medallions and diptychs issued in commemoration, and much like a piece of specially composed music today. So conventional (not to say trite), and so divorced from anything so mundane as mere facts are most of the themes of most such panegyrics that it is hard to believe that they could have had much influence on the conduct or beliefs of either Emperor or subjects. What mattered more than the content was the form and the execution.[4] The panegyrist was applauded and rewarded not, in general, for what he said, but for how he said it.

Before turning to the panegyric itself, we must first consider the very serious situation created by the death of Theodosius. The Empire was now divided between his two sons. Of these, Honorius was a mere child, and Arcadius, though 18, was a dull, lethargic youth, barely capable of ruling his own half, let alone his brother's as well. Yet with a barbarian menace on every frontier, a strong hand at the helm had never been more necessary. Furthermore, a serious uprising in the West had only been suppressed three months earlier, and the wounds had not yet closed over. The loyalty, too, of Alaric and his Visigothic federates was not above suspicion.[5] What was to happen to the West?

---

[1] L. K. Born, *AJPh* lx (1939), 20 f.
[2] J. A. Straub, *Vom Herrscherideal in der Spätantike* (1939).
[3] Cf. Oswyn Murray, *CR* xvi (1966), 104–5, and R. MacMullen, *Art Bulletin* xlvi (1964), 437.
[4] See below, pp. 254, 377 f.
[5] On Alaric, see Ch. VII.

In Rome, probably in October 394, and certainly before he realized that he was dying, Theodosius had appointed Stilico regent for Honorius, with full command of all troops stationed in Honorius' portion of the Empire, which was to comprise Gaul, Spain, Africa, and Italy.[1] A regent was clearly necessary even while Theodosius lived, for he was hoping to be able to return to the East as soon as the situation in the West—and his health—permitted. His presence there was urgently required: hordes of Huns had burst across the Danube into Thrace and across the Caucasus into Syria, and the Marcomanni were devastating Pannonia down as far as the Adriatic coast. The obvious choice for regent of the West seemed to be Stilico: not so much for his military ability[2] as for his connection with the Imperial house. For he was the husband of Theodosius' favourite niece and adopted daughter Serena. This would at once give him a better claim than a mere *privatus* on the loyalty of both troops and civilian population alike, and would also (or so it might be hoped) prevent him treating Honorius like a puppet, as Arbogast had Valentinian II. Especially since, as the son of a Vandal chieftain, he had barbarian blood in his veins, and so could not aspire to the purple himself.

But the moment Theodosius was dead, Stilico suddenly announced that with his dying breath the Emperor had appointed him regent not of Honorius alone, but of *both* his sons.[3] That a regent should be appointed for the 10-year-old Honorius was reasonable enough: but Arcadius was 18, quite old enough, it might have seemed—certainly by Roman standards—to rule in his own right. And that such a momentous pronouncement should have been confided to Stilico alone at the very last minute, without a single witness present, was even more surprising, not

---

[1] Historians have all, hitherto, neglected this earlier stage in Stilico's regency, though it is clearly attested by Zosimus (iv. 59. 1 f.), whom there is no reason to doubt. There are other arguments too, which I have assembled in 'Theodosius the Great and the Regency of Stilico', in *Harvard Studies* lxxiii (1968), 247–80.

[2] See below, p. 55.

[3] For this interpretation, the only one to which our sources (especially Zosimus, v. 4. 3) lend any support, see again my paper in *Harvard Studies* lxxiii (1968), 274 f.

to say downright suspicious. It will be seen from the following chapters that there is reason to believe that Stilico's claim was indeed greeted with frank scepticism in many quarters. Modern historians have been prepared—often unquestioningly—to give Stilico the benefit of the doubt. It is hard to see why. It is true that St. Ambrose in his funeral oration on Theodosius says that the Emperor 'commended' both his sons to Stilico,[1] but what else could he say? It was a question of either accepting what Stilico said, or calling him a liar: and this would be to run the risk of precipitating another civil war less than a year after the last, and putting Honorius' life in danger. In any case it might be pointed out that Ambrose could hardly have said less than he did on this crucial topic, and could so easily have been more explicit had he wished. There is no need to doubt that as he lay dying Theodosius said to his closest male kinsman something to the effect: 'commendo tibi filios meos.' Precisely what sort of a relationship he had in mind when making such a statement, whether he either intended or envisaged Stilico using it to set himself up as *de facto* ruler of the whole Empire for an indefinite period—this is quite another matter. Mommsen long ago pointed out that there could in any event be no question of Stilico being appointed legal guardian of either Emperor. Both had already been crowned Augustus, and there were no provisions in constitutional law for a period of minority during which an Augustus could not rule in his own right.[2] In practice, of course, Theodosius must have intended that Stilico should rule for Honorius until it was decided (presumably by Theodosius) that he was old enough to take his own decisions. It was a purely informal arrangement. But is it really conceivable that Theodosius would have asked Stilico to rule in this way for Arcadius, 18 years old, and Augustus for eleven years already? In civil law *tutela* ceased at the age of 14. If Arcadius was not old enough to rule in his own right at 18, when would he be? And, perhaps more important, who was going to decide? It is hardly less doubtful whether Theodosius

---

[1] *De Ob. Theod.* 5.
[2] *Hermes* xxxviii (1903), 101 f. (= *Ges. Schr.* iv. 516).

had intended Stilico to rule for Honorius in quite the manner he did. But, whatever the truth of the matter, when Claudian arrived at court in Milan some time in the course of 395, Stilico was engaged in trying to convince the world at large that Theodosius really had declared him regent of both Honorius and Arcadius.

So, early in January 396, we find Claudian reciting another panegyric, but this time before the Emperor himself:

> iam dominas aures, iam regia tecta meremur,
>   et chelys Augusto iudice nostra sonat
>   (*pr. III Cons.* 17–18).

But if there had been a shortage of deeds to praise with the consuls of 395, the shortage was still more acute with the even younger and even more insignificant consul of 396. Though consul now for the third time, he was still only 10. However, as before, the deeds of the father were more than enough to make up for the shortcomings of the son.

After skipping briefly through the first three subdivisions of the formal panegyric (προοίμιον, γένος, γένεσις), Claudian lets himself go in the section for ἀνατροφή, and paints a vivid (if wholly fictitious) picture of the baby Honorius in his father's camp:

> reptasti per scuta puer, regumque recentes
>   exuviae tibi ludus erat . . . (22 f.).

Bolder than the young Astyanax

> aspera complecti torvum post proelia patrem (24).

Like Cato the Censor, the proud Theodosius taught his willing son

> frigora saeva pati, gravibus non cedere nimbis,
> aestivum tolerare iubar, transnare sonoras
> torrentum furias, ascensu vincere montes . . .
> in galea potare nives . . . (44 f.).

The young prince drank in his father's precepts more eagerly than Achilles at the feet of Cheiron the centaur. In fact, of course, Honorius is a sad but classic example of an heir to the throne corrupted and demoralized by the stifling atmosphere of a palace education. Court eunuchs are a poor substitute for a mother who died when he was only one, and a father continually absent on campaigns.

It happened that Honorius had been consul in 394 as well as 396, so Claudian skilfully assigned to him the credit for his father's victory over Eugenius (this he could do now Theodosius was safely dead), because technically it had been won under Honorius' auspices as consul (an interesting piece of antiquarian information for an Egyptian to have at his finger-tips in the late fourth century):

> victoria velox
> auspiciis effecta tuis: pugnastis uterque,
> tu fatis, genitorque manu (87 f.).

He represents the young Emperor burning with desire to accompany his father into battle and hear the longed-for clang of the trumpets and trample the corpses underfoot, 'quae tibi tunc rabies . . .' One hopes that the audience managed to keep a straight face.

A little less imaginary perhaps is his picture of Honorius' triumphant entry into Milan:

> quanti[1] tum iuvenes, quantae sprevere pudorem
> spectandi studio matres, puerisque severi
> certavere senes . . . (126 f.).

But those among Claudian's audience who were beginning quietly to nod off to sleep despite the brilliance of his rhetoric must have been woken up with a start when he came to relate the death of Theodosius. No longer were they being treated to a vacuous if entertaining panegyric of their youthful Emperor.

Now Claudian's commission had been merely to panegyrize Honorius. All that was required of the panegyrist was to recount the praises of his subjects under the various accepted headings. It was an entirely formal affair, and more often than not the panegyrics of the later Empire contain a maximum of empty and

---

[1] *Quanti* = *quot*, as often in late Latin.

insincere rhetoric and a minimum of hard facts. Their authors normally confined themselves to the conventional common-places of the genre, and steered well clear of controversial issues: it was safer to avoid politics and stick to harmless eulogy. Thus it was by no means inevitable that Claudian should have touched on the burning issue of the day. Yet he did so, and in a manner that left no doubt where his allegiance lay.

After Honorius' triumphal entry into Milan, the scene changes to Theodosius' death-bed. After bidding all but Stilico leave the room, Theodosius instructs him as explicitly as anyone could wish to act as guardian and regent of *both* his sons. With Stilico as their *custos*, says the dying Emperor, he will die happy: 'iamiam securus ad astra | te custode ferar' (158–9); whatever disasters may threaten the Empire, 'opposito Stilicone cadent' (162).

Now since Stilico is the central theme of virtually all Claudian's poetry from now on, whatever the ostensible subject, it is of the greatest importance to be perfectly clear about the precise nature of Claudian's relationship to him. It is often said that this poem represents Claudian's first 'bid for Stilico's favour', and that all his subsequent poems were either similarly designed to flatter Stilico in the hope of personal gain or advancement, or else dictated by sincere admiration for 'le dernier défenseur de Rome'. There is an element of truth in both these explanations, but they do not go far enough.

In my opinion, there can be no doubt whatever that Claudian was acting as Stilico's official propagandist; that the lines just quoted and similar passages in all of his nine other major political poems were written at the instigation or with the approval of either Stilico himself or those close to him, with the deliberate intention of publicizing and justifying his policies and actions.

It would be hard to imagine a much clearer presentation of Stilico's claim than the speech assigned to Theodosius in this poem. But no less significant than the speech itself are the two lines which introduce it:

> ut ventum ad sedes cunctos discedere tectis
> dux iubet, et generum compellat talibus ultro (142–3).

Claudian actually admits that no one else was present when Theodosius was alleged to have made this speech. Now it is incredible that Theodosius should deliberately have confided such a momentous decision to Stilico alone. The best that can be said for Stilico's claim is that Theodosius did tell Stilico in private of his decision but died before he was able to make it public. But Claudian does not say this. He represents Theodosius as deliberately dismissing all possible witnesses, Honorius himself evidently included. Why? The only possible explanation is that he was making a virtue of necessity. Every single person in Claudian's audience knew that there had been no witness but Stilico: had Claudian said that Theodosius made the speech in open court, or even in front of Honorius, he would have been discredited at once. There was no point in asserting what every one knew to be false. So he made the best of the uncomfortable but undeniable truth by implying (without giving it) that Theodosius had a perfectly good reason for not wanting any witnesses.[1]

The speech opens with a fulsome eulogy of Stilico's martial prowess. Claudian's concentration on this particular virtue of Stilico (not perhaps his strongest suit) gains in significance when it is realized that his expedition against Alaric in the autumn of 395 had in fact been singularly unsuccessful and ineffective.[2] All the more reason therefore to stress that he was a good general nevertheless—and that Theodosius had thought so too.

Stilico himself could not have stated more clearly than Claudian does, in the lines that follow, that his regency included both Emperors:

> *tu* curis succede meis, *tu* pignora solus
> nostra fove: *geminos* dextra *tu* protege fratres (152–3).

Stilico is to succeed to all Theodosius' responsibilities—that is to rule the whole Empire just as Theodosius had done. A detail worth dwelling on is the word *solus*. Why should Claudian feel it necessary to say that *only* Stilico was to be regent?

---

[1] I have argued the point more fully in *Harvard Studies* lxxiii (1968), at 275 f.
[2] See below, pp. 160 f.

Whether or not Theodosius had really appointed Stilico regent
of both his sons, he had certainly not appointed anyone else.
Nevertheless Rufinus, praetorian prefect of the East, had dis-
puted Stilico's eastern pretensions, and since Theodosius' death
had himself acted as *de facto* regent of the feeble Arcadius.
The Rufinus affair will be dealt with in Chapter IV: but it may
be observed here that Rufinus' assassination took place on
27 November 395. Claudian's poem was recited on or soon after
1 January 396. It will have taken about three weeks for a messenger
to reach Milan overland from Constantinople in winter,[1] so the
news of Rufinus' death will have been very much in the fore-
front of people's minds when they came to listen to Claudian
perform. There can be little doubt that Claudian was warning
anyone else who might be thinking of standing in Stilico's way
that it would be the will of Theodosius he was opposing.

   In the very next line Claudian reminds his audience of Stilico's
exceptional credentials. Was he not the son-in-law of Theodosius
himself? Theodosius appeals to him

> per consanguineos thalamos noctemque beatam,
> per taedas . . . (154 f.),

and 'reminds' him that the Empress Flaccilla herself had been
a matron of honour at his wedding. This was a qualification that
not even Rufinus could match—though not for want of trying.[2]

   All this is not mere conventional flattery, a 'bid for Stilico's
favour'. Indeed, considering what a wholly conventional genre
the panegyric was, what is most striking about Theodosius'
speech is precisely the fact that it does not contain a single conventional theme. Claudian confines himself exclusively to the
matter of Stilico's regency and his qualifications for it. Nor is the
speech just a profession of faith in Stilico's claim, a vote of confidence, or an indication that Claudian was on Stilico's side. It
is nothing less than a careful and deliberate defence of Stilico's
position.

---

[1] On the speed of couriers, see A. M. Ramsay, *JRS* xv (1925), 60 f.; Bury,
LRE i². 225; Jones, *LRE* i. 402, iii. 91 f.   [2] See below, p. 64.

And the propaganda line is just as clear cut in this, Claudian's first political poem, as it is in any of his later work. It is difficult to see on what grounds Romano can claim *Ruf.* (396–7) as Claudian's first political poem,[1] or Fargues that he did not become 'poète officiel' until 398, two whole years later.[2] Others postpone his entry into politics till 399,[3] or even 400, when he declaimed the eloquent three-book panegyric on Stilico.[4] But Claudian was no less committed to the policies of Stilico in January 396. None of his poems, from 396 on, can be properly understood unless this elementary fact is fully appreciated.

[1] p. 71. [2] p. 18.
[3] N. Martinelli, *Misc. G. Galbiati* ii (1951), 59.
[4] It was not till then, according to E. S. Ducket, *Latin Writers of the Fifth Century* (1930), 19, that Claudian could 'boldly step forward as an official panegyrist'.

III

TECHNIQUES OF THE PROPAGANDIST

THE crucial distinction between mere flattery and actual propaganda has too often been either blurred or denied. Influential among the sceptics was G. Boissier, who objected that on occasions Claudian goes further than even Stilico can have wished, and cannot therefore have been writing to a brief.[1] This objection will not stand up to scrutiny. In the first place one example (and Boissier could find only one example) is hardly sufficient to establish his case. What official organ, even today, does not on occasion overreach itself, whether through excessive enthusiasm or defective information, and embarrass its party? In the second, Boissier's one and only example[2] in fact proves exactly the reverse of what he thought.

Claudian accords considerable prominence to Stilico's son Eucherius, several times emphasizing that royal blood flowed in his veins and hinting unmistakably at a royal marriage for him. This, Boissier argues, can only have embarrassed Stilico, for it was widely rumoured (as we know from Orosius and Zosimus) that Stilico was planning to make Eucherius Emperor of the East instead of the infant Theodosius II. It was also believed that Eucherius was a crypto-pagan, and intended when Emperor to persecute the Christians.

[1] *Fin du paganisme* ii (1891), 291, cf. Glover, *Life and Letters in the Fourth Century* (1901), 229. Most recently, F. Paschoud claims (*Roma Aeterna* (1967), 135) that 'il est impossible d'identifier absolument Claudien à Stilicon', and insists that Claudian 'a conservé une certaine autonomie'. He produces neither evidence nor argument in support. The tract of Steinbeiss which is all he cites (n. 6) contains nothing relevant.

[2] It is also sometimes alleged that the appeal of Aurora at the end of *Eutr.* ii must have exceeded Stilico's instructions (J. H. E. Crees, *Claudian as a Historical Authority* (1908), 124), but this is entirely to misunderstand Claudian's purpose here (see pp. 141 f.).

But the mere mention of Theodosius II dates these rumours after the death of Arcadius in May 408, for it would not have made sense to talk of deposing Theodosius while his father was still alive. This accusation, then, is no more than one of the many slanders sedulously spread by Stilico's enemies in the course of the propaganda campaign which led to his fall and execution in August of that same year. But the poems of Claudian in question (*Stil.* ii and iii, *VI Cons.*) were recited in 400 and 404 respectively, the first before Theodosius was even born and when Eucherius was only 11.

If we turn to the poems themselves, we shall find that Claudian says no more in them than what Stilico himself had claimed before the death of Arcadius. At *Stil.* iii. 176 f. Claudian describes how Eucherius was born in Rome in 389, and shown there to his 'grandfather' Theodosius I, who 'sustulit in Tyria reptantem veste nepotem'. Now *tollo* is the technical term for acknowledging a child as legitimate: so Theodosius himself, according to Claudian, publicly acknowledged Eucherius as his grandson, born in the Imperial purple. In fact, there is no good reason to doubt that something of this sort did happen. It seems likely that Eucherius is represented together with Arcadius and Honorius on one side of the base of the great obelisk of Theodosius in the Hippodrome of Constantinople (where it still stands today).[1] This would clearly indicate that he was officially recognized by Theodosius himself as a member of the Imperial family.

At *Stil.* ii. 341 f., in the course of a description of the figures embroidered on Stilico's consular robe, Claudian hints at a marriage between Eucherius and a princess, who can only be Galla Placidia. Also represented on the robe are his two sisters, Maria (by then Honorius' wife, and optimistically portrayed in an

---

[1] See G. Bruns, *Der Obelisk und seine Basis auf dem Hippodrom zu Konstantinopel* = *Istanbuler Forsch.* vii (1935), 71–2, and (against the objections of J. Kollwitz, *Gnomon* xiii (1937), 423 f.) Mazzarino, pp. 101–3, n. 4; W. Hartke, *Römische Kinderkaiser* (1951), 238–9. Note also in this connection the fact that all Stilico's children were named after members of (Serena's branch of) the house of Theodosius: Eucherius (her great-uncle), Maria (her mother), and Thermantia (her grandmother and her sister as well). See stemma, p. xiv.

advanced stage of pregnancy: see p. 153), and the young Thermantia. A dynastic passage, certainly. But have we any good reason to doubt that precisely this scene really was represented on Stilico's consular robe?

In the cathedral treasure at Monza, there is an ivory diptych issued by Stilico to commemorate the award of the *insignia* of some public office to Eucherius.[1] Since the only post Eucherius held was that of tribune and notary (like Claudian), it can only be this. Eucherius is the principal figure, represented as holding a scroll in one hand and standing between Stilico and Serena. Maria is not accorded the prominence which would have been her due after her marriage to Honorius in 398, and since Eucherius was born in 389 and is represented as a boy of obviously less than 10, a date before 398 may be regarded as certain. Moreover, according to R. Delbrück, the two Emperors portrayed on Stilico's shield (i.e. Arcadius and Honorius) are both represented as consuls, which points to their joint consulate in 396. Thermantia is not represented at all, presumably because she was still a baby at the time. But she does appear on another interesting item, a *bulla* found (in 1544 at Rome) in what is very probably the sarcophagus of Maria herself, bearing the legends: 'Honori, Maria, Stelicho, Serena, vivatis!' and 'Stelicho, Serena, Thermantia, Eucheri, vivatis!' (*ILS* 800). Stilico clearly liked parading Eucherius, and it was after all only natural that, in view of his own marriage to Serena and Maria's to Honorius, he should have thought of himself and his family as part of the Imperial family. We have no reason to suppose that Stilico was not well pleased with the two passages of Claudian under discussion.

Lastly, at *VI Cons.* 554 f. Claudian emphasizes that despite his 'regius undique sanguis' Eucherius did honour to Honorius like a

---

[1] See frontispiece, or (better) R. Delbrück, *Die Consulardiptychen* (1929), Tafeln, no. 63. For full commentary see the Textband, pp. 242–8. The old view (still prevalent) that it commemorates one or other of Stilico's two consulates in 400 or 405, must be abandoned, because (*a*) Stilico is not represented in the *trabea*, and (*b*) after her marriage to Honorius in 398, Maria would have been represented more prominently than Eucherius (in any case it is clearly Eucherius, not Stilico, who is the principal honorand).

common soldier, that Stilico's 'dura pietas' denied his own son the favours he freely granted to senators. This too is perfectly true: at Stilico's death four years later Eucherius was still only a tribune and notary.[1] Stilico had carefully resisted the temptation to promote his only son to an early prefecture or consulate. Thus it can be seen that his policy with regard to Eucherius was on the one hand to foster the notion that he was a prince of the blood royal and destined for great things (in which he had actually been encouraged by Theodosius), but nevertheless not to give him any too flagrantly preferential treatment. It can hardly be just a coincidence that we find precisely this double attitude in Claudian. Perhaps after all Claudian knew better what Stilico wanted than M. Boissier.

It may well be that Stilico was unwise to flaunt Eucherius' royal blood and his own dynastic pretensions in this way. It may even be that these passages of Claudian provided Stilico's enemies with welcome ammunition in later years. But that is another matter.

Perhaps the clearest proof of Claudian's commitment is the consistency and coherence of the devices he employs to publicize and justify Stilico's acts and aims. By this I do not mean the slanted manner in which he represents—or misrepresents—particular facts in individual poems; this will be discussed at length in later chapters. I mean the motifs which recur again and again in his political poems over a period of years. A brief survey of these themes will clear the ground for more detailed analysis of the individual poems.

First and most obvious, Claudian harks back again and again to Stilico's alleged regency. We have seen already how this theme made its début in 396. In 397 it reappears just as emphatically:

> iamque tuis, Stilico, Romana potentia curis
> et rerum commissus apex, tibi credita fratrum
> utraque maiestas geminaeque exercitus aulae (*Ruf.* ii. 4–6).

---

[1] Zosimus v. 34. 7; cf. too Oost, *Galla Placidia* (1968), 72–3.

In 398 again:

> . . . quem fratribus ipse
> discedens clipeum defensoremque dedisti
>
> (*IV Cons.* 437–8),

and

> dignus cui leges, dignus cui pignora tanti
> principis, et rerum commendarentur habenae
>
> (*Nupt.* 307–8).

And in 399:

> defensor utrique
> sufficis . . .
> unaque pro gemino desudet cardine virtus
>
> (*Eutr.* ii. 599 f.).

Still in 400:

> nec pignora curas
> plus tua quam natos, dederat quos ille monendos
> tutandosque tibi (*Stil.* ii. 53 f., cf. i. 140 f.).

The very fact that Claudian dwells so often and so emphatically on this point gives (or should give) rise to the gravest suspicions concerning the truth of Stilico's claim. While not, perhaps, sufficient in itself actually to disprove the claim, it certainly indicates clearly enough that there must have been many at the time who did not believe it, and needed constant 'reminding'.

So accustomed indeed have we become to the refrain, that it comes as a surprise to find that it does not reappear in his last two poems, recited respectively in summer 402 and January 404. In view of its monotonously regular occurrence in every year up to 400, this cannot be written off as mere coincidence. Nor can we be satisfied with the explanation that Claudian simply got tired of trotting out the same old cliché. The answer is that by 402 Stilico had virtually abandoned all hope of ever establishing his regency over the then 26-year-old Arcadius. In 404 Claudian writes, addressing Stilico:

> illumque diem sub corde referres
> quo tibi confusa dubiis formidine rebus
> infantem genitor moriens commisit alendum
>
> (*VI Cons.* 581 f.).

When we reflect how invariably Claudian had linked Arcadius' name with Honorius' whenever he had touched on Stilico's regency in all his earlier poems, it is very striking—and suggestive —that he here alludes to Honorius alone. There was no longer any point in including Arcadius.[1]

Next we may turn to Claudian's repeated insistence on the essential unity of the two halves of the Empire. The reality of the situation was that after the death of Theodosius the two halves were administered quite separately; the West by Stilico in Honorius' name, the East by the ministers of Arcadius—Rufinus, Eutropius, Aurelian, Anthemius—who steadfastly refused to acknowledge, and often actively resisted, Stilico's eastern pretensions. Stilico's supreme goal was to unite both halves under his regency.[2] So Claudian duly emphasizes the excellent relations which, it was alleged, existed between the two Emperors. In 396 they are 'unanimi fratres' (*III Cons.* 189): in 398, after the conclusion of the Gildonic war, which had stretched relations between the two courts almost to breaking point, he proclaims that 'concordia fratrum | plena redit' (*Gild.* 4–5). Earlier in 398, before the outcome of the war was known, he had prayed that as a symbol of unity the brothers might soon take the consulate together:

> tempus erit, cum tu trans Rheni cornua victor,
> Arcadius captae spoliis Babylonis onustus,
> communem maiore toga signabitis annum
> *(IV Cons.* 652 f.).

In 399, referring to the period immediately after the fall of Rufinus, he writes that 'fraterno coniungi coeperat orbis | imperio' (*Eutr.* ii. 546–7).

Correspondingly, Stilico's enemies are always represented as demons of discord, whose only aim is to destroy this unity. Stilico's army is made to denounce Rufinus with the words:

> quid consanguineas acies, quid dividis olim
> concordes aquilas? (*Ruf.* ii. 237–8).

---

[1] Not that Stilico ever completely abandoned his dream: cf. below, p. 155.

[2] The unfounded modern hypothesis of his designs on eastern Illyricum will be discussed below, pp. 59 f.

In a later poem we are told that:

> Rufinus origo
> prima mali; geminas inter discordia partes
> hoc auctore fuit (*Eutr.* ii. 539 f.).

Eutropius is asked bitterly:

> geminam quid dividis aulam
> conarisque pios odiis committere fratres? (*Eutr.* i. 281–2).

Naturally the same reproach is levelled at Gildo the Moor:

> in fratres medio discordia Mauro
> nascitur (*Gild.* 236–7).

This attitude is also reflected in the inscription to the equestrian statue of the two Emperors erected in the forum in commemoration of Gildo's defeat: 'Imperatoribus invictissimis felicissimisque DD. NN. Arcadio et Honorio fratribus . . .' (*CIL* vi. 1187). The fact that the revolt had been instigated in the name of Arcadius and suppressed without his help is tactfully passed over in silence. Again, it is suggestive that the *concordia* motif is absent from Claudian's last two poems. In 404 Claudian describes the equestrian statue just mentioned: significantly enough, however, he writes as though there were only one horseman—Honorius.

Arcadius' ministers Claudian lashes with all the ample resources of vituperation at his disposal. But his attitude to Arcadius himself is quite different and most instructive. Stilico had supposedly been appointed regent of Arcadius by Theodosius, and claimed always to be acting in Arcadius' best interests. So Claudian is always very careful to dissociate Arcadius from the alleged crimes of his ministers: and even more careful not to suggest for a moment that Arcadius might share their hostility to Stilico. In *de bello Gildonico* he pretends that Arcadius was misled by specious promises from Gildo, whom he at once renounced on learning the 'truth'. Rufinus he represents as forcing Arcadius with threats to forbid Stilico access to eastern territory. But he does not attempt to make out that Eutropius coerced Arcadius. We happen to know from other sources that Arcadius was in fact devoted to Eutropius, and wept at his fall. Claudian could not of course admit this, since it would imply that Arcadius sympathized with Eutropius' anti-Stiliconian policy. So he solves his problem by simply saying nothing at all about their relationship.

In *Stil.* i he damns the whole eastern court in the warmest terms. But in Bk. ii he is very careful to add, after his usual reaffirmation of Stilico's regency over Arcadius:

> nec si quid iners atque impia turba
> praetendens proprio nomen regale furori
> audeat, adscribis iuveni [i.e. Arcadius] (*Stil.* ii. 78 f.).

Did Claudian perhaps feel—or did Stilico perhaps point out—that he had gone just a little too far in Bk. i? No one could mistake his warning that the policy of the eastern court was nothing but the machinations of a corrupt cabal sheltering behind the name of their unwilling, or unknowing, Emperor.

There is only one passage which constitutes a partial exception to this otherwise remarkably consistent attitude to Arcadius throughout Claudian's political poems. In his epithalamium for Honorius, Claudian makes the young Emperor proudly deny that he had chosen his bride from a picture:

> non ego luxuriem regum moremque secutus
> quaesivi vultum tabulis ut nuntia formae
> lena per innumeros iret pictura penates (*Nupt.* 23–5).

Now we learn from Zosimus that Arcadius' interest in the future Empress Eudoxia was indeed aroused by pictures of her, shown to him secretly by the cunning Eutropius.[1] There can be little doubt that this is what Claudian is alluding to. But it is a harmless enough sally, with no direct bearing on the relationship between Arcadius and Stilico: excused, moreover, by the facts (*a*) that it entails a compliment to Honorius and (*b*) that it is indeed placed in the mouth of Honorius. Perhaps too it was aimed not so much at Arcadius as at Eutropius and Eudoxia. Consider Claudian's prayer at the end of the poem:

> sic puer Eucherius superet virtute parentem;
> aurea sic videat similes Thermantia taedas;

[1] v. 3. 3.

> sic uterus crescat Mariae; sic natus in ostro
> parvus Honoriades genibus considat avitis (*Nupt.* 338 f.).

How could Thermantia make a 'similar' match to Maria, wife of Honorius? Only it would seem, by marrying Arcadius. Was Stilico perhaps hoping that when he had managed to bring about Eutropius' fall, Arcadius might be induced to divorce Eudoxia, Eutropius' nominee, and marry Thermantia instead? Compare now with this passage the other dynastic passage in Claudian concerning Stilico's family: their representation on the embroidery of Stilico's consular robe. Here Claudian makes much capital out of the marriages between Stilico and Serena and Honorius and Maria, and hints at the forthcoming match (in fact fated never to take place) between Eucherius and Galla Placidia. But all he says of Thermantia, two years later, when she was much more nearly marriageable than in 398 and in a context wholly devoted to past and future dynastic marriages of the house of Stilico, is that she smiled at her brother:

> Eucherius trepido iam flammea sublevat ore
> virginis; adridet retro Thermantia fratri (*Stil.* ii. 358–9).

Why does Claudian not repeat here, in more precise and emphatic terms, the hope that Thermantia might equal her sister's good fortune? Surely because by 400 Eudoxia had survived—indeed in large measure engineered—the fall of Eutropius (August 399) with increased power, and now dominated her feeble-minded husband. There was no longer the slightest possibility of Arcadius divorcing her for Thermantia or anyone else. Thus it was pointless for Claudian to repeat the fond hopes he had expressed in the earlier poem. But it can now be seen that the one apparently uncharacteristic allusion to Arcadius there may well have had a very specific contemporary justification and purpose: to discredit, not Arcadius, but Arcadius' marriage to Eudoxia.

Claudian constantly, of course, praises Stilico's military prowess. This might seem so obvious a feature of any panegyric on any general as not to be worth mentioning as a specifically propagandist theme. Yet once more Claudian does not confine himself to mere general eulogy (though naturally there is much of this as well). Already in 396, as we saw in the last chapter, he had stressed that Stilico had been at Theodosius' side in every one of his victories:

> quid enim per proelia gessi
> te sine, quem merui te non sudante triumphum?
> Odrysium pariter Getico foedavimus Hebrum
> sanguine, Sarmaticas pariter prostravimus alas . . .
> (*III Cons.* 146 f.).

Cf. too *Nupt.* 220 f.,

> quicquid ab innumeris *socio Stilicone* tremendus
> quaesivit genitor [sc. Theodosius] bellis . . .

And in 398, in another speech placed in the mouth of Theodosius, now speaking from the world of the dead in a dream:

> ut sileam varios mecum quos gesserit actus,
> quae vidi post fata loquar . . . (*Gild.* 291 f.).

Claudian subtly implies that Stilico's earlier achievements together with Theodosius are too well known to need recapitulation. In fact, with the one exception of his expedition against the Bastarnae in 392, which terminated in a negotiated treaty, not a battle, there were no earlier achievements in this sphere. Whatever he may have thought of Stilico's abilities in other directions, Theodosius does not seem to have valued him highly as a general. It was not till the last months of his life that he promoted Stilico to commander of all western forces, and this only because he had decided, by virtue rather of his connection with the Imperial house than his military virtues, to make him Honorius' regent. We know of at least one major expedition of Theodosius' in which Stilico did not take part, and if he did take part in all the others (and there is no evidence that he did) it will have been very much in a subordinate role.

It seems in fact to have been part of official Stiliconian propaganda to emphasize at once Stilico's outstanding military ability and Theodosius' recognition of it. For we find precisely the same tendentious claim on official inscriptions, where he is described as 'comiti divi Theodosi Augusti in *omnibus* bellis adque victoriis' (*CIL* vi. 1730, in 398), and compare *CIL* vi. 1731 (in 406), 'socio bellorum *omnium* et victoriarum' of Theodosius. One critic has argued that these inscriptions show that Claudian was merely reflecting a popular theme of the day.[1] But it is naïve to suppose that Stilico would have allowed stone-cutters to inscribe just what they pleased on the base of statues of himself erected in the Forum of Rome.

Again in *Laus Serenae* (*c.m.* xxx) 179 f. Claudian claims that it was for his outstanding military achievements that Theodosius chose Stilico as husband for Serena: and at *Stil.* i. 71 that he chose Stilico 'simul imperioque ducem nataeque maritum', as though already in 384 Theodosius had been looking for someone to play the role Stilico did in fact play after Theodosius' death. But at this date Stilico had neither displayed nor had any opportunity to display any such martial prowess. Theodosius does not seem to have entrusted him with an independent military command until as late as 392. It would seem as if it was Serena herself, not Theodosius at all, who chose Stilico for her husband—one of those very rare events in a royal family, a love match. Theodosius must have given his blessing, but he did not show Stilico any special marks of favour until some years after the marriage.[2] But it was very necessary for Claudian to represent Stilico's past military achievements in the most favourable light possible, and to underline the confidence Theodosius had placed in his generalship, since in the years following Theodosius' death, his military record had been lamentable. He did not win a single decisive victory until Faesulae in 406.[3]

Naturally enough, Claudian loses no opportunity of drawing attention to Stilico's marriage with Serena, Theodosius' favourite

---

[1] Fargues, p. 60, n. 2, and cf. Hartke, *Röm. Kinderkaiser* (1951), 237–8.

[2] See Demougeot, pp. 129 f. for all details of Stilico's career, though on his supposed presence in Italy in 388/9, see *Harvard Studies* lxxiii (1968), 266, n. 41.

[3] Nor, it seems, did he ever actually direct his battles in person: cf. Fargues p. 124.

niece and (after her own father's death) his adoptive daughter. The titles *socer* and *gener* appear in Claudian almost as often as in Lucan.

Mommsen argued[1] that Serena was never actually adopted by Theodosius, on the basis of *CIL* vi. 1730, where Stilico is styled '*progener*', not '*gener*' of the blessed Theodosius. If this were true, Claudian would stand convicted of a grave misrepresentation of the truth, for at *Laus Serenae* (*c.m.* xxx) 104–5 he explicitly describes the adoption:

> defuncto genitore tuo sublimis *adoptat*
> te patruus . . .

But Mommsen is almost certainly wrong. Here is the relevant part of the inscription:

. . . progenero divi Theodosii, comiti divi Theodosii Augusti in omnibus bellis adque victoriis et ab eo in adfinitatem regiam cooptato . . .

Unless the inscription was drafted more carelessly than it would be safe to assume in a compliment to such an important man, an attempt is being made to distinguish between two different Theodosii, Theodosius Augustus, the Emperor, and his father, Count Theodosius. Before as after her adoption, Serena had been the elder Theodosius' granddaughter, and since 'progener' properly means 'husband of a granddaughter', surely then 'progener divi Theodosii' describes Stilico's relationship to the elder Theodosius.[2] Thus there is no sufficient reason to question the adoption. But the capital Claudian makes out of Stilico's marriage is none the less significant for being justified.

It was only to be expected, then, that Claudian would exploit to the full the subsequent marriage of Maria to Honorius. Not only was Stilico an Emperor's son-in-law, he was father-in-law of an Emperor as well. Claudian was not slow to make the point:

> gener Augusti pridem fueras,
> nunc rursus eris socer Augusti (*Fesc.* iii. 8–9).

---

[1] *Hermes* xxxviii (1903), 102, n. 1 (*Ges. Schr.* iv. 517, n. 1).
[2] Cf. too Mazzarino, p. 104, n. 4.

In the same year Theodosius is represented as appealing to Arcadius to respect Stilico's wishes with the words:

> at soceri reverere faces, at respice fratris
> conubium, pignusque meae regale Serenae (*Gild.* 309–10).

When appealing to his troops, in 402, Stilico invokes 'quam sanctum soceri nomen, quam dulce mariti . . .' and of course his 'carior omni | luce gener' (*Get.* 318 f.).

Up till Honorius' marriage, Serena had been (after her adoption) Honorius' sister. A useful enough relationship to the Emperor, and naturally Claudian exploits it. But after the marriage she became his mother-in-law, a rather closer and still more useful relationship. Significantly enough, Claudian never mentions the sister relationship after 398.[1] Even in the epithalamium she is praised for being more of a mother than a sister to him all along (*Nupt.* 38 f.).

Another motif, linked to this one, to which Claudian constantly recurs, is the continuity of policy between Stilico and Theodosius. Stilico is always represented as the loyal servant of Theodosius while he lived, and as the loyal executor of his wishes after his death. Theodosius is made to say of Stilico:

> hunc solum memorem solumque fidelem
> experior . . . (*Gild.* 305–6).

The destruction of Gildo is represented as something Theodosius had been on the point of doing when he died; the marriage of Honorius to Maria had been long since planned by Theodosius. . . . The fact that Stilico did in general adhere closely to the policies of Theodosius does not detract from the significance of the manner in which Claudian draws attention to it. Propaganda does not have to be false.

Lastly, not the least important of Claudian's devices is simple omission. Very often what he does not say is just as significant, sometimes more so, than what he does. Two examples must suffice. The most important single event of 397 was Eutropius' declaration of Stilico as *hostis publicus* in the name of Arcadius:

---

[1] See below, p. 407.

naturally this put Stilico in a highly embarrassing and delicate position. Claudian wrote no fewer than four full-length poems in 397-8, in none of which did he suggest for a moment that there was the slightest hitch in relations between Arcadius and Stilico. Another eloquent omission is his complete failure to mention in a single one of his poems the Goth, Gainas, who played such an important part in the fall of both Rufinus and Eutropius, not to mention the revolt of Tribigild to which Claudian devotes so much of Bk. ii of the *In Eutropium*. Again this must be deliberate.[1]

I propose then to work on the assumption that Claudian was Stilico's official propagandist. The importance of this should be obvious, but it has seldom been fully appreciated or stated in so many words. It means that Claudian's poems can, with all due caution of course, be used to reconstruct Stilico's policies: or—perhaps more interesting and certainly no less important—how Stilico wished his aims and actions to appear to contemporaries. In short, they offer a unique opportunity to see how a Roman government justified its policy to its subjects year by year—and on occasions month by month. More generally they make it perfectly clear what the basic goal of Stilico's policy was during all the period in which Claudian served him—that is to say from 396 to 404.

For a long time it was widely believed that the keynote of Stilico's policy was to wrest control of the diocese of Illyricum from the eastern government. This view (first proposed by Mommsen)[2] finds no direct support in our sources. It is a retrojection to 395 of the intention Olympiodorus ascribed to Stilico in 405 (according, that is, to the rather incoherent abstract of Olympiodorus made by Photius).[3] That this was Stilico's aim in 405 seems likely enough: but there is no reason to suppose it was also his aim in 395. Indeed there is every reason to suppose that it

[1] These 'omissions' are discussed at length in later chapters.
[2] For full bibliography on the Illyricum question, see V. Grumel, *Rev. Ét. Byz.* ix (1952), 5 f., whose conclusions, in essentials, I accept.
[3] Olympiodorus, frag. 3 (cf. Zosimus v. 26. 2), *FHG* iv. 58 *b*.

was not. Nowhere in all the ten political poems Claudian wrote between 396 and 404 (three in two or more books) is there the faintest suggestion that Stilico wanted to gain control of Illyricum. On the contrary, in two passages Claudian writes as though Alaric's devastation of eastern Illyricum was a disaster which affected the *eastern*, not the western court (*Gild.* 311 f., *Eutr.* ii. 142 f.).[1]

A refinement of this view is that at the death of Theodosius all Illyricum actually belonged to the West, but that in 395 Stilico was obliged to cede the eastern part to the East, and thereafter tried continually but unsuccessfully to recover it. Certainly by 396 eastern Illyricum was administered by the eastern government. The true explanation however, is that at Theodosius' death all Illyricum belonged to the East, and that the East ceded western Illyricum to Stilico. There is one decisive piece of evidence that Stilico could not lay claim to any of Illyricum in 395: a speech Claudian places in the mouth of Rufinus. Rufinus is protesting about Stilico's ambition:

> succumbere poscit [sc. Stilico]
> cuncta sibi: regit Italiam Libyamque coercet;
> Hispanis Gallisque iubet (*Ruf.* ii. 153 f.).

Rufinus is trying to make the point that Stilico controls quite enough of the Empire already and should not be trying to encroach on Arcadius' share: hence his list of the areas Stilico controls is exhaustive. Had Stilico controlled in addition only western Illyricum (modern Austria and Yugoslavia), let alone eastern Illyricum as well (the whole of the Balkan peninsula), an area as large as Gaul and Italy together, then Claudian could not have failed to include it in Rufinus' list.[2] And if Stilico had had any designs on eastern Illyricum at this period, then it is surely inconceivable that his propagandist—and so skilful a propagandist

[1] Note also that at *Eutr.* i. 196 Claudian assigns to Eutropius jurisdiction over all the territory between the Tigris and Mt. Haemus.
[2] Cf. also *Ruf.* ii. 304 f., which clearly implies that the closest Stilico could get to Constantinople in 395 without crossing into Arcadius' territory was the frontier of Italy.

as Claudian—should have openly admitted that he had no right even to western Illyricum. Moreover, if Stilico had ceded eastern Illyricum, then, as Baynes observed,[1] Claudian would have certainly praised him for his generous sacrifice in the interest of concord between the two brothers—just as he praises him for his loyal obedience in ceding half his army to the eastern government at about the same time as he is supposed to have ceded eastern Illyricum (*Ruf.* ii. 197 f., *Stil.* ii. 95 f.).

That Stilico did control western Illyricum from 396 on we know from one very explicit passage in Claudian. In his panegyric on the consulate of Mallius Theodorus in 399, he carefully enumerates all the lands administered by Theodorus as praetorian prefect of Italy, an office in which he is first attested in January 397. The list is as follows:

> prima [sc. habena, i.e. rein of his judicial carriage] Padum Thybrimque ligat, crebrisque micantem
> urbibus Italiam; Numidas Poenosque secunda
> temperat; *Illyrico se tertia porrigit orbi*;
> ultima Sardiniam . . . (*Theod.* 200 f.).

And in 400 Claudian lists among the lands which had experienced the benefits of the Stiliconian regime, Gaul, Africa, and western Illyricum ('Pannonius potorque Savi', *Stil.* ii. 192). But there is no mention of the eastern part of Illyricum. Most striking of all, perhaps, is the list of provinces urging that Stilico should accept the consulate for 400; only Spain, Gaul, Britain, Africa, and Italy.[2] Claudian did not even bother to include Pannonia or Dalmatia. Had it really been Stilico's one overriding ambition at this period to get control of eastern Illyricum, then Claudian must have included it in such lists, or in some other way made it perfectly clear that by right, if not in fact, it should have been there. It is

---

[1] *JRS* xviii (1928), 224, and against Levy, *Invective In Rufinum* (1935), 34, see Mazzarino, p. 65, n. 3 (on p. 66).

[2] This cannot, however, be used as evidence that Stilico did not control even western Illyricum in 400, since, even if not too much weight can be laid on *Stil.* ii. 192 (cf. Grumel, *Rev. Ét. Byz.* ix (1952), 31, n. 2), *Theod.* 200 f. must be held decisive in this respect.

out of the question that he should have so misunderstood Stilico's aims, or expressed them so carelessly, as to concede the very fact that Stilico was trying so hard to deny: that eastern Illyricum was in fact firmly in the control of the East.

The only possible conclusion to be drawn from Claudian's references to Illyricum is that in 395 Stilico neither controlled nor apparently had any designs on any part of Illyricum: and that although he administered western Illyricum from 396 on (no doubt ceded to him by Eutropius for defence purposes), he did not apparently attach any particular importance to the fact and did not publicize it unduly. At no time up to 404 did he lay any claim to eastern Illyricum. In short, that for the whole of the period from 395 to 404, control of Illyricum was not a live political issue.

Our only reliable guide for Stilico's intentions during this period is Claudian. And it is perfectly clear from Claudian that Stilico's one ambition was simply to unite the two halves of the Empire. Nominally, of course, under the joint rule of Arcadius and Honorius, but Claudian's insistence in poem after poem on the regency—even as late as 400, when Honorius was 20—shows clearly enough that the real ruler was to be Stilico himself. In Claudian's eyes the crime of the eastern government was not to have obstructed Stilico's claim to eastern Illyricum (in fact he not only never makes this accusation, but openly concedes that it belonged to the East), but to have opposed the unification of the Empire, and to have promoted discord instead of concord be-tween East and West.

Had Stilico entertained only the far less grandiose ambitions ascribed to him by Mommsen and his followers, then it is im-possible to believe that he would have allowed Claudian to mis-represent him so seriously and so consistently in virtually every poem he wrote.

IV

RUFINUS

NOTHING is known of the early career of Flavius Rufinus, but by 388 we find him in Constantinople as master of offices. He rapidly became Theodosius' most trusted minister, and in 392 was honoured with the consulate.

The consulate was the supreme mark of Imperial favour, but the most important civil magistracy was the praetorian prefecture of the East. In 392 this was held by Tatian, consul the year before, whose son Proculus was city prefect. Rufinus managed to secure the dismissal of both men, and was himself appointed prefect of the East in Tatian's place. Once in office he engineered their trial and condemnation as well: Proculus was actually executed, but at the last minute Theodosius commuted Tatian's sentence to exile.[1]

With the fall of the house of Tatian, Rufinus was supreme. But his supremacy was not to the liking of all. Theodosius' military leaders (notably Promotus and Stilico) were especially resentful of the ascendancy this upstart civilian exerted over the Emperor. Indeed, feeling between Rufinus and Promotus ran so high that on one occasion Promotus actually struck Rufinus in public. Rufinus soon secured Promotus' banishment from court, and shortly afterwards he died fighting in Thrace. Thus Stilico and Rufinus had been personal enemies for some while before the death of Theodosius made them political rivals.

On Theodosius' death Rufinus became effective ruler of the

---

[1] For all sources concerning the career of Rufinus see, in addition to the standard works (Bury, Seeck, Stein, Demougeot, and *PLRE*, no. 18), the excellent account in the introduction to H. L. Levy's edition of the *In Rufinum* (N.Y., 1935), pp. 1–26. I have not thought it worth while to document any but controversial statements.

East. But his supremacy was now far from secure. For his success so far he had been entirely dependent on the favour of Theodosius. Arcadius, however, did not share his father's confidence in Rufinus. A telling illustration of this is provided by the affair of Lucian, count of the East.

Eucherius, a great-uncle of Arcadius, had asked an unreasonable favour of Lucian, which Lucian very properly refused. Eucherius complained to Arcadius, and Arcadius blamed Rufinus (Lucian being Rufinus' protégé). Rufinus set off post-haste to Antioch (the residence of the count), where he had Lucian condemned, tortured, and put to death all at dead of night, for fear of his popularity with the people of Antioch. This at any rate is how Zosimus reports the affair.[1] It may be, as Zosimus implies, that Rufinus' motive was anxiety to repair his crumbling credit with Arcadius. But the punishment was out of all proportion to the offence, and why did Rufinus need to go to Antioch in person? There was surely more to it than this. Perhaps Rufinus had reason to believe that Lucian was directing (or at any rate privy to) some conspiracy against himself. This alone would explain why it was necessary that he should be put to death. But however the incident is interpreted, the drastic measures Rufinus took are clear evidence of his insecurity.

Even before this, Rufinus had apparently been hoping to strengthen his uncertain position by marrying his daughter to Arcadius. According to Zosimus,[2] his plans were foiled by the cunning eunuch chamberlain, Eutropius, a man no less ambitious than Rufinus, and enjoying the advantage of a position which kept him closer to the Emperor than that of praetorian prefect. Zosimus' story is as follows. Eutropius looked out a rival bride for Arcadius, a girl who had been brought up in the house of Rufinus' bitterest enemy, Promotus, since the death of her father (another of Theodosius' generals). He secretly persuaded Arcadius that this girl, Eudoxia, would make him a better wife than Rufinus'

---

[1] v. 2. 3 (Zosimus calls Eucherius Arcadius' uncle, but he must in fact have been a great-uncle: cf. J. R. Martindale, *Historia* xvi (1967), 254, and stemma, p. xiv).
[2] v. 3.

daughter. It was not till the wedding day itself, when the Imperial carriage drew up outside the house of Promotus instead of his own, that Rufinus learnt what had happened.

Clearly we cannot accept this just as it stands (though many have). It is all a little too dramatic. Could Rufinus have survived such a humiliating public blow to his already tottering position? But a modified version may still be retained. In view of his position it is likely enough that Rufinus may at least have hoped to marry his daughter to Arcadius, and when it became known that Eutropius' protégée was to become the new Empress, people would inevitably have construed it as a setback for Rufinus. Zosimus' story is no doubt a written up and dramatized version, put about by Rufinus' enemies. But it must surely be a contemporary story, for what would have been the point of inventing it after Rufinus' fall?

With his influence at home rapidly waning, Rufinus was faced with two serious external threats. First, there was Stilico's claim to the regency over Arcadius which Rufinus had been exercising *de facto* since Theodosius' death. And given their personal relationship, Rufinus had not much to hope for if Stilico returned to Constantinople to take up the regency in person.

Secondly, a wave of barbarian invasions had suddenly descended on the eastern provinces. Apart from the Hunnic and Marcoman inroads already mentioned, the Visigoths, whom Theodosius had settled inside the Danube frontier in Moesia, had revolted under the energetic leadership of their new king, Alaric,[1] and were devastating Dacia and Macedonia. Indeed Alaric advanced to the walls of Constantinople itself. With the eastern army still in Italy where Theodosius had led it in 394, Rufinus was helpless to deal with any of these dangers. After some negotiations (and presumably the payment of a large subsidy) Alaric withdrew from Constantinople: but he did not return to Moesia, and the devastation of eastern Illyricum continued.

It was only natural that Stilico, who had under his command all Imperial forces and was eager, moreover, to establish his authority

[1] See below, p. 156, n. 4.

over Arcadius, should have taken this opportunity of intervening in eastern affairs. In about September 395 he arrived in Thessaly at the head of both eastern and western armies, and soon ran Alaric to earth. The Goths were surrounded and blockaded behind the defences they had hurriedly thrown up.

Exactly what happened next is uncertain, but, for whatever reason, Alaric was allowed to retreat with his army still more or less intact. (The matter will be discussed in detail in Chapter VII.) Stilico then dispatched the eastern forces back to Arcadius: while Stilico returned to Italy, the eastern army, under the command of Gainas, marched to Constantinople. On its arrival there Arcadius came outside the city to inspect the troops, accompanied by Rufinus. Why this particular occasion was chosen, and to what extent the deed was planned in advance is far from clear, but the army literally tore Rufinus to pieces on the spot.

Thus perished in spectacular fashion the only man (so Stilico fondly hoped) who stood in his way. It cannot have caused much surprise in Milan when, early the next year, Stilico's newly acquired propagandist delivered a slashing invective on the fallen minister, a justification, indeed a glorification of the murder.

Now it so happens, as a result of the deficiencies of our other authorities, that we are thrown back on the *In Rufinum* for most of our knowledge of both Rufinus and the events of 395. But just because it is an important historical source, that is no reason why it should be treated, as it too often is, as history. Few nowadays would go so far as one nineteenth-century German scholar, who postulated a lacuna in Bk. ii on the ground that the text as it stands omits a stage of Stilico's march to Thessaly. It would be dangerous enough to posit a lacuna in the text of a historian just because he does not tell us quite all we think he ought to have told us, but to treat a poet like this is nothing short of absurd. Yet even P. Fargues, one of Claudian's more sympathetic commentators in modern times, after stating firmly enough that Claudian is a poet, not a historian, goes on to reproach him for lacking 'les qualités morales et scientifiques d'un historien', and for not appreciating 'les faits d'un ordre social et économique qui explicaient la faiblesse de l'empire'![1] It is clear that, for all his *caveats*, Fargues too was under the impression that Claudian was trying to write a history of his times, but failed. One does not need to read far into *In Rufinum* to see that nothing was further from his mind.

Book i opens with a brilliant mock-solemn exordium, in which it is claimed that Rufinus' fall has justified the dealings of God with men:

> iam non ad culmina rerum
> iniustos crevisse queror: tolluntur in altum
> ut lapsu graviore ruant.

The poem proper opens with a council of the Furies in Hades. Allecto speaks first, complaining that it is high time that the prosperity brought to Earth by Theodosius came to an end. She suggests that the Furies venture forth together into the light of day and do their worst. Then Megaera takes the floor: she has a much better idea. For some time now she has been seeing to the education of a creature of unprecedented and unimaginable wickedness:

> prodigium cunctis immanius hydris,
> tigride mobilius feta . . . (89 f.).

His name—what but Rufinus? So ready a pupil did he prove that before long he had outstripped even his teacher in the black arts, Megaera herself: 'ipsa quidem vinci fateor' (109). In short, she concludes: 'solus habet scelerum quicquid possedimus omnes' (111). The surest way to bring the Empire to disaster, she suggests, is to make Rufinus a minister at court. The Furies are delighted, and abandon their original plan. Megaera gives Rufinus his instructions, and he sets off for Constantinople, where he makes his evil influence felt at once.

We are then treated to a lively, if hackneyed, catalogue of Rufinus' crimes and vices. He betrayed secrets, deceived his clients, sold offices, and was no more sated by the gold that kept

[1] pp. 45 and 40.

tumbling into his coffers than Ocean is by the rivers which continually flow into it. (The tirade is interrupted by a rather unseasonable homily on Rufinus' folly in preferring Tyrian purple to the green sward: 'Vivitur exiguo melius . . .') We then return to Rufinus' greed, his shamelessness, his perjury, his savage fury, more deadly when foiled than a Hyrcanian tiger or that other favourite of Latin poets, the wounded Gaetulian lioness. He delights to torture his victims: the brutality of such stock monsters as Sinis and Sciron, Phalaris (bull and all) and Sulla naturally pales into insignificance beside that of Rufinus:

> o mites Diomedis equi! Busiridis arae
> clementes! iam Cinna pius, iam, Spartace, segnis
> Rufino collatus eris! (254 f.)

Fargues reproaches Claudian for exaggerating Rufinus' vices, and solemnly concludes that 'le jugement de Claudien dans son ensemble est d'une sévérité excessive et d'une partialité manifeste, puisqu'il ne tient compte que des vices de Rufin et omet systématiquement les qualités qu'il devait avoir.' This is entirely to misunderstand the point of the *In Rufinum*. It might be a fair enough comment had Claudian been writing a biography of Rufinus. But he was not. He was writing an invective, and the invective was a recognized literary genre of its own. One has only to read, for example, Cicero's *In Pisonem* to see that the author of an invective did not feel himself bound by the same standards of veracity or relevance as the historian. It was thought perfectly legitimate to make the most startling allegations of vice, cruelty, and corruption without the remotest degree of justification or plausibility—or, apparently, the slightest fear of exposure or refutation. Claudian's audience naturally came expecting a display such as he gave them—not a balanced assessment of Rufinus' career taking into account all the relevant social and economic factors. And they certainly will not have taken Claudian's accusations as seriously as many modern scholars. Such inventions 'were meant to cause pain or hilarity, not to be believed'.[1] Terms like 'judgement' and 'partiality' are simply not

[1] R. G. M. Nisbet, Cicero, *In Pisonem* (Oxford, 1961), 191.

appropriate to an invective. Claudian, like the modern cartoonist —and his technique often resembles that of the political cartoonist —is not giving a 'judgement', partial or otherwise: this was not the point of the exercise. He was writing an invective, in which— and his audience knew this as well as he did—it was just not done to allow the possibility that the victim might have any good qualities. It was an exercise in the art of vituperation. The historian would naturally have preferred a balanced assessment: but he must not reproach Claudian for not doing what he did not set out to do.

It is worth noting that throughout this tirade Claudian only cites three concrete illustrations in support of his allegations, two of which are different aspects of the Tatian affair (and the Tatian affair is not really a good illustration of Rufinus' cruelty, for which Claudian cites it). All the rest is elegant, if often commonplace, variation on the stock themes of invective. But to relieve the monotony of a mere list of such *exempla*, Claudian conceived the original and entertaining idea of lifting Rufinus' wickedness far above the level of ordinary mortal transgressions. He represents him as the nursling of the powers of Evil, sent into the world to destroy it. This note of fantasy runs through the whole poem. At the end of Bk. i Megaera puts in another appearance, crowing over all the turmoil and distress her pupil has been causing. And at the end of Bk. ii, after his death, Rufinus is haled before the judgement seat of Minos in Hades, where it is decreed that the run-of-the-mill punishments suffered by such cosmic convicts as Tantalus and Tityos are quite inadequate for Rufinus: he is sentenced to be hurled below the prison of the Titans, below Tartarus, below the foundations of deepest Night for evermore.

One advantage accruing from this alleged demonic quality in Rufinus' wickedness is that, when Claudian is stuck for a motive for some action he ascribes to him (and many of Rufinus' alleged misdeeds do seem singularly pointless on any rational calculation), he can always fall back on sheer delight in evil (e.g. ii. 62 f.). Another and more substantial advantage is that he can gloss over the means whereby Rufinus insinuated himself into Theodosius' favour in the first place. After all, it did not reflect much credit on an Emperor to place so much power in the hands of so unworthy a minister as Claudian paints Rufinus. It is clear that Claudian did feel this to be a problem. For he makes Megaera conclude her plan of unleashing Rufinus on the Imperial court with the words:

> Sit licet ipse [sc. Theodosius] Numa gravior, sit denique Minos,
> cedet, et insidiis nostri flectetur alumni (114–15).

If Rufinus' elevation to Theodosius' right hand is the result of a plot by the powers of darkness against humanity, then Theodosius can hardly be held responsible for his crimes in the ordinary way. Thus Claudian is enabled neatly to sidestep the awkward circumstance that Theodosius had in fact evidently preferred Rufinus even to Stilico himself. He had made Rufinus consul, but not Stilico (it is significant that Claudian is careful never to mention Rufinus' consulate:[1] contrast the capital he later made out of Eutropius' ill-starred consulate).

However, like the cartoonist again, Claudian did have a serious purpose in writing the *In Rufinum*. But he did not hope to achieve this purpose by heaping accusations of greed and cruelty on Rufinus' head. Fargues devotes several pages to these topics, collecting the evidence of other writers on Rufinus' addiction to these two particular vices, and concluding that they confirm the essential accuracy of Claudian's picture. But if Rufinus used his position to line his own pockets, so did every other Roman magistrate of the day. Indeed to judge by the sermons St. Ambrose addressed to the same Milanese grandees who formed Claudian's audience, they were by no means strangers to this vice themselves.[2] And if Rufinus was cruel, the fourth century was a cruel age. We read in the pages of Ammian and the *Code* of hair-raising tortures being employed simply as a matter of course: both Theodosius and his father were guilty of acts of brutality far

---

[1] Thus Platnauer is wrong to translate ii. 82 'One who drives a consul's chariot': Claudian is alluding to the chariot of the praetorian prefect, frequently mentioned in honorific epigrams of the period: cf. *CQ* N.S. xviii (1968), 393.

[2] Cf. Homes Dudden, *St. Ambrose* ii (1935), 465 f.

exceeding anything Rufinus did. Rufinus may well have been unusually cruel and avaricious, but Claudian would certainly have made just the same accusations even if he had not been. And he surely did not expect to stir up any very deep indignation in his audience this way. We must try to distinguish between the mud which he slung merely to entertain, and the mud he intended to stick.

A good example of the latter is his accusation that Rufinus repeatedly betrayed the Empire to barbarians: a skilful mixing of fact and fiction to produce some very neat propaganda. Claudian details three separate acts of treachery.

First, it was Rufinus, he claims, who in 392 whipped up the Bastarnae—or as Claudian preferred to have it, Sarmatians and Dacians, Massagetae drinking mares' blood jostling with Alans fresh from breaking the ice on Lake Maeotis and, of course, some tattooed Geloni—to destroy Promotus. As with his allusions to Tatian and Lucian (p. 80), Claudian does not mention Promotus by name:[1] the most oblique allusion was sufficient for such a recent and notorious event:

> iamque Getas Histrumque movet Scythiamque receptat
> auxilio, traditque suas hostilibus armis
> reliquias (i. 308 f.).

In the context *reliquias* must mean 'that which was left over or spared' from his savagery: that is to say Promotus, who was spared the fate of Lucian, Tatian, and Proculus only to be handed over to Rufinus' barbarian 'friends'. That Rufinus did actually betray Promotus to the Bastarnae is almost inconceivable (other considerations apart, it is difficult to see how a civilian in Constantinople could have helped a barbarian tribe in Thrace to defeat a Roman army, even had he wished). But to contemporaries it might have seemed too much of a coincidence that Rufinus' bitterest enemy should have perished so very opportunely so

---

[1] But he does so when retelling the story at *Stil.* i. 94 f.: eight years after the event it was advisable to be more explicit if his readers were not going to miss the allusion.

very soon after Rufinus had persuaded Theodosius to send him
out to the frontier.

Second, when Stilico was sent out to revenge Promotus' death,
Rufinus (so Claudian alleges) anxious to protect his 'friends' the
Bastarnae tricked Theodosius ('eluso principe', 320) into for-
bidding Stilico to finish them off when he had them in his power:

> vetat ille domari,
> innectitque moras et congrua tempora differt (314–15).

His motive, according to Claudian, was to allow some Huns
(whom he had also 'invited') time to come up and reinforce the
Bastarnae. Stilico, of course, easily defeats their combined forces:
Mars himself lent a hand, and together they routed the foe, 'et
clipeis et mole pares' (351).

Claudian is curiously reticent in *In Rufinum* about this 'delay'
Rufinus engineered. Four years later he gives more details:
Stilico had the Bastarnae at his mercy,

> extinctique forent penitus, ni more maligno
> falleret Augustas occultus proditor [sc. Rufinus] aures,
> obstrueretque moras strictumque reconderet ensem,
> solveret obsessos, praeberet foedera captis (*Stil.* i. 112 f.).

One can only admire the skill and audacity with which Claudian
has twisted the facts to serve his purpose.[1]

When Theodosius came to the throne in 379, the Empire was
faced with perhaps the most serious barbarian danger in its
history.[2] The year before the Romans had suffered at the hands of
the Goths their most crushing defeat since Cannae, the whole
Roman army having been almost annihilated. Theodosius, realizing that he could not hope to defeat the Goths in battle, tried to
win them over by peaceful means. His policy of heaping gifts and
honours on the Gothic optimates soon paid dividends: many of
them went over to the Romans (Gainas for one), and the rank
and file of the Goths were settled in Moesia and Scythia, where
Theodosius had been able to call upon their services as federates
for his armies. Since therefore it was Theodosius' standard policy

---

[1] Bury, for example, *LRE* i². 107, n. 3, uncritically accepts this version.
[2] For more details, see below, p. 156.

not to destroy barbarians in battle if he could negotiate with them, settle them within the Empire, and use them to supplement the depleted Roman armies, it did not require deceitful advice from Rufinus[1] or anyone else to persuade Theodosius to conclude a treaty with the Bastarnae. And Stilico, whom subsequent events reveal to have held essentially the same views as Theodosius on the barbarian question,[2] must obviously have been acting from the beginning on orders from Theodosius to negotiate with the Bastarnae if possible. Both were doubtless well satisfied with this conclusion to the Bastarnae menace. Such 'philo-barbarism', however, was highly unpopular with the greater part of the population of the Empire, peasant and noble alike. So Claudian neatly transferred this particular blot from the copy-book of Stilico and Theodosius to that of Rufinus. It was Rufinus, he claims, who had tricked them into sparing the Bastarnae.

The third alleged instance of Rufinus' treachery is the claim made at the beginning of Bk. ii that it was Rufinus who sparked off all the barbarian invasions which followed the death of Theodosius—especially of course Alaric's devastation of the Balkans and siege of Constantinople. This accusation is, if anything, even less plausible than the other two. What Rufinus, already unpopular enough with most sectors of the population, could possibly have hoped to gain by inviting the Goths to attack Constantinople and then paying them to go away again, Claudian does not attempt to explain. He paints instead a fantastic picture of Rufinus joyfully gazing down from the battlements of the besieged city at the Goths laying waste the suburbs and surrounding countryside:

> obsessa tamen ille ferus laetatur in urbe
> exultatque malis summaeque ex culmine turris
> impia vicini cernit spectacula campi:
> vinctas ire nurus, hunc in vada proxima mergi
> seminecem, hunc subito percussum vulnere labi
> dum fugit, hunc animam portis efflare sub ipsis

---

[1] Mazzarino accepts this (p. 256, n. 1), but exclusively on the strength of the false reading *exceptis* for *praeceptis* at *Ruf.* ii. 71: on this see *CQ* N.S. xviii (1968), 392.   [2] pp. 370 f.

           . . . immensa voluptas
et risus plerumque subit; dolor afficit unus,
quod feriat non ipse manu! (61 f., 68 f.)

He openly boasted that the Goths were his friends, and when
he went to parley with them, actually wore Gothic costume.
(Whether or not Rufinus did wear Gothic costume, Claudian
knew what he was doing in exploiting the accusation. A year or
two earlier the pro-Gothic bishop Valens of Pettau had caused
great offence by wearing Gothic dress,[1] and in the very year in
which Claudian was writing Honorius had forbidden the wearing
of any barbarian dress by Roman citizens under the stiffest of
penalties—a ban reissued two years later.)[2]

Yet the three accusations prop each other up. And though few
modern scholars have taken them seriously (Romano however
appears to accept all three),[3] all our ancient sources, whether
dependent on Claudian or not, pagan or Christian, agree that
Rufinus was in league with the barbarians.

It is important to realize that Claudian's contemporaries did not
understand why it was that fresh barbarian hordes kept batter-
ing at the frontiers of the Empire, and were perfectly satisfied with
the explanation that someone had invited them. This is plainly
illustrated by the monotonous frequency with which barbarian
invasions are blamed (usually falsely and often absurdly) on
individual treachery throughout the later Empire. There had been
many barbarian attacks since Rufinus had come to power, and
many Romans had perished as a result. Surely someone was to
blame? A few may perhaps have been satisfied with the view of
Christian apologists, that it was all a judgement of God on the
vices of Rome. But most were looking for a more tangible
scapegoat. And why not Rufinus—especially now he was dead
and unable to defend himself?

This is surely one of the pieces of mud which Claudian in-

[1] Ambrose, *Epp.* 10. 9–10.
[2] *Cod. Theod.* xiv. 10. 1–2.
[3] pp. 72, 79: for a more sceptical view, É. Demougeot, 'Le préfet Rufin et les
barbares', *Mélanges Grégoire* ii (1950), 185 f.

tended to stick. It was not enough to assassinate a man just because he was cruel or avaricious. But if he could be shown to have betrayed Rome to the barbarians, that was a very different matter. Precisely the same accusation, ironically enough, was later used to justify the murder of Stilico himself.

Claudian says much about cruelty, greed, and barbarians. We come now to what he does not say. A suggestive example is the affair of Arcadius' marriage. However exaggerated Zosimus' story, we have seen that it must be contemporary. What grist to Claudian's mill! What clearer proof of Rufinus' boundless ambition, of his alleged plan to have himself declared co-Emperor? In short, a gift to anyone writing an invective on Rufinus. How well Claudian could have depicted Rufinus' baffled rage and humiliation as the Imperial carriage stopped at the wrong door.

Yet he did not touch it. The omission is certainly deliberate, since an allusion in a later poem proves that he was familiar with the event (p. 53). Two reasons, equally cogent, can readily be supplied.

First, it was Eutropius, not Stilico, who foiled this particular plan of Rufinus. Not only this: the affair revealed that Stilico was not, as Claudian so emphatically proclaimed, the only man who had dared to stand up to Rufinus. In fact there was a strong anti-Rufinian faction in Constantinople. It was no coincidence that Eutropius happened to choose a girl brought up in the house of Promotus to oust Rufinus' daughter from the Imperial bed. Eutropius exercised greater influence over Arcadius than Rufinus did, and Eudoxia, too, soon learnt how to dominate her feeble husband: indeed, four years later she prevailed upon him to depose Eutropius, the author of her own elevation. So it is not surprising that Claudian, anxious to ascribe all the dubious glory of Rufinus' grisly end to Stilico alone, is careful not to betray the extent and source of the home opposition to Rufinus. Hence too his citation of the Lucian affair merely in passing as an illustration of Rufinus' cruelty: it is a much better illustration of his waning influence and his insecurity.

The other point which cannot but have weighed with Claudian is the long-planned match between Honorius and Stilico's daughter. By the time Claudian wrote *Ruf.* ii (p. 78), Stilico must already have decided that the date might have to be advanced. And if it was to be a crime for Rufinus to try and marry a daughter to his Emperor, why should it be all right for Stilico to do the same? Much better to keep quiet about the whole thing.

Study of *Ruf.* has hitherto been impeded by the assumption that the two books were conceived together and form a unity. In fact Bk. ii has a very different character and purpose from that of Bk. i, and was written and recited a year after it.

The preface to Bk. ii alludes clearly to the outcome (according to Claudian successful)[1] of Stilico's second expedition to Greece in 397, and is actually addressed to Stilico. Plainly, therefore, it cannot have been written before Stilico's return from Greece in mid 397, more than eighteen months after Rufinus' death. Hence J. Koch contended that both books of the poem were first recited in mid 397. He argued that Claudian had wanted to perform them in front of Stilico himself, and that, Stilico having been kept busy campaigning since Rufinus' death, mid 397 was the first opportunity he had had. But it is impossible to believe that Stilico was away from Milan for the whole eighteen months up till then: indeed, there is positive evidence that he paid at least two visits there during this period.[2] Moreover, an invective on a fallen political rival would surely lose much of its point if not published as soon as possible after Rufinus' fall: eighteen months later Rufinus' fall was history, and the political situation quite different. And why is Stilico addressed only in the preface to Bk. ii?

Fargues[3] offers a different explanation: both books were recited early in 396, as soon as Claudian had finished them—and then again in mid 397. The preface to Bk. i he assumes to have been the original preface to both books for the first recitation: and

---

[1] For all details, Ch. VII.
[2] Demougeot, pp. 162–3: one such return is clearly attested by *CLE* 907.
[3] pp. 15–16.

since it names neither Honorius nor Stilico, he deduces that the
first recitation was given in the absence of both (it seems to have
been Claudian's standard practice to mention the fact in his preface
if his audience included either). The preface to Bk. ii he assumes
to have been added for the second recitation before Stilico.

This view does at least have the advantage of doing away with
the implausible eighteen months delay, but it is still open to the
serious objection, why was this new preface placed before Bk. ii?
A preface belongs at the beginning of a work, not half-way
through it. Surely it would have been easy enough to write a
new preface to Bk. i, or simply to add the apostrophe to Stilico
to the original preface. It is hard to see why Stilico should have
been made to sit through the whole of Bk. i and the now out-of-
date preface addressed only to the rank and file of the court
('sacra caterva', line 16) before being addressed himself and hearing his recent 'victory' hailed.

Koch[1] alone comments on what he regarded as the curious
anomaly of this apostrophe to Stilico being placed before Bk. ii
instead of Bk. i. He admits that he cannot explain it, but offers
three parallels: the only preface to the two books of *Eutr.* is
placed before Bk. ii, the only preface to the three books of *Stil.*
before Bk. iii, and though Bk. i of *Rapt.* has a preface, the preface
which names the dedicatee is placed before Bk. ii. Koch concludes,
mystified, that for some reason known only to himself, Claudian
did not like placing the preface to a work before the first book
of that work.

This would indeed be very strange—if it were true. In fact
there is a perfectly obvious and simple explanation of the phenomenon. The second book of *Eutr.* was written at least six months
after Bk. i, *Rapt.* ii probably several years after Bk. i, and *Stil.*
iii several weeks at least after i and ii. Clearly then each of these
books was delivered at a separate recitation from the earlier book
or books of the same poem. And since they were delivered
at a separate recitation, naturally enough they were equipped
with separate prefaces of their own, called forth by the new

---

[1] *Rhein. Mus.* xliv (1889), 582 f.

circumstances attending this recitation, or the different audience there addressed.[1]

Thus the explanation of our difficulty is that *Ruf.* ii, together with its preface, was written and recited in the summer of 397,[2] while Bk. i was written and recited early in 396, its preface being the preface to Bk. i alone.

Nor is it in the least surprising that Bk. ii should have been written as much as a year after Bk. i. Compare once more the stages of composition of *Eutr.* Book i was published very early in 399 when Eutropius was at the height of his power. Book ii was not recited till after his fall[3] in August 399. Evidently Claudian waited for new developments before continuing his poem. To take another example, Claudian wrote Bk. i of *Gild.* as soon as news of Gildo's defeat reached Milan. But as a result of events which happened after the publication of that book, he never wrote the other book or books which he must at one time have intended to complete the poem: as it stands it is clearly unfinished. It would seem to have been Claudian's normal practice when undertaking a work which was likely to run into more than one book to recite each book as he wrote it, before even thinking about what he was going to say in the next book. The political situation could (and did) change very rapidly, and a political journalist—and Claudian may fairly be so described—could not

---

[1] Cf. P. Friedlaender, *Johannes von Gaza* (1912), 121, on the prefaces to the prose recitations of the fifth- and sixth-century sophists of Gaza, quoting examples of *meletai* being recited over two sittings, with a fresh preface for each sitting. Cf. too the numerous prefaces to the separately published individual books of (e.g.) Statius' *Silvae* and Martial's *Epigrams*.

[2] No one, I hope, will wish to revive the characteristically drastic and arbitrary solution of Jeep (following Koenig), that the preface to Bk. ii belongs to a lost panegyric on Stilico's campaign of 397 (Koch, *Rhein. Mus.* xliv (1889), 582; Fargues, p. 16, n. 2; A. Kurfess, *Hermes* lxxvi (1941), 94–5). It may be confidently assumed that Claudian never wrote any such panegyric: *Ruf.* ii was what he wrote instead (below, p. 87).

[3] Cf. Demougeot, p. 220. T. Zawadski, *Studii clasice* v (1963), 249 f. bases a theory on the date of the *Historia Augusta* in large measure on the mistaken assumption that both books of *Eutr.* were recited after Eutropius' fall: cf. *Latomus* xxiv (1965), 156–7. On the complicated circumstances surrounding the composition of Bk. ii, see below, pp. 136–8.

plan his editorial too far in advance or he might be saying all the wrong things.

The fact that *Ruf.* i, ending as it does with a prophecy of Rufinus' fall, is obviously unfinished and looks forward to Bk. ii, is no argument against the suggestion that Bk. ii did not appear till eighteen months after Bk. i. *Eutr.* i ends with an exhortation to Stilico to crush Eutropius, no less obviously looking forward to the next book. But nine months passed before *Eutr.* ii appeared. And *Eutr.* ii ends with another such appeal, looking forward to a third book, which the changing political situation soon rendered impossible.[1]

Before discussing the change in the political situation which called forth *Ruf.* ii, I propose to outline some of the important (but hitherto ignored) differences in structure and technique between the two books which both illustrate and confirm my contention that they were not conceived as a unity.

The most obvious difference is the complete disregard of chronology in Bk. i contrasted with its careful observance in Bk. ii. Book ii presents what, for all its factual distortions and omissions, purports to be, and in essentials is, a continuous narrative of the events of 395 from the death of Theodosius to Rufinus' murder. In Bk. i on the other hand there is no attempt at a narrative: after he has introduced Rufinus, Claudian makes no attempt to depict his gradual rise to power and the means he used to rid himself of possible rivals. He launches straight into a timeless portrait of Rufinus as he was (or rather as Claudian claimed he was) at the height of his power: the type of the cruel avaricious tyrant.[2] (Note in this respect the contrast with *Eutr.*, which offers a detailed—though naturally distorted and highly selective—account of Eutropius' early years and rise to power.)

In Bk. i Claudian writes as a contemporary for contemporaries, as one who did not feel himself bound to give detailed documentation

---

[1] See p. 149.

[2] Similarly, *Stil.* iii, written separately from Bks. i and ii, is different in both structure and conception from Bks. i and ii, which form a closely knit unity: cf. below, p. 149, n. 2.

and chronology for events which he could expect his audience to be perfectly familiar with already. He did not need to dwell at length on the exile of Tatian and execution of Proculus: enough to refer allusively to the affair in passing, merely as an example of Rufinus' cruelty, unmoved by either youth (Proculus) or old age (Tatian):

> iuvenum rorantia colla
> ante patrum vultus stricta cecidere securi;
> ibat grandaevus nato moriente superstes
> post trabeas exsul (i. 246 f.).

No names or details, but Tatian was the only exiled ex-consul whose son Rufinus had had executed. In similarly allusive fashion Claudian touches on another of Rufinus' more notorious crimes:

> cetera segnis,
> ad facinus velox, penitus regione remotas
> impiger ire vias: non illum Sirius ardens
> brumave Riphaeo stridens Aquilone retardat (i. 239 f.).

It seems natural to take this as an allusion to Rufinus' sudden journey to Antioch early in 395 to have Lucian put to death.

The order in which Claudian alludes to these two events illustrates the positive chronological disorder of this book. Failure to appreciate this has been a frequent source of error. For since Claudian mentions the Lucian affair before the Tatian affair, most scholars have dated it before the death of Proculus (6 December 392),[1] in spite of the fact that Zosimus, our only narrative source, clearly places it between the death of Theodosius (17 January 395) and the marriage of Arcadius (27 April 395). Yet we must surely accept Zosimus' date: the incident fits perfectly into the period immediately following Theodosius' death when Rufinus was beginning to feel his ascendancy threatened by Eutropius. The speed with which he acted—the only detail which interested Claudian—was prompted by his anxiety for his own position.

---

[1] e.g. Seeck, *Rhein. Mus.* lxxiii (1920–4), 84 f.; G. Downey, *A Study of the Comites Orientis* (Diss. Princeton, 1939), 13; and, most recently, A. F. Norman, *Libanius' Autobiography* (Oxford, 1965), 227.

Claudian does not even purport to be recording the events in chronological order: he quotes them merely as illustrations of Rufinus' cruelty, whereas he could easily (and to better purpose) have used the Tatian affair to illustrate the methods Rufinus used to oust all rivals for the Emperor's favour.

Nor does this example stand alone. Seventy lines after mentioning the death of Proculus in December 392, Claudian turns to Stilico's campaign against the Bastarnae earlier in the same year. And at lines 230 f. he describes with splendid *crescendo* effect how it was not enough for Rufinus to vent his wrath on the person of his victim alone, nor even on his wife, his sons, his relatives, his friends:

> exscindere cives
> funditus, et nomen gentis delere laborat.

This can only be an allusion to the extraordinary decree (obviously inspired by Rufinus) by which all inhabitants of Lycia (Tatian's home province) were deprived of all dignities and of the right of holding any Imperial office. The decree has given rise to no little astonishment. Levy finds it hard to believe that 'this absurd and iniquitous law . . . had no other motive than that of manifesting the Emperor's displeasure against the Lycian Tatian', but admits that he has been unable to 'find a clue as to any other motive'.[1] Certainly we should be reluctant to assume that Rufinus was motivated by mere petty spite. In fact, a much more substantial motive may readily be discerned. The reason Rufinus banned Lycians from holding posts in the administration is surely quite simply because Tatian, while prefect, had packed the administration with a disproportionate number of Lycians. This was a common phenomenon in the later Empire: under Valentinian, we find a disproportionate number of Pannonians in high office, under Gratian, Aquitanians,[2] under Theodosius, a clique of Spaniards.[3] Tatian had doubtless taken many fellow Lycians up the ladder of success with him. The only such appointment we

---

[1] Op. cit., p. 18: we learn of the law from *Cod. Theod.* ix. 38. 9, repealing it.
[2] Cf. A. Alföldi, *Conflict of Ideas in the Late Roman Empire* (Oxford, 1952), 15 f.
[3] A. Chastagnol, in *Les Empereurs romains d'Espagne* (Paris, 1965), 269–90.

know of—that of his own son to the prefecture of Constantinople —is striking enough. And the hypothesis that he was more devoted to the interests of his native province than to those of his diocese as a whole is strongly supported by the fact that he administered his duties as prefect *in absentia* from his home in Lycia.[1] Obviously, when Rufinus ousted Tatian as prefect, for his own security he had to eliminate the whole of the Lycian faction, both for the present and the future, to prevent one of Tatian's protégés doing what Rufinus himself had done—securing the Emperor's ear and working for Rufinus' fall in turn. Thus Rufinus' edict, outrageous though it might seem, was perfectly understandable under circumstances such as these. Our pagan sources regard the fall of Tatian and his dependants as a perversion of justice and a disaster. Most contemporaries (especially non-Lycians), while not perhaps approving of Rufinus' methods, may have viewed with less concern the ruin of this flamboyant, overpowerful pagan, who made such unscrupulous and ostentatious use of his wealth and patronage.[2]

What matters for our present purpose, *Ruf*. i. 230 f. does indeed allude to the decree banning all Lycians from holding public office. Thus from the point of view of chronology it should follow, not precede, the section on the fate of Proculus and Tatian, at lines 246 f. But it suited Claudian's purpose to treat it as an entirely separate example of Rufinus' cruelty—which suggests of itself that he was rather short on hard facts to bolster up his accusations. Naturally, it should come as no surprise that Claudian takes a hostile view of Rufinus' destruction of the Lycian faction. But it is suggestive that he makes such limited and allusive use of the affair, merely as an example of senseless cruelty.

The whole of the section *Ruf*. i. 175–300 is devoted to elaboration

---

[1] Zosimus iv. 45. 1. See too Addenda, p. 490.

[2] Cf. e.g. his erection of statues of the Emperors in most of the large cities of Asia Minor, the inscriptions from many of which survive (conveniently collected by L. Robert, *Hellenica* iv (1948), 47–53). In most Tatian's name was erased after his *damnatio memoriae* in 392, but at least two escaped the chisels of Rufinus' minions. For Tatian's policies while prefect, cf. C. Zakrzewski, *Le parti théodosien et son antithèse* (*Eus*, Suppl. xviii, 1931), 16 f.

of the theme of Rufinus' cruelty and greed, 301–31 to his treachery and intrigues with barbarians. None of the very few facts Claudian intermingles with his fiction and rhetoric is intended to be in any sort of order: their purpose is solely to illustrate Rufinus' character. The comparison between Rufinus and Stilico which starts at i. 259 f. is likewise timeless. Rufinus is portrayed as the power of darkness, Stilico of light. Claudian is not depicting Stilico's opposition to Rufinus at any particular time: his motive is solely to contrast their characters. This emerges very clearly from i. 297 f.:

> certamen sublime diu, sed moribus impar
> virtutum scelerumque fuit; iugulare minatur,
> tu [sc. Stilico] prohibes; ditem spoliat, tu reddis egenti;
> eruit, instauras; accendit proelia, vincis.

Such a σύγκρισις is a regular feature of the formal rhetorical ψόγος (as it is also of the ἐγκώμιον).[1]

This brings us to the key to the differences between the two books. For Bk. i, if not a full-blown formal ψόγος in its entirety (cf. p. 255), is both in conception and treatment strongly influenced by the pattern of the rhetorical ψόγος. Whereas Bk. ii is conceived and treated as a straightforward historical epic. The 'rules' for the ψόγος are the same as those for the ἐγκώμιον, only with each of the subdivisions serving as an opening for vituperation instead of eulogy. Of the principal subdivisions Bk. i lacks only the section for γένος: and the reason for this omission is plainly that, being a Gaul, Rufinus no doubt came of perfectly respectable stock which did not provide an opening (especially in front of a western audience) for ridicule and contempt. (Contrast *Eutr.*, where Claudian makes the most of the servile birth of the unfortunate Eutropius.) The rhetors made special provisions for the omission of a subdivision if, as in the case of Rufinus' γένος, there was no suitable material for it.[2] But, γένος apart, Bk. i can show a προοίμιον, sections on ἀνατροφή and πράξεις (κατ᾽ εἰρήνην and

---

[1] Cf. L. B. Struthers, *Harvard Studies* xxx (1919), 83 f.; and for examples from the Panegyrici Latini, W. S. Maguinness, *Hermathena* xlvii (1932), 45 f.

[2] Cf. Levy, *TAPhA* lxxvii (1946), 60.

κατὰ πόλεμον), a σύγκρισις, and an ἐπίλογος—and all in the prescribed order. It may be added that there are, too, several minor (μερικαὶ) συγκρίσεις inside the other subdivisions, just as Menander had laid down: e.g. the comparison between Rufinus' avarice and extravagance and the simple tastes of Fabricius, Serranus, and Curius (i. 196 f.), under the πράξεις κατ' εἰρήνην heading.[1]

This is why Claudian touches on the Lucian and Tatian affairs both out of order and out of context: his only concern was to classify them under the appropriate heading, not to date them or explain their significance.

Yet in Bk. ii he *is* concerned to narrate events in their proper order: nothing is out of place: everything, in fact, is relevant both to its immediate context and to the gradual, dramatic unfolding of Rufinus' doom. The fundamental difference between an invective (or panegyric) and a historical epic (and *Ruf.* ii may fairly be so classed) is that in the former, the subject's actions are only recorded in so far as they reflect praise or blame on him: in the latter, they are recorded for their own sake. Naturally there is a certain amount of vituperative material in Bk. ii, but such as there is is not arranged under formal headings (of which there are none) but arises naturally in the course of the narrative: for example the denunciation of Rufinus, at ii. 385 f., is couched in the form of a speech by the eastern army, explaining the motives which allegedly drove them to assassinate him.

Book i, then, was written as an invective, early in 396, presumably almost at once after the murder. What then of the circumstances which called forth Bk. ii more than a year later? When Claudian was writing Bk. i, with the death of Rufinus

---

[1] On the influence of the rhetorical ψόγος on *Ruf.* see Levy's excellent article in *TAPhA* lxxvii (1946), 57 f., though he makes the basic error of taking the two books together as a unit. It is quite implausible to claim the epilogue to Bk. ii as the epilogue to the ψόγος as a whole—while dismissing ii. 1–453 as a digression, a digression more than twice as long as that part of Bk. i which answers to the description of the ψόγος! It would be much more satisfactory to regard the epilogue to Bk. i as the epilogue to a ψόγος consisting of Bk. i alone: and to treat Bk. ii as an entirely separate poem, basically an epic.

and the surrender of Alaric the peace and unity of the Empire seemed assured at last. But before 396 was very old, it became clear that this was not so.

In Constantinople Eutropius stepped into Rufinus' shoes and inherited both his immense wealth and his opposition to Stilico. This opposition did not become apparent at once. Zosimus remarks that for a spell Eutropius 'worked in concert with Stilico in all things' and Claudian himself admits in 399 that immediately after Rufinus' death 'fraterno coniungi coeperat orbis | imperio' (*Eutr.* ii. 546–7).[1] But it cannot have been very long before Stilico realized that Eutropius was no man of straw. Early in 396 Eutropius took steps to rid himself of all rivals: Timasius and Abundantius, two loyal and senior generals of Theodosius, were convicted on trumped up charges and exiled.[2] It was to Abundantius that Eutropius owed his place in the Imperial household.

In Illyricum, as soon as Stilico was back in Italy, and the huge Roman army of 395 safely split up between East and West, Alaric turned on his heels and crashed through the poorly defended pass of Thermopylae into Greece. Thebes, Athens, Megara, Corinth, the whole Peloponnese fell to the Goths.

It could hardly be denied that this disastrous state of affairs was the direct result of Stilico's failure to destroy Alaric in 395. Whatever his reasons for allowing Alaric to retreat unharmed from Thessaly when he had him apparently at his mercy,[3] Stilico had seriously miscalculated. Men must have been beginning to wonder already whether perhaps it was not Rufinus after all but Stilico who was in league with the barbarians.

During the whole of 396 Alaric was given a free hand in eastern Illyricum. Neither Stilico nor Eutropius lifted a finger to defend the wretched Greeks; meanwhile,

> Geticis Europa catervis
> ludibrio praedaeque datur frondentis ad usque

---

[1] Cf. too Demougeot, p. 169.

[2] The reason he did not get rid of Gainas was not, as Demougeot supposed (p. 164), because 'Il ne pouvait toucher à Gainas, l'homme de confiance de Stilicon, d'ailleurs barbare sans prestige et perdu à Constantinople'. Gainas had become 'l'homme de confiance' of Eutropius: cf. p. 147.   [3] Cf. pp. 160 f.

Dalmatiae fines: omnis quae mobile Ponti
aequor et Adriacas tellus interiacet undas
squalet inops pecudum, nullis habitata colonis,
instar anhelantis Libyae, quae torrida semper
solibus humano nescit mansuescere cultu.
Thessalus ardet ager; reticet pastore fugato
Pelion; Emathias ignis populatur aristas (ii. 36 f.).

It was not till spring 397[1] that Stilico set out once more for the Balkans, and before long he had run Alaric and his army to earth again and blockaded them on Mt. Pholoe in Arcadia. Once more, however, Alaric contrived to escape: the exact circumstances are no less obscure than in 395, but Stilico can hardly be said to emerge from the affair very creditably.[2] Suspicion that Stilico was in league with the barbarians can only have increased, however unjustified it was. Eutropius—presumably for this reason[3]—went so far as to declare Stilico *hostis publicus*. Being at the time fully engaged containing the Huns in Asia Minor, Eutropius was unable himself to cope with Alaric, and solved the problem for the time being by the ignoble expedient of simply appointing him *magister militum per Illyricum*, thereby legalizing his possession of the Balkans.

It was probably not till after the recitation of *Ruf.* i that the full consequences of Stilico's treatment of Alaric in 395 became apparent (though it may be that the somewhat irrelevant, and certainly tendentious, emphasis laid on Stilico's victory over the Bastarnae at the end of Bk. i was designed to counter talk that Stilico was too well disposed to barbarians). As 396 progressed, on the one hand the situation in Illyricum steadily deteriorated, on the other, it was becoming more and more obvious that the elimination of Rufinus had diminished rather than increased Stilico's prospects of establishing his regency over Arcadius. Under these circumstances there might not seem to be much point in continuing *Ruf.* Claudian probably decided to wait,

---

[1] Cf. Demougeot, p. 170.
[2] Cf. pp. 169 f.
[3] Cf. p. 176.

and write instead an epic on Stilico's hoped-for victory over Alaric in 397. But what was he to do when this victory failed to materialize, when the fiasco of 395 repeated itself? When, furthermore, in the eyes of the eastern government it was now Stilico who was the *hostis* and Alaric the Roman general? Clearly none of this could be admitted. Yet to keep silence indefinitely would be as good as admitting it. So he decided instead to evade the necessity of either revealing the events of 397 or distorting them too flagrantly to escape exposure, by going back to 395 again. True, there had been no glorious victories in 395 either, but he could at least have another crow over Rufinus, and 'remind' his readers of Stilico's services in ridding the world of that monster at any rate. Moreover, it was a good deal easier to justify Stilico's failure in 395 than his second and even more inglorious failure in 397. The result was *Ruf.* ii.

The campaign of 397 he alludes to very briefly in the preface, in what might be described as a 'stop-press' notice, as if the news had reached him too late to do any more: but what more could he have done? We are treated to confident but conveniently vague clichés about the Alpheus and Arethusa running red with Gothic blood—but no details, of course. Stilico is exhorted to lay aside his spear for a brief moment and take a well-earned rest from his mighty labours.

The book proper opens with a very pointed recapitulation of Theodosius' last wishes. Theodosius had left Stilico in charge of both his sons and both the eastern and the western armies. A very necessary 'reminder' now that Eutropius had turned out a much more serious rival for the power behind Arcadius' throne than even Rufinus.

We then turn at once to Rufinus. The moment Theodosius was dead he began to stir up discord on all sides. Seeing that he was without the support of Emperor, people, or army, he exclaims:

> quid restat nisi cuncta novo confundere luctu
> insontesque meae populos miscere ruinae?
> everso iuvat orbe mori; solacia leto

> exitium commune dabit nec territus ante
> discedam: cum luce simul linquenda potestas (17 f.).

There follows a vivid account of all the various barbarians Rufinus invited to invade and destroy the Empire, and a brilliant description of the siege of Constantinople, of which part has already been quoted. The scene changes to Stilico setting off from the West in spring 395 to deal with Alaric. No sooner had Stilico arrived in Thessaly than Alaric in fear gathered his men together behind some rapidly thrown up fortifications. On learning this Rufinus was terrified:

> audit iter [sc. Stiliconis] numeratque dies spatioque viarum
> metitur vitam (137–8).

So he forces Arcadius (naturally Claudian cannot let it seem that Arcadius agreed of his own accord) to send a message ordering Stilico to raise the blockade, retreat from Illyricum at once, and return the eastern army to Constantinople. Rufinus represents Stilico as intending to march on the capital after finishing off Alaric, and claims that this will mean not only Rufinus' death but Arcadius' as well: 'haec cervix non sola cadet' (166). Arcadius reluctantly agrees, and just as Stilico is delivering his final harangue to his troops before they join battle, the message arrives. Stilico is thunderstruck:

> obstupuit; simul ira virum, simul obruit ingens
> maeror, et ignavo tantum licuisse nocenti [i.e. Rufino]
> miratur. dubios anceps sententia volvit
> eventus: peragat pugnas an fortia coepta
> deserat? Illyricis ardet succurrere damnis;
> praeceptis obstare timet (197 f.).

But being a loyal son of Rome, naturally he obeys his Emperor, and tells his men to replace in their scabbards the swords they have already drawn in readiness:

> taceant litui. prohibete sagittas.
> parcite contiguo—Rufinus praecipit—hosti (218–19).

The troops are no less indignant than Stilico himself. Their spears, athirst for barbarian blood, 'sponte volant', their scabbards refuse to sheath the swords not stained with blood. Stilico loyally persuades them to accept his decision, and much against their will the eastern army is dispatched back to Constantinople, professing undying loyalty to Stilico and muttering dark threats against Rufinus.

Strangely enough, this tissue of tendentious falsehoods has been generally believed.[1] They will be exposed in Chapter IX. For our present purpose it will suffice to point out that it is carefully designed to deflect from Stilico on to Rufinus all responsibility for the Gothic devastation of the Balkans in 396. This motive emerges especially clearly from ii. 187 f.; if Stilico had been allowed to join battle with Alaric, Claudian affirms,

> prodita non tantas vidisset Graecia caedes,
> oppida semoto Pelopeia Marte vigerent,
> starent Arcadiae, starent Lacedaemonis arces;
> non mare fumasset geminum flagrante Corintho
> nec fera Cecropiae traxissent vincula matres.

It was Rufinus who prevented Stilico destroying Alaric, not Stilico's own miscalculations or inability.

The rest of Bk. ii is devoted to the murder, and the events leading up to and following it. The account of the murder itself is a dramatic masterpiece. So sure was Rufinus that this day would see his elevation to the purple, so eagerly was he awaiting Arcadius' announcement to the assembled troops, that he did not notice the long columns gradually circling around him till he was surrounded, and there was no escape!

Did Rufinus really have designs on the purple? Most of our other sources agree with Claudian here, not of itself decisive in such a matter. Levy[2] regards it as perfectly plausible, Demougeot[3]

---

[1] It will be appreciated that I find it difficult to concur in Romano's solemn judgement that in *Ruf.* as a whole 'i dati storici principali non sono alterati' (p. 79). Fargues displays a more healthy scepticism, but not thorough-going enough. Almost all historians have accepted *Ruf.* ii as basically historical. It is in fact virtually pure fiction—but a fiction more suggestive than the facts.

[2] Edition of *Ruf.*, pp. 20–5.   [3] pp. 156–8.

as perfectly implausible. It is impossible to decide. Rufinus was in a desperate position, and might well have calculated that only desperate measures could save him. Certainly more ill-judged usurpations are attested in the long and varied annals of Imperial Rome. But how many can have known Rufinus' real intentions at the time? Certainly not Claudian, 1,000 miles away. And it was inevitable that Rufinus should have been accused of such designs by his enemies to justify their action. It is true that, with unusual restraint, even Claudian only accuses Rufinus of wishing to be co-Emperor with Arcadius (cf. *Ruf.* ii. 315, '*in partem* mihi regna dari', 383, '*participem* sceptri, *socium* declaret honoris'). But it does not necessarily follow from this that the accusation was justified. After all, nobody would have believed that Rufinus had been so foolish as to intend to kill Arcadius and rule in his place—leaving Honorius (backed by Stilico) with the inescapable duty of taking vengeance. But as co-Emperor he could reasonably have hoped to rule the East with Arcadius, the senior Augustus, as sleeping partner, leaving Stilico and Honorius with no legitimate or peaceful remedy. Emphasis has sometimes been laid on Claudian's allegation that Rufinus had had coins carrying his own head ready minted as a donative for the troops (ii. 342). Proof indeed —if true. But it is just the sort of circumstantial detail that would have been invented afterwards by Rufinus' enemies—not necessarily by Claudian himself, who may even have believed it.

Much more important is the question of the responsibility for Rufinus' death. Here again, all is not quite so straightforward as has usually been supposed. Claudian certainly wishes to claim for Stilico the credit for the fall of Rufinus. Yet he is careful not to say in so many words that Stilico was directly responsible for the deed. Assassination, though useful and sometimes even beneficial, is not the most creditable of political weapons. So Claudian represents the eastern army as both planning and executing the deed without any direct prompting from Stilico, but inspired nevertheless by loyalty to Stilico. As they leave their beloved general to return to Constantinople, they drop dark hints of their intentions:

tu mihi dux semper, Stilico, nostramque vel absens
experiere fidem. dabitur tibi debita pridem
victima: promissis longe [from afar] placabere sacris
(ii. 275 f.).

All the way back they hatch their plans, telling not a soul right
up to the fateful day. And then the man who strikes Rufinus first
cries out:

hac Stilico, quem iactas pellere, dextra
te ferit: hoc absens invadit viscera ferro (ii. 402–3).

A very neat way of ascribing to Stilico the credit of ridding the
world of Rufinus, but not the discredit of the means whereby it
was done.

Who really was responsible? 'There can be no reasonable doubt
that the assassination of Rufinus was instigated by Stilico', wrote
J. B. Bury,[1] and this has indeed generally been taken for granted.
One wonders. The first thing every good detective looks for,
so we are told, is the motive: *cui bono?* Stilico might certainly
have hoped to profit by the removal of Rufinus. But the one man
who certainly did profit was undoubtedly Eutropius. And Eutropius was on the spot when Rufinus was killed, while Stilico was
1,000 miles away. But the question of the actual responsibility for
the deed is perhaps not very important. It might have been
Stilico; it might have been Eutropius; it might easily have been
both in concert; nor can we rule out altogether the possibility
that the soldiers really did lynch Rufinus on their own initiative
(Philostorgius says they killed him in indignation because he
treated them scornfully). What matters for our present purpose,
however, is the very fact that Claudian does claim the credit for
Stilico (it was not inevitable that he should do this, even granted
that he was combining eulogy of Stilico with vituperation of
Rufinus in the same poem). His purpose is surely to ascribe to
Stilico the credit claimed by Eutropius.

Whether or not Eutropius was behind the assassination, he had
certainly been working against Rufinus some time before it (witness the Eudoxia affair) and stepped into his shoes immediately

[1] *LRE* i². 113.

after. Moreover, we know that Eutropius, unlike Rufinus, enjoyed the confidence and even the affection of Arcadius. Rufinus' end was too spectacular to be glossed over. So it must have been represented in the East, as it was by Claudian in the West, as a merciful and timely release from tyranny. And in the East at any rate the credit will inevitably have been taken by Eutropius. Claudian, of course, does not mention Eutropius. More significant still, he does not mention him in any of the other poems he wrote during the period of the rivalry between Stilico and Eutropius.[1] And in *Gild.*, written when this rivalry was at its height, Claudian claims the credit of the fall of Rufinus for Stilico even more openly than before. Theodosius (as a ghost) is extolling Stilico to Arcadius (significant choice of interlocutors), late in 397:

> Rufinumque tibi, quem tu tremuisse fateris,
> depulit (*Gild.* 304–5).

It is surely very striking—and suggestive—that Claudian is at such pains to ascribe the credit for this sordid murder to Stilico as late as two years after the event; and to try and make out that Theodosius himself would have approved of the deed. As so often with Claudian, it is not so much whether what he says is true that matters. Whether or not Stilico had a hand, however remote, in the deed itself, what is significant is that it was clearly important for him to claim the credit afterwards. At all costs he had to be represented as the *only* protector of both Emperors. So it must be Stilico who saves Arcadius from Rufinus. And until Stilico is able to 'save' him from Eutropius as well, no one must know about Eutropius at all.

---

[1] Until, that is, *Eutr.* i broke the unnatural silence with a vengeance.

V

GILDO

THE declaration of Stilico *hostis publicus* in summer 397 made it perfectly clear that Eutropius was now a far more formidable rival for Stilico than Rufinus had ever been. His ascendancy over Arcadius was complete—'lording it over him like an ox', as Zosimus picturesquely put it.[1] Since, moreover, unlike Rufinus, he was able to count on the support of the army, he was complete master of the eastern Empire.

Nor was his ambition confined to the East. In 397 Eutropius opened negotiations with Gildo, an African prince whom Theodosius had (unwisely) entrusted with full civil and military powers in Africa, and invited him to transfer his allegiance from Honorius to Arcadius. This was no ordinary attempt at territorial encroachment. Rome was now almost wholly dependent on Africa for her corn supply. Before the foundation of Constantinople Rome had drawn on the twin granaries of Africa and Egypt, but after Constantine had instituted *frumentationes* in his new Rome on the model of the old, Africa alone was left: Egypt was reserved for Constantinople. So dependent indeed was Rome on Africa that only a few days' delay in the arrival of the African corn ships could, and too often did, lead to famine and riots.[2]

Both Gildo and Eutropius stood to gain by the transference of Africa to the East. Gildo would naturally prefer the nominal suzerainty of distant Constantinople to the tighter rein of nearby Rome: and Africa would be freed from the crippling obligation of exporting most of its corn to Rome. Eutropius, by cutting off the corn on which Rome was so dependent, hoped to destroy

---

[1] v. 12. 1.

[2] For further discussion of the corn supply of Rome, I refer to my commentary on *De Bello Gildonico* (forthcoming).

Stilico's credit there and impose his own terms on Honorius—
terms which would naturally include the removal of Stilico, and
would, in effect, bring about the extension over Honorius of the
ascendancy which Eutropius already exercised over Arcadius. He
would then have fulfilled the ambition Stilico had been cherishing
since 395: as *de facto* regent of both Emperors he would be effective
ruler of the whole Empire.

In the course of 397 Gildo began to reduce African exports to
Rome, and in late autumn suspended them altogether. What was
Stilico to do? Though generalissimo and guardian of one Emperor, he was in the embarrassing position of having been declared
a public enemy by the other. How could he lead an expedition
against Gildo in the name of Honorius, when Gildo could claim
that he was a loyal servant and legitimately appointed magistrate
of Arcadius? And how could he do this without causing an open
breach between the two Emperors and being obliged, even if
successful, to renounce for ever his aim of uniting them both under
his influence? Yet swift action had to be taken if he was going to
survive the crisis at all. The longer it lasted the more serious would
grow famine in Rome, and the greater the pressure on Honorius
from all quarters to sacrifice Stilico to avert starvation and civil
war. And history suggested that a war against an African chieftain
on his own ground would not be over quickly. One has only to
think of the long-drawn-out and troublesome Roman campaigns
against Jugurtha and Tacfarinas: or, a much more recent example,
the three frustrating and hard-fought years it had taken Theodosius' father to crush the rebellion of Gildo's own brother Firmus.

But Stilico was more fortunate than he could possibly have
dared to hope. By a singular stroke of luck he was able to make
use of the services of another brother of Gildo, named Mascezel,
who had recently sought asylum in Milan to escape Gildo's
clutches. Gildo had attempted to murder Mascezel, and had in
fact succeeded in killing his two sons—a deed in comparison with
which, so Claudian assures us, the crimes of the house of Atreus
pale into insignificance. Mascezel saved the situation for Stilico
by bringing about Gildo's total defeat and capture in an astonish-

ingly short space of time. His expedition left Pisa in November 397, and Gildo was defeated within weeks of its arrival in late February 398. So quickly, in fact, that Eutropius had not yet had time to consider whether he ought—or dared—to send a force to support Gildo. Thus an open breach was prevented, and the uneasy peace restored.

In the meanwhile Stilico, who could not have been expecting such a rapid conclusion to the war, had taken the precaution of marrying his daughter Maria to Honorius, despite the fact that Honorius was still only 14 and Maria barely 12.

Nor was this the only step Stilico took to strengthen his position at court. Throughout the crisis he was ably supported by a re- markable series of poems from Claudian. Indeed the poems Claudian wrote during and immediately after the Gildonic war offer a unique opportunity of watching the situation change month by month. *IV Cons.* and *Nupt.* were both recited during the crisis: *IV Cons.* early in January 398, *Nupt.* a month or so later, and *Gild.* as soon as the news of Gildo's defeat reached Milan, probably in April.

In January 398, with Mascezel's expedition having left Italy but not yet arrived in Africa, there was little of use Claudian could say about the African situation. Thus it is hardly surprising that, although *IV Cons.* is by far his longest poem to date (656 lines), Claudian nowhere refers to either Gildo or Eutropius. In fact he nowhere alludes directly to the war at all:[1] the closest he gets is at 436 f., where in a eulogy of Stilico he claims,

> *Libyae* squalentis harenas
> audebit superare pedes madidaque cadente
> Pleiade Gaetulas intrabit navita Syrtes.

Towards the end he elaborates at length on the coincidence that Theodosius had won a great victory both times he had made Honorius consul (386 and 394):

> quotiens te cursibus aevi
> praefecit, totiens accessit laurea patri (621 f.).

---

[1] Though it is significant that the list of territories ruled by Honorius at *IV Cons.* 392 f. does not include Africa.

But during this, his fourth, consulate (Claudian tactfully passes over Honorius' third consulate, during which nothing of any moment happened),[1] he will win a great victory in his own right:

> sed patriis olim fueris successibus auctor,
> nunc eris ipse tuis (638–9).

There was no need to say over whom this hoped for victory would be won.

Lastly, it is perhaps no accident that so much prominence is accorded to the African campaign of the elder Theodosius (lines 25–40). Not that the subject is dragged in out of season. As grandfather of Honorius, the elder Theodosius had an un-impeachable claim to a mention in the section devoted to γένος. Yet he is barely mentioned in either of Claudian's other two panegyrics on Honorius. There was no harm in reminding his no doubt anxious and apprehensive audience at this juncture that the last African rebel, Gildo's brother Firmus, had been suppressed by Honorius' grandfather.

The rest of the poem is for the most part straightforward panegyric: interesting enough in its own right as an illustration of Claudian's skill as a panegyrist—the poem as a whole has been described (with some exaggeration: see p. 254) as an almost perfect example of the rhetorically constructed ἐγκώμιον, and contains a particularly instructive section on kingship—but irrelevant for our present purpose. All that concerns us here is the section on Stilico's recent military achievements. Claudian justifies the section by including the achievements among Honorius' πράξεις κατὰ πόλεμον, but there is no doubt who gets the credit for them. First he extols some minor mopping up operations along the Rhine frontier. Sygambri abased their flaxen locks before Stilico, Franks prostrated themselves, followed by Bastarnae, Bructeri, and Cimbri specially resurrected for the purpose together with Cherusci

---

[1] Claudian's silence about the military side of Honorius' third consulate rules out of court completely the once popular view that Stilico's second expedition to Greece took place in this year. So (decisively) J. Koch, *Rhein. Mus.* xliv (1889), 572 f., and cf. Appendix C.

fresh from the pages of Tacitus.[1] But Claudian's predilection for hyperbole undermines the impression he is trying to convey. Drusus' conquest of Germany was won only at the cost of warfare and disasters: Stilico did not need even to draw his sword:

> nobilitant veteres Germanica foedera Drusos,
> marte sed ancipiti, sed multis cladibus empta.
> quis victum meminit sola formidine Rhenum?
> quod longis alii bellis potuere mereri,
> hoc tibi [sc. Honorio] dat Stiliconis iter (455 f.).

Clearly there was no actual fighting at all. Stilico merely marched down the frontier obtaining professions of loyalty and (more important) recruits.[2]

Next, Claudian continues, still addressing Honorius:

> hortaris Graias fulcire ruinas (460).

The most recent commentator on the poem observes that 'hortaris' is a device to give Honorius the credit for Stilico's exploit. This is true enough, but it is not the whole reason. When we recall that Stilico's campaign in Greece had ended with Arcadius declaring him a public enemy, we can see at once why Claudian is really so anxious to make out that Stilico was only acting under orders from Honorius. He was matching the order of one Emperor against the order of the other.

Claudian's account of the 397 campaign is, if longer, no less vague and rhetorical than the few lines in the preface to *Ruf.* ii. We hear of wagons swimming with blood, skin-clad youths being mown down, and even of the blockade of Alaric on Mt. Pholoe— but no details, and not even a clear statement that Stilico had won a victory (thereby stopping short of an outright lie).

The poem ends with a pious wish that before long Arcadius and Honorius might hold the consulate together, a symbol of that unity which had never been more sorely strained than at that very moment. Instead of commenting on their disunity, Claudian asks for an even more glorious proof of their unity.

---

[1] See below, p. 346.   [2] On the question of recruits, see below, p. 375.

But before this final prayer, there is an unmistakable hint of Honorius' forthcoming marriage. 'Quae gaudia mundo', Claudian innocently[1] exclaims,

> per tua lanugo cum serpere coeperit ora,
> cum tibi protulerit festas nox pronuba taedas! (642 f.).

Who will be the lucky bride? If only it could fall to Claudian's lot to sing the marriage song!

It cannot have caused much surprise when a month or so later it was duly announced that the young Emperor was going to take a wife. Nor when the name of the bride was disclosed—nor the name of the poet chosen to sing the marriage song. Claudian did the young couple proud, with a full-scale epithalamium and four suitably licentious[2] *Fescennines*. The *Fescennines* build up to a clever climax. The first, much the most peaceful in tone and general in content, ends: 'beata quae te mox faciet virum | primisque sese iunget amoribus' (i. 41–2), as if the identity of the bride was still unknown. The second drops the hint that her mother came from Spain (ii. 27), which narrowed the field considerably. The third revealed that Stilico was the future father-in-law (which hardly left much room for doubt). But it was not until the very last triumphant line of the fourth, much the most passionate and erotic of the four, that she is actually named:

> haec vox per populos, per mare transeat:
> 'formosus *Mariam* ducit Honorius' (iv. 36–7).

The third *Fescennine* reveals all too clearly the political import of the marriage—and its reason: hostility and opposition to Stilico. The poem is addressed to Stilico himself:

> gener Augusti pridem fueras
> nunc rursus eris socer Augusti.

---

[1] I cannot accept the common view that Claudian was unaware how soon the marriage would take place when he wrote *IV Cons*. (e.g. Mazzarino, p. 266, n. 5). On the contrary, he was preparing the ground.

[2] We know from St. Chrysostom that Christian weddings in Claudian's day were just as (superficially) licentious as weddings in Republican times: see the passages collected by W. G. Holmes, *Age of Justinian and Theodora*[2] (1912), 117, n. 4.

> quae iam rabies livoris erit ?
> vel quis dabitur color invidiae ?
> Stilico socer est, pater est Stilico!

The epithalamium, too, is highly charged politically. The propaganda themes are skilfully interwoven into the structure of the poem together with Venus and her band of Cupids and all the other traditional paraphernalia of the genre. However obvious it might have seemed, Claudian could not admit that Stilico had arranged the match for his own purposes. No, Claudian assures us, it had in fact been arranged long since by Theodosius himself: indeed it had been his dearest wish. From the very first line Maria is a 'promissa virgo'. It had merely been a question of waiting till the pair was old enough. Of course with the groom still only 14 it was only too obvious that this time had not yet arrived. But Claudian vigorously denies that Stilico had anything to do even with the advancing of the happy day; indeed, he had actually been opposed to it. The 'real' reason for the suddenness of the marriage was the passion Honorius felt for Maria, which he discovered he could no longer contain. He had lost all interest in his hunting, and thought of nothing but Maria:

> quotiens incanduit ore
> confessus secreta rubor, nomenque beatum
> iniussae scripsere manus! (*Nupt.* 8–10)

But Stilico was adamant. 'Quonam usque verendus', protests the lovelorn youth,

> cunctatur mea vota socer?[1] quid iungere differt
> quam pepigit, castasque preces implere recusat? (20 f.)

After the indirect criticism of his brother's recent choice of bride discussed above (p. 53), Honorius decides to try Serena instead: perhaps she will prove less inexorable. This means of attributing all initiative in the marriage to

---

[1] On this anachronism, see below, p. 109.

Honorius instead of Stilico might have seemed too transparent
an artifice to take anyone in; but if it deceived Gibbon, who
thought Claudian was merely flattering Honorius' erotic prowess,
it may well have deceived at least some of the less politically
alert among Claudian's original audience.[1]

The scene changes to Venus' palace in Cyprus, built of gold
and precious stones, and positively reeking with all the rarest
odours. Cupid interrupts his mother as she sits at her toilet to tell
her the news: Honorius himself has fallen a victim to Cupid's
arrow. Venus well knows, of course, the bride-to-be, daughter of
the man who is the bulwark of Gaul and Italy. She drops everything and sets off for Italy at once on Triton's back, accompanied
by winged Cupids and naked Nereids, who profess undying
loyalty to Stilico: was it not they who had carried Stilico's
'victorious' fleet across to Greece for his campaign against Alaric
in 397 (178–9)? At Venus' arrival in Milan the soldiers rejoice,
their standards sprout forth blossom, their spears give forth green
shoots—beneath all the fantasy an ominous sign of a city preparing
for war. While Hymen chooses the festal torches, Gratia picks
flowers, and Concordia weaves garlands, the Cupids are set to
work to decorate the marriage bed: among the decorations Venus
is careful to include all the spoils gathered in innumerable victories
by Theodosius—of course with Stilico as always at his side.
Venus herself breaks the news to Maria, who is quietly studying
the classics with Serena, unaware of her destiny:

> Salve sidereae proles augusta Serenae,
> magnorum suboles regum *parituraque reges* (252–3).

This is not the only allusion in the poem to the hoped for fruit
of the marriage—a son who in time would succeed to the purple:
nor need this have been postponed till his father's death. Honorius
had been crowned Augustus when 9, Arcadius when only 6,
both in their father's lifetime. Who could oppose Stilico then?
It was traditional for an epithalamium to close with a prayer for

---

[1] Romano, too, naïvely supposes (p. 86) that *Nupt.* represents a temporary
return from contemporary poetry to poetry of purely literary inspiration,
apparently quite unaware of its highly political character.

a fruitful marriage: but Claudian's prayer has an added—and un-mistakable—significance:

> sic uterus crescat Mariae; sic natus in ostro
> parvus Honoriades *genibus considat avitis* (341–2).

It is Stilico, not Honorius, who will dandle the little Augustus on his knee. It was not the least of Stilico's tragedies that the wretched Honorius was incapable of fathering this child.[1]

All this could be justified within the traditional framework of the epithalamium. But the same can hardly be said for the section immediately preceding, a long eulogy of Stilico, making per-fectly clear the two pillars on which his authority rested: the will of Theodosius and the support of the army. The speech is placed, ominously enough, in the mouth of the army itself—not the usual chorus in a wedding song. 'Dive parens', they cry, addressing Theodosius,

> en *promissa* tibi Stilico iam vota peregit;
> iam gratae rediere vices; cunabula pensat;
> acceptum reddit thalamum natoque reponit
> quod dederat genitor. numquam te, sancte, pigebit
> iudicii, nec te pietas suprema fefellit.
> dignus cui leges, dignus cui pignora tanti
> principis et rerum commendarentur habenae (300 f.).

They could sing at length, they claim, of Stilico's military prowess and achievements, but this is not the place ('prohiberet Hymen', line 312). Instead they tell of his other virtues:

> iustissime legum
> arbiter, egregiae pacis fidissime custos (332–3).

At a time when Stilico was a *hostis publicus* in the eyes of the eastern government, Claudian defiantly calls him 'iustissime *legum* arbiter'. And at a time when the two governments were on the brink of open war, Stilico is '*pacis* fidissime custos': Claudian is making it clear, for those who can read between the lines, that

---

[1] On the question of the consummation of Honorius' two marriages, see below, p. 153, n. 1. Gibbon's devastating characterization of the unhappy Emperor is, alas, all too just.

Stilico at least was trying to preserve the peace: the 'aggressor' was Eutropius. Three lines earlier he emphasizes that Stilico had never stained his sword in civil war ('nec infecti iugulis civilibus enses'): this was what Eutropius was proposing to do.

Hardly had the wedding taken place when the news of Gildo's defeat arrived, and Claudian's services were in demand once more:

> conubii necdum festivos regia cantus
> sopierat, cecinit fuso Gildone triumphos.
> et calidis thalami successit laurea sertis,
> sumeret ut pariter princeps nomenque mariti
> victorisque decus (*Stil.* i. 3 f.).

De bello Gildonico is an excellent illustration at once of Claudian's art as a poet and of his skill as a propagandist. The artistic aspects of the poem will be dealt with later (pp. 263 f.): for the moment it is the political side which concerns us. By way of preliminary it might be observed that, in contrast with Claudian's only other historical epic, *De bello Getico*, very little is said about the antecedents (still less the cause) of Gildo's revolt. We are treated instead to a series of impressionistic denunciatory speeches, imparting remarkably little in the way of facts. This can hardly be fortuitous. For to go into the antecedents of the war would have entailed revealing (or necessitated concealing) the extent of opposition to Stilico in the East. And this (as we shall see) Claudian was at pains to avoid throughout the poem.

The poem opens with a triumphal cry: Africa has been recovered! 'Concordia fratrum | plena redit'—not that Claudian had admitted for a moment in *IV Cons.* or *Nupt.* that this *concordia* had ever been in danger (see above, p. 52). Next Claudian makes what might seem to be a perfectly straightforward statement:

> patriis solum quod defuit armis,
> tertius occubuit nati virtute tyrannus (5–6).

'The third tyrant has fallen before the prowess of Honorius—the only victory that failed to grace the arms of Theodosius.'

Yet we must remember that Constantinople not only continued to recognize Gildo as a properly appointed Roman magistrate, but actively supported the policy he was pursuing. Eutropius would have complained—and probably did—that an attack on Gildo was implicitly an attack on Arcadius himself. But Claudian dismisses Gildo bluntly as a *tyrannus* (the word bears the quite specific meaning 'usurper' at this period). Moreover he calls him the *third* tyrant, thereby explicitly putting him on a par with Magnus Maximus and Eugenius, the two undoubted usurpers Theodosius had defeated in 388 and 394 respectively. Claudian suppresses Gildo's eastern backing, and represents his defeat by Honorius as the natural continuation and completion of Theodosius' policy of putting down usurpers—thus completely glossing over the delicacy of the situation, and the dubious legality of Stilico's action. Later in the poem Theodosius is made to claim that he had been on the point of crushing Gildo himself had not death cut short his plans (253 f.). In justification of this claim Claudian makes much play with Gildo's alleged treachery to Theodosius during Eugenius' revolt. But at *Gild.* 247 f. he makes Theodosius bewail the fact that Gildo had *not* been openly disloyal to him: 'si signa petisset | obvia, detecto summissius hoste dolerem' (247 f.). Instead he sat on the fence, waiting to see who would win ('restitit in speculis fati . . . seseque daturus victori')—an understandable, if reprehensible, policy under the circumstances. Whatever Claudian may imply elsewhere in the poem, this is a clear admission that in 394 Gildo had not in fact done anything which could justify regarding him as a *hostis*.[1] It is not till six years later, in *VI Cons.*, that Claudian can say outright that Gildo actually refused allegiance to Theodosius (108 f.). It suited Claudian's case to build up Gildo as a monster of treachery, and we should be careful not to swallow his allegations too uncritically.

It will be both relevant and instructive to note here an earlier instance of Gildo's treachery to Theodosius which Claudian actually fails to mention. According to Claudian the Gildonian regime in Africa lasted for twelve years ('bis senas hiemes', line 154):

[1] Cf. Mazzarino, p. 265, n. 4 and Addenda, p. 490.

twelve years from 397 (the dramatic date of the poem) takes us back to 385 (or 386, counting inclusively). Now it is certain that Africa supported Magnus Maximus against Theodosius in 387–8. If Gildo was already then count of Africa, obviously he must have been disloyal to Theodosius. Why then does Claudian fail to exploit a fact which could only, it might have seemed, strengthen his case?[1]

S. I. Oost[2] has recently challenged the accepted view that Gildo was appointed count in 385, for two reasons: (*a*) he cannot believe that Theodosius would have left Gildo in a position of such power if he had supported Maximus; (*b*) Gildo's adherence to Eugenius, he writes, 'is depicted in the blackest colours. It is the argument from silence at its most convincing to conclude that Claudian would have listed two cases of disloyalty had there actually been two.' He simply dismisses Claudian's unambiguous twelve years on the ground that we should not 'press such a statement of a poet interested more in poetic or courtly effects than in precise chronological accuracy'. Yet if Claudian had been more interested in poetic effects, why did he not pick the round number ten ('bis quinas'—a common and metrically identical poetical periphrasis)—which would have been exactly accurate according to Oost's calculations, for he thinks that Gildo was in fact appointed in 388, after Maximus' fall? Claudian's omission is in fact to be explained by precisely that consideration which prompted Oost to challenge the date 385. It *was* a blunder of the first order for Theodosius to have left Gildo in charge of Africa after his disloyalty in 387–8—and we may be sure that Theodosius' many detractors said so at the time, and again, more loudly, after Gildo's dubious conduct in 394—and yet again after his revolt in 397. To a poet who was at pains to represent Stilico as Theodosius' political heir, it was undesirable to accord more prominence than was necessary to Theodosius' blunders—especially to a blunder

---

[1] Similarly, six years later, at *VI Cons.* 103 f., Claudian says that Gildo and Alaric 'saepe' refused allegiance to Theodosius. But the only example of Gildo's disloyalty he cites is that of 394.

[2] *Class. Phil.* lvii (1962), 27 f.

which Stilico was now faced with undoing. Moreover, if Claudian was going to represent Gildo as in Theodosius' eyes merely another usurper to be dealt with summarily like Maximus and Eugenius, how could he reconcile this with the fact that Theodosius had displayed remarkable clemency towards Gildo? For we learn from a chance remark in a letter of St. Jerome that, to secure Gildo's loyalty after 388, Theodosius gave a nephew of his first wife Flaccilla to Gildo's daughter in marriage. Thus Gildo too, like Stilico, could claim a connection with the Imperial house. It is hardly to be wondered at that Claudian does not mention this little detail. It was something Theodosius' heir would prefer to be quietly forgotten. The solution to all these problems was obvious enough: Claudian must simply omit the matter of Gildo's disloyalty in 387–8.[1] He had a good enough case against Gildo already. This was not the first or last time Claudian glossed over or covered up for the blunders or unpopular policies of Theodosius.[2]

After a few introductory lines expressing astonishment at the rapid conclusion to the war ('congressum profugum captum vox nuntiat una . . . quem veniens indixit hiems, ver perculit hostem'), the poem proper opens in the best epic manner with a *concilium deorum* on Mt. Olympus. Roma, no longer the proud goddess who used to lay down laws for the Britons and quaking Indians, but a thin emaciated figure, with sunken cheeks and failing voice, her helmet sitting crooked over her grey hair and her spear all rusty, makes supplication to Jupiter. In a heart-rending speech (justly admired by Gibbon), she vividly depicts the plight of the great city which had once ruled the world, now reduced to famine by a Moorish brigand. She implores Jupiter to relieve her distress: better the Tarquins, better Brennus than this—'cuncta fame leviora mihi' (line 127). Jupiter is on the point of granting her

---

[1] Oost argues (op. cit. 28) that Claudian could easily have explained away the implications of Gildo's overlooked disloyalty in 387–8 by praising 'the mercy and clemency of the Emperor, so ill-rewarded by the ingrate'. A possible way out, it is true, but Claudian must have known as well as his audience that it was criminal irresponsibility for an Emperor to rely on gratitude as a safeguard of loyalty.

[2] See below, pp. 371 f.

request when Africa appears, similarly dishevelled, to add her laments (the purpose of this, of course, being to suggest that Gildo's actions did not represent the will of the inhabitants of Africa as a whole—all loyal to Honorius). She chronicles in outraged detail the enormities Gildo has been committing in her fertile land. Happier the sun-scorched Sahara! Gildo, we hear, is assailed by the most contradictory vices, which lend each other mutual support:

> quodcumque profunda
> traxit avaritia, luxu peiore refundit.
> instat terribilis vivis, morientibus heres,
> virginibus raptor, thalamis obscenus adulter. . . .
> divitibusque dies et nox metuenda maritis (163 f.).

Africa's accusations are for the most part commonplace, and should not be taken too seriously. For example it is more than doubtful whether it is legitimate to deduce from lines 197–8—

> proturbat avita
> quemque domo; veteres detrudit rure colonos

—that Gildo 'undertook an agrarian reform',[1] still less, with a recent Marxist scholar, that he brought about 'radical changes in the property structure of North Africa'.[2] These are stock accusations levelled at any *tyrannus*. For example Pacatus claims that Maximus' lieutenants turned people out of their 'avitis patrimoniis' (*Pan. Theod.* xxix. 3), and Claudian himself uses almost exactly the same words of Rufinus: 'laribus pellit, detrudit avitis | finibus . . .' (*Ruf.* i. 191).[3] Yet no one has ever suggested that Maximus and Rufinus were agrarian reformers. Moreover, even if we do press Claudian's words here, the natural meaning of the word *coloni* is not big landowners: surely they would have to be the poor peasants, often of Donatist sympathies, in whose interests Gildo is supposed to have been working? In fact the phrase is

---

[1] C. Courtois, *Les Vandales et l'Afrique* (1955), 146.

[2] H. J. Diesner, *Theologische Literaturzeitung* 85 (1960), 503.

[3] Similarly, Claudian elsewhere denies that such things were ever done by Stilico: 'non dives sub te pro rure paterno | vel Laribus pallet' (*Stil.* ii. 119–20).

probably no more than an echo of Vergil's 'veteres migrate coloni' (*Ecl.* ix. 4).

Jupiter assures both goddesses that 'communem prosternet Honorius hostem' (205), and straightway Roma becomes her own vigorous self again, her hair no longer grey, her helmet no longer crooked, her spear shining once more as the rust falls off.

Jupiter's solution is to send two ghosts down to the world, Theodosius, the lately deceased Emperor, and his father Theodosius *comes*, the ill-fated[1] general of Valentinian, to speak to Arcadius and Honorius in their sleep. Both descend from heaven through all seven of the planetary spheres, Theodosius the Emperor, alighting in Constantinople to address Arcadius, Theodosius *comes* in Milan to address Honorius. Now Claudian's choice of the two Theodosii as his heavenly messengers was no random decision—nor was it a random decision that the Emperor should address Arcadius, and the *comes*, Honorius. Twenty years before, Theodosius *comes* had suppressed another African rebel, Gildo's own brother Firmus. The conqueror of Firmus was thus a particularly appropriate person to tell his grandson Honorius that it was the destiny of the house of Theodosius to destroy the house of Gildo and Firmus—'hoc generi fatale tuo' (341):

> iungantur spoliis Firmi Gildonis opima . . .
> una domus totiens una de gente triumphet.
> di bene, quod tantis interlabentibus annis
> servati Firmusque mihi fraterque nepoti (343 f.).

The house of Theodosius naturally included Arcadius, and the obvious implication is that he too should have shared the 'sacred

---

[1] Theodosius the elder was executed in 376, an event the details of which were not disclosed at the time and were naturally glossed over after the unexpected accession of his son to the purple three years later. Claudian, of course, is too tactful to say anything of this unfortunate event. Instead he praises Theodosius' exploits *passim* (cf. Birt's index, s.v., p. 456), and at *IV Cons.* 190 even calls him *divus* (a title normally reserved for dead Emperors—Christians included: cf. *CR* N.S. xvii (1967), 62). In this, as in so many other such details, he is following the official line: cf. Pacatus, *Pan. Theod.* 8, 'pater divinus', and *CIL* vi. 1730 (of 398) 'divi Theodosii'—an inscription quoted above, p. 56, to illustrate another of Claudian's propaganda themes.

duty' of his family to destroy Gildo—instead of actually supporting him.

In addition, Theodosius' appeal significantly misrepresents an
important detail in Gildo's early career, parallel to the matter of
his treachery in 387-8. For during the rebellion of Firmus, Gildo
had fought for the Romans against Firmus. Indeed his aid had
largely contributed to Firmus' defeat, and it was for this very reason
that Theodosius had appointed Gildo count of Africa in the first
place. Naturally enough, Claudian entirely suppresses Gildo's, on
this occasion, pro-Roman role. Not only this. He implies—without actually saying it in so many words—that Gildo had fought
for Firmus against the Romans! 'Do the Moors dare to oppose
Rome once more, and join battle "victoris cum stirpe sui"?' (333 f.)

> Firmumne iacentem
> obliti Libyam nostro sudore receptam
> rursus habent? ausus Latio contendere Gildo
> germani nec fata timet? nunc ire profecto,
> nunc vellem, notosque senex ostendere vultus:
> nonne meam fugiet Maurus cum viderit umbram?

Admittedly, at the beginning of the passage the subject is the
Moors in general, but after 'Gildo' at line 335, it might seem natural
to assume that the 'Maurus' of 338 is Gildo too (it is clearly so
taken, for example, in V. Crépin's French translation): and that
'notos . . . vultus' in line 337 means 'the face he [i.e. Gildo]
knows but too well' (as indeed it is taken by both Crépin and
M. Platnauer, in the only other modern translation of Claudian).
When at line 340 Theodosius exclaims 'captivum mihi *redde* meum',
the *suggestio falsi* becomes unmistakable. The casual reader would
inevitably infer that Gildo had taken part in Firmus' revolt, and
on Firmus' side, and that he had been captured once by Theodosius
already.

Nor is even this the end of Claudian's distortion of vital
details in the Firmus saga. For while Gildo had fought for the
Romans,[1] Mascezel had, on that occasion, fought against them,

---

[1] Similarly, Claudian is careful never to reveal that Alaric had fought on
Theodosius' side at the Frigidus.

and rendered Firmus valuable assistance. Yet in 398 here was Stilico using Mascezel against Gildo! An anomalous situation— and one not entirely to the credit of the house of Theodosius. This too was best glossed over. Instead, we are merely told that Mascezel ('illi [sc. Gildoni] patribus, sed non et moribus isdem', 389) was cruelly wronged by his monstrous brother. Not a word of Mascezel's treachery in 373; but then no untruthful allegations that he had always been loyal to Rome either. Claudian simply concentrates on the obvious advantage to the Romans of Mascezel's personal grudge against Gildo. It was now more than a quarter of a century since Firmus' revolt. The chances are high that very few among Claudian's listeners could recall off-hand which side either Gildo or Mascezel had fought on. If they could, no harm was done. Claudian had told no outright lies. But if they could not, and instead drew the natural (if mistaken) inference from Claudian's words, so much the better.

Naturally, Claudian does not fail to make the most of Honorius' recent marriage to Maria. He tells how Theodosius entered their room

Tyrio quo fusus Honorius ostro
carpebat teneros *Maria cum coniuge* somnos (327-8).

When Honorius wakes up and summons Stilico, 'iubet acciri *socerum*' (352), and Theodosius the Emperor appeals to Arcadius 'respice fratris conubium' (309-10). Yet at the dramatic date of the poem the marriage had not yet taken place. In order to gain the maximum political capital out of it Claudian coolly antedated the marriage, which had only taken place a month or less before he wrote, by four months. Some scholars, not realizing what he was up to, have been led to date the departure of the expedition much too late, in the belief that it took place after the wedding.[1] This is certainly wrong: the expedition left in November 397, the wedding took place probably in February 398. A bold anachronism, but the less startling when it is noticed that already at *Nupt.* 21

---

[1] So Mazzarino, p. 266, n. 5: but see Demougeot, p. 183, n. 337.

Claudian takes the liberty of calling Stilico *socer* in anticipation,[1] in the very sentence where he is represented as refusing to grant his permission for the marriage.

The speech of Theodosius the Emperor to Arcadius is no less tendentious. Claudian treads very carefully here. He could have reproached Arcadius for letting Eutropius talk him into instigating the revolt, or attacked Eutropius directly. Instead he makes out that all the initiative in the revolt had come from Gildo, who had promised to transfer Africa to Arcadius. Theodosius is merely made to reproach Arcadius for being taken in by Gildo's specious promises. He warns him that since Gildo has been disloyal to both Theodosius himself and now Honorius, he will surely betray Arcadius too before long. The two brothers must pull together and help each other against their respective enemies; united they will be irresistible:

> debueras etiam fraternis obvius ire
> hostibus, ille [sc. Honorius] tuis. quae gens, quis Rhenus et Hister
> vos opibus iunctos conspirantesque tulisset? (311 f.)

As soon as Theodosius has finished Arcadius at once agrees:

> iussis, genitor, parebitur ultro.
> amplector praecepta libens, nec carior alter
> cognato Stilicone mihi. commissa profanus
> ille [sc. Gildo] luat. redeat iam tutior Africa fratri (321 f.).

Now there can be no question of Arcadius saying anything of the sort in September 397, the dramatic date of the poem. But by the time Claudian was writing, with Gildo defeated and Honorius' authority firmly re-established in Africa, he might well have wished that he had. Stilico was anxious only that the whole unfortunate affair should be forgotten once it was over, and had no wish to make capital out of his success at Arcadius' expense. So his propagandist duly prepared the way for reconciliation. If he could put all the blame for the revolt on Gildo, then with Gildo gone no obstacle remained to the longed-for *concordia fratrum*. But

---

[1] Cf. p. 99.

to admit that the eastern government had been responsible was to admit that, although the revolt was over, the *discordia* still existed. Had Eutropius been prepared to accept Stilico's olive branch, then Claudian's listeners need never have known of the part played by the East in the revolt. One line in Theodosius' speech is particularly instructive in this connection:

Sed tantum permitte cadat. nil poscimus ultra (314).

Now that the revolt is over, all Stilico wants is for Arcadius to dissociate himself from it.

Naturally Theodosius' speech contains fulsome praise of Stilico —Claudian's by now familiar device of putting praise of Stilico in Theodosius' mouth. As usual, however, the praise is not mere stock flattery. Theodosius says emphatically that he has found Stilico '*solum* memorem *solumque* fidelem' (305): 'memor', mindful of Theodosius' wishes, 'fidelis', steadfastly loyal in observing them —the implication being that Eutropius, who was at this very time trying to secure for himself the position Stilico had been claiming since 395, was neither *memor* nor *fidelis*. Stilico is praised for coping with the aftermath of the civil war of 394 and the ill feeling between the now combined armies of Theodosius and Eugenius (ill feeling which Claudian had hitherto hotly denied: see p. 164). He has of course been like a father to Arcadius since Theodosius' death: did he not get rid of Rufinus, whom Arcadius admits he had been frightened of? Once more Claudian is careful to assign the credit for the murder to Stilico—and for the same reason as before. Only this time it receives the sanction and praise of Theodosius—who had in fact placed unlimited confidence in Rufinus.

One other remark in the speech deserves closer scrutiny: 'When', says Theodosius, 'did Stilico not obey an order?' ('quando non ille iubenti | paruit?', 289-90). One critic thinks that this is meant to illustrate the presence in Stilico of 'altrömische Disziplin';[1] but there is more to it than this. Claudian is alluding to Stilico's two expeditions against Alaric. On each occasion, it will

---

[1] H. Steinbeiss, *Das Geschichtsbild Claudians* (Diss. Halle, 1936), 34.

be recalled, Alaric had managed to escape Stilico. Claudian's version, however, was that on each occasion Stilico had been right on the point of exterminating Alaric completely (as earlier the Bastarnae), when he was ordered in Arcadius' name to hold his hand and withdraw.[1] It is *this* alleged obedience of Stilico, in sacrificing certain victory to his loyalty to Arcadius, that Claudian is evoking here.[2]

A scholar who studied Claudian's speeches from a purely literary point of view criticized this one for inappropriateness: Arcadius must, he says, have been perfectly well aware of the state of the Empire at Theodosius' death, and it was therefore quite unnecessary for Theodosius to remind him in such detail.[3] But quite apart from the fact that better writers than Claudian have found it necessary to make their characters 'remind' each other, for dramatic purposes, of things which in real life they must have known already, the real point is that Arcadius would have claimed that the state of the Empire at his father's death, as *he* remembered it, was very different from the 'reminder' Claudian places in the mouth of Theodosius.

Day dawns, and the ghosts disappear. Honorius wakes and summons his 'father-in-law'. He has decided to emulate his grandsire's African triumph, and is indeed himself ready to cross in the first ship. Stilico tactfully dissuades him from this rash project: it would be beneath Honorius' dignity to go in person, and why give a Moorish rebel the honour of falling to the hand of an Emperor? Honorius agrees, accepts Stilico's suggestion that they send Mascezel instead, and sets to work to get an expedition ready. Before it sails from the harbour of Pisa, Honorius addresses a few rousing words to his men to speed them on their way. Significantly enough he tells them to prove their loyalty to him by winning a great victory—thereby washing away the stains of civil war. Once more, an admission that the scars of the civil war were

---

[1] For full discussion of this, below, pp. 159 ff.
[2] Cf. too *Stil.* ii. 95–7.
[3] A. Parravicini, *Studi di retorica sulle opere di Claudio Claudiano* (Milan, 1905), 20.

not yet healed, and that there had been serious disunity in Stilico's army. Even more significantly, he continues:

> sciat orbis Eous
> sitque palam Gallos causa, non robore, vinci (430–1).

The Gauls in question are the western troops who had fought for Eugenius (and many perhaps for Maximus too) against Theodosius in 394. Honorius calls on them to show the East that they did not surrender to mere force of arms, but to the better cause. The defiant undertone in 'sciat orbis Eous' is unmistakable. It would seem that Eutropius had been trying to turn to his own advantage the disunity between the eastern and western elements in Stilico's army. For confirmation of this conjecture we may turn to *Stil.* i, where Claudian at last reveals Eutropius' part in the revolt (see pp. 151 f.): 'illinc', he then claims (sc. from the East), 'edicta[1] meabant | corruptura *duces*' (lines 277–8). So Eutropius did attempt to undermine the loyalty of Stilico's army: but in *Gild.*, still hoping for a *rapprochement* with the East, Claudian contents himself with an oblique allusion.

Demougeot was struck by the prominence accorded to Honorius in Claudian's account of the preparations for the expedition, and hazarded the guess that Honorius had already begun to resent Stilico's domination, and manifested a certain independence on this occasion, which Claudian was obliged to represent in his poem.[2] But this will hardly do. In his panegyrics on both the third and fourth consulates of Honorius Claudian had pretended that, when only 9, the young Emperor had begged Theodosius to let him march against Eugenius in 394, and had then expressed a most ardent desire to wield a sword and trample underfoot the corpses of the enemy. It is scarcely likely that the lethargic 9-year-old really expressed these sentiments on that occasion: it was merely an elegant way to flatter the boy. Similarly I see no reason

---

[1] *Edicta* must cover something more than private attempts to create disaffection. Claudian is understandably less than explicit, but presumably they were official edicts in Arcadius' name condemning Stilico as a *hostis*, and with him all army personnel who opposed Gildo.

[2] p. 180, n. 320.

to suppose that when he was 13 he was any more eager to lead the expedition against Gildo. He displayed no such martial ardour in the remaining thirty years of his reign, despite the abundant opportunities it offered. In fact Honorius does not seem to have shown any signs of independence until, at the death of Arcadius in 408, he realized that he was now senior Augustus. But on this occasion Claudian's motive was not, or at any rate not principally, to flatter Honorius. The real explanation is that Claudian carefully avoids imputing any initiative in the campaign to Stilico, and for the reason already noted, that he was, being a *hostis publicus* in the eyes of Arcadius, in no position to take any such initiative. At the very beginning of the poem Claudian assigns the glory of the victory to Honorius, not Stilico, and just as in *Nupt.* he had played down Stilico's part in the hasty marriage by playing up Honorius', so in *Gild.* he represents Honorius both as proposing to send the expedition and actually wishing to lead it in person. Similarly in *IV Cons.* Claudian had said that Honorius ordered Stilico to rescue Greece (above, p. 97). In all his poems written during the Gildonic crisis, and indeed so long as there was any chance of a *rapprochement* with Eutropius, Claudian consistently assigns the initiative for everything Stilico does to Honorius. There is no suggestion in *Gild.* that Stilico ever considered going to Africa himself, redoubtable warrior though he was supposed to be: he merely advises Honorius to send Mascezel. And if we turn again to Theodosius' speech to Arcadius, we find that at its climax Theodosius praises Stilico not for his military prowess, but for his *consilium*: even if Gildo should retire behind the Atlas Mountains into the Sahara,

> novi *consilium*, novi Stiliconis in omnes
> aequalem casus *animum*: penetrabit harenas,
> inveniet virtute viam (318–20).

That Claudian was here reproducing official Stiliconian policy in assigning all the initiative and glory of the campaign to Honorius and only some rather vaguely evoked 'consilium' to Stilico, can be deduced from two contemporary inscriptions, from the base of statues of Honorius and Stilico respectively, erected in the Forum at Rome. First that of Honorius:[1]

armipotens Libycum defendit Honorius [orbem].

Then that of Stilico:[2]

Fl[avio] Stiliconi | ... progenero divi Theodosi, comiti divi | Theodosi Augusti in omnibus bellis | adque victoriis et ab eo in adfinitatem | regiam cooptato itemque socero d[omini] n[ostri] Honori Augusti Africa *consiliis* eius et *provisione*[1] liberata, ex s[enatus] c[onsulto].

This inscription also emphasizes three other themes to which Claudian was careful to accord due prominence: Stilico's marriage connections with both Theodosius and Honorius, and his alleged presence at Theodosius' side in all his victories (p. 56).

De bello Gildonico i takes the expedition no further than the storm which caused the Imperial fleet to put in at Cagliari after leaving Pisa. Thus even without explicit manuscript evidence that what has come down to us is only 'liber primus', it would in any case be clear that the poem is unfinished. What happened to Bk. ii? In spite of the conviction of some that it was lost in the course of the Middle Ages,[3] it is in fact almost demonstrable that Claudian either never wrote it, or committed his draft unpublished to the flames. For in describing the campaign itself and the battle, Claudian could hardly have avoided giving Mascezel the greater

---

[1] *CIL* vi. 31256.   [2] *CIL* vi. 1730.

[3] Jeep argued that Bk. ii fell out of the archetype of extant MSS., in the course of a far-fetched essay in Überlieferungsgeschichte. First, he claims (on inadequate grounds) that the archetype had twenty-nine lines to the page. Next, that *Gild.* started with a fresh page, and that its 526 verses filled exactly eighteen pages. By assuming that Bk. ii also filled up an exact number of *folia*, he is able to explain neatly how it disappeared without either leaving a trace or taking the end of Bk. i or the beginning of the next poem with it. It did not, of course, escape Jeep's notice that eighteen pages carrying twenty-nine lines each do not, in fact, make a total of 526, but of 522 lines. But he coolly remarks that anyone familiar with the ways of scribes will readily agree with him that the four lines left over must have been written in the margin of one of the eighteen pages! Such a theory does not deserve even its, in all conscience, remote enough possibility of being true, but perhaps merits chronicling as an extreme example of the legacy of Procrustes.

part of the credit. This would not have been pleasing to Stilico—the more so since Mascezel claimed on his return to Milan that he owed his success to a posthumous intervention of St. Ambrose (Ambrose had died in April 397: he seems to have made a number of such appearances in the first twelve months or so after his death). Mascezel had further advertised his orthodoxy by holding up the expedition while he fasted and prayed with some Catholic monks on the island of Capraria.[1] It looks as if he was trying to ingratiate himself with the powerful Catholic party at court in Milan—a group Stilico was beginning to alienate himself from by his lenience towards heretics and pagans (Claudian, for example).[2] Stilico had an easy solution to the ambitions of Mascezel: he had him pushed off a bridge while they were crossing a river together. It was alleged that he was seen to smile as Mascezel drowned.[3] After this, we may be sure, he indicated to Claudian that *De bello Gildonico* ii would not be required.

Even in Bk. i Mascezel's part is belittled. The only motive Claudian gives for his being put in command of the expedition is that it would be a nice case of poetic justice if Gildo met his end at the hand of the brother he had wronged. He waxes eloquent over the murder of Mascezel's sons—but only as an example of Gildo's inhuman savagery. Stilico appeals to Honorius to give Mascezel this opportunity for his revenge:

> te perdita iura,
> te pater ultorem, te nudi pulvere manes,
> te pietas polluta rogat . . . (402 f.).

In fact there were a number of excellent reasons for sending Mascezel rather than Stilico, even if the political situation had not compelled it. As an African chieftain like his brother, Mascezel could and probably did call on local support to strengthen his

---

[1] Orosius vii. 36. 5.

[2] So too at this date, perhaps, was Longinianus (for his career, cf. Chastagnol, *Fastes de la préfecture de Rome au Bas-Empire* (1962), 255 f.), if he is to be identified with the pagan correspondent of St. Augustine (Aug. *Epp.* 233 f.).

[3] Zosimus v. 11. 5.

expeditionary force. In particular, it is clear from Claudian's very lucid and detailed list of Mascezel's troops (only 5,000 men), that he took no cavalry with him at all. Now if the Romans had learnt anything from past experience of campaigning in Africa, it was that cavalry was essential to cope with the formidable Numidian horsemen. Mascezel must have been reckoning on raising some after he arrived. Second, as a fervent Catholic he might, and apparently did, cause the desertion of such Catholics as had been forced to fight under the banner of Gildo, who had become, in some sense, the secular champion of Donatism in North Africa.[1] Lastly, and when we recall the difficulties experienced by Roman armies against African chieftains in the past, by no means least, he knew the terrain and had had experience of fighting on it. Indeed, twenty-five years earlier when fighting against the Romans there, he had raised a considerable force for Firmus.[2] Stilico was no doubt counting on him being able to do the same again in 398.[3]

Of all these qualifications not a hint in Claudian. Gildo's troops he represents as cowardly, untrained, and inadequately armed— the obvious implication being that Mascezel's victory over them will be no very great achievement: a mere formality, as it were, once Stilico and Honorius have taken the really important step of deciding to send the expedition. No one would guess from Claudian's description that the nucleus of Gildo's forces consisted of the Roman infantry and cavalry he had at his disposal as count of Africa.

Though *Gild.* ii is lacking, we do have a long section devoted to the latter stages of the campaign in the first book of the panegyric on Stilico's consulate. Though hopelessly vague and rhetorical, this account is nevertheless of the very highest interest. First, the mere fact that Claudian devoted such a disproportionate amount of space to the war here is strong confirmation of the hypothesis

[1] W. H. C. Frend, *The Donatist Church* (Oxford, 1952), ch. xiv with H. J. Diesner, *Klio* xl (1962), 178 f., and E. Tengström, *Donatisten und Katholiken* (1964).
[2] Amm. Marc. xxix. 5. 14.
[3] Claudian was well aware that Theodosius the elder had used native troops against Firmus (*IV Cons.* 35).

that he never wrote *Gild*. ii, and took this opportunity of round-
ing off the campaign he had so obviously left unfinished there.
Second and more important (though so far unnoticed), are the
striking differences of emphasis between *Gild*. and *Stil*. i. Most
scholars have simply combined details from the two versions
into one composite picture as though they were merely complementary.

Yet much had changed between summer 398 and January 400.
The Gildonic crisis had been over for eighteen months, and
Eutropius was now disgraced and dead. Things could be viewed in
a different perspective now. Mascezel is not mentioned at all. No
need to pretend that all initiative came from Honorius: Stilico
was no longer *hostis publicus*, but consul.[1] Hence if the victory is
to be Stilico's, not Mascezel's, it can now be magnified instead of
belittled. We are treated to an impressive and fearsome list of
Gildo's African auxiliaries (still no mention of his Roman troops,
of course), concluding with a comparison of the swarthy Gildo
at the head of his dusky warriors to Memnon arriving at Troy, and
to Porus leading his mighty host of Indians against Alexander.
Naturally, just as Memnon was laid low by Achilles and Porus
by Alexander, so Gildo met his match in Stilico. The reader is so
carried away by the power of Claudian's rhetoric that he almost
forgets for the moment that Stilico had stayed behind in Italy all
the while. Very different is the picture Claudian had drawn in
Gild. of Gildo marching forth to war. He had staggered along half
drunk at the head of his demoralized and debauched band of
villains, reeking with unguents, decked out with garlands fresh
from a carousal, and wincing—a nice touch—at the raucous sound
of the bugle. The victory, dismissed in *Gild*., as being won merely
'without a hitch' ('nullis victoria nodis | haesit', 10–11) and as-
signed to Honorius, is now extolled as greater than the defeats of

---

[1] The only passage where Claudian alludes (though even here obliquely) to the
embarrassing interlude while Stilico was *hostis publicus* is *Stil*. i. 297 f., where he
describes how Stilico remained 'securus, quamvis et opes et rura tenerent |
insignesque domos. levis haec iactura, nec umquam | publica privatae cesserunt
commoda causae.'

Tigranes, Mithradates, Pyrrhus, Antiochus, Jugurtha, Perseus, and Philip V; and the glory is all Stilico's:[1]

> quis Punica gesta,
> quis vos, Scipiadae, quis te iam, Regule, nosset,
> quis lentum caneret Fabium, si iure perempto
> insultaret atrox famula Carthagine Maurus? . . .
> restituit Stilico cunctos tibi Roma triumphos (380 f.).

To the obvious objection that all Stilico had done was stay behind while Mascezel did all the fighting for him, Claudian has a ready answer: not explicitly so formulated, of course, but an answer none the less. We did not risk all on the one battle, he claims: if anything had gone wrong, a second fleet was ready to leave with a greater general at its head:

> non uni certamina pugnae
> credidimus, totis nec constitit alea castris
> nutatura semel; si quid licuisset iniquis
> casibus, instabant aliae post terga biremes;
> venturus dux maior erat (364 f.).

That is to say, Stilico was not pinning all his hopes on Mascezel. Nor did he remain idle while waiting for the outcome of Mascezel's expedition. In all three books of *Stil.* (i. 308 f., ii. 393 f., iii. 91 f.) as well as a year earlier at *Eutr.* i. 401 f., Claudian praises the vigour and efficiency with which Stilico contrived to make good the loss of the African harvest with corn from such unwonted sources as Gaul and Spain ('quis Gallica rura | quis meminit Latio Senonum servisse ligones? . . .', *Stil.* iii. 91–2).

But why was it that Stilico did not go himself? One reason, as we have seen, was that Stilico was careful to take a back seat while proscribed by the eastern government—no doubt to avoid compromising Honorius. In addition he was probably anxious to stay where he could keep an eye on Honorius: he could not risk his enemies (nor were they lacking) taking advantage of what might be a prolonged absence to alienate the affection of his newly

---

[1] Note also that whereas at *Gild.* 415 f., Honorius levies and equips the expedition, at *Stil.* i. 306 f. Stilico does it.

acquired son-in-law, and persuade him to accede to Eutropius' demands. Valid enough motives, to be sure: but hardly such as could be openly admitted to critics. It seems clear from Claudian's far-fetched attempt to explain it away both that Stilico's failure to go gave rise to comment and that Claudian was unable to provide a satisfactory explanation. The reason, so Claudian solemnly claims, is that Stilico did not want to frighten Gildo by going in person! For Gildo might then retreat into the desert and evade pursuit:

> consilio stetit ira minor, ne territus ille
> te duce . . . in harenosos aestus zonamque rubentem
> tenderet . . . res mira relatu,
> ne timeare times! (*Stil.* i. 335 f.)

But the most significant difference of emphasis between *Gild.* and *Stil.* i is that the East is now blamed quite openly for the revolt.[1] While Eutropius was supreme Claudian had suppressed his part in the affair in the hope of a *rapprochement*. But now Eutropius was dead, all the guilt could safely be fixed on him, in the hope that the *discordia* he had fostered would perish with him, cf. *Stil.* i. 7–8: 'Libyae post proelia crimen | concidit Eoum.' He could be depicted as a second Rufinus, the only obstacle to the *concordia* which, with his removal, could blossom forth between the brothers once more. So Claudian no longer needed to pretend that it was Gildo who made overtures to the East; he can admit that

> coniuratus alebat
> insidiis Oriens: illinc edicta meabant
> corruptura duces (276 f.).

Eutropius' attempt to cause disaffection in Stilico's army has been discussed above (p. 113). We learn also of other dark intrigues, and even attempted assassination:

> quid primum, Stilico, mirer? quod cautus ad omnes
> restiteris fraudes, ut te nec noxia furto
> littera nec pretio manus inflammata lateret? (291 f.)

---

[1] Note, however, that Eutropius is not yet blamed in either book of *Eutr.*: see below, p. 151.

Naturally, however, it is made perfectly clear that Arcadius himself had nothing to do with the wicked machinations of his ministers. In *Stil.* ii Claudian refers contemptuously to the 'iners atque impia turba | praetendens proprio nomen regale furori' (79–80). The rest of this passage is most revealing. Stilico is praised because at the height of the *discordia*, though 'saepe lacessitus probris gladiisque petitus' (83), he never sought to take vengeance on the frenzy he endured by unholy war,

. . . causamque daret civilibus armis (85).

Claudian now admits that the two *partes* had been on the brink of civil war. Nevertheless all the time, firm on the bed-rock of Stilico's loyalty,

mediis dissensibus aulae
intemeratorum stabat reverentia fratrum (86 f.).

The next few lines seem innocent enough at first sight. Stilico is praised for sharing equally between Arcadius and Honorius the treasure of Theodosius—jewel-studded belts, breastplates encrusted with emeralds, helmets flashing with sapphires, etc. But turn back to the denunciation of Stilico placed in the mouth of Rufinus at *Ruf.* ii. 156 f. Stilico is accused there of appropriating for his own purposes all Theodosius' treasure.[1] It is surely legitimate to conjecture that Stilico really was accused of keeping Theodosius' wealth for himself, and that to refute this charge he ostentatiously sent half (or as much as he could spare) back to Constantinople—taking care, of course, that his magnanimity was adequately publicized. That Claudian was thinking at the end of this passage of the *tempora Rufiniana* rather than Eutropius is proved by the fact that he goes on immediately to praise Stilico for loyally returning the eastern troops to Constantinople in 395 despite the signs of nascent civil war: 'hostem muniri robore mavis | quam peccare fidem' (96–7).

Perhaps most significant of all are the closing lines of the passage. Stilico, claims Claudian, accedes to every 'reasonable' request

---

[1] Presumably Theodosius had brought a large part of the Imperial reserves with him on his expedition to Italy in 394.

Arcadius makes ('permittis *iusta* petenti'), and refuses only that the withholding of which Arcadius himself will shortly approve, and that which it would be shameful to obtain:

> idque negas solum, cuius mox ipse repulsa
> gaudeat, et quidquid fuerat deforme mereri (98–9).

That is to say, if Stilico appeared, despite his protestations of loyalty to Arcadius, to be acting at times against Arcadius' wishes, this was only because Arcadius had not yet come to realize what was 'really' best for him.

One last example from the *reprise* of the Gildonic war in *Stil.* i. Stilico is praised for giving haughty answers to the demands of the eastern government—answers which he soon made good:

> responsa quod ardua semper
> Eois dederis, quae mox effecta probasti (295–6).

Now it may well be that Stilico did give haughty replies to ultimata from the East about Gildo:[1] but if so he was very careful not to publicize the fact at the time. At all events, as we have seen, Claudian betrays no hint, in *Gild.*, that there were any such ultimata. And though Stilico certainly made good any such replies he may have given, he did not make capital out of this at the time either. Nothing was further from Claudian's mind as he wrote *Gild.* than to crow over the discomfited East: on the contrary, the keynote of the poem was reconciliation with the East.[2]

One modern historian followed Claudian's earlier version, in *Gild.*, and believed that it was Gildo who made the overtures to Eutropius.[3] But we cannot just choose whichever of Claudian's two versions suits our own reconstruction of events best. Claudian

---

[1] Though this hardly squares with Claudian's praise of Stilico at *Stil.* iii. 81 f., because 'iam non praetumidi supplex Orientis ademptam | legatis poscit Libyam'. But it does illustrate his skill as a pleader *in utramque partem*.

[2] 'The whole poem is an eirenicon between East and West', N. H. Baynes, *Byzantine Studies* (1955), 335. Despite one or two clear errors and a too close adherence to Mommsen, these few pages of Baynes (originally part of a review of Bury, *LRE*², in *JRS* xii (1922), pp. 207 f.) are perhaps the most intelligent contribution ever made to the understanding of Claudian. It is thus unfortunate that they have been generally overlooked.

[3] O. Seeck, *Gesch. d. Untergangs d. ant. Welt*, v (1913), 285.

had a motive for misrepresenting the affair in the earlier poem which was no longer present when he wrote the later. Formally, *De Bello Gildonico* must be classed as a historical epic; but it should by now be clear that the whole conception of the poem is dictated by political considerations and propaganda motives, rather than by the desire simply to present an account of the war in verse. One recent history of later Latin literature states that 'Claudian shows a quite uncourtierlike love of truth. He keeps closely to facts in his narrative.'[1] It will be appreciated that I do not find it easy to accept this verdict. Claudian had little concern for facts, unless it happened to be more profitable—or quite harmless—to state them rather than to conceal or distort them: and for a very good reason. Throughout the Gildonic crisis Stilico had been in serious danger. If Mascezel had failed, Stilico might have fallen before the year was out. And Stilico's danger was Claudian's danger too. When Stilico eventually fell in 408, all his close associates perished with him in a bloody massacre. Had Claudian still lived at the time, he would not have escaped. His own interests were inextricably bound up with those of the man he had chosen to serve, and so it is not surprising that he should have taken such pains to serve him well.

[1] F. A. Wright and T. A. Sinclair, *Hist. of Later Latin Literature* (1931), 33.

VI

EUTROPIUS

WITH the fall of Gildo, Stilico could breathe again. The immediate crisis was over, but the problem of his relationship with Eutropius remained. How the East greeted Gildo's fall we do not know: but Stilico's policy towards the East is clearly mirrored for us in *Gild.*: in a word, reconciliation. Not a word of Eutropius, or of his support for Gildo, still less of Stilico's compromised status as *hostis publicus*. It is often supposed that Eutropius quietly withdrew his decree outlawing Stilico after the collapse of Gildo's revolt. But it is difficult to see what motive he could have had for so doing. Gildo's fall had spoilt one plan he had hoped would rid him of Stilico; but this does not mean that he abandoned the attempt. Indeed, as we shall see, there is every reason for believing that the decree remained in effect.

It was now fifteen years since Stilico had married into the Imperial house, and three since he had become master of the West and 'regent'. Yet so far (unlike even Rufinus) he had never held the consulate. The defeat of Gildo and recovery of Africa might have seemed the obvious occasion: and that Stilico would have liked, or was expected, to enter on the consulate for 399 is unmistakably implied by several passages in Claudian. At *Stil.* ii. 258 f., Africa personified is made to say that she had hoped Stilico would assume the consulate immediately after Gildo's fall, and yet he still refuses:

> sperabam nullas trabeis Gildone perempto
> nasci posse moras. etiamnunc ille repugnat . . .

And throughout the panegyric on the consulate he eventually took in 400, Stilico is hailed above all as the victor of Gildo (cf. especially Bks. i and iii and the preface to Bk. iii). No doubt is left that this is his title to the *fasces*. Again in *VI Cons.*, Roma personified twits Honorius with not taking the consulate himself after Gildo's fall: Honorius replies that he sent Stilico instead. Yet the fact remains, Stilico did not take the consulate in 399: he waited till 400. In 399 the western consulate was given to Mallius Theodorus, a Milanese lawyer with a brilliant career behind him who had been living in retirement, devoting himself to philosophy, for sixteen years. Why? It cannot have been that Stilico could not persuade Honorius to consent. But while still a *hostis publicus* in the eyes of the East, he could hardly expect Arcadius to recognize him as consul. Obviously Stilico could not risk another such blow to his prestige, so the loyal and suitably distinguished Theodorus was offered the year instead.[1]

In the East, however, Eutropius too had been covering himself with military glory. In summer 398 he had decided to take the field himself against the Huns who had been creating such havoc and distress in Asia Minor. For our knowledge of the campaign, we are unfortunately thrown back entirely on the hostile and maliciously distorted report of Claudian, but even he cannot altogether conceal that it was a success. Eutropius was hailed in Constantinople as a victor—much to Claudian's affected disgust. But perhaps the best proof of the effectiveness of the campaign is the fact that the Huns gave no more trouble for the next twenty-five years.[2] It also emerges from Claudian's account that it was for this success that Eutropius was awarded the consulate for 399:

> gestis pro talibus annum
> flagitat Eutropius, ne quid non polluat unus,
> dux acies, iudex praetoria, tempora consul (i. 284–6).

This was more than Stilico could take. Yet at the same time it provided him with an opportunity to hit back openly at last. For the news of Eutropius' nomination was not well received in the

---

[1] For Theodorus' career, see Mazzarino, pp. 338–42 (and *PLRE*, s.v.).
[2] Cf. Demougeot, p. 190.

West. Claudian complacently describes the mixture of horror, disbelief, and derision with which it was greeted. Of course he is exaggerating. Symmachus, for example, an aristocrat and himself consul in 391, makes no mention of this 'pollution' of the *fasces* in any of the numerous letters he wrote in the course of 399. Nevertheless, it is safe to assume that a substantial body of conservative opinion was indeed shocked at the prospect of a eunuch holding the consulate. It was not in accord with the *mos maiorum*. Stilico refused to allow it, Eutropius' consulate was not recognized in the West, and Claudian's fervent and oft-repeated prayer that Eutropius' name should not be allowed to infect the *fasti* was granted.[1] At last there was a current of hostility to Eutropius in the West which Stilico could exploit. He was quick to make the most of his opportunity, such as it was, and Claudian was set to work at once. The result was the *In Eutropium*, the cruellest invective in all ancient literature.

Claudian had in fact a double commission. For he had already undertaken to write the customary panegyric for Theodorus. Stilico was no doubt aware of and in favour of this project, but it may be allowed that Claudian was prompted in the first instance by friendship or respect for Theodorus himself. As his minor poems and *Rapt.* attest, Claudian's pen was not reserved exclusively for the service of Stilico. Nevertheless, no one could fail to be impressed by the contrast between Claudian's pictures of the two consuls of 399: one the lecherous, treacherous, and corrupt eunuch of servile birth; the other a lawyer, philosopher, and man of letters who had led a most distinguished administrative career. In short, a man who possessed every qualification Eutropius so signally lacked for the supreme honour of the Roman world.

The panegyric on Theodorus is a graceful piece, tracing Theodorus' career through all its stages according to the traditional pattern, and dwelling at length on his philosophical attainments. Of great interest from the point of view of Claudian's cultural attitudes and attainments,[2] but of no contemporary political

---

[1] Some later chroniclers give Mallius Theodorus sole consul, some 'Mallius *et* Theodorus'!   [2] See below, p. 323.

content except for just five lines towards the end which stand right
out of their context, and explain at once why Stilico later included
it in his omnibus edition of Claudian's political works:[1]

> nil licet invidiae, Stilico dum prospicit orbi
> sidereusque gener. non hic violata curulis,
> turpia non Latios incestant nomina fastos;
> fortibus haec concessa viris solisque gerenda
> patribus, et Romae numquam latura pudorem
> (*Theod.* 265 f.).

The allusion to Eutropius and to the scandal of his consulate is unmistakable. Yet even so he is not named. But Claudian's audience
did not have much longer to wait. A few weeks later, in Milan,
he recited Bk. i of the *In Eutropium*. Gone is all Claudian's earlier
restraint. Gone the discreet suppression of Eutropius' support of
Gildo.[2] Claudian bursts out into a savage, hysterical flood of invective more eloquent than anything since Juvenal.

For the moment our concern is solely with the political aspects
of the poem. The pervading theme of Bk. i is the enormity, the
monstrous portent, of a eunuch assuming the consulate. Other
accusations are of course made, but the main burden of Claudian's
attack throughout is simply the bare fact that he had dared to
become consul. 'Let the world cease to wonder', it begins, 'at
monstrous creatures that terrify their own mothers, at wolves
howling by night in cities, at talking cattle, at wells running with
blood. . . . All portents pale before a eunuch consul.'

> omnia cesserunt eunucho consule monstra (8).

Only his death can purify the *fasces*:

> consule lustrandi fasces, ipsoque litandum
> prodigio (21-2).

Then follows a brilliantly savage account of Eutropius' early
years, in which a minimum of fact is skilfully interwoven with

---

[1] See below, p. 252.

[2] It is thus no mere coincidence that it is not till after the collapse of Gildo's
revolt that Zosimus remarks that ἐντεῦθεν ἡ μὲν Εὐτροπίου δυσμένεια καὶ Στελίχωνος
ἀνεκαλύπτετο, καὶ ἐν τοῖς ἁπάντων στόμασιν ἦν.

a maximum of fiction and innuendo. He was castrated straight from the womb by an Armenian 'edoctus mollire mares': should we praise or curse the hand that robbed him of his manhood? He would still have been a slave had he remained a man. He was dragged from one market to another, sold and resold as successive owners tired of him, till at last, 'postquam deforme cadaver | mansit et in rugas totus defluxit aniles', they found they could only give him away, and foisted him off on unsuspecting friends. Countless times he was stripped while a buyer consulted the doctor to see if he was fit.

We then progress to his (alleged) career as a pander and pervert, till the day he was introduced to the Imperial service by Abundantius, consul in 393, and, appropriately enough, as Claudian is quick to point out, the first of Eutropius' victims after his rise to power. But there is one stage, the crucial stage, in Eutropius' rise which Claudian is careful to omit: the means he used to win and keep the unquestioning trust and favour of Arcadius. It was said that he lorded it over Arcadius as though he had been an ox, and it is well attested that Arcadius was absolutely devoted to Eutropius. Claudian had been able to claim, and probably not without some degree of truth, that Arcadius' hand had been forced by Rufinus. Unable to make the same claim in the case of Eutropius, he understandably decided simply to omit the whole subject: Arcadius is nowhere mentioned in either book of the *In Eutropium*.[1]

In his attack on Eutropius' administration Claudian has, as in the case of Rufinus, remarkably little genuine ammunition. The accusations of every sort of perversion and trade in vice we may probably ignore. Eutropius' orthodoxy and piety were notorious, and allegations of this nature were a regular feature of invective literature. It is possible that on occasions he was cruel (i. 181 f.), but there is no supporting evidence from other sources and much humane legislation was issued during his supremacy.[2] The very

---

[1] Thus we must accept *domini*, not *dominus* at *Eutr.* i. 311, as argued in *CQ* N.S. xviii (1968), 401–2.

[2] Cf. Mazzarino, pp. 196 f.

brevity and half-heartedness of Claudian's section serves only to confirm its lack of foundation. That he was avaricious is more than likely ('hoc uno fruitur succisa libido', i. 191), but hardly a very serious or even an uncommon accusation against a high official of the day. Perhaps the best illustration of the unscrupulous methods he employed is the outrageous decree issued after Rufinus' death proclaiming that since those whom Rufinus had robbed did not claim their property back during his lifetime, it was now forfeit to the treasury![1] It is probable enough that he did make extensive confiscations (i. 168 f.): Fargues has collected all the references to greed and confiscations in other sources (p. 87).

But at the same time we should beware of simply taking it for granted that Eutropius' purpose was to amass all this wealth for himself alone. Naturally this is what our violently hostile sources say. Yet after the costly wars and heavy barbarian subsidies of Theodosius, not to mention the terrible Hunnic looting and devastation of Asia Minor since his death, the eastern treasury must have been pretty empty—the more so since Theodosius took what he had left with him to Italy in 394.[2] In addition to the other expenses Eutropius had to meet, large subsidies were required to keep Alaric and Tribigild quiet—and by 399 Tribigild, at least, was being kept short (see below). It was only natural that a minister who tried to fill the treasury should be accused of personal avarice by interested parties. It was only natural too that such accusations should go down well with the landed gentry of the West to whom Claudian addressed himself. Stilico had never dared to milk them in this way.[3] It was precisely this failure of successive western governments to take a strong line with the landowning aristocracy, who absorbed such a dangerously high proportion of the resources of the West, which reduced the West to bankruptcy while the eastern treasury was still full—a factor of no small importance for the survival of the eastern Empire after the collapse of the West. That Eutropius' administration was a good deal less self-interested than our hostile literary sources imply

---

[1] *Cod. Theod.* ix. 42. 14.   [2] See above, p. 121.
[3] See below, pp. 233–4.

is clearly illustrated by his legislative activity, which reveals a
valiant attempt to curb the growing encroachment of Church
and landowners on the power of the central administration.[1]
Eutropius may have been cunning and unscrupulous, his low
ways may have offended the nobility (Claudian refers with contempt to the days he and his cronies spent at the mime and circus),
and he doubtless lined his own pockets very liberally: but he
served his Emperor better than is generally allowed.

One reproach Claudian makes much of is Eutropius' sale of
provincial governorships. He represents them as being held up for
auction to the highest bidder. 'One man buys Asia with his villa,
another Syria with his wife's jewels, a third repents of exchanging
his family mansion for Bithynia. Above the open door of Eutropius' residence is a placard listing the provinces and their prices:
so much for Galatia, so much for Pontus and Lydia: if you want
Lycia, so much: if Phrygia, a little more. . . .' (i. 196 f.). No doubt
Eutropius did accept money for such posts. But quite apart from
the benefit accruing therefrom to the treasury, Claudian's audience
must have known perfectly well that this had been common, indeed almost normal, practice since at least the days of Constantine.[2]
It was certainly rife under Constantius II, and though Julian
tried to discourage it, Theodosius went so far as to decree that
a compact whereby money or land was promised in return for
a post was legally enforceable.[3] According to Zosimus,[4] offices
were openly sold under Theodosius—not surprisingly, under the
circumstances.

At the end of Bk. ii, Claudian returns to the subject with an
interesting new detail—something Eutropius had done since the

---

[1] Mazzarino, pp. 199 ff.

[2] Bury, *LRE* i[2]. 117, was exaggerating when he wrote: 'The greatest blot on
the ministry of Eutropius . . . was the sale of offices.' See A. H. M. Jones, *LRE* i.
393–4.

[3] *Cod. Theod.* ii. 29. 2, cf. Jones, *LRE* iii. 87, n. 56. According to Eunapius,
frag. 87, governorships were auctioned under the pious Pulcheria, and Zeno's
praetorian prefect Sebastian is reported to have shared the profits with the
Emperor (Malchus, frag. 9).

[4] iv. 28.

publication of Bk. i—which provides an excellent illustration of his malicious cartoon technique. He alleges that in order to recoup himself for the revenues he had lost from the provinces devastated by Tribigild and his Goths, Eutropius divided the remaining provinces into two so that he had twice as many governorships to sell:

> ne quid tamen orbe reciso
> venditor amittat, provincia quaeque superstes
> dividitur, geminumque duplex passura tribunal
> cogitur alterius pretium sarcire peremptae (ii. 585 f.).

Now clearly this cannot be sheer fiction. Claudian could hardly have made such a specific accusation if it had no basis whatever. But it is equally clear that Eutropius cannot have halved *all* the eastern provinces—and indeed did not. In fact it had been general governmental policy since Diocletian, and even earlier, to divide the provinces into smaller units in order to achieve greater administrative efficiency.[1] Once more it was a practice followed by Theodosius, who had divided both Cappadocia and Armenia into two.[2] Hence there is nothing at all outrageous or even out of the ordinary in Eutropius doing the same (presumably only one or two provinces were involved in any case). But Claudian seized on the fact, and deliberately gave it a humorous misinterpretation.

To return to Bk. i, Claudian continues with the reproach that Eutropius meddled in legal and judicial matters.[3] But his only objection is that a eunuch has no business here:

> quibus umquam saecula terris
> eunuchi videre forum? (i. 233–4)

Then he even had the audacity to command an army in battle! Mars blushed and Bellona turned aside and smiled. The enemies

---

[1] Mazzarino, pp. 196 f., arguing, however, that the purpose was to reduce the possibility of military rebellions rather than to increase administrative efficiency. That the first consideration was much less important than often supposed has been shown by Jones, *LRE* i. 45–6.

[2] *Cod. Theod.* xiii. 11. 2, in 386.

[3] Eutropius' judicial activity is attested too by Zosimus v. 9.

of Rome rejoiced. Eutropius' business should be with Minerva's other role:

> Tu potes alterius studiis haerere Minervae,
> et telas, non tela, pati (i. 273–4).

The result (so Claudian alleges) was disaster. The countryside was ravaged, the women of Cappadocia carried off, the youth of Syria enslaved. However, as observed above, not even Claudian's sneers can altogether obscure the fact that Eutropius' campaign against the Huns succeeded. Once more, Claudian's real objection here is only that Eutropius was a eunuch. And though there were as yet no precedents, there was no particular reason why a eunuch should not have the ability to command an army, and there are certainly many later examples. Narses was one of the greatest of Byzantine generals, and, like Eutropius, had remained a civilian until past middle age: in later times it became quite common.[1] But Claudian is merciless where the wretched Eutropius' physical shortcomings are concerned.

We are treated to more portents—none of course equal to a eunuch consul, judge, or general. Then to a description of Eutropius in his consular robes, a hideous sight, as if a small boy had dressed a monkey up in silken clothes but left his buttocks bare to amuse the guests at dinner. The senate, some of them perhaps his former masters,[2] accompany the dishonoured *fasces* in solemn procession. It would be less of a disgrace if a woman had taken them: many lands have seen a woman ruler—but none a eunuch.

There was no longer any point in glossing over Eutropius' support of Gildo:

> Gildonis taceo magna cum laude receptam
> perfidiam, et fretos Eoo robore Mauros (i. 399–400).

Having introduced Gildo, Claudian rather irrelevantly inserts a brief eulogy of the energetic means whereby Stilico kept Rome

---

[1] For eunuch generals in the later Byzantine period (particularly common, significantly enough, under Empresses), see R. Guilland, *Études byzantines* i (1943), 197 f. Then there is the great Chinese eunuch general of the fifteenth century, Chêng-Ho.   [2] Cf. *CQ* N.S. xviii (1968), 401.

supplied with corn while the African supply was withheld; an excerpt, no doubt, from the second book of *Gild.* which he had been unable to finish. The mention of Gildo's eastern backing provides a transition to another disaster from the East, less terrible but more shameful—Eutropius' consulate once more. The rest of the book is wholly given over to variations on this already much exploited theme. Was it for this that Horatius kept the bridge and Mucius braved the flames? Eutropius' name appears on the same *fasti* as one of his former masters, Arinthaeus (cos. 372). The book ends with an exhortation from Roma to Stilico to destroy Eutropius: she assumes that he is only hesitating out of disgust. But what need of weapons? Eutropius' guilty back will cringe before the familiar sound of the whip!

It should be clear enough by now that Claudian rests his case almost entirely on the one fact that Eutropius was a eunuch. His attack on his judicial and military activity and above all his consulate neither have nor were felt to need any further justification. Rufinus he had portrayed as a primeval force, a power of darkness. Eutropius is merely disgusting, a joke—and a bad joke. Claudian simply exploits to the full (and beyond) the universal dislike and contempt in which eunuchs were held[1]—an attitude which was probably even stronger in the West, where eunuchs were less common and less influential. At the other end of the spectrum, the consulate was still generally felt to be the highest honour to which a private citizen could aspire. It could be traced (and of course Claudian predictably traces it) right back to the first year of the Republic, 900 years ago, and had been held by most of the famous men in Roman history over that period. Claudian knew what he was doing when he decided to concentrate, in front of a western audience, on the theme of the eunuch consul.

The result, however, is that as a political manifesto, the poem has astonishingly little content.[2] Now Claudian's skill as a political

[1] Keith Hopkins, 'Eunuchs in politics in the later Roman Empire', *Proc. Camb. Phil. Soc.* 189 (1963), at pp. 78–80.

[2] F. J. E. Raby, *Secular Latin Poetry* i² (1957), 91, writes of *Eutr.* that, for all his rhetoric, Claudian 'has proved very little'. He did not ask himself whether Claudian was trying to 'prove' anything.

writer cannot be doubted after *Gild.* The lack of content is deliberate. Claudian's purpose was merely to arouse hatred and
contempt against Eutropius. No one could have guessed from
Eutr. i alone that Eutropius was a more dangerous rival to Stilico
than Rufinus had ever been. There is still no revelation of Eutropius' hostility to Stilico, of his attempts to disaffect the western
troops, and even on Stilico's life, that first appear in *Stil.*, twelve
months later. Above all, still no hint of the decree outlawing
Stilico. *Ruf.* had been designed to clear Stilico and convict Rufinus
of some very specific accusations. *Eutr.* i had the very limited
objective of simply creating an unfavourable climate of opinion.

Like *Ruf.*, *Eutr.* too was a serial. As usual, however, Claudian
did not write Bk. ii at once. He waited for fresh developments.
And what eventually prompted him to publish Bk. ii, about six
months later, was not, as often supposed, the fall of Eutropius,
but his failure to deal with Tribigild's rebellion.

Tribigild was a Goth, apparently a kinsman of Gainas, who had
been placed in command of some Gothic federates settled in
Phrygia, with the rank of *comes.* It was the usual story. Eutropius
had been cutting down Tribigild's subsidies—or else not increasing them to the amount Tribigild demanded. It may be too that
Tribigild wanted a higher rank for himself, like Alaric. And if
Alaric could get what he wanted by rebelling, why should not
Tribigild try his hand? The precedent of Alaric was dangerous
enough, and it was imperative that Tribigild should be suppressed.
Eutropius sent out two armies, one under Gainas to the Hellespont
region to stop the revolt spreading or reinforcements coming
from that direction: the other under Leo, a man of low origins
(Claudian makes the most of the fact that he had once been a
wool-carder), and evidently of little ability. Leo's army was overwhelmed and Leo himself killed. Gainas came up, but refused to
engage Tribigild. He kept sending reports back to Constantinople
saying that Tribigild was very formidable and it would be best to
negotiate. Not unnaturally in view of his kinship with Tribigild,
it was assumed (then as now) that the two were in league with
each other, and that the whole revolt had been planned in advance

by Gainas. This seems on the whole unlikely. It may be that Gainas really was heavily outnumbered by Tribigild, whose army was swelling daily with deserters and discontents from all sides. After all, Tribigild had disposed of Leo's army without much trouble. And it must be remembered that Gainas' troops were predominantly, if not exclusively, Goths themselves. It may well be that Gainas was unwilling to risk them against their fellow Goths. In any case, Gainas did parley with Tribigild, and wrote to Constantinople again, reporting that Tribigild would only return to his allegiance if Eutropius was deposed. Since there was already a party working for Eutropius' fall inside Constantinople, headed by the Empress Eudoxia herself, it was not long before Arcadius had to consent. For the time being Eutropius' life was spared, and he was sent to exile on Cyprus: but before long he was executed on a charge of treason.

If Stilico had imagined that he would profit by Eutropius' fall, he was soon disillusioned. The government of the East was taken over by Aurelian, a fanatical barbarophobe who was no more prepared than his predecessors to give way to Stilico's eastern pretensions. In March 400 Gainas staged a short-lived military *coup*, to which he had been pushed, no doubt, by the anti-barbarian policy of Aurelian (consul in 400, though, like Eutropius, not recognized by Stilico). But by December Gainas was dead, and though little is known of the men who directed eastern affairs thereafter, John, Caesarius, Eutychian, Anthemius, they seem to have been united in one matter at least—their common opposition to Stilico. An illustration of this is provided by a tantalizing fragment of Eunapius in which Fravittas, a Romanized Goth who had defeated Gainas and been rewarded with the consulate for 401, accuses John of deliberately trying to wreck the *concordia fratrum*, that central theme of Claudian's attack on successive eastern governments. It seems reasonable to conjecture that Fravittas may have favoured a reconciliation with Stilico. It is significant that he was put to death at once by the party of John and Caesarius.[1]

[1] Eunapius, frag. 85 (*FHG* iv. 51): cf. Mazzarino, p. 224; Demougeot, pp. 263 ff.

It is usually supposed that *Eutr.* ii was inspired by Eutropius' fall—a hasty and mistaken inference from the undoubted fact that it was recited after his fall.[1] The elegiac preface is entirely devoted to Eutropius' exile on Cyprus, where, claims Claudian,

> scindere nunc alia meditatur ligna securi
> fascibus et tandem vapulat ipse suis (*pr. Eutr.* ii. 7–8).

The first paragraph of the poem itself also betrays knowledge of the exile. Fargues points out that when writing the preface Claudian seems to have heard only that Eutropius was on his way to Cyprus, whereas in the poem he writes as if he had now arrived. From this he infers that the poem was written after the preface.

The observation is good and true—but the inference (if natural) is paradoxical. It would be strange indeed if Claudian had written the preface before the poem. The preface is the last thing any author writes, and Claudian's, dealing as they mostly do with the circumstances of the recitation and those present in the audience, are no exception.

The truth is that the preface was (as usual) written after the poem—but the first paragraph of the poem (which I shall call the proem to distinguish it from the preface) was tacked on after even the preface. This might appear an extreme hypothesis, but its truth can readily be demonstrated. For if we except the few brief lines in the proem alluding to Eutropius' exile, the whole of the rest of the poem plainly presupposes that he was still in power.

The book ends with an appeal to Stilico from Aurora, referring in the present tense to Eutropius' halving of the provinces (discussed above), and begging Stilico:

> eripe me tandem, servilibus eripe regnis (ii. 593).

Throughout the poem Claudian has used *famulus, servus, servilis*, and similar words to designate the ex-slave Eutropius,[2] and there can be no doubt that this is an appeal for Stilico to save the East

---

[1] That is to say, when the edict condemning Eutropius to exile (probably to be dated to 17 August: Demougeot, p. 230, n. 575; A. H. M. Jones, *JRS* liv (1964), n. 4 to the table on p. 81) reached Milan.

[2] Similarly, 'servilibus arvis' at *Stil.* iii. 126 alludes to the East under Eutropius' rule.

from the rule of Eutropius. Claudian would hardly have ended his poem on such a note if he had begun it after Eutropius' fall, to which (as we shall see) Stilico contributed nothing; nor does Claudian dare to suggest that he did when recounting the fall in the preface.

This discrepancy between the first and last paragraphs did not escape the acute but perverse Jeep.[1] But he cut the knot in his usual cavalier fashion: after toying with the notion of positing a massive lacuna at the end of the book for the actual fall, he finally decided that the lines alluding to the exile in the proem must be an interpolation. The preface too must be an interpolation—or rather a separate, later poem on Eutropius' exile which a scribe had mistakenly inserted before *Eutr.* ii, left without a preface by Claudian himself. It was this scribe, in fact, who interpolated the allusion to the exile in the proem, to bring the poem up to date with the preface he had just given it.

It is easy to poke fun at Jeep's methods, but for once he has put his finger on a genuine problem, or rather complex of problems. He was even right to feel uneasy about the preface—three or four times as long as most of Claudian's prefaces, and unlike them in other respects too. Indeed, though there seems no reason to doubt that Claudian intended it to stand as a preface, it is really a separate invective in its own right, covering new and different ground from the poem itself.

A less drastic solution than Jeep's will suffice. Claudian had already completed the bulk of his poem when the news of Eutropius' fall reached him. For both artistic and political reasons the poem could not simply be brought up to date. Yet at the same time it could hardly just be recited as though nothing had happened. So Claudian dealt with the new development in a separate work, cast into the form of an extended preface.

But he then added some lines to the proem as well. Why another addition? Why not, it might be replied. As it happens, there is an answer. Claudian had received a fresh bulletin from the East.

---

[1] See his edition, i (1876), xxiv–xxvi.

It has been remarked that the fall of Eutropius did not bring about the desired improvement in Stilico's relations with the eastern government. Claudian knew this by the time he wrote the lines in the proem. He did not when he wrote the preface.

The burden of the poem as a whole is that Eutropius is the source of all eastern troubles, and the only obstacle to peace and concord between the two courts. The implication is that once he has gone, all will be well. And this, a natural first reaction, is the theme of the preface, a veritable hymn of triumph on the fallen eunuch. But the tone of the proem is strikingly different. Eutropius' fall is now too late and too little. It will make no difference:

> Quid iuvat errorem mersa iam puppe fateri? (7)

When an ulcer has penetrated to the bone, it is no use just treating the surface: it must be cut right out if the rest of the body is going to be restored to health (11–19).[1] In the preface he had exclaimed exultantly that

> abluto penitus respirant nomine fasti,
> maturamque luem sanior aula vomit (13–14).

In the proem he retracted the latter claim with some vehemence and no little bitterness. The 'aula' had *not* become more healthy merely through the exile of Eutropius:

> At vos egregie purgatam creditis aulam,
> Eutropium si Cyprus habet? (20–1).

Claudian knew better now.

It may be that no more than a couple of days separated the proem from the preface, and both were probably written only a week or so after the completion of the rest of the poem. But in a rapidly changing political situation, a few days can make all the difference.

The body of the book was left unchanged. Like the concluding paragraph, its tenor and purpose throughout presuppose that Eutropius was still conducting the affairs of the East. Only in this light can it be understood aright.

The proem aside, Bk. ii opens with a recapitulation of the

---

[1] *CQ* N.S. xviii (1968), 405–7.

portents which followed Eutropius' consulate: earthquakes, fires, and floods. For once not mere poetic fancy: the earthquakes are confirmed by other sources.[1] Naturally Claudian made the most of this evident celestial manifestation of disapproval. This was heaven's answer to the monstrous scandal of the eunuch consul—and worse was to follow. Next comes a section illustrating (a) the luxury and frivolity to which Eutropius has allegedly abandoned himself; and (b) the adulation in which the people of Constantinople hold him, senator, general, and commoner alike. This prompts Mars to turn in despair to Bellona, and lament the effeminate ways into which the East has now fallen. 'Argaeus reeks with heaps of still warm Cappadocian dead, yet the Byzantines have forgotten already. They have chosen a eunuch consul.' It would have been all over with the consulate had a similar spirit prevailed in the West as well. But Stilico, 'memor imperii . . . morumque priorum', kept Rome unsullied by the crime. The eastern court is as bad as their consul. Do they express any disapproval, silently, if not out loud? No. They applaud him, the 'Byzantini proceres, Graiique Quirites':

> o patribus plebes, o digni consule patres (136–7).

Mars decides to teach the East a lesson by bringing fresh war down upon them. Not in Thrace or Macedonia this time: he will stir up Tribigild and his Ostrogoths and Gruthungs. Let a barbarian teach the unwarlike East not to knuckle under to a eunuch. Bellona then assumes the form of Tribigild's wife and, catching him just returned from an audience at court with empty pockets, goads him to revolt. She tells him that he need have no fears. In the old days Rome used to reward services rendered and punish rebellion. But nowadays it is the man who breaks treaties who gains. Alaric, the 'vastator Achivae gentis', has been put in charge of Illyricum. It is not as if Tribigild will have *men* to face up to:

> alter in armis
> sexus, et eunuchis se defensoribus orbis
> credidit (223 f.).

---

[1] Seeck, *Gesch. d. Untergangs* v (1913), 305, 563.

It should be clear that Claudian's aim is to show that Tribigild's revolt is the direct consequence of Eutropius' consulate and the demoralizing effect it has been having on the eastern Empire as a whole.

At first, claims Claudian, Eutropius pretended to pay no attention to the revolt, and covered up its effects, hiding his head in the sand like an ostrich. But when he found he could no longer buy Tribigild off, he called a council of his cronies, wanton youths and lecherous old men, whose sole concern is their stomachs, who find even silk robes too heavy; skilful dancers, and experts on charioteers. Some of them risen from the dregs, with the marks of fetters still on their ankles and the brands still on their foreheads. It seems clear from passages such as this that Eutropius had been relying on new men, men who owed everything to him, rather than on men of birth and standing. Claudian makes the most of the opportunities offered by Hosius' former profession as a cook and Leo's as a wool-carder. He describes with relish how they assembled to take counsel at this crisis—and then promptly forgot all about it once assembled, and started to argue about the circus instead! The only one of Eutropius' lieutenants really put to the test was Leo, and he certainly failed miserably against Tribigild. But it is unlikely that they were all so corrupt and frivolous as Claudian paints them.

After the news of Tribigild's success against Leo, came other and hardly less terrible news: a new king in Persia,[1] who was planning to invade the Empire. No such invasion in fact materialized, but we cannot doubt that for a short while rumours to this effect were current at the time. Claudian exploits them to his own end once more. It is all Eutropius' doing, he who was behind the plot to assassinate the new king's predecessor!

We come now to the last part of the poem, which has usually been misinterpreted, with the result that not only Claudian's art and purpose, but the entire historical situation has been misunderstood. For Claudian claims that on the failure of Leo and the news

---

[1] On the text here (*Eutr.* ii. 481), see *CQ* N.S. xviii (1968), 409–10.

of the impending Persian invasion, the easterners began to turn against Eutropius:

> infensos tandem superos et consulis omen
> agnovere sui . . . accepta clade queruntur
> et seri transacta gemunt. iam sola renidet
> in Stilicone salus (487 f., 500 f.).

They confess they deserve punishment for deserting Stilico and entrusting themselves to slaves. The lictors shudder and throw away their *fasces*, like Maenads returning to Thebes and recognizing the results of their folly. It is this reaction which provides the context for the supplication of Stilico by Aurora. Aurora had been hoping that all would be well between East and West after Rufinus' fall, but then (a fine phrase) 'Rufini castratus prosilit heres' (550). After yet another tirade against Eutropius and his associates, the book ends with the appeal to Stilico to save and protect the East as he does the West already:

> clipeus nos protegat idem
> unaque pro gemino desudet cardine virtus (601–2).

Birt takes this as an allusion to Eutropius' fall. Yet as we have seen already the conclusion of Aurora's appeal presupposes that he is still in power. What Claudian is describing, or alleging, is a *decline* in Eutropius' power following the consequences of his policies, which as yet comes short of his fall. That Eutropius' position was already crumbling before his fall is likely enough. But what of this eastern appeal for Stilico's help? Did it actually take place, or is it mere wishful thinking on Claudian's part?

Many authorities, including Seeck, Zakrzewski, and even Demougeot, assume that, faced with this decline and anxious for his personal safety, it was Eutropius himself who appealed to Stilico.[1] Such a view is difficult to credit even on *a priori* grounds. After his conduct towards Stilico over the past two years, can Eutropius really have imagined that Stilico would protect him? He must have realized that Stilico had been waiting for just such

---

[1] Stein, *Bas-Empire* i. 235, writes vaguely that 'on y aspirait aussi à une entente avec Stilicon'.

an invitation ever since the death of Theodosius—and could hardly
be expected to make use of it in any but his own interests. Moreover, the upholders of this view are then faced with the problem
of explaining why Stilico refused this longed-for opportunity: for
it is certain that he never went. Demougeot suggests that he was
perhaps relying on Gainas to destroy Eutropius for him, concluding weakly (and implausibly) that he 'crût politique de négliger
l'appel de l'Orient' (p. 229). But there is no evidence that Stilico
could any longer rely on Gainas—if he ever could (see below).
The most decisive objection to the view is that Claudian—and
the view is entirely based on this one passage in Claudian: no
other source lends any support whatever—neither says nor implies any such thing. Had Eutropius, Stilico's bitterest enemy,
been reduced to pleading for Stilico's help to save his skin, Claudian
would certainly have said so quite explicitly—and made the most
of such a come-down for the haughty eunuch consul of a few
months before. Yet all he does is place this appeal in the mouth of
a vague personification like Aurora—who complains all the time
about Eutropius. A strange way to describe an appeal by Eutropius! Nor is it any the more likely that the appeal came from
Arcadius, as sometimes suggested. Arcadius would not have
acted without either Eutropius or Eudoxia, and neither would
have consented to such an appeal. In any event, had Arcadius
issued an appeal to Stilico, then we may be confident that Claudian
would have left his listeners in no doubt at all about the matter, and
seized this opportunity of dissociating Arcadius from the policies
of Eutropius (something which he was in fact clearly unable to do).

The truth is that there never was any such appeal, and it is a
misunderstanding of Claudian's method to suppose that there was.
Compare the opening scene of *Gild.*, an impassioned appeal by
Africa for help against the ravages of Gildo. Yet no one surely
would wish to suggest that this was a genuine appeal sent by
Gildo or anyone else in authority in Africa. If Africa in this scene
stood for anything concrete in Claudian's mind, then it was the
oppressed people of Africa as a whole. Similarly with Aurora
in *Eutr.* ii: she represents, if anything, the ordinary oppressed

easterners, suffering from Eutropius' maladministration. But there can be no question of a real appeal, even from them. Similarly again with the appeals of Spain, Gaul, Britain, Africa, and Italy that Stilico should take the consulship for 400 (*Stil.* ii. 218 f.). It is merely Claudian's usual picturesque way of representing what he believed—or rather wished to be believed—was public opinion in those areas.

What then was the purpose of *Eutr.* ii—that is to say the original Bk. ii, minus the preface and the additions to the proem? Clearly to paint as dark a picture as possible of the state of the eastern provinces, all of course the result (direct or indirect) of Eutropius' consulate, so as to give Stilico a good pretext for claiming that his intervention alone could save them from total disaster.

When Claudian wrote he knew only that Eutropius had so far utterly failed to check Tribigild; that Leo's army was destroyed and Gainas' afraid even to engage Tribigild—and that there was the possibility of war with Persia. At this time and under these circumstances Stilico might reasonably have expected (or at least hoped) that before long Eutropius would be *forced* to summon him back to the East with his army to suppress Tribigild and help in the war against Persia. Book ii prepared the ground for such an intervention on Stilico's part, just as *Gild.* had prepared the ground for Stilico's conciliatory eastern policy of mid 398. It may even be that Stilico was planning to intervene uninvited if the eastern situation deteriorated far enough (though there was Alaric in Illyricum to be reckoned with). This is why, for the first time in Bk. ii, Claudian does not restrict the lash of his invective to Eutropius alone, but takes in all his administration, the eastern senate, and even the people of Constantinople. His aim is to show that the entire core of the eastern Empire has gone rotten—and that only Stilico can cut it out and put the East to rights.

But with Eutropius' fall the whole situation was changed at one stroke. By coming to terms with Tribigild and obliging Arcadius to accept those terms, Gainas had effectively brought the rebellion to an end. The false alarm of a Persian invasion seems also to have subsided, for we hear no more of it. Stilico's hopes of intervention in the east were dashed—and *Eutr.* ii, as a political weapon, became irrelevant overnight.

For the circumstances of Eutropius' actual fall we must turn back again to the preface. The most important passage is the couplet where Claudian alludes in tantalizingly vague terms to its immediate cause:

> concidit *exiguae* dementia vulnere *chartae*;
> confecit saevum *littera* Martis opus (19–20).

What is this 'scrap of paper'? One obvious possibility is Arcadius' (surviving) decree condemning Eutropius to exile. Seeck objected[1] that Claudian would not have referred to an Imperial decree in such disrespectful terms: this argument has generally been accepted,[2] but it should be obvious that it is beside the point. Claudian does not, of course, mean that the letter in question was 'exigua' as such: merely that any letter was a small thing to have had such a result when compared with a full-scale war. The obvious alternative possibility is the letter Gainas sent on behalf of Tribigild demanding Eutropius' deposition.[2] Seeck will not have this either, and postulates a third letter, the letter Stilico sent in reply to the appeal Seeck believes Eutropius sent him. This suggestion is elaborated further by Zakrzewski,[3] who even knows what the letter said: 'A n'en pas douter il déclara qu'il [sc. Stilico] entreprendrait la pacification des provinces d'Asie et assumerait la conduite d'une guerre avec la Perse, à la condition qu'Eutrope donnerait sa démission.' We have seen already that this eastern appeal is of itself a fiction, so hypotheses erected upon it have a grave initial disadvantage.

Furthermore, this hypothesis entails the assumption view that Stilico played a leading part in Eutropius' fall. This historians in general have been perfectly prepared to accept. Yet Claudian, the decisive witness on such a matter, lends no support to it. It is most striking that Stilico is not even named in either the preface or the introduction, much less praised as the author of Eutropius' fall.

---

[1] *Gesch. d. Untergangs* v (1913), 565.
[2] So Mazzarino, p. 212, n. 2.
[3] *Le Parti théodosien et son antithèse* (*Eus* Supplementa xviii, 1931), 54.

And the tirade against the eastern court in the introduction, for realizing its own folly too late, and for supposing that all would be well now that Eutropius was gone, strongly suggests that the East alone was responsible. Now if Stilico had played a leading part, would Claudian have not only refrained from saying so, but actually given the impression that it was an exclusively eastern affair? Compare his emphatic attempts to claim the glory of Rufinus' fall for Stilico.[1] And any such role in Eutropius' fall as Seeck and his followers postulate for Stilico would have been far more creditable than his role in Rufinus' fall. Claudian could have had no motive for suppressing or glossing over it. Moreover both books of *Eutr.* actually end with an appeal for Stilico to destroy Eutropius and save the East, thereby preparing the ground for his intervention. Thus Claudian's silence on the point when actually describing Eutropius' fall can only mean that Stilico played no such part.

This argument from silence becomes much stronger when we turn from *Eutr.* to *Stil.*, recited only three months later. As remarked at the beginning of this chapter, throughout all three books Stilico's claim to the consulship is his triumph over Gildo— not his saving of the East. Indeed the only two passages which might at first sight seem to imply such a claim, in fact imply the contrary. First, *Stil.* i. 8–9:

> oriente subacto
> consule defensae surgunt Stilicone secures.

But though Stilico is said here to have 'defended' the consulate, this defence consists in having now taken the *fasces* himself— not, perhaps, a very ambitious claim. Again at *Stil.* ii. 279 f., Roma tries to persuade the allegedly reluctant Stilico to take the *fasces* with a speech which begins as follows:

> servatas, Stilico, per te, venerande, curules
> ornatas necdum fateor. *quid profuit anni*
> *servilem pepulisse notam?* defendis honorem
> quem fugis . . .

---

[1] See above, p. 91.

At first sight the italicized words do look like precisely the claim under discussion. But if we read on (especially lines 291–311), we discover that Claudian's words are in fact to be taken quite literally. Stilico has kept the year free from stain only because he refused to recognize Eutropius' consulate: and not only because he refused to recognize it himself, but because he refused to allow the senate even to debate the matter. 'Pars sceleris dubitasse fuit': 'even to have hesitated would have been to share Eutropius' guilt' (ii. 301). Here, if anywhere, was the place for Claudian to expatiate on Stilico's role in saving the East from the monster he had attacked so bitterly only three months before. Yet all he can claim is that Stilico refused to recognize Eutropius' consulate. This, surely, is one of the rare cases where the argument from silence is decisive.

What then is the 'exigua charta'? I am inclined to give my verdict for Arcadius' decree. The argument against identifying it with Gainas' letter is again an argument from silence: but it is a silence which has always been felt to be especially significant. Nowhere in all his output from 396 to 404 does Claudian either name or even allude indirectly to Gainas. It seems clear that, whatever Stilico's ultimate responsibility, Gainas played a leading role in the plot against Rufinus. Yet when Claudian comes to the actual deed, it is only an anonymous 'vox ingens' which cries out as Rufinus is stabbed. Gainas played an even more decisive part in Eutropius' fall: yet again Claudian ignores him. Everyone who has ever written on Claudian has remarked how 'significant' his silence is here. Yet no one has ever explained what it is significant of. Crees's view (that Gainas' 'deeds were too dark, his character too foully stained for even the epic of the fourth century to heroize. Either as protagonist or as a foil to Stilico he was an impossible character and Claudian knew it', p. 125) is hardly satisfactory. It is, of course, based on the common belief that Gainas was and always had been a creature of Stilico. Yet there is no evidence at all for this belief beyond Eunapius'[1] allegation that Stilico used Gainas to get rid of Rufinus. Even this can only

---

[1] Cf. Appendix C, p. 475.

have been an inference: a very natural inference, in view of Stilico's attempt to claim the credit for Rufinus' fall, but not necessarily the truth.[1] Even if it was true, there is neither evidence, nor even probability, that Gainas continued to work for Stilico. It is surely far more likely that he came to terms with Eutropius. Eutropius owed his rise to Gainas' elimination of Rufinus, and it would be naïve to suppose that Gainas was without ambition for himself. Whereas, too, Eutropius soon took steps to rid himself of the other Theodosian generals, Timasius and Abundantius, he continued to use and rely on Gainas. After all, what could Stilico offer Gainas that Gainas could not get equally, or indeed better, from Eutropius? For Gainas could never have hoped to play anything more than second fiddle to Stilico, while as senior surviving eastern general with a loyal army of fellow Goths, he might well have reckoned to dominate the civilian Eutropius. Is it likely that Eutropius would have used Gainas against Tribigild if he had known that he was a creature of Stilico?

The reason Gainas ultimately turned on Eutropius is not, as usually supposed, because he was working for Stilico, but because he was working for himself. As Zosimus observed (v. 17. 4), Gainas was jealous of all the honours Eutropius was assuming. And he no doubt suspected that before long Eutropius would eliminate him: the example of Abundantius had shown that Eutropius' gratitude towards the authors of his own good fortune was short-lived. So Gainas seized the opportunity of ruining Eutropius before Eutropius ruined him.

The best proof, however, that Gainas' aim was to benefit, not Stilico, but himself, is provided by his *coup* the following year. He seized power to protect himself against the anti-barbarian cabal of Aurelian. There is no evidence that his regime was any more favourable to Stilico than Eutropius' or Aurelian's. He certainly did not invite Stilico to come to Constantinople and exercise his regency over Arcadius. Yet this is surely what he should have done had he really been Stilico's creature all the while. Interestingly enough it was Gainas' conqueror, Fravittas, who

[1] Above, p. 90.

favoured reconciliation with the West. Gainas was not Stilico's creature: he was his rival. This, surely, is why Claudian is so careful not to mention him. How could he mention the real author of the fall of both Rufinus and Eutropius? A discreet silence was the best policy—the same policy he had employed with Eutropius till the latter took the consulate.

For the same reason (among others) I cannot follow Seeck's interpretation of *pr. Eutr.* ii. 21–2:

> mollis feminea detruditur *arce* tyrannus,
> et thalamo pulsus perdidit imperium.

Seeck[1] accepted the much less well attested *arte* for *arce* in line 21, and took 'feminea ars' as an allusion to the part played in Eutropius' fall by Eudoxia. Yet if Claudian could not give Stilico the credit, and suppressed Gainas' role, is he likely to have given it to Eudoxia, the ally of Aurelian and—so rumour had it—the lover of John? And quite apart from its better manuscript authority (though admittedly *c* and *t* are virtually indistinguishable in minuscule hands), *arce* is far preferable on stylistic grounds. Eutropius' 'kingdom', as a eunuch chamberlain, was the bed-chamber, a 'feminea arx' for a 'mollis tyrannus'. This interpretation is confirmed (*a*) by the reference to the eunuchs' 'femineas latebras' at *Eutr.* i. 466 (cf. too *Eutr.* ii. 553), and (*b*) by line 21. The pentameter, as so often in developed Latin elegiac poetry, is merely a restatement of the hexameter in different terms. The 'imperium' is what Eutropius had wielded as a 'tyrannus', and 'thalamus' exactly parallels 'feminea arx'.

So the 'exigua charta' cannot be the letter of Gainas. And in any case, while Gainas' letter gave Aurelian and Eudoxia a lever to use on Arcadius, it was not the direct cause of Eutropius' fall. Arcadius' decree was. Also, it is probable that the first Stilico and Claudian heard of Eutropius' fall was when Arcadius' decree reached Milan. It would thus be perfectly natural for Claudian to have spoken of it as the 'charta' which brought Eutropius low. Moreover, if, as suggested above, Claudian wrote the preface

---

[1] *Gesch. d. Untergangs* v. 565.

to *Eutr.* ii immediately on receipt of the news, he had probably not even heard yet of the continued eastern opposition to Stilico. Perhaps then he wrote before learning of the circumstances of Eutropius' fall, his information being restricted to Arcadius' decree. If so, he may not even have known then of Gainas' ultimatum and the petticoat pressure brought to bear on Arcadius to consent to the decree.

Seeck argued that *Eutr.* was unfinished, that Claudian originally intended to devote a third book to the fall of Eutropius. It should by now be clear that he was no more able to write *Eutr.* iii than *Gild.* ii. In any event, not long after the appearance of *Eutr.* ii he received a fresh commission. With Eutropius' fall his decree against Stilico seems to have been withdrawn,[1] and so Stilico decided to take the consulate for 400. Naturally a panegyric was called for; and since Stilico was now the nominal as well as the actual subject of Claudian's praises, the one book that the Anicii, Honorius, and Theodorus had had to be content with was not enough. Stilico was honoured with no fewer than three. Books i and ii form a whole, the first extolling Stilico's warlike, the second his domestic virtues, and were recited in Milan early in January 400: Bk. iii is really a separate poem, and was recited on the occasion of Stilico's triumphal entry into Rome a month or so later.[2]

Some features of this poem have been discussed at length in earlier, some will be discussed in later chapters. What concerns us here is the light it casts on Stilico's policy towards the East in the period immediately following the fall of Eutropius. Books i and ii were recited four months later, but Claudian presumably started work on them as soon as Stilico's decision (not perhaps quite so reluctantly made as Claudian would have us believe) became known, probably in September.

Book i covers in rhetorical and impressionistic fashion all Stilico's military exploits—his campaigns against the Bastarnae,

---

[1] Or perhaps, rather, it simply lapsed automatically after the decree (*Cod. Theod.* ix. 40. 17) revoking all Eutropius' *acta*.

[2] Birt had assumed (p. xli) that all three formed a unity and were recited together, but against see Seeck, *Forsch. z. deutsch. Gesch.* xxiv (1884), 178, and (decisively) Arens, *Quaestiones Claudianeae* (1894), 8 f. Briefly, Fargues, p. 25.

the two against Alaric, the campaign on the Rhine frontier in 396, and above all the Gildonic war. The relative amounts of space allotted to each are most instructive. Claudian's never very plausible earlier claims of a great victory over Alaric in 397 are not strengthened by the few vague lines the campaign receives here, compared with the detailed coverage of the Bastarnae campaign. It is in fact interesting to compare Claudian's *Stil.* version of the Bastarnae campaign with his earlier version in *Ruf.*, four years before. In *Ruf.* he had represented the affair as a resounding victory for Stilico, the more glorious in that he had defeated some Huns who came to the Bastarnae's aid as well. In *Stil.* he reveals that though Stilico did gain some sort of military advantage over the Bastarnae, the campaign nevertheless terminated in a negotiated settlement, which he blames on the malicious intervention of Rufinus, anxious to rob Stilico of the glory of a full victory. Claudian's motive is obvious enough. In 396, as yet insecure in his new position, Stilico badly needed a victory behind him—especially after his failure in 395. So Claudian made the most of his success against the Bastarnae, without mentioning the little matter of the treaty. But in 400, with his position consolidated and the defeat of Gildo to his credit, there was no longer any need for such subterfuges. In addition, his claim that Rufinus treacherously stopped Stilico exterminating the Bastarnae is suspiciously similar to his claim that Rufinus treacherously stopped Stilico exterminating Alaric in 395. Since both claims were gross distortions of the truth, there was little point in making this more obvious than was necessary by juxtaposing them in the same poem. In *Stil.* he reserves it for the Bastarnae, keeping a discreet silence about the campaign against Alaric. It had been necessary to justify Stilico at the time; four years later it was better not to bother.

But it is to the Gildonic war that most space is devoted. Throughout all three books Claudian recurs again and again to the defeat of Gildo as Stilico's greatest achievement, his title to the consulate, to a place among the heroes of Rome. This of itself is significant. For while we may accept that Stilico organized the campaign well and kept the situation in Italy under control, the actual defeat of Gildo was due entirely to Mascezel. Nor was it even the result of a battle, but of treachery and desertion on the part of Gildo's supporters, engineered by Mascezel. Nevertheless it was Stilico's greatest success so far. Once more, too, as in *Eutr.* i, Claudian devotes a disproportionate amount of space to Stilico's measures to keep Rome supplied with corn during the crisis: naturally enough, since this was Stilico's main personal contribution to the war effort.

But the most interesting feature is the striking difference of emphasis from the account of the war in *Gild.* already illustrated at length in Chapter V. Claudian goes much further than he had done even in *Eutr.* in revealing the extent of Eutropius' support for Gildo. In *Eutr.* he had still been very careful not to suggest that Eutropius was a serious danger. All that he had there disclosed is that Eutropius did support Gildo. It is not till *Stil.* that we hear of the cold war between Milan and Constantinople, of Eutropius' attempt to disaffect the loyalty of Stilico's troops, of attempts even at assassination:

> ut te nec noxia furto
> littera, nec pretio manus inflammata lateret (i. 292–3, cf. ii. 214).

> discordia quippe
> cum fremeret, numquam Stilico sic canduit ira,
> saepe lacessitus probris gladiisque petitus,
> ut bello furias ultum, quas pertulit, iret
> illicito, causamque daret civilibus armis (ii. 81 f.).

And for the first time we now find a discreet allusion (possible now it had lapsed) to the decree declaring Stilico a *hostis publicus*:

> quamvis et opes et rura tenerent
> insignesque domos? levis haec iactura; nec umquam
> publica privatae cesserunt commoda causae (i. 297 f.).

For all the savagery of Claudian's attack in both books of *Eutr.*, he had never betrayed any hint of the real insecurity and personal danger in which Stilico stood during and after the Gildonic crisis.

But if *Stil.* is more explicit in some ways, there is one significant omission: the revolt of Tribigild. This will appear the more striking when it is reflected that, less than four months before, Claudian had devoted nearly 500 lines to it, breaking off with the revolt at its height, and the East at Tribigild's mercy. Since *Stil.* has so much to say about eastern affairs, one might perhaps have expected Claudian at least to mention, if only in passing, the outcome of such an apparent catastrophe. Yet there can be little doubt why he did not complete the story. The thesis of *Eutr.* ii had been that Stilico alone could save the East. As it turned out, the eastern government managed to suppress the revolt on its own, with the help, not of Stilico, but of Gainas— thus refuting Claudian's entire thesis. As far as Stilico was concerned the revolt of Tribigild was an irretrievably lost opportunity, better forgotten.

It is striking too that in 400, with Honorius now 16 and Arcadius 23, Stilico had still not retreated a jot from his claim to the regency of both. Bk. ii contains an even longer development of the theme than before (53–99): moreover Claudian reaffirms the regency over Arcadius with even greater emphasis now:

> fratrem levior nec cura tuetur
> Arcadium; nec, si quid iners atque impia turba
> praetendens proprio nomen regale furori
> audeat, ascribis iuveni (ii. 78 f.).

No one could mistake this desperate attempt to dissociate Arcadius from the policy of his ministers. This vicious cabal that Claudian attacks so hysterically is presumably, rather than the now dead and discredited Rufinus and Eutropius, the party of Aurelian, John, and Caesarius, which was opposing Stilico at the time (Gainas' *coup* had not taken place by January 400).

How far all this eastern hostility had damaged Stilico's position in the West is uncertain. But it is worth observing that when comparing Stilico's achievements with those of Marius and Pompey, Claudian singles out as the major difference between them the fact that whereas Pompey and Marius were unpopular with some sections of the population—Pompey with the people,

Marius with the senate—Stilico was equally popular with all classes alike:

solus hic *invidiae* fines virtute reliquit
humanumque modum. quis enim *livescere* possit . . . (iii. 39 f.).

One cannot but recall the similar development in Claudian's third *Fescennine*:

> gener Augusti pridem fueras
> nunc rursus eris socer Augusti.
> quae iam rabies *livoris* erit?
> vel quis dabitur color *invidiae*?
> Stilico socer est, pater est Stilico.

Against this background it comes as no surprise that Claudian should have made the most of a possibility which, had it been realized, would enormously have strengthened Stilico's position: the birth of a son by Maria, a grandson for Stilico, and a future Emperor. At ii. 239-40, Stilico is praised 'quod pulchro Mariae fecundat germine regnum, | quod dominis speratur avus'. Then at ii. 341 f. Maria's pregnancy, labour, and even the birth of a son are described at length as one of the scenes embroidered on Stilico's consular robe (see p. 47):

> rutilis hic pingitur aula columnis
> et sacri Mariae partus; Lucina dolores
> solatur; resident fulgente puerpera lecto;
> sollicitae iuxta pallescunt gaudia matris.
> susceptum puerum redimitae tempora Nymphae
> auri fonte lavant: teneros de stamine risus
> vagitusque audire putes. iam creverat infans
> ore ferens patrem: Stilico maturior aevi
> Martia *recturo* tradit praecepta nepoti.

Naturally the latter details are wishful thinking (never to be fulfilled), but it seems natural to conjecture that they had some basis in fact. Was it rumoured at the time that Maria was pregnant?[1]

---

[1] Orosius' allegation that Honorius' marriages to both Maria and Thermantia remained unconsummated, I would dismiss as a stupid guess based on the fact that neither gave birth to a child, and designed to save Honorius from some at least

But whether or not Claudian knew the rumour to be false when he wrote, he made the most of its potentialities.

This description of Stilico's consular robe is the most blatant expression of Stilico's dynastic ambitions in all Claudian's work. Another of the *tableaux* is the projected marriage of Eucherius, the third union between the house of Stilico and the house of Theodosius (ii. 354 f.). The unnamed bride, described as 'progenitam Augustis Augustorumque sororem' can only be Galla Placidia. Another hope that was never to be fulfilled—but who could then have guessed that Placidia would marry a Visigothic king? We have seen above that there is no good reason to suppose that Claudian was exceeding his brief in laying such emphasis on Stilico's dynastic aims. Stilico was anxious to 'remind' his subjects that he was not just another general or politician like those who were dominating Arcadius in the East. He alone had received his commission from Theodosius. He alone was son-in-law, father-in-law,[1] and now prospective grandfather of Emperors.

Unfortunately Claudian's pen fails us for the next two years. And when he picks up the thread again for us in summer 402, his concern is with the Gothic war of that year. However, while it is understandable enough that he should have concentrated entirely on the war in *De bello Getico*, it was not quite so inevitable that he should have treated only western affairs in *VI Cons.* eighteen months later. *III Cons.* and *IV Cons.* had both served as vehicles for Stilico's eastern claims. And at *VI Cons.* 581 f., when recalling the day Theodosius entrusted Honorius (now aged 20) to Stilico, he passed up what might have seemed an obvious opening to include Arcadius as well under Stilico's *tutela*. With a writer like Claudian his silences must be given at least as much weight as

of the ignominy of two successive marriages to daughters of the hated Stilico. The rumours of a pregnancy reflected in Claudian are enough to scout the even more stupid story that Serena deliberately prevented consummation. She must have wanted a grandson as much as Stilico, and in any case, had she really acted thus, Claudian would not have written as he did. Cf. also now S. I. Oost, *Galla Placidia* (1968), 66.

[1] At *Stil.* iii. 122 Claudian makes the extravagant assertion that Stilico was a truer father to Honorius than Theodosius had been ('verior Augusti genitor')—perhaps his boldest claim so far.

his statements. There is perhaps just enough evidence to warrant the conjecture—in any case likely enough on general historical considerations—that, faced with the capable as well as resolute opposition of Aurelian and his successors, especially after the fall of Gainas, his eastern counterpart, Stilico temporarily shelved his eastern pretensions.

Not that he abandoned them for good. With Arcadius in his late twenties the hope of the regency might have seemed altogether gone. But in 408 Arcadius died unexpectedly, leaving the 7-year-old Theodosius II as his successor. Stilico had already persuaded Honorius, now senior Augustus, to let him go to Constantinople and exercise the new eastern regency, when his plans were cut short by the plot which cost him his life.

VII

ALARIC

I

In 378 the Romans suffered a disastrous defeat at Adrianople. But the Visigoths did not follow it up, and Theodosius turned their internal dissensions to the Roman advantage, and was able, by skilful diplomacy and lavish gifts, to split the leadership and settle the body of the Goths in Moesia and Scythia.[1] For the moment this might have seemed, to optimists at least, a satisfactory conclusion to the Gothic menace. In fact it only posed the same problem in different terms. What sort of *modus vivendi* could be established between 'Gothia' and 'Romania'?

In 394 Alaric commanded a band of Visigothic federates for Theodosius at the Frigidus.[2] But what he wanted was a proper Roman command, such as Stilico, Bauto, Arbogast, and other men of barbarian stock had enjoyed. This Theodosius was not prepared to grant: as yet Alaric was fit only to command other barbarians.[3] Alaric was naturally disgruntled, and when in 395, still in his twenties, he was elected king[4] of his people, he seized the opportunity of the crisis brought about by Theodosius' death and revolted.

Stilico engaged Alaric four times. On each occasion Alaric managed to extricate himself, and still remained a force to be reckoned with. Indeed, in 405, Stilico was preparing to enlist his aid when first Radagaisus, next Constantine III ruined his

---

[1] Cf. E. A. Thompson, 'The Visigoths from Fritigern to Euric', *Historia* xii (1963), at pp. 107 f.

[2] Socrates, *HE* vii. 10 (presumably from Eunapius: cf. Appendix C, p. 475).

[3] Thompson, art. cit., p. 110.

[4] I use the term 'king' for convenience, though Alaric's position was probably not so strong as the title might suggest (cf. Thompson, *Nott. Med. Studies* v (1961), 22 f. = *The Visigoths in the Time of Ulfila* (Oxford, 1966), 44 f.).

plans. Then in 408 Stilico was murdered, and Honorius refused to honour Stilico's bargain with Alaric. The result was an event which shook the world and spelled the doom of the western Empire—Alaric's sack of Rome in 410.

Naturally enough, men writing after 410 did not fail to point out that if Stilico had succeeded in what might have seemed his obvious and easy duty on any one of these occasions, Rome might never have been sacked. Thus for Orosius, the Christian, and Rutilius, the pagan, alike, Stilico was the arch traitor who betrayed Rome to the barbarians. And on the face of it, it was not without some justification that Orosius, looking back over this series of indecisive engagements, indignantly exclaimed: 'taceo de Alarico rege cum Gothis suis saepe victo, saepe concluso, semperque dimisso' (vii. 57. 1). Many modern historians too have been prepared to accept—albeit with widely varying interpretations— that Stilico had some sort of understanding with Alaric from the start. Bury and Seeck, for example, took an almost Orosian line: Stilico secretly protected Alaric (cf. Orosius' 'occulto foedere fovens') so that he could later make use of him for his own ends. And even those with a much more favourable estimate of Stilico's character and achievement (Mazzarino, for example) praise him for attempting, like Theodosius before him, to use in this way the more Romanized among the barbarians in the interests of Rome.

In my view there were no such agreements, secret or otherwise, between Stilico and Alaric before 405. Careful examination of the relevant poems of Claudian will support an alternative explanation of Stilico's failures which, if less than wholly favourable to Stilico's ability, at any rate does not call his loyalty or judgement into question. Claudian's evidence is of especial importance here, because we are fortunate enough to possess what he wrote after each one of Stilico's four engagements before the next had occurred. Thus Claudian alone among our sources was not writing with the distorting hindsight of even so much as a year, let alone the events of 410.

We have seen already that the view that Stilico's one desire, from 395 on, was to wrest control of eastern Illyricum from the

eastern government is a retrojection to 395 of an intention he
formed only in 405. It is my belief that the view that he made
a pact with Alaric in 395 or 397, or even 402, is a similar retrojection. With Claudian failing us after January 404, the reasons
for Stilico's new policy towards Illyricum can only be conjectured,
but it seems likely that one of the most important was the ever
increasing need for a new and more abundant recruiting ground.[1]
To achieve this end, an understanding with Alaric was essential.
For four years (397–401) Alaric had controlled eastern Illyricum
for the East, and when he tired (or was relieved)[2] of this command
he had invaded the West. Expelled from the West in 402, he
had been hovering ever since in a limbo between them, a potential
danger to both. So, to gain control of Illyricum, Stilico must,
since he could not eliminate Alaric, enlist him on his side before
the East re-enlisted him on theirs.

Thus Stilico's decision to make use of Alaric in 405 was intimately bound up with his intention to recover eastern Illyricum
from the East. Before he formed this intention he had no need
of Alaric, and accordingly no motive for all these alleged secret
pacts. He had no call to take the risk of protecting Alaric and
deliberately allowing him to escape. It is not as if either Alaric
or the Visigoths were promising allies. Nor, *pace* Mazzarino,
could it be said that Stilico had the precedent of Theodosius to
guide him here. The Visigoths in general and Alaric in particular
had a bad record. They proved troublesome and disloyal right
from their settlement in Moesia in 382. When Theodosius tried
to use them against Maximus in 388, he discovered that they had
been bribed by Maximus, whereupon they at once deserted.[3]
In 391 Alaric attacked Theodosius on his return to the East,[4] and
though he fought with him at the Frigidus in 394, he deserted
and rebelled again in 395. It is difficult to believe that Stilico was
prepared to take the tortuous risks ascribed to him by modern

---

[1] See N. H. Baynes, *Byzantine Studies* (1955), 337. It may be observed that
Claudian was well aware of the value of Illyricum as a source of cavalry (*c.m.*
xxx. 62). For his awareness of the urgency of the recruiting problem in general,
see below, p. 375.   [2] See below, p. 178.

[3] Zosimus iv. 45. 3.   [4] Ibid., 48. 1 f., with Mazzarino, p. 256, n. 1.

historians to win himself such an ally. We may well believe that it was only with reluctance that Stilico finally took the step in 405.

The campaign of 402 is relatively unproblematical. We have a fairly clear idea of what happened. It is very different with 395 and 397. Since both campaigns were unsuccessful, Claudian glosses over them in more than usually rhetorical and misleading fashion, and though what he does (and does not) say is nevertheless of the very highest importance, we are thrown back on the epitomators of Eunapius for some of the basic facts. Unfortunately they let us down rather badly here. Both Zosimus and John of Antioch telescope the two expeditions into one. Their agreement on this point probably means that Eunapius made the same confusion,[1] but this is of little comfort. Fortunately, however, it is reasonably certain that the actual campaign they both describe is that of 397, though they place it before the return of the eastern troops to the East and the death of Rufinus.

II

Let us now turn to the expedition of 395. According to Claudian, Stilico's men were just on the very point of rushing on the Goths to exterminate them utterly when a message arrived from Arcadius (extorted from him with threats by Rufinus) ordering Stilico to hold his hand and return the eastern army at once. With minor modifications and reservations this version has been accepted by such authorities as Mommsen, Seeck, Bury, Stein, Mazzarino, Demougeot, and now Jones. I can only repeat my verdict expressed in an earlier chapter (p. 89), that it is a tissue of tendentious falsehoods.

To begin with, is it not a strange coincidence that, according to Claudian, this is the way Stilico's campaign against the Bastarnae ended in 392? Stilico was just on the point of attacking them, and

> extinctique forent penitus, ni more maligno
> falleret Augustas occultus proditor [sc. Rufinus] aures
> (Stil. i. 112–13).

[1] Cf. Appendix C.

Even more remarkable, exactly the same thing happened yet again in 397. 'Extinctusque fores', says an old Goth to Alaric before Pollentia, 'ni te sub nomine legum | proditio regnique favor texis-set Eoi' (*Get.* 516–17). What extraordinarily bad luck that on three separate occasions Stilico was robbed of certain victory over barbarians by the treacherous intervention of his enemies!

That this is certainly not true of the Bastarnae campaign has already been demonstrated above (p. 71). That it is equally false of the 397 campaign will be shown below (p. 173). There is surely little reason to suppose that it happened in 395 either.

No Roman army had defeated the Visigoths since Adrianople, and Alaric, as the events of the next fifteen years were to show, was an able and vigorous king. It was thus imperative that his rebellion should be crushed as soon as possible. However low our estimate of Rufinus, it is hard to believe that he would have deliberately prevented Stilico putting an end to Alaric. After all, only a few months previously Alaric had laid siege to Constanti-nople itself, and if Stilico let him go, might be expected to return, or at least to continue his devastation of the Balkans. This could only have further damaged Rufinus' already crumbling position in the East. Nor was there any prospect of Rufinus himself being able to redeem the situation, lacking as he did the support of the military—and an army too. It is always said that Rufinus acted as Claudian alleges that he did, because he was afraid that if Stilico won a victory over Alaric, he would march on Constanti-nople in triumph and eliminate Rufinus. But granted that Rufinus could reckon on Stilico obeying the order at all (and this in itself must have seemed a long shot), why should he have supposed that Stilico would be more likely to obey it before fighting than after? If he let Stilico dispose of Alaric first, then he would at least have rid himself of one of his two most serious problems. The other way he left himself with both—Stilico and Alaric— still to face. If the combined eastern and western armies held back from attacking Alaric, for whatever reason, then Alaric would inevitably have concluded that they did not dare—as also, no doubt, would the eastern and western armies themselves. This could only have had the effect of raising Gothic, and lowering Roman morale. It would also—as both Rufinus and Stilico must have realized—have caused deserters and discontents to flock to Alaric's banner from all sides,[1] so that he would be even harder to tackle the next time, when the now combined armies were divided.

Under these circumstances, it is just as hard to believe that Stilico would have obeyed such an order from Arcadius. It is always said that he did obey because not to do so would have been to abandon his claim that he was really acting in Arcadius' best interests in accordance with the wishes of Theodosius. Yet in *Ruf.* Claudian has no hesitation in representing Rufinus as coercing Arcadius to issue the order in question. If Claudian felt able to take this line after Rufinus' death, why could not Stilico have taken it before? He could simply have ignored the message (alleging that it was extorted under duress), defeated Alaric, marched on Constantinople, and put Rufinus to death. Arcadius would have had no option but to agree that Rufinus had been coercing him and admit that Stilico had been in the right—just as Honorius, too, had no option but to acquiesce in Stilico's policies and submit to two successive marriages to daughters of Stilico. Stilico must have known from his spies that Rufinus could not last much longer in any case, and there is some evidence that Arcadius really was afraid of Rufinus. However strong Stilico's loyalty to Arcadius, it would have been very misguided loyalty to obey an order which amounted to abandoning the Balkans to Alaric for an indefinite period.

In the absence of any account of the actual campaign in Zosimus, we can never be sure what really happened. However, there are suggestive hints in Claudian which point, in spite of himself, to a very different answer from Claudian's own—and one which is intrinsically more likely.

Zosimus claims that in 397 Stilico's failure was due to the indiscipline of his troops. To this point we shall return (pp. 169 f.).

---

[1] As they did to Tribigild's in 399 (Zos. v. 13. 4)—as Claudian well appreciated (*Eutr.* ii. 222).

What concerns us at present is the prominence Claudian accords to the topic of the loyalty and discipline of Stilico's troops in 395. It is most striking to see how often and how emphatically he feels it necessary to draw attention to the matter. In *Ruf.* ii. 105 f., he describes how Stilico set out for Thessaly at the head of his two armies:

> Gallica discretis Eoaque robora turmis.

He stresses the very different character of the eastern and western contingents, curly-haired Armenians side by side with fiery Gauls etc., but nevertheless

> mens eadem cunctis, animisque recentia ponunt
> vulnera: non odit victus victorve superbit.
> et quamvis *praesens* tumor et civilia nuper
> classica bellatrixque *etiamnunc* ira caleret
> in ducis eximii[1] conspiravere favorem.

For all Claudian's insistence to the contrary, the clear implication of the passage is that ill will and bad blood might at any rate have been expected between the two armies. It was only Stilico's exceptional qualities which kept them in check. Compare now *Gild.* 293 f., written a year later. Theodosius, addressing Arcadius in a dream, harks back to the moment of his death:

> res incompositas (fateor) tumidasque reliqui.
> stringebat vetitos *etiamnum* exercitus enses
> Alpinis odiis, alternaque iurgia victi
> victoresque dabant. vix haec amentia nostris
> excubiis, nedum puero rectore quiesset.
> heu! quantum timui vobis, quid libera tanti
> militis auderet moles cum carcere moto
> ferveret iam laeta novis. dissensus acerbus
> et *gravior* consensus erat.

Once more Claudian singles out for especial comment Stilico's achievement in keeping the dissensions of the two armies under control. Only here the gravity of this dissension becomes more apparent. It can be described as *amentia*, both sides were causing trouble, there was talk of civil war breaking out afresh. The last

---

[1] For the reading, cf. *CQ* N.S. xviii (1968), 394.

sentence implies that the aftermath of the civil war was worse than the war itself: a hyperbole of course, but all the same very suggestive.[1]

Again, in his panegyric on Stilico five years later, Claudian recurs to the theme, devoting 17 lines to it this time (*Stil.* i. 151 f.):

> nil inter geminas acies, ceu libera frenis,
> ausa manus . . .

He describes at colourful length the diversity of the various contingents, and emphasizes the total absence of any signs of dissension on Theodosius' death. In addition he gives explicit instances of what did *not* happen: no looting, no violence, no rape, etc. It rather looks as if Claudian protests too much. To return to *Ruf.*, Claudian lays enormous and absurdly exaggerated emphasis on the devotion shown by both armies to Stilico when Arcadius' message arrived. They refused to be separated:

> quid consanguineas acies, quid dividis olim
> concordes aquilas? non dissociabile corpus
> coniunctumque sumus . . . (ii. 237 f.).

They will follow Stilico wherever he leads them, be it frozen Thule, the burning sands of Libya, or any other of the distant and inhospitable localities so beloved by the Roman poets. What profit to return to their homes and children if it means leaving the side of their beloved Stilico? The eastern army trudges back to Constantinople in deep and bitter indignation, plotting Rufinus' death as it goes: its sole motive, so Claudian claims, was to prove its loyalty to Stilico. Now we have seen already that it is most unlikely that Rufinus' assassination was really the result of a spontaneous plot on the part of the army.

Obviously it is natural enough to praise a general for the good discipline he kept—and to dilate a little on the affection and esteem in which he was held by his men. But there is clearly more than this to these particular passages of Claudian. On his own admission in *Gild.* there *was* grave dissension between the two armies

---

[1] This is not the only time the fondness of the poet and *rhetor* for hyperbole leads the politician to make points he might better have suppressed. Cf. p. 177, n. 3 below.

for some while after the Frigidus, which serves only to underline the significance of the fact that in *Ruf.* and *Stil.* he denied that there was. And since he introduces the motif twice into his account of the 395 campaign itself (*Ruf.* ii. 105 f., 237 f.), it seems legitimate to wonder whether perhaps Stilico did after all have trouble with indiscipline and even disloyalty in his army.

That there should be such ill feeling was only to have been expected. For some time by 395, Theodosius had been enrolling Goths and other barbarians into his armies with more enthusiasm than judgement—and on more favourable terms than Roman citizens, severely punishing all who discriminated against them.[1] Naturally, this policy gave rise to much criticism—especially, it may be conjectured, among the more conservative elements in the army. Nor was this mere prejudice on the part of Theodosius' critics. It is clear from several incidents related by Zosimus that these Goths proved undisciplined and unreliable from the first.

The armies Theodosius had led against both Maximus and Eugenius contained a dangerously high proportion of barbarians.[2] It is easy to appreciate that Theodosius, and after him Stilico, found it no easy task to amalgamate these troops with the defeated remnants of the much more Romanized western army: the more so, since the battle between them had lasted for two bitterly fought days, with terrible casualties on both sides. It was only decided in the end by the combination of a sudden hurricane which blinded the western army, and of treachery. Some of Eugenius' officers agreed to go over to Theodosius if he guaranteed them high commands in his army.[3] Against this background it becomes the more significant that forty days after Theodosius' death St. Ambrose, too, in his funeral oration, should twice have appealed to the loyalty of the army.[4]

Suppose, then, we accept the natural implication of Claudian's

[1] Cf. Thompson, *Historia* xii (1963), 108.

[2] Cf. the sources collected by Jones, *LRE* iii (1964), 29, n. 54.

[3] Homes Dudden, *St. Ambrose* ii (1935), 430.

[4] *De Ob. Theod.* 2 and 8, with J. R. Palanque, *S. Ambroise et l'empire romain* (1933), 301.

exaggerated insistence on the unity and reliability of the combined armies in 395: that Stilico did in fact experience difficulty in controlling them. It now becomes much easier to explain both his failure to deal with Alaric and his return of the eastern army, without having recourse to implausible interventions from the East—still less to secret pacts or treachery.

Naturally, if Stilico had felt that he could not rely on his army, he could not have risked giving battle. The Romans could not afford another Adrianople. It may be that it was the strong Gothic element in the eastern army which caused him most concern:[1] could they be trusted to fight to the death against their own countrymen? It is significant that the officer under whose command Stilico returned them—and whose very name Claudian so conspicuously and consistently suppresses—was a Goth, Gainas. Moreover, as we have seen already, there is little basis for the common view that Gainas was Stilico's loyal henchman. On the contrary, on his return to the East he became Stilico's rival. It may be that his disagreement with Stilico dates even from before his return—and in part at least explains the events of 395.

We must presumably accept that Stilico came within striking distance of Alaric. Claudian would hardly have represented him as on the point of engaging battle if every man in that part at least of the army which returned to the West had been prepared to testify that they never even sighted the enemy. But the rank and file could not have known why they did not engage: here at least there was room for invention.

This brings us to the problem of the return of the eastern army, which has scarcely so far received the attention it deserves. Indeed no one yet seems to have appreciated that it is a problem. It is not merely that there are intrinsic difficulties and implausibilities in Claudian's version. We have to contend with the very different version (so far ignored) of the Eunapian tradition,[2]

---

[1] In addition, the eastern troops were probably anxious to rejoin the wives and families they had not seen for eighteen months: it is suspicious that Claudian explicitly denies any such desire on their part (*Ruf.* ii. 266-7).

[2] Cf. Appendix C.

represented for us by both Zosimus and John of Antioch. For Claudian, the return of the eastern army is an intimate, in fact the most important, part of the order received from Arcadius on the point of battle (cf. *Ruf.* ii. 161 f.). But both John and Zosimus relate it quite separately from the conclusion of the expedition itself.[1] Zosimus, moreover, so far from bearing out Claudian's claim that Arcadius ordered Stilico to return the troops, assigns the initiative to Stilico, and represents him as persuading Honorius to allow him to return them. I have yet to discover a historian who has preferred this version: yet considerations of intrinsic probability aside, it should be observed at once that Claudian, writing as he was in defence of Stilico, had every motive to misrepresent the affair, Zosimus none. Of course Zosimus (that is to say, Eunapius) may have made a mistake: but it would be a very careless mistake indeed to have confused Arcadius ordering Stilico with Stilico persuading Honorius.

Claudian repeats his version in an even more extreme form at *Stil.* ii. 95 f.:

> mittitur et miles, quamvis certamine partes
> iam tumeant. hostem muniri robore mavis
> quam peccare fidem.

Once more Claudian protests a shade too much. To arm one's enemy on the brink of civil war is not the act of a loyal patriot, it is the act of a fool: and Stilico was certainly not a fool.

Perhaps the most unsatisfactory feature of Claudian's version is his failure to suggest any real motive for the return of the troops. Yet both John and Zosimus suggest what might have seemed a perfectly satisfactory and sufficient motive: the growing need of the eastern government for more troops to defend the much harried eastern provinces. That Arcadius was in desperate need of reinforcements there can be no doubt. But in Claudian this consideration is completely suppressed: neither Stilico nor Rufinus is represented as giving it a moment's thought. The return of the

---

[1] It may be added that Socrates' reference to the return of the eastern army (*HE* vi. 1) lends no support to Claudian's version, though not too much can be made of this, since Socrates does not mention Stilico.

troops is just a part—an unquestioned and unexplained part—of Rufinus' wicked plan to save himself from the wrath of Stilico and betray the Empire to the barbarians.

Now it is clear that *Ruf.* ii is an apologia for Stilico's conduct in 395. But what sort of criticism was Claudian answering? After setting out with two armies to punish one barbarian rebel, Stilico had returned with only one army and the rebel still at large and causing more damage than before. Men must have been asking why it was that he had sent one of his armies away before using it to destroy Alaric. And even if Stilico pleaded the defence of the eastern frontier, the question still remained, why send half the army away *before* destroying Alaric? This had after all been the object of his expedition.

Surely, then, Claudian took the line he did because his purpose was to conceal the fact that Stilico had returned the eastern troops *voluntarily*. For once this fact was admitted, then there was no creditable explanation. Of the possible alternatives, the obvious one, treachery, would have been scarcely less creditable in the eyes of hostile critics than the truth, that the unreliability of the eastern troops had made battle impossible, and that, in order both to conceal this and to prevent such a fiasco recurring, Stilico had seized on the pretext of Arcadius' defence requirements to rid himself of them.

As I hope to have shown above (pp. 89 f.), the purpose of *Ruf.* ii as a whole was to deflect from Stilico to Rufinus responsibility for Alaric's occupation of Greece. As emerges even from Claudian's version, the return of the eastern army was a central factor in Stilico's failure in 395—a failure which allowed Alaric to penetrate into Greece. Moreover (as will be argued in the next paragraph) without the eastern troops Stilico was unable to defend Greece until he had recruited a new, western, army. So if Claudian's justification of Stilico's conduct was to succeed, it had to explain at one stroke both the failure of the expedition and the return of the eastern army. And this is precisely what it does. It is not surprising that eastern writers (the Eunapian tradition) should have thought that Stilico's motive was solicitude for the eastern frontier:

this is no doubt how he explained his action to the eastern government (who had doubtless been genuinely requesting the troops anyway). Claudian's version was designed to explain it in the West. Once Claudian had decided to assign the initiative in the return to Rufinus, then clearly it was best to say nothing about the question of eastern frontier requirements. Solicitude for the eastern frontier could only seem a point in Rufinus' favour—and opposition to it an act of disloyalty on Stilico's part.

III

Throughout 396 and early 397 Alaric was allowed a free hand in Greece. Why? Why did Stilico not take steps to stop him in 396, instead of waiting till 397? It is always said that Stilico was not in a position to intervene in Greece, since it fell within Arcadius' half of the Empire, into which Stilico dared not penetrate uninvited. But if he had really been appointed regent of Arcadius, then he could easily have claimed that he did not need an invitation. In any event he did go in 397—and certainly without an invitation from Arcadius, since Claudian is at pains to attribute the initiative in the campaign to Honorius (*IV Cons.* 460). So on any hypothesis this was clearly not an overriding consideration with Stilico. Moreover, in at least the early part of 396, Stilico and Eutropius were on good terms: Eutropius was biding his time and consolidating his position. Eutropius must have been as anxious as anyone to have an end put to Alaric's depredations, which had become, by the end of 396, perhaps the worst invasion Greece had sustained for a millennium. But he was no better able than Rufinus to deal with the problem himself: his own forces were fully engaged dealing with the Hunnic inroads into Asia Minor.

Claudian reveals, in *IV Cons.* 439 f., and *Stil.* i. 188 f., that what Stilico did in 396[1] was to tour the Rhine frontier: and it emerges from *Stil.* i. 231 f. that his purpose was to gain recruits. His preoccupation with this problem is confirmed by several constitutions issued between April and June of the same year

---

[1] Cf. Mazzarino, p. 127, n. 3.

concerning deserters and the provisioning of troops.[1] Left as he now was, with only the remnants of the army Theodosius had defeated at the Frigidus, Stilico could not face Alaric again before he had rebuilt his army. This, I would suggest, is the primary reason he waited a whole year before turning his attention again to Alaric. That Stilico was reduced to such straits by the loss of the eastern army is further confirmation that he must have had a more substantial motive for returning it than Claudian suggests.

Claudian makes it perfectly clear that there was no fighting at all in the 395 campaign. But he frequently recurs to the theme of Arcadia piled high with Gothic dead and barbarian wagons swimming with blood in 397. This time there must at least have been a battle. Significantly enough, however, Claudian nowhere actually lays claim to a Roman victory in so many words. The only details given are in *IV Cons.*, where he describes how (once more) Stilico ran Alaric to earth and blockaded him:

> uno colle latent [sc. the Goths]. sitiens inclusaque vallo
> ereptas quaesivit aquas, quas hostibus ante
> contiguas alio Stilico deflexerat actu,
> mirantemque novas ignota per avia valles
> iusserat averso fluvium migrare meatu (479 f.).

It is most striking, however, that he then changes the subject abruptly, without even saying whether or not the Goths were actually starved into surrender! It is Zosimus (i.e. Eunapius) who finishes the story for us, taking up exactly where Claudian had left off. 'And Stilico would easily have destroyed Alaric through lack of provisions', he writes, 'if he had not given himself up to luxury, mimes, and loose women, and allowed his men to plunder what the barbarians had left, thus giving the enemy the opportunity to escape to Epirus with all their booty and loot the cities there' (v. 7. 2). This is usually dismissed as a cheap and obvious slander by a hostile source. But is it so very obvious? It is surely significant that Eunapius, a hater of Stilico who, like Orosius and Rutilius, wrote after Stilico's fall, assigns his failure on this occasion only to lack of discipline. What one might have expected is an

[1] *Cod. Theod.* vii. 18. 9, vii. 4. 22–3: cf. Demougeot, p. 163.

accusation (or at least insinuation) of treachery. Bury argued that Zosimus' account could not be pressed because 'a phrase he uses is borrowed from Julian's *Misopogon*'.[1] But the fact that Zosimus (i.e. Eunapius) used a borrowed phrase does not mean that he was writing fiction. Why after all should it have occurred to him to borrow this particular phrase of Julian unless it had seemed appropriate? The detail about Stilico's loose women is no doubt a rhetorical embellishment, but embellishment of a fact: indiscipline.

That Alaric did indeed escape to Epirus, where he continued his looting, is actually confirmed by Claudian himself in a later poem, where he describes Alaric as

vastator Achivae

gentis et *Epirum nuper populatus inultam* (*Eutr.* ii. 214–15).

Even the detail about Alaric taking all his booty with him is confirmed by Claudian. In 399 he represents the Goths as still being in possession of the spoils of Greece, waited on by Spartan handmaids (*Eutr.* ii. 199 f.). In 402 he describes how the Romans recovered after Pollentia what the Goths had stolen from Argos and Corinth (*Get.* 611 f.).

When Claudian so obviously and so suspiciously refrains from disclosing how the blockade ended, what grounds have we for rejecting Zosimus' explanation—which is certainly one Claudian would understandably have kept quiet about? The more so since once again Claudian himself betrays a few hints in later poems which support such an explanation.

We have seen already that he was probably answering similar criticisms of indiscipline concerning the 395 campaign. In one of the passages cited above in that connection he vigorously denied that any of Stilico's men had ever stooped to plundering vineyards and farms. At the beginning of the section Claudian was thinking of 395, but by the end he was writing in more general terms of Stilico's control over his men: and the detail about vineyards points to Greece rather than Thessaly. Another

---

[1] Cf. his edition of Gibbon, vol. iii (1897), App. 14, p. 496.

suggestive but so far wholly neglected text is *Get.* 87–8. After
Pollentia Claudian crows over Alaric, the man who had destined
the women of Rome for his lusts, but whose own wife and family
had now been captured by the Romans: Alaric, *who once tried to
corrupt the Roman army with gold* ('nostri quondam qui militis
auro | adgressus temptare fidem'), now deserted by his own men.
This must allude to either 395 or 397, and presumably 397, since
in 395 Alaric would hardly yet have been able to accumulate the
booty necessary for such a project: by 397 he had the riches of
Greece at his disposal. Claudian, of course, implies that Alaric's
attempt failed: but then he naturally would. Once the story had
got about, Stilico would have to take this line. It is significant
(though understandable) that Claudian does not mention it in
any earlier poem. Yet in 402, four years after the event, he obviously expected his audience to pick up this brief allusion. He
must have thought that after Pollentia it was no longer necessary
to suppress this evidently notorious detail. Things which Claudian
first mentions in his later poems are usually things he did not dare
to say earlier: either because they were too flagrantly false—or
else, as here, too painfully true.

Compare the allusions to Eutropius' attempt to corrupt Stilico's
army during the Gildonic crisis, in the period immediately following his return from Greece (p. 113). Perhaps Eutropius too had
reason to believe that there was a chance of such an attempt meeting
with success. With the wealth of Greece in his possession, Alaric
was in a good position to bribe Stilico's hastily recruited barbarian
mercenaries, and it is perhaps asking too much of the loyalty Stilico
could yet command to suppose that all were able to resist the
temptation.[1] In *IV Cons.* too, written towards the end of 397,
Claudian recurs twice to the loyalty of his armies to Honorius—
a loyalty that will last, since it is not *bought* ('perdurat non *empta
fides*', 501, cf. 120–1). Nor should we forget the emphatically

---

[1] In 376 Visigothic optimates bribed the Roman commanders on the Danube
(cf. E. A. Thompson, *The Visigoths* (1966), 49). After Pollentia, on Claudian's own
admission they tried similar methods to prevent the Romans following up their
victory (*Get.* 604 f.). Again, Claudian says unsuccessfully, but one wonders how
far, e.g., the Alans (cf. p. 186) really managed to resist the temptation.

loyal speech placed in the mouth of the army early in 398 (*Nupt.* 300 f.).

Let us now turn to some of the modern explanations of Stilico's second failure. The most popular is that Stilico deliberately let Alaric go, after concluding a (or another) pact with him in the hope of making use of him later. But once granted that Stilico had no designs as yet on eastern Illyricum, then he had as yet no need of Alaric. Moreover—and perhaps most important—what could he offer Alaric? Gold was no doubt always acceptable, but Alaric probably had more of it at the moment than Stilico, and the only thing he really wanted was a proper Roman command. And this is the one thing Stilico, like Theodosius before him, was clearly not prepared to grant. It was Eutropius who eventually capitulated and gave Alaric his command in Illyricum, after which he gave no more trouble for several years.

It surely passes belief that Stilico went to all the trouble and expense of transporting an army by sea to the Peloponnese, running Alaric to earth, blockading him—and then let him go to continue his devastation elsewhere. If Stilico had for whatever reason been unwilling to destroy Alaric, then why go to Greece at all, thereby raising the natural expectation that he did intend to destroy him? After all, no one was forcing him to go. Indeed, strictly he had no right to be there at all. But to go into Arcadius' dominions uninvited, and then achieve nothing, especially after his exactly similar failure (for whatever reason) in 395, this was simply to cry out for accusations of incapacity or treachery—or both. Moreover, had Stilico come to any sort of agreement with Alaric, Claudian would have played his cards rather differently. As it is, though clearly very embarrassed about the outcome of the expedition, he does try to make out, however unconvincingly, that it was a military success. If Alaric had made a negotiated withdrawal, Claudian would surely have represented him begging Stilico for mercy on his knees or else protesting tearfully that he would rather by far have perished on the field of battle than suffer the ignominy of being pardoned, just as he does with reference to the negotiations between the two after Pollentia (below, p. 185).

Similarly, when describing the *foedera* concluded between Stilico and barbarians along the Rhine frontier (*IV Cons.* 445 f.), Claudian portrays them prostrating themselves before Stilico and begging for favourable terms.

It is sometimes alleged that Stilico lifted the blockade and returned to Italy because he had heard of Gildo's projected rebellion in Africa.[1] Now if Stilico had heard the news while he was still in Greece, then it is certainly quite understandable that he should have felt that his place was in Italy and that the Goths could wait. The seriousness of Gildo's revolt has been underlined above. But if this is what happened, then why did Claudian never say so? It is the only explanation of Stilico's failure in Greece which completely absolves him of any blame or suspicion of treachery. Not only this; Claudian could have praised Stilico for putting the safety of Rome above the punishment of a mere barbarian rebel—precisely the line he was to take about Stilico's reluctance to tackle Alaric again after Pollentia (below, p. 183).

Even if this is not what happened, why did it not occur to Claudian to say that it did? The answer must be: chronology. Gildo's revolt did not break out till late autumn of the year. As will be argued below, Eutropius' negotiations with Gildo, which preceded the revolt, must be placed after Stilico's return to Italy. Thus there can be no question of Stilico getting wind of the revolt while he was still in Greece. Had Claudian pretended that he did, the subterfuge would have been seen through at once.

Mazzarino[2] and Grumel[3] accept Claudian's allegation at *Get.* 516–17 that Alaric was protected by an intervention from the East. Now it is clear from *Eutr.* ii. 216 ('praesidet [sc. Alaric] Illyrico') and also from the words put into Alaric's mouth before Pollentia, 'at nunc Illyrici postquam mihi tradita iura' (*Get.* 535 f.), that Alaric was appointed to a command (presumably *magister militum*) in Illyricum by the eastern government. Mazzarino and Grumel argue that it was precisely in order to prevent Stilico attacking Alaric that Eutropius gave Alaric this command.

---

[1] e.g. Stein, *Bas-Empire* i. 231, and cf. 542, n. c. 72.
[2] p. 262.   [3] *Rev. ét. byz.* ix (1951), 36.

But it is very hard to believe in this third occasion on which Stilico was robbed of victory by such a last-minute intervention. Nor is Eutropius' alleged motive—fear of Stilico marching on Constantinople after his victory—any more convincing for Eutropius in 397 than it was for Rufinus in 395. Nor on this hypothesis can one explain Alaric's continued devastation of Epirus after he had escaped from Greece. For it is clear from *Eutr.* ii. 214 f. that the devastation of Epirus preceded Alaric's appointment to the Illyrican command: and not even Claudian alleges that Alaric continued to devastate Illyricum after he had become its legal governor.

Nor is it really very likely that Stilico would have refrained from delivering his *coup de grâce* for such a reason. After all, later that same year he was in exactly the same position with regard to Gildo, who was recognized by Eutropius as legitimate governor in Arcadius' name of Africa. This did not stop Stilico sending an expedition—successful this time—against Gildo. To hold back, for whatever reason, could only have laid him open to the same accusations of treachery and incapacity—as indeed it did. It must have been a moot point whether this would damage his credit more than to disobey Arcadius.

Furthermore, Claudian writes of this alleged eastern intervention in only the vaguest of terms, and even then not till 402, when 397 was past history. Why no hint of it in earlier poems, when Stilico's failure still urgently required both explanation and justification? That he says nothing in *Ruf.* ii, *IV Cons.*, or *Gild.* is of no significance. As we have seen already,[1] Claudian never mentions Eutropius in these poems, and minimizes eastern hostility to Stilico throughout. But why no reference in *Stil.* i, especially since he does in fact devote a section of the poem to the 397 campaign—just a rehash of his earlier rhetoric, Alpheus choked with Gothic dead *et sim*? And why not in *Eutr.* ii, where Claudian comments on the irony of the fact that, now a legitimate Roman governor, the 'vastator Achivae gentis'

iam quos obsedit amicos

---

[1] Above, pp. 92, 120, 124.

ingreditur muros, illis responsa daturus
quorum coniugibus potitur natosque peremit
(*Eutr.* ii. 216–18)?

Why not include among all Eutropius' other crimes, real and
imaginary, his treacherous protection of Alaric from Stilico's
revenge? The same charge fills a very large part of Claudian's
indictment of Rufinus.

Moreover, the passage in *Get.* must be read in context. It
comes in a speech by an old Goth, before Pollentia, designed to
persuade Alaric to abandon his invasion of Italy and retreat. He
reminds Alaric that no one has ever successfully challenged Rome,
that Stilico has already piled Arcadia high with Gothic dead, and
that they were only saved from total defeat in 397 by 'proditio
regnique favor . . . Eoi'. We simply cannot press these words in
a speech aimed at belittling Gothic successes, against Claudian's
earlier silence. The principal interest of the passage lies in the fact
that it is a (belated) admission that 397 was not really a victory
at all.

I would suggest then that we have no good reason to reject
at least the kernel of Zosimus' explanation of Alaric's escape:
indiscipline on the part of Stilico's troops, quite probably brought
about in large measure by Gothic gold. But this does not necessarily mean that the expedition was a total failure. That there was
at least a certain amount of fighting seems certain: Claudian
could not have alluded so often to his rivers of Gothic blood if not
a drop had in fact been spilt. However, it cannot have been decisive,
and Alaric escaped with most of his men and his booty intact.
But Stilico did at least succeed in ridding the Peloponnese of
Alaric, and it was not entirely without justification that Claudian
claimed that, by Stilico's efforts,

resurgens
aegra caput mediis erexit Graecia flammis (*Stil.* i. 186).

Claudian's first reference to the campaign (*pr. Ruf.* ii), written
within weeks probably of Stilico's return from Greece, is especially
skilful. Nothing he says in it about the savage foe no longer
profaning Castalia's spring is actually false. It is simply not the

whole truth. It is clear that Stilico's line on his return was that he had saved the Peloponnese, and thus achieved the immediate object of his expedition. After all Alaric was not a menace to the West in any case.

IV

But he remained very much a danger to the East. It is against this background that we must try to understand the subsequent conduct of Eutropius. Eutropius was well aware of Stilico's eastern pretensions,[1] and it is clear that he did not actually invite Stilico to make his expedition to Greece in 397. However, he would no doubt have been very grateful to have Alaric out of the way, with his own forces fully occupied elsewhere for the time being. What must he have thought when Stilico came to Greece uninvited, and then went away again leaving Alaric apparently unharmed? Not unnaturally he suspected collusion of some sort, and at once declared Stilico *hostis publicus*. No doubt he was genuinely apprehensive that Stilico might be intending to make use of Alaric against him. His answer was to outlaw Stilico in the East and open up negotiations with Gildo to transfer Africa to the jurisdiction of the East, with the object of destroying Stilico's credit in the West. But what was he to do about Alaric?

Eutropius took the only course left open to him. He granted Alaric the one thing he wanted, and the one thing he had not been able to obtain from either Stilico or Theodosius. He legitimized his *de facto* rule of the Balkans by appointing him *magister militum per Illyricum*. At one stroke the Gothic problem was solved. That Eutropius' motive was sheer desperation,[2] rather than (as often supposed) a cunning plot to use Alaric against Stilico, is strongly suggested by the fact that there is not the slightest evidence that he ever did use Alaric in this way.[3] Had this been

---

[1] Cf. Zos. v. 11. 1. And at *Eutr.* ii. 502 f., Claudian represents the Byzantines as terrified if they hear that Stilico has advanced even so far as the Alps.

[2] Cf. also *Cod. Theod.* ix. 14. 3 of 4 Sept. 397, aimed to protect 'viri inlustres' (i.e. Eutropius) against conspiracy by soldiers, private persons, or barbarians (cf. Bury, *LRE* i[2]. 118; Demougeot, p. 173).

[3] Indeed, it seems that Alaric continued sporadically to cause trouble to

Eutropius' intention, Claudian would surely have said so some-where in *Eutr.*, *Stil.*, *Get.*, or *VI Cons.* In general it is interesting to note how little capital Claudian made out of Eutropius' dis-creditable if understandable solution to the Gothic problem.[1] His reason is presumably that this was rather a delicate subject for Stilico. After all, whatever the means he employed, Eutropius had succeeded where Stilico had failed.

It is often alleged that Alaric's agreement with Eutropius was followed by a treaty between Alaric and Stilico, by the terms of which Alaric undertook not to invade the dominions of Honorius. This view is wholly based on two passages in Claudian. The first is *Get.* 496 f., where the old Goth laments Alaric's rashness:

> saepe quidem frustra monui, servator ut icti
> foederis Emathia tutus tellure maneres.

What is this *foedus* according to which Alaric undertook to remain in 'Emathia tellus', and which he evidently violated to invade Italy? According to Mazzarino and Grumel it is a non-aggression pact between Stilico and Alaric. Grumel places it immediately after, as Stilico's answer to, the agreement between Alaric and Eutropius;[2] Stilico's motive was apprehension that Eutropius would use Alaric against him. Mazzarino feels obliged to put it two years later, on the ground that Claudian's reference to Alaric as 'vastator Achivae gentis' late in 399 is 'too harsh' for such an agreement to have been in existence at that time.[3]

Eutropius in eastern Illyricum if his subsidies were not paid: cf. Demougeot, p. 267.

[1] The allusion to the 'vastator Achivae gentis' who 'praesidet Illyrico' (*Eutr.* ii. 214 f.) is no exception. It does not come in an attack by Claudian *in propria persona*, but in a trouble-making speech by Bellona inciting Tribigild to revolt because Eutropius has not treated him the same way. And in *Eutr.* i. 241–2 Claudian alludes in remarkably non-committal terms to the occasions when Eutropius 'arbiter . . . belli pacisque recurrit | adloquiturque Getas' (contrast the capital he had made out of Rufinus' parleys with the Goths). I cannot accept that Fargues (Commentary on *Eutr.* ii. 215) was justified in claiming on the evidence of *Get.* 535 f. that Eutropius' conduct 'a été l'objet de vives critiques de la part de Stilichon'. Even here the criticism is very indirect—and long after the event.

[2] *Rev. ét. byz.* ix (1951), 36, with n. 3.

[3] p. 69: against, cf. Grumel, loc. cit. It might be observed in any case that there

But is there the slightest ground for supposing that the old Goth is alluding either to a non-aggression pact, or to a pact at all between Stilico and Alaric? Surely what he has in mind is the agreement between Alaric and Eutropius. After all, so long as Alaric remained in the service of the East as *magister militum* in Illyricum, he remained 'tutus in Emathia tellure'.[1] To cross over into Honorius' territory would be to violate the terms of his agreement with the eastern government. Whether or not the eastern government would have cared about this is quite irrelevant for Claudian's purpose: the point the old Goth is trying to make is that the Goths were safe while Alaric stayed peaceably in Illyricum as its lawful governor—safety they have now abandoned to turn bandits once more.[2]

Mazzarino argues that Claudian must have been alluding to some such pact between Stilico and Alaric as he postulates, because when Alaric invaded Italy in 401 he had already been relieved of his Illyrican command by the East. But this is quite uncertain:[3] and what matters for our present purpose is that Claudian did not seem to think so. Immediately before Pollentia, Alaric is made to say:

> at nunc Illyrici postquam mihi tradita iura
> meque suum fecere ducem, tot tela, tot enses,
> tot galeas multo Thracum sudore paravi (*Get.* 535 f.).

The use of the perfect tenses suggests that Claudian thought that

are other examples where Claudian's inability to resist the temptation of writing a good speech leads him to dangerous admissions. For example, Rufinus' condemnation of Stilico's ambition at *Ruf.* ii. 144 f. is a little too eloquent for (Stilico's) comfort—and in fact makes several good points. Alaric's exhortation to his men before Pollentia, 'Romanamque manum tantis eludimus annis' (*Get.* 490), is rather damaging to Claudian's earlier claims of a Roman victory in at least 397. Thus Demougeot was unjustified in deducing from 'vastator Achivae gentis' that relations between Stilico and Alaric were 'assez mauvais depuis 397 pour justifier une aggression' (i.e. in 401–2).

[1] I see no objection (*pace* Mazzarino, p. 69, n. 2) to Claudian having used 'Emathia tellus' loosely for the sphere of Alaric's command.

[2] In fact Claudian's remark is very similar to what Socrates says about Alaric's revolt in 395: although Ῥωμαϊκῇ ἀξίᾳ τιμηθείς, οὐκ ἤνεγκε τὴν εὐτυχίαν (*HE* vii. 10).

[3] Cf. Demougeot, p. 267.

Alaric remained *magister militum* in Illyricum right up till his invasion. He may have been mistaken in this, but granted that he did think so, then it was natural for him to write as he did about Alaric remaining safe in 'Emathia' till he broke his *foedus.*

The second passage used to support this mysterious non-aggression pact, is from a speech made to his own men before Pollentia, where Stilico condemns Alaric because 'foedera fallax | ludit et alternae periuria venditat[1] aulae' (*Get.* 566–7). This again is taken to imply the existence of a treaty between Alaric and Stilico. But let us recapitulate Alaric's career to date. Nothing is known of him before 391, when he led a revolt against Theodosius; in 395 he led another revolt, looted the Balkans for two years, and even laid siege to Constantinople. Then for four years he ruled the same area for the East, until he seized the opportunity offered by Stilico's absence coping with another barbarian invasion in Raetia to cross the Alps and march on Rome. This, surely, is enough to justify Claudian accusing Alaric of treachery to both East and West[2] without postulating a separate treaty between Stilico and Alaric which Alaric violated in 401. Moreover, it is clear from an earlier passage in the same poem that the immediate act of perfidy towards the West which Claudian had in mind, is no more than Alaric's descent on Italy during Stilico's absence in Raetia. For at *Get.* 278 f. he writes:

> *perfidia* nacti penetrabile tempus
> inrupere Getae, nostras dum Raetia vires
> occupat, atque alio desudant Marte cohortes.

In any case, what did either party stand to gain by such a treaty? There was nothing Stilico could offer Alaric, who had now got the one thing he wanted from Eutropius. And Stilico must have been realist enough to see that so long as Alaric remained in Arcadius' service, the West would be safe anyway: and if Arcadius withdrew

---

[1] A phrase borrowed from Juvenal (xiv. 218)—missed by Birt.

[2] And in any case the treachery of Germanic peoples was an ethnographic commonplace, to be invoked at will without specific acts of treachery being required in justification: cf. A. Leiprecht, *Der Vorwurf d. german. Treulosigkeit in d. antiken Literatur* (Diss. Würzburg, 1932).

Alaric's command or Alaric himself laid it down, no mere treaties would suffice to stop him invading the West if he chose to. It was not till after Pollentia and Verona had shown that Roman armies simply could not destroy Alaric that Stilico first formed the idea of allying himself with Alaric. My conclusion, then, is that nothing Claudian says, whether at the time or later, lends support to the view that there was any pact, secret or otherwise, between Stilico and Alaric, whether in 395, 397, or 399; on the other hand, that what he does say is much easier to reconcile with the view that there was not.

V

Fortunately, we are much better informed about the campaign of 401–2. Not indeed that Eunapius or his epitomators help us here. Zosimus passes over the whole campaign in silence, and we have no fragment of either John or Eunapius. Western chroniclers lend some slight assistance, but we are almost entirely dependent on Claudian for all details. This time, however, owing to the happy circumstance that Stilico actually defeated Alaric in battle, Claudian has much more to say than hitherto. But even so there are some interesting omissions, and the way he says what he does say is most illuminating.

In *De bello Getico*, recited probably a month or two after the battle of Pollentia (April 402), he describes Alaric's crossing of the Alps, his initial victory over a Roman force at the river Timavus, and his siege of Milan. Then Stilico's relief of Milan, the battle, the flight of the Goths, and the capture of their spoil and women. Eighteen months later Claudian returned to the theme in *VI Cons.* The primary purpose of the poem was to celebrate Honorius' entry into his sixth consulate in January 404.[1] The unwarlike Emperor had cautiously waited a year just to make sure Alaric

---

[1] Gabotto argued that Honorius came to Rome in 404 to celebrate his Decennalia. If so, it is remarkable that Claudian does not mention it when alleging that Honorius' sixth consulate was more memorable than the other five (*VI Cons.*, *fin.*). And the proper time to celebrate Decennalia would have been 403, since Honorius became Augustus in 393 (cf. Mazzarino, p. 104, n. 3).

would not return, before holding a triumph in Rome (his first visit to the capital since 389), where Claudian recited his poem. As in the panegyric on the fourth consulate, more space is devoted to Stilico than to his feeble son-in-law, and hence to a *reprise* of his most recent achievements, culminating in the battle of Verona (July/August 402)—but with much new detail, and with some interesting differences of emphasis.

Perhaps the most striking feature about *Get.*—though one which has passed almost unnoticed—is that Claudian devotes hardly any space at all to the actual battle. He does not reach it till line 580, and even then we only get 17 lines. This of itself is suggestive.[1] And even more suggestive is the one and only detail he gives about it. On the death of their leader, who was (so Claudian alleges) eager to wipe away all suspicion of disloyalty even at the cost of his life, a troop of Alan auxiliaries were on the point of deserting when Stilico came up just in time to rally them. It emerges from this (*a*) that there were suspicions before the battle that the Alans would be disloyal, and (*b*) that in the battle they did let Stilico down. Once again, Claudian reveals in spite of himself that Stilico could not rely on his troops. And though he turns the event to Stilico's credit, it looks as though a disaster was only narrowly averted. This is all Claudian has to say about the battle.

That Pollentia was a Roman victory can hardly be doubted. But the evidence of Prudentius, regarded as decisive by Fargues, is worth little. This section of his poem is hardly less of a panegyric of Stilico and Honorius than Claudian's, and writing as he was within months of the battle while Stilico was still supreme, it is hardly surprising that he should have extolled the Roman victory. More reliable is the grudging testimony of the anti-Stiliconian Orosius, writing after Stilico's death. But we learn from other sources that it was bitterly fought with heavy slaughter on both sides, and, as is well known, Gothic writers of the next century

---

[1] Fargues, p. 111, rather naïvely ascribes this to the fact that Stilico 'ne dirigeait pas lui-même les opérations', but then he did not command in Africa in 398 either, nor did Honorius command in any of the campaigns Claudian credits him with in *III* and *IV Cons.*

claimed it as a Gothic victory. Claudian's description of the battle suggests that it was little more than a favourable draw.

This impression is only increased when we turn back to the beginning of the poem. After the usual proem, the narrative proper opens with a description of Alaric's retreat after the battle. The goddess Roma is asked to reflect on the reason why Alaric has been *spared*. 'Surely it is noble to spare the wretch, and a kind of punishment to see him on his knees. What vengeance greater than when terror breaks the spirit of the once haughty. But Stilico's clemency was inspired rather by another motive: consideration of Rome. It was anxiety for her that caused a way of retreat to be opened up to the cornered enemy ('inclusis aperire viam', 97), lest, faced with certain death, Gothic frenzy should grow more savage still when confined. To risk Alaric getting any closer to Rome would have been too high a price to pay for the destruction of the Goths. May Jupiter prevent any barbarian profaning by so much as a glance the shrine of Numa and the temple of Romulus.'[1]

By appealing to carefully chosen historical *exempla*, Claudian argues that in the old days, when the senate depended on *citizen* armies ('proprio late florerent milite patres', 106), Romans only fought aggressive wars abroad. In Italy, they were always too concerned with the safety of Rome to hazard all on one battle. He cites the example of Curius, who drove Pyrrhus from Italy (an interesting choice: Pyrrhus had *defeated* the Romans in battle!), thereby winning more glory than Decius and Fabricius who had checked him in battle. Again, though Fabius had delayed and Marcellus defeated Hannibal (who, again, had defeated the Romans on more than one occasion), it was Scipio who actually drove him out of Italy (Stilico, Claudian characteristically adds, combined the achievements of all three). And what was more, it took five years before Pyrrhus was driven out, and seventeen before Hannibal went. Stilico expelled Alaric in only one.

It is only too obvious that all this is an answer to criticism. Nor is it too difficult to see what this criticism was, and what gave

[1] A condensed and simplified translation.

rise to it. As Claudian's description of the actual battle has led us to suspect already, while Stilico may have won the day, Alaric nevertheless retired from the field with his army little damaged. Indeed, to anticipate, eighteen months later when Stilico had defeated Alaric again at Verona, and there was no longer the same need to gloss over this fact, Claudian admits it quite openly. After Verona, Alaric is made to say:

> non me Pollentia tantum
> nec captae cruciastis opes . . . non funditus armis
> concideram: *stipatus adhuc equitumque catervis*
> *integer* ad montes [the Apennines] reliquo cum robore cessi
> (*VI Cons.* 281 f.).

Claudian is not so outspoken in *Get.*, only a month or two after Pollentia. But it is still clear enough there that after the battle Alaric remained a dangerous force—and still inside Italy. It is equally clear that up till the time Claudian wrote *Get.* Stilico did not venture to attack him again, and was criticized for not doing so. Claudian defends him by arguing that it was more important to keep Rome safe and be content with driving Alaric out of Italy, than to risk another battle. The implication of this line of reasoning—an implication which Claudian is careful not to formulate in so many words—is that to attack Alaric again, even after Pollentia, might be to court defeat.[1]

Claudian lays great emphasis on his claim that Alaric's one overriding aim was to take Rome. Alaric himself is made to say that he has been urged on by the gods themselves with a clear promise that 'penetrabis ad urbem'. Claudian vividly depicts the panic at Rome when news came of Alaric's approach. The walls, long neglected, were hastily repaired (a detail confirmed by archaeology), all manner of omens were observed (eclipses,

---

[1] Similarly Gainas claimed that Tribigild was too formidable to attack. Treachery and collusion were alleged, naturally enough, but it may well be that Gainas really was unable to rely on his mainly Gothic troops to attack their fellow Goths.

showers of stones, fires, comets, etc.) which were duly interpreted as portending the imminent destruction of the eternal
city. And Alaric's three sieges between 408 and 410 would
certainly seem to indicate a desire to make himself master of
Rome.[1] Yet it is perhaps unlikely that he ever really wanted to
take the city. It meant the failure, not the fruition, of his plans
when he finally did. The *threat* of capture was an effective
counter in his negotiations with Honorius—so long as he did
not spend it. But Rome was too proud to recognize herself as
just a counter, and in Claudian we see the birth of the flattering
myth of Alaric as the heroic barbarian who saw the sack of the
eternal city as his destiny. It is surely no accident that Claudian,
reciting his poem in Rome, so carefully fosters the myth. How
better to underline the gratitude due to Stilico merely because
Rome still stood?

In *VI Cons.* Claudian takes up again this same theme of Stilico
preferring to drive Alaric out of Italy without risking battle to
protect Rome—but with a significant change of emphasis. He
now claims that Stilico had spared Alaric after Pollentia in order
to lure him back over the Po and then, with Rome safe, pounce.
He explains this plan of Stilico's very carefully, twice (*VI Cons.*
210 f., and 301 f.). Now this, if true, is clearly a much better
defence against the criticisms levelled at Stilico. Why then did
Claudian not make use of it in *Get.*? Surely it is because he wrote
Get. before Verona.[2] This is in any case likely enough. *Get.* will
obviously have been written not more than a month or two after
Pollentia (not much sooner, since it reflects the criticism directed
against Stilico in the weeks following the battle). And Verona did
not take place till probably July or August.[3] *Get.* should probably

---

[1] Cf. too Socrates, *HE* vii. 10 *ad fin.*

[2] Baynes, *Byzantine Studies*, p. 328, wrongly argues that Claudian deliberately
omitted Verona in *Get.* Birt too, p. lii, pointed out that Claudian does not mention
Verona in *Get.*, but wrongly inferred that Verona did not take place till 403.

[3] No one is likely to maintain Birt's once fashionable dating of Verona to 403:
cf. Baynes, *Byzantine Studies*, pp. 326–9; Müller, *Claudians Festgedicht* (1938), 17–22;
Mazzarino, p. 274, n. 4; Demougeot, p. 279. I infer July/August from 'anni vapor'
and 'aestivo pulvere solis' (*VI Cons.* 241 and 215).

then be placed in about June. And when Claudian wrote it, there was as yet no prospect of Stilico risking another battle.

There is one very significant difference, so far, I believe, unnoticed, between Claudian's defence of Stilico in the two poems. In *Get.* Claudian implies, mainly by skilful use of historical *exempla*, that Stilico was taking steps after Pollentia to accelerate Alaric's departure from Italy. But in *VI Cons.* he reveals that Stilico had made an agreement with Alaric. We now learn that Verona came about because Alaric 'rursus *pacta* movet' (204), and committed '*periurum* . . . furorem' (206). Stilico eagerly seized the opportunity of renewing the battle 'violato *foedere*' (210). Later in the poem Alaric is made to lament Stilico's cunning pretence of sparing him until he was safely over the Po (there had been nothing in *Get.* about Stilico's clemency being feigned). Naturally this *foedus* is usually interpreted as yet another of the pacts (treacherous or far-sighted according to taste) which Stilico concluded with Alaric. But it is hardly conceivable that Stilico would have dared to play such a dangerous game—especially after his failures in 395 and 397—with an enemy now far more formidable (see below) than in 395 and 397: and an enemy not now in the far-off Balkans, but a menace to Italy itself. Are we to suppose that Stilico deliberately called his men off before Alaric's army could be dealt a mortal blow?[1] Obviously the *foedus* was no more than a safe-conduct out of Italy. Stilico must have undertaken not to attack Alaric again if he in turn undertook to march straight out of Italy. The perjury of which Claudian accuses Alaric must mean that he went back on the agreement, and stopped to loot on the way (all his previous plunder had been recaptured by the Romans at Pollentia).

Now in *Get.* there is no hint of any such *foedus*. This cannot be just chance. Stilico evidently did not want it publicized at this period. Claudian was being pushed to extremes of special pleading as it was, explaining Stilico's reluctance to attack Alaric again.

[1] The same arguments apply here as for the 395 and 397 campaigns. What could Stilico have offered Alaric? Little enough, if Alaric was prepared to break the treaty at once merely for the sake of a little plunder.

And to have to justify this safe-conduct as well would have been too much. It may have been a prudent enough step for Stilico to take under the circumstances. He was unwilling to risk another battle, and the sooner Alaric was out of Italy the better. But the aristocracy of Rome could not be expected to look kindly on a general who negotiated with a defeated enemy. Especially if there were rumours flying about already of earlier such 'negotiations'. But after Verona, the *foedus* could be revealed and exploited as a cunning device to postpone, until Rome was safe, the battle Stilico had been planning all the time—as if Stilico could have known in advance that Alaric would break the *foedus*!

However, Verona was to prove hardly more decisive than Pollentia. Once more Alaric escaped with a substantial body of men. Claudian alleges that he would have been captured but for the rashness of the Alans ('calor incauti male festinatus Alani', 224). This may be an excuse of a sort—but once more it reveals Stilico's inability to control his own army. And again it is the Alans who let him down. (It is interesting in this connection to turn to Orosius' account of the period after Pollentia: 'taceo de ipsorum inter se barbarorum crebris dilacerationibus, cum se invicem Gothorum cunei duo, *deinde Alani* atque Huni variis caedibus populabantur.' No wonder Claudian was embarrassed at their conduct.) But Claudian professes himself glad that Alaric escaped; that way he can be a living witness to the Roman victory—'i, nostrum vive tropaeum' (228)!

The ineffectiveness of Verona is betrayed at once by Claudian himself. For he goes on to describe how Alaric, his spirit not yet broken (229 f.), tried to strike out a new path across the Alps and fall suddenly on Gaul or Raetia. Stilico of course stopped him, though Claudian gives no details. Nevertheless it looks as if the Goths still had a dangerous striking force even after Verona. Claudian naturally tells of deserters leaving their camp in droves, while Alaric, in tears, desperately but vainly tries to call them back. Alaric laments, in an eloquent and pathetic speech, Stilico's cunning and skill that have ruined him: would that he had died in battle rather than be left alive, disgraced and deserted, with nowhere to flee! It is not known where Alaric did spend the next two years, but by 404–5 he was still undisputed king of the Visigoths, and still at the head of just as formidable a force as before.

Claudian's unique value as a historical source is well illustrated by these two poems. If we read attentively enough we discover not only what happened, but how it was received and how justified. It must be acknowledged, however, that much of the criticism Claudian was at such pains to answer was essentially unreasonable. Backward-looking Roman senators expected a Roman general to march out and defeat the Goths just as Marius had the Cimbri and Teutones. But Stilico could no longer call on the highly trained regular armies of earlier days—nor were Alaric and his Goths an ordinary barbarian horde. The greatest single advantage the Romans had always possessed over barbarians was their sheer technical superiority, their better armour and weapons. Barbarians normally fought virtually naked.[1] It was partly at least, no doubt, for this reason that Stilico found the huge Ostrogothic horde of Radagaisus easy enough meat in 406.[2] But many of Alaric's men had fought as Roman federates, and by 402 Alaric had put to good use the armament factories of Illyricum. Of this Claudian was perfectly well aware. In *Get.* 534 f. Alaric is represented as making precisely this point: the Goth did well enough 'nullis cum fideret armis', but now Alaric has forced the Thracian smiths to forge him 'tot tela, tot enses, | tot galeas'.[3] It may well be that at Pollentia the Goths were better armed than Stilico's hastily recruited barbarian levies. We should not belittle Stilico's achievement. It was a great service to Rome merely to have held Alaric at bay and forced him out of Italy. It should not

---

[1] Cf. E. A. Thompson, *Early Germans* (1964), ch. iv.

[2] Not, as Mazzarino supposed, because Stilico had no compunction about destroying the savage Radagaisus, but preferred to try to use the half-Romanized Alaric.

[3] A good example of Claudian's keen awareness of important factors in the contemporary military situation—giving the lie to the common view that he lived only in the past.

be forgotten that if Stilico was unable to inflict a decisive defeat on Alaric, his successors were utterly helpless before the renewed Gothic invasions of 408–10. Alaric carried all before him after Stilico's death. And if Stilico's main achievement in 402 was only, as Claudian claimed, to have saved Rome, this is more than his successors were able to do in 410. Paradoxically, men blamed Stilico for the sack of Rome, instead of reflecting that if he had lived, Rome might never have fallen.

VI Cons. was Claudian's last poem. For the last four years of Stilico's supremacy we are deprived of the unique illumination his poems cast on the first nine. Regrettably we do not possess his presentation and justification of Stilico's new policy towards Alaric in 405. But I hope to have shown that this was a new attitude to Alaric on Stilico's part, intimately bound up with his new policy towards eastern Illyricum. I cannot find any support in Claudian, the decisive witness, for the view that Stilico pursued either policy before 405, nor any support for the much quoted and approved verdict of F. Lot,[1] that in all his dealings with Alaric, Stilico 'semble l'avoir ménagé dans l'arrière-pensée de l'utiliser un jour'.

---

[1] *Fin du monde antique*² (1951), 236.

VIII

THE PAGAN AT A CHRISTIAN COURT

I

THE question of Claudian's attitude to Christianity has evoked much discussion over the years, yet it can hardly be said that it has so far received a satisfactory treatment. To some it has seemed necessary to suppose that Claudian was a Christian, to others that he was a pagan propagandist, spokesman of the pagan aristocracy of Rome. But before passing on to discuss the passages on which these contradictory views are based, let us pause to consider the significance of some obvious enough but hitherto neglected facts.

We have seen already that Claudian's departure from Alexandria probably coincided with the mass exodus of pagan intellectuals thence, in 391, following the over-rigorous execution of Theodosius' anti-pagan laws by the patriarch Theophilus. Curiously enough his arrival in Italy in 394 coincided with the collapse of the last pagan revival in the West. After his victory over Eugenius at the Frigidus Theodosius had visited Rome in triumph, and exhorted the pagan aristocracy to embrace Christ.[1] But there were no forced conversions: Theodosius was far too astute to antagonize more than was necessary those enormously wealthy landowners whose co-operation with the Imperial government was essential for the administration of Italy. It was made clear that there would continue to be a place for the Roman aristocracy in the running of the Empire—but only if they abandoned their paganism. And as a symbol of this new pattern for the future, he designated as consuls for the following year two members of the most illustrious

---

[1] It has been much debated whether or not Theodosius really did visit Rome in 394. For the case for and against (cautiously inclining to the former) cf. *Harvard Studies* lxxiii (1968), at pp. 249–65.

senatorial family in Rome—but a family that had been Christian for a generation: the Anicii.

Whom now did Claudian first approach as patrons when he arrived in Rome at such a moment? One of the old pagan families? No; he offered his services to the Anicii, and was rewarded with a commission to hymn the Christian consuls of 395, the symbol of a Christianized aristocracy of the future. And in this panegyric he dismissed the pagans who had fought and died for their beliefs at the Frigidus as 'Furiae rebelles' (*Prob.* 138). Pagan Claudian may have been, but not of the sort to die for *his* beliefs. The man who had deserted the sinking ship in Alexandria was not going to board it again in Rome. Such considerations could not be allowed to interfere with the choice of the right patrons for a rising young poet.

And to whom did Claudian transfer his services after the Anicii? To the Catholic court in Milan. Honorius was very devout, and Stilico was certainly a Christian too, if not tough enough with pagans and heretics to please the bigots. Serena was one of the bigots: in 394 she had incurred the undying hatred of the pagan aristocracy by profaning in a most offensive way the shrine of the Magna Mater in Rome. After Stilico's death, they took terrible vengeance on her.[1] Yet at Claudian's hands she receives the most fulsome eulogies, no less than Stilico and Honorius. Indeed at *Laus Serenae* 223 f. Claudian praises her for her devotion to prayer whenever Stilico was absent on a campaign:

> numinibus votisque vacas et supplice crine
> verris humum: teritur neglectae gratia formae
> cum proprio reditura viro.

Pagans would have needed no telling which god and what sort of prayers these were. Whatever Claudian's own religious beliefs may have been, we must always bear in mind that, politically at any rate, he was irrevocably tied to the party of Stilico and Serena.

---

[1] Zosimus v. 38 (she was strangled by order of the senate during the siege of Rome in 408-9).

This seems to me a grave objection *ab initio* to the view that he was the spokesman of the pagan aristocracy. In their eyes he must have been fully identified with the Christian party.

Next we must consider the evidence of Augustine and Orosius. At the end of Bk. v of his *De civitate Dei*, Augustine relates Theodosius' miraculous victory over Eugenius, and then adds: 'unde et poeta Claudianus, quamvis a Christi nomine alienus, in eius tamen laudibus dixit', quoting from *III Cons.* 96 f., though he telescoped three lines into two by neatly excising two half lines alluding to the pagan god Aeolus. Augustine quoted them to show that even the pagan Claudian admitted that Theodosius had received divine assistance (though curiously enough Claudian was not in fact referring to Theodosius, but to Honorius, to whom, now that Theodosius was dead, he ascribed all the credit for the victory). Birt ingeniously argued that by 'a Christi nomine alienus' Augustine meant only that Claudian never actually names Christ (which is true enough in his major poems). Unfortunately, however, Augustine uses exactly the same phrase elsewhere in a context where it can only mean just 'pagan'.[1]

Orosius quotes the same lines of Claudian in the same context with the same telescoping and making the same error about their subject: the only difference is that he goes further than Augustine and calls Claudian 'paganus pervicacissimus'.[2] On the face of it, it might seem legitimate to dismiss this as no more than an exaggeration of Augustine, and allow Orosius' testimony no independent value. However, Augustine and Orosius were contemporaries and friends, and though Orosius was undoubtedly just copying out Augustine here, it would be rash to deny the possibility that he nevertheless had independent access to the information on which Augustine had based his judgement.

But what evidence did Augustine have? It is sometimes alleged that his statement is no more than an inference from the 'pagan character' of Claudian's poetry—i.e. that he had no more to go

---

[1] *Enchir.* 4 (*PL* xl. 233): 'his qui contradicit aut omnino a Christi nomine alienus est aut hereticus.'

[2] *Adv. pag.* vii. 35. 21.

on than we have. But Augustine was a rhetor and poet himself, and would not have been so naïve as this. Moreover, he was born some ten or fifteen years before Claudian, and wrote the book in question less than ten years after Claudian's death. Claudian was a celebrity in his day, and it is perfectly possible that Augustine met many people who had known him. We happen to know that St. Ambrose's future biographer, Paulinus, present in Milan during Claudian's heyday there, later went to Africa to meet Augustine. Claudian himself visited Africa for perhaps a year or so at the turn of the century.[1] It would be rash indeed to rule out the possibility that Augustine had spoken to people who knew Claudian well.

Whether what they told him about Claudian was true or not is another matter. If Stilico's enemies could spread rumours that his son Eucherius was a pagan (an unlikely story, but swallowed by Orosius for one), then it was almost inevitable that they should have made the same allegations to discredit his propagandist. And with much greater chance of success. Everybody knew that these Egyptian poets were usually pagan,[2] and the 'pagan character' of his poetry provided an obvious enough handle for such accusations.

Almost the only Egyptian poet of the day we can be reasonably sure was a Christian is Cyrus of Panopolis. He can be shown to have had some knowledge of recent developments in Mariology, he founded a famous church of the Virgin in Constantinople, and later in life wrote an epigram (which survives) on the *stēlē* of St. Daniel the Stylite. Yet when his enemies (the Emperor Theodosius II chief among them) grew jealous of his power and popularity, they accused him—of all things—of paganism.[3]

Thus the evidence of Augustine and Orosius may be held to prove that Claudian was believed by contemporaries to have been a pagan, but not necessarily that he was.

[1] Cf. p. 413.

[2] Certainly pagan: Ammonius, Eudaemon, Helladius, Horapollon, Olympiodorus, Palladas, and Pamprepius. Very probably so: Andronicus, Christodorus, Nonnus. For the details, see *Historia* xiv (1965), 472–7.

[3] See my *Early Byzantine Epigrams in the Greek Anthology.*

II

What now of this alleged 'pagan character' of Claudian's poetry, which has seemed so decisive to many critics? 'Claudian writes', remarks H. L. Levy, 'as if the old Roman state religion were in full bloom throughout the empire.'[1] Perhaps so: his pages are certainly full of Jupiters, Marses, and Romas. But does this prove that he was a pagan? We must not forget that many of the Christian poets of the fourth and fifth centuries continued to deck out their verses with all the old epic paraphernalia. As long as Vergil remained the staple diet in the school of the *grammaticus*, this was inevitable.

The most obvious subject for comparison is Sidonius Apollinaris, later Bishop of Auvergne. His panegyrics on three successive emperors, Avitus, Majorian, and Anthemius, in 456, 458, and 468 respectively, are very much in Claudian's style—indeed they are closely based on Claudian, both in general structure and in verbal echoes.[2] Claudian's *Gild.* opens with Roma and Africa pleading their case before Jupiter, who agrees that Gildo shall be destroyed. Half a century later the same parties perform the same service in honour of Majorian and Anthemius. Jupiter is still 'pater superum' for Sidonius (*c.* vii. 17) as much as he had been for Claudian. For Sidonius too, as in Claudian, when Roma has finished her speech, Mars and Venus stand by while Juno weeps (ib. 121 f.). This epic machinery obviously had no 'religious' significance for Sidonius. Did it have any for Claudian? Christian poets soon transferred to Christian matters epithets formerly reserved for things pagan. The Christian heaven becomes Olympus, Jehovah 'Tonans' and 'superi regnator Olympi': hell is Tartarus, Avernus, Erebus.[3]

Let us take an example of a literary genre well represented among both Claudian and the Christian poets of the period: the

---

[1] *TAPhA* lxxxix (1958), 345: cf. Demougeot, p. 288, 'il chantait avec trop de ferveur la mythologie pour ne pas être païen de cœur', and many similar verdicts.

[2] Geisler's list of verbal borrowings in Luetjohann's edition does not bring out the full extent of Sidonius' debt. It will be apparent enough to anyone who has read both poets.

[3] Cf. H. Hagendahl, *Latin Fathers and the Classics* (1958), 382 f.

epithalamium. We possess two by Claudian, of which the one on the marriage of Honorius is of especial interest. In addition to Honorius and Maria themselves, the parents of both bride and groom were all Christians: yet the poem is wholly pagan in inspiration. Cupid flies to Venus' magic palace to tell her of Honorius' passion for Maria. Venus rides to Italy on the back of Triton, followed by a crowd of Nereids to prepare Maria. Yet it does not follow that this is a manifestation of Claudian's paganism. Claudian was court poet: he would not have written like this had he thought for a moment that it would offend the Christian susceptibilities of his audience. The answer is that he wrote this way, not because he was a pagan, but simply because this was the accepted and acceptable way to write an epithalamium. That this is so can easily be proved by a reading of the epithalamia of Sidonius, Dracontius, and Ennodius. The form and treatment are exactly as in Claudian, and Claudian's model, Statius: the lovers are always brought together by Cupid and Venus, who waltz through the air in dove-drawn chariots pursued by flocks of Nymphs and Amoretti. Even Venantius Fortunatus in the late sixth century follows the same formula in his epithalamium for Brunhilda, both poet and subject canonized saints of the Catholic church.[1] Clearly neither poet nor audience thought of Cupid, Venus, and the rest, as representatives in this connection of 'the Roman state religion'. They were no more than an expected feature of the genre.

In the tradition of the epithalamium there was only one dissentient voice. Paulinus of Nola did disapprove, and wrote a truly Christian epithalamium to show that it could be done:

> absit ab his thalamis vani lascivia vulgi,
> Iuno Cupido Venus, nomina luxuriae . . .
>   (*Carm.* xxv. 9 f.).

Yet he could not change the fashion. It was to Claudian and

---

[1] For a detailed study of the late Latin epithalamia, see C. Morelli, *Stud. ital.* xviii (1910), 319–432. Cf. also R. Keydell, 'Epithalamium', in *RAC* v (1962), 927 f.; Z. Pavlovskis, *Class. Phil.* lx (1965), 164 f.; P. Dronke, *Medieval Latin and the Rise of European Love-lyric* i (1965), 193 f.

Statius, not to Paulinus, that Sidonius, Dracontius, and the others looked as their models. In any event, there would inevitably be some difference between the practice of an avowed ecclesiastic and a secular Christian writer, such as Sidonius. But it might be worth inquiring whether there was a limit beyond which even the most liberal Christian would not have gone. Is there, in fact, any noticeable difference between the practice of Claudian and the Christian secular poets?

Fargues[1] observes that if our knowledge of the period were based on Claudian alone, we should never have guessed that Theodosius and Honorius were Christians—or even that Christianity existed at the time he wrote. This is very nearly true. Yet it is equally true of Sidonius: no one could have guessed from Sidonius alone that Avitus, Majorian, and Anthemius were Christians, or even lived in a Christian world. Fargues also finds it significant that among all the *topoi* in his voluminous panegyrics Claudian refrains from praising the piety of Stilico and Honorius. As he observes, some of the prose panegyrists of the age do make vague allusions to a divine power which might have satisfied a Christian Emperor. But not all. There is nothing in Ausonius' *Gratiarum actio* to the pious Gratian to suggest that either Ausonius or Gratian were Christians. Yet both certainly were. Apart from a closing appeal to a vague 'supremus ille imperii et consiliorum tuorum deus conscius et arbiter et auctor' (§ 83), in the body of the speech he compares Gratian successively to a Vestal virgin, a pontifex, and a flamen (§ 66)! In any event, the conventions of poetry were not the same as those of prose. Sidonius nowhere says a word about the piety of any one of his three Emperors. Thus, strange as the omission might seem, nothing can be built upon it. And if Claudian has nothing to say about the piety of Stilico and Honorius, he does at least praise Serena for her devotion to prayer.

Another similar 'omission' in Claudian (not mentioned by Fargues) to which it is worth drawing attention, is his failure, throughout several tirades against Alaric and his Goths, to make any capital out of the fact that Alaric was a detested Arian heretic.

[1] p. 154.

The same applies for Gildo, according to official propaganda champion of Donatism in North Africa—though himself, according to one source, a pagan. But Sidonius, in the course of two tirades against Gaiseric the Vandal (v. 327 f., ii. 348 f.) nowhere reveals that Gaiseric too was an Arian, and a persecutor of Catholics as well: indeed the restoration of Catholic rule was one of the principal pretexts for Justinian's reconquest of Africa. All these omissions must be explained on stylistic, not religious grounds. Poets writing, as were Claudian and Sidonius, within the classical tradition, were reluctant to spoil the purely classical flavour of their work by introducing discordant modern notes.

R. Helm tried a different line of approach.[1] He pointed out that while the Christian poets made liberal use of the traditional epic machinery, and all the traditional clichés of the epic tradition (e.g. metonymy such as Mars for War), they never refer to a plurality of gods when writing *in propria persona*. Claudian, however, and the certainly pagan Rutilius Namatianus[2] do. Claudian, for example, writes '*dis* proximus ille' (*Theod.* 227), 'sola *deos* aequat clementia nobis' (*IV Cons.* 277), 'secundis | fide *deis*' (*Get.* 52–3), 'gravis ira *deum*', (ib. 171), 'infensos tandem *superos* . . . agnovere' (*Eutr.* ii. 487–8), and several other examples. From Rutilius, compare ii. 40, i. 39–40, 'sollicitosque habuit Roma futura *deos*', i. 96, 'ipsos crediderim sic habitare *deos*.' Helm might have added that Claudian hardly ever uses *deus* or *numen* in a monotheistic sense,[3] not even to the extent of Ammianus Marcellinus, who uses the words in singular and plural with equal and apparently indifferent frequency. It has sometimes been claimed that despite this fact Ammianus was 'really' a monotheist.[4] But Ensslin[5] was surely right to detect a personal note in passages such

---

[1] 'Heidnisches und Christliches bei spätlateinischen Dichtern', *Natalicium J. Geffcken* (1931), 1–46.

[2] On Rutilius' paganism, cf. most recently *JRS* lvii (1967), 37–8.

[3] Cf. *Ruf.* i. 7, 'consilio firmata dei'—followed up immediately by 'deos', at line 21.

[4] A. Demandt, *Zeitkritik und Geschichtsbild im Werk Ammians* (1965): cf. *CR* N.S. xvii (1967), 62.

[5] *Klio*, Beiheft xvi (1923), 52–3.

as 'exstructis aris caesisque hostiis, consulta *numinum* scitabamur' (xxiv. 8. 4). Nor is there any mistaking the significance of the plural when Symmachus remarks with pleasure that at Beneventum '*deos* magna pars veneratur' (*Ep.* i. 3).

Would we be justified in concluding that Claudian too really was a polytheist? Perhaps we would; but there are three reservations. First, none of the poets Helm cites, except Sidonius, wrote full-scale formal panegyrics like Claudian: their usage is not therefore strictly comparable. Moreover, of these poets Ausonius does occasionally use phrases like 'pia cura deum' (*Epigr.* ix. 11). While it may be that such passages occur mainly in Ausonius' earlier poems, it is implausible to postulate a pagan and a Christian period in his literary activity: there is no evidence that he was ever anything but a Christian. And even Corippus, who wrote his epic from an openly Christian point of view, with frequent references to Christ himself, lets an 'o superi!' slip out at *Joh.* ii. 140. Second, though it might seem decisive that for once Sidonius provides no exact parallel, in fact too much should not be made of this. There is only one such reference to an unspecified divine power in his three panegyrics, and while it does happen to be in the singular—'si mea vota deus perduxerit' (ii. 542)—it should not be overlooked that the plural would not have scanned. One example like this is hardly enough to sustain a generalization. We cannot rule out the possibility that it is pure chance he never uses the plural. One passage Helm does not quote is ii. 317–18 (cf. 481–2), where Sidonius says that after his death the western Emperor Severus 'auxerat . . . *divorum* numerum'. No one, surely, would wish to suggest that Sidonius really thought that an Emperor joined the Pantheon after death: yet he obviously felt that it would cause no offence within the backward-looking context of his epic style. This is an instructive example, since it has sometimes been regarded as indicative of Claudian's paganism, as of Ammian's, that they too speak of dead Emperors as gods.[1] Third, there is surely something artificial in separating off colourless

[1] e.g. L. K. Born, *TAPhA* lxix (1938), xxxi: cf. (on Ammian) *CR* N.S. xvii (1967), 62.

references to a plurality of gods from open allusions to the Olympians. For, once Claudian had decided (though 'decided' implies a more conscious choice than actually took place) to write within the traditional epic framework with its divine machinery, then it was natural enough that, even when not naming specific Olympians, he should nevertheless refer to gods in the plural. Even Milton, writing a Christian epic in the same tradition, refers to the angels who surround God in heaven collectively as 'gods'. It may be that Claudian was a pagan. But I feel that it would be unsafe to regard this feature of his work as a direct manifestation of his paganism.

Let us take some examples where no one surely would wish to press the polytheistic implication of Claudian's words. 'Quo precor haec effecta deo?', he exclaims of the victory over Gildo (*Gild.* 14). To those who knew that this supposed champion of heresy in North Africa had been defeated (or so Mascezel alleged) with the divine aid of the recently deceased St. Ambrose, the answer to this question was only too obvious. Claudian cannot have expected his listeners to have taken it as anything more than a stylized form of exclamation. Nor can he possibly have intended to imply that the bigoted Serena was a polytheist when he praised her for her devotion to 'numinibus' (*Laus Serenae* 223). Compare also *Prob.* 71-2, where he appeals to the Muse:

> Tu, precor, *ignarum* doceas, Parnasia, vatem,
> *quis deus* ambobus tanti sit muneris auctor.

Claudian must have known perfectly well that it was precisely their Christianity that had brought Probinus and Olybrius their consulates. Similarly, we cannot press his exclamation 'nunc pateras libare *deis*' later in the poem (line 247).

Nor can he have expected or intended that anyone should take him seriously when he represented Stilico as praying to Mars before battle (*Ruf.* i. 334 f.),[1] or paying his respects to the Lares of his palace in Constantinople (*Stil.* i. 118). For the purposes of the genre it was considered natural by both poet and audience

---

[1] Birt's 'allegorical' interpretation (*Charakterbilder Spätroms* (1919), 475-6, n. 45) of Mars here as standing for Gainas is altogether fantastic.

for Stilico to do anything Aeneas might have done. More particularly, it is worth emphasizing that the panegyric on Probinus
and Olybrius, recited within months of the extinction of the last
pagan stand in the West and for an occasion of such obvious
Christian significance, is not a whit less 'pagan' in character than
any of his later poems. When he likened Proba, dowager of the
leading Christian family in Rome, to Juno 'summoned by sacred
incense' (*Prob.* 196), it was intended, and no doubt taken, as a
compliment, not an insult, to that venerable lady. In any event,
the poem went down so well that he was invited to court at once,
where he continued to write for audiences whose most important
members were all Christians. It was in Claudian's interest to win
and retain their favour, and this he clearly did.

It is inadequate to explain the 'pagan character' of Claudian's
work, as Birt and later Mazzarino did, as a reflection of the tolerant
attitude of the Stiliconian regime in such matters. Tolerant
Stilico may have been, but *Prob.* was performed while the persecutor Theodosius, basking in his victory over paganism, was
still alive and holding court only 300 miles away at Milan. The
answer is that in literature the old mythology had long since
become merely decorative, and in any case bore so little relationship to contemporary paganism, that none but a few extremists
gave its pagan associations a thought. St. Ambrose, preaching to
much the same audiences as Claudian, made frequent use of
examples from mythology in his sermons. Only the Arians complained.[1]

III

The inference that, since Claudian writes as though the Roman
state religion were in full bloom, he must have revered the old
Roman gods, is based on a naïvely unitarian view of the amor-
phous and many-sided conglomeration of beliefs which went to
make up late paganism. Claudian was an Alexandrian, and paganism in late fourth-century Alexandria was very different from

[1] Homes Dudden, *St. Ambrose* i (1935), 9.

paganism in late fourth-century Rome. It is unlikely in the highest degree that an Alexandrian of Claudian's day would have felt any religious attachment to the figures of the Roman pantheon. It seems likely that they did mean a lot to a deeply Roman pagan like Symmachus:[1] but even Symmachus was probably in a minority among his fellow aristocrats, most of whom (when not Christian, of course) were devotees of one or more of the Oriental religions.[2] If Claudian was a religious man at all, one might certainly have expected his allegiance to lie with Isis and Serapis, like so many other pagan intellectuals who left Alexandria at the same time as he did.

The culmination of the anti-pagan persecution at Alexandria in 391 was the destruction of the great Serapeum, one of the marvels of the ancient world. Evidently it was felt to be the bastion of paganism in Alexandria: 'caput ipsum idololatriae', crowed Rufinus.[3] Yet for a century or more after that, pagan intellectuals remained firm in their devotion to Isis, despite sporadic Christian persecution. Those two mines of information on paganism in fifth-century Alexandria, the life of Severus by the Christian Zacharias and the life of Isidore by the pagan Damascius, confirm each other on this point. The religious attitude of Palladas, who lived and taught in Alexandria during Claudian's schooldays, has given rise to almost as much discussion as that of Claudian himself. He refers often and slightingly to the old Olympians, but it is significant that the only god he represents as having an effect on man's everyday life is Serapis.[4] His sombre and pessimistic

---

[1] On the Roman character of Symmachus' paganism, cf. Baynes, *Byzantine Studies* (1955), 364 f. (= *JRS* xxxvi (1946), 176 f.).

[2] Cf. especially H. Bloch, *Harv. Theol. Rev.* xxxviii (1945), 199–244, with a table of priesthoods held by aristocrats.

[3] *Hist. Eccl.* ii. 24. There is a miniature from an Alexandrian chronicle showing Theophilus trampling the Serapeum under foot. For sources on the destruction of the Serapeum and the events of 391 see *JHS* lxxxiv (1964), 54 f.; *Byz. Zeit.* lvii (1964), 287 f.; and *JRS* lv (1965), 21 f. Cf. also J. Schwartz, 'La fin du Sérapéum d'Alexandrie', *Essays in Honor of C. B. Welles* (1966), 97 f. (who does not use Palladas).

[4] Cf. *Anth. Pal.* ix. 174 and 378, with *JHS* lxxxiv (1964), 61 (with references to Damascius and Zacharias).

poems proclaim that he was not basically a religious man. Claudian too may not have been a regular temple-goer. But it is against this sort of pagan religious background that both are likely to have been brought up, among these academic circles that both moved. So it is for traces of a specifically Egyptian paganism that we should be looking.

At *IV Cons.* 570 f. Claudian compares the child Honorius being carried on a golden throne in his consular procession to a tiny statue carried by Egyptian priests during a procession at Memphis:

> numina Memphis
> in vulgus proferre solet: penetralibus exit
> effigies, brevis illa quidem, sed plurimus infra
> liniger imposito suspirat vecte sacerdos,
> testatus sudore deum: Nilotica sistris
> ripa sonat, Phariosque modos Aegyptia ducit
> tibia, summissis admugit cornibus Apis.

Now we learn from Macrobius that 'the Egyptians' carried out of his sanctuary, at the winter solstice, a figure of a small boy, representing the sun at his smallest when the day is shortest. At the spring equinox he was represented by a statue of a youth, growing as the days lengthen out, and at the summer solstice by a statue of an adult with a beard.[1] It is tempting to conjecture that Claudian is referring to the winter celebration of this very festival. He may well have seen one during his youth in Egypt. The comparison between the child Honorius carried on the shoulders of his courtiers and the child Sun-god carried on the shoulders of his priests is striking, and unlikely to have occurred to one who had not himself seen this strange procession at Memphis.

We must not take Claudian's description too literally. Ancient poets seldom wrote autobiography. More often they offer a core of observation embellished with literary reminiscences. In the present case, while the musical accompaniment is acceptable enough, the presence of Apis raises a doubt. For it is generally

[1] *Sat.* 1. 18. 10.

(and doubtless correctly) thought that the last Apis bull was the one specially looked out for the Apostate Julian in 362, when it is implied that the ceremony was already long since obsolete.[1] Yet he is bellowing away merrily in Claudian's simile.

With or without Apis, Claudian may, of course, have been no more than a bystander at the time. But evidently the procession made an impression on him strong enough for it to recur to his mind as he watched Honorius' procession a few years later.

It was Norden who saw the connection between these two passages of Claudian and Macrobius.[2] And he found further confirmation in line 8 of a late syncretistic hymn to Luna identified with Isis, 'tu sistro *renovas brumam*'.[3] This hymn is ascribed in the tenth-century manuscript, which alone preserves it, to an otherwise unknown Claudius. Claudian's full name was Claudius Claudianus, and several manuscripts of his works (including the earliest), and entries in medieval library-catalogues style him simply Claudius.[4] From the stylistic and metrical point of view, though no masterpiece, the hymn could certainly have been written by Claudian. Thus it was not wholly without justification or probability that Norden suggested that it was written by him.

A suggestion worth making, it might be objected, but hardly to be regarded as more than an attractive hypothesis. Yet an additional argument can now be brought in its favour. In the course of a recent discussion of the motif of the wheel of Fortune, P. Courcelle has pointed out that Claudian is the very first writer to represent Fortune as actually turning the wheel herself.[5] Interestingly enough Claudius uses the very same motif in the last

---

[1] A. Hermann, *JbAC* iii (1960), 46, n. 94, thinks that since the bull found for Julian was 'zweifellos ein Jungtier', it might still have been alive twenty years later for Claudian to have seen during his schooldays. I am told that twenty years would be a not unreasonable age for a bull, but I still incline to dismiss him as literary embellishment.

[2] *Die Geburt des Kindes* (1924), 25, n. 3, and cf. especially E. H. Kantorowicz, *Selected Studies* (1965), 32–3.

[3] *AL* Riese 723. [4] Cf. Birt, p. i.

[5] *La Consolation de philosophie dans la tradition littéraire: antécédents et postérité de Boèce* (1967), 134 (Claudian identifies Fortuna with Nemesis, on which cf. Courcelle, loc. cit.).

line of his hymn. 'Ce poète,' writes Courcelle, 'est-il antérieur ou non à notre Claudien?' Perhaps he *is* our Claudian. It would be an odd (though not, of course, impossible) coincidence if two roughly contemporary poets, both interested in Egypt, both bearing the name Claudius, had both used this same unusual theme.

Further confirmation would be at hand if we could be sure about the authenticity of *c.m. app.* xi, another address to Isis, this time more specifically on the festival of the *Navigium Isidis* held every 5 March.[1] This poem too is preserved in only one manuscript, but is directly ascribed to Claudian. Its authenticity has been questioned, together with the other twenty-one poems which constitute the so-called *carminum minorum appendix*, because, though sometimes quoted in manuscripts together with the genuine *carmina minora*, they do not appear in the majority of these manuscripts, thus giving rise to the suspicion that they did not feature in the official edition of Claudian's minor poems.[2]

That some of these poems are not by Claudian seems certain.[3] The 'Laus Herculis' (ii) is disfigured by no fewer than four false quantities, of which only two can plausibly be removed by emendation. Nos. vi, vii, and viii have six false quantities between them, all irremovable. But some at least of the rest could have been written by Claudian, and four or five look as if they were. No. iv, on a present from Serena to Arcadius is almost certainly genuine.[4] No. ix, on a hippopotamus and a crocodile, is a very obvious theme for an Egyptian poet. No. x is on an ornamental table top, just the sort of curiosity that caught Claudian's eye.

We shall see later that Claudian's minor works were published hastily after his death at the orders of Stilico.[5] Short poems like these, often in only 4 or 6 lines, written specially for some particular occasion, would have been 'published' on a single sheet of

---

[1] On the poem, cf. A. Alföldi, *JbAC* viii–ix (1965–6), 65.

[2] For the evidence, cf. Birt, pp. clxiii–clxxii.

[3] D. Romano, *Appendix Claudianea: questioni d'autenticità* (1958), accepts virtually all as authentic, but his criteria are not sufficiently rigid. His elaborate comparisons of the metrical technique of the poems with Claudian's genuine works are vitiated by ignorance of prosody.

[4] See below, p. 407.   [5] See p. 418.

paper or papyrus, or even a card,[1] for many years existing perhaps in just the one copy Claudian himself had sent to the friend for whom he had written it. It goes without saying that some at least of the *nugae* Claudian dashed off and distributed in this way are likely to have escaped the notice of this slapdash editor.

I should be inclined to accept no. xi as authentic too. Here is the poem:

> Isi, o fruge nova quae nunc dignata videri
>   plena nec ad Cereris munera poscis opem—
> nam tu nostra dea es nec te deus ipse tacendi
>   abnegat, expertus quis tua vela ferat:
> namque tibi Zephyrus favet ac Cyllenius ales—
>   ne nostra referas de regione pedem.

Verbal parallels between two works can often prove that one depends on the other; but seldom that both were written by the same writer. However, there is one interesting parallel between this poem and *Rapt.* i. 77, 'Cyllenius adstitit *ales*'. Mercury is often 'Cyllenius' or 'Cyllenia proles' to Latin poets, but there is only one other example of 'Cyllenius ales'.[2] Like many late poets, and especially late Greek epic poets,[3] Claudian tends to repeat phrases; perhaps this is such a case. It is possible, of course, that the poem was simply ascribed to Claudian in error: but if so, it would be an odd coincidence for it to have contained a phrase borrowed from Claudian. And with the formula 'dignata videri' compare 'visere . . . dignatus' at *VI Cons.* 62, with similar ellipse (very common in Claudian) of 'es'.

The poem suggests that its author had actually seen the *Navigium Isidis* performed. If Claudian is the author, this could have been in Egypt before the ban on pagan festivals in 391. But the use of the Latin language and the local reference in the last line points rather to Italy. With so many of the city and praetorian prefects

---

[1] See O. Seeck, *Gött. Gel. Anz.* xiii (1887), 502 f., and S. Prete, *Stud. z. Textgesch. und Textkritik* (1959), 219 f. (both discussing the publication of Ausonius' minor poems).

[2] Val. Flacc., iv. 385. Claudian is particularly fond of the word *ales*: Birt, *index verb.*, s.v.

[3] It is a very marked feature of Nonnus' style.

still pagans,[1] there is no reason to doubt that Isiac festivals were still conducted from time to time. As late as 417, Rutilius Namatianus witnessed the great autumnal festival of the *Heuresis* of Osiris at Faleria.[2] Clearly, if Claudian had written one address to Isis, he might easily have written another. It is only too easy to see an additional reason why these poems might have been left out of the original official edition of the minor works. The influence of tradition was so strong in literary matters that few were likely to take offence at the superficially pagan mythological imagery in Claudian's major poems. But hymns to Isis were a very different matter. It may well be that the decision that both should be excluded was deliberate.

But let us return to firmer ground. One of the most intriguing passages in Claudian is the closing fifty lines of *Stil*. ii. The Sun (Phoebus) yokes his chariot and visits the cave of Time (Αἰών), which is surrounded by a serpent devouring its own tail. By the entrance sits Natura (Φύσις), while the old man himself writes down the laws which govern the orbits of each of the planets:[3]

> mansura verendus
> scribit iura senex, numeros qui dividit astris
> et cursus stabilesque moras, quibus omnia vivunt
> ac pereunt fixis cum legibus. ille recenset
> incertum quid Martis iter certumque Tonantis
> prospiciat mundo; quid velox semita Lunae
> pigraque Saturni; quantum Cytherea sereno
> curriculo Phoebique comes Cyllenius erret (433–40).

Inside the cave are all the ages, past and future, fashioned variously in bronze, iron, silver, and a very few in gold. It is one of the gold ones[4] that Phoebus selects to be the year of Stilico's consulship,

> aureus et nomen praetendit consulis annus (474).

---

[1] Cf. *JRS* lv (1965), 241–2.   [2] *De Red.* i. 373 f.: cf. *JRS* lvii (1967), 36.
[3] For (overlong) commentary on the astronomy of the passage, see W. H. Semple, *CQ* xxxi (1937), 164–7.
[4] On this symbolism of the golden year, see Norden, *Geb. des Kindes* (1924), 25; H. Gressmann, *Zeitschr. f. Kirchengesch.* xli (N.S. iv) (1922), 175 (though cf., too, Nock, *Harv. Theol. Rev.* xxvii (1934), 88).

It used to be thought that the notion of deified Time was Iranian in origin.[1] This is no longer generally accepted,[2] but in any event, nowhere is Claudian more likely to have come across such ideas than in his native Egypt, more particularly Alexandria. Αἰών features extensively in the Hermetic corpus, those curious works attributed to the Egyptian god Thoth, and even more so in Egyptian magical papyri, where he is found represented, as in Claudian, surrounded by the serpent devouring its own tail (οὐροβόρος), the symbol of never-ending time.[3] We hear more than once from Damascius of the worship of Aion/Osiris by pagan intellectuals in fifth-century Alexandria, and a statue of Aion (identified with Osiris and Adonis) was still an object of cult there (and occasional visitations by the deity himself) three quarters of a century after Claudian.[4] So it would be a mistake to look for one particular source from which Claudian might have derived this wide-spread conception. But there is one text, written precisely in late fourth-century Alexandria, which does provide a particularly striking parallel.[5] It is an astrological poem (or fragment of a poem)[6] by Theon, a description of the seven planets wheeling round heaven. Just as in Claudian, it is Aion who lays down the paths they are to follow:

> ἑπτὰ πολυπλανέες κατ' Ὀλύμπιον ἀστέρες οὐδὸν
> εἰλεῦνται, καὶ τοῖσιν ἀεὶ κανονίзεται Αἰών ...

[1] e.g. Reitzenstein, *Das iranische Erlösungsmysterium* (1921).

[2] e.g. Nock, *Harv. Theol. Rev.* xxvii (1934), 79 f.

[3] A. J. Festugière, *Révélation d'Hermès Trismégiste* iv (1954), 152–99.

[4] *Vitae Isidori Reliquiae*, ed. C. Zintzen (1967), 75. 7, 147. 7, with Nock, art. cit., pp. 91–2.

[5] Latest edition (and a bad one) by Heitsch, ii. S. 4, from Stobaeus, i. 5. 14, and an unknown source used by Aldus for his edition of the *Anthology* (1503). Heitsch (who used only Jacobs's edition, App. Plan. 40), carelessly inferred that Aldus's source was Planudes' autograph. In fact it was probably *B.M. Add.* 16409 (C. Gallavotti, *Boll. Acc. Lincei* vii (1959), 35–6), but (unknown to Heitsch—or Jacobs) the poem is preserved in Planudes' own hand nonetheless, at f. 81ʳ of *Cod. Ven. Marc.* 481. Line 7 also appears as *Anth. Pal.* ix. 491. I shall be publishing a more securely based text in a forthcoming study, 'Planudea'.

[6] Like the similar list of the planets in John of Gaza, i. 198 f.; Nonnus, xxxviii. 226 f. (cf. Stegemann, op. cit. (p. 208, n. 5), pp. 32 f.)—and of course Claudian. Claudian omits the sun from his list because the sun is already present in another capacity, visiting Aion.

What makes this poem so relevant is that Theon, like Palladas, taught in Alexandria during Claudian's schooldays. Claudian was keenly interested in both astronomy and astrology (the difference was not very clear by his day), and it is overwhelmingly probable that he attended the great Theon's lectures—or at least, being a poet himself, read his poetry.

Claudian, of course, as befits a real poet, has improved on the feeble fumblings of Theon. But is the result any more than a fine purple passage? Despite the authentic detail of the δράκων οὐρο-βόρος, so great an authority as A. D. Nock could see here only 'an imaginary allegorical picture'. 'Aion', he objects, 'should properly speaking be superior to the sun. As it is, he is a mere janitor, or rather caretaker, for Nature is the janitress.'[1] So perhaps we should see Claudian's Aion as merely a personified abstraction, on a level with the many others—Clementia, Justitia, Gallia, Britannia—which conspire to do honour to Stilico throughout *Stil.* ii. Its function, like that of the others, is purely decorative. It is surely for this reason that it appears in later poets too,[2] perhaps deriving from Claudian himself. We have seen already that Claudian's combination of Aion and Physis, and the visit to the cave of Time, can be closely paralleled in Nonnus.[3]

Nevertheless, it is obviously significant for Claudian's literary

[1] Op. cit., p. 88.

[2] John of Gaza, i. 137–9 (though differently described: cf. Friedlaender's commentary, pp. 177–9); Christodorus, *Anth. Pal.* ii. 135. M. L. West (*Gött. Gel. Anz.* ccxv (1963), 171) makes the attractive suggestion that Aion is the subject of the fragmentary line 36 of Heitsch XXXV. 3 (Pamprepius), and (*CQ* N.S. xviii (1968), 291) corrects †ναίων at *Orph. H.* 12. 10 to Αἰών (retaining φολίσιν). For the prominence of Αἰών even in Nonnus' Paraphrase of St. John, see J. Golega, *Studien über die Evangeliendichtung des Nonnos* (*Bresl. Stud. z. hist. Theol.* xv; 1930), 63–5; and for Αἰών in later Neoplatonic writings, E. R. Dodds, on Proclus, *Elements of Theology*² (1963), p. 228; for the *ouroboros* in late texts, J.-G. Préaux, *Hommages W. Deonna* (1957), 393 f.

[3] Above, p. 11. Aion and Helius were frequently identified (see Nock, op. cit., p. 84): it is thus the more significant that Nonnus (*Dion.* xii. 23–5), like Claudian, is careful to distinguish them. For other parallels for the combination of Aion and Physis, cf. Mesomedes, *Hymn* iv (Heitsch I. 4), and Lydus, *De Mens.* iv. 17 and iv. 61 (with Nock, p. 87). For Αἰών as a snake, *Orph. H.* 12. 10 (West, *CQ* 1968, 290).

if not religious interests, and certainly for the milieu in which he grew up, that when in search of a suitably majestic finale for his poem he should have thought of this theme and no other.

It has been inferred from this and other passages referring to the stars and planets that Claudian was an 'astral fatalist'.[1] Certainly, he was interested in astrology, and knew a little about it. But in the fourth century who was not? Besides, a smattering of astrological lore was a standard part of the poet's equipment. Sidonius and his Christian friends half a century later knew at least as much as Claudian.[2] Naturally enough, the subject was especially popular in Egypt: in addition to the writings of Theon, handbooks by Hephaestion of Thebes (a Christian) and Paul of Alexandria appeared there probably during Claudian's lifetime (the latter rapidly running into a second edition—a great success with Christians and pagans alike).[3] The stars bulk larger in Claudian, perhaps, than in his Latin predecessors:[4] but considerably less than in Nonnus. And Nonnus' astrology is often so garbled and incomprehensible that it is uncertain how far it was merely a source of literary embellishment (or rather obfuscation) for him too.[5] It would be going too far to see Claudian as a slave of the stars.

Much has been made of the fact that he represents the souls of the great as dwelling in the stars, traversing all seven of the planetary spheres to get there. Yet this would have seemed perfectly

---

[1] G. Martin, *Studies . . . Ullman* (1960), 71 f.; Fargues, p. 175.

[2] Cf. C. E. Stevens, *Sidonius Apollinaris* (1933), 7–8; Miremont, *RÉA* xi (1909), 301–13.

[3] Christ–Schmid–Stählin, *Gesch. d. griech. Literatur* ii. 2⁶. 1073. Christian scribes tried to tone down some of the more overt pagan features of Paul's work: cf. E. Boer's edition (Teubner, 1958), p. xii. For the second edition, cf. Paul, ib., p. 1. 6 f. Palladas mocked the Alexandrian *rhetor* Gessius for believing astrologers (*A.P.* vii. 687–8). Note also that Claudian lampooned an astrologer in *c.m.* xliii–xliv, and invents some spoof astrological explanations of the wayward ways of the man's son.

[4] Fargues, p. 175; Rolfe, *TAPhA* l (1919), 147 f.

[5] See the useful notes in the Loeb edition by Rouse and Rose, especially (e.g.) vol. i, pp. xvi, 42–3, 240–3; cf. also V. Stegemann, *Astrologie und Universal-geschichte: Studien zu . . . Nonnos* (1930), which is perhaps too favourable to Nonnus.

acceptable to a contemporary Christian audience. Since Christians accepted the traditional cosmic geography, how could they deny that souls had to traverse the planetary spheres in order to reach Heaven? And had not St. Paul himself spoken of a man being borne up to at any rate the third heaven (2 Cor. 12: 2)?[1] Many contemporary Christian epitaphs refer to the dead as dwelling among the stars. 'Rettulit ad Chr[istu]m celsa per astra gradum', wrote Claudian's Christian friend Mallius Theodorus on his sister's tomb.[2] A stone erected in Rome in 392 proclaims that its owner '[proxima] sed Cristo sidera celsa tenet'.[3] Nor is it likely that Claudian would have sent the souls of Honorius' mother, father, and grandfather anywhere that was likely to have offended the pious Emperor.

Much play has been made with terms like 'Orphic', 'Pythagorean', and 'Neoplatonic' in connection with the passage at *Ruf.* ii. 481–93, where Claudian gives a fascinating account of the transmigration of souls, describing with examples how the soul of man passes after death from one animal to another for 3,000 years, till it finally returns to human form after being purged in Lethe. This is certainly at variance with current Christian teaching. Among contemporary writers, Ambrose in particular had made it clear that no Christian could accept that the soul of a man could pass into a brute beast.[4] But it would be rash to suppose that Claudian himself actually believed in metempsychosis. Or that either he or his audience saw in this episode anything more than

---

[1] Ambrose was of the opinion that pagan philosophers had only been 'imitating' David's allusion to 'coeli coelorum' at Ps. 148 when 'quinque stellarum et solis et lunae globorum consonum motum introduxerunt' (*Hexaem.* ii. 6).

[2] *CLE* 1434. 8 (cf. Courcelle, *RÉA* xlvi (1944), 66 f.).

[3] *CLE* 1345. 6 (for further examples from Christian funerary epigrams, cf. B. I. Knott, *Vig. Christ.* x (1956), 77: oddly enough it seems to be confined to Latin epitaphs, cf. R. Lattimore, *Themes in Greek and Latin Epitaphs* (1942), 312). On the Christianization of this motif, see also H. Lietzmann, *Hist. of the Early Church* ii (Engl. trans. 1949), 310 f.; P. Lejay, *Rev. Phil.* xxxvi (1912), 201–2; F. Cumont, *Afterlife in Roman paganism* (1912), 109; S. Sambursky, *Physical World of Late Antiquity* (1962), 174.

[4] Courcelle, *Conflict between Paganism and Christianity* (ed. Momigliano, 1963), 161 f.

a picturesque detail skilfully grafted on to the traditional picture of underworld judgement. For once having suggested metempsychosis as a possible punishment for Rufinus, Claudian rejects it as too mild, and considers instead combining the fates meted out to Sisyphus, Ixion, Tantalus, and Tityos—before rejecting even that as too mild! Clearly we are not meant to take any of this very seriously. In any case, it is interesting to note that while metempsychosis was accepted by the earlier Neoplatonists (Plotinus and the young Porphyry), in later years Porphyry rejected it, and after him Iamblichus and his followers denied altogether the possibility of human souls passing into animals.[1] So whatever Claudian's source (surely poetical rather than philosophical), by c. 400 the doctrine of metempsychosis was no more acceptable to pagan thinkers than to Christians.

Further 'Orphic' traces have been found in *Rapt.*[2] In fact it is clear from Claudian's own frequent references to Orpheus that he was familiar with Orphic writings.[3] Nevertheless, *Rapt.* is in no sense an Orphic poem. There is no trace in Claudian of the Orphic saga of the rape of Persephone by Zeus, Persephone's son Dionysus torn to pieces by the Titans, Zeus' vengeance on the Titans, and Man born from their sooty smoke. The poem is unfinished, of course, but the brief summary of its proposed scope at the beginning of Bk. i makes it clear that Claudian had no intention of treating the eschatological aspects of the myth. He announces that he is going to tell:

> qua lampade Ditem
> flexit Amor; quo ducta ferox Proserpina raptu
> possedit dotale chaos, quantasque per oras
> sollicito genetrix erraverit anxia cursu;
> *unde datae populis fruges* et glande relicta
> cesserit inventis Dodonia quercus aristis (i. 26 f.).

It was the material benefits conferred by Demeter, not her

---

[1] H. Chadwick, *Early Christian Thought and the Classical Tradition* (1966), 167, n. 85.

[2] E. Bernert, *Philologus* xciii (1939), 352 f.

[3] See pp. 309 f.

mysteries, which concerned Claudian. There is not the slightest reason for supposing that the poem would have ended with the mysteries, still less with the Orphic anthropogony.

It is to go to the other extreme to believe with Birt and Fargues that Claudian only chose the subject as a compliment to the dedicatee of the poem, Florentinus, then in charge of the corn supply of Rome in his capacity as city prefect.[1] Apart from the intrinsic improbability of such an explanation, the books dedicated to Florentinus were not published till long after Florentinus had ceased to be prefect—deposed for his failure to deal with the corn supply during the Gildonic crisis. It is enough to say that Claudian's motives were purely literary. It was a good subject, that had never been treated before at length in a separate epic. And this, surely, is why the god he invokes at the beginning of Bk. i is Phoebus, the god of poesy in general. We have seen already that the other major mythological theme Claudian treated (twice) in a separate poem, the *Gigantomachia*, was also selected for purely literary reasons.[2]

There is, however, one brief passage in *Rapt.* which might profitably detain us for a moment. At iii. 27–8 Jupiter exclaims:

> haut equidem invideo—neque enim livescere fas est
> vel nocuisse deos—sed . . .

Now the jealousy and anger of the gods is a theme beloved by the poets and historians of Greece and Rome. Elsewhere indeed Claudian himself writes in the traditional manner of 'gravis ira deum'.[3] Why then does he for once deny here such a commonplace poetical motif? Could it be that a crack in the stylized rhetoric of late Imperial epic is for once allowing us a glimpse of an opinion Claudian really held? For whatever the poets might say, pagan thinkers had long felt the idea of a god being subject to any such degrading emotion to be monstrous.[4] 'Hoc commune est omnium philosophorum,' wrote Cicero (*De Off.* iii. 102),

---

[1] See Appendix A, pp. 454 f. [2] See above, p. 15.
[3] *Get.* 172, cf. *c.m.* xxii. 39.
[4] See (briefly) P. de Labriolle, *Hist. de la Litt. Lat. Chrét.* i³ (1947), 307 f.

'. . . numquam nec irasci deum nec nocere.' But it was a fundamental tenet of Christianity that God was a jealous God, and did
visit his wrath on sinners and unbelievers. Early Christian thinkers
tried to wriggle out of a conclusion they found so repugnant to
their philosophical training, but Lactantius made the point clear
in his *De Ira Dei*: 'sine ira Deum esse credentes dissolvunt omnem
religionem' (xxii. 2). The Apostate Julian poured scorn on such a
doctrine:[1] οὐδαμοῦ χαλεπαίνων ὁ θεὸς φαίνεται, οὐδ' ἀγανακτῶν,
οὐδ' ὀργιζόμενος . . . ὡς ὁ Μωϋσῆς φησι. It would appear that
Claudian shared this view. Whether he too was attacking the
Christian view must remain uncertain (he may not have known it).
It does not necessarily follow. I should prefer to compare another
aside, this time at *Stil.* ii. 26 f., where Claudian compares Stilico's
clemency to that of the heavenly father (Jupiter, of course):

> aetherii patris exemplo, qui cuncta sonoro
> concutiens tonitru Cyclopum spicula differt
> in scopulos et monstra maris *nostrique cruoris*
> *parcus* in Oetaeis exercet fulmina silvis.

Jupiter dispatches his thunderbolts over rocks and sea monsters
and the forests of Oeta—but not at human beings. Here too we
find the same idea that Jupiter either cannot or should not cause
harm to mankind.

There is no polemical purpose in either passage. It is just that
Claudian shared the belief common to many pagans of his age in
a just and beneficent divine power. A simple concept, vague
enough to be consistent with both mono- and polytheism, but
none the less noble or sincere for that. A healthy if shallow optimism, quite different from the bleakness implied by his supposed
subservience to astral fatalism.

The gods are just. Thus the fall of Rufinus disproves the notion
that they allow unrighteousness to prosper,[2] while it is the
righteousness of Marcus Aurelius that won him the favour of

---

[1] *Contra Christianos*, ed. Neumann (1880), p. 190, 5 f. (with R. Asmus, *Julians
Galiläerschrift* (1904), 19–20). So too Iamblichus, A. D. Nock, *Sallustius* (1926),
lxxxii.

[2] *Ruf.* i. 20 f.

heaven.[1] The universe is held together by love.[2] Clemency is frequently extolled. It is the greatest of the virtues, the oldest of the gods.[3] It dwells, not in temples, but in the heart of man.

> prima Chaos Clementia solvit
> congeriem miserata rudem, vultuque sereno
> discussis tenebris in lucem saecula fudit (*Stil.* ii. 9–11).

It is clemency alone which raises us to the level of the gods—once more the motif of the beneficence of the gods. All is in accordance with a divine plan:[4]

> omnia rebar
> consilio firmata dei, qui lege moveri
> sidera, qui fruges diverso tempore nasci,
> qui variam Phoeben alieno iusserit igni
> compleri Solemque suo, porrexerit undis
> litora, tellurem medio libraverit axe.

Of course this is very much a *topos*.[5] But that does not mean that Claudian did not believe it. When contemplating the remarkable warm springs of Aponus, he was moved to a very similar reflection:[6]

> quidquid erit causae, quocumque emitteris ortu,
>   *non sine consilio* currere certa fides.
> quis *casum* meritis adscribere talibus audet?
>   quis negat auctores haec statuisse deos?
> ille pater rerum, qui saecula dividit astris,
>   inter prima poli te [the springs] quoque sacra dedit
> et fragilem nostri miseratus corporis usum
>   telluri medicas fundere iussit aquas (*c.m.* xxvi. 79–86).

---

[1] *VI Cons.* 349–50.

[2] *IV Cons.* 284 f.: there follows a section on the equilibrium of the universe like those discussed below.

[3] *Stil.* ii. 6 f.

[4] *Ruf.* i. 6 f.; on this passage see further p. 328.

[5] 'An mundus providentia regatur?' (Quintilian iii. 5. 6, v. 7. 35, xii. 2. 21, and esp. vii. 2. 2: cf. Theon, *Rh. Gr.* i. 2. 42 f. Walz. Similar developments in Marcus Aur., *Med.* vi. 10, vii. 32, etc.).

[6] This too, of course, is a *topos*: cf. the almost verbally identical reflections of *Ep. Bob.* 1 'In Aquas Maternas'—though I suspect that this poem, written *c.* 400 (cf. Munari's edition, 1955, pp. 27 f.) was directly inspired by Claudian's.

Claudian may have consulted his horoscope regularly. Isis and
Serapis may have kept a special place in his heart. But this, surely,
is the central article of his faith. The Church did not have
a monopoly on optimism: but Claudian's is an optimism so
lacking in content that it is easy to see why sooner or later it
was bound to yield to Christianity.

IV

We have seen that, whether or not Claudian was a pagan at
heart, he was evidently not a pagan prepared to be a martyr for
his beliefs. Now many such men deemed it the safest and simplest
course to profess a nominal Christianity at this period. Was
Claudian among their number? The fact that Augustine and
Orosius thought him a pagan is not necessarily inconsistent with
such a view. After all, whatever he professed, people may not have
believed him. There is one poem which certainly seems to support
the conjecture: *c.m.* xxii, an Easter hymn entitled *De Salvatore*.
Scholars have often found it disconcerting to see an Easter hymn
among Claudian's works, and most have taken the easy way out
by denying its authenticity—or at least alleging that it is 'not
beyond question'. In fact the one and only reason for questioning
it is the conviction that Claudian was a 'paganus pervicacissimus'
and as such could not have written such a poem. But there is
equal superficiality on the other side: some (notably Shelley)[1]
have supposed that its author must have been a sincere Christian,
and thus that to accept Claudian's authorship entails accepting
that he was a sincere Christian. Let us consider the matter a little
more deeply.[2]

[1] With interesting consequences: see p. 450.
[2] Recent discussions by W. Schmid, *RAC* iii (1957), 161 f.; L. Alfonsi, *Riv. Fil.*
xxxiv (1956), 173 f.; and S. Gennaro, *Da Claudiano a Merobaude* (1959), *passim*.
Lines 7–8, 'quemque utero inclusum Mariae mox numine viso | virginei tumuere
sinus', have caused much difficulty (cf. Schmid, *Stud. ital.* (1956), 517–18). Koch
took the drastic and implausible course of expelling line 8 (cf. Schmid, p. 518). All
difficulties are removed if we adopt L. Havet's forgotten but certain correction
(*RÉA* xviii (1916), 24) of *tumuere* to *timuere*. *Tumuere* is grammatical nonsense

First, the question of authorship. The strongest single argument —in my opinion, decisive—in its favour, is quite simply the fact that it is ascribed to Claudian at all. Orosius was one of the most widely read writers of the Middle Ages, and so the one thing literary people of the Middle Ages knew (or believed) about Claudian was that he was 'paganus pervicacissimus'. Moreover this particular chapter of Orosius was taken over into the *Historia Romana* of Paulus Diaconus in the eighth century, and thence into a number of other medieval works. Why then should anyone from Claudian's own lifetime to the eighth century (the date of the very earliest manuscript of Claudian, in which *De Salv.* is already present) have ascribed by conjecture a Christian hymn of all things to a 'paganus pervicacissimus'? The only plausible explanation for the fact that *De Salv.* was included among Claudian's writings is quite simply that he wrote it. From the linguistic and stylistic point of view there can be no objection. There is nothing at all to be said for the popular view that it is a work of Merobaudes. The fact that Merobaudes wrote a similar poem is no argument: so did Helpidius Rusticius and Sedulius, both of whom were clearly familiar with *De Salv.* It is likely that all three were imitating Claudian. To ascribe it to Damasus,[1] is to pay the worthy pope an undeserved compliment. It has been argued that Augustine and Orosius would not have called Claudian a pagan had they known of this poem: therefore they did not know of it: therefore Claudian did not write it. Not one of these inferences is sound. In particular, we have no reason to suppose that either took the trouble to read everything Claudian wrote. I propose then to work on the assumption that the poem is genuine.

What prompted Claudian to write it? The answer is provided by the last two lines:

> Augustum foveas, festis ut saepe diebus
> annua sinceri celebret ieiunia sacri.

and a feeble anticipation of 'stupuit compleri viscera partu' in line 9. The hyperbole *timuere* is eminently characteristic of Claudian (for other examples cf. *CQ* N.S. xviii (1968), 408), and fear is an appropriate reaction after 'numine viso'.

[1] Cf. Schmid, *RAC* iii. 162.

It is not a genuine hymn, but a *pièce d'occasion* to wish Honorius a happy Easter. The last line and a half—may he often celebrate the annual fast—is merely a neat way of wishing him a long reign. The poem as a whole is more notable for its verbal conceits than for its depth of piety. After the annunciation ('numine viso') the 'innupta mater' (an odd phrase to the modern ear)

> arcano stupuit compleri viscera partu,
> auctorem genitura suum.

It is hard to resist the suspicion that Claudian was more interested in the verbal potentialities of the motif of the unwed mother giving birth to her own creator than to the theological implications of the event. He goes on to develop the equally promising motif, 'latuitque sub *uno* | pectore qui *totum* late complectitur orbem.' 'Death where is thy sting?' had its possibilities too: 'mortemque fugares | morte tua'. Not exactly a moving confession of faith, but this of itself is hardly sufficient to warrant the conclusion that Claudian was insincere. What is interesting is that at line 4 he writes,

> impia tu *nostrae* domuisti crimina vitae

and at line 17,

> ut *nos* surriperes leto.

The clear implication is that Claudian considered himself, or at any rate wished to be considered, among the number of the faithful. It does not seem to me that we would be justified in disregarding this implication. It would certainly have made things a lot easier for Stilico if Claudian had at least been prepared to let it be believed that he was a Christian. No one was likely to take much exception to the 'pagan character' of his poetry. But Stilico could hardly have afforded to protect a professed pagan.[1] Nor is it likely that the pious Honorius would have permitted a professed pagan to write him an Easter hymn.[2]

---

[1] Fl. Macrobius Longinianus, one of Stilico's closest lieutenants and murdered with the other Stiliconians at Pavia in 408, a pagan at one stage of his career, appears as a Christian by 402 (cf. Chastagnol, *Fastes*, pp. 255–7).

[2] The pagan *rhetor* Bemarchius gave a recitation at the inauguration of a church

Another passage in which Claudian pays some deference to the God of his patrons is *III Cons.* 93 f., where he describes the miraculous aid the elements lent Theodosius' arms at the Frigidus.

> gelidis Aquilo de monte procellis
> obruit adversas acies revolutaque tela
> vertit in auctores et turbine reppulit hastas.
> o nimium dilecte deo, cui fundit ab antris
> Aeolus armatas hiemes, cui militat aether
> et coniurati veniunt ad classica venti.

The fact that Claudian introduces a superficial touch of pagan imagery cannot obscure his adhesion to the official Christian line. Theodosius had claimed that the hurricane which blinded Eugenius' men and decided the issue was sent directly by God to punish the unbelievers: that he had won, as Augustine put it, 'magis orando quam feriendo'. Augustine and Orosius at any rate were certainly of the opinion that Claudian, for all his paganism, did accept the Christian miracle. Compare also *IV Cons.* 99 f., where Claudian claims that Theodosius' victories over both Maximus and Eugenius,

> praesentes docuere deos: hinc saecula discant
> indomitum nihil esse pio, tutumve nocenti.

Another bit of literary polytheism. Again, the pagan implication cannot possibly be pressed,[1] for pagans would naturally have denied that Theodosius' victories 'praesentes docuere *deos*'.

Moreover, there is some evidence that Claudian was not wholly ignorant of Christian writings. Naturally his epics and panegyrics were not the place to air such knowledge, but *De Salv.* reveals a certain minimal familiarity with the life and teachings of Christ. Indeed, the poem shows some acquaintance not only with the Gospels (e.g. the opening of John), but also with the Pauline

built by Constantius (J. Bidez, *Vie de Julien* (1930), 48, with n. 24 on p. 365). But things had changed since the reign of Constantius.

[1] Paschoud's claim (*Roma Aeterna* (1967), p. 146) that 'la pirouette la plus audacieuse de Claudien, c'est de rendre profane, mythologique, la victoire chrétienne de 394' seems to me entirely misconceived.

Epistles. If, with Schmid,[1] we accept the variant *mancipii* for *supplicii* at line 16,

> quin et mancipii nomen nexusque subisti,

Claudian would be alluding to Philippians 2: 7, 'took upon him the form of a servant' (μορφὴν δούλου λαβών in the original, 'formam servi accipiens' in the Vulgate).

> mergatur, volucres ceu Pharaonis equi'

in *c.m.* l (discussed further below) shows some knowledge (if only at second hand) of the Old Testament. Various other possible echoes of Old and New Testament phrases were adduced by Glover, but all are very questionable.[2] However, it might be observed that the list of saints enumerated in *c.m.* l is not restricted to the most familiar ones. Along with Peter and Paul, Thomas and Bartholomew, we find Susanna and Thecla. But there is no need to suppose Claudian a student of hagiography. All were commemorated in cities where Claudian had spent some time. The only attested shrine of Susanna in the West was at Rome; the older of the two cathedrals of Milan was dedicated to Thecla, and the only attested western shrine of Bartholomew was at Ravenna[3]—thereby offering some slight confirmation for the view expressed below that the poem was not written till the period 402–3, after court had moved from Milan to Ravenna.[4]

It has been alleged that Claudian knew Minucius Felix and Lactantius, but the attempt to prove it must be acknowledged a failure.[5] However, it is likely enough that he would have taken the trouble to read some Christian poetry. A case has been made out for his use of Juvencus, and while it falls short of proof, the possibility cannot be ruled out. That Prudentius had read Claudian seems certain, but there is also a possibility that Claudian had read some at least of Prudentius' earlier poems.[6] There are several

---

[1] *Stud. ital.* (1956), pp. 498 f.: Sedulius, *hymn.* 2. 6 'servile corpus induit' is surely a direct echo of Claudian's poem here (cf. Schmid, p. 517, n. 2).

[2] *Life and Letters*, p. 242.

[3] H. Delehaye, *Les Origines du culte des martyrs*[2] (1933), pp. 275–6, 325, 339.

[4] Below, p. 226, cf. 415.　　　　　　　　　　　　　　　　[5] See p. 331.

[6] See Appendix B. On Juvencus, A. K. Clarke, *Augustinus* xiii (1968), 126–7.

close parallels between *Prob.* and a (secular) poem by another contemporary Christian writer, Augustine's friend and pupil Licentius.[1] Both poems were written at Rome early in 395. *A priori* it might seem likely that Claudian was the imitator, since at the time he was an unknown (at least in the West), whereas Licentius had been writing poetry for at least ten years. But it is impossible to decide on the basis of the parallels alone. There are in addition two close parallels between the poem and passages in *Rapt.* ii and iii.[2] There can, I think, be no doubt that *Rapt.* ii–iii were written some time after 395,[3] so here at least there would seem to be no doubt.

Parallels have also been adduced with the writings of Ambrose.[4] Again, they fall short of certainty, but again it is likely enough that when in Milan Claudian will have gone, if only out of curiosity (like the young Augustine before his conversion),[5] to hear a sermon by perhaps the most celebrated man in all the West.

'Unam pro mundo Furiis concedimus urbem' at *Eutr.* ii. 39 has (no doubt quite unintentionally) a curiously Christian ring ('sacrifice for the sins of the world'). But contrast the allusion at *Stil.* ii. 342 to 'sacri Mariae partus'. Maria is in fact Stilico's daughter Maria, not the Virgin, and her (in the event falsely) anticipated confinement is 'sacer' because everything to do with the Imperial family was spoken of as 'sacer' in Claudian's day. But a more truly Christian writer might have avoided the *double entendre*. Glover objects that the cult of the Virgin was not as yet officially recognized.[6] Perhaps not, but according to the most recent scholarly survey of the Virgin birth in the theology of the early church, 'of all the early fathers the most productive and interesting from "Marian" points of view is undoubtedly Ambrose'.[7]

---

[1] For full discussion, Clarke, op. cit. 127 f. and *Stud. Patr.* viii (1966), 174–5.

[2] Cf. Clarke, op. cit. 129.   [3] Appendix A.

[4] Clarke, op. cit. 130–1.

[5] Augustine, *Confess.* v. 13. 23. At *In Ps.* xxxvi. 61 (*CSEL* lxiv. 118. 25) Ambrose himself implies that pagans attended his sermons.

[6] *Life and Letters*, p. 242.

[7] H. von Campenhausen, *The Virgin Birth in the Theology of the Early Church* (*SCM* Press, 1964), 76 (= *Sitz.-ber. Heidelb. Akad.* 1962, phil.-hist. Klasse 3, p. 59).

The Milanese might well have been more conscious of the Virgin than other contemporaries. Even so, it is hardly likely that many would have been offended by Claudian's words.

Naturally a Claudian who paid at least lip-service to Christianity cannot easily be reconciled with the anti-Christian Claudian of Fargues and Mazzarino. Let us examine their arguments.

Mazzarino lays much weight on the allusion at *Get.* 231–2 to what can only be the Sibylline books:

> quid carmine poscat
> fatidico custos Romani carbasus aevi.

Now, as is well known, Stilico had the Sibylline books burnt— in Rutilius' eyes the worst of all his crimes.[1] And Zosimus records that Stilico despoiled the temple of Capitoline Jupiter for the gold on its doors.[2] As Mazzarino points out, this is where the Sibylline books were kept, and accordingly he connects the two events. He further observes that at *VI Cons.* 44 f. Claudian alludes to the 'caelatas fores' of this same temple. Mazzarino assumes that by 404 Stilico had already burnt the books and despoiled the temple, and regards these passages in Claudian as pagan propaganda:[3] that is to say, he thinks that Claudian is taking the side of the pagan party here in glorifying the Sibylline books. But É. Demougeot has now shown that Stilico did not in fact burn the books till 407–8.[4] Since Claudian's words were written in 402, his allusion to the books is of no particular significance. In any case, by Claudian's day the Sibyl was by no means an exclusively pagan concern. A full century before, Lactantius had been prepared to accord her authority in matters of prophecy second only to holy writ. An example of perhaps the very oracle Claudian had in mind is given in the *Lausiac History* of Palladius—quoted by a Christian saint. Shortly before the sack of 410, St. Melania the elder left the city, prophesying that 'Ρώμη would soon become

---

[1] *De Red.* ii. 52.
[2] v. 38. 4.
[3] *Rend. Ist. Lombardo* (1938), 249 f.
[4] *RÉA* liv (1952), 83–92 (missed by G. Alföldy, op. cit. (p. 221, n. 2), pp. 14–15).

a ῥύμη (village), 'as the Sibyl had foretold'. This very prophecy is to be found in our extant collection of *Sibylline Oracles*.[1] But there is an even more decisive objection. The lines have been taken out of context. Claudian quotes the oracle along with numerous other portents and prophecies of doom which were circulating in the weeks before Pollentia—all of them *falsified* by the result of Pollentia. He goes on to praise Stilico for dismissing all this defeatist propaganda as 'muliebres querellae'. So not only is the Sibylline oracle of *Get*. 231–2 very probably not pagan at all[2] but Christian, but Claudian mentions it not to glorify but to refute it.

Fargues, observing at least that Claudian did not accept these prophecies, drew the wider inference that Claudian viewed omens and portents in general with an 'élégant scepticisme'.[3] Naturally he is sceptical of the omens he records here, because they were falsified by indisputable facts. But the mammoth series of portents he records at the beginning of *Eutr.* i he professes to believe. Naturally, again: for it was his purpose there to persuade people that they really did portend the ills which befell the East during the year 399—all, so Claudian alleges, the direct result of Eutropius' assumption of the *fasces*. What he really felt about such things himself we have no means of knowing. But it is unlikely that he was wholly free of the superstition and credulity of his age.

Mazzarino claims as another piece of 'pagan propaganda' in Claudian his fondness for describing circus games.[4] A few years later Andreas Alföldi advanced a similar though more general view: that representations of circus themes on contorniate issues were 'propaganda' put out by pagan aristocrats.[5] In fact, of course,

---

[1] Cf. Demougeot, op. cit., 89 f.: *Sib. Or.* iii. 50 f., viii. 142 f. Geffcken.

[2] As taken for granted (e.g.) by G. Alföldy, 'Barbareneinfälle und religiöse Krisen in Italien', *Historia-Augusta-Colloquium Bonn 1964/65* (1966), p. 12—an error which leaves little of his strange theory that *HA Aur.* 18. 2–21. 4, on the invasion of the Marcomanni in 270–1, is 'really' a disguised account of the invasion of Radagaisus in 405–6.

[3] p. 179.

[4] *Rend. Ist Lomb.* (1938), p. 244.

[5] *Die Kontorniaten* (1943), 43 f. (47, n. 79 for Claudian): see the criticisms of J. M. C. Toynbee, *JRS* xxxv (1945), 118 and Mazzarino, *Doxa* iv (1951), 119 f.

they prove little more than that the inhabitants of Rome still took a keen interest in the games. It is true enough that Christian writers often expressed strong disapproval of such entertainments, but it would be absurd (and certainly false) to suppose that it was only pagans who watched and enjoyed them. It was precisely the fact that so many Christians went that caused such anxiety to the Church Fathers. And some pagans disliked them just as much.[1] Of the three sets of games Claudian describes, it looks as though the ones given by the Christian Theodorus were the most lavish. And it happens to be attested that Theodosius himself watched the games at Milan the day before he died.[2]

Gladiatorial games were in a slightly different category. In 399 Honorius passed a law closing the gladiatorial schools in Rome. But three years later Prudentius still felt it necessary to appeal to Honorius to have gladiatorial contests abolished. Taking a leaf out of Claudian's book he put the appeal in the mouth of Theodosius, explaining Theodosius' own failure to take the step with a diplomacy and ingenuity worthy of Claudian: 'partem tibi, nate, reservo'![3] Whether or not Honorius responded is uncertain:[4] but it is significant that in *VI Cons.*, recited some eighteen months later, Claudian concludes his account of the military manoeuvres performed at Honorius' games at Rome in 404, with the words:

> Ianus bella premens *laeta sub imagine pugnae*
> armorum *innocuos* paci largitur honores (638–9).

It seems natural to deduce that Claudian was deliberately drawing attention to the bloodless character of Honorius' games—in other

---

[1] See Ville's article (n. 4, below) at pp. 298 f.

[2] Socrates, *HE* v. 26.

[3] *Contra Symm.* ii. 1119. The poem shows several verbal echoes of Claudian, and it is not surprising that Prudentius should have picked up some of Claudian's other techniques as well.

[4] For all aspects of this question see now G. Ville's illuminating study 'Les jeux de gladiateurs dans l'Empire Chrétien', *Mélanges d'arch. et d'hist. de l'école franç. de Rome* (1960), 273–335 (curiously enough missing the passage from *VI Cons.*), and A. Chastagnol, *Le Senat romain sous le règne d'Odoacre* (1966), 20–2.

words that he was reflecting the current Christian attitude rather than indulging in pagan propaganda.

Fargues calls attention to Claudian's allusion to the miraculous rain storm that saved the army of Marcus Aurelius during his campaign against the Quadi in 173:

> flammeus imber in hostem
> decidit . . . mortalis nescia teli
> pugna fuit: Chaldaea mago seu carmina ritu
> armavere deos, seu, quod reor, omne Tonantis
> obsequium Marci mores potuere mereri (342 f.).

It is notorious that Christians claimed that the rain storm came in answer to the prayers of some Christian soldiers in Marcus' army. According to Fargues, Claudian makes it clear ('quod reor') that he believed the pagan version. This is an oversimplification. There were at least four different explanations of the miracle:[1] the result of prayers by (*a*) Christian soldiers, (*b*) Julian the Chaldaean theurgist, (*c*) Arnuphis an Egyptian magician, (*d*) Marcus himself. It is not true, as Fargues implies, that Claudian rejects the Christian version: he chose between two of the rival pagan versions—and rejected the one most likely to be offensive to his Christian audience. In any event is it likely that Claudian would have gone out of his way to take up an anti-Christian stand on such a point when his immediate purpose was merely to compare Honorius' triumphal entry into Rome with Marcus' return from the Quadi? It will probably be suggested (if it has not already) that the very choice of Marcus, especially styled '*clemens Marce*', is of itself an anti-Christian sign. For in Christian history Marcus went down as a persecutor. All it really proves is that Claudian derived his knowledge of Marcus from pagan sources, which was in any event almost inevitable. In Claudian's day there was no readily accessible Christian history: Orosius did not appear till 417, and it is hardly likely that a man with Claudian's literary inclinations would have spent his time reading Eusebius or

---

[1] For the various versions and modern views, see most conveniently A. B. Cook, *Zeus* iii. 324 f. (also J. Guey, *Rev. Phil.* xxii (1948), 16 f.). Fargues' discussion is at pp. 162–3.

Jerome's *Chronicle* (380–1). Indeed, for this very reason it is possible that Claudian did not even know of the version which ascribed the rain miracle to the prayers of Christian soldiers: the same may have been true of many of even the Christians in his audience. It is perhaps not surprising that there is one Christian version which accepts (*d*) too: the twelfth of the *Sibylline Oracles* (196 f.) says, in vague terms reminiscent of Claudian, that *theos ouranios* granted Marcus' prayers because of his *eusebia*.

Fargues finds another proof of Claudian's pagan sympathies in his frequent praise of L. Junius Brutus.[1] Christian writers hotly criticized Brutus for the execution of both his sons—an act much admired by the callous Romans of earlier times. Hence Claudian's praises, claims Fargues, are inspired in part at least by religious preoccupations. But quite apart from the fact that all but one of the texts he cites were written after Claudian's death, this is surely to credit Claudian with far too positive and calculating a motive. Was he not quoting Brutus almost without thinking merely as a traditional example of old Roman virtue? More significant is the sign at *IV Cons.* 403 that Claudian himself was undergoing the influence of the changing ethical standpoint of his age. Christians naturally expressed equal horror at Manlius Torquatus for having his son put to death. Yet Claudian, in a speech placed in the mouth of Theodosius, advises Honorius, 'Torquati *despice* mores'. If we are to attach any importance to such indications (which I doubt), then Claudian would appear to be following the Christian line here.[2]

The only poem of Claudian which is arguably anti-Christian in sentiment[3] is *c.m.* l, *In Iacobum magistrum equitum*:

> per cineres Pauli, per cani limina Petri,
>   ne laceres versus, Dux Iacobe, meos.
> sic tua pro clipeo defendat pectora Thomas,
>   et comes ad bellum Bartholomaeus eat;
> 5 sic ope sanctorum non barbarus irruat Alpes,

---

[1] pp. 163, 250.
[2] See too O. Skutsch, *Studia Enniana* (1968), 52–3.
[3] See Appendix B, p. 472.

sic tibi det vires sancta Susanna suas;
sic quicunque ferox gelidum transnaverit Histrum,
mergatur volucres ceu Pharaonis equi;
sic Geticas ultrix feriat romphaea catervas
10   Romanasque regat prospera Thecla manus;
sic tibi det magnum moriens conviva triumphum
atque tuam vincant dolia fusa sitim;
sic numquam hostili maculetur sanguine dextra:
ne laceres versus, Dux Iacobe, meos.

T. R. Glover translated the poem as follows:

By the threshold of Peter, the ashes of Paul
My verses, duke Jacob, misquote not at all;
So the saints from the Alps the invaders repel:
So Susanna the chaste lend her forces as well;
So Thomas be with you instead of a shield;
So Bartholomew go as your squire to the field;
So whoever shall swim the chill Danube to fight,
Like the horses of Pharaoh be lost to your sight;
So the sword of your vengeance lay Gothic hordes low;
So the blessing of Thecla add strength to your blow;
So your guest by his death yield the glory to you;
While the bottles outpoured shall your dryness subdue;
So your hand ne'er be stained by the blood of a foe;
Those verses, duke Jacob, I pray you let go.

According to Fargues[1] (among many others) the poem proves beyond doubt that Claudian viewed Christianity with disfavour. In fact all it proves is that Claudian viewed Jacob with disfavour, and was prepared to be flippant about his misplaced piety. Before we could interpret the poem with confidence, we should need to know rather more about Jacob than we do. For example, is Claudian, as Fargues claims, levelling against Jacob the stock pagan accusation that Christianity weakens a man's warlike instinct and undermines his patriotism: or is he alluding to a specific, and perhaps notorious, occasion on which Jacob had failed in his duty in some way because of his excessive piety? Birt[2]

---

[1] p. 161: so too Mazzarino, *Rend. Ist. Lombardo* (1938), 244, and (most recently) Paschoud, *Roma Aeterna* (1967), p. 138.   [2] p. lxii.

argues from line 5 that the poem was written immediately before the Goths crossed the Alps (i.e. before *c*. November 401). Yet if so, he ought also by parity of reasoning to have accepted from line 7 that it was written before they crossed the Danube too—which they had in fact crossed thirty years earlier. The line seems to me to have more bite if the Goths had already crossed the Alps: and if Jacob had been the officer in charge of the Roman force which was unable to prevent the Goths entering Italy. Otherwise, since Alaric's invasion was a surprise, we should have to suppose the poem written during the bare week or so when it was known that Alaric was intending to cross but had not yet done so.

Claudian was obviously driven to write the poem by Jacob's criticism of his poetry (cf. lines 2 and 14). His poetry in general, or a particular poem? Might it not be *De Bello Getico*?[1] This would nicely explain why, by way of reply to Jacob's criticism, Claudian ridiculed the ineffective part Jacob himself had played in the same war. Claudian did not attack the cult of saints as such: he attacked Jacob's excessive and untimely devotion to it.[2] Since we do not know to what extent, and how culpably, Jacob put this devotion before his military responsibilities, and in particular how other Christian contemporaries viewed his behaviour, we can hardly assume that Claudian's poem would have been construed by contemporaries as a pagan manifesto. Some may have construed it so, and it may even have done Claudian some harm. But he need not have intended it as an attack on anything more than the bibulous and superstitious Jacob.

No one ever took very seriously O. Seeck's far-fetched conjecture that Claudian was executed for participating in the now forbidden pagan sacrifices.[3] But the notion that his paganism was responsible for his sudden end has been revived in a more subtle

---

[1] If so, the epigram probably belongs in 402–3, as suggested above, p. 218.

[2] Cf. Ammian's rather similar mockery of Sabinianus for putting devotion to 'Edessena sepulchra' (i.e. worship of martyrs)—and dancing—before *his* military responsibilities (xviii. 7. 7). Yet Ammian was certainly not in general hostile to Christianity.

[3] *Gesch. d. Untergangs* v (1913), 295, 559: fairly characterized as a 'Roman' by Schanz, *Gesch. d. röm. Lit.* iv. 2 (1920), 5.

formulation by Mazzarino. He argues that the pagan propaganda he claims to detect in Claudian (in particular the allusions to Victoria[1] and the Sibyl), builds up to a climax in his latest poem, *VI Cons.*—a climax that Christians found intolerable. Such was the outcry that Stilico was forced to abandon Claudian to his enemies. In addition to this, Mazzarino uses Claudian's poems as evidence— his only evidence—that during the earlier part of his supremacy Stilico allowed pagans to express even anti-Christian sentiments quite openly, but after Claudian's fall was obliged to tighten up his censorship.[2] That Stilico's regime became less tolerant of heretics is clearly revealed by his legislation: but there is no corresponding evidence that he became less tolerant of pagans. Equally, once it is seen that there is no pagan propaganda in Claudian, this earlier period of complete religious tolerance must vanish. The strongest single argument against Mazzarino's view, as against any view that Claudian was disgraced or executed for his paganism, is the fact that immediately after Claudian's death, Stilico took the trouble to have all his political poems—including *VI Cons.*—republished in an omnibus edition: furthermore, he saw to the publishing of all Claudian's minor and unfinished work as well—including the epigram which, like Fargues, Mazzarino finds so decisively anti-Christian, the lampoon against Jacob. We have seen that there is just a possibility that he ordered the exclusion of two poems on Isis. But it seems clear that he found nothing either compromising or offensive from the religious point of view in any of the poems that were included.

[1] Discussed at pp. 237–41.   [2] Op. cit. 251.

IX

CLAUDIAN'S AUDIENCE

IF then Claudian's poems reveal not simply indiscriminate flattery, not even straightforward bias, but skilful and clear-cut propaganda, then one obvious question suggests itself: at what audience was this propaganda aimed? According to H. L. Levy: 'However much Stilico may have needed or wanted to influence the powerful churchmen of Italy, Claudian, "paganus pervicacissimus" as Orosius calls him, could have been of no help in this direction. The one group with which it was both feasible and possibly advantageous for Claudian's pen to support Stilico's sword was the pagan aristocracy of Rome.'[1]

Claudian may have been a pagan, or at any rate been believed to be a pagan (for our present purpose it makes little difference which). But, as we have seen, the specifically pagan character of his work has been much exaggerated. And it is important to bear in mind that no fewer than eight out of Claudian's ten major political poems were recited, not in Rome, the last stronghold of paganism, but in Milan, the home of uncompromising Christian orthodoxy. If Stilico, himself a Christian, had felt that the pagan character of Claudian's poetry was doing his cause no good with the devout Catholics of Milan, we may be sure that he would have warned Claudian to tone it down a little, instead of allowing, indeed encouraging, him to repeat the mixture as before in eight consecutive recitations. When Claudian shows himself so skilful and sensitive an interpreter of Stilico's views and aspirations elsewhere, it would be very strange if he had failed him in this respect. Whatever attitude some of the more uncompromising of the Fathers might profess towards pagan literature, most good Christians continued to read and enjoy the

[1] *TAPhA* lxxxix (1958), 339.

old poets, and no doubt expected Claudian to give them councils
of the gods on Olympus and Mars standing at Stilico's right
hand in his battles. Mallius Theodorus, consul in 399 and later
one of the leading members of the faction that eventually brought
about Stilico's fall,[1] was panegyrized by Claudian in a poem no
less pagan in character than any of his others, nor is there the
least reason to suppose that this caused any offence. We possess
from the hand of Theodorus an epitaph on his sister couched in
language of a strikingly pagan flavour.[2]

One critic has observed that among all the reproaches he heaps
on Rufinus, Claudian nowhere alludes to the fact that he was
a persecutor of pagans and heretics;[3] true enough—but let us
reflect a moment. What most damned Stilico in the eyes of the
pious Milanese was his tolerance of pagans and heretics: the fact
that Rufinus persecuted them would have seemed a point in his
favour rather than the reverse. Eutropius too was a persecutor,
and Mascezel made an ostentatious display of his orthodoxy. It
may have been a cause of satisfaction to Stilico rather than regret,
that Claudian's *lex operis* enabled him to steer clear of such delicate
topics. There is, I would suggest, no *a priori* reason why Stilico
should not have had every confidence that Claudian's propaganda,
for all its superficially pagan character, might win him valuable
support among the devout Christians who would have formed the
greater part of Claudian's audience at court in Milan.

What now of the claim that Claudian was making a bid for
the support of the pagan members of the senatorial aristocracy of
Rome? This is, I believe, partly true. But I would make at least
two important preliminary reservations.

First, we must remember that the first eight of Claudian's
ten political poems were recited in Milan, and we have Claudian's
own word for it that for the five years between 395 and 400 he
did not set foot in Rome.[4] Now if Stilico had really decided that

---

[1] Mazzarino, pp. 245, 285, 340 f.

[2] *CIL* v. 6240 (= *CLE* 1434), brilliantly studied by P. Courcelle, in *RÉA* xlvi
(1944), 66 f.

[3] Levy, *Invective in Rufinum* (1935), 22: cf. also Paschoud, *Roma Aeterna* (1967),
138.   [4] *Pr. Stil.* iii. 23–4.

the only group Claudian might be able to conciliate to his policies was the senators of Rome, why did he let him recite the greater part of his work in Christian Milan?

Second, we must disabuse ourselves of the common misconception that the senatorial aristocracy comprised a tightly-knit, homogeneous group of die-hard pagans. Prudentius claims that after Theodosius' appeal to the senate in 394,[1] the pagans blushed, tore off their pontifical robes, and 600 families were converted on the spot. An exaggeration, of course. Nevertheless, there is abundant evidence that by *c.* 400 a large number of senatorial families were wholly or largely Christian. Thus an appeal by Claudian to senatorial interests would not be an appeal to exclusively pagan interests. We shall thus view with some scepticism the claim that Claudian was a mouthpiece for pagan propaganda.

Even the most cursory glance at the passages adduced in support of this view should have revealed the significant fact that all of any importance occur in Claudian's last three poems, *Stil.*, *Get.*, and *VI Cons.* Of these, while *Stil.* i and ii were recited in Milan (but see below), *Stil.* iii, *Get.*, and *VI Cons.* were all recited in Rome. Claudian's earlier poems, all but *Prob.* performed in Milan, reveal a lively interest in the glorious past of Rome, like most writings of the age, but little that could be said to show any particular partisanship for the senate. One especially instructive example of the much greater concern Claudian displayed for senatorial interests in his last three poems is provided by his account in *Stil.* i of an incident that took place in the Gildonic war.

Stilico was in an exceedingly delicate position at the time, above all because Eutropius had had him declared *hostis publicus*: a move for which he had cleverly obtained the sanction of the senate of Constantinople.[2] Stilico answered these tactics by prevailing

---

[1] *Contra Symm.* i. 562 f., cf. *Harvard Studies* lxxiii (1968), 257. Cf. too *Perist.* ii. 516, 521 (*senatus lumina* and *illustres domos* praying in the Basilica of St. Hippolytus). See P. R. L. Brown's excellent study (*JRS* li (1961), 1 f.) of the Christianization of the aristocracy—a more fruitful and important subject than the pagan reaction, of which we have perhaps heard too much in the studies of, for example, Straub and Alföldi.

[2] Zosimus v. 11. 1.

upon the Roman senate to declare Gildo *hostis publicus*. Thereby
he killed two birds with one stone: the senate, unaccustomed now
to be consulted on a matter of such importance, was naturally
flattered, and Stilico was able to shelter behind their authority
without compromising Honorius. Claudian has an eloquent
section on Stilico's action in *Stil.* i (325–32):

> hoc quoque non parva fas est cum laude relinqui
> quod non ante fretis exercitus adstitit ultor
> ordine quam prisco censeret bella senatus.
> neglectum Stilico per tot iam saecula morem
> rettulit, ut ducibus mandarent proelia patres
> decretoque togae felix legionibus iret
> tessera. Romuleas leges rediisse fatemur,
> cum procerum iussis famulantia cernimus arma.

No one has ever challenged Boissier's remark that though this
move of Stilico's was 'a mere formality, it overwhelmed Claudian
with joy'.[1] But first, as we have just seen, Stilico's consultation
of the senate was not a mere formality: he badly needed their
authority, and not only this; a declaration of war on Gildo would
entail complete stoppage of the African corn quota, with no
prospect of any more till the war was over. If previous Roman
experience with African rebellions was anything to go on, this
might be several years—or so at any rate it must have seemed at
the time. As soon as the *plebs* realized this, corn riots would
follow: faced with starvation, they would take their revenge
on those responsible, the rich senators in their fine Trastevere
villas, instead of Honorius and Stilico. And this is precisely what
happened: Symmachus and many of his friends were obliged to
flee from the city with their villas in flames.[2] Thus Stilico's move
was neither a formality nor indeed such an unmixed compliment
to the senate as might have seemed.

The second objection to Boissier's view is that if Claudian was

---

[1] *Fin du paganisme* ii. 290, cf. Steinbeiss, *Geschichtsbild Claudians*, 59, and many
others: most recently, Paschoud, *Roma Aeterna* (1967), 146; Wes, *Ende des
Kaisertums* (1967), 38.

[2] Seeck, *Symmachus*, lxx; McGeachy, *Symmachus*, 16; and cf. Jones, *LRE* i. 329.

really so delighted by Stilico's deference to the senate as Boissier supposed, why is it that he allowed two years to elapse before manifesting his joy? For there is not a word about the consultation of the senate in Gild.: and since Gild. is entirely concerned with the preparations for the war, one might have expected Claudian to mention it here rather than in the later poem, which only deals with the war as a whole in the most general terms. Yet not only does Claudian not do this; in Gild. (44 f.) he makes Roma lament the passing of the good old days when

> armato quondam populo patrumque vigebam
> conciliis,

with the obvious implication that this happy state of affairs no longer existed. With an ironic allusion to the 'bellator senatus' of the principate, Roma describes how since Augustus' day

> lapsi mores, desuetaque priscis
> artibus in gremium pacis servile recessi (51–2).

We have seen already that in Gild. Claudian assigns all the initiative in the war to Honorius, without so much as mentioning the senate in this connection. The conclusion seems inescapable that in mid 398, when Gild. was recited in Milan, Stilico had no particular wish to make capital out of his consultation of the senate: or rather, perhaps, that there was little point in trying to make capital out of it in Milan. Two years later, however, he evidently was anxious to make the most of it. Stil. i was not actually recited in Rome, but it was recited in front of much the same audience that might have been expected in Rome, for Stilico sent out very pressing invitations to members of the aristocracy to attend the celebration of his consulate in Milan. The man who acted as spokesman of the senate when the declaration of war was made was Symmachus: we possess the letter he wrote to Stilico announcing the senate's 'decision'. Now many of Symmachus' letters survive from the last few years of his life, and it is possible to compile a tolerably complete chart of his movements and whereabouts at this period. Virtually the whole of the period during which Claudian's earlier work was being performed at

Milan, Symmachus spent in or about Rome. But in January 400, in response to Stilico's invitation, he did make the trip to Milan.[1] Symmachus himself, then, was present in Claudian's audience to hear the glowing account of the part played by the senate in the suppression of Gildo. It was no doubt with Symmachus in particular in mind that Claudian refers at ii. 410 f. to veteran ex-consuls[2] braving the long journey and winter weather to be there for the great occasion.

It is my view that these and similar passages to be discussed below were designed to present Stilico's actions in a favourable light to the senatorial aristocracy. Throughout the period of his supremacy one of the main goals of Stilico's policy was to obtain the co-operation of these men. Not, as sometimes naïvely supposed, out of the natural admiration of the simple barbarian for the hallowed traditions of the senate, but quite simply because the co-operation of a body of men who between them absorbed a major part of the resources of Italy, Gaul, Spain, and Africa was essential for the administration of the western provinces. On the whole he lost the battle. Perhaps the best example of the conflict is provided by another aspect of the Gildonic crisis. Stilico urgently needed recruits for the war. The senate urgently wanted the war to be over and the normal supply of corn to the capital to be resumed so that *la dolce vita* could continue there. The senators also had thousands of able-bodied men on their estates. But they refused to let Stilico have them for his armies. They protested bitterly to the Emperor, and in the end Stilico was forced to allow them to make a cash payment and keep their retainers.[3] Thus the senate was prepared to declare war on Gildo—but not to provide the armies to fight him with. It will be realized that Stilico had to make the attempt to conciliate these selfish, short-sighted, but

[1] Seeck, *Symmachus*, pp. lx f., with the conclusion at p. lxv: 'paene quadriennium continuum a. 398–401 . . . Symmachus Romae permansit, quae assiduitas semel tantum evocatione Stilichonis interrupta est.'

[2] Excluding Theodorus (who lived at Milan) and the two young Anicii, there were perhaps only two other ex-consuls still alive in 400 (Atticus and Neoterius, *coss.* 390 and 397). Symmachus had been consul in 391.

[3] McGeachy, *Symmachus*, 47–8.

immensely rich and powerful men. His attempt can be traced in the series of laws in which he alternately granted and withdrew concessions to their order. Against this background it is easy to understand why Claudian dwells so carefully on Stilico's consultation of the senate in 397.

In Bk. iii (recited in Rome itself this time) Claudian introduces with a similar fanfare of trumpets another act of Stilico concerning the Gildonic war:

> hoc quoque maiestas augescit plena Quirini,
> rectores Libyae populo quod iudice pallent
> et post emeritas moderator quisque secures
> discrimen letale subit . . . tremuit quos Africa nuper
> cernunt rostra reos (iii. 99 f.).

Once again it is Stilico who has restored to *SPQR* its ancient rights of prosecuting erring magistrates and meting out due punishment to the guilty. It seems that what he did was to turn over to the long since defunct jurisdiction of the senate, and to the even longer defunct *iudicia populi*, such of Gildo's subordinates as had been taken alive. An inexpensive enough concession—and perhaps, again, more than a mere concession. Some of these men were no doubt themselves of senatorial families and popular with the people: moreover, they were still magistrates recognized by the eastern government. Rather than risk the odium of executing them as traitors himself, Stilico made a great show of restoring the control once exercised by the *populus Romanus* over its provincial governors. Claudian makes the most of it once more:

> fallitur, egregio quisquis sub principe credit
> servitium. numquam libertas gratior extat
> quam sub rege pio. quos praeficit ipse regendis
> rebus, ad arbitrium plebis patrumque reducit
> conceditque libens, meritis seu praemia poscant
> seu punire velint. posito iam purpura fastu
> de se iudicium non indignatur haberi (iii. 113–19).

From this one trivial incident Claudian does not hesitate to proclaim the restoration of the principate—nay the Republic itself[1] (even the *princeps* had been *supra leges*).

That this was very far from being the case is revealed by another passage in the same poem (ii. 296 f.). Claudian is praising Stilico for not recognizing Eutropius' consulate in the West. He adds:

> in quo vel maxima virtus
> est tua, quod, nostros qui consulis omnia patres,
> de monstris taceas. pellendi denique nulla
> dedecoris sanctum violant oracula coetum
> nec mea funestum versavit curia nomen.

> [Roma, as usual, is speaking.]

Claudian praises Stilico for not allowing the senate even to debate about recognizing Eutropius. He goes on to praise him further for destroying all missives from the East concerning Eutropius' consulate before they could pollute the ears of Italy. Now this is surely very suspicious. It was one thing for Stilico to prevail upon Honorius to refuse to recognize Eutropius: but quite another to prevent the senate even discussing the matter. Surely Stilico cannot really have cared a jot whether the senate discussed it— so long as they came to the right conclusion. It would no doubt have suited him very well if the senate had condemned Eutropius. For example, it had suited him very well for them to condemn Gildo. Claudian's contorted and sophistic argument strongly suggests that the senate had in fact wanted to debate the matter— and that Stilico prevented them because he was afraid that they might come to the wrong decision. Naturally he could not risk them recognizing Eutropius. So Claudian had to make the best of the matter and argue, implausibly enough, that Stilico's one concern was to save the senate the ignominy of having even entertained the idea: 'pars sceleris dubitasse fuit.' It was not an easy thing to reconcile with the image of a Stilico 'qui consulis omnia patres', but Claudian did his usual ingenious best.

This passage alone is enough to put out of court the view that Claudian was a senatorial spokesman.[2] Would one whose aim

---

[1] On this passage, see below, p. 379.

[2] Espoused most recently by Wes, *Ende des Kaisertums* (1967), who at p. 32 calls

was to speak up for the interests of the senate have defended Stilico against the charge of putting a restriction on those interests? It is in any event hard to reconcile this view with the fact that these three poems, like all Claudian's other political poems, are indisputably full of propaganda for Stilico. Are we really to suppose that Claudian combined in the same poems propaganda for two quite distinct and mutually conflicting parties?

In Bk. iii he returns to the theme of the senate's declaration of war ('spectant aquilae decreta senatus', 86). No longer, he exclaims, does Rome regret the passing of the Republic, now that it awards the *fasces*, now that it gives the word for war. He then repeats his account of the miraculous means by which Stilico kept Rome provisioned during the crisis. Naturally enough: this was a subject very close to the heart (though from different points of view) of senate and people alike. Through Stilico, he continues, its rightful power has been restored to Rome, power long since weakened and almost transferred, forgetful of itself, an exile in lands of servitude (iii. 125 f.). What he means is that Stilico has restored to Rome the role of capital of the Empire which was being at once usurped and degraded by Constantinople. Once more we have the theme of the effeminate and servile East, so prominent in *Eutr.* ii: this too could be expected to go down well in Rome. There follows perhaps the most eloquent eulogy of Rome in all ancient literature (*Stil.* iii. 138 f.), much quoted and much admired. It is certainly a splendid passage, but before building too much on it, we should perhaps bear in mind that the whole purpose of Claudian's panegyric, and above all this third book, was to extol Stilico as the saviour of Rome and restorer of all her past glories ('restituit Stilico cunctos tibi, Roma, triumphos', i. 385). It is not necessary to doubt Claudian's admiration for the achievement of Rome:[1] but it will be appreciated that it was in his interest to magnify it, in order to magnify correspondingly the

Claudian one of the 'Koryphäen' of the Roman aristocracy, and at p. 37 so far insults him as to write: 'Die politische Anschauungen und Ideale des Claudianus liegen völlig auf derselben Linie wie die der *Scriptores Historiae Augustae*'!

[1] See below, p. 354.

achievement of Stilico. Nor should it be forgotten that Bk. iii was recited in Rome.

The two crucial passages for the view (most forcibly championed by S. Mazzarino)[1] that Claudian was a pagan propagandist, concern the goddess Victoria. For centuries an altar of Victoria had stood in the senate house at Rome: offerings were made at it before all meetings of the senate. But in 382, among other, in themselves far more important, measures against paganism, Gratian ordered the removal of this altar. Pagan senators, led by Vettius Praetextatus and Symmachus, made a series of appeals to three successive Emperors begging for its restoration—all in vain. We are fortunate enough to possess both the eloquent plea delivered to Valentinian II by Symmachus in 384, and two Christian rejoinders, the first by St. Ambrose, the second the two books of Prudentius' *Contra Symmachum*. Then as now the affair achieved a notoriety exceeding its intrinsic importance, and the altar of Victoria came in a sense to symbolize the struggle for paganism itself.

So when Claudian, by common consent a pagan, alludes to Victoria on two occasions with marked enthusiasm, it might indeed seem that he was entering the controversy on the senatorial side. A closer inspection of both passages will show that he was doing something much more sophisticated than this.

First, *Stil.* iii. 202 f.:

> quae vero procerum voces, quam certa fuere
> gaudia, cum totis exsurgens ardua pennis
> ipsa duci [i.e. Stilico] sacras Victoria panderet aedes!
> a palma viridi gaudens et amica tropaeis
> custos imperii virgo, quae sola mederis
> vulneribus . . .
> adsis perpetuum Latio, votisque senatus
> adnue, diva, tui.

Birt (followed by many to this day) thought this an allusion to an

[1] *Rend. Ist. Lombardo* lxxi (1938), 243.

otherwise unattested restoration of the altar of Victoria by Stilico,
approved of by Claudian. From *pr. Stil.* 19 he felt able to infer that
the restoration took place, precisely, in 400:

> advexit *reduces* secum Victoria Musas,

which he explains as follows:[1] 'scilicet tum simul Musa Claudiani
et Victoria redux fuit', that is to say that Claudian's return to
Rome coincided with the 'return' of the altar of Victoria. An
ingenious and attractive suggestion—until we look at the context
and discover that the Muses there are the Muses of Ennius,
returning to Rome with Scipio Africanus![2]

Nor is any support to be won from the passage in *Stil.* iii.
Nothing is said about an altar, much less the restoration of an altar
(or of anything else, for that matter). Claudian is plainly referring
to a *temple* of Victory, presumably the one on the Palatine.[3]
Naturally, there can be little doubt that Claudian did have the
struggle over the altar in mind. His description of Victoria as
'amica tropaeis' unmistakably recalls Symmachus' reference to
her 'amicum triumphis patrocinium' (*Rel.* iii. 3). But he is very
careful not to name the altar itself. And he is certainly not pleading
the cause of pagan senators, for he continues:

> *Stilico* tua saepius ornet
> limina, teque simul rediens in castra reducat.

What he is doing is evoking the name (though not the altar) of
the goddess in order to stress the deep veneration in which Stilico
held her. He is trying to suggest that Stilico too respected what
the pagan senators held dear—even if he was not able to restore
the altar for them. The propaganda line of the passage is in
Stilico's favour, not the senate's.

As a further argument for his date of 400 for Stilico's alleged
restoration, Birt pointed out that Claudian does not refer to

---

[1] p. lviii, n. 1.
[2] Cf. Birt's similar, though again mistaken, interpretation of the preface to
Rapt. ii (p. 455).
[3] I. Lugli, *Fontes ad topographiam veteris urbis Romae pertinentes* viii. 1 (1960),
103 f.

Victoria in any earlier poem up to and including 399. The point is certainly suggestive—though not for this reason. None of these earlier poems was recited in Rome.

Four years later, and again in Rome, Claudian writes of the speech Honorius made to the senate, adding that

> adfuit ipsa suis ales Victoria templis [i.e. in the senate house]
> Romanae tutela togae: quae divite penna
> patricii reverenda fovet sacraria coetus,
> castrorumque eadem comes indefessa tuorum [i.e. Honorius']
> nunc tandem fruitur votis atque omne futurum
> te Romae seseque tibi promittit in aevum (597 f.).

It has often been alleged that this is another allusion to the restored altar.[1] It must be admitted that we are certainly now in the senate house. But it is a *statue* Claudian is talking about this time, not an altar. And it was an altar, not a statue, that all the fuss was about.[2] This is not an equivocation. Naturally it was the altar, fuming with incense, that offended Christians, not the statue it stood in front of. True, fanatical monks had destroyed pagan statues at Alexandria in 391, but in 399 Honorius issued a law specifically ordering the preservation of pagan statues as works of art. Prudentius too, following the official line,[3] makes Theodosius

---

[1] Mazzarino, *Rend. Ist. Lomb.* (1938), 239, rejecting Birt's view about the restoration of the altar, still thinks it was Claudian's purpose 'risvegliare la questione pagana, dando così una prova del suo paganesimo e della libertà di pensiero che Stilicone gli concedeva'. At p. 246, n. 1 he argues that Claudian took up a position 'nettamente anticristiano' on the matter. Neither claim seems to me justified.

[2] It is thus seriously misleading when (e.g.) Raby writes (*Secular Latin Poetry* i[2]. 54): 'The venerable *statue* of Victory disappeared for ever from the Senate house.' Romano, *Carattere e significato del 'Contra Symmachum'* (1955), 32, n. 36, argues that there is no difference between the statue and the altar (cf. too J. J. Sheridan, *L'Ant. class.* xxxv (1966), 206): but see (decisively) Paschoud, *Historia* xiv (1965), 218, n. 19, *Roma Aeterna* (1967), 78, n. 30 (and add A. Alföldi, *Festival of Isis* (1937), 41, n. 77). It does not seem to me that there is any reason even for supposing (with the majority of scholars) that the statue was removed in accordance with *Cod. Theod.* xvi. 10. 19 of 408, which only orders the removal of cult statues 'in templis fanisque', which hardly applies to Victoria in the senate house, quite apart from the fact that most such laws were ignored.

[3] See F. Solmsen's acute analysis of this passage in *Philologus* cix (1965), 310 f.

himself concede this point in his refutation of Symmachus' case. So long as the pagans give up their sacrificing,

> liceat statuas consistere puras,
> artificum magnorum opera . . . (*Contra Symm.* i. 503 f.).

So there is no reason to suppose that the statue of Victoria was ever moved from the senate house together with the altar, and no evidence here either for Stilico's supposed restoration of the altar.

One last prop remains. It has often been argued[1] that Prudentius would not have written his refutation of Symmachus when he did, in June or July 402, eighteen years after Symmachus' *Relatio*, unless the issue of the altar had been raised again more recently. Indeed, that he was directly inspired by a fresh attempt. An attractive and powerful argument at first sight. Yet closer inspection of Prudentius' poem as a whole proves the very reverse. Both verbal parallels and the method and content of his arguments put it beyond doubt that Prudentius had open in front of him as he wrote a copy of both Symmachus' *Relatio* and Ambrose's refutation of it. No modern reader will be able to appreciate the poem to the full without first reading Symmachus and Ambrose. But he will not need anything else: Prudentius confines himself entirely to the arguments presented by Symmachus in 384. The one thing he does not do is bring them up to date. He is fighting again the battle of 384—won for him when the pagan senators tear off their fillets and bow to Christ after Theodosius' appeal to them in 394. There is no suggestion that the old danger has recurred in Prudentius' own day.

The poem closes with an impassioned appeal to Honorius. Now if Symmachus' attempt had just been renewed, if this is why Prudentius wrote his blow by blow refutation, then why not appeal to Honorius not to listen: implore him not to restore the accursed altar? Yet instead Prudentius appeals for the abolition of gladiatorial games. A worthy cause, to be sure; but scarcely

---

[1] Most recently by Romano, *Carattere* (p. 239, n. 2), *passim*, and W. Schmid, *RAC* iii (1957), 161.

weighty enough to pre-empt the restoration of the altar. I must confess that Prudentius' silence on this point seems to me decisive.

In any event, it is unlikely in the highest degree that either Stilico or Honorius would have consented to such a restoration. Not only would it have been to reverse the policy of Theodosius, who had refused an appeal from Symmachus in 389–90. It would have finished Stilico with the Catholic element at court—and probably offended many Christian senators of Rome as well. But there was nothing too compromising in Claudian paying the *statue* of the venerable lady a compliment, and proclaiming that she would look after the destiny of Rome for ever. It was only her altar that was a pagan symbol. Victoria herself continued to feature prominently in Christian art, and was a common coin type under Christian Emperors. 'Quis ita familiaris barbaris', Symmachus had exclaimed (*Rel.* iii. 3), 'ut aram Victoriae non requirat?' Stilico could not afford to restore the altar, but after his sorry record against Alaric the least he could do to answer Symmachus' question was to show her statue a little respect, and hope that this would do as well. In fact the gesture probably failed to please the Symmachi and antagonized instead the Catholics. But Stilico could not please all parties, and he probably calculated that it was worth making the attempt.

Yet we must not overestimate the significance of Claudian's attempt to win Stilico favour in Rome. We must remember that it is almost restricted to the poems recited in Rome: it is not a theme which runs all through his work. A blatant, if trivial, example of this tendency to curry favour for Stilico with the Romans when in Rome is the claim at *Stil.* iii. 225 f. that though Stilico had given magnificent games in Milan, 'Romae *maiora* reservat.' However, it is interesting to note that, judging by his own account of Stilico's Roman games, they were not a patch on Theodorus' games at Milan the preceding year as Claudian himself had described them (*Theod.* 270 f.).

It is obvious enough, if only from the language in which they are written and the places where they were performed, that

Claudian's poems were aimed in the first instance at western audiences. For it seems clear that by the end of the fourth century Latin was no longer the everyday language of Constantinople.[1] It lingered on for a century and more in official usage, and naturally there was the odd scholar who knew the language well: but by the middle of the fifth century Sidonius could take it for granted that a western ambassador to Constantinople would require the services of an interpreter.[2] It may be conjectured that Rufinus' unpopularity owed not a little to his imperfect command of Greek.[3]

But much of Claudian's propaganda does concern Stilico's eastern policy. To what extent, if at all, is it likely that Claudian had an eastern audience in mind? And how much was he read in the East?

The answer to the first question must be almost entirely negative. Claudian's treatment of eastern affairs is aimed at western rather than eastern audiences. As far as Stilico's standing in the East between 397 to 399 is concerned, by far the most important factor was his declaration as *hostis publicus*, following the failure against Alaric in 397. Yet so far from defending Stilico against the charge of collusion with Alaric, and protesting at Eutropius' decree, Claudian glosses over the outcome of the 397 expedition and entirely suppresses all reference to the decree. He writes throughout this period as though nothing had happened to cause any deterioration in relations between East and West. Plainly his object was to conceal the failure of Stilico's foreign policy from home readers. He could hardly have expected to achieve much in the East this way. Nor would his attack on the eastern senate and indeed the people of Constantinople as a whole have gone down very well in Constantinople. Nor his praise of Stilico for restoring to Rome the pre-eminence that was

---

[1] See most recently B. Hemmerdinger, 'Les lettres latines à Constantinople jusqu'à Justinien', *Polychordia . . . F. Dölger (Byz. Forsch*, i, 1966), 174 f., who omits, however, the important evidence collected by E. Stein, *Bas-Empire* i (1959), 295–6. Both missed the fact that Socrates could evidently read Latin (cf. *HE* ii. 1). On bilingualism, I. Ševčenko, *Synthronon . . . A. Grabar* (1968), 32–3.

[2] C. xxiii. 228 f.   [3] Libanius, *Epp.* 784, 1025.

being usurped and degraded by the new Rome. The supposed appeal of the East for Stilico's aid against Eutropius must again have been aimed at a western audience, who would not know, as an eastern one would, that it did not correspond with reality.

There were, of course, a number of themes Claudian might have wished to reach an eastern audience as well. For example, his constant dwelling on Stilico's loyalty to Arcadius, the continuity of his policy with Theodosius', his marriage connections with the house of Theodosius (no eastern minister could match this claim), and (above all) the double regency and the desirability of *concordia fratrum*. But the other themes must inevitably have detracted greatly from the acceptability and credibility of these.

The poem which most concerns the East is *Eutr.* Now Eutropius was very unpopular by the time of his fall: he had to flee for his life to the refuge of a church, and was only saved from a lynching by the intercession of the patriarch, St. John Chrysostom. Obviously Claudian's poem cannot have created this unpopularity, but it might possibly have had some influence on some of the more conservative and pro-western elements in Constantinople. For example, the decree exiling Eutropius makes much play with the wretched eunuch's pollution of the consulate: to quote just one phrase, 'divinum praemium consulatus lutulentum prodigium contagione foedavit' (*Cod. Theod.* ix. 40. 17). *Eutr.* i was almost wholly devoted to this theme, and much of the language of the edict could be paralleled from it: Eutropius' consulate is a 'prodigium' at both i. 22 and 232, and for 'contagio' cf. i. 489–90, 'contagia fascibus oro | defendas.' A century and a quarter later Marcellinus *comes*, an Illyrian chronicler writing in Constantinople under Justinian, turned to *Eutr.* to enliven his dry record of the year 399, reflecting precisely Claudian's thesis of the calamitous consequences and terrible uniqueness of a eunuch consul:

Eutropius omnium spadonum primus atque ultimus consul fuit, de quo Claudianus poeta 'omnia cesserunt eunucho consule monstra' (*Eutr.* i. 8).

It may be then that Claudian's concentration on this theme did do something to increase the resentment of those who had disapproved all along of a eunuch becoming consul. But hardly more. The primary purpose of the poem was beyond doubt to create a current of hostility to Eutropius in the West[1]—the more necessary if, as suggested above, the senate had been prepared to consider recognizing Eutropius' consulate.

It is likely enough that Stilico saw to it that copies of Claudian were disseminated in Constantinople, and equally likely that they found a few readers. But there is little evidence that they had much influence.

Among Eastern writers, Zosimus, John of Antioch, the church historians, and Marcellinus *comes* all reflect Claudian's accusation that Rufinus had deliberately invited the barbarians to invade the Empire, and J. Koch for one argued that they all derived it from Claudian. But there is no evidence and little likelihood that Eunapius, probably the ultimate source of most if not all of the Greek writers named, could read Latin. And we cannot be sure, nor is it *a priori* very likely, that Claudian originated this charge. Rufinus had plenty of enemies in Constantinople.[2]

St. Jerome, in Bethlehem, seems to have got hold of *Eutr.* soon after it appeared: but if so, he was not taken in by the propaganda, for he wrote an attack on Stilico in his commentary on Daniel, published during Stilico's lifetime.[3]

Interestingly enough the only eastern centre where we do have some evidence, if only from the sixth century, is Constantinople. Mainly, of course, among the few to whom Latin was still a first language, the grammarian Priscian and Marcellinus *comes*, but there is also the antiquary John from Lydia. And while Priscian merely borrowed the odd tag to adorn his own feeble verses, Marcellinus used *Eutr.* at least as a historical source. Naturally,

---

[1] See above, p. 134.   [2] Mazzarino, p. 252, n. 1.
[3] *Vig. Christ.* xix (1965), 111 f., and E. Demougeot, *RÉA* liv (1952), 83 f. Levy made out a good case for *Ruf.* ii being known to Jerome (*AJPh* lxix (1948), 62 f.), but the later date for that book suggested above (p. 78) would rule this out. But *Ruf.* ii may possibly have been known to the author of *De Vita Christiana*, written by Pelagius or one of his followers, it is uncertain when (? *c.* 400) or where (cf. W. Liebeschuetz, *Latomus* xxvi (1967), 442 f. for details).

this is not evidence for Claudian's lifetime, but what is suggestive is John's contemptuous reference to him as a Παφλαγών, 'windbag'. Is this not perhaps a sign of the hostility to Claudian we might after all have expected to find in the city he attacked so warmly? Might not Παφλαγών be the sobriquet his prolific pen earned him from contemporary Constantinopolitans?

Stilico's opponents in the East were quick to find an answer to the propaganda of Stilico's 'windbag'. After the fall of Gainas a protégé of Aurelian named Eusebius wrote an epic *Gainea*. It would have been instructive to compare his poem with Claudian's, but unfortunately it is lost. However, Socrates drew his account of Gainas' rebellion from it, and it is fairly clear that he must have presented his audience in Constantinople with as distorted a version of the facts as Claudian concocted for his audiences in Rome and Milan. Another propagandist of Aurelian was Synesius of Cyrene, who wrote an extraordinary allegory of the circumstances of Aurelian's rise to power and exile under Gainas' regime. Aurelian emerges as the prince of light, his 'brother' and rival Eutychian as the prince of darkness, and Gainas as his dupe.[1] In another propaganda piece, *De Regno* (§ 18), Synesius mentions that he had written poems in Aurelian's honour too—and even refers to 'many others' who had also written such poems. The most striking feature of Synesius' propaganda from our point of view is that it is wholly concerned with the struggle for power in the East: there is no mention of western affairs, still less of Stilico. Did Aurelian's propagandist have any knowledge of Stilico's? It might seem *a priori* likely that he should have—though there is no evidence that Synesius could read Latin. It has been argued that he modelled his *De Regno* on Claudian's *IV Cons*. It must be admitted that there are some striking parallels between the two works: but then kingship literature is a very traditional genre, and a common source is a perfectly adequate, perhaps even preferable, explanation.[2] But even if

---

[1] I hope to elucidate this work (*De Providentia*) elsewhere: meanwhile see A. H. M. Jones, *JRS* liv (1964), 81, on the identification of Typhos with Eutychian. Ammonius too wrote a poem on Gainas (Socrates, vi. 6). [2] See p. 322.

Synesius did read Claudian's poem, then it was only some common-places concerning kingship which he imitated: for the political content of *De Regno* was the very antithesis of the policy of Stilico. It was the policy of Aurelian, nothing less than the complete de-Germanization of the state and the dismissal of all barbarian soldiers and officers.

On the whole then, whether or not Claudian found many readers in the East, his propaganda is not likely to have had much more effect there than communist propaganda in western capitals today.

What chance was there, whether with pious Christians in Milan or unrepentant pagans in Rome, that Claudian's propaganda would succeed in the West? On the face of it a very good chance. Stilico's ministers were not required to give statements to an independent press whenever his relations with the ministers of Arcadius took a new turn, and it must have been easy enough for Stilico to keep back news for months, if not indefinitely, and spread about his own version instead.

This is not mere conjecture. Here is what Eunapius wrote when he came to relate the period of Eutropius' supremacy for his history:[1]

It was impossible to discover any accurate information concerning the West. Owing to the length of the voyage, news took a long time to arrive, and was distorted when it came. Travellers and soldiers with access to information about affairs of state spoke according to their own personal likes or dislikes. If you collected three or four of them together with their rival versions as witnesses, quite a quarrel would ensue, beginning with questions like 'What was your source for that?', 'Where did Stilico see you?', 'And where could you have seen the eunuch?' So that it was a job to decide between them. Merchants told nothing but lies, or what would bring them some gain. . . .

This, of course, refers to the difficulty of getting western news in the East, but there is every reason to believe that it was just as difficult to get eastern news in the West. By 408 Stilico had banned all eastern shipping from western ports, as we know from

[1] Frag. 74 (*FHG* iv. 46*b*).

the law issued soon after his death revoking the ban: 'Hostis publicus Stilico novum atque insolitum reppererat, ut litora et portus crebris vallaret excubiis, *ne cuiquam ex Oriente ad hanc imperii partem pateret accessus.* . . .'[1]

It will be remembered too that in 400 Claudian praises Stilico for destroying communications from the East before they could be even debated by the senate in Rome. For Claudian to have felt obliged to mention this, the senate must presumably have got wind of what was happening and protested. But how many other communications did Stilico suppress that no one got to hear of? Even without deliberate suppression of news, there were probably a good many people in Milan and Rome who knew little if anything about the political situation in Constantinople or Africa. True, many Roman nobles owned vast estates in Africa, but they were, almost without exception, absentee land-lords who had seldom, if ever, set foot in Africa,[2] and probably knew next to nothing about the activities of Gildo. In any case, if the evidence of Symmachus' letters is anything to go by, many Italian aristocrats of the late fourth century were quite apathetic about politics, and mindful of little beyond what concerned their own immediate personal interests. As Samuel Dill observed: 'Either the government was very reticent, or Symmachus and his friends were very unobservant or careless of public affairs.'[3] On either count Claudian stood to gain. Symmachus in particular appears to have known almost nothing about the East—at any rate he almost never mentions it in his letters. Rufinus' fall he mentions once in passing, calling him a 'praedo annosus' (*Ep.* vi. 14. 1), Eutropius he never refers to at all. No doubt many of Claudian's listeners had a shrewd suspicion that they were being fed a doctored version, but had no means of distinguishing truths from half-truths, or of knowing when Claudian was simply suppressing something. He may not have been able to convince them of all Stilico's more extravagant claims, but he may well have

---

[1] *Cod. Theod.* vii. 16. 1.
[2] C. Courtois, *Les Vandales et l'Afrique* (1955), 132 f.
[3] *Roman Society in the Last Century of the Western Empire* (1899), 145.

succeeded in concealing, for example, the extent of eastern opposition to Stilico.

It remains to inquire how far Claudian did succeed in the West. Naturally, there is little positive information. The only directly contemporary writer we know to have read Claudian and paid him the compliment of imitation is, surprisingly enough, Prudentius:[1] surprisingly, that is, for those who think that as a pagan Claudian would not have been read by Christians. This is the more remarkable in that Prudentius was a much older man than Claudian, and wrote while Claudian was still alive. Eloquent testimony of the charm Claudian's poetry exercised on the mind of one at least of his contemporaries. It would, of course, be implausible to trace Prudentius' eulogy of Pollentia to *Get.*, but his emphasis on Alaric's supposed inner compulsion to sack Rome (*Contra Symm.* ii. 697 f.) may perhaps have been influenced by Claudian (cf. p. 184). Much more significant is Prudentius' adaptation of Claudian's picture of Roma. In *Gild.*, Claudian had drawn a pathetic, aged Roma bewailing Gildo's seizure of Africa, who was restored to her pristine vigour and youth at once on Jupiter's promise to restore Africa to the rule of Honorius. In Prudentius' *Contra Symm.* (ii. 655 f.) we have a very similar portrayal of the rejuvenation of Roma, certainly under the influence of Claudian. But this time Roma is rejuvenated because she sees so many of the old senatorial families bowing their heads to Christ. A neat Christianization of a motif from the 'paganus pervicacissimus'.

Augustine, we know, read and admired Claudian as a poet. Yet he distrusted Stilico for his weakness with the Donatists.[2] Orosius too professed to admire Claudian. But although he reproduces Claudian's line that Rufinus had invited the barbarians, he was bitterly hostile to Stilico.

What then of the aristocracy of Rome? In 400 a bronze statue was erected to him in the forum of Trajan 'senatu petente' as the inscription states, dedicated in the names of Arcadius and

---

[1] See Appendix B, pp. 469–73.   [2] Cf. Aug., *Ep.* 97. 2–3

Honorius (the addition of Arcadius' name is purely formal: it is unlikely that he was consulted—and improbable that he would have agreed). In the preface to *Get.* (line 9) Claudian himself writes of it,

> annuit hic princeps titulum poscente senatu.

But did the senate honour him spontaneously—or just to please Stilico?[1] We might have expected to hear of it in a letter of that doughty patron of the liberal arts, Q. Aurelius Symmachus. Yet not only does he not mention the statue: he never even mentions Claudian. It is often claimed or assumed that Claudian must have belonged to the so-called 'circle of Symmachus'.[2] But there is no evidence. We have seen already that Claudian spent his first five years as Stilico's propagandist at Milan, while Symmachus was more or less continually at Rome: and Claudian spent perhaps a large part of the last two years of Symmachus' life (400–2) in Africa.[3] Moreover not one of Claudian's epigrams mentions or is addressed to Symmachus, just as Symmachus never mentioned or wrote to Claudian. Indeed, though in *Stil.* Claudian paid Symmachus a nice oblique compliment (above, p. 233), in an epigram he styles an orator friend called Gennadius 'Romani fama *secunda* fori'. Second after Symmachus, according to Birt, but surely in fact second after Cicero[4]—i.e. implicitly rating Gennadius *above* Symmachus. This would certainly not have pleased Symmachus, if he ever saw it. And surely Symmachus' failure to mention Claudian is very striking. Symmachus prided himself greatly on his love for and on his patronage of letters:

[1] 'Omitto senatus consulta', wrote Suetonius of the honours the senate voted Augustus, 'quia possunt videri vel necessitate expressa vel verecundia' (*D. Aug.* 57. 1). And cf. C. E. Stevens's similar reservations about the sincerity of the senatorial reaction to Sidonius' panegyric on Avitus half a century later (*Sidonius Apollinaris* (1933), 35).

[2] Most recently, U. Knoche, *Symb. Colon. J. Kroll Oblata* (1949) 159; W. Schmid, *RAC* iii (1957), 160–1; G. Martin, *Studies . . . B. Ullman* (1960), 70.

[3] See below, p. 412.

[4] Similarly, in *Pan. Const.* (iv) xiv. 2, Fronto is styled 'Romanae eloquentiae non secundum, sed alterum decus': i.e. 'non point la seconde, mais l'une des deux' (Galletier, Budé ed., ad loc.). Again, the first, or other, is obviously Cicero.

the footling poetic trifles of his friends[1] he praised to the skies—
but he shows no knowledge even of the existence of the one poet
of the day who 'soared above the heads of his feeble contemporaries
and placed himself, after an interval of 300 years, among the
poets of ancient Rome'.

Mazzarino has, I think, greatly overrated the degree of intimacy
between Symmachus and Stilico:[2] I would regard their relationship as no more than an uneasy alliance of convenience. K. F.
Stroheker has drawn attention to a curious alliance between the
pagan aristocracy and the barbarian marshals of the earlier fourth
century.[3] But there is a vital difference between Stilico and these
earlier barbarian marshals. They were all pagans: Stilico was a
Christian—and husband of Serena. Symmachus was obliged to
correspond with Stilico himself over affairs of state—and pay
court to him when he wanted favours only Stilico could grant.
But he was not obliged to have anything to do with his Egyptian
upstart of a propagandist.

After Symmachus we might look to another poet, representing
the same senatorial interests, though a Gaul instead of an Italian:
Rutilius Namatianus. It is plain from his famous little poem
De Reditu Suo, written a dozen years after Claudian's death and
seven after Alaric's sack of Rome,[4] that Rutilius was very familiar
with Claudian's poetry. There are several certain verbal echoes.[5]
Yet so far from Rutilius taking over Claudian's picture of Stilico
as a second Camillus, his poem contains the most vehement attack

---

[1] The recent discovery of the *Epigrammata Bobiensia* has done little to enhance
our opinion of the poetic attainments of Symmachus' friends.

[2] e.g. p. 236.

[3] *Historia* iv (1955), 314–30, now reprinted in *Germanentum und Spätantike*
(1965), 9 f.

[4] i.e. 417, as I hope to have established in *JRS* lvii (1967), 31 f.

[5] J. Vesserau, *Cl. Rutilius Namatianus* (1904), 387 f., is certainly wrong to deny
direct imitation by Rutilius (cf. R. Helm, *Natalicium J. Geffcken* (1931), 41 f.). His
argument, 'à vrai dire il est bien difficile de croire que deux contemporains se
soient imités l'un l'autre jusqu'à pouvoir se faire accuser de plagiat' (pp. 399–400),
is at once to misunderstand completely the purpose of poetic imitation in antiquity, and seriously to underestimate the chronological gap between Claudian and
Rutilius. Claudian had been dead thirteen years when *De Reditu* was written.

on Stilico that has come down to us. Indeed it is ironic—and surely no accident—that Rutilius uses in denouncing Stilico the very same motifs Claudian had used to defend him. Claudian had explained Stilico's reluctance to risk a second battle with Alaric after Pollentia by his anxiety to prevent Alaric getting any closer to Rome, to prevent

> ut delubra Numae sedesque Quirini
> barbaries oculis saltem temerare profanis
> possit, et *arcanum tanti deprendere regni* (*Get.* 101-3).

Compare Rutilius ii. 41-2:[1]

> quo magis est facinus diri Stiliconis acerbum,
> proditor *arcani* quod fuit *imperii.*

It was precisely the words 'proditor imperii' that Claudian had used of Rufinus, in his accusation that Rufinus invited the barbarians to attack Rome (*Ruf.* i. 319). Now it was Stilico who stood accused, not merely of inviting the Goths to attack Rome, but of treacherously introducing them into the very bosom of Rome and protecting them:

> immisit Latiae barbara tela neci;
> visceribus nudis armatum condidit hostem
> illatae cladis liberiore dolo (ii. 46-8).

With 'visceribus nudis' compare *Get.* 577-8, 'visceribus mediis ipsoque in corde videtis | bella geri.' No doubt too it was from Claudian that Rutilius derived his use of the adjective 'pellitus' to describe the Goths. But for Rutilius they are Stilico's 'pelliti *satellites*' (ii. 49). I cannot believe it a coincidence that Rutilius so neatly turned Claudian's propaganda for Stilico against him.

It seems likely, then, that Claudian's propaganda had no lasting effect among the senatorial circles of Rome, even with those who read and admired his poetry. In Milan he may have succeeded for a while at least in winning for Stilico, if not the active support, at least the acquiescence and co-operation of the predominantly

---

[1] Cf. P. Courcelle, *Hist. litt. des grandes invasions germaniques* (1948), 217, n. 2 on p. 30. Paschoud's interpretation of this passage (*Roma Aeterna* (1967), 162) is certainly wrong.

Christian element at court. He may have played an important role in tiding Stilico over the Eutropian crisis. But in the end it became obvious that Stilico had fallen between three stools. His eastern pretensions had met with total failure. And in the West, he was too Christian for the pagans, and too tolerant of pagans and heretics for the Christians.[1]

In the hope that Claudian's eulogies might do him some good even after the poet's death in 404, Stilico had all the poems which dealt with himself collected and republished together—hence the poems that do not concern him have a different manuscript tradition. But in vain. The counter-propaganda of Stilico's enemies prevailed over even Claudian's eloquence, and Stilico was beheaded at Ravenna on 22 August 408.

Claudian continued to be read and admired throughout late antiquity and the Middle Ages. But as a poet, or (later) as a teacher of moral and political wisdom.[2] After a few generations had passed the constant recurrence of the name Stilico seemed merely a blemish amidst such artistry. What clearer proof could there be than the entry 'Stillicio' in the late thirteenth-century *Repertorium* of Conrad of Mure: 'proprium nomen cuiusdam, de quo satis dicit Claudianus'?

[1] On ancient criticisms of Stilico, see now L. Várady, *Acta Antiqua* xvi (1968), 413–32, and L. Cracco Ruggini, *Riv. di storia e lett. relig.* iv (1968), 433–47.
[2] See below, pp. 431 f.

X

TECHNIQUES OF THE POET

I

THAT Claudian was a 'rhetorical' poet there is no gainsaying. But as usual with this term (abusive rather than descriptive), little has been done to clarify the implications of such a judgement. For, as has often been remarked,[1] 'rhetoric' need not have the pejorative associations usually conjured up in the mind of the modern reader.

For example, too much has perhaps been made of Claudian's debt to the Greek rhetorical handbooks for his panegyrics. The influence of Menander, Aphthonius, and lesser names is indeed plain, both in the general structure of the panegyrics—προοίμιον, γένος (if noble), γένεσις (portents, omens), ἀνατροφή, πράξεις (elaborately classified), συγκρίσεις, ἐπίλογος (suitable prayers)—and in the treatment of individual *topoi*.[2] And while Claudian never reaches the self-consciousness of one fourth-century panegyrist,[3] who refers openly to what the rules allow (ὡς οἱ νόμοι θέλουσι τῶν ἐγκ[ωμί]ῳ[ν]), he does follow their hints very closely, often down to quite trivial details.

This is an interesting and important discovery, to be sure—but not one that can simply take the place of criticism. A conventional form is not in itself vicious—nor even inappropriate for

---

[1] e.g. H. Fränkel, *Ovid: A Poet between Two Worlds* (1945), 167 f., and E. J. Kenney, 'Juvenal: satirist or rhetorician?', *Latomus* xxii (1963), 706 f.

[2] O. Kehding, *De panegyricis Latinis capita quattuor* (1899); L. B. Struthers, *Harvard Studies* xxx (1919), 49–87; Fargues, ch. vi; and (for *Eutr.*) W. Suess, *Ethos* (1910), 264 f.

[3] Heitsch XXVII, recto, 19 (not in Page)—a preface to a hexameter poem, not an iambic encomium in its own right as assumed by Heitsch: cf. *CQ* N.S. xx (1970).

a ceremonial occasion. It is at least as important to inquire whether Claudian was master or slave of his medium.

Certainly, his panegyrics follow the broad lines laid down by Menander, but they are by no means so monotonously similar even in structure as the neat tables of Fargues and Struthers might suggest. Under analysis both *IV Cons.* and *VI Cons.* emerge as perfect specimens of the genre. Yet a third of *VI Cons.* (127–330) consists of an account of Pollentia and Verona—narrative, not the topical treatment proper to a panegyric. *IV Cons.* 214–418, again a third of the poem, is a perfect miniature περὶ βασιλείας, skilfully grafted into the panegyric pattern under the guise of the advice Theodosius supposedly gave Honorius on his elevation as Augustus in 393, split in two by an interruption from Honorius to relieve the monotony (and implausibility) of an unbroken monologue. In order to diversify the rigidity of the pattern, Claudian has combined quite distinct genres, overstepping the boundaries between rhetoric and philosophy, epic and panegyric.

This excessive concentration of earlier studies on Claudian's debt to the Greek rhetorical tradition has tended to overshadow what is new in his panegyrics. In the first place, if the form is Greek, the spirit is Roman. Claudian is no less familiar with the Latin panegyrists, from Pliny to his own contemporary Pacatus. The virtues he praises, the *exempla* he cites, are all Roman (see Ch. XII).

Secondly, they are in verse. Verse panegyrics are not unknown in Latin, but as the *corpus* of the Panegyrici Latini shows, till Claudian prose had been the invariable medium for consular inaugurations and similar ceremonies. Greek verse panegyrics were becoming relatively common in the fourth century (p. 23), but there does not seem to be any example of a Greek *consular* panegyric in verse, and Claudian is certainly the first to use verse for such occasions in the West. His success was immediate and overwhelming, and in the next three-quarters of a century only one Latin prose panegyric is known.

Thirdly, abstract personifications. In earlier panegyrics they are employed occasionally, for a special vivid effect. Even Menander only recommends them as one device among many to be used in the πράξεις section.[1] In Claudian, however, personifications play a major part in the action of the panegyric—a counterpart to the divine machinery of epic. The only Greek parallel for this development comes from a fragmentary panegyric of the fifth century,[2] and I suspect that the main influence here is Latin epic, above all Statius. For example, the descent to earth and speech of Virtus in *Theb.* x. 632–82, and the descriptions of, and altercation between, Pietas and Tisiphone in *Theb.* xi. 457–96, strikingly foreshadow much in Claudian. Claudian's panegyrics are a new and hybrid form, children of the marriage between Greek panegyric and Latin epic.

The real value of the rhetorical pattern in Claudian is well illustrated by a comparison with his Latin successors.[3] For there was no Latin Menander, it seems, and Merobaudes and Sidonius modelled their panegyrics directly on Claudian—unaware, however, of the pattern Claudian himself had followed and exaggerating some features out of proportion to others. The result is that individual *topoi* take over from the over-all structure, and nothing can happen without one personification haranguing another. The rhetor in Claudian would have disowned such disciples.

In his invectives Claudian diverges more widely from the rhetorical pattern. In theory the invective was simply an inversion of the panegyric, with each subdivision serving as an opening for vituperation instead of eulogy. Yet of the four books (two each) of *Ruf.* and *Eutr.* the only one which fits this pattern even approximately is *Ruf.* i. And not even *Ruf.* i could be adequately described as just a run-of-the-mill invective. It is true that the opening underworld scene could be classified loosely within the pattern as the section on upbringing, since it is Megaera who sees to Rufinus'

---

[1] *Rhet. Gr.* iii. 374 Sp.

[2] Heitsch XXXVI. 4. 9 f. (Page 143. 37 f.), one city reproaching another.

[3] I am much indebted here to Oswyn Murray's illuminating study 'Panegyric and Advice to Rulers in Late Antiquity and the Early Middle Ages', to appear in *Journ. Warb. Inst.* xxxiii (1970). See too pp. 490–1, below.

upbringing. But the underworld setting goes much further and deeper than this. Megaera's account of Rufinus' education is only part of her plan to destroy the upper world, which in turn is only one of two such plans put to the infernal council. And Rufinus is represented as a spirit of evil and discord throughout the poem. Megaera reappears at the end of Bk. i to glory in Rufinus' crimes—and to be told by Justitia that Stilico will surely put a stop to them. It *may* be (but we are here in the realms of conjecture) that it was preliminary pondering on the ἀνατροφή section which first suggested the possibility of making Rufinus a nursling of the Furies. But if so the notion soon transcended these limitations and formed the central theme of the poem as a whole: evil (personified by Rufinus) versus justice. So while it is true enough that a large part of the book is classified according to the invective pattern,[1] it would be a gross oversimplification to leave the matter there. The thread of the supernatural which runs through the poem gives a unity and coherence to what otherwise might really have been no more than a list of neatly classified crimes and vices.

As for Bk. ii of *Ruf.*, we have seen already that it would be more accurately described as an epic. Naturally vituperation of Rufinus and eulogy of Stilico hold a not inconsiderable place, but arising out of the narrative, not distributed under headings.

The two books of *Eutr.* are less disparate in character. Book ii, like *Ruf.* ii, is basically an epic (the revolt of Tribigild and Eutropius' unsuccessful attempt to crush it)—though not accorded epic treatment. Indeed, there is much that is deliberately unepic, almost a parody of epic. Eutropius holds a council of war with his peers, in the best epic tradition—but of course it is a farce, quickly degenerating into gossip about the races. The battle fought by Leo is the very antithesis of an epic combat. Poor Leo is already running away when he mistakes the rustle of a leaf for the whistle of an arrow and drops dead on the spot from sheer fright. Yet Bk. i, while hardly an epic, is not really a rhetorical invective

[1] See Levy, *TAPhA* lxxvii (1946), 57–65, with my reservations, above, p. 79.

either. For instead of Eutropius' crimes being catalogued by topics (as, by and large, Rufinus' are in *Ruf.* i), we are treated to a chronological record of Eutropius' rise from castration in the cradle through all the slave markets of the Levant to a career as pervert, pander, chamberlain, and finally master of the East. The list of his crimes when established in power is more in the invective manner, but (unlike Rufinus') they are still narrated rather than catalogued: his treatment of opponents, his greed, sale of provinces, arrogation of judicial powers, campaign against the Huns, and finally his consulate and its reception in the West. There is an obvious suggestion of his enormities gradually rising to a climax. Scarcely qualified, by either subject-matter or treatment, as an epic, but basically a narrative all the same.

But more important than the difference between the individual books of each poem is the contrast between the two poems themselves. The tone of *Ruf.* is elevated and solemn throughout. Rufinus is wicked, monstrous. His eventual punishment matches his crimes: torn limb from limb on earth, and then hurled beneath Tartarus for all time. *Eutr.* is quite different. Right from the start Eutropius is vile, disgusting, comic were it not for his power and his crimes. The difference can be well illustrated by considering the treatment of the motif of avarice in both poems. Rufinus' greed brings about the ruin of innocent persons, the confiscation of ancestral estates (Claudian is writing for a predominantly landowning audience!), treachery, perjury, torture, murder . . . (i. 179 f.). All is grim. In *Eutr.* all is comic: the man who buys Asia with his villa, Syria with his wife's jewels, the placard outside Eutropius' house advertising the price of each province on a sliding scale. His alleged motive, too, is deliberately absurd: having been sold so often himself, he wants to sell everything else (i. 196 f.).

There are at least two reasons—different but converging—for this contrast. In the first place, it should be obvious that the invective was a much more flexible genre. For unless the writer was prepared to risk offending the honorand (especially if the latter happened to be the Emperor), a panegyric had always to be dignified. There was little opportunity for levity or humour. Eulogy, however well written, however sincere, can hardly fail to become monotonous in the strict sense of the word (hence Claudian's attempts to diversify *IV Cons.* and *VI Cons.* with an admixture of epic and philosophy). The invective, on the other hand, allowed a variety of approaches: straightforward attack, satire, buffoonery, innuendo—not to mention unlimited freedom for downright invention. Thus an invective offered Claudian the opportunity to vary his technique. It is no coincidence that *Ruf.* and *Eutr.* are his two best poems.

Classic invectives such as the *In Verrem* and *In Pisonem* employ all or most of the techniques in turn. As too does Claudian in the two miniature invectives on Gildo in *Gild.* The first is a straightforward attack on Gildo for his crimes and his cruelty, the second draws a comic picture of him staggering forth to battle half-asleep from a carousal, wincing at the bugle. There is no such variation within *Ruf.* and *Eutr.* The buffoonery, innuendo, comedy, even downright obscenity that so characterize *Eutr.* are wholly absent from *Ruf.* Not a hint (however baseless) of even the milder sexual perversions, or even of anything so relatively innocuous as the gluttonous banquets Gildo is accused of. In short, nothing which would mar the picture of Rufinus as a demon of evil. For a demon, however wicked, must have a certain dignity if he is going to inspire the appropriate emotion—fear.

At this point it is well to bear in mind yet again (nor yet for the last time) that political considerations are seldom absent from the conception of Claudian's contemporary poems. The point has been illustrated in detail already in the case of *Gild.*, and here too politics and art go hand in hand. Quite apart from the artistic desirability of making *Eutr.* different from *Ruf.*, its political purpose was quite different too. Both books of *Ruf.* were written after Rufinus' fall, to celebrate and justify it. Both books of *Eutr.* *preceded* Eutropius' fall (p. 136), and were designed (hopefully) to pave the way for it—or at least to create a climate of hostility against Eutropius in the West. Since Rufinus was already dead when Claudian wrote, it was possible to reveal, even exaggerate, the extent of his hostility to Stilico and his ambitions; to represent him as a truly fearsome figure whom Stilico alone had been able to destroy. But while Eutropius was still supreme and Stilico powerless against him, a different technique was called for.

Eutropius' case must in any event have suggested different treatment from the start: if Claudian was going to succeed in creating this hostility, the obvious course was to concentrate on his physical shortcomings, his servile origin, his low habits, and—above all—the unparalleled horror of a eunuch defiling the *fasces*. Anxious as he was to conceal at all costs the fact that Eutropius was a real danger to Stilico, Claudian chose to treat him throughout merely as a figure of fun. He was not to be taken seriously: hence the buffoonery and innuendo. Note particularly the prevalence—in this alone of Claudian's poems—of extended and heavy puns, a sure sign of the 'low' style. Hosius the ex-cook who cooks the books,[1] Leo the ex-weaver who makes a speech full of allusions to his former profession (I spare readers the details), and the ingenious but crude run of obscene innuendoes about Eutropius' sex life.[2]

And it is political considerations, I suspect, which in part at least determined the change from invective to epic in *Ruf.* ii, the epic form of *Eutr.* ii, and the narrative sections of *VI Cons.* For the major purpose of *Ruf.* ii was to put over the official version of what 'really' happened between Stilico and Alaric in 395. Since this version differed in several material respects from what had actually happened, a narrative was obviously the best way of putting across the official sequence of events. In *Eutr.* ii Claudian's purpose was to represent Eutropius' handling of Tribigild's revolt as a total failure, necessitating Stilico's intervention. Here too narrative was the best way to bring out this alleged sequence of events. In *VI Cons.* Claudian was attempting to explain (and justify) what had taken place between Stilico and

---

[1] See *CQ* N.S. xviii (1968), 409.

[2] *Eutr.* i. 358 f., explained in the decent obscurity of an elegant Latin footnote (for the sake of clarity, not prudery, he claims) by Birt, *Zwei politische Satiren* (1888), 45, n. 1: cf. also A. C. Andrews's commentary (Diss. Philadelphia, 1931), ad loc. One or two details remain obscure.

Alaric after Pollentia in 402: here again the topical impressionistic technique of the panegyric was less suited than a narrative to bring out the all-important sequence of events: Stilico
had only made the agreement with Alaric to get him across the
Alps; *then* he could—and did—pounce. Even in *Gild.* the switch
to a comic treatment of Gildo marching to battle serves the
purpose of making Gildo appear easy meat to a Roman army—
hence reducing Mascezel's credit (p. 118). It would be wrong, of
course, to concentrate on political to the exclusion of purely
artistic considerations. Obviously Claudian wanted his poems to
be read and enjoyed as poems. Nevertheless, it is no less obviously
no accident that so often his choice of literary techniques happens
to suit his political purpose better than other techniques he might
have chosen. A purely literary approach to Claudian's literary
techniques is doomed to failure.

II

Let us return now to the epics and panegyrics. In theory the
two were of course quite distinct, and Claudian himself certainly
so distinguished them. What he considered to be panegyrics he
entitled (e.g.) *Panegyricus de tertio* (*quarto, sexto*) *consulatu Honorii*,
what he considered epics *De bello Gildonico, De bello Getico.*
The subject-matter of the epic was, traditionally, war—'res
gestae regumque ducumque et tristia bella'.[1] Yet when, as often
happened, the epic celebrated the campaigns of a living general or
Emperor, and was moreover actually recited (as were Claudian's)
in his presence, it was almost inevitable that the epic should
have come to take on some of the characteristics of the
panegyric. Thus it is hardly surprising that (e.g.) *Get.*, recited
within a couple of months of the victory at Pollentia, should
descend at times into outright eulogy of Stilico. There is a similar
eulogy (disguised as a speech of Theodosius to Arcadius) in *Gild.*
   When publishing one of the contemporary papyrus fragments
to which reference has often been made already, Wilamowitz

---

[1] Horace, *Ars Poetica,* 73.

observed that from such a brief sample it was hardly possible to say whether the poem from which it came had been an epic or a panegyric.[1] One can go further. Sometimes the decision is not clear-cut even when the entire poem survives. Claudian still distinguished them by title and gives at least the appearance of narrating events in his epics, while merely classifying them in his panegyrics. But there does not appear to be any material difference between George of Pisidia's *Heraclias*, a panegyric on Heraclius, and his *Bellum Avaricum* and *Bellum Persicum*, poems on Heraclius' Avar and Persian wars. The two latter are scarcely less panegyrics than the *Heraclias*. By contrast, Corippus' *In Laudem Justini* is scarcely less a narrative than his *Johannis*, an eight-book account of John Troglita's campaign against the Vandals in 543-8. The 'panegyric' is in fact a detailed narrative in four books of the events of the first few weeks of Justin's reign, containing remarkably little eulogy.[2]

One of the most interesting of the papyri in this category contains fragments from two poems: one obviously a Πάτρια, the other describing a war against Persia under Diocletian.[3] J. Bidez at once made the attractive suggestion that the author was Soterichus, known from Suidas to have written a Πάτρια of his native Oasis and a panegyric of Diocletian.[4] Keydell has now shown that the Πάτρια is in fact the foundation legend of Hermupolis.[5] Since the two papyrus fragments were probably written by the same author, and since Soterichus is not known to have written a Πάτρια of Hermupolis, the probability that he is the author of the other poem is correspondingly diminished. But Keydell may have gone too far in ruling it out completely on the ground that Soterichus' poem on Diocletian is described as a panegyric whereas the lines of the papyrus fragment appear to be narrative. If a hundred or so lines from the narrative portions of *Ruf.* and *VI Cons.* had turned up on a papyrus, they would inevitably

---

[1] *Berliner Klassikertexte* v. 1 (1907), 107.
[2] Cf. H. Nissen, *Hermes* lxxv (1940), 298-325 on George and Corippus.
[3] Heitsch XXII and XXIV (= Page 135-6).
[4] *Rev. de Phil.* xxvii (1903), 81-5.   [5] *Hermes* lxxi (1936), 465-7.

have been identified as part of an epic. While there is nothing beyond chronology and geography in favour of assigning the lines
to Soterichus, it would be rash to deny the possibility that they
could come from a panegyric as easily as from an epic.

With Claudian, however, this fusion of panegyric and epic
does not manifest itself only in the inclusion of panegyrical
sections in an epic or narrative sections in a panegyric. It also
affects what purports to be narrative in a deeper way. For example, at *Get.* 319 f. Stilico makes a forced march to Raetia to
nip a rebellion in the bud. The country was hard, meals hurried;
no soft bed, sleep snatched in a wild beast's den, shield for a
pillow. . . . We are up in the clouds. This is not narrative: it is the
style of panegyric. Compare a passage from the panegyric on
Stilico (i. 126 f.), where we hear how Stilico scales the snowy
peak of Athos, Rhodope his rocky bed. . . . Such hyperbole is
not even meant to be taken seriously: it is just a figurative and
emphatic way of underlining Stilico's selfless devotion to duty.
Another passage of *Get.* describes how the Goths burst into Greece:

> nil Rhodope, nil vastus Athos, nil profuit Haemus[1]
> Odrysiis; facili contemptum Strymona saltu
> et frustra rapidum damnant Haliacmona Bessi.
> nubibus intactum Macedo miratur Olympum
> more pererratum campi (*Get.* 177–81).

Obviously the Goths did not ride up to the top of Olympus.
Again, Claudian is not even attempting to *describe* the Gothic
advance. Rhodope, Athos, and Haemus are the traditional strong-
points of the Thraceward area (at least to the poets and rhetors),[2]
and all Claudian is doing is to underline symbolically the completeness of the Gothic conquest of the Balkans.

But there is another, still deeper, cause for the breakdown of the
epic style which is clearly visible in Claudian and complete by
George of Pisidia. To put it bluntly, Claudian is almost incapable
of writing true narrative. It is hardly an exaggeration to say that
all Claudian's major poems, epics no less than panegyrics and

---

[1] For the reading, cf. *CQ* N.S. xviii (1968), 404.
[2] Cf. *CQ* N.S. xviii (1968), 404.

invectives, consist of little but a succession of speeches and descriptions.[1]

Gild. is a good example. Ostensibly the first book of a narrative of the war against Gildo, in fact it contains less narrative than some of the formal panegyrics and invectives. After a proem the poem opens with the appeals of Roma and Africa, both duly described before they speak. Both descriptions and speeches are highly effective. Africa's speech, which otherwise balances Roma's perfectly, is cut short by Jupiter ('iret adhuc in verba dolor, ni Juppiter...'). Much to his credit Claudian resisted the temptation to round the speech off with a peroration according to the text-books, so that Jupiter's contribution really does appear to cut Africa off in mid flow. After these two impassioned appeals, Jupiter's reply (only four lines) comes as something of an anti-climax. He merely tells them that Honorius will remedy the situation. The scene now changes. The two Theodosii descend from heaven (again, more description than narrative), and speeches follow from each to Arcadius and Honorius respectively. Theodosius the Emperor addresses Arcadius for nearly 90 lines (236–320), and (again) a rather lame four-line assent follows. Within five lines we are listening to the other Theodosius haranguing Honorius. Six lines after he has finished, Honorius is awake and haranguing Stilico. Only one line separates Honorius' speech from Stilico's reply, then a bare three lines of narrative before a description of the army and another speech from Honorius, this time to the army. Then after another description, this time of the favourable omens which followed Honorius' speech, there is a loyal 'speech' by the army as it sails away. It is worth quoting a few of the 20 lines of 'narrative' which close the book:

> iam classis in altum
> provehitur; dextra Ligures, Etruria laeva
> linquitur et caecis vitatur Corsica saxis.
> humanae specie plantae se magna figurat

[1] Something of this tendency is foreshadowed already in Statius' *Thebaid*: cf. G. Krumbholz's study in *Glotta* xxxiv (1955), at pp. 247 f. On the Greek side Nonnus is as good an example as Claudian: cf. Wifstrand, *Von Kallimachos zu Nonnos* (1933), 151 f.

> insula (Sardiniam veteres dixere coloni),
> dives ager frugum, Poenos Italosve petenti
> opportuna situ: quae pars vicinior Afris,
> plana solo . . .

Once again, within three lines Claudian has abandoned narrative proper for description.

Claudian goes through the motions. He uses all the traditional divine machinery of epic, dream visitations, epic similes, and so forth—but he is not really writing epic at all.

This is not a characteristic of the contemporary poems alone. *Rapt.* too is constructed on the same pattern of speeches and descriptions, linked by passages of seldom more than a dozen or so lines of narrative.[1] No sooner has Claudian mentioned Ceres' hideout for Proserpina in Sicily, than he must describe Sicily. Aetna, of course, is in Sicily: how then can we avoid weighing the various theories on the cause of volcanic eruptions? Proserpina is embroidering: obviously the pattern must be described. In the next book she wears an embroidered dress, a different one, of course, again described. The plain of Henna too must be described, its trees and flowers catalogued. . . . Some of these descriptions are very beautiful of their kind (the speeches on the whole less so),[2] but their frequency and length cannot but hold up the flow of the narrative.[3]

---

[1] There are some interesting remarks on this in the section 'Die Illustrationen des älteren vatikanischen Virgil und der spätrömische Stil um 400', of F. Mehmel's *Virgil und Apollonius Rhodius* (1940), 99–132—but he pushes too far his thesis of the lack of a sense of time in late fourth-century poetry (taking in, for example, even the precisely chronicled *De Reditu* of Rutilius).

[2] The silliest speech in all Claudian is the one Proserpina makes while being abducted by Pluto (naturally she could not submit to such treatment in silence): in tones which recall nothing so much as the shrewish ravings of Nonnus' Semele (*Dion.* ix. 208 f.), she finds time as she is being whisked away to contrast her lot with other kidnapped heroines: at least they were allowed to stay in the upper world. Poor Proserpina loses both virginity and daylight (ii. 250–72). Pluto, oddly enough, is moved to tears by this inappropriate outburst.

[3] The most obtrusive such description occurs in *VI Cons.* (286 f.), where Alaric breaks off an exciting account of the retreat of his defeated army across the Alps to describe the Alps: he had stopped to ask an 'incola' how far they stretched, whether they divided Italy in two. . . . Compare a similarly obtrusive digression

This is a criticism which the modern reader would feel bound to make. To Claudian it would probably have seemed misdirected. There can be little doubt that, in practice if not in principle, he considered the episode more important than the whole.

It is obvious from the preface to Bk. i that Claudian considered *Rapt.* his most ambitious work. And it is obvious too that much care has been lavished on the luxuriant descriptive passages. Yet the opening scenes are a structural disaster. Out of the blue Pluto bursts into a paroxysm of rage because he has no wife. All hell is in a ferment. The Furies assemble as in *Ruf.*, and Pluto is on the point of releasing the Titans and declaring war on Jupiter. Then Lachesis suggests that he tries *asking* Jupiter first: 'posce Iovem; dabitur coniunx.' Pluto has apparently not thought of this. He calms down, asks Jupiter—and gets a wife (or at least the promise of one).

Further comment on the feebleness of the 'plot' would be superfluous. More interesting to inquire why someone of Claudian's undoubted ingenuity did not take the trouble to come up with something better. The answer is (I suspect) that he did not think it sufficiently important. So long as he had a framework on which to hang his speeches and descriptions, that was enough. This is well illustrated by the positively Ovidian vandalism with which he resurrected from *Ruf.* i a pale ghost of his brilliant infernal council and underworld in revolt to support Pluto's protest against Jupiter.[1] Obviously he was pleased with the idea and thought that it would be appropriate in a poem largely about the underworld. But it is only superficially appropriate. The myth required that Jupiter should *agree* to Pluto's request, so the revolt peters out into an anticlimax, unlike the climax in *Ruf.*, where the revolt is abandoned only for what is represented as an even deadlier blow to mankind—Rufinus! Things in *Rapt.* are not improved by the immediate sequel.[2] Pluto sends a long speech to

(on the causes of plagues) which breaks up Ammian's exciting account of the siege of Amida (xix. 4. 2–7). It is clear that contemporaries must have reacted differently to what we cannot help but regard as mere interruptions.

[1] For the priority of *Ruf.* over *Rapt.* see Appendix A, p. 459.

[2] See too A. K. Clarke, *Proc. Class. Assoc.* xxvii (1930), 38–41, for some brief

Jupiter via Mercury, pathetically contrasting his lonely celibate state with the chequered sex life and numerous children of Jupiter. As with the complaints of Roma and Africa in *Gild.*, Jupiter receives the message, ponders it, and assents, all within four lines, and then the scene changes.

III

Both speeches and descriptions merit closer study. First the speeches.

Direct speech occupies a larger, and different, role in Claudian than in his Latin (and Greek) predecessors. A few statistics[1] will help to make these differences clearer. That post-Vergilian epic became progressively more 'rhetorical' is of course a commonplace. Yet it is not always sufficiently appreciated that rhetoric is not the same as making speeches. As it happens, not one of the Silver Age epics reaches the proportion of direct speech in the *Aeneid* (38 per cent). The closest is Statius, with 37 per cent: Lucan has only 32 per cent. Claudian's epics, however, give an average of 41 per cent, with *Gild.* rising to 75 per cent.

But if the post-Vergilians do not have as much direct speech as Vergil, or so many individual speeches, they tend to make the speeches they do have longer. And significantly enough, despite his high total proportion of direct speech, Claudian has proportionately fewer speeches than any poet of the Silver Age. Naturally it follows that those he does have are longer (the average length for a speech in Claudian's epics is 24 lines, as against 11 in Vergil, 14 in Statius, and 21 in Lucan, his nearest rival).

Hand in hand with this tendency to fewer but longer speeches

but useful remarks on *Rapt.*—though her interpretation of *mens congesta* at Bk. i. 4 as a mind full of poetical echoes which must be unloaded is strained: it is surely no more than an allusion to the poet's traditional divine frenzy (so E. R. Curtius, *European Literature*, 474, with many parallels).

[1] Drawn, with supplements of my own, from H. C. Lipscomb, *Aspects of the Speech in the Later Roman Epic*, and G. W. Elderkin, *Aspects of the Speech of the Later Greek Epic* (Diss. Baltimore, 1909 and 1906 respectively).

goes another, related, tendency, to reduce the interchange of speeches. At *Aen.* i. 321–409 Aeneas and Venus exchange six speeches. In Valerius and Statius we still find as many as 4 or 5, in Silius only 3. In Claudian's epics there are only four examples of the first speaker being allowed to reply, and then usually only a brief assent to the second speaker (e.g. *Gild.* 321–4). A similar tendency is clearly observable in Nonnus. Direct speech had been in sharp decline throughout Hellenistic and early Imperial Greek epic: as against the 50 per cent of Homer, Apollonius of Rhodes has 29, Quintus 24, Triphiodorus 20, and the Orphic Argonautica only 12 per cent. Nonnus, with 36 per cent, and his disciples Musaeus and Colluthus with 34 and 37, return to something approaching the Homeric proportion—though there is little else that is Homeric about their speeches.[1] In Nonnus we find the same tendency as in Claudian to reduce exchange of speech to a minimum, often with a bare assent from the second party.

The effect of all this should be obvious enough. In Claudian, speeches no longer arise naturally and frequently out of the narrative.[2] The tendency is rather to long set speeches, either single, virtual declamations, or (much less frequently) in pairs, either complementary or contrasting. There is almost no genuine dialogue.

One particular manifestation of this (even clearer in Nonnus than in Claudian) is the monologue, often so dissociated from its context that it is addressed to no one in particular.[3] And

---

[1] On Nonnus' speeches, see Wifstrand, *Von Kallimachos zu Nonnos* (1933), 142 f.; on Musaeus', T. Gelzer, *Mus. Helv.* xxv (1968), 22 f.

[2] Another detail of technique, small in itself but pointing in the same direction: unlike all the other Latin epic poets but Lucan, Claudian hardly ever inserts more than a bare *dixit* into a speech in parenthesis (cf. Lipscomb, *Aspects*, pp. 30–6); i.e. we never find in Claudian a speech opening like the following (from *Aen.* xi. 459 f.): ' "immo," ait, "o cives", arrepto tempore Turnus, | "cogite . . .".' This can only accentuate the impression of formality, of lack of spontaneity. On the other hand Claudian shows no increased tendency over his Latin predecessors to begin and end speeches within the line: 29 per cent of his speeches end before the line end, 38 per cent begin after its beginning.

[3] Wifstrand, *Von Kallimachos*, 149 f.

a further refinement of this sort of speech is the *ethopoiia*. Of characterization proper there is little trace in Claudian. We should hardly expect it, of course, in the panegyrics and invectives. There Claudian's object was to represent Stilico, not as he really was, but as the ideal warrior and statesman he wished to appear. And if Stilico is all white, Rufinus and Eutropius are naturally all black: Rufinus is the archetypal scheming villain, Eutropius the lecherous incompetent buffoon. But there is little attempt at characterization in the epics either. In fact the nearest approach to characterization (as in Nonnus) is the *ethopoiia* speech, the monologue (often addressed to a very vaguely defined audience) composed on the τίνας ἂν εἴποι λόγους pattern. Rufinus, when terrified of Stilico, makes a speech expressing dismay: when exultant, thinking (mistakenly) that he has got rid of Stilico, he makes a boastful speech. Alaric too makes a boastful speech before Pollentia, a pathetic one after, when defeated. Stilico makes three speeches in *Get*. Not one of them rings true as the sort of speech Stilico is likely to have made on any of the three occasions. He stops the panic at court in Milan, he brings the rebellious Alans back to their allegiance (by a lecture on Roman history, according to Claudian), and encourages his men to fight at Pollentia: each is designed exclusively to represent him, in different ways, as the bulwark and saviour of Rome. There are no personal touches, nothing that one could say was characteristic of Stilico rather than of a Camillus, a Scipio, a Cato. For it was Claudian's aim, precisely, to present Stilico as a Camillus, a Scipio, a Cato. Indeed, though we hear time and again in the 6,000 odd lines Claudian wrote over nearly 10 years, of Stilico's bravery, loyalty, patriotism, foresight, statecraft, honesty, popularity; paradoxically we learn nothing whatever of Stilico the man. The one and only personal detail we can extract is a purely external one: Stilico had grey hair.

Theodosius' speeches, too, reveal him only as the ideal Emperor and father. Naturally he is the obvious choice for the role of Honorius' instructor in the duties of kingship, but once launched on this congenial theme Claudian pays scant attention to what a Spanish gentleman of very modest education might really have said to a 9-year-old boy interested in little but hunting. Lectures on kingship aside, the only other subject Theodosius brings up in his speeches, more than once and not without some warmth, is his unbounded admiration and affection for Stilico!

Some remarks now on the descriptions. Claudian's method could hardly be characterized better than it was almost 70 years ago by T. R. Glover:[1]

Virgil's method is that of suggestion; it is that of appeal to the heart, and it requires something from the reader, as music does from the listener. Claudian on the other hand leans more to painting than to music, appealing rather to the eye. Thus he lingers fondly over his work, seeking to bring before the eye the presentment of his conception by massing colour upon colour, making his picture splendid as one of Honorius' toilets. The reader *sees* in Claudian's case and *feels* in Virgil's.

Two examples will show what he means. First father Tiber,[2] as he leaves his couch of green leaves, his mossy bed, and entrusts his urn to his attendant nymphs. Grey eyes flecked with blue shine out from his shaggy countenance, recalling his father Oceanus; thick curled grasses cover his neck and lush sedge crowns his head. This the Zephyrs may not break nor the summer sun scorch to withering; it lives and burgeons around those brows immortal as itself. From his temples sprout horns like those of a bull; from these pour babbling streamlets; water drips from his breast, showers pour down his hair-crowned forehead, flowing rivers from his parted beard. There clothes his massy shoulders a cloak woven by his wife Ilia, who threaded the crystalline loom beneath the flood.

Not much has been left out. Claudian can never resist giving a river god his traditional horns, and the detail of Ilia's underwater loom, eminently logical in an underwater ménage but scarcely poetical, is very characteristic.[3] More successful all round

---

[1] *Life and Letters* (1901), 224.

[2] *Prob.* 212 f. (Platnauer).

[3] Part of the humanization of divine behaviour which is especially noticeable in *Rapt.*—unavoidable, perhaps, if an epic with no mortal characters was to have any 'human' interest, though the effect is often unfortunate. To obtain torches to

is his first description of Roma as she leaps on to her chariot.[1]
Note especially the emphasis on colour:

Her right side is bare; her snowy shoulder exposed; her brooch fastens
her flowing garments but loosely and boldly shows her breast: the
belt that supports her sword throws a strip of scarlet across her fair skin
. . . her threatening helm of blood-red plumes casts a dark shadow and
her shield challenges the sun in its fearful brilliance, that shield which
Vulcan forged with all the subtlety of his skill. In it are depicted the
children Romulus and Remus, and their loving father Mars, Tiber's
reverent stream, and the wolf that was their nurse; Tiber is embossed
in amber, the children in pure gold, brazen is the wolf, and Mars
fashioned of flashing steel.

It is as though Claudian was describing a statue or painting—and
just like the painter, he cannot leave the job half done. Every
detail, every colour must be there. When Triton carries Venus
on his back,[2] he arches his tail to shade her as she sits on scarlet
coverlets, her snow-white feet trailing in the foam. Very pretty,
but we cannot leave them alone in the middle of the picture.
We must have a swarm of Cupids gambolling above her head and
summon up Nereid after Nereid to chase after her, each riding
a different sea animal, and each holding a different present for
Maria's wedding. Not an inch of the canvas is left. Venus is meant
to be skimming across the water at great speed. But Claudian's
picture is stationary.

   At the beginning of *Rapt*. iii Jupiter convenes an assembly to tell
the gods his plans for Proserpina. Iris has carried out her instructions to the letter, and every deity there ever was is present:
'arranged and grouped almost, as it were, for the photographer'.[3]

light her search Ceres chooses the highest trees she can find, and then hoists up her
skirt, rolls up her sleeves ('cincta sinus, exerta manus') and chops them down
(with a two-headed axe). Then panting (as well she might) she climbs Aetna with
one in each hand and dips them down the crater for a light—turning her head
aside to avoid the smoke. Scylla's dogs stopped barking at the glare—or rather
some did: the others happened to be looking the other way and carried on barking as before (*Rapt*. iii. 332–448).

   [1] *Prob*. 87 f. (Platnauer).   [2] *Nupt*. 149 f.
   [3] T. S. Duncan, *The Influence of Art on Description in the Poetry of Statius* (Diss.
Baltimore, 1914) (a useful work), p. 39.

They sit in order of rank: heavenly gods at the front, then sea gods, then river gods. Water-nymphs have to sit on their fathers' laps, and a thousand minor rivers just have to stand like the commoners they are: 'plebeio stat cetera more iuventus, | mille amnes.' The pictorial character of *Rapt.* was clearly recognized by its first English translator, Leonard Digges (1617), who dedicated his version to his sister, to serve 'as a Patterne for a piece of Needlework', for which purpose, he remarked, 'no Poeticall Authour will with more variety furnish you, than Claudian'.

The pictorial character of *Nupt.* is so marked that the whole poem could ber epresented pictorially in just four tableaux. (A) The love-lorn Honorius soliloquizing about Stilico's (alleged) refusal to advance the wedding date. (B) Venus' magic palace, built all of precious stones and heavy with the odour of rare spices, Amoretti splashing about in two running streams, one sweet, the other bitter. The description (inspired by Statius, but more lush and extravagant at every point)[1] is delightful of its kind and was a favourite of eighteenth-century translators. (C) Venus' trip on Triton. (D) Venus breaking the news to Serena while various attendants make preparations for the wedding and the army sings its congratulations.

Similarly there is very little in *Gild.* that could not be expressed in a series of tableaux.[2] I am not suggesting that such tableaux actually existed, but it is interesting to compare Claudian's description of a real series of tableaux (in prospective—and unfulfilled—chronological order), those depicted on Stilico's consular robe. (A) Maria in labour in the Imperial palace, while Serena looks on, anxious but happy. (B) Nymphs wash the new baby

---

[1] For a comparison of the two passages see Z. Pavlovskis, *Class. Phil.* lx (1965), 166–7 (Statius, *Silv.* i. 2 [the epithalamium on Stella] 147 f., and *Nupt.* 85 f.). Both palaces are extravagant, but while Statius' is built of material not beyond the pocket (or taste) of an eccentric Flavian millionaire, Claudian's is pure fantasy.

[2] Prudentius' *Psychomachia* consists of a similar series of tableaux, and from probably as early as the fifth century was indeed illustrated, with the Virtues and Vices painted just as Prudentius had described them. Sixteen illustrated manuscripts exist (A. Katzenellenbogen, *Allegories of the Virtues and Vices in Medieval Art* (1939), 3 f.).

in a gold basin. (C) Stilico dandles his grandson on his knee. (D) Eucherius practises his riding. (E) Venus unites the two houses for the third time (i.e. the wedding of Eucherius and Galla Placidia), while Thermantia smiles at the groom. Claudian need only have described each scene, each person, at his customary length, and equipped them with some speeches (e.g. Stilico lecturing his grandson on statecraft as Theodosius had Honorius) and he would have had a full-length poem, just like most of his others. And just as on Stilico's robe we pass straight from one scene to another, so in *Nupt.* scant attention is paid to the linking of the scenes. We hear no more of Stilico's reluctance to allow the marriage after the opening scene, where it happened to be dramatically (and politically) appropriate. By the last scene (still, apparently, on the same day) the wedding is on the point of taking place. A small inconsistency, easily rectified by an allusion to Stilico being won over. But Claudian just could not be bothered. It was the pictures that mattered. A tiny detail like this could be left to the listener's imagination.

Of course this is in large measure the result of the concentration of the Imperial age (in both East and West) on the writing of *ecphraseis*, descriptions of isolated scenes, captured at a particular moment in time. When the writer of *ecphraseis* turned his hand to a more ambitious work, such as an epic, inevitably it tended to consist of a series of *ecphraseis*. In Claudian's case it is easy to trace the influence of Statius,[1] one of the masters of the genre, an influence that shows itself not merely in the borrowed turn of phrase but in a generally Statian attention to detail and colour.

As so often, Claudian just pushes the tendency further. But there is something new as well. A tendency to depict what is living and moving in static terms, a tendency that is visible even in a historian like Ammian. Indeed it has recently been remarked of Ammian, and Julian too, that they 'often render the historical scene immobilised as on a relief, rather than in a lifelike narrative form'.[2] Not only does Ammian depict the combatants in a battle

---

[1] But a thorough study of Statian influence on Claudian would be welcome.
[2] Larissa Warren Bonfante, *Parola del passato* xix (1964), 420.

scene as though they were actors on a stage: on occasions he explicitly draws the parallel himself. Julian's soldiers at the battle of Strasbourg stand on the bank watching 'just as in some theatrical scene, when the curtain displays many wonderful sights' as the defeated Alamanni try desperately to escape across the river.[1] Even the participants are represented as seeing themselves as spectators of a tableau.

The fourth century loved spectacles and shows, and one especially striking spectacle which both Ammian and Claudian describe is the *clibanarii*, literally 'oven-men', mailed cavalry: they made a fearsome sight, covered as they were from head to toe in closely interlocking iron plates (the horse too), each man's face covered by a brightly painted or gilded visor. 'You might have supposed them statues polished by the hand of Praxiteles, not men' ('crederes simulacra, non viros'), exclaimed Ammian. 'credas simulacra moveri | ferrea, cognatoque viros spirare metallo', echoed Claudian. Julian too twice explicitly likens them to statues. There is no need to suppose that Claudian is dependent on either Ammian or Julian for this reaction to a sight he must often have seen himself. It is just that all three (and others too) were struck by the same quality about them, the quality of dramatic immobility.[2]

IV

That some of Claudian's descriptions of mythological figures closely resemble actual representations of those same figures on coins, paintings, etc. of the Roman period has long been recognized. Since it is one of a scholar's duties to apportion credit where due among his predecessors, it is appropriate to record the priority of Joseph Addison here over a German dissertation of 1878. 'The three figures you have here shown us', says Eugenius (one of the interlocutors in *A Dialogue of Medals*), 'give me an idea of a

[1] xvi. 12. 57 (cf. L. Warren Bonfante, art. cit. 422).
[2] Amm. Marc. xvi. 10. 8; Claud. *Ruf.* ii. 357 f.; Jul. *Or.* i. 37CD (i, p. 54 Bidez); *Or.* ii. 57C (i, p. 126); and cf. *Pan. Lat.* x (iv) 22. 4: see Ramsay MacMullen, *Art Bulletin* xlvi (1964), 440.

description or two in Claudian that I must confess I did not before know what to make of. They represent Africa in the shape of a woman, and certainly allude to the corn and headdress that she wears on old coins.' 'I think', replies Philander, 'there is no question but the poet has copied out in his description the figure that Africa made in ancient sculpture and painting.' And again, '[I] will give you a passage out of Claudian, where the compliment to Stilico [a *corona civica*] is the same that we have here on the medal. I question not but the old coins gave the thought to the poet.' In many cases the similarity is very close indeed. Notably Roma, where Claudian's description (quoted above) corresponds in every detail with the 'medals', down to the position of her brooch and the baring of one breast. There is a further correspondence in a later description. In *Gild.* the aged and ailing goddess 'plenamque *trahit* rubiginis hastam'. The point can be appreciated a little better when it is realized that Roma is very frequently represented carrying a reversed spear.[1] It is not a far step from carrying a reversed spear to dragging it when you are tired.

Addison wrote in an age when numismatic commentaries on ancient authors were all the vogue, and of course he pushed his case much too far. 'Copied' is hardly the right word at best, and it is certainly a misconception to picture Claudian composing in front of a coin cabinet. The reason the poet and the coins give us the same figure is not because either is copying the other. It is simply that this was the accepted figure. It is interesting, certainly, to have this numismatic commentary on Claudian (it will be remembered that Addison's contemporary Hardouin dismissed as forgeries all texts not so confirmed), and one might legitimately reproach art historians for failing to make use of Claudian's minute descriptions.[2] But it would perhaps be more worthy of comment if the poet and the coins had given us *different* pictures. Long before Claudian's day the characteristics of the major

---

[1] Cf. J. M. C. Toynbee, *Studies . . . D. M. Robinson* ii (1953), 271.

[2] Claudian is ignored, for example (together with Rutilius), both by Miss Toynbee in her studies of Roma in late antique art in *JRS* xxxvii (1947), 135–44, and *Studies . . . D. M. Robinson* ii (1953), 261–77, and by C. C. Vermeule, *The Goddess Roma in the Art of the Roman Empire* (1959).

goddesses[1] and personifications were far too firmly established for
such as Claudian to depart from them except in details. For example, the broken-down Roma of *Gild.*, with a wisp of grey hair
poking out from her crooked helmet, presupposes for its impact an
audience familiar with all the details of the conventional picture.
A slightly different line of approach may be more illuminating.
Let us consider some of the consular diptychs of the age. As we
might have expected, there is a close parallelism between their
representations of Roma and Claudian's. But more interesting is
the parallelism between the diptych as a whole and some of
Claudian's consular panegyrics as a whole. On the diptych of
Basilius, consul in 480, Roma stands with the *fasces* in her left
hand, her right hand on the consul's shoulder, evidently investing
him with his regalia and hence his office.[2] The motif appears
elsewhere in a fascinating passage from Prudentius' poem on the
martyr St. Laurence:[3]

> illic [in heaven] inenarrabili
> allectus urbi municeps
> aeternae in arce curiae
> gestas [like Stilico] coronam civicam.

> videor videre inlustribus
> gemmis coruscantem virum,
> quem *Roma caelestis* sibi
> legit *perennem consulem.*

Heaven is a very Roman place. What concerns us here is the
celestial Roma who chooses the eternal consul—a heavenly counterpart to the 'earthly' Roma who chooses the regular consuls, in both
the diptychs and Claudian's panegyrics. It should now be clear that
there is more to her recurring role in Claudian's panegyrics than
either burning patriotism[4] or mere lack of imagination.

---

[1] Claudian much prefers goddesses to gods, 'sans doute', as Fargues remarks,
'parce que sa Muse recherchait de préférence les couleurs riantes et les formes
gracieuses' (p. 288).

[2] Cf. Toynbee, *Studies . . . D. M. Robinson* ii (1953), 274.

[3] *Perist.* ii. 553 f.: for the motif of the 'perpetual consul' see *JThS* N.S. xix
(1968), 213–15.   [4] Below, pp. 363 f.

In *Prob.* Roma flies to the Frigidus to beg Theodosius to appoint the two young Anicii consuls for 395, in *Stil.* she begs Stilico to accept the *fasces* for 400, in *VI Cons.* she begs Honorius to inaugurate his consulate for 404 in Rome. To the modern reader this repetition, this self-plagiarism, can only seem proof of lack of originality. But are not Claudian's panegyrics in some sense a literary counterpart to the consular diptychs, both different but parallel manifestations of the ceremonial that formed so vital a part of the consular inauguration?[1] Contemporary listeners would take Roma's appearance for granted in such a context— indeed they would half expect her.

This is not the whole answer, of course. Roma was not quite *de rigueur* even in consular panegyrics. She does not appear, for example, in *III Cons.* or *IV Cons.*, or in *Theod.*, where Justitia (in all but name identical with Roma) does the honours for Theodorus because of his long-standing connection with the law. And Roma does appear in non-panegyrics, like *Gild.*, where she begs Jupiter to destroy Gildo, and *Eutr.*, where, indefatigable as ever, she flies to Milan to beg Honorius to send Stilico against Eutropius. Here Claudian is extending the scope of his formula— though Roma's speech in *Eutr.* is really only an inversion of her consular speech. Usually she recommends someone *for* the consulate: here she begs that it be taken away from Eutropius because he has defiled it.

The rest of our answer is that having once established a satisfactory formula, Claudian is quite content to re-use it time and again. Just so long as it provided a workable framework within which he could concentrate on his speeches and descriptions.

V

We have seen already that in addition to both the human and the more venerable divine creatures which people Claudian's poems there are many abstract personifications. In itself, this is nothing new. To go back no further than Vergil, and to choose

[1] See the text volume of R. Delbrück's *Die Consulardiptychen* (1929), *passim*.

a passage which Claudian happens directly to imitate, there is the sombre group standing 'primis in faucibus Orci' in *Aen.* vi: Luctus, the Curae and Morbi, Senectus, Metus, Fames, Egestas— 'terribiles visu formae'. They were all still there in Claudian's day, though (like all things) they had moved with the times, bigger and brighter than before (p. 281). Not only have they grown: they have taken on a new role, actors rather than scenery. Roma, Africa, and Tiber we have met already. Britannia, Gallia, Oenotria, and Hispania queue up to plead Stilico's case before Roma. Justitia begs Theodorus to accept the consulate, Aurora Stilico to save her from Eutropius.[1] Especially remarkable is the concluding scene to *Stil.* ii, the cave where old man Time sits while dame Nature guards the door and an encircling snake unceasingly devours his own tail (the symbol of never-ending time). Nature appears elsewhere too, 'age-old, but fair of face', a powerful figure, intermediary between Jupiter and the other gods, with some of the attributes of Physis in contemporary Orphic poetry.[2]

On the whole, however, the allegory does not go very deep. In *Ruf.*, certainly, Megaera and her protégé Rufinus stand for the powers of evil, Justitia and Stilico for the powers of good. And the sorry state of Rome in autumn 398 is vividly portrayed by the grey-haired distraught old hag barely recognizable as the proud goddess who once made the world tremble.[3] But there is no real moral allegory. Nor any trace of a deeper meaning to either the *Gigantomachia* or *Rapt.*[4]—myths which certainly lent themselves to allegorical interpretations. Many of Claudian's personifications serve as little more than lay figures for a colourful description, or as mouthpieces for a necessary speech. To turn from Claudian

---

[1] For a list (though not much more) of Claudian's personifications, see A. Marsili, *Antiquitas* i (1946), 49–55.

[2] See Curtius, *European Literature*, 106–7, for references. Curtius insists that Natura is a 'religious experience' for Claudian rather than just a 'personification of an intellectual concept', but I feel sure that what we have in Claudian is little more than the decorative traces of such a religious experience. Her role in the cosmological section at *Rapt.* i. 249 f. is clearly derived wholly from Ovid, *Met.* i. 5 f. For the ambiguity of her status as Time's janitress, see above, p. 207.

[3] On Roma, see below, pp. 363 f.

[4] See above, pp. 15, 210–11.

to the full-scale battles between the Virtues and Vices in the exactly contemporary *Psychomachia* of Prudentius, is to enter another world.

The difference between the allegory of Prudentius and Claudian can be well illustrated by the prefaces with which both (in the contemporary fashion)[1] introduced most of their poems. It is Claudian's regular practice to hint at the subject-matter of his poem through an appropriate myth, sometimes drawing the parallel explicitly, sometimes not. The preface to *Nupt.*, for example, describes the preparations for the wedding of Peleus and Thetis, to take place on the seventh day of the festivities. The 'seventh day' is the only intrusion into the myth of the reality of Honorius' wedding. In the preface to *Ruf.* i Claudian tells of Python slain by Phoebus—adding at the end the news that 'another Python' has now fallen. And just as Claudian depicts the present through the mythical past, so Prudentius sees it through the biblical past. But there is a basic difference in both literary origin and purpose over and above the religious difference. Prudentius is working inside a long established tradition of biblical allegory, and his purpose was moral. Claudian's prefaces have grown out of the rhetorical tradition, the comparison of the ruler to a god. Honorius is another Peleus, his son will be an Achilles. Stilico is a new Apollo, Rufinus a new Python. His purpose was to vary artistically the themes of compliment[2]—though the preface to *Rapt.* i is an interesting example of the extension of this method to a non-panegyrical theme. It tells of the sailor who grows bolder little by little till at last he ventures into the open sea. It was not necessary to add the key: that the sailor is Claudian, his latest

---

[1] For a useful collection of material, O. Schissel, *Berl. Phil. Woch.* xlix (1929), 1073 f. Claudian's, like those of most Latin poets of the age, are in elegiacs: 'comic' iambics were the rule for Greek poets (cf. my paper in *CQ* N.S. xx (1970)).

[2] See R. Herzog, *Allegorische Dichtkunst des Prudentius* (1966), 119–35—an interesting comparison, though not all of Claudian's prefaces fit his generalizations (C. Gnilka, *Gnomon* xl (1968), 368–70): see A. Parravicini, *Athenaeum* ii (1914), 183 f., for a useful classification of Claudian's prefaces. *Pr. Eutr.* is *sui generis* for special reasons (p. 137, above).

voyage *Rapt*. Worlds away still from Prudentius, but a fascinating illustration of the parallel development of two different modes of thought.

V I

The question of Claudian's borrowings from earlier poets has been touched upon already. It is a large subject, as yet not fully explored, though much material has been collected. Within the compass of this book it is not possible to do more than make a few general observations.

The analysis of poetical borrowings is more complex than is often assumed. A full classification, indeed, would occupy another whole volume, but for our present purpose it will suffice to glance at just three categories, often overlapping and certainly not the only possible subdivisions, but (it is hoped) a helpful illustration[1] none the less of the different ways in which Claudian made use of his predecessors.

First, we have borrowings or adaptations of isolated phrases. Of these, naturally, there is a very large number. Many of the more trivial variety are doubtless unconscious, interesting only in so far as they attest the wide and catholic knowledge of earlier poetry from which they derive. To list them (not in itself a useless occupation) would merely be to illustrate the traditionalism and tenacity of Latin poetic diction.

A recent study of the influence of Lucan on Claudian suggests that 'before setting to work on his regular poetic stint he had a slave read out a passage of Lucan that seemed relevant to what he contemplated putting into verse'.[2] This seems to me no less fundamental a misunderstanding of Claudian's method of composition than another recent suggestion, that Claudian's

---

[1] More helpful, I think, than the three different categories proposed by A. K. Clarke, *Proc. Camb. Phil. Soc.* clxxxi (1950/51), 5, or the three more used by V. Cremona, *Studi italiani pubbl. dell'Istituto di Filologia classica di Bologna* (1948), pp. 40 f.

[2] R. T. Bruère, *Class. Phil.* lix (1964), 253 (exaggerating Claudian's conscious debt to Lucan).

borrowings from poems he was less familiar with (allegedly the
Georgics, Lucan, and Statius' *Achilleid*) were obtained by turning
over methodically the pages of a codex open in front of him as he
wrote. Support for this view is claimed in an apparent progression
in the references to these works in *Rapt.*[1] But quite apart from the
fact that no attempt is made to distinguish conscious from unconscious, certain from uncertain, trivial from significant among
the 'parallels' listed (many of which are very uncertain), such
a theory seems to me to rest on an outrageously oversimplified
view of the nature of poetic imitation—even in an age of iron.
Claudian certainly knew the major poets, if not by heart, at
least as well as an Ausonius, who could throw his *Nuptial Cento*
together in one day—a remarkable tribute to his memory, if
not his taste. As often as not the appropriate phrase would just
spring to Claudian's mind unbidden.

Rather than simply list even a selection of such echoes, let us
just consider one or two in which Claudian uses the borrowed
phrase in a different meaning, an old Hellenistic trick of which
there are several famous examples in Vergil. One good example
in Claudian is *Rapt.* i. 263, where at the top and bottom of her
cosmological weaving Proserpina portrays the two frozen zones,

et aeterno *contristat frigore* telas,

'portraying in her weaving the gloom of never ceasing cold'
(Platnauer). Obviously an echo (surely conscious) of a famous
line from the *Georgics* (iii. 279), 'pluvio *contristat frigore* caelum'—
but with an imaginative extension of meaning.[2] At *Ruf.* i. 107
he takes 'discrimina vocum' from Vergil's 'obloquitur numeris
septem discrimina vocum' (*Aen.* vi. 646), a musical context, and
applies it to the different languages spoken by the different ethnic
units in Stilico's army. When suggesting the possibility that Gildo

---

[1] O. A. W. Dilke, *Rev. belge de phil. et d'histoire* xliii (1965), 60–1. The case
from progression of references is hardly strengthened by the fact that Dilke is
obliged to explain away discrepancies by postulating that Claudian read Lucan and
Statius' *Achilleid three* times in this mechanical way while composing *Rapt.*

[2] On Claudian's freer use of words, cf. Clarke, *Proc. Class. Assoc.* xxvii (1930),
40–1.

'praetentis Syrtibus armet' (*Gild.* 315), Claudian obviously had 'praetentaque Syrtibus arva' from *Aen.* vi. 60 at the back of his mind: is the alteration deliberate, or did he perhaps only half remember the phrase?

Now two examples (from many) of a rather different sort. When Claudian writes of Diana at *Rapt.* ii. 27–8, 'et multus in ore | frater erat' ('there was much of her brother in her face'), beyond doubt he was adapting a phrase from his favourite Statius (of Achilles), 'et plurima vultu | mater inest' (*Ach.* i. 164). Yet they have only the *et* in common. It is typical of Claudian's often quite independent attitude to his models to take the thought or structure of his original and clothe it in new words. Lastly, a fusion of originals. Juvenal, disapproving of mixed marriages, had written contemptuously of the 'decolor heres' an Aethiopian son-in-law would father on a Roman girl (vi. 600). Lucan, writing of prodigies in the form of deformed births, had said 'matremque suus conterruit infans' (i. 563). Combining both Claudian struck out a fine hyperbole of his own, again of marriages between Roman girls and Aethiopians: 'exterret cunabula discolor infans' (*Gild.* 193).

The second category is deliberate imitation, often in fact emulation, of a whole passage. Both purpose and technique are different here. The listener is meant to recognize the original and admire the variation. And the poet will not be 'borrowing' phrases: usually he will do his best to vary the actual phraseology of the original. A good example is Claudian's version of the band which awaits 'primis in faucibus' of Vergil's Underworld—an excellent illustration too of the different techniques of the two poets. Vergil conjures up a grim vision, but he succeeds in doing so without elaborate pictorial effects. Indeed only one of his fifteen personifications is described in any detail, Discordia, the last,

> vipereum crinem vittis innexa cruentis.

Luctus unqualified had opened Vergil's list: Claudian has 'scisso maerens velamine Luctus'—an interesting example of how he infuses a characteristic Statian echo into his Vergilian imitation, for Statius had written of 'sanguineo *discissus* amictu | Luctus' (*Theb.* iii. 125–6). In Vergil Egestas had been merely *turpis*: for Claudian she is 'infelix humili gressu' and she is the bosom companion of 'Luxus populator opum'. Senectus becomes 'leto vicina' instead of just 'tristis', and we have a newcomer, 'caeco praeceps Audacia vultu'—perhaps just a shade too obviously the sort of way one would expect Audacia to behave. In Vergil 'ultrices posuere *cubilia* Curae'. The beds seem to have struck Claudian as inappropriate, for his Curae are insomniacs: clinging to the foul bosom of their mother Avaritia, in a fine golden line,

> insomnes longo veniunt examine Curae.

By the standards of the Silver Age, Claudian has improved on Vergil: but the gain in colour is more than offset by the loss of the sense of foreboding, the suggestion of the sombre in Vergil.

Another example, more briefly. When Pluto brings his new bride down to Hades there is a temporary suspension of the infernal torments in celebration. So Claudian rewrites the famous passage in *Aen.* vi, making the appropriate adjustments. Tantalus gets a drink at last, and Tityos does the human thing, he *stretches* the limbs that have hitherto been pinioned down over nine acres. In fact the only one who isn't pleased is the vulture, robbed of its food supply:

> invitus trahitur lasso de pectore vultur
> abreptasque dolet iam non sibi crescere fibras (ii. 338–9).

The macabre has become the grotesque.[1]

The last category is the use of words or phrases selected (unlike the first) not for the appropriateness of the borrowed words alone, but for the associations of the original context as well. Appreciation of such a passage depends on the recognition of both. When Claudian writes '*unus* in hoc Stilico . . . *cunctando* vicitque manu victumque [sc. Alaric at Pollentia] relegat' (*Get.* 142 f.), clearly we are meant to think at once of the most famous

---

[1] Cf. Cremona, op. cit. 43—though he does not note another characteristic Statian infusion: *Theb.* xi. 15, 'dum miserae crescunt in pabula fibrae'.

line in all Ennius, '*unus* homo nobis *cunctando* restituit rem'.[1]
But the echo is more than merely literary. Fabius' delaying tactics
had the sanction of antiquity and success. Stilico's current policies
were not yet obviously successful, and certainly not popular.
The Ennian echo is a subtle and emotional way of equating the
two policies.

At *Gild.* 231 f. the recently dead Theodosius appears to Arcadius
in a dream:

> *unde* tuis *optatus* ades [cries Arcadius] . . . quis tale removit
> praesidium terris? *ut te* mortalia pridem
> implorant longeque pium fortemque requirunt.

The verbal parallels are slight, but no one could fail to appreciate
the evocation of Aeneas' words to Hector, again recently dead and
appearing to him in a dream:

> quae tantae tenuere morae? *quibus* Hector *ab oris*
> *expectate* venis? *ut te* post multa tuorum
> funera defessi aspicimus . . . (*Aen.* ii, 282 f.).

Having once recognized the allusion the listener cannot but come
to Claudian with all the emotional associations of the Vergilian
passage in his mind. Theodosius' speech will open with the
urgency of Hector's appeal 'heu, fuge, nate dea' ringing in his
ears. A year before Claudian had tried to capture some of this
for Stilico, by calling on him, 'vel solus *sperate veni*' (*Ruf.* ii. 98).[2]

The fall of Eutropius came too late, thunders Claudian:

> *tunc decuit* sentire nefas, tunc . . .

All who like the young St. Augustine had wept over the sad fate
of Dido in school would at once recall *Aen.* iv. 596–7:

> infelix Dido, nunc te facta impia tangunt?
> *tunc decuit*, cum sceptra dabas . . .

Rufinus is at the height of his power and crimes: all are cowed,

> at non magnanimi virtus Stiliconis eodem | fracta metu . . .

---

[1] Not that this necessarily implies any wide knowledge of Ennius on the part of
either Claudian or his audience.

[2] And he used it again, less successfully, at *Rapt.* iii. 80 f., Proserpina appearing
in a dream to Ceres (cf. Cremona, op. cit. 46 f.).

Readers of Lucan would at once recognize the implications of the echo of Lucan ii. 234–5:

> at non magnanimi percussit pectora Bruti | terror . . .

An example of a rather different sort. Claudian is poking fun at the low theatrical tastes of Eutropius' cronies:

> hi tragicos meminere modos; his fabula Tereus,
> his *necdum commissa choro* cantatur *Agave* (*Eutr.* ii. 363–4).

The 'parallel' from Juvenal's famous section on Statius (vii. 87) has long been noted. For all his popularity Statius will starve.

> intactam[1] Paridi nisi vendit *Agaven*.

Nevertheless Claudian's line has been misunderstood. 'Il s'agit ici d'une nouvelle pièce sur ce sujet si connu' (the story of Agave), comments Fargues. Birt solemnly infers from 'necdum commissa choro' that Statius' play was no longer known in Claudian's day. The point is, of course, that Claudian was writing for an audience which knew its Juvenal backwards (Ammian remarks that they read little else); they had already savoured many a Juvenalian echo in the preceding book and a half of *Eutr.*[2] There was no new Agave. Claudian's Agave is 'necdum commissa choro' purely because Juvenal's had been 'intacta'. The line is meant to be a literary puzzle, for Juvenal connoisseurs only.

VII

Coleridge remarked admiringly in his *Table Talk* on Claudian's 'power of pleasingly reproducing the same thought in different language'—echoing perhaps Addison's praise of the 'great fruitfulness of the poet's fancy, that could turn the same thought to so many different ways',[3] for both cited the same poem, *Phoenix*, in illustration.

---

[1] i.e. not yet performed, though in the context there is probably a *double entendre* (G. Highet, *Juvenal the Satirist* (1954), 271, n. 5).

[2] Birt, *Zwei pol. Satiren* (1888), 52 f., and Fargues's commentary (1933), 6 f.: and cf. p. 328, below.

[3] *Treatise on Medals* (ed. G. W. Greene) ii (1856), 42.

hic [sc. the phoenix] neque concepto fetu nec semine surgit,
sed pater est prolesque sui nulloque creante
emeritos artus fecunda morte reformat
et petit alternam totidem per funera vitam . . .
o felix heresque tui! quo solvimur omnes,
hoc tibi suppeditat vires; praebetur origo
per cinerem, moritur te non pereunte senectus
                    (*c.m.* xxvii. 23 f., 101 f.).

There is much more in the same vein, variations on the theme of
life from death. Certainly it is all very clever. Many examples
from other poems could be cited as well—but the result is not
always so pleasing. For it is not so much a facility on Claudian's
part as a compulsion. If seven, or ten variations on his current
theme sprang to that fertile mind, he did not, could not, select
the more from the less appropriate: he used them all. As Abraham
Cowley remarked to Thomas Hobbes, when Claudian 'met with
a phancie that pleas'd him, he could not find it in his heart to
quit or ever to have done with it'.[1] Just one illustration will suffice.
After a pretty explicit insinuation at *Eutr.* i. 62 that Eutropius had
played Ganymede to the Zeus of one of his early masters, Ptolemaeus, Claudian continues at 64–5,

            cum fastiditus abiret,
     quam gemuit, quanto planxit *divortia* luctu.

Not even the most obtuse listener could miss the implication of
divortia. Here one might have hoped that he would stop: the point
has been made, and the listener will laugh or not according to
taste. But Claudian has not finished yet. Not because he fears that
he has not been sufficiently explicit, but merely to demonstrate
his facility at varying the theme.

        haec erat, heu, Ptolemaee, fides? hoc profuit aetas
        in gremio consumpta tuo, *lectusque iugalis*
        et ducti totiens inter praesepia somni?
        libertas promissa perit? *viduumne* relinquis
        Eutropium tantasque premunt oblivia *noctes*,
        crudelis? generis pro sors durissima nostri!

    [1] In a note to his Pindaric ode dedicated to Hobbes.

Nor has he sucked it quite dry even yet:

> femina, cum senuit, retinet conubia partu,
> uxorisque decus matris reverentia pensat.
> nos Lucina fugit, nec pignore nitimur ullo.

To the modern reader this is not only tedious: it submerges and ruins the original joke.

The same tendency is manifested in Claudian's inability to resist the temptation of making a list. The list of fourteen Roman worthies whom Honorius must emulate, the even longer list of the same scandalized at Eutropius' tenure of the consulate,[1] the list of disasters Roma has survived in the past only to be starved out by Gildo. . . . Tiresome, certainly, but no worse than many such lists in Lucan—or indeed Ovid. Worse, far worse, was to come. Anyone who thinks the list of philosophical schools in *Theod.* excessive should turn to Sidonius' imitation, the list of 34 names in 36 lines in the panegyric on Avitus (156 f.). And the list of rivers in the panegyric on Majorian (208–9),

> Rhenus, Arar, Rhodanus, Mosa, Matrŏna, Sequana, Ledus,
> Clitis, Elaris, Atax, Vacalis; Ligerimque . . .

is exceeded only by the list of 'Scythian' tribes a little later in the same poem (474 f.):

> Bastarna, Suebus,
> Pannonius, Neurus, Chunus, Geta, Dacus, Halanus,
> Bellonotus, Rugus, Burgundio, Vesus, Alites,
> Bisalta, Ostrogothus, Procrustes [!], Sarmata, Moschus . . .

It was no doubt passages such as these which inspired Raby to claim that Claudian killed ancient poetry.[2] The seeds of Sidonius (and Nonnus too) are all there in Claudian. But they are still (to mix the metaphor) under control. Claudian still belongs with Lucan and Statius. Sidonius and Nonnus are in another world: they are unreadable.

---

[1] On the historical *exempla*, see below, pp. 350 f.
[2] *Secular Latin Poetry* i[2] (1957), 92.

VIII

The criticisms of Claudian's poetry advanced in the preceding pages would probably for the most part have puzzled both Claudian and his contemporary critics. This must be obvious to anyone who has listened for long to the after-dinner conversation of the guests assembled by Macrobius for the Saturnalia of 384. And such as Servius taught their pupils to criticize a poem, not as a whole, nor even episode by episode, but 'vers par vers', as Marrou writes, 'que dis-je, mot par mot!'[1] Interestingly enough, however, one of Claudian's epigrams[2] is a reply to contemporary criticism— a typically pedantic criticism of the sort, generally speaking, one might have expected. But it is a surprising criticism of Claudian.

> Quae tibi cum pedibus ratio? quid carmina culpas?
> scandere qui nescis, versiculos laceras?
> 'claudicat hic versus; haec', inquit, 'syllaba nutat';
> atque nihil prorsus stare putat podager.

How can a man with 'gout' in his own feet dare to criticize Claudian's? But more interesting than Claudian's reply is the mere fact that anyone should ever have thought to criticize his prosody at all. For he wrote the purest and most correct Latin poetry since the Silver Age. He can be convicted of only one false quantity (and that venial): *ferītura*.[3] One has only to turn again to Prudentius to see Claudian's achievement in this field in perspective. I suspect, in fact, that our critic had picked Claudian up, not for *feritura*, but for his very occasional lengthening of a short syllable at the strong caesura: e.g. at *Gild.* 87, 'Carthago ter victa ruīt? hoc . . .'—one of only two certain examples in the major poems.[4] What leads me to suggest this is the fact that

---

[1] *S. Augustin et la fin de la culture antique*[4] (1958), 25.

[2] *C.m.* xiii.

[3] Venial, that is, in comparison with *petītura, verĕcunda, locŭtura, rogătura* (with similar shortening between primary and secondary word accents) in other contemporary poets (cf. Birt, p. ccxi, and L. Mueller, *De re metrica*, p. 365).

[4] Birt, p. ccxi.

Claudian has allowed himself precisely this licence in the very line which describes his supposed metrical shortcomings, 'claudicat hic versūs; haec', inquit, 'syllaba nutat.' In view of the extreme rarity of this phenomenon in Claudian, it is hard to believe it a coincidence in this of all lines. Claudian does not defend himself: he just replies with a counter accusation. If the original accusation had been what I suggest, how neat to repeat the same licence defiantly in his reply, just to show the pedant that he didn't care!

This criticism is illuminating, since a modern critic would make the reverse accusation. The fault of Claudian's versification is precisely that it is flawless—too flawless. He has weeded out almost all the 'licences' which disfigure the pages of Vergil. The tendency to smoothness at the cost of variety which distinguishes almost all post-Augustan poetry is pushed even further in Claudian. Some more statistics will help to give a clearer picture.

Vergil repeats the same combination of dactyls and spondees once every 12·4 lines, Lucan once every 11·4 lines: Claudian does it once in ten lines, more frequently than any Latin poet of consequence but Valerius Flaccus (1:8·6). More interesting is the concept of 'repeat clusters' introduced by G. E. Duckworth: repetition of the same combination six or more times within sixteen or fewer consecutive lines—an arbitrary definition, of course, but a useful indication none the less. Such 'repeat clusters' occur once in 200·1 lines in Vergil, once in 101·1 lines in the *Thebaid*, in Valerius (the most metrically monotonous of all Latin poets) once in 44·7. Claudian, with one every 73·3 lines, is closer to Valerius than any other major poet. Oddly enough Sidonius, in so many other respects Claudian's monotonously servile ape, differs from him very sharply here: he repeats the same combination in consecutive lines less often than any other Latin poet but Vergil, and has 'repeat clusters' only once in 190·3 lines.[1]

---

[1] G. E. Duckworth, *TAPhA* xcviii (1967), 77–150, continuing his series of metrical studies in the same journal (xcv (1964), 9–65, xcvi (1965), 73–95, xcvii (1966), 67–113). Claudian also repeats the reverse of his favourite patterns to an unprecedented degree (i.e. SSDS and SDSS).

The feature in which Claudian differs most markedly, not only from Vergil, but even from Ovid and Lucan, is in his avoidance of elision. Elision occurs about once every two lines in Vergil, once in three and a half lines in Ovid, once in six in Lucan. In Claudian the average is once in eighteen lines: there are only fourteen in the 526 lines of *Gild.* And when he does tolerate elisions, they are usually very light ones, mostly short syllables, hardly ever monosyllables. Indeed it has been remarked that if we exclude simple suppression of -*que*, -*ve*, and -*ne*, Claudian uses elision proper, not nine times less frequently than Vergil, but seventeen times less frequently.[1] Elision between the fifth and sixth feet is almost entirely avoided: *moriensque Ephialtes* (*Get.* 75) is one of only three examples. (The quadrisyllabic ending is rare too—virtually confined, as in the 'best' models, to Greek proper names. *Spondeiazontes*—four only—are entirely restricted to Greek proper names.[2])

As far as the caesural break is concerned, the most interesting development is the higher proportion of trochaic breaks in the third foot—always accompanied, of course, by a strong break in both second and fourth feet: *Inferni* | *raptoris* || *equos* |. There are no more than six examples per hundred in Vergil: the proportion rises to 16 per cent in Lucan and 22 per cent in Valerius. According to Plessis's statistics[3] (based, I suspect, on an insufficient sample), the proportion in Claudian is 21 per cent. My own figures are much higher: 24·5 per cent over the 526 lines of *Gild.*, 28·6 per cent over the 287 lines of *Rapt.* i. In both these poems every other line but one has the third foot strong break (the other one in each case is the fourth foot strong break), only once blurred by an elision. The trochaic break leads to a certain jerkiness, involving, as it tends to do, coincidence of verse ictus and word accent in the middle of the line followed by conflict in the fourth foot—the latter being particularly affected by Claudian.[4]

---

[1] F. Plessis, *Traité de métrique grecque et latine* (1889), § 99.
[2] Cf. Birt, p. ccxv. See too p. 466, below.   [3] Plessis, § 90.
[4] Birt, p. ccxiv (as usual exaggerating the tendency: cf. S. Axelson, *Studia Claudianea* (1944), 52) and Duckworth, *TAPhA* xcviii (1967), 124.

For example, he adapts 'Emathiis *quod solum* defuit armis' from
Lucan ix. 1017 to 'patriis *solum quod* defuit armis' at *Gild.* 5.
An unconscious change, perhaps, but significant none the
less.

There are other rhythms, fine in themselves, which tend to
recur a shade too often. He much affects a heavy pentasyllabic
word before a final bacchius: *debellavisse bipenni, libertatemque
comarum.* Less than 20 times in Vergil, more than a hundred times
in Claudian. Again, tricola such as

> cincta sinus, exerta manus, armata bipenni,
> caede madens, atrox gladio, suspecta veneno.

Clever and attractive—but rather too artificial to bear overmuch
repetition.

'All the versification', as Dryden succinctly remarked, 'and
little variety of Claudian is included within the compass of four
or five lines, and then he begins again in the same tenor.'[1] Dryden
added yet another recurring pattern, in a famous phrase which
perhaps few who quote it know was applied to Claudian: 'that
verse commonly which they call golden, or two substantives and
two adjectives, with a verb betwixt them to keep the peace'.
Claudian has 24 examples in the 287 lines of *Rapt.* i, 21 in the 372
lines of *Rapt.* ii—more even than Lucan, who also affects it greatly,
with 24 in the 695 lines of *Phars.* i.[2] The effect is accentuated (as
Dryden noted) by the fact that the golden line tends to close its
period. So Claudian's lines succeed each other, to quote one which
makes the point in sense as well as structure,

> continuum simili servantia lege tenorem.[3]

It has been remarked already that there are certain clear stylistic

---

[1] *Preface to Sylvae* (1685).
[2] I interpret the concept 'golden line' more strictly than (e.g.) W. B. Sedgwick,
Speculum v (1930), 50, who seems to count any combination of two epithets, two
nouns and a verb—though less strictly than L. P. Wilkinson, *Golden Latin Artistry*
(1963), 216, for whom chiastic order of nouns and epithets counts only as 'silver'.
[3] *Prob.* 17.

differences between *Ruf.* and *Eutr.* But there is no difference in metrical technique. Claudian frequently borrows or echoes ideas and phrases from Juvenal in *Eutr.*, but there is no trace of the freer satiric hexameter that Juvenal and Horace before him had used to such effect. There were some things Claudian could vary—but even for the lowest comedy, the most excruciating puns, it must be the same polished vehicle that served him for dignified Imperial panegyrics and elevated mythological epics alike.

But the monotony of Claudian's verses does not lie in stylistic and metrical features alone. There is no variation of intensity. He is always straining at full power, never slowing down even to a trot between gallops. One purple passage follows another without pause, and then a third almost before we have had time to regain our breath.

However, Claudian's monotony is not the monotony of contemporary Greek epico-panegyrical poetry, as one might perhaps have expected from a Greek who had won his spurs in that medium. There is no trace of the tendencies of contemporary Greek versification. Greek epic notoriously became progressively more dactylic. Claudian's verse is not at all dactylic: the proportion of spondees in the first four feet is 55·1 per cent—very much the same (for once) as Vergil (56 per cent), and noticeably heavier than Statius (50·6 per cent) and Valerius (46·7 per cent). The third-foot trochaic caesura overwhelmingly predominates in late Greek epic, but Claudian's fondness for it must surely be seen as an extension of the tendency clearly visible already in Lucan and Valerius. Not least because in all but three cases in Claudian's major poems the trochaic caesura is followed by a strong fourth-foot caesura (often with sense pause too)—quite alien to Greek epic, and giving an entirely different effect. Contrast, for example, the first line of the *Dionysiaca*,

Εἰπέ, θεά, Κρονίδαο διάκτορον αἴθοπος αὐγῆς,

with *Rapt.* i. 1,

Inferni raptoris equos afflataque curru.

There are not noticeably fewer fourth-foot trochaic caesurae in Claudian than in any other Latin poet—the notorious Hermann's bridge, eschewed by every self-respecting Greek poet for almost a thousand years. The strong fourth-foot main caesura,

accipiat patris exemplum || tribuatque nepoti (*Theod.* 336),

completely rejected by Nonnus, is rare in Claudian, but no rarer than in Lucan (there are between 40 and 50 examples).[1] As for the golden line which Claudian so cultivates, it is almost unknown to Greek epic: no example in all Homer, one only in Callimachus, two in Apollonius. Nor is the story different in Imperial times: not one in Quintus and the Oppians, one only in Triphiodorus.[2] That there is no example in the 77 surviving lines of Claudian's Greek *Gigantomachia* is hardly significant. Oddly enough against such a background, Nonnus much affects it, and since he seems to have read some at least of Claudian's Latin works, we should perhaps allow the possibility that it was from Claudian that he learned the possibilities of this attractive configuration. But however this may be, there can be no doubt that Claudian was influenced by a Latin tradition going right back to Ennius.[3] That Claudian's Latin poetry has much in common with Nonnus (and no doubt his own Greek works) is undeniable. But in all the basic details of versification, it is entirely Latin. It is not a little remarkable that he was able to keep the two techniques so separate.

IX

It has been observed before now that the poets of late Antiquity show greater interest than their predecessors in the description of natural phenomena for their own sake. The examples of Ausonius' *Mosella* (or at least parts thereof) and the little fragment

---

[1] Birt, p. ccxiii, argues that Claudian used it when he wanted an effect of 'durities quaedam ac robur': this may be true of some cases, but it is not of all, and since the fourth-foot caesura tends to give this effect anyway (at least by contrast) inferences as to intention are labile.

[2] Wifstrand, *Von Kallimachos*, 139–40.

[3] C. Conrad, *Harvard Studies* lxix (1965), 234 f.

of Tiberianus are well known.[1] Less known, perhaps, is Quintus' interest in mountain scenery,[2] and despite its preposterous Nonnian bombast even Pamprepius' *Autumn Day* shows a feeling for nature generally lacking in his master. In an anonymous and sadly mutilated fragment of another follower of Nonnus stands out a striking description of the way a mountain deceives the traveller about its true distance, fleeing before him as he approaches, chasing him as he goes away again. A simple enough observation— but one no other ancient poet saw fit to put into words.[3] Despite the verdict of Mackail there are traces of this deeper awareness of nature in Claudian too. Only traces. Many of his descriptions of scenery are very much in the traditional classical manner. The grove through which Proserpina and her friends wander picking flowers is none other than what Curtius has christened the 'ideal mixed forest',[4] a landscape with a long past and a future no less long—though it is interesting to note, in view of his weakness for the list, that Claudian's forest has fewer trees than those of either Ovid or Statius. But with this stereotyped picture of the oak dear to Jupiter, the pine useful for seafaring, etc., contrast the touch of sentimentality in the picture of the very shrubs and trees whispering sweet nothings to each other in the garden of Venus (*Nupt.* 65–8):

> vivunt in Venerem frondes, omnisque vicissim
> felix arbor amat; nutant ad mutua palmae
> foedera, populeo suspirat populus ictu
> et platani platanis alnoque adsibilat alnus.

The nearest parallel is from a poem usually thought worlds apart from Claudian: the *Pervigilium Veneris*, where (76)

> rura fecundat voluptas, rura Venerem sentiunt.

---

[1] See the interesting discussions of E. E. Sikes, *Roman Poetry* (1923), 130 f., and E. R. Curtius, *European Literature* (1953), 196 f. (emphasizing the strict structure of Tiberianus' poem).

[2] Cf. Glover, *Life and Letters*, 84–5.

[3] Heitsch XXXIV. 1 verso, 41 f. (= Page 144. 17 f.—who unfortunately misunderstands the passage: cf. Wifstrand, *Von Kallimachos*, 200).

[4] Cf. Curtius, *European Literature*, 195.

The description of Zephyrus wooing the buds with the dew that drips off his wings as he paints the year with flowers recalls another passage in the *Pervigilium*.[1] Then, more in the classical manner but delightful none the less, there is the comparison of Maria and Serena to a young laurel growing in the shade of its parent tree, or to two roses on one stem,

> haec largo matura die saturataque vernis
> roribus indulget spatio; latet altera nodo
> nec teneris audet foliis admittere soles (*Nupt.* 248–50).

There are more traces of this other Claudian in some of his minor poems. One cannot but deplore many aspects of the concentration on ecphrastic poetry which in general they manifest, both for itself and for its effect on other sorts of poetry, but there is another side to the matter. There is perhaps more to forgive in the *Thebaid* than the *Silvae*. In the *Silvae* we are at least in touch with the age in which Statius lived, and with Statius' own reactions to it.[2] So too (less so, unfortunately) with some of Claudian's minor poems (as with some of the descriptions enshrined in the major poems). 'The choice of subjects,' as Raby has remarked, 'dictated at first by convention, was wide enough to suggest new possibilities, and these exercises tended to keep the versifier close to things that had a real meaning and relevance—a landscape, a river, a building, a statue, or even an unusual phenomenon of nature.'[3] The poet did not altogether renounce personal observation for Valerius Maximus, Menander Rhetor, and the *Corpus poetarum*.

The slightly misnamed 'Old Man of Verona'[4] has come in for much admiration over the years—misnamed, because the point of the poem is that the old man lives in a suburb of Verona

---

[1] Cf. Gladys Martin, *Class. Journ.* xxx (1935), 536 f., an interesting discussion, though one need not accept her (tentative) conclusion that Claudian wrote the *Pervigilium Veneris*.

[2] Cf. most recently J. Cancik, *Untersuchungen zur lyrischen Kunst des Statius* (*Spudasmata* xiii) 1965 (with the reservations of E. J. Kenney, in *CR* N.S. xvi (1966), 331–3).

[3] *Secular Latin Poetry* i² (1957), 95.

[4] *C.m.* xx: for modern translations, see p. 439.

and has never actually been to the 'big city' itself. There are some nice touches—the oak-tree he remembers as an acorn—but much too that is banal:

> non freta mercator tremuit, non classica miles,
> non rauci lites pertulit ille fori.

And one could wish away the strained conceit with which it closes. The old man is happier by far than the restless globe-trotter:

> plus habet hic vitae, plus habet ille viae.

More interesting is the hundred-line poem[1] on the warm springs of Abano, which contains some minute and (for the late fourth century) relatively clear and simple description of the gentle hill in which the hot lake is set, crystal clear yet untouchable and undrinkable. When a breeze dispels for a moment the pall of steam you can see the glint of spears at the bottom (presumably dropped in by generations of spectators looking over the edge like Claudian). Particularly skilful is the description of what I take to be a sort of translucent film or crust which surrounds the lake, seemingly treacherous under foot and insubstantial, but in fact quite solid:[2]

The ground floats lightly with slender film ('levis exili cortice terra natat'); never will it give way beneath the visitor's weight, upholding his timorous feet, trusty though seeming so unsure ('sustentat trepidum, fida ruina, pedem').

Statius himself could have done no better—though the touch *fida ruina* is Claudian's own signature.[3]

---

[1] For 'numerical composition' in late Antiquity and the Middle Ages, cf. Curtius, *European Literature*, 502 f. Birt (p. ccxix) somewhat exaggerates the 'significant' subdivisions of the larger poems.

[2] *C.m.* xxvi. 45 f.

[3] The slave given his liberty with the traditional cuff departs 'grato . . . securior ictu', the cuff itself is a 'felix iniuria', the oven-men are 'metuenda voluptas | cernenti pulcherque timor' (*IV Cons.* 615, 618; *Ruf.* ii. 363–4). As Addison remarked, 'there is none of the poets that delights so much in these pretty kinds of contradictions as Claudian . . . some of his greatest beauties as well as faults arise from the frequent use of this particular figure' (*Works*, ii, ed. Greene, p. 54).

Different again, but especially clear and precise is the vivid description of the turns booked by Theodorus for his consular games. Just a part may be quoted in translation:

Let the clown be there to move the people's laughter with his happy wit, the mime whose laughter is in his nod and in the movement of his hands, the musician whose breath rouses the flute and whose fingers stir the lyre . . . him too whose light touch can elicit loud music from those pipes of bronze that sound a thousand diverse notes beneath his wandering fingers and who by means of a lever stirs to song the labouring water. Let us see acrobats who hurl themselves through the air like birds and build pyramids that grow with swift entwining of their bodies, to the summit of which pyramid rushes a boy fastened by a thong, a boy who, attached there by the foot or leg, executes a step-dance suspended in the air (*Theod.* 312 f.).

Praise of the skill of pantomime dancers (highly paid stars) is common in writers of the age, especially in Nonnus (whose phraseology closely parallels Claudian's),[1] and we possess a famous epigram on the hydraulic organ ascribed to the Emperor Julian.[2] Addison was delighted to see precisely the acrobatic trick Claudian describes still being performed at Venice on Holy Thursday, and duly quoted the passage in his *Remarks on Italy* (1705).

x

It is a commonplace that Homer reveals more of his own world in his similes than in his narrative. It might seem merely paradoxical to make the same claim for a contemporary poet like Claudian. Yet Claudian's similes do in fact tell us more about Claudian and his world than is the custom of epic similes in Latin poets. It will be worth examining them a little more closely than has been done hitherto.

---

[1] Cf. L. R. Lind, *CW* xxix (1935), 21, for references from Nonnus, and on the phraseology (missing this passage of Claudian) see O. Weinreich, *Epigramm u. Pantomimus* (Sitzb. Heidelberg, 1948), 102 f. For the frequency of metaphors from the stage in contemporary writers, see MacMullen, *Art Bulletin* xlvi (1964), 453.

[2] *AP* ix. 365 (see Beckby's note), and Bidez, *Juliani Epp. Legg. Poem.* (1922), 218.

There are more similes in Claudian than in any of his Latin predecessors:[1] 145 in the 8,468 lines of the major poems, as against 105 in the *Aeneid* (9,898 lines) and 119 in the *Pharsalia* (8,157 lines). Often they occur in batches of brief ones, tossed out in quick succession as one image after another flashed into Claudian's ready mind, deriving from the rhetorical tradition of the σύγκρισις rather than the epic tradition proper. Stilico will remind Claudian of Hercules or Mars, Honorius of Phoebus, Jupiter, or Bacchus.

There remain a number of epic similes proper. Many (of course) are variations on traditional themes: no epic would have been complete without plenty of bulls and storms; a variety of things recall to him lions retreating before huntsmen, and Ceres robbed of Proserpina (naturally) suggested that old favourite the Hyrcanian tigress—though Claudian adds (this time to Statius) the characteristic embellishment that her cubs had been carried off to be playthings of the Persian King.[2] But Claudian's similes tend to be longer than those of his predecessors: 36 of from 6 to 8 lines, 14 of 9 lines or more. Not surprisingly they frequently hold the narrative up by their length, rather than genuinely help it along. In fact, here again Claudian seems often more interested in the simile for its own sake, as yet another episode within an episode. It had, of course, long been common to develop an epic simile a stage beyond what was required by the comparison, but Claudian pushes it much further. Proba, preparing the consular robes for her two sons, is compared to Leto:

As fair Latona gave scarlet garments to her divine offspring when they returned to the now firm-fixed shrine of Delos their foster-mother, Diana leaving the forest glades and bleak Maenalus, her unerring bow wearied with much hunting, and Phoebus bearing the sword still dripping with black venom from the slaughtered Python. Then their dear island laved the feet of its acknowledged deities, the Aegaean smiled more gently on its nurslings, the Aegaean whose soft ripples bore witness to its joy (*Prob.* 183–91).

[1] For figures I depend on C. Müllner, *De imaginibus similitudinibusque . . . Claudiani* (1892): cf. too Fargues, pp. 320 f., with further bibliography.
[2] *Rapt.* iii. 263 f.: cf. Statius, *Theb.* iv. 315 f.

The point of comparison is slight enough to begin with: both give robes to their two children—but Proba's children are both male, and not twins. Nor is there any way in which they could be said to resemble Diana returning from the hunt or Apollo from slaying Python: indeed the whole burden of the simile is the *return* of the two deities to Delos—a detail in no way relevant to the comparison. I suspect that having drawn in his mind's eye the picture of Proba equipping her children with robes, Claudian was reminded of a painting he had once seen of Leto welcoming hers to Delos in like fashion—an illustration (if so) of the way his mind worked in pictures. But however this may be, clearly the simile has become a miniature *ecphrasis* in its own right.

Cranes are a familiar sight in epic poetry, and Claudian's are a good example of a fusion of literary similes. Honorius' soldiers leave for Africa

> pendula ceu parvis moturae bella colonis
> ingenti clamore grues (*Gild.* 474–5 f.).

As the cranes fly they form a letter in the sky. There can be no doubt that Claudian was directly imitating a simile of Lucan's (v. 711 f.): Caesar's orderly fleet dispersed by a storm is likened to the letter the cranes form in the sky being broken up by a breeze. But Claudian's cranes stay together: his letter is irrelevant to the comparison, and serves only to embellish—or to recall Lucan to attentive listeners. Lucan, almost restrained for once, had passed up the pygmies, more relevant to Claudian's comparison. Claudian's *moturae* was perhaps suggested to him at a phonetic level by Lucan's '*poturae* te, Nile, grues', but the combination of the participle, the dative after *bella*, and the *clamore* suggest that Homer himself rather than any of the Latin versions supplied the details:

> κλαγγῇ ταί γε πέτονται ἐπ' Ὠκεάνοιο ῥοάων
> ἀνδράσι Πυγμαίοισι φόνον καὶ κῆρα φέρουσαι (*Il.* iii. 5–6 f.)

Claudian himself is left with the slightly arch description of the pygmies as 'parvi coloni', and 'pendula bella'—'pendula' not because 'doubtful' (Platnauer), but because the cranes do their fighting airborne. Possibly an echo of the closest Latin parallel, 'pendentia bella' in Manilius (iv. 288), where however the reference is to naval battles, fought on the uncertain surface of the sea: perhaps from some now lost Greek source—though we might even allow Claudian himself the credit. At all events an interesting mingling of models.

A theme which is new to Latin epic, but still of literary origin (because untrue) is the whale preceded by its tiny pilot-fish: catch the fish and the whale is helpless. Claudian compares the eastern army successively to a riderless horse, a ship without its helmsman, and a whale without its pilot-fish (*Eutr.* ii. 423–31). His source must be Oppian (*Hal.* v. 67–110) who alone (in a didactic section, not a simile) has Claudian's detail that it is the movements of the fish's tail that guide the whale. Without its fish the whale is 'rationis inops' in Claudian, ἀμήχανον in Oppian. Furthermore, Oppian then adds a simile comparing the abandoned whale to a ship without its helmsman, and even uses the same metaphor as Claudian as well as the same simile: for Claudian the ship is '*orba* magistro', for Oppian χηρωθὲν . . . ἡνιόχοιο. Confirmation of the extent of Claudian's familiarity with Imperial Greek poetry, and a good illustration of his technique: he adapts a theme from didactic poetry into a simile while taking over as well Oppian's own simile and adding a third of his own to make a characteristic *congeries* of successively longer comparisons.

But Claudian's imagination was by no means confined within the walls of his library. 'Scholars are sometimes so scholarly', it has recently been remarked, 'that they forget the obvious, the things that come instantly to the common mind when in search of a phrase to convey excitement, ferocity, color, or danger.'[1] So when Claudian likens Rufinus' shock when surrounded by a circle of drawn swords to a wild beast, lately torn from its mountain lair and thrust into the arena, gazing in astonishment at

[1] MacMullen, *Art Bulletin* xlvi (1964), 443. It is significant of Fargues's approach that he is interested only in similes with a literary pedigree where he can quote sheafs of parallels: the others he dismisses in half a dozen lines, remarking that 'Claudien n'a pas eu un grand mérite à employer ces images qui devaient être fréquentes dans la langue familière' (p. 323).

the packed tiers of the amphitheatre,[1] we are surely bound to assume that he is writing from real life. The one and only reflection of contemporary life in that most conventional of all Greek epics, the *Posthomerica* of Quintus, is a simile drawn from the amphitheatre (vi. 532–6). Another brings a touch of life to Oppian's fish encyclopedia (ii. 350–6).[2] Claudian himself devotes much space and colour elsewhere to the wild beast shows given at their consular games by both Theodorus and Stilico—passages aimed at the cultivated upper classes, not the city *plebs*.

One of the most vivid of Claudian's similes is the comparison of Eutropius incongruously clad in his consular robes to a monkey which a small boy has dressed up in silk to amuse dinner guests—leaving his buttocks bare![3] Who can doubt that this was a typical dinner *divertissement* in the elegant circles of Claudian's day—or at least one Claudian himself had witnessed?

When Eutropius at first deals with Tribigild's revolt by pretending that it has not happened, he is compared to the ostrich, who buries his head in the sand at the first sign of danger.[4] So trite a comparison today that we are in danger of forgetting that Claudian is the first (? the only) ancient author to use it. And since he refers to the ostrich just as the 'Libyan bird', it may be, once more, that he was writing from experience (whether heard or seen) in his native continent.

We might add a creature who is no stranger to Latin poetry, but appears in a different context in Claudian. Alaric, watching his Goths desert in droves after Pollentia, is likened to an old beemaster watching his bees swarm, and desperately trying to call them back with a gong.[5]

Other similes that are less obviously drawn from direct personal experience but are still original, or at least new in extant ancient poetry; the irresponsible Byzantines faced with danger are like small children enjoying themselves free from care while father

---

[1] *Ruf.* ii. 393 f.

[2] On Oppian's simile see A. W. James, *Proc. Cam. Phil. Soc.* cxcii (1966), 34–5.

[3] *Eutr.* i. 300 f. (metaphorical apes are apparently uncommon in ancient literature: cf. Curtius, *European Literature*, 538 f.).

[4] *Eutr.* ii. 310 f.   [5] *VI Cons.* 259 f.

is away—till sudden danger threatens, when they cry out for him in fear.[1] When Eutropius tries to persuade his council to get down to serious business, he is like a raucous old forewoman telling factory girls who are begging for a day off to get on with their weaving (ii. 370 f.). Alaric meets more than he had bargained for at Pollentia, like the pirate ship which attacks a man-of-war in error for a cargo-boat (*VI Cons.* 132 f.). Rome decking herself out for Honorius' visit is like a mother fussing over her daughter's clothes when a boy friend is expected (ib. 523 f.). All are the sort of simile (unlike Statius', for example) which really help the narrative out, instead of merely adorning it.

It is no accident that the majority (though by no means all) of these more unusual similes occur in *Eutr.* For as Fargues has illustrated at (perhaps too) abundant length, there was an immense stock of traditional material available and indeed almost required for the genres in which Claudian was writing. Epic similes and dreams, panegyrical *topoi*, *topoi* for the invective (the tyrant, his torturers, his greed . . .). Much of this Claudian could use for *Eutr.*, but it would not do alone. For obvious reasons *Eutr.* is in some respects unique: it was possibly the first formal invective on a eunuch, certainly the first on a eunuch consul. And it was precisely Eutropius' eunuchhood to which Claudian devoted most of his attention. Rufinus is a fine creation, destined to a long and distinguished future in European literature: but it is the very stylization that is so successful. This is why Alan of Lille called his poem about the perfect man *Antirufinus*—the antithesis to Claudian's perfect villain. This too is why Rufinus could serve as many a future tyrant figure in the ages to come.[2] But the human and individual features which Rufinus did not need were essential for Eutropius—at least if Claudian was going to bring him before his listeners' eyes in all his squalor. So Claudian was forced to take a step to which few poets of the age were reduced: he had to rely on his own observation and native wit. The result can only occasion regret that elsewhere he was (inevitably, in his age) content to vary traditional material.

---

[1] *Eutr.* ii. 509 f.   [2] See below, pp. 423, 430, 440 f.

Eutropius appears to have suffered from a form of ringworm, which leaves bald patches on the scalp, and a residue (I learn) of 'broken stumps of hairs and a fine white powdering of desquamated epidermic scales'. Both the latter details are brilliantly evoked by Claudian's comparison with 'patches of parched stalks gleaming among the starved beards in the thirsty fields'.[1] As Andrews explains in his note: 'The drought-parched bearded stalks are here and there lightened by patches of shorter stalks wholly without beards.' Anyone familiar with a parched Italian cornfield would instantly have a picture of poor Eutropius' scalp. What with this and his face 'more wrinkled than a raisin' ('rugosior uva'), his cheeks which flap like a sail in the wind, it is not surprising that he frightened children and turned the stomach of dinner guests,

> aut pueris latura metus, aut taedia mensis (i. 124).

Who can help but wince even today as he pictures Eutropius being stripped in the slave market while a prospective purchaser consults with a doctor. Or when his last owner cannot even give away this 'totiens venale cadaver', and turns him loose, just as the shepherd turns out a mangy old sheepdog no longer able to guard the flock—but takes the collar off first, so as to save that at least! The comparison is apt, since it had been Eutropius' duty to guard his master's house. The last detail goes beyond the point of comparison, of course, but it is clearly relevant at an emotional level, a devastating final touch. We can almost hear this pathetic creature with his voice 'more effeminate than effeminacy's self' ('verbis . . . ultra nequitiam fractis'), wiping the tears from his eyes as he speaks, making sobbing and sighing noises between each word—like some parched old woman who has come to visit her daughter-in-law: no sooner has she arrived than she gasps for a drink.[2]

There has always been a tendency to regard *Rapt.* as self-evidently Claudian's only important and worthwhile poem.

---

[1] *Eutr.* i. 113 f.
[2] *Eutr.* i. 35, 130 f., 262 f. (Platnauer).

Claudian himself certainly hoped that it would be his master-piece—another *Thebaid* or *Aeneid*. Yet for all its fine descriptions (much admired by Walter Pater), it has all the faults both of structure and detail of the contemporary poems. The Furies' council which introduces Rufinus owes much of its effectiveness to a subtle pervading strain of mock solemnity and fantasy: the serious treatment of the theme in *Rapt.* is a failure. Hardly less brilliant in its different way is the debate of Eutropius and his cronies on how to deal with Tribigild: certainly it is more memorable than Jupiter's council of the gods in *Rapt.* iii, challenging comparison with the council of Domitian in Juvenal iv (on which it is loosely modelled). It is legitimate to wonder whether Claudian's real forte did not lie in the direction of satire,[1] where his keen observation, his caricaturist's eye for the grotesque, and his power to coin a striking epigram, could be put to their best use.

XI

Above all, however, Claudian's art brings before our eyes late fourth-century society in all its pomp and show, its vulgarity and excess. The splendour, the colour, of court at Milan, the last triumphal procession ever held in Rome: these things live for us as otherwise they never could have.

It has sometimes been doubted whether the consular robe Claudian describes for Stilico really existed. Nobody who has seen surviving representations of consular robes of the age would feel it necessary to share this scepticism (though art may have improved on reality: it is easier to work with words than gold thread). Amidst all the magnificence of the embroidery there is no word of encrusted jewels; but Honorius' consular robe in 398 is described as heavy with emeralds and amethysts. Precisely this difference between the *trabea* of an Emperor and a subject is illustrated by the painting of Constantius II and his Caesar

---

[1] It is because they see but do not understand this that critics claim *Rapt.* as a 'youthful' work, falling short of the 'maturity' of *Ruf.* and *Eutr.* (e.g. N. Martinelli, *Misc. G. Galbiati* ii (1951), 59, n. 36). In fact most of it is later than both invectives (Appendix A).

Gallus together in full consular regalia: Constantius alone has the jewels.[1] Further proof of the general accuracy of Claudian's descriptions will hardly be necessary. Ceremonial clothing was of enormous importance in the eyes of Claudian's contemporaries.

More interesting from our point of view 'is their conviction that for one's role, one should dress the part. An Emperor should look like an Emperor . . . chamberlains should not dress like lawyers, nor lawyers like consuls.'[2] Only against this background can we appreciate *why* Claudian finds the sight of Eutropius in consular robes so outrageous. For obvious physical reasons nobody looked his role more than a eunuch chamberlain: to contemporaries he simply *could* not carry off the *trabea*. Just as fourth-century artists pay 'less attention to plasticity and individuality in order to focus on the insignia of a role',[2] so does Claudian concentrate on the insignia of Stilico and Honorius, in all their minute detail. Nor merely because he was paid to. It was a recognized function of contemporary art to capture for posterity the magnificence of the present.

Rapt. differs only in subject-matter from the contemporary poems. Proserpina's robe could have come from the same fourth-century workshop as Stilico's or Honorius'. Diana's,[3] with a floating Delos embroidered in gold, certainly did. The gods on Olympus in *Rapt.* iii and the demons of Hell in *Ruf.* i alike assemble in due order according to precedence, just like the senators and courtiers at Honorius' consular ceremony in Milan.

To read Claudian is to read, not a latter-day Valerius or Silius, breathing feeble life into a tired and irrelevant medium, but, with its virtues as well as its faults, an authentic manifestation and perhaps the most eloquent representative of that era of tradition and innovation which is the fourth century—a strange fusion of the styles and conventions of the past with the freshness and theatricality which stamps his own age.

[1] Cf. the reproductions (after a fifteenth-century copy of a ninth-century copy of a fourth-century original) in H. Stern, *Le Calendrier de 354* (1953), pls. xiv, xv, with pp. 153 f.

[2] MacMullen, *Art Bulletin* xlvi (1964), 448.

[3] *Rapt.* ii. 34–5.

XI

DOCTUS POETA

'Scivit, credo, Claudianus, quidquid tum sciebant homines, et multo plus quam vulgo sciebant, etiam qui docti habebantur' (M. Gesner, *Claudiani quae extant* i (1759), vi).

FEW perhaps have been quite so enthusiastic as Gesner in their praises of Claudian's erudition, but the level of his culture has commonly been held to be very substantial, at any rate for the age in which he lived.

Recent researches on the culture of contemporary figures, such as Libanius, Symmachus, Augustine, and Jerome,[1] have shown that what appears to be wide erudition is all too often superficial and derived at second hand. The range of Claudian's culture certainly appears wide: he was hailed by contemporaries as 'inter *ceteras decentes artes* praegloriosissimus poetarum'.[2] What we must do is to make an attempt, remembering all the while that Claudian was writing poetry, not history, natural history, philosophical, medical, literary, scientific, geographical, or astronomical treatises, to assess the depth of his culture.

We must remember too that in Claudian's day culture meant, in effect, rhetoric. Such was the dominance of rhetoric that all other subjects had become little more than its handmaidens, the source of suitable allusions with which to deck out a speech, a poem, or a letter. They were usually taught by the *rhetor* too. For higher education was almost entirely in his hands. Philosophy was much less widely studied: in general it was reserved for a very

---

[1] To name only the most substantial contributions, Marrou's *S. Augustin* (1938—together with the notable *Retractatio* of 1949); Courcelle, *Lettres grecques en occident*[2] (1948); Hagendahl, *Latin Fathers and the Classics* (1958) and *St. Augustine and the Latin Classics* (1967); Norman, 'Libanius' Library', *Rhein. Mus.* cvii (1964), 158–75.

[2] *CIL* vi. 1710 (*ILS* 2949).

few, who would normally have studied rhetoric already for some while—a sort of post-graduate course.[1] Alexandria, where it may be presumed Claudian did much (if not all) of his studying, was famous for its schools of medicine and mathematics as well. During Claudian's youth, the celebrated mathematician Theon (father of Hypatia) and the doctor Magnus taught there.[2] But everywhere it was the *rhetores* who drew the largest classes, everywhere rhetoric the key that opened every door.

This does not, of course, mean that we are entitled simply to assume that Claudian's culture was purely rhetorical. It does mean, however, that it is likely to have been so; that we cannot simply assume that Claudian had a thorough first-hand knowledge of all the varied subjects to which he alludes from time to time. Scepticism must not be pushed too far, or a 'rhetorical commonplace' claimed wherever two writers happen to say the same thing. Nevertheless, we must be on our guard.

I

Before attending the lectures of the *rhetor*, Claudian will have studied with the *grammaticus*—with *grammatici*, in his case, of both Latin and Greek. The *grammaticus*' province was the elucidation of the classical poets, 'poetarum enarratio'. Unfortunately, too little of Claudian's Greek work survives for us to be able to form any firm judgement on the extent of his acquaintance with Greek poetry—with one obvious exception. That he knew his Homer backwards is apparent not only from the Greek *Gigantomachia*, but also from the Homeric similes in his Latin poems. But it would be far more worthy of note if he had not been influenced by Homer. Birt lists numerous supposed 'parallels' with Callimachus, Theocritus, Apollonius, Moschus, Aratus, Oppian, and Dionysius Periegetes.[3] It is likely enough that Claudian had read

---

[1] *Cahiers d'histoire mondiale* x (1967), 658 f.; *Proc. Camb. Phil. Soc.* cxcv (1969).

[2] See my entries in *PLRE*, s.vv. Magnus received the unique testimonial of a compliment from Palladas (*Anth. Pal.* xi. 281).

[3] p. lxxii: on Oppian, see above, p. 299.

most if not all of these poets, but (with the exception of Oppian) the resemblances are unfortunately too tenuous and isolated to amount to the necessary proof.

Palladas refers to Homer very frequently, but mentions Callimachus and Pindar too among the books he used for his classes.[1] Papyrus finds show that both Pindar and (especially) Callimachus were still being read in late fourth-century Egypt, and most Greek writers of the day show some knowledge of the early lyric poets, particularly Anacreon.[2] And we may be confident that Claudian had read some at least of the Classical dramatists (certainly Menander, much quoted by Palladas). *Eutr.* i. 90 f. seem to echo a famous epigram by Plato.[3]

But Claudian is not likely to have confined his reading to the poets of the Classical or even Hellenistic periods. He is bound to have read some of the numerous and prolific poets of the Roman age, most of whose works have perished. Not merely the surviving didactic poems, like those of the Oppians and Dionysius, but (in view of his own interests) mythological poets like the other Dionysius, Nestor of Laranda and his son Peisander, Triphiodorus and Quintus of Smyrna. Or those who wrote contemporary epics and panegyrics as well, especially fellow countrymen like Soterichus of Oasis under Diocletian, and Andronicus of Hermupolis, still alive *c.* 380.[4] We have seen already that the Greek

---

[1] *Anth. Pal.* ix. 175, 165–9, etc.

[2] Synesius knew Pindar, and apparently one or two other of the lyric poets (Lacombrade, *Syn. de Cyrène* (1951), 22), as too did Libanius (Norman, *Rhein. Mus.* cvii (1964), 162 f.). Another contemporary Alexandrian, Horapollon, wrote commentaries on Alcaeus and Sophocles as well as Homer (Suidas, s.v.). Himerius had quite a wide acquaintance with early lyric (see the testimonia in Colonna's edition). Julian quotes Sappho and Simonides. Sappho, indeed, was a favourite with the rhetoricians of the late Empire (see R. Browning, *CR* N.S. x (1960), 192–3; G. Moravcsik, *Studia Byzantina* (1967), 399 f.), and was recommended by Menander as a model for epithalamia (*Rhet. Gr.* iii. 402. 17 Sp.). Much more research on the culture (Greek and Latin) of Greek writers of this period is required. Themistius in particular would repay study.

[3] *Anth. Pal.* vi. 1, translated too by Ausonius(*Epigr.* liii, p. 210 Schenkl), and still known to Olympiodorus, teaching in Alexandria two centuries after Claudian (*Comm. in Alcib.* i. 31). On Palladas and Menander, see *CQ* N.S. xv (1965), 228.

[4] Cf. *Historia* xiv (1965), 500.

Gigantomachia shows traces of other and more recent influences than Homer or even the Hellenistic poets.

We have seen also that Claudian may have read an astrological poem by Theon of Alexandria. And it is worth adding that Theon also wrote a work on the sources of the Nile: under the circumstances a more likely 'source' for Claudian's unfinished poem on that subject than most others suggested so far.[1] Theon will still have been teaching at Alexandria in Claudian's day, as too will Palladas. And if Claudian did not attend their classes, he certainly knew Palladas' poetry. At *c.m.* xxiii. 6, a lampoon addressed to Alethius the quaestor, he envisages a series of unpleasant prospects: crossing Ethiopia in summer, Scythia in winter, sailing the Ionian Sea in a storm, or

irati relegam carmina grammatici.

Who is this angry *grammaticus* to re-read whose poems will prove such a penance? Alethius himself, according to many. But though Alethius was clearly a poet, he was a quaestor, not a *grammaticus*. And the lampoon is cast in the form of a (mock-serious) assurance that Claudian had not meant to criticize Alethius' poems, and will never do it again:

en moveo plausus! en pallidus omnia laudo!
et clarum repeto terque quaterque sophos!

It would be quite inconsistent with the sarcastic tone of the poem if Claudian had said that it would be a penance to read Alethius' poems. The re-reading of this *grammaticus'* poems is one of the penances Claudian calls down on his head if he is not telling Alethius the truth.

Now a very high proportion of Palladas' epigrams are biting lampoons, and most of those which are not are characterized by extreme bitterness of tone. 'Iratus grammaticus' would be an entirely appropriate description of him. Claudian had read Palladas' bitter poems once, and humorously classes the prospect of repeating the experience with crossing Ethiopia in summer.

To have made such a joke Claudian must have been confident

[1] See Suidas, s.v. Θέων.

that his audience would be familiar with Palladas' work. And such confidence would have been justified. Despite the decline of Greek studies in the West, Palladas' epigrams were evidently popular in western literary circles at the end of the fourth century. Several of Ausonius' epigrams are loose translations or adaptations of Palladas, as are two of the recently discovered *Epigrammata Bobiensia*,[1] emanating from the same circles (one of the authors was a friend of Symmachus, another Claudian's friend Probinus). Nevertheless, it seems natural to assume that Claudian had read Palladas (for the first time) in Alexandria. The epigram was not really Claudian's forte, but just occasionally (e.g. *c.m.* xxi) he shows a Palladan bite.

Among other Greek works of the Imperial age, Claudian was evidently familiar with a poem or poems passing under the name of Orpheus (presumably, like the surviving Orphic poems, of relatively recent composition). This is not surprising. Theon gave lectures on the Orphic poems, and it must have been during this period that Syrianus, later scholarch of the Academy at Athens, and a firm believer, like his successors, in the divine inspiration of the Orphic writings, was studying at Alexandria. It is about this period that various extant pseudo-Orphic writings, the Orphic *Argonautica*, and a *corpus* of hymns, were written.[2] Thus it is hardly surprising that Claudian should have been familiar with such works. He frequently refers to Orpheus, and note especially his description of the studies of young Maria:

> Latios nec volvere libros
> desinit aut Graios, ipsa genetrice magistra,
> Maeonius quaecunque senex, aut *Thracius Orpheus*
> aut Mytilenaeo modulatur pectine Sappho (*Nupt.* 232 f.).

He simply takes it for granted that *Orphica* would feature on any Greek reading-list. This does not mean, however, that Claudian necessarily believed in their divine inspiration (though of course

---

[1] See the *index scriptorum* in Schenkl's edition, p. 267, and add *App.* v. 30 (p. 261), based on *Anth. Pal.* xi. 255. On the *Ep. Bob.*, see *CQ* N.S. xv (1965), 223, 225–6.

[2] Keydell, *PW* xviii. 1333 f.

he may have done). The *Orphica* could be studied at two levels. Either with the *grammaticus*, simply as a specimen of (supposedly classical) literature (as Maria is alleged to have done), or at one of the rare seminars at which Syrianus expounded their secret meaning to his special pupils.[1] There is no reason to suppose that Claudian read them at the second level rather than the first.

Much ink has been expended on the problem of the sources Claudian used for his *De Raptu Proserpinae*. He was obviously familiar with Ovid's account, but this does not seem to have been his 'Hauptquelle'. The most recent inquiry postulates two 'Hauptquellen': (1) an Orphic poem, and (2) an Alexandrian poem.[2] Why two poems rather than just one Alexandrian Orphic poem[3] is not altogether clear, but let that pass. We have seen that Claudian was familiar with Orphic poems. But why is it necessary to postulate an Alexandrian source? For no better reason than the naïve assumption that it was only the Alexandrians who wrote learned mythological works. No doubt some of Claudian's material goes back ultimately to an Alexandrian poem, but his direct source is far more likely to have been some such work as the mammoth Ἡρωϊκαὶ Θεογαμίαι of the early third-century poet, Peisander of Laranda. Though almost entirely lost now, Peisander's poem was widely read in late Antiquity, and it is as certain as any such conjecture can be that it heavily influenced Nonnus' *Dionysiaca*. Nonnus, for example, like Peisander, places the battle of the Gods and Giants before the flood, describes how Cadmus helped Zeus defeat the Giants, and lists a whole series of Zeus' unions with mortal women, the main theme of Peisander's poem (though we are told that he took in almost all the rest of ancient mythology as well in the course of his sixty books—twelve more than even the *Dionysiaca*!).[4] Peisander's starting-point was the

---

[1] Marinus, *V. Procli*, 26.   [2] E. Bernert, *Philologus* xciii (1939), 352 f.

[3] Callimachus, for example, seems to have used Orphic writings (cf. Pfeiffer on frags. 466 and 302).

[4] R. Keydell, 'Die Dichter mit namen Peisandros', *Hermes* lxx (1935), 301 f. (with the criticisms of F. Vian, *Recherches sur les Posthomerica de Quintus de Smyrne* (1959), 99–100). The fragments and testimonia are conveniently reproduced in Heitsch ii. S. 6 (his bibliography omits Vian).

wedding of Zeus and Hera,[1] so he did not confine himself entirely to matches with mortal women.

Naturally, such a suggestion can only be put forward very tentatively. It is easy—and safe—to postulate lost works as sources for what survives. But just because the principle is so often abused, this does not mean that we can leave out of account so well-known and influential a work as the Ἡρωϊκαὶ Θεογαμίαι simply because it no longer survives. It would be surprising if a Greek poet of Claudian's day had not read and been influenced by it. In addition to Nonnus, Claudian's contemporary, Olympiodorus of Thebes, certainly knew the poem,[2] and it was still being widely read and quoted in the following century.[3]

As for the 'Orphic source', there was an Orphic version of the rape by Pluto alongside the regular Orphic saga, and it may be that Claudian knew it. Yet while some details in Claudian accord with the Orphic version, others do not. As for other Orphic poems, the cave of Aion in *Stil.* ii. 426 f. more closely resembles the cave of Night in the so-called *Rhapsodic Theogony* (*Orph. fr.* 105 Kern) than (e.g.) the cave of Sleep in Statius, *Theb.* x. 84 f. Adrasteia makes laws for the gods in the cave of Night just as Aion makes laws for the planets in Claudian. Aion himself, however, may come from elsewhere (see p. 206).

It would be rash to suggest particular sources for Claudian's evident fascination with the Gigantomachy theme (p. 468), but it bulked large in Peisander,[4] as later in Nonnus. And there was also the *Gigantias* of Dionysius, still being read in fourth- and fifth-century Egypt.[5]

Claudian's debt to his Latin predecessors is so obvious and well

---

[1] Macrobius, *Sat.* v. 2. 4, with Keydell, p. 304, and Vian, p. 99.

[2] Zosimus v. 29. 2–3 (drawing here on Olympiodorus' history, whence his citation of Peisander: cf. Mendelssohn's note).

[3] Quoted by Evagrius, John Lydus, John Philoponus, Olympiodorus (the philosopher), Stephanus of Byzantium, and Stobaeus (Heitsch ii. S. 6. 6–20). There is no reason to doubt that at least the first four were quoting at first hand.

[4] Keydell, *Hermes* lxx (1935), p. 306.

[5] For imitations by Nonnus and Musaeus (and probably Quintus), see Wifstrand, *Von Kallimachos*, pp. 178–9. A probably fourth-century papyrus contains a few wretched fragments (Heitsch XIX. 15–26). More awaits publication.

documented that it is worth drawing attention to a few neglected passages where it is possible to trace the influence of the contemporary Greek epic tradition. At *Stil.* i. 176 f. Claudian writes of the loyalty of Stilico's men:

> tu si glaciale iuberes
> vestigare fretum, securo milite ducti
> stagna reluctantes quaterent Saturnia remi;
> si deserta Noti, fontem si quaerere Nili,
> Aethiopum medios penetrassent vela vapores.

The obvious implication is that *Saturnia stagna* is the name of a 'glaciale fretum' (a name is badly required to balance the Nile and Aethiopia, representing the other extreme Stilico's men will brave under his leadership). W. H. Semple,[1] however, confidently informs an unwary public that *Saturnius* (Κρόνιος in Greek) is never applied to a northern Sea. Not by Latin poets, perhaps, but it is common in Greek poets of the Imperial age.[2] Cf. Dionysius Periegetes, 31–2:

> πρὸς βορέην ἵνα παῖδες ἀρειμανέων Ἀριμασπῶν
> πόντον μιν καλέουσι πεπηγότα τε Κρόνιόν τε.

Compare also the Orphic *Argonautica*, 1085–6, describing how on its return journey the Argo sailed northward up a river leading out of Lake Maeotis:

> ἔμπεσε δ' Ὠκεανῷ· Κρόνιον δέ ἑ κικλήσκουσι
> πόντον Ὑπερβόρεοι μέροπες . . .

Not surprisingly Nonnus too follows suit, at *Dion.* ii. 412. The geography of ancient poets was very traditional (p. 345), and it is to the Greek, not the Latin tradition that the 'Kronian' Sea[3] belonged.

---

[1] *CQ* xxxi (1937), 164. Semple's own interpretation ('waters as cold as Saturn') is both implausible (a proper geographical name is essential) and unoriginal (it was so taken by both Birt and Platnauer).

[2] And even Pliny: cf. *NH* iv. 104, 'A Thyle unius diei navigatione mare concretum a nonnullis *Cronium* appellatur'; and Triedler, *PW* Supp. x. 352.

[3] J. R. Bacon, 'The Geography of the Orphic Argonautica', *CQ* xxv (1931),

We have seen that Claudian knew poems which he at least
believed to be written by Orpheus. Could it be that the extant
Orphic *Argonautica* was among them? There is one other slight
indication. In a detailed thirty-line comparison of Stilico to the
Argonauts, Claudian describes how Athene fitted the Argo out
with its talking figure-head from the grove of *Tomarian* Jupiter.[1]
Why Tomarian? From Tomarus, a mountain close to Dodona,
whence the famous talking tree had come. Other tellers of the
tale content themselves with a more straightforward Δωδωνίδος
... φηγοῦ (Apollonius, i. 527) or 'Dodonida quercum' (Valerius, i.
303). Yet 'Orpheus' twices offers a Τομαριὰς φηγός (266, 1161).
And it might be pointed out in addition that while for Claudian
and 'Orpheus' alike the mountain was 'Tomarus', all other Latin
poets use the form 'Tmarus'.

Another small linguistic detail. When referring to Cadmus'
battle against the Spartoi, springing up from the earth ready
armed, Claudian writes of their 'cognatos . . . gladios' (*Stil.* i.
322). No Latin poet before Claudian felt able to use *cognatus*
('born together with them')[2] in this way: even so elegant a
writer as Ovid felt obliged to say 'secum natis . . . telis' when
writing of the similar exploit of Jason (*Her.* xii. 47). Yet compare
Nonnus' account of Cadmus' battle with the Spartoi:[3] *Dion.* iv.
438, ὁμόγνιον ἔγχος; 458, ὁμογνήτῳ . . . σιδήρῳ; cf. 436, τεύχεσιν
αὐτοφύτοις. It is not impossible that Nonnus was directly imitating Claudian, but a common model is more likely: Peisander, for
example, who seems to have covered the Theban saga in much
the same detail as Nonnus.[4]

At the very end of the *In Rufinum* Claudian says that Rufinus

180, suggests that it may be 'the gulf of Riga, which would be accessible down the
riven Dwina'. It is obviously one of these poets who influenced Claudian here,
not Pliny. See too now E. D. Phillips, *Cl. et Med.* xxvii (1966), 184 f.

[1] *Get.* 18 f., with Birt's app. crit., ad loc.
[2] Indeed no Latin writer at all before Claudian except St. Hilary (died 366): cf.
ThLL iv. 344. 69–73.
[3] The parallel with Nonnus was drawn to my attention by Ursula Keudel.
[4] Cf. Heitsch ii. S. 6. 15 and 8 (the Astakides of 8 must be Melanippus, one of
the Seven: cf. Gow and Page, *Gr. Anthology, Hellenistic Epigrams* ii (1965), 193).

will remain in the abyss of darkest night 'dum rotat astra polus' (ii. 527). No one has ever quoted a Latin parallel for this phrase, but a strikingly close Greek one is provided by an anonymous epigram from the reign of Justinian: ὑμετέρην ἀρετὴν . . . αὐδήσει χρόνος αἰέν, ἕως πόλος ἀστέρας ἕλκῃ.[1] Late honorific epigrams of this sort draw heavily on the vocabulary of late epic,[2] and it seems a not unreasonable conjecture that this was a formula of the genre ('so-and-so will last so long as . . .').

A little earlier in the same poem (ii. 112) he briefly alludes to the (alleged) Germanic custom of throwing new-born babies into the Rhine: the legitimate ones floated, the bastards supposedly sank. Now as it happens this belief is not mentioned by any Latin poet, or for that matter by any extant Latin writer. Yet it is a commonplace in Greek poetry (especially epic) of the fourth century and later. Claudian wrote of the babies 'quos *explorat* [tests] gurgite Rhenus' (*Ruf.* ii. 112). Compare Nonnus:[3] νέων βρεφέων καθαρὴν ὠδῖνα δικάζων | ῾Ρῆνος; Pamprepius:[4] θεμιστοπόλου ποταμοῖο . . . δικασπόλον οἶδμα; an anonymous fragment from a probably fourth-century epic:[5] κεκριμένον λουτροῖσιν ἐλεγξιγάμου ποταμοῖο; George of Pisidia (early seventh century):[6] γενοῦ δικαστὴς Κελτικοῦ ῾Ρήνου πλέον. In every case the idea is expressed in very similar terms. All these writers, except perhaps the anonymous one, wrote after Claudian, but we find allusions to the same custom a generation before Claudian in Julian, Libanius, and Gregory Nazianzen, all three strangers to Latin literature. An example from one of Gregory's interminable effusions is as close to Claudian as any of the secular poets quoted above:[7]

Κελτοὶ μὲν κρίνουσι γόνον ῾Ρήνοιο ῥεέθροις.

[1] *Anth. Pal.* ix. 821 (cf. 820 for the date).
[2] Cf. *Early Byzantine Epigrams in the Greek Anthology.*
[3] *Dion.* xlvi. 55, and again at xxvi. 94 f.
[4] Heitsch XXXV. 4. 10 f. (Page 140b. 10 f.).
[5] *Anth. Pal.* ix. 125 (11 hexameters: not an epigram proper, as Wifstrand showed, *Von Kallimachos*, pp. 163–4, but a fragment from an epic. Style and metric point to the fourth century.). See too p. 492, below.
[6] *Exp. Pers.* i. 41, ed. A. Pertusi, *Stud. Patr. et Byz.* vii (1960), p. 86.
[7] *c.* ii. 2. 4. 143: cf. Wifstrand, pp. 163 f., and *CQ* xviii (1968), 393–5.

It seems clear that Claudian too stands within the Greek tradition here. The example from George of Pisidia is particularly interesting in this connection, for it has been shown that there are a number of often rather close parallels between George's panegyrics and the Latin panegyrics of Claudian, both in general structure and individual *topoi*.[1] There can be no question of George imitating Claudian, nor of postulating any particular intermediary. It is just that both were writing in the same late Imperial Greek tradition of contemporary poetry.

No doubt Claudian knew the major Hellenistic poets well, but it is suggestive (if not perhaps surprising) that it is more recent works that have left the most obvious traces.

II

His familiarity with the major Latin poets is too obvious to require demonstration. It will be enough to list the writers, imitations and echoes of whom fill his every page. There are traces not merely of such school authors as Vergil, Horace, and Ovid, but of Lucretius too, and the whole of 'Silver' epic: Lucan, Statius, Valerius, and even Silius.[2] Birt wanted to add Lucilius and Ennius to the list, but this is perhaps unlikely.[3] But there can be no doubt about Catullus, Propertius, Tibullus, Manilius, and an author neglected for centuries and only recently restored to favour in Claudian's own day: Juvenal.[4] Nor about even so recent a poet as Ausonius, perhaps still alive when Claudian arrived in Italy. Many more less certain echoes of lesser poets have been adduced from time to time, and though they cannot be held decisive, this does not prove that Claudian had

---

[1] T. Nissen, 'Historisches Epos und Panegyrikus in der Spätantike', *Hermes* lxxv (1940), 298–325; cf. also Pertusi's edition (1960), 35, with a convenient list of parallels at n. 7.

[2] In addition to the collections beneath the text in Birt's edition and in the preface to vol. ii of Jeep's edition, see the works of Bruère, Cerrato, Clarke, Cremona, Eaton, and Fletcher listed in the bibliography.

[3] I shall be discussing the matter in my forthcoming commentary on *Gild*.

[4] *Hermes* xcii (1964), 369.

not read them. Naturally, he did not have to 'imitate', whether consciously or unconsciously, every poet he had read.

Thus Claudian's knowledge of Latin poetry is by any standards very extensive. And it will be shown below that he had some knowledge (much less extensive, however) of Latin prose authors too. It is likely that he read or re-read some of these works after his arrival in Italy (Ausonius, for example, and probably Florus: see below), but the very first poem he recited in Italy reveals the same easy familiarity with Vergil, Lucan, Statius, Ovid, Valerius, Silius, and Juvenal that we find in his later and more ambitious Latin poems. This he must presumably have acquired already in his native Alexandria. Before progressing any further we must consider the significance of this phenomenon.

We have seen already that there were probably quite adequate facilities for learning Latin in Alexandria, and that Claudian was not alone among his fellow Egyptians in his familiarity with Latin poetry. No doubt he was not alone either in being able to write Latin poetry, though we do not happen to know of another. Twenty years or so before Claudian arrived in Rome, Andronicus from Hermupolis sent a copy of his poems to Symmachus. But it is clear from Symmachus' acknowledgement that they were all in Greek.[1]

However, if Claudian stands alone (at least for us) in the field of poetry, by a strange (though not unnoticed) coincidence the only other really talented secular writer of the day, the last Roman historian, just as Claudian is the last Roman poet, was likewise a Greek: Ammianus Marcellinus.[2] This is a commonplace of literary histories. Yet to the best of my knowledge no one has ever undertaken a serious comparison of their achievement.

Ammian, born and educated at Antioch, spent most of his active life as a regular soldier before retiring to Rome, a decade or so before Claudian's arrival, and writing there, in Latin, a history of the Roman Empire from Nerva to the death of Valens.

---

[1] *Ep.* viii. 22.
[2] On Ammian's culture, see now the useful sketch in P.-M. Camus, *Ammien Marcellin* (1967).

As a historian, Ammian can claim an honourable place alongside Sallust, Livy, and Tacitus—especially writing, as he was, in an age that actually admired the wretched epitomes of Victor and Eutropius. In portrayal of character he is outstanding. Yet as a stylist, for all that he often strikes out a vivid and memorable phrase, he betrays on every page that he writes in the late fourth century. Any given page of Claudian, on the other hand, might easily pass for Lucan or Statius. Why is it that of these two highly talented Greeks, both of whom handled the Latin language to such effect, one might have written in the first century while the other could only have written in the fourth?

We may surmise that Claudian learnt his Latin exclusively from books—from books, moreover, written in classical Latin. He had probably had little contact with the spoken Latin of the fourth century before his arrival in Italy. If, then, his reading was confined to classical writers, it is hardly surprising that he wrote classical Latin himself. It must inevitably have been more difficult for one who spoke the language continuously, with both educated and uneducated alike, to avoid in his writings every pitfall of popular speech. Thus the secluded young ladies of Pliny's circle were reckoned to speak a purer Latin than their menfolk,[1] and aristocrats in fourth-century Roman Britain, long cut off from the more debased popular speech of Italy and the other western provinces, spoke a purer and more 'classical' Latin than their other western contemporaries.[2]

It used to be popular to explain Ammian's stylistic shortcomings by claiming that he learned the language in the ranks. This is an absurd exaggeration. He will doubtless have studied with a *grammaticus* and *rhetor* in the usual way, though possibly not with such expert teachers as Claudian enjoyed. We happen to know that there was no chair of rhetoric in Latin at Antioch till 388,[3] so Ammian may have had to go elsewhere once he

---

[1] *Ep.* i. 16. 6 (cf. Cic., *De Or.* iii. 45): see J. C. Rolfe, *CR* xv (1901), 452–3, and *TAPhA* l (1919), 137.

[2] K. Jackson, *Language and History in Early Britain* (1953), 108 f.

[3] A. F. Norman, *Libanius' Autobiography* (1965), 223—not in 356, as claimed by

had passed the elementary stage. And however pure the Latin he had learned at school, fifteen years' *sermo castrensis* cannot but have left its mark.[1] Even so, this is not a sufficient explanation of the difference between the two men's writings. For Ammian's curious prose style cannot be even partially explained by the supposition that it represents the colloquial, still less the camp Latin of a foreigner. It is a literary Latin none the less, and indeed it is by no means peculiar to Ammian. As M. L. W. Laistner wrote: 'One need only turn to the prose writings of Sidonius, Avitus, or Ennodius, to see a similarly ornate, overloaded manner of expression and a vocabulary largely poetical . . . and Latin was the mother tongue of all three.'[2] The style of even such a Roman of old Rome as Symmachus is not strikingly purer or more classical than Ammian's. The key to the difference between Ammian and Claudian is, quite simply, that Ammian wrote in prose, Claudian in verse.

Four centuries earlier Cicero had remarked that 'difficilius est oratione [= prose] uti quam versibus, quod in illis certa quaedam et definita lex est, quam sequi sit necesse' (*Orator*, 198). If this was true in Cicero's day, it was even truer by the fourth and fifth centuries. Sidonius' verse, for example, while precious and monotonous in the extreme, is a good deal less bombastic and hybrid than his prose letters. The same holds of Venantius Fortunatus and Ennodius. In small doses their verse is not altogether unpleasing: yet their prose can often scarcely be made to yield a meaning at all. A particularly instructive case is Sedulius. Having written (around the middle of the fifth century) a *Paschale Carmen* in five books of hexameters, a few years later the fancy took him to rewrite the work in prose. Thus a direct comparison is possible.

(among others) P. Petit, *Libanius et la vie municipale à Antioche* (1955), 365, n. 3.

[1] For the odd traces of 'sermo castrensis' (not to be exaggerated) see G. B. Pighi, *Studia Ammianea* (1935), 65 f. Not that Claudian's latinity is purely 'classical' throughout: there are several examples (for instance) of *quod* for accusative and infinitive, *tanti* for *tot*, etc. (C. Paucker, *Rhein. Mus.* xxxv (1880), 605 f.).

[2] *The Greater Roman Historians* (1947), 148.

The prose work (*Opus Paschale*) reveals the same quest for the recherché and allusive, the same excessive ornamentation and the same horror of using a proper name where a learned periphrasis lay to hand, that characterize all late Imperial prose, Greek and Latin alike. The *Carmen*, while far below Claudian's standards, is nevertheless much simpler and more 'classical' by comparison.[1]

Much the same applies to the Greek literature of the age. There is a similar distinction between the Greek poetry of the fourth century and the rhetorical prose of (e.g.) Himerius. Nonnus, of course, and his successors in the next century were a good deal more bombastic, but even so they are easier to understand than sophists like Aeneas and Procopius of Gaza. A century later again Agathias could toss off epigrams that sometimes rival Callimachus in their elegance—but his prose, as manifested in a history of the later wars of Justinian, is an odd mixture of echoes from such different models as Herodotus, Thucydides, Polybius, and Diodorus of Sicily, jumbled up together with an indiscriminate admixture of poetical words from a similar range.

In writing poetry there was 'certa quaedam lex, quam sequi sit necesse'. In Claudian's case, as for every Latin poet of the Empire, the supreme model was, inevitably, Vergil. No prose author in either language had ever won the same degree of authority. Thus it is that we find in Ammian a combination of Ciceronian *abundantia* with Tacitean *varietas* and *inconcinnitas*, together with a high proportion of poetical words.[2] In consequence, it was much easier by dint of assiduous practice to turn out a recognizably Vergilian set of hexameters than a recog-

---

[1] de Labriolle, *Hist. de la litt. lat. chrét.* ii³ (1947), 735; Curtius, *European Literature* (1953), 460 f.

[2] Little of importance has appeared on Ammian's style since H. Hagendahl's *Studia Ammianea* (Uppsala, 1921), and 'De abundantia sermonis Ammianei', *Eranos* xxii (1924), 161–216. More recently, see E. Auerbach, *Mimesis* (1953), 43 f.; L. Warren Bonfante, *Par. del Passato* xix (1964), 401 f.; R. MacMullen, *Art Bulletin* xlvi (1964), 435 f. It is perhaps in the striving after *varietas* that his high literary ambitions are most evident: e.g. the twenty-nine different expressions for 'die', and no fewer than thirty-five for 'at dawn' (see Hagendahl's excellent discussion, *Stud. Amm.*, pp. 100 f.).

nizably 'classical' piece of prose. Moreover, the emphasis in the school of the *grammaticus* fell almost exclusively on the poets. Pupils spent most of their time reading Vergil aloud, and answering detailed questions about the quantity of each syllable, the number and type of caesurae, the names of the various figures and tropes employed, etc.[1] The overwhelming preponderance of Vergil papyri in Egypt is a clear enough sign of his influence, even there, as a stylistic model. Indeed, his influence on the Latin prose of the age is hardly less than his influence on the poetry. Ammian is a typical case in point.[2] Naturally enough, however, the effect of Vergilian influence on prose was to make it less, rather than more classical. Whether the prose writers of the age realized how unlike their classical models their work really was is a nice question. But evidently they were perfectly, indeed in many cases inordinately, happy with the results they achieved.

It would be an oversimplification to suppose that Claudian succeeded where Ammian failed. By contemporary standards both succeeded. We must be careful not to belittle Claudian's achievement: as a poet, he stands head and shoulders above his contemporaries. But from the purely technical point of view he had a much easier, or at any rate simpler, task than Ammian. Writing, like the schoolboy composer today, in a language he had learned from books according to strict rules, he had only to follow those rules. Anyone who has written Latin verses himself knows that it is, paradoxically, easier to write Ovidian than Vergilian hexameters, precisely because Ovid is stricter. This is why the Silver poets follow Ovid rather than Vergil in their metrical practice—a tendency carried even further by Claudian. Thus purity of diction and precision of caesurae are really no more surprising in Claudian than they are in the modern schoolboy. It is much to be regretted that we have no prose work from his hand for comparison. It may be just a coincidence, though it is worthy of comment, that when the proconsul Aeternalis asked

---

[1] Cf. Marrou's *S. Augustin*, ch. i.

[2] Hagendahl, *Stud. Amm.*, 1–15; Fletcher, *Rev. Phil.*[3] 11 (1937), 382–3.

Claudian to write him a prose work, Claudian politely, but firmly, declined:

Quidquid Castalio de gurgite Phoebus anhelat,
quidquid fatidico mugit cortina recessu,
carmina sunt: sed *verba* negant *communia* [i.e. prose] Musae.
carmina sola loquor: sic me meus implet Apollo (*c.m.* iii).

Perhaps Claudian was shrewd enough to recognize his own limitations.

III

Let us return now to Claudian's studies with the *rhetor*. Here too he was clearly an excellent pupil. Several special works have illustrated in great (perhaps excessive) detail his familiarity with the precepts of the third- and fourth-century rhetorical manuals on the composition of the formal orations called forth by different occasions like weddings (p. 194), addresses to the Emperor (p. 253), or panegyrics on a city (p. 354). No western writer was ever again to reveal this degree of familiarity with Greek rhetorical theory.[1]

The only Greek prose writer with whom the parallels so far adduced are sufficiently close to warrant the hypothesis of direct imitation on the part of Claudian is Aelius Aristides. Significantly enough, a *rhetor*. And even here it may be only that both were following a similar rhetorical model (p. 355).

Birt[2] drew attention to a number of parallels, often quite striking, between Claudian's panegyric on Honorius' fourth consulate and Synesius' *De Regno*, concluding that it was Claudian who had 'imitated' Synesius. Unfortunately, later research has proved conclusively that *De Regno* appeared a year after *IV Cons.* The obvious alternative hypothesis—that Synesius imitated Claudian—has recently been embraced by C. Lacombrade.[3] But quite apart from the fact that there is no evidence that Synesius knew Latin (not perhaps a decisive objection in view of what has

---

[1] O. Kehding, *De panegyricis Latinis* (1899), cap. ii; L. B. Struthers, *Harvard Studies* xxx (1919), 49–87; above, p. 255.
[2] *De Moribus Christianis* (1885), xv–xxii.
[3] *Pallas* iv (1956), 15–26.

been said above of Latin studies in fourth-century Egypt), the distribution of the parallels between the two works is against such a view. *IV Cons.* is a βασιλικὸς λόγος, a formal address to the Emperor, composed according to the rhetorical pattern for the genre, into which Claudian has inserted, in the form of a speech from Theodosius to Honorius, a περὶ βασιλείας, a semi-philosophical discussion with no set rules on the merits and duties of the ideal king. *De Regno* is not a βασιλικὸς λόγος, but something rather akin, a στεφανωτικὸς λόγος, an address accompanying the offering to the Emperor of *aurum coronarium*. But Synesius has in addition taken the opportunity of delivering what amounts to a περὶ βασιλείας. It deals in generalities: what Arcadius ought to do, rather than what he has done or is doing.

All the substantial parallels between Synesius and Claudian are confined to the περὶ βασιλείας section in *IV Cons.*[1] This is the more striking when it is recalled that Synesius was the spokesman of Stilico's political enemies. If he had really read Claudian's poem, then it might surely have been expected that, so far from simply imitating its rhetorical commonplaces, he would attack its political doctrines. As it is, we are asked to believe that he used *IV Cons.* merely as a guide to compose his own περὶ βασιλείας, ignoring the rest of the poem. Do these facts not point rather to the conclusion that both were following a similar tradition for the περὶ βασιλείας? The likelihood of this hypothesis is only increased when it is recalled in addition that Synesius and Claudian were exact contemporaries, and both studied in Alexandria. If, then, the possibility of direct influence of one work on the other can be excluded, we are left with additional proof of Claudian's close familiarity with Greek political as well as rhetorical theory. Synesius' model, we

---

[1] Lacombrade, p. 23, feels the allusion to consular dress at *De Regno* 15 (p. 32. 14 f. Terzaghi) decisive ('visiblement déplacée' in a speech delivered in late summer). But as my friend Oswyn Murray (from whose advice this paragraph has greatly benefited) has remarked to me: 'Synesius mentions consular dress, not because he is copying from a consular panegyric, but because it is precisely when the Emperor appears in the senate among the *homotimoi* [see Synesius, loc. cit.] that his special regalia is most obnoxious: it makes a farce of the whole tradition of *homotimia*.'

know, was Dio of Prusa. It seems a fair assumption that Dio was among Claudian's sources too—though, as we shall see, Claudian certainly had Roman sources as well (pp. 383 f.).

IV

Let us turn now to Claudian's knowledge of Greek philosophy. It is here that the large claims made for Claudian's cultural attainments are at their weakest. The most important passages come from the panegyric on Theodorus,[1] himself a philosopher of some distinction in his day.

At *Theod.* 67–83 Claudian gives a brief poetical résumé of the teachings of a whole series of early Greek philosophers:

namque aliis princeps rerum disponitur aer [i.e. Anaximenes];
hic confidit aquis [Thales]; hic procreat omnia flammis [Heraclitus] ...

A German dissertation solemnly lists quotation after quotation from Diels's *Vorsokratiker*, Claudian's 'sources'. Yet by Claudian's day, not even philosophers read the Pre-Socratics at first hand: the doxographical tradition had long since displaced the original texts. Claudian's list comes, surely, from the section 'de placitis philosophorum' in some rhetorical manual.

Courcelle, however, argues that they came from a history of Greek philosophy by Theodorus: or rather not a history by Theodorus himself, but Theodorus' Latin translation of a history by a certain Celsinus of Castabala, a translation which (he claims) was also used by St. Augustine.[2] In fact, however, it is very uncertain whether Augustine did use Celsinus (in either the original or translation). That Theodorus translated him into Latin is the purest conjecture (even his dates are quite uncertain). Courcelle

---

[1] Cf. Barth's exaggerated comment ad loc.: 'Eruditissimum, eloquentissimum hunc librum, humanae sapientiae mysteria magnam partem indicantem, si enarrare ex merito velis, Graeciae Latiique penetralia omnia necesse erit ut excutias.'

[2] *Lettres grecques*, pp. 123, 179–81. Courcelle also claims (pp. 240–1) that this work was used by Sidonius too. But as Diels saw (*Doxographi Graeci* (1879), 173), Sidonius' list corresponds exactly with Augustine's (see text), which was surely his source. Courcelle's argument that Sidonius' 'Arcesilas' derives from a 'texte corrompu', since Augustine's text offers 'Arcesilaus' is unhappy: obviously Sidonius deliberately shortened the name to fit his metre.

bases his (admittedly attractive) hypothesis on an alleged parallelism between Claudian's list of philosophers and a similar list in Augustine, *De Civ. Dei* viii. 2. Augustine's list is as follows: Pythagoras, Thales, Anaximander, Anaximenes, Diogenes of Apollonia, Archelaus, Socrates, Plato. Claudian's is: Anaximenes, Thales, Heraclitus, Empedocles, Democritus, Epicurus, Plato, Anaximander. Courcelle admits that the lists do not coincide exactly, remarking that 'L'ordre adopté par Claudien est poétique et manque de rigueur, tandis qu'Augustin suit l'ordre historique.' Let us be frank: the only names they have in common are Thales, Anaximander, Anaximenes, and Plato. Courcelle adds that 'leurs notices sur Anaximandre concordent textuellement'. Claudian says 'parturit *innumeros* angusto pectore *mundos*', Augustine 'credidit . . . *innumerabiles mundos* gignere'. Yet this is hardly very striking: how else could one describe Anaximander's views? And in any case Augustine's source here is surely Cicero, *De Nat. Deor.* i. 10. 25, 'Anaximandri autem opinio est . . . *innumerabiles* esse *mundos*.'

Moreover, though it is clear from *Theod.* 84—'Graiorum obscuras Romanis floribus artes | inradias'—that Theodorus did write a work on Greek philosophy in Latin, this line follows the passage just discussed. Thus it is the section which follows, lines 85 f., that is supposed to represent Theodorus' work. Lines 67–83 bear no relation to anything Theodorus wrote: they are merely Claudian airing his own rather hackneyed knowledge of 'placita philosophorum'.

Furthermore, there is nothing in what Claudian says to suggest that Theodorus' book was a translation. He continues (85–6):

> vicibus gratis formare loquentes
> suetus et alterno verum contexere nodo.

—'skilled to shape speech in happy interchange and weave truth's garland with alternate knots' (Platnauer). That is to say, it was cast in the form of a dialogue. Courcelle, solely on the ground that lines 67–83 suggest a work of continuous exposition, denies the clear allusion in lines 85–6 to a dialogue. Once it is appreciated that lines 67–83 do not even refer to Theodorus' work, Courcelle's case falls to the ground.[1]

As for the section which follows lines 84–6, a long and admittedly very skilful and entertaining summary of almost every aspect of philosophy, mathematics, and physics, even Courcelle admits that 'il n'en faudrait pas conclure que Théodorus a écrit un traité spécial sur chacun de ces questions: Claudien ne fait que développer un lieu commun oratoire.' Later, however, he partially retracted this sensible judgement, and suggested that at any rate lines 95 f. refer to a book on morals whose existence he infers from another uncertain passage in Augustine.[2]

But whether or not these vague and allusive words of Claudian do have any reference to actual books by Theodorus, what is far more striking is that Claudian has nothing to say about Theodorus' principal title to fame as a philosopher. As we learn from some this time unmistakable passages in Augustine, Theodorus was, though a Christian, a celebrated Neoplatonist. Indeed, as Courcelle has more convincingly argued,[3] it was Theodorus who introduced Augustine to Plotinus in 386 at Milan. Thus he was an important contemporary philosopher. No one could have guessed this from Claudian. Claudian praises Theodorus, tritely enough, for combining in himself all that was best in the rival schools— a courtly compliment which might have been paid to any hack philosopher. Courcelle detects an allusion to Theodorus' Neoplatonism in *Theod.* 93–4,

> nobiliore magistro
> in Latium spretis Academia migrat Athenis.

Yet this too is a facile cliché, giving no inkling of Theodorus'

---

[1] For some different objections to Courcelle's case see A. Solignac, *Rech. Augustin.* i (1958), 125–6 (cf. 138 f.), and in his notes to the *Confessions* in the series *Œuvres de S. Augustin* (14, 2), viii–xiii (1962), 533 f.

[2] *Recherches sur les Confessions de S. Augustin* (1950), 209. Similarly, Peter Brown, *Augustine of Hippo* (1967), 125, is perhaps unwise to infer from 'innumeros mundos' that Theodorus had popularized the doctrine of an infinity of worlds, recently condemned as a heresy by Filastrius of Brescia.

[3] *Recherches*, 153 f., 208 f.

devotion to Plotinus,[1] in whose person the Academy had migrated from Athens to Latium more than a century before Theodorus (Plotinus, like his successor Porphyry, had taught in Rome). The answer seems obvious. Claudian did not himself know any more about philosophy than his list of the famous names of olden days and a word or so each on their respective teachings. Thus he was incapable of saying anything meaningful about a contemporary Neoplatonist.

Before we can embrace such a conclusion with full confidence, it will be necessary briefly to consider the other passages where it has been alleged that Claudian shows knowledge of Neoplatonic doctrines.

Courcelle claims that it was from a Neoplatonic commentator that Claudian derived his view of the transmigration of human souls into animal bodies after death.[2] Yet such views were current long before the Neoplatonists. And though they were accepted by some early Neoplatonists, by Claudian's day even that school had abandoned such a view as degrading.[3] Of course, we cannot rule out the possibility that Claudian had read an early Neoplatonic work. But much of his underworld scene is beyond doubt based on the underworld scene in *Aeneid* vi, and it seems more natural to assume that the non-Vergilian details come from some such later poetical account of this theme obviously so congenial to a poet.[4] A strictly philosophical source seems much less likely.

At *IV Cons.* 228 f., Claudian describes at length the threefold division of the soul as a preliminary to exhorting Honorius to exercise firm control over the two irrational elements:

> tunc omnia iure tenebis
> cum poteris rex esse tui (261–2).

According to Courcelle, Claudian 'admet la tripartition platoni-

---

[1] It has been argued (A. K. Clarke, *Augustinus* xiii (1968), 131) that the 'nobilior magister' of line 93 is Plotinus. If the passage is read as a whole, it will be seen that he can only be Theodorus himself.

[2] *Lettres grecques*, 121, n. 6.   [3] See p. 209.

[4] There is a brief underworld scene in the third-century hymn to Dionysus, Heitsch LVI (Page 129), 52 f. See too p. 492.

cienne de l'âme'; 'admet' implies much too positive a decision on Claudian's part. Next to the notion of the philosopher king there can have been few features of Platonic philosophy more familiar to the educated lay public than the threefold division of the soul. Compare St. Jerome's remark 'legimus in Platone, *et philosophorum dogma vulgatum est*, tres esse in humana anima passiones . . .', continuing with a development not unlike Claudian's.[1] In view of the italicized words, it is most unlikely that Jerome had in fact 'read it in Plato', any more than the many other writers of the age who allude to the doctrine. Of these the most relevant for our present purpose is Synesius, who in his *De Regno* advises Arcadius, just as Claudian had Honorius, to subdue τὰς ἀλόγους τῆς ψυχῆς μοίρας[2] —a parallel between the two works curiously missed by Lacombrade. Since, as we have seen, there can be no question of either work 'imitating' the other, it seems legitimate to infer that it was a commonplace of the περὶ βασιλείας to embroider the topic of the self-control of the king in this semi-philosophical way.

The question might also be raised, where is Claudian likely to have studied Neoplatonism? For there is little evidence that it was even taught at Alexandria between Plotinus' teacher Ammonius Saccas and Proclus' pupil Hermias in the mid fifth century. Claudian's contemporary and probably fellow student Synesius seems to have known very little of either Plotinus or Porphyry.[3]

S. Gennaro[4] has recently claimed that Claudian was strongly influenced by an even older pagan school of thought: Epicureanism. This would certainly be both interesting and important if true, since there is no other evidence that Epicureanism was still alive by the end of the fourth century. Gennaro is confident

---

[1] *In Matth.* ii. 13. 33 (*PL* xxvi. 91B). Cf. Courcelle, *Lettres grecques*, 58, n. 1; M. L. W. Laistner, *Christianity and Pagan Culture* (1951), 78, 139, n. 36 for many further examples.

[2] 10 (p. 21 Terz.).

[3] J. M. Rist, 'Hypatia', *Phoenix* xix (1965), 216 f. Though it might be observed that Synesius was acquainted with that Bible of the later Neoplatonists, the Chaldaean Oracles (cf. W. Theiler, *Schriften der Königsberger Gelehrten Gesellschaft* xviii. 1 (1942), 1–41).

[4] *Lucrezio e l'apologetica latina in Claudiano* (1958).

that it was;[1] but, long since despised by Christians, Epicureanism was despised too by all pagan thinkers of whom we have any information in the fourth century.[2] By Claudian's day St. Augustine wrote of both Stoics and Epicureans that 'iam certe nostra aetate sic obmutuisse conspicimus, ut vix iam in *scholis rhetorum* [N.B.] commemoretur tantum quae fuerint illorum sententiae.'[3] Indeed, it would be very singular if such an essentially rational philosophy had still satisfied the generation after Iamblichus and Maximus of Ephesus.

Gennaro bases his argument solely on echoes of Lucretius in Claudian. But in the first place he devotes almost all his attention to only twenty-four lines, the proem to *Ruf.* i. And in the second, though it is clear that Claudian knew his Lucretius well, none the less even here there are many much closer parallels in other authors, with whom Claudian was just as familiar: Vergil, Ovid, Lucan, and Tacitus.[4] Indeed, anyone who takes the trouble to compare the passages will see at once that this whole section of Claudian is directly inspired by Juvenal, xiii. 86 f. Not only are there several close verbal parallels (the text of Claudian can actually be established with Juvenal's help), but the subject-matter too is identical: the Epicurean, who does not need to fear

---

[1] Op. cit., pp. 45–6: this is a favourite theme of the Catania school as a whole, notably E. Rapisarda.

[2] Julian, for example, forbade his reformed pagan clergy even to read Epicurus (*Ep.* 89b, p. 169. 15 Bidez). For Themistius, Epicurus was the type of the pure sensualist, σαρκὸς ἡδονὴν τεθαυμακώς (*Or.* xxxiv. 30), as much as he was for Augustine (*Ep.* 167. 4). Macrobius writes of 'Epicureorum tota factio aequo semper errore a vero devia' (*Comm.* i. 2. 3). The common view that Palladas was an Epicurean (cf. W. Peek, *PW* xviii. 3. 159) is unfounded.

[3] *Ep.* 118. 21: their views, he claims, had been 'eradicata atque compressa' even in the universities of Greece, having been refuted by the Platonists as well. Cf. too ib. 12, 'ne ipsorum quidem . . . Epicureorum cineres caleant'. Gennaro cites none of the texts in this or the preceding note: all he can produce is Aug., *Conf.* vi. 16. 26, which proves nothing. Moreover, the phrase there 'de finibus bonorum et malorum' betrays clearly enough the source of Augustine's information. H. Hagendahl firmly (and I am sure rightly) denied that Epicureanism was a living force even in Arnobius' day a century earlier (*Latin Fathers*, pp. 9–88). Gennaro's remarks in *Da Claudiano a Merobaude* (1959), 9–10 in no way answer Hagendahl's case.

[4] See Birt ad loc., and Gennaro himself, p. 6, n. 8.

the just retribution of God on his misdeeds.[1] Knowledge of Lucretius does not in any case entail acceptance of Epicureanism, as the examples of Arnobius and Lactantius show. Gennaro does adduce a few Lucretian echoes from Claudian's brief survey of philosophical systems at *Theod.* 70–112. But as it happens not one of these echoes has anything to do with Epicureanism: indeed, where they are not merely verbal they concern the other systems, which Lucretius had only discussed in order to refute. Claudian used Lucretius merely as a convenient doxographical source: Epicureanism itself he barely mentions.

Gennaro criticizes earlier scholars for concentrating on merely linguistic parallels and failing to notice 'il senso misterioso ed inafferrabile della vita e l'incertezza del destino' which Lucretius had inspired in Claudian. In fact it is Gennaro who has been led astray by verbal parallels without paying sufficient attention to what Claudian actually says even in the passage to which he devotes almost all his attention. After dilating at length on the *topos* of the argument from design, Claudian claims that

> omnia rebar
> consilio firmata dei, qui lege moveri
> sidera, qui fruges diverso tempore nasci . . . (*Ruf.* i. 6 f.).

Claudian then confesses to finding this conviction shaken by that well-known stumbling-block, the evident prosperity of the wicked. At this, he says,

> rursus labefacta cadebat
> religio, causaeque viam *non sponte* sequebar
> alterius, vacuo quae currere semina motu
> affirmat, magnumque novas per inane figuras
> fortuna, non arte, regi, quae numina sensu
> ambiguo vel nulla putat vel nescia nostri (ib. 14–19).

That is to say, Claudian embraced Epicureanism for a while. It is clear that *alterius* is Epicurus, and that lines 16–19 are at once a clever pastiche of Lucretian phrases and a brief summary of

---

[1] *CQ* N.S. xviii (1968), 388.

Epicurean doctrine. However, Claudian continues, the punishment of Rufinus dispelled all these hesitations:

> abstulit hunc tandem Rufini poena tumultum,
> absolvitque deos. iam non ad culmina rerum
> iniustos crevisse queror: tolluntur in altum
> ut lapsu graviore ruant.

So Epicureanism was something Claudian turned to against his will—'non sponte'—while temporarily disenchanted with his former belief in a just and beneficent providence—only to reject it at once when the tidings of Rufinus' fate restored his faith in divine justice.[1] So much for Claudian's Epicureanism!

It is certainly a remarkable passage ('avait-on rien écrit,' wrote Gaston Boissier, 'depuis Juvénal, de plus ferme et de plus brillant que cette tirade?').[2] Yet it should be obvious that Claudian is writing with tongue in cheek. He pretends that the whole question of divine justice and all the doubts he had ever entertained concerning the ordering of the universe were settled definitively for him by just the death of Rufinus—*parturiunt montes!* The Lucretian colouring on which Gennaro lays so much emphasis was (of course) deliberately designed to heighten the mock solemn effect. Obviously Claudian did not really abandon his faith during the few months of Rufinus' supremacy. If anything at all is to be deduced from the passage concerning Claudian's true *Weltanschauung*, it is surely that he did believe in a just and beneficent providence, and thought Epicureanism merely good for a laugh, the only faith consistent with the prosperity of the wicked.

It has also been alleged that Claudian was influenced as well (still in this same one passage) by Christian Apologetic. This would certainly be both interesting and important[3]—if true.

---

[1] See Himerius' attack on Epicurus for denying providence (*Or.* iii): obviously it was a regular declamation theme.

[2] *Fin du paganisme* ii (1891), 279. Gibbon pronounced the passage beautiful (ed. Bury iii. 229, n. 34). There is an interesting discussion in Bayle's *Dictionnaire critique*, 'Rufin', note E. Its humour was clearly perceived by the author of *The Stumbling Block* (see p. 443).

[3] I have argued elsewhere (*JRS* lv (1965), 21 f.) that Palladas (exceptionally) *was* familiar with some of the apologetical themes.

However, the passages cited are all simply developments in Lucretian terms on the same *topos* of divine providence. There is nothing specifically or even noticeably Christian in a single one of them, much less any sentiment characteristic of Apologetic in particular. Texts of Lactantius and Minucius Felix are alleged to have inspired a line for which several Lucretian parallels are also cited, and Lucretius is actually cited at length in one of the passages from Lactantius.[1] More economical (and more sensible) to dispense with the Apologists, and suppose that Claudian was echoing Lucretius direct.

V

Next, we turn to the extent and character of Claudian's knowledge of Roman history. The only comprehensive work on the subject is an 1889 dissertation by E. Stoecker, a pupil of Birt's.[2] Stoecker argued that Claudian had a detailed and first-hand knowledge of Sallust, Livy, and Tacitus, as well as of the handbooks and epitomes of later times, Florus, Victor, and Eutropius. There is nothing intrinsically absurd in such a claim, despite the fact that Claudian was a Greek. His contemporary and fellow Greek Ammian had certainly read Sallust, Livy, and Tacitus, as well as Cicero and several other Latin prose writers.[3] But then Ammian was a historian. Claudian (despite the pious confidence of modern historians) was not. He was a poet, and thus it is only natural that his literary interests should have differed from Ammian's. The converse is equally true, of course. While thoroughly acquainted with the historians and prose writers, Ammian is less

---

[1] e.g. with the passages cited on pp. 39 and 43 of Gennaro's monograph, compare those on pp. 33–4. It is arbitrary to claim that *Ruf.* i. 12–13 'tolluntur in altum | ut lapsu graviore ruant' must have been inspired by Minucius Felix xxxvii. 7, 'in hoc altius tolluntur ut decidant altius' (p. 43, n. 107). The *topos* is ubiquitous. Some parallels are quoted by Birt ad loc., more by L. Sternbach, *Festschr. T. Gomperz* (1902), 396, n. 2, and cf. J. Moreau on Lactantius, *De mort. pers.* i. 22 (p. 191): add Amm. Marc. xxx. 5. 10.

[2] *De Claudiani veterum rerum Romanarum scientia* (Marburg, 1889).

[3] G. B. A. Fletcher, *Rev. Phil.*[3] xi (1937), 377–95 (with full earlier bibliography).

influenced by the Latin poets—with the inevitable exception of Vergil. For this reason it is worth subjecting Stoecker's results to a closer scrutiny.

Let us turn first to Livy, and to the history of Republican Rome. Stoecker fills fifty-six pages with 'parallels' between Claudian and Livy or the Livian epitomators, concluding that Claudian had read both Livy himself and his epitomators. It might seem odd of itself that anyone who had waded through the original text should waste his time on such as Florus and Eutropius:[1] but let that pass. I have carefully considered each one of the parallels between Livy and Claudian on its own merits, and must confess that barely one seems to me to have probative value. Of course, the absence of definite verbal parallels with Livy does not necessarily prove that Claudian had not read Livy. Absence of echoes from (say) Lucan or Juvenal (in fact there are many) might legitimately have been judged significant in this respect. For both are 'rhetorical' poets one might have expected to be very congenial to Claudian, and both strike out many a memorable phrase one might have expected to be echoed by later poets. Things are rather different with a prose writer not noted for the brilliance of his epigrams. For this reason it is perhaps significant that the only parallel between Livy and Claudian which does impress me is an epigram. With the phrase 'contemptu . . . tutus' at Livy i. 56. 7 ('safe because he was despised') cf. *Eutr.* i. 132, where Claudian writes that Eutropius 'contemptu iam liber erat.' I would be quite prepared to allow the possibility that Claudian had read Livy i—and perhaps several more books as well. What I do dispute is that he had read all or even a large part of Livy, and that this was the major source of his knowledge of Republican history.

What now of Claudian's knowledge of the Livian epitomators? Here a much stronger case can be made out—but one which suggests a conclusion other than Stoecker's own. At *Get.* 396 Claudian says that M. Valerius Laevinus was consul when he

---

[1] Though Ammian did (Fletcher, op. cit., 383–6, 392), and perhaps Augustine too (Hagendahl, *Augustine and the Latin Classics*, pp. 650 f.).

commanded against Philip V of Macedon in 214 B.C. In fact
Laevinus was propraetor at the time. Livy of course knew this
perfectly well. But Florus says that he was consul (i. 23. 6). At
Get. 291 Claudian writes of Rome's revenge for the Gallic sack:
'[Ausonia] Senonum restinxit sanguine flammas.' Compare the
strikingly similar phrase in Florus (i. 7. 17): '[Camillus] omnia
incendiorum vestigia *Gallici sanguinis inundatione* deleret'. At
Gild. 108, Roma exclaims, referring to the size of her Empire,
'ipsa nocet moles.' Stoecker compares Livy, *pr.* 4: '[Roma] iam
magnitudine laboret sua'. In fact the idea is a commonplace,
but by far the closest verbal parallel to Claudian's words is Florus
again, 'ipsa moles exitio fuit' (ii. 21. 5). And it is surely from Florus
that Claudian derived the cliché of the comparison of the ages of
Rome with the life of man. According to this simile (first recorded
in a lost work of Seneca quoted by Lactantius), Rome's infancy and
childhood fell under the kings and early Republic, her youth in
the period of her great conquests, and her old age under the
Empire. The aged Roma bulks large in *Gild.* (17 f., 208 f.), and
at 114–15 f. she exclaims:

ast ego quae terras iuvenis[1] pontumque subegi,
deseror: emeritae iam praemia nulla senectae.

Cf. Florus (i. 18. 1): 'domita subactaque Italia, populus Romanus
. . . vere robustus et *iuvenis* . . . Africam, Europam, Asiam, totum
denique orbem terrarum bellis victoriisque peragravit.' Apart
from Seneca, an unfashionable author in pagan circles in Claudian's
day,[2] the only other extant writer to use the simile is Ammian
(who almost certainly got it from Florus).[3] Claudian clearly
referred to Ammian's description of the Huns,[4] and for the

---

[1] Barth's in my opinion certain correction of the MSS. *humeris*, which I shall
be justifying in my commentary ad loc. For the simile, see most recently Demandt,
Zeitkritik Ammians (1965), 118 f., and A. Momigliano, *History and Theory* vi
(1966), 13–14.
[2] *JRS* lvii (1967), 31–2.
[3] Not from Lactantius, as alleged by Demandt; cf. *CR* xvii (1967), 63.
[4] O. J. Maenchen-Helfen, *AJPh* lxxvi (1955), 384 f., *Byzantion* xvii (1944–5),
237 (doubted, unnecessarily, by R. Syme, *Ammianus and the Historia Augusta*

purposes of *Gild.* may well have looked up Ammian's section on the revolt of Firmus (the only available account). In view of his apparent lack of interest in Imperial history (below, p. 340), it would be interesting to know whether he had read much more of Ammian's very detailed and bulky work.

In view of the difficulties, already mentioned, in establishing that a poet had read a prose writer of undistinguished style, these four passages suggest that Claudian had read Florus rather carefully. Moreover, it is worth noting that two each of these Floran echoes occur in Claudian's two historical epics, *Gild.* and *Get.*, the two poems which demanded, with their (at least sometimes) carefully chosen historical parallels, more precise historical knowledge on Claudian's part. It would be attractive, and not over fanciful, to suggest that Claudian brushed up his Republican history with Florus while writing these poems. Laevinus, for example, compared with the other heroes who parade through Claudian's pages, is a very minor figure. Claudian might well have felt it necessary to check up on the details of his command in a handbook like Florus. Florus may perhaps then be regarded as Claudian's major historical source for Republican history—though (as will be shown below) his primary sources for Republican history were probably not histories proper at all.

What now of Tacitus and Sallust? It is *a priori* much more likely that Claudian would have read some Sallust, who had long been one of the most popular of all school authors. Livy, on the other hand, was much less popular—mainly, no doubt, because of his immense bulk. Hence the vogue in Claudian's day of Livian epitomes. It is hardly surprising that Livy himself was outstripped by these less demanding competitors.

At the factual level, it seems certain that Claudian had read (or re-read) his *Bellum Jugurthinum* for African 'background' when drafting *Gild.* For example, his section on African battle tactics owes a lot to the numerous indications in Sallust (though other sources have contributed here as well), and his claim that

(1968), 14: Ammian can actually be used to establish the text of Claudian at one point, *CQ* N.S. xviii (1968), 390).

the Africans were polygamous (*Gild.* 441 f.) presumably derives from *BJ* 80. 6. His allusion to Adherbal's pitiful appeal to the senate is also surely inspired by *BJ* 14 f. It would be tedious to enumerate all the verbal parallels between Claudian and Sallust listed in Stoecker's dissertation. Few are striking, and the effect is cumulative, rather than immediately apparent from one or two examples. We may probably, then, assume with some confidence that Claudian had read his Sallust.

All the same, it is interesting and instructive to observe that it is colourful details and linguistic points that Claudian takes from Sallust, rather than basic historical judgements. For example, senatorial tradition assigned most of the credit for Jugurtha's defeat to Metellus, robbed of the fruits of his labours by the upstart Marius.[1] Sallust, though without unduly depreciating Metellus, gave Marius his due. Yet Claudian clearly reflects the senatorial tradition, the version, significantly enough, of the Livian epitomators—and Florus:

> *fractumque Metello*
> traximus immanem Marii sub vincla Iugurtham (*Gild.* 91–2).

It would certainly be both interesting and important if it could be shown that Claudian had read (even some) Tacitus, and a good case can certainly be made out. First, the verbal echoes; at *Hist.* v. 6 Tacitus describes the snow-capped peak of Mt. Lebanon as 'mirum dictu, tantos inter ardores opacum *fidumque nivibus*'. It is surely this rather unusual phrase that Claudian had in mind when he wrote of the peak of Aetna, 'quamvis nimio fervens exuberet aestu, | scit *nivibus* servare *fidem*' (*Rapt.* i. 164–5). With *Gild.* 247 'fluitante fide', compare *Hist.* ii. 93 'fides fluitasse'; with *pr. Nupt.* 4 'continuare dies epulis', compare *Germ.* 22, 'diem noctemque potando continuare'; and with *Eutr.* ii. 147 'Thracum Macetumque ruinis | taedet, et in gentes iterum saevire sepultas', compare *Hist.* iii. 35, 'sepultae urbis ruinis'.[2]

---

[1] Cf. Syme, *Sallust* (1964), 151.
[2] Platnauer curiously takes *iterum* with *sepultas* instead of *saevire*. For a further clear Tacitean echo, see below, pp. 346–7.

Much more significant, however, is the influence of Tacitus the thinker. Cf. *Gild*. 49 f. (Roma is speaking):

> postquam iura ferox in se communia Caesar
> transtulit, et lapsi mores desuetaque priscis
> artibus in gremium pacis servile recessi.

All commentators and translators have taken it for granted that the 'Caesar' of this passage is Julius Caesar, the dictator. Yet it must in fact be Augustus. Claudian is recalling the words of *Ann*. i. 2, 'Caesar . . . insurgere paullatim, munia senatus magistratuum legum *in se trahere*', where Tacitus too had styled Augustus simply Caesar. Tacitus, it should be noted, continues his account of Augustus 'pacem sine dubio post haec, vero cruentam' (ib. i. 10), just as Claudian goes on with 'gremium pacis servile'. Moreover, it should now be clear that Platnauer's 'proud Caesar' for 'ferox Caesar' is mistaken; 'cruel' would be nearer the mark. It is probably no coincidence that the most servile of Claudian's imitators, Sidonius Apollinaris, writes '*trux* Auguste' at *Pan. Avit*. 93. The Tacitean Augustus has left his impression elsewhere in Claudian as well. Tacitus had noted cynically that Augustus' 'pietatem erga parentem' was 'obtentui sumpta' (*Ann*. i. 10. 1). Claudian likewise dwells on his hypocritical *pietas*:

> pavit Iuleos inviso sanguine manes
> Augustus, sed falsa *pii* praeconia *sumpsit*
> in luctum patriae civili strage parentans
> (*VI Cons*. 116 f.).

Yet while it is important to assess Claudian's familiarity with the Roman historians, it would be an error of method to suppose that it was historians whom Claudian read to learn Roman history. It is abundantly clear that the periods which most interested Claudian were the early and mid Republic: less so the late Republic, hardly at all the Empire. Yet we have now seen that of the three major Roman historians, it is only Sallust and Tacitus, the historians of the late Republic and early Empire, of whom Claudian had any real first-hand knowledge.

Anyone who has given the countless historical allusions in

Claudian's work (especially his later work) more than passing attention will have realized at once that his interest in the past is not historical at all, but rhetorical. For Claudian, the great Roman heroes are personifications of virtue, quoted solely to illustrate that virtue. He uses history exclusively to 'point a moral or adorn a tale'. If it is a question of noble poverty (a contrast to the luxurious ways of Rufinus or Eutropius), then immediately Fabricius, Serranus, Curius Dentatus spring to his mind—the dictator who leaves his plough for battle, and returns to it after victory. If bravery, then the Decii Mures flow automatically from his pen; for generalship, Camillus, Marcellus, Aemilius Paullus, the Scipiones . . . Or if caution needs to be advocated (or defended), who but Q. Fabius Maximus Cunctator? The great enemies of Rome— Brennus, Pyrrhus, Antiochus, Hannibal—attain similar status, a fit match for Stilico or comparison for his enemies.

There is nothing new here, of course. Since late Republican times the history of the early and middle Republic had been viewed as a Golden Age, untouched by corruption. It is an attitude which requires no further illustration for anyone familiar with the literature of the principate, above all Lucan, Seneca, and Juvenal.[1] The poets, understandably, were less concerned with the historical facts than with the emotive power of the great names. Thus it was not long before they were saved the trouble of ransacking the historians for suitable examples. Handbooks with heroes and villains alike (foreigners as well as Romans) neatly classified according to all the desirable virtues and vices began to appear. The best known surviving example is that of Valerius Maximus, destined to become a much thumbed *vade mecum* among the poets and rhetors of the fourth century.

That it was from some such source that Claudian drew much of his historical material requires little demonstration. Consider the following passage, designed to illustrate Rufinus' cruelty:

> quid tale immanes umquam gessisse feruntur
> vel Sinis Isthmiaca pinu vel rupe profunda

[1] See H. W. Litchfield's still invaluable study 'National *Exempla Virtutis* in Roman Literature', *Harvard Studies* xxv (1914), 1–71.

> Sciron vel Phalaris tauro vel carcere Sulla?
> o mites Diomedis equi! Busiridis arae
> clementes! iam Cinna pius, iam Spartace segnis
> Rufino collatus eris! (*Ruf.* i. 251 f.)

By a curious whim of posterity, Sulla was a monster of cruelty to
the Imperial age, while Marius, guilty of proscriptions far worse
than Sulla's, was the hero of his day. This conventional (and
unhistorical) assessment of the two men is faithfully reflected
in Claudian, who frequently evokes Marius as a hero, while
Sulla is for him an author of murder and treachery.[1] And here
we find Sulla rubbing shoulders with a very motley crowd.
Mythological characters like Sinis, Sciron, and Busiris, a figure
from Greek history (Phalaris)—and Spartacus. Roman history
being rather thin on monsters of cruelty, Spartacus is improperly
transferred from the rubric under which he belongs, *hostes
publici Romani*. The whole list has probably come straight from
a chapter 'de crudelitate' in a rhetorical handbook, where (as in
Valerius Maximus) Roman examples were listed together with an
appendix for 'exterarum gentium'.

But the clearest proof by far of the origin and character of
Claudian's use of *exempla* is the long passage *IV Cons.* 396–418,
where Theodosius the Great is advising Honorius on his historical
reading. It is made perfectly clear throughout that the purpose of
studying history is solely to learn what to imitate and what to
avoid in one's own conduct:

> interea Musis animus, dum mollior, instet
> *et quae mox imitere legat*; nec desinat umquam
> tecum Graia loqui, tecum Romana vetustas.
> antiquos evolve duces, adsuesce futurae
> militiae, Latium retro te confer in aevum.

Then follows a list of *exempla*, with a brief phrase characterizing
the virtue (or vice) of each:

> libertas quaesita placet? mirabere Brutum.
> perfidiam damnas? Metti satiabere poenis.

---

[1] Cf. Birt's *index nom.*, s.v.

triste rigor nimius? Torquati despice mores.
mors impensa bonum? Decios venerare ruentes.
vel solus quid fortis agat, te ponte soluto
oppositus Cocles, Muci te flamma docebit;
quid mora perfringat, Fabius; quid rebus in artis
dux gerat, ostendet Gallorum strage Camillus.
discitur hinc nullos meritis obsistere casus:
prorogat aeternam feritas tibi Punica famam,
Regule; successus superant adversa Catonis.
discitur hinc quantum paupertas sobria possit:
pauper erat Curius, Pyrrhi cum sperneret aurum:
sordida dictator flexit Serranus aratra.

The handbook origin of these *exempla* is too obvious to need
further comment. That Claudian (like Lucan)[1] actually used
Valerius Maximus himself (no doubt among other such manuals)
is suggested by a close verbal parallel from another poem:

primus fulmineum lento luctamine Poenum
compressit Fabius, campo post ausus aperto
Marcellus vinci docuit, sed tertia virtus
Scipiadae Latiis tandem deterruit oris (*Get.* 138 f.).

Cf. Val. Max. iv. 1. 7, 'Marcellus . . . Hannibalem vinci . . . posse
docuit.'

But in addition to such works as these, the practice of earlier
poets must have influenced Claudian at least as much as any strictly
historical works he had read. The merest handful of examples
must suffice. With *Eutr.* i. 447, 'attonitum tranavit Cloelia Thybrim', Stoecker compared Livy, ii. 13. 6, 'Cloelia . . . Tiberim
tranavit'. As soon as it is realized that *tranare* is the standard Latin
word for 'swim across', and that neither proper name could very
well have been dispensed with if the story was to be told at all,
the parallel vanishes. In fact the *attonitum* suggests that Claudian
was echoing Silius x. 493–4, '*mirantem* interrita Thybrim [sc.
Cloelia] | *tranavit.*' Similarly, it was probably not, as Stoecker
suggests, from Livy that Claudian learnt that Tanaquil had second

---

[1] Cf. M. P. O. Morford, *The Poet Lucan: Studies in Rhetorical Epic* (1967), 65,
n. 1—though Lucan had certainly read Livy as well.

sight (*c.m.* xxx. 16), but Silius again (xiii. 819 f.). A very close
verbal parallel shows that he derived his version of the punishment
of Mettius (*Gild.* 254 f.) from *Aen.* viii. 642 f. Stoecker claimed
that *Gild.* 81 f., 'iam proximus Hannibal urbi | . . . noctesque
cruentas | Collina pro turre tuli' derived from Livy (xxvi. 9 f.),
because only Livy (or so he alleged) tells of a battle by the Colline
gate. At best this is a dangerous sort of argument, since (especially
with popular stories from Republican history) plainly Claudian
may have had access to works which no longer survive.[1] In this
case it is perfectly clear that he was directly imitating Juvenal,
vi. 290–1: '*proximus urbi* | *Hannibal,* et stantes *Collina turre* mariti'.

Fargues, noting particularly Claudian's debt to Lucan in this
respect, regards Lucan as one of Claudian's historical 'sources'.
As examples of events Claudian 'learnt of' from Lucan he cites[2]
'la guerre de Véies, la défaite de l'Allia, la guerre contre Pyrrhus,
la bataille de Cannes, l'invasion des Cimbres et des Teutons,
l'invasion des Gaulois, la campagne de Scipion en Afrique'. Yet
to admit that Claudian was influenced by the passages of Lucan
Fargues cites, is not at all the same as saying that he derived his
knowledge of the events from Lucan and no other source. We
have seen that Claudian had read at least some Livy, and almost
certainly studied Florus. It is not the events which Claudian derives
from Lucan (Vergil, Silius, Juvenal, or whoever), but the idea of
using a particular event in a particular way in a particular context.

Claudian refers freely to Republican history, but has very little
to say of the Empire. This apparent lack of interest in the Empire
is not to be ascribed to a mere personal whim on Claudian's part.
It is a taste he shares with almost all other writers of his day, indeed of the Imperial age in general. At a very early date it was
accepted that the canon of *exempla virtutum* ended with the Republic. Various factors contributed to shape this attitude, the most
important probably being the belief that the virtues which had

---

[1] The late fourth century was much given to potted Roman histories (cf. *JRS*
liv (1964), 17). That of Nicomachus Flavianus, conveniently lost, has been
invoked to explain a multitude of sins.

[2] p. 251.

made Rome great disappeared with Cato at Utica.[1] This is why moralists of the early principate—notably Juvenal—so often produce Republican *exempla* precisely in order to reproach the age in which they lived. As a result, almost no citizen-subject of the Empire (not even the 'Stoic saints', Thrasea Paetus and Helvidius Priscus) ever succeeded in getting into the canon (Claudian mentions neither). A very few of the early Emperors made it, but on a slightly different footing. Panegyrists regularly exhorted their addressees to imitate the virtues of the 'good' Emperors, Trajan and Titus, Pius and Marcus—and avoid the vices of their 'bad' counterparts, Nero and Tiberius. Claudian fits exactly into this pattern. Emperors are divided up into good or bad, and only the stock examples of each quoted. Of the good ones, he has most to say about Trajan, but this is for the special reason that, as a Spaniard, Trajan was by a courtly fiction held to be a distant ancestor of Theodosius and Honorius.

Claudian's divergences from this conventional attitude to the principate are for the most part slight and unimportant. The story of Marcus and the Thundering Legion[2] is no real exception, since it is quoted as an illustration of Marcus' virtue. Nor is his allusion to the death of the Emperor Carinus in the *Epithalamium* on Palladius and Celerina (74 f.), for it is only introduced because an ancestor of Celerina's was allegedly offered the vacant throne. This is no doubt a detail which Claudian first discovered when doing his research on the pedigree of bride and groom—a necessary part of his trade. His extended eulogy of the Roman Empire at *Stil.* iii. 130 f. is no real exception either, since this belongs to a different rhetorical tradition, the *Laudes Romae*.[3] His only notable divergence from the pattern is to use Augustus as an *exemplum* of hypocrisy and false piety—a role he does not seem to play elsewhere in the rhetorical tradition. This perhaps supports the suggestion made above that Claudian derived it from Tacitus. Thence too, perhaps, derives the citation of Narcissus as a parallel to Eutropius—both ex-slaves who came to dominate an Emperor.

[1] Cf. Litchfield, op. cit. 53 f.
[2] See p. 223.   [3] See p. 354.

If I am not mistaken this is the only private citizen of the Imperial period whom Claudian mentions.

Thus with few and insignificant exceptions Claudian's knowledge of and attitude to the history of both Republic and Empire is entirely conventional, determined by the prevailing attitude of Latin writers of the Empire as a whole. It is the poets and rhetoricians of the early principate to whom he owes most.

It may be presumed that his knowledge of and attitude to Greek history were broadly similar, though not surprisingly in poems written in Latin for western audiences he finds little occasion to allude to Greek history. The few trite allusions we do find are for the most part *exempla* again, and confined to the strictly Classical period, closing with Alexander. For example, Solon and Lycurgus are *exempla* of lawgivers (*IV Cons.* 507 f.). The allusions are too few to allow any safe generalizations, but the analogy of other Greek poets and panegyrists of the later Empire suggest that even if we had more, Claudian's range would still have been restricted to the Classical period. It is to Miltiades and Plato that Pamprepius compares Theagenes.[1] To Aristides, Peisistratus, Themistocles, Cyrus, Agesilaus, Philip II, and Alexander that Procopius of Gaza compares Anastasius.[2]

In his eulogy of Rome in *Stil.* iii Claudian briefly runs through the series of world empires (including the unhistorical Median Empire)[3] and the successive hegemonies of Athens, Sparta, and Thebes in Greece. But in the context this is merely a conventional *topos* of the *Laudes Romae*—the unfavourable comparison of all previous empires to that of Rome.

Claudian refers several times to Alexander—and to his most glamorous adversary, Porus the Indian. Birt thought he could detect verbal echoes of Quintus Curtius. But they are very flimsy,

[1] Heitsch XXXV (Page 140b), 40–1.

[2] *Pan. Anast.* 14 and 25 f. Countless other examples could be cited: merely *exempli gratia,* Aristides Εἰς Ῥώμην, and the anonymous encomium on Philip the Arab, [Aristides] *Or.* xxxv Keil; cf. L. J. Swift, *Greek, Rom. and Byz. Studies* vii (1966), 271.

[3] A commonplace in the chronographical tradition: Claudian cannot be reproached for this particular misconception.

and there is something *a priori* improbable about an Alexandrian whose native tongue was Greek reading a Latin history of Alexander, when there were so many Greek ones available. Fargues goes to the other extreme (p. 252) and thinks that Claudian knew of Alexander only from the rhetorical textbooks, because 'L'histoire d'Alexandre fournissait de nombreux sujets de *suasoriae*.' No doubt, but we must not forget that Claudian was an Alexandrian—and proud of it. He writes to his fellow Alexandrian Hadrianus that Alexander was 'conditor . . . *patriae*' (*c.m.* xxii. 20). Thus his interest in Alexander may well have gone deeper than Fargues supposed. He is surely very likely to have read one or more of the numerous Greek poems or histories about Alexander during his Alexandrian schooldays. It is probably no coincidence that his estimate of Alexander is so favourable—despite the fact that there was a very strong rhetorical tradition that Alexander was merely a power-mad tyrant, reflected above all in Lucan,[1] who influenced Claudian so strongly in so many other respects.

VI

It will not be necessary to discuss the other sides of Claudian's erudition at length: astronomy, natural science, medicine, geography etc.[2] It is, of course, the erudition of the poet, but in general it is less inaccurate than is customary with ancient poets.

Claudian's astronomy is on the whole very accurate. Like Latin predecessors such as Lucan and Greek successors such as Nonnus, naturally enough he inserted astronomical passages for their ornamental value. But unlike them, he took the trouble to get his astronomy correct.[3]

[1] Cf. Morford, op. cit., ch. ii.

[2] For knowledge of these subjects in late Antiquity, see especially the masterly pages in Marrou's *S. Augustin et la fin de la culture antique*, part i. For Claudian's disciple Sidonius there is much of interest in A. Loyen, *Sidoine Apollinaire et l'esprit précieux en Gaule aux derniers jours de l'empire* (1943). More generally, W. H. Stahl *Isis* l (1959), 95–124; J. O. Thomson, *H. of Ancient Geography* (1948), 351 f.

[3] See Semple's two articles in *CQ* xxxi (1937), and xxxii (1938), with pp. 205–9, above, and Appendix A below, pp. 461–3.

As for natural science, Claudian is knowledgeable about such things in the way poets usually are. He likes to talk about the causes of earthquakes, volcanoes, comets, and winds, and wrote special poems on the sources of the Nile, the powers of the magnet, and a sphere of Archimedes.[1] He knows the true cause of eclipses (*Get.* 235) and tides (*Theod.* 107). R. Eisler in his learned *Weltenmantel und Himmelszelt* suggests recondite Orphic sources for the cosmogony which Proserpina (like Harmonia in Nonnus, xli. 295 f.) weaves into her robe—the globe of the earth formed by gravity from chaos, with its two habitable zones (*Rapt.* i. 248 f.). Every detail comes from the opening section of Ovid's *Metamorphoses.*

Like most educated men of his day, Claudian had a smattering of medical knowledge (we have seen already that Alexandria was one of the few centres where it was studied at an academic level). There are similar medical allusions in the poems of western writers like Prudentius and Paulinus of Nola. And interestingly enough both, like Claudian, even though they are writing poetry, are careful to use medical terminology, as though to advertise their expertise.[2] But it is no less interesting to note that George of Pisidia, whose panegyrics have so much in common with Claudian's, makes even more frequent use of medical imagery and terminology—especially of technical terms.[3] Evidently this was a stock feature of the contemporary Greek epico-panegyrical tradition. We need not, of course, deny Claudian a lively and genuine interest in medicine for its own sake, but obviously for the purposes of his poetry he viewed it primarily as a source of imagery—and a convenient handmaiden to rhetoric. Compare his double account of the 'best' way to treat an ulcer (an image also used by George, *Exp. Pers.* ii. 191 f.). When advocating strong measures against Eutropius, he remarks that deep ulcers require drastic treatment:

> non leviore manu, ferro sanantur et igni (*Eutr.* ii. 14 f.).

---

[1] See Fargues, pp. 313 f. for full discussion—but unduly hard on Claudian.
[2] See the passages quoted in CQ N.S. xviii (1968), 406–7.
[3] See A. Pertusi's edition (1959), pp. 41–2.

When deprecating strong measures against Alaric (*Get.* 120 f.), he warns instead that a surgeon

> *cautius* ingentes morbos et proxima cordi
> ulcera . . . tractat.

Claudian's geographical knowledge is again essentially the knowledge of the poet. Most of the places he mentions had been mentioned many, many times by other poets before him. Here too, as in the case of historical *exempla*, the poet of late Antiquity had convenient handbooks to tell him, the easy way, which were the 'poetical' rivers, lakes, mountains, etc. in the various areas of the world: witness the surviving minuscule manual of Claudian's contemporary Vibius Sequester, *De fluminibus, fontibus . . . quorum apud poetas mentio fit.* The Vergilian commentator Tiberius Claudius Donatus planned a similar work. Claudian refers widely to distant outposts of the Empire—but always to its traditional poetic boundaries, Maeotis and Meroe, the Nile and the Danube, Cadiz and the Caucasus, the Libyan desert, the 'mollis Arabs', the Sarmatians, distant Thule, and even the Orkneys.[1] There can be little doubt that his major 'source' in this sphere was the poets, not his own experience as a traveller.

But it is perhaps going too far, with A. Loyen, to claim that most of these names were nothing but names to him. For example, when Claudian proclaims, addressing Honorius,

> tu licet extremos late dominere per Indos,
> te Medus, te mollis Arabs, te Seres adorent
> (*IV Cons.* 257–8 f.),

Loyen assumes that Claudian had no idea how far away China and India really were, and really believed that they formed part of Honorius' realm.[2] It may well be that Claudian did have a rather hazy idea of the exact location and extent of China and India—as, too, probably, of vaguely conceived areas such as 'Scythia'. But

[1] See, for example, the mass of passages collected under the rubrics 'Völker-kataloge' and 'Flusskataloge—Grenzen' in F. Christ, *Römische Weltherrschaft in der antiken Dichtung*, Tüb. Beitr. z. Altertumsw. xxxi (1938), 29–53. For Claudian's dependence on Lucan's geography see Fargues, p. 52. See too above, p. 3.

[2] *Sidoine Apollinaire* (1943), 22.

surely in this case he was merely echoing the courtly flatteries of the Augustans. If Vergil and Horace had envisaged Augustus as the conqueror of India and China, could Claudian do less for Honorius? It does not follow that he believed his own hyperboles.

The vagueness of his knowledge of more distant areas is better illustrated by his references to the Elbe. Claudian praises Stilico's pacification of the Rhine frontier:

> ut iam trans fluvium [i.e. the Rhine], non indignante Caüco,
> pascat Belga pecus, *mediumque* ingressa *per Albim*
> Gallica Francorum montes armenta pererrent (*Stil.* i. 225 f.).

The implication is that the Elbe is just a tributary of the Rhine. Some have tried to save Claudian, by assuming instead a reference to a river Alve, a tributary of the Meuse, others a mountain range on the far side of the Rhine apparently known in Antiquity by the same name as the Alps.[1] In vain: Claudian twice elsewhere uses *Albis* to stand for a large and distant river. And what can this be but the river we know as the Elbe? The answer is simply that he did not realize quite how far from the Rhine it was. Compare too *IV Cons.* 452, where at Stilico's call

> paludibus exit
> Cimber, et ingentes Albim liquere Cherusci.

Both Cimbri and Cherusci had of course been long extinct by Claudian's day: they stand for Germanic tribes in general. But even when they did exist, the Cherusci lived nowhere near the Elbe. Why then did Claudian think that they did? The answer is simple but revealing. He was misled by some passages of Tacitus,[2] welcome further proof of his familiarity with that author.

Several passages in *Annals* i and ii refer to the Cherusci as living 'between the Rhine and the Elbe' (i. 59. 4, ii. 22. 1, ii. 41. 2). And at *Ann.* ii. 19. 1 the defeated Cherusci debate the advisability

---

[1] For full reference to all these discussions see A. Loyen, *RÉL* xi (1933), 203 f., 321 f.

[2] Pointed out by Loyen, *RÉL*, 208–9.

of fleeing across the Elbe. The inference that the Cherusci actually lived on the Elbe, if hasty, is perhaps pardonable.[1] Claudian assumed that they did cross—and had been waiting on the other side ever since for Stilico's call.

But there is one passage where Claudian has been wrongfully accused of geographical error. At *Stil.* i. 53–4 he describes how Stilico, on an embassy to the Persian king, crossed both Tigris and Euphrates to get to Babylon. It has long been pointed out that only the Euphrates would have to be crossed by someone coming from Constantinople. Hence an error by Claudian. Yet it has not been asked why Stilico should have wanted to go to Babylon. All he would have found there, like Trajan before him, is a pile of ruins. He went, of course, to the Persian capital at Ctesiphon. Ctesiphon *is* on the far side of the Tigris. But it is also a cretic, barred from the hexameter line. So Claudian did what he does elsewhere (*III Cons.* 201, *IV Cons.* 653), and used the older name of Babylon. Babylon may never have been the capital of Persia, but it was one of the great cities of the Achaemenid Empire, and both geographically and phonetically close to Ctesiphon.

In fact, like most writers of his age, Claudian usually preferred to use archaic in preference to modern names—often names (especially in the case of foreign peoples) that no longer even had a reference, such as the Cimbri and Cherusci met above. Thus Herodotus' Massagetae course over the same pages as Vergil's painted Geloni—and the very real Huns. Naturally enough Claudian's information on foreign peoples is usually little more than ethnographical commonplaces, a practice so normal even for historians (Ammian, for example) that criticism for 'lack of original research' would be entirely inappropriate. Even so we find exceptions. While Gildo's Africans are depicted (after Sallust) as polygamous—in a country that had been Christian for centuries—by contrast we find an up-to-date and vividly detailed description of the Huns, clearly taken from Ammian[2] (an author one might

---

[1] The more pardonable when we recall Tacitus' complaint that already by his day the Elbe 'flumen inclutum et notum olim, nunc tantum auditur' (*Germ.* xli).
[2] See above, p. 333, n. 4.

not have expected to find on Claudian's bookshelf, and a warning not to underestimate the width of his reading).

What then should our judgement be on the extent and depth of Claudian's culture as a whole? Somewhere, probably, between the extremes of Gesner on the one hand (perhaps not quite the most learned man of his day) and Fargues on the other (for whom everything was reduced to rhetorical commonplaces). Claudian had read very widely, and not only in his own field, the poetry of Greece and Rome, but in historical, political, and rhetorical writings in both Latin and Greek. Of philosophy he knew little, and of geography, natural science, medicine, astronomy, etc., not much more (though certainly no less) than any well educated man of his day might be expected to have at his finger tips. The difference is that Claudian knew it all in two languages. A rare achievement in an age when Ammian, himself bilingual, felt it worth drawing special attention to anyone he had occasion to mention who could even speak both Latin and Greek, much less boast a familiarity with their literatures. In fact the only parallel to Claudian's knowledge of both literatures is Ammian himself. The obviousness of this one parallel tends to make us forget that there is no other. And if by sophisticated modern standards much of Claudian's culture outside the field of poetry might seem superficial, there can be no doubt that—and not by the standards of his own age alone—he more than lived up to the ancient ideal of *doctus poeta*.

XII

CLAUDIAN AND ROME

'Of all the writers of this time none shows a greater appreciation of Rome's history than Claudian. Although an Hellenic Alexandrian who turned to composition in Latin somewhat late, he has expressed the feeling of his age more adequately than any other. He often offends us by his extravagant flattery and by his attempts to give nobility through his polished verse to trifling and petty subjects; but when he deals with the grandeur of Rome he shows the true insight of the poet, is sincere and noble. Like Rutilius he understood the service which the city had been to the nations.' Though written sixty years ago,[1] these words may still be taken as reflecting the generally accepted view of Claudian's attitude to Rome.

They are not untrue, but they need to be qualified in a variety of ways. Claudian's attitude in this matter is considerably more complex than has so far been realized. Here, as always with Claudian, it is impossible (or unwise) to forget that he was not a free agent, expressing his own personal views. Moreover, this *communis opinio* has commended itself in the past more because it is congenial to modern admirers of Rome than because it is based on a dispassionate assessment of the evidence. People have been (understandably) loath to believe that Claudian really thought Stilico and (above all) Honorius the supermen he paints them. Yet they dearly want to believe that he did feel deeply, even uncritically, about Rome, that such loyalty could still be kindled in the breast of an Alexandrian Greek in the fifth century after Christ.

I hope to show that Claudian's attitude to the Empire of his day was in fact something far more interesting and perceptive

---

[1] C. H. Moore, 'Rome's heroic past in the poems of Claudian', *Class. Journal* (1910), 110.

than the blind admiration for which he has so often been alternately reproached and praised.

I

First, Claudian's attitude to the Roman past. We have seen in the last chapter that Claudian's actual knowledge of Roman history is much more limited than usually supposed: more particularly, it is conventional. For the most part it derives, not from histories proper, but from poets and rhetorical handbooks. Indeed, it is hardly an exaggeration to say that for Claudian the Republic was little more than an anthology of *exempla virtutis et vitii*.

There are times when he seems merely to be playing with his *exempla*. For example, Stilico had to cross the Addua to raise the Gothic blockade of Milan. The thought of the river at once suggested Horatius Cocles: not that Stilico had held a bridge, but he had crossed a river (though not alone, and not by swimming!). And once Horatius had been introduced, naturally Stilico must surpass his achievement; we pass from the merely inappropriate to the positively grotesque. Horatius swam the Tiber to escape Porsenna: Stilico the Addua to get to grips with Alaric:

> sed cum transnaret, Etruscis
> ille [Horatius] dabat tergum, Geticis hic pectora bellis
> (*VI Cons.* 489–90 f.).

The occasional effectiveness of these comparisons is often marred by too indiscriminate application. For example, Claudian has no hesitation or scruple about proclaiming that the two wholly insignificant teenage consuls of 395 excel the Decii and Metelli, the Scipios and even Camillus (*Prob.* 147 f.). And the effect of one well-chosen example is too often blunted by the addition of a whole series of remoter parallels. It is clear, in fact, that he is more concerned to demonstrate his skill at piling example on example than in selecting the one historically appropriate comparison. In *Eutr.* i he lists[1] every Roman hero he could think of

[1] Cf. p. 286.

who had held the consulate, all of them allegedly now horrified at Eutropius' pollution of the office. Not surprisingly it is a very long list: so long, indeed, that he absent-mindedly includes Brutus and Dentatus twice! This very piling up of parallels, which in many cases are not parallels at all, reveals a lack of any true historical perspective. One gets the impression that Ammian, for example, is always much more in control of his historical *exempla*. When he soberly records, at the very end of his vivid account of the disaster at Adrianople, 'nec ulla annalibus praeter Cannensem pugnam ita ad internecionem res legitur gesta' (xxxi. 13. 19), one feels (as one seldom does with Claudian) that he has considered and rejected other disasters too before concluding that Cannae alone was comparable.[1]

But caution is required here. Just because the use to which Claudian put Roman history was almost entirely rhetorical, it does not follow that he was therefore insincere. It was hardly possible for any writer of Claudian's day not to be rhetorical, and so not to use *exempla* in this way. Yet many must have been perfectly sincere. Consider some sensible remarks of E. J. Kenney on this use of *exempla*: 'Because without a very great effort of the historical imagination they have little or no emotional appeal to us—this in itself is a relatively recent phenomenon, born of the Romantic movement in literature—we tend to dismiss their employment as "frigid"; to Juvenal [the subject of Kenney's paper] it is clear that mention of Sejanus or Messalina, hackneyed as these particular examples may have been, was profoundly evocative and moving.'[2]

Need we doubt that in many cases at least the *exempla* which Claudian quotes had just such associations both for himself and for his audience? For example, after the defeat of Alaric, the greatest threat to Rome since Hannibal, it might well have seemed that Stilico deserved to be compared with Fabius

---

[1] For the *exemplum* in Ammian, see Chapter iv of C. P. T. Naudé's *Ammianus Marcellinus in die lig van die antieke Geskiedskrywing* (Diss. Leiden, 1955), with full bibliography. For some well-chosen *exempla* in Claudian, above p. 182.

[2] *Proc. Camb. Phil. Soc.* 188 (N.S. 8; 1962), 38: cf. id., *Latomus* xxii (1963), 718–19.

Maximus, Marcellus, and the younger Scipio (*Get.* 139 f.)—though here too the rhetorician's touch is betrayed by the characteristic embroidery that Stilico had excelled the achievements of all three combined: Stilico alone had delayed, conquered, and expelled the Goths! For an audience which honoured every name in the list of consuls in *Eutr.* i, their very accumulation in such a context may actually have heightened the emotional effect. And if Claudian lacked what we should call historical perspective, we may be sure that most of his listeners did too. The strongly moralizing cast of the Roman tradition made it all but impossible to view the Republic in any but a moral light.

The most quoted and (justly) admired passage in all Claudian is his eulogy on Rome at *Stil.* iii. 130–60. It is indeed perhaps the most eloquent extant statement of Rome's achievement in all ancient literature. Hence I make no apology for quoting it at length, for only thus can its character and power be fully appreciated:

> proxime dis consul, tantae qui prospicis urbi,
> qua nihil in terris complectitur altius aether,
> cuius nec spatium visus nec corda decorem
> nec laudem vox ulla capit; quae luce metalli
> aemula vicinis fastigia conserit astris:
> quae septem scopulis zonas imitatur Olympi;
> armorum legumque parens quae fundit in omnes
> imperium primique dedit cunabula iuris.
> haec est exiguis quae finibus orta tetendit
> in geminos axes parvaque a sede profecta
> dispersit cum sole manus. haec obvia fatis
> innumeras uno gereret cum tempore pugnas,
> Hispanas caperet, Siculas obsideret urbes
> et Gallum terris prosterneret, aequore Poenum,
> numquam succubuit damnis et territa nullo
> vulnere post Cannas maior Trebiamque fremebat
> et, cum iam premerent flammae murumque feriret
> hostis, in extremos aciem mittebat Iberos
> nec stetit Oceano remisque ingressa profundum
> vincendos alio quaesivit in orbe Britannos.

haec est in gremium victos quae sola recepit
humanumque genus communi nomine fovit
matris non dominae ritu, civesque vocavit
quos domuit, nexuque pio longinqua revinxit.
huius pacificis debemus moribus omnes,
quod veluti patriis regionibus utitur hospes,
quod sedem mutare licet; quod cernere Thulen
lusus, et horrendos quondam penetrare recessus;
quod bibimus passim Rhodanum, potamus Orontem:
quod cuncti gens una sumus. nec terminus usquam
Romanae dicionis erit. nam cetera regna
luxuries vitiis odiisque superbia vertit:
sic male sublimes fregit Spartanus Athenas
atque idem Thebis cecidit; sic Medus ademit
Assyrio Medoque tulit moderamina Perses;
subiecit Persen Macedo, cessurus et ipse
Romanis (*Stil.* iii. 130–66).

'Consul, all but peer of the gods, protector of a city greater than any that upon earth the air encompasseth, whose amplitude no eye can measure, whose beauty no imagination can picture, whose praise no voice can sound, who raises a golden head amid the neighbouring stars and with her seven hills imitates the seven regions of heaven, mother of arms and of law, who extends her sway o'er all the earth and was the earliest cradle of justice, this is the city which, sprung from humble beginnings, has stretched to either pole, and from one small place extended its power so as to become co-terminous with the sun's light. Open to the blows of fate while at one and the same time she fought a thousand battles, conquered Spain, laid siege to the cities of Sicily, subdued Gaul by land and Carthage by sea, never did she yield to her losses nor show fear at any blow, but rose to greater heights of courage after the disasters of Cannae and Trebia, and, while the enemy's fire threatened her, and her foe [sc. Hannibal] smote upon her walls, sent an army against the furthest Iberians. Nor did Ocean bar her way; launching upon the deep, she sought in another world for Britons to be vanquished. 'Tis she alone who has received the conquered into her bosom and like a mother, not an empress, protected the human race with a common name, summoning those whom she has defeated to share her citizenship and drawing together distant races with bonds of affection. To her rule of peace we owe it that the world is our home, that we can live where we please, and that to visit Thule and explore its once dreaded wilds is but a sport; thanks to her all and sundry may drink the waters of the Rhone and quaff Orontes' stream, thanks to her we are all one people. Nor will there ever be a limit to the empire of Rome, for luxury and its attendant vices, and pride with sequent hate have brought to ruin all kingdoms else. 'Twas thus that Sparta laid low the foolish pride of Athens but to fall herself a victim to Thebes; thus that the Mede deprived the Assyrian of empire and the Persian the Mede. Macedonia subdued Persia and was herself to yield to Rome' (Platnauer).

By any standards a superb piece of writing. But is it any more? Taken by itself, everything Claudian says here had been said before—many, many times. In 1918 W. Gernentz collected together under the title *Laudes Romae* everything in praise of Rome that he could find in Greek and Latin literature, classified according to the rules of the rhetoricians for the ἐγκώμιον πόλεως. Of this very passage of Claudian he specifically remarks, 'nullum fere versum non ex arte rhetorica petitum esse cognoscemus' (p. 47). In 1938 F. Christ performed a similar though more restricted service for the ancient poets (*Die römische Weltherrschaft in der antiken Dichtung*), illustrating at length what solid poetical precedent there was for most of what Claudian has to say. This need not affect our judgement of the passage as literature. Nor need we assume for a moment that Claudian was not sincere. Yet it must have some bearing on our assessment of Claudian's supposed 'understanding' of the Roman achievement. What the passage illustrates is, not so much a personal historical judgement of the Roman achievement, as Claudian's skill in assembling the *topoi* of a genre.[1]

A true assessment is hampered by the curious fact that there is only one formal panegyric on Rome extant for comparison—the (much overrated) Roman oration of Aelius Aristides. It may well be that Claudian had read Aristides,[2] though there must

---

[1] F. Paschoud's brief and rather unsatisfactory discussion of the 'rhétorique du patriotisme' (*Roma Aeterna* (1967), 14–15) fails to appreciate this point.

[2] The parallels are collected by O. Kehding, *De panegyricis Latinis capita quattuor* (1899), 44–7.

surely have been many other such works written in the four centuries before Claudian, which he will have known as well (or instead). What matters is that both employ precisely the same *topoi*. Rome the *communis patria*, the lawgiver, she who spares and welcomes the defeated as citizens, the bringer of peace and ease of communication, the Empire which surpasses all others.

This is not the place to discuss the sincerity (usually taken for granted) of Aristides' oration, but it may legitimately be observed (*a*) that Aristides did, after all, like Claudian, recite it in Rome in front of a Roman audience; and (*b*) that it was his practice to recite such panegyrics in every important city he visited—panegyrics which in some respects closely resemble the Roman oration. It is greatly to be regretted that we do not have any of the poems Claudian must have written on other cities for comparison with his eulogy of Rome.

For if the second century had been the age of the wandering sophists, the fourth and fifth were the age of the wandering poets, ready (for a suitable reward) to pen panegyrics or Πάτρια on each city they visited.[1] We have seen already that there are reasons for believing that Claudian had written Πάτρια of Berytus, Tarsus, Nicaea, and Anazarbus. Naturally, before arriving in Italy, he will have taken care to prepare himself to write on the Roman past, familiarizing himself with the appropriate *exempla* and traditions. We know of only one other Greek poet of the age who visited Rome: Claudian's fellow countryman Olympiodorus. It is interesting to note that the first time Olympiodorus mentioned Ravenna in his *History*, he appended a digression on its foundation; a colony of the Thessalians, he claimed, named after 'Romus', the brother of Romulus.[2] Possibly the abstract of a Πάτρια he had recited at court there during his Italian stay. The only surviving line of his poetry,

εἷς δόμος ἄστυ πέλει, πόλις ἄστεα μύρια κεύθει,

which he himself quoted in the course of a description of Rome

---

[1] Cf. *Historia* xiv (1965), 484–9.

[2] Zosimus v. 27, expressly citing Olympiodorus—and refuting him from Asinius Quadratus (cf. E. A. Thompson, *CQ* xxxviii (1944), 45, n. 3).

in his *History*, conforms to one of the standard *topoi* of the *Laudes Romae*.[1] Is it a fragment, perhaps, of a panegyric, like Claudian's, embodying a eulogy of Rome?

Compare too the fragmentary panegyric of Claudian's other fellow countryman, Pamprepius, on the Athenian grandee Theagenes.[2] The historical and mythological comparisons he employs are all Greek—and for the most part Athenian. It may be doubted whether Pamprepius would have employed all this Athenian colouring back in his native Panopolis—or in the poems he recited a few years later in Constantinople. Clearly he was adjusting his *exempla* to suit his Athenian patron and Athenian audience. Claudian would doubtless have done exactly the same in Athens.

It is worth emphasizing how unusual it would be if the enthusiasm for Rome and use of Roman *exempla* that so characterize his Latin poems had been present already in the Greek poems Claudian wrote before his arrival in the West. We have no extant body of Greek poetry on contemporary themes for purpose of comparison, but we do have numerous fragments from such works surviving on papyrus (all, like Claudian's, from Egypt), which present a remarkably uniform picture.

There is not a single allusion to Roman myth or history in any of them. The historical parallels are exclusively Greek—more precisely from classical Greek history. A fifth-century panegyric referring to a campaign against Persia compares its subject, not to Trajan or Julian, but to Themistocles—an inappropriate as well as a distant parallel, since Themistocles had repelled a Persian invasion, not invaded Persia.[3] All these poems are stuffed with Greek mythology. Indeed, one goes so far as to call Roman legionaries by the names of Homeric warriors.[4] A fragment of a panegyric on Theodosius II by another contemporary Egyptian

---

[1] Frag. 43 (*FHG* iv. 67*b*); cf. Gerentz, op. cit. p. 50.
[2] Heitsch XXXV. 4. 32 f. (Page 140). Compare too (e.g.) the opening of Julian's *Letter to the Athenians*.
[3] Page 141 (omitted—like much else (cf. West, *Gött. Gel. Anz.* 215 (1963), 164 f.)—from Heitsch i; but added in vol. ii as S. 10).
[4] Heitsch XXXII (Page 142).

poet, Cyrus, presumably recited in Constantinople, compares the Emperor successively to Achilles, Teucer, Agamemnon, Odysseus, and Nestor.[1] It is plain that the mythological poets of the day too, Quintus, Triphiodorus, Nonnus, Colluthus, Musaeus, and the lesser figures represented on papyrus fragments, drew their inspiration exclusively from Greek mythology.[2] Both Nonnus and Quintus, it is true, do refer to Rome. And Nonnus has been credited with an 'unbounded faith in the civilizing mission of the Roman Empire'.[3] But little can in fact be made of either of their references.

Quintus makes Calchas warn the victorious Greeks not to harm Aeneas, since he is fated:

Θύμβριν ἐπ' εὐρυρέεθρον ἀπὸ Ξάνθοιο μολόντα
τευξέμεν ἱερὸν ἄστυ καὶ ἐσσομένοισιν ἀγητόν (xiii. 337–8).

The temptation for anyone writing under the Empire to insert such a prophecy at this point must have been irresistible, whatever he thought of Rome. In a similar prophecy, Nonnus makes Venus forecast the future fame of the Berytus law school:

σκῆπτρον ὅλης Αὔγουστος ὅτε χθονὸς ἡνιοχεύσει,
'Ρώμη μὲν ζαθέῃ δωρήσεται Αὐσόνιος Ζεὺς
κοιρανίην, Βερόη δὲ χαρίζεται ἡνία θεσμῶν,
ὁππότε θωρηχθεῖσα φερεσσακέων ἐπὶ νηῶν
φύλοπιν ὑγρομόθοιο κατευνήσει Κλεοπάτρης (xli. 389–93).

'When Augustus shall hold the sceptre of the whole world, Ausonian Zeus will give sovereignty to holy Rome, but to Berytus he will grant the reins of law, when, protected by her shielded ships, she shall pacify the strife of Cleopatra who fights by sea.'

Is he saying any more than that the law school dated from soon after Actium? It is Berytus Nonnus is interested in, not Rome: Rome is only mentioned because it was, after all, Roman law for

---

[1] *Anth. Pal.* xv. 9 (discussed in *Early Byzantine Epigrams in the Greek Anthology*).
[2] Cf. too mythological exercises such as *Anth. Pal.* ix. 451 f. (cf. *BICS* xiv (1967), 58 f.).
[3] H. J. Rose, Loeb edition of Nonnus, i (1940), xvii.

which Berytus became famous. And if the prophecy looks forward to Augustus, it is at least interesting to observe that it looks forward too to his great rival Cleopatra, the last queen of Nonnus' native Egypt.

If we turn to the Greek prose writings of the age, the picture is much the same. Libanius knew not a word of Latin, and throughout his long life remained completely and ostentatiously ignorant of Roman literature, thought, and history.[1] In his *Antiochicus* (*Or.* xi) he skips straight from the Seleucids to his own day.[2] The culture of Julian, an Emperor, was almost entirely Greek: his knowledge of Roman history comes to him for the most part from Greek sources, Dionysius of Halicarnassus and Plutarch.[3] Procopius of Gaza confines his historical *exempla* entirely to the period which closed with the death of Alexander.

Even Aristides provides only a partial parallel to Claudian in this respect. For while the similarities between their eulogies on Rome are striking and obvious enough, it is no less instructive to draw attention to the differences. And there is one very striking difference. As far as Aristides is concerned the Republic might never have happened. He quotes numerous historical parallels—but they are all drawn from classical Greek history, the usual pattern for a Greek writer of his age. It is clear that he is not interested in the means whereby the Romans had won their Empire.[4] He merely talks in very general terms about the benefits of the Empire. Claudian, on the other hand, except for the one passage in *Stil.* iii, virtually ignores the Empire, and concerns himself almost entirely with the Republic.

[1] J. Palm, *Rom, Römertum und Imperium* (1959), admits and dismisses these gaps as no more than might have been expected of a Greek writer of the Empire, maintaining that Libanius was a Roman patriot. He seems to me to underestimate the significance of the fact that Greek writers of the Empire *were* so ignorant of Roman history and literature, and is in general content to equate absence of overt hostility to Rome with positive loyalty.

[2] Cf. (e.g.) A. F. Norman, *Rhein. Mus.* cvii (1964), 169.

[3] Cf. C. Lacombrade, *Pallas* ix (1960), 158–9; W. E. Kaegi, *Proc. Amer. Philos. Soc.* cviii (1964), 35 (with a list of Julian's references to Roman history); and J. F. Gilliam, *AJPh* lxxxviii (1967), 203–8.

[4] Though his familiarity with Polybius shows that he must have known.

The only other Greek writer of the age to manifest a similar interest in, knowledge of, and admiration for the Republic, is Ammian. And like Claudian, Ammian not only lived for a long time in the West (at least ten years). He wrote in the Latin language.

It would, of course, be putting the cart before the horse to suppose for a moment that Ammian wrote so enthusiastically about the Roman past just to please western audiences. After all, he did not have to come to Rome. He could easily have remained in his native Antioch and written his *History* in Greek. Indeed it is very strange that he did not. Ammian has recently been described as a 'typical Romanized Greek'.[1] Nothing could be further from the truth. Ammian is an unknown quantity, a mystery. No Latin history proper had been written since Tacitus, and since then the tradition of writing the history of Rome in Greek had become firmly established, with Appian, Dio, Herodian, Dexippus, and finally Ammian's contemporary, Eunapius. Even Dio, twice consul and senator, had written in Greek. Yet Ammian, a Greek, solemnly undertook the task, not attempted by any Latin writer for more than two and a half centuries, of continuing Tacitus up to his own day. A work conceived and executed on the grand scale,[2] the fruit of many years of research, reflection, and labour. It is a work which would not be 'typical' if it had been written by a Roman senator at the close of the fourth century, much less a Greek ex-soldier. Thus we must not simply assume that Ammian's attitude towards Rome can be regarded as typical of his Greek contemporaries.

The situation of Claudian, however, does provide a close parallel. It was remarked in Chapter I how many of the 'wandering poets' of the fourth and fifth centuries gravitated to Constantinople, in contrast to those of late Republican and early

---

[1] Palm, op. cit., p. 99. Without any explanation Palm omits not only Claudian (while including Ammian), but all Greek Imperial poetry from his scope.

[2] I am wholly convinced by H. T. Rowell's restatement of H. Michael's suggestion that what we possess is the second half of only one of two histories written by Ammian, both on a similar scale (*A.M.*, *Soldier Historian* (1964), chapter 1, and in *Mél. Carcopino* (1966), 839 f.).

Imperial times, when all roads had led to Rome. Yet it was to Rome that Claudian went. We know of only one other Greek poet who made the trip as late as this, Olympiodorus. Oddly enough Olympiodorus also wrote a contemporary history somewhat in the manner of Ammian's. Yet unlike both Ammian and Claudian, he wrote neither poetry nor history in Latin. Nor, so far as we know, did he stay in the West as long as either Ammian or Claudian. And to judge from remarks in his *History* and the one surviving line of his poetry, it was the material splendour of Rome with its huge senatorial palaces that impressed him most.

The length of Claudian's stay is easily understandable. Life at court had its attractions, and as Stilico's propagandist he was doubtless a man of consequence—and wealth. But the decision to try Rome before he knew what lay in store for him there, when the Greek world might have seemed his more natural oyster, suggests not merely that he had confidence in his command of the Latin language (in which, as we have seen, he may not have been unique), but also that he felt himself sufficiently at home in the Roman cultural and political tradition to be able to interpret it to the satisfaction of his future audience, the Roman aristocracy. This need not mean, of course (though it is often assumed), that Claudian abandoned his former loyalties, or even that they took second place to Rome. Alexandrian pagans of the fifth century looked back with pride not merely to their Ptolemaic origins as a Greek city and the cultural tradition of Alexandria, still the third city of the Empire, but further, to the Pharaonic hey-day of their country, a millennium before the rise of Rome.[1] But success in this must have required much more than the procedure followed by Pamprepius at Athens—the tactful insertion of a few references to local heroes and deities: it meant nothing less than the adoption of the traditional Roman values.

It is not just a coincidence that Ammian and Claudian both combined this love of Rome with a wide knowledge of Roman literature and the ability to add to it themselves. For it was through the literature that they discovered Rome. This is why the Rome

---

[1] Cf. J. Maspéro, *Bull. de l'Inst. franç. d'arch. orient. du Caire* xi (1914), 186 f.

they discovered was the Rome of the past. It was the standards and achievements of the heroic past that Ammian held dear. It is only too apparent that he was sadly disillusioned, indeed scandalized by the state of the Empire in his own day. Not only were the inhabitants of the eternal city itself (senate and people alike) no true heirs of what Claudian, with similar nostalgia, called 'ille diu miles populus'. Injustice and corruption were everywhere: and not only discipline, but the very will to serve had vanished from the army, the prop of the entire Empire.[1] Claudian, as we shall see, had no more illusions about the present state of affairs than Ammian. But it was by the standards of the past, learnt from books, that both judged the present.

And as soon as they had begun to write in Latin, they could not help but take over, not just the phraseology of their Latin models, but their Roman outlook and *exempla* too. Though he was still writing in the tradition of Greek contemporary poetry, by turning to Vergil, Lucan, and Juvenal instead of to the Greek poets as his stylistic models, Claudian could not help but look back with them to Republican Rome instead of mythological Greece.

It is not surprising that, despite the shortcomings of its inhabitants, the decaying magnificence of the eternal city was still able to cast its spell on both our Greeks—as it was to again a few years later on Olympiodorus. Ammian has left us an unforgettable picture of the effect on the Emperor Constantius II of his visit to Rome (xvi. 10). Brought up in the East, the Emperor was dumbfounded by the splendour of the buildings and the enthusiasm of the crowds. It may be conjectured that some of Ammian's own first impressions went into this picture. Of all the sights of Rome Ammian himself was impressed most by the forum of Trajan (xvi. 10. 5). It was here that Claudian's statue was erected in 400. A bronze statue erected in the forum by the senate and Emperors of Rome. Not bad for a Greek poet not yet 30. We

---

[1] For Ammian's attitude to the contemporary scene, see F. Paschoud, *Roma Aeterna* (1967), 40–69.

may well imagine that it was with genuine excitement and enthusiasm that he described the huge crowds that filled the slope between the Palatine and the Milvian bridge, hanging from the very rooftops to catch a glimpse of Honorius' entry into Rome in 404. So also when he exclaimed in 400:

> septem circumspice montes,
> qui solis radios auri fulgore lacessunt,
> indutosque arcus spoliis aequataque templa
> nubibus, et quidquid tanti struxere triumphi
> (*Stil*. iii. 65 f.).

All this we may readily concede. But it is a very different matter to claim that some such natural and genuine admiration blinded Claudian to the comparative insignificance of Rome in the late fourth century, long since superseded by Trier, Milan, and finally Ravenna as the administrative capital of the West. Yet many scholars have taken literally such outbursts as *VI Cons*. 39 f.:[1]

> non alium certe decuit rectoribus orbis
> esse Larem, nulloque magis se colle potestas
> aestimat, et summi sentit fastigia iuris.

'It is astonishing', one leading historian has recently remarked, 'that anyone could entertain such illusions twenty years after Adrianople and only ten before the sack of Rome by the Goths.' And, again, that Claudian 'has succumbed to the drug of his own poetry and eloquence'.[2]

Even *a priori* this is most unlikely. As the confidant and propagandist of Stilico Claudian must have known better than most that the centre of power and decision lay, not with Rome and its senate, but wherever Stilico happened to be. That he was fully aware that the senate was a mere cipher is amply and decisively illustrated by his attitude to its role in the Gildonic war. In *Gild.*, written at the time and recited in Milan, Claudian ignores completely the part played by the senate in the declaration of war on Gildo. Indeed he represents the declaration as a joint decision of

---

[1] e.g. Laqueur, *Probleme der Spätantike* (1930), 19 f.; Wes, *Ende des Kaisertums* (1967), 20–1.

[2] J. Vogt, *The Decline of Rome* (1967), 189, 190.

Honorius and Stilico, and refers slightingly to the senate. Yet two years later he devoted disproportionate space and enormous emphasis to the role of the senate—in a poem recited in Rome.[1] His purpose was to suggest, by emphasizing this one example, that Stilico always deferred to the senate. In fact, of course, it is clear from the way Claudian labours this example, and from his obvious embarrassment at Stilico's refusal to allow the senate even to debate recognition of Eutropius' consulate,[2] that this was the only example he could quote. Yet Romano can write of Claudian's 'sogno politico di una diarchia tra senato e impero'.[3] Naturally this is what Claudian wanted the senators to believe—though it may be doubted whether many even of them were sufficiently simple-minded to do so.

Much has been made of Claudian's insistence in *Get.* and *VI Cons.* on the paramount importance of the safety of Rome during the Gothic invasion. Yet again, as explained in Chapter VII, one of Claudian's primary purposes in both *Get.* and *VI Cons.* was to excuse Stilico's reluctance to engage Alaric again after Pollentia on the ground that Stilico was playing the Fabius Maximus to protect Rome. To this end it was essential that he should lay great stress on the necessity of saving Rome, so as to convince the Roman audience in front of which he recited both poems that the safety of Rome was more important than the defeat of the Goths. This does not mean that we can discount what Claudian says: but it would certainly be naïve to assume that he was simply stating his personal view of the matter.

The feature about Claudian's attitude to Rome which has been most misunderstood is the fact that what bulks largest in his poems is, not the Romans (past or present), nor even the city of Rome, but the symbolic figure of Roma personified. Roma first appears in literature during the early Augustan period,[4] a mere shadow of what she was to become in later centuries. As the reality of Roman power dwindled, so Roma grows in stature in

---

[1] See pp. 231 f.   [2] See p. 235.   [3] p. 134.
[4] Cf. U. Knoche, 'Die Augusteische Ausprägung der Dea Roma', *Gymnasium* lix (1952), 324–49.

the literature of Rome. It may be, indeed, that Roma as she appears in Claudian is to some extent Claudian's own creation. Certainly it is under the influence of Claudian[1] that she bulks so large in the Christian Prudentius and pagan Rutilius alike, and even larger in Sidonius, who straddles both worlds. But was she anything more than a literary creation to Claudian? Many think so. 'An actual divine power, more real than the Gods of Olympus', according to E. R. Curtius.[2] For F. Paschoud, most recently, Rome 'est pour Claudien une réalité si vivante que sans cesse il la personifie'.[3] But is she really more of a reality than the Africa he depicts just as vividly and pathetically in *Gild.*, or the Aurora of *Eutr.* ii? Or the cluster of provinces, Spain, Gaul, Britain, and Italy, who beg Roma to persuade Stilico to take the *fasces* for 400 in *Stil.* ii? We have seen already that, new as Claudian's Roma may be to Latin poetry, she is no more than the Roma of contemporary artistic representations transferred to another medium.[4] Group personifications of provinces too, similarly represented as female figures, are common in the art of the period —the best known example is the painted insignia of the *Notitia Dignitatum*, copied ultimately from a work compiled within a decade or so of Claudian's death.[5] Roma surrounded by her sister provinces is no more than *prima inter pares*. She appears so frequently in Claudian, not because he was obsessed with her or worshipped her, but rather because she was dramatically the most appropriate figure to exhort Stilico to save the East from Eutropius or Africa from Gildo or (above all) to officiate in a consular panegyric.

To think differently is not merely to misunderstand Claudian's

---

[1] A. Marsili's 'Roma nella poesia di Claudiano', *Antiquitas* 1946, 3–24, is of little value. More useful (though mainly concerned with Rutilius) is Knoche's paper in *Symbol. Colon. J. Kroll.* (1949), 143 f.

[2] *European Literature,* 104.

[3] *Roma Aeterna*, 152.   [4] See pp. 274 f.

[5] There are sketches of some of the illustrations in the Munich MS. in the editions of Böcking and Seeck, and those in the Paris MS. were published in 1911 by O. Omont. Those in the Oxford MS. (the best) are mostly still unpublished: cf. E. A. Thompson, *Roman Reformer and Inventor* (1952), 15–18 (on the date of the *Notitia*, cf. now Jones, *LRE* iii. 344 f.).

artistic technique and method of composition (p. 277). It is to be misled by the splendour and frequency of Roma's appearance in Claudian's poems into ignoring the insignificance of the actual role she plays therein. She is for Claudian the personification of the city of Rome, no more and no less.[1] And how faithfully she mirrors the sorry state of Rome in the late fourth century, a city of memories, accorded the honour of a visit by its Emperor but three times in 100 years! Claudian's Roma, like the city, is reduced to starvation and humiliation by Gildo's stoppage of the corn supply and has to beg Jupiter for his aid. She cannot even appoint her own consuls: all she can do is submit her requests to Theodosius or Honorius. She even has to beg Honorius to visit her in 404, rehearsing her disappointment that he had gone back on an earlier decision to come in 400. A fine simile suggestively compares her preparations for the visit to a mother anxiously getting her daughter ready when a suitor is expected. Time was when such anxiety would not have been necessary. Often as Roma appears in the pages of Claudian, it is always as a suppliant, like the city she represents deserving respect for her age and past achievements, but no longer able to take independent action.

In fact it is precisely because Roma *was* only a personification that she was able to serve as one of those cultural bridges which in an intangible and yet very real way contributed to the surprisingly rapid and complete Christianization of the pagan aristocracy of Rome. The appeal of the aged Roma in *Gild.* is almost certainly inspired directly by the appeal of a similarly aged Roma in Symmachus' famous third *Relatio*, pleading for the relaxation of Gratian's anti-pagan laws. For this and other reasons it is clear that Claudian's Roma is the personification of a basically pagan city. Yet Roma herself is (so to speak) religiously neutral. Prudentius can without absurdity use the same motif of the aged Roma—only rejuvenated[2] this time by Christianity. And by the

[1] Rutilius' picture of Roma is, in Knoche's formulation (*Symbol. Colon. J. Kroll*, 162), 'der Ausdruck eines keineswegs religiösen, sondern eines humanistischen Glaubens'.

[2] For some interesting remarks on this rejuvenation motif, cf. Curtius, *European Literature*, 104—underestimating, however, the antiquity of the theme of the

beginning of the fifth century we find many unmistakably Christian Romas on coins, medallions, and diptychs—most notably on the mosaics on the triumphal arch of the church of Santa Maria Maggiore in Rome.[1] The new Christians, embracing Christ mainly perhaps because he now seemed better able than Jupiter to ensure the survival of a minimum of *Romanitas* in a dangerous age,[2] could do so with a better will if Roma came across with them.

Claudian sings the praises of Rome loud and long. But he has some very different things to say about Constantinople and the East in general. These passages have always been regarded as important evidence of the growing gulf between East and West, in particular of the jealousy of the old Rome for the new. When Claudian writes contemptuously of the 'Byzantinos proceres Graiosque Quirites' (*Eutr.* ii. 136) who are 'Romam contemnere sueti' (ib. 339), he is held to be the spokesman of the senate of old Rome, resentful of the upstart senate of Constantinople.[3] That such a gulf, that such jealousy was coming into being at this period is possible. In addition to the political division of the Empire created by the death of Theodosius, the cultural and especially linguistic differences were growing wider.[4] But it would be

rebirth of Rome. In addition to the common ROMA RENASCENS coin type, cf. Martial, v. 7. 3, 'taliter exuta est veterem nova Roma senectam', and Florus, *praef.* 8, 'sub Traiano principe . . . senectus imperii quasi reddita iuventute revirescit'; and cf. too R. MacMullen, *Enemies of the Roman Order* (1967), 333. For a grey-haired Roma who stays that way, Lucan, i. 186 f.

[1] J. M. C. Toynbee, *JRS* xxxvii (1947), 135 f. and in *Studies . . . D. M. Robinson* ii (1953), 261 f.

[2] Cf. P. R. L. Brown, 'Aspects of the Christianisation of the Roman Aristocracy', *JRS* li (1961), 11, and 'Pelagius and his supporters', *JTS* N.S. xix (1968), 95 f.

[3] Fargues, p. 139. The subtitle of Marsili's article quoted on p. 364, n. 1 is 'Romanità occidentale contrapposta a quella orientale'. Most recently (and emphatically), Wes, *Ende des Kaisertums* (1967), 16 f.; Paschoud, *Roma Aeterna* (1967), 147 f. On the other hand I can see nothing in favour of Mazzarino's assertion (pp. 242–4) that the Roman senate identified itself with the eastern senate: 'Il senato [romano] si opponeva alla politica "estera", ossia antibizantina, di Stilicone: ed era opposizione tacita [i.e. unsupported by evidence], ma non per ciò meno violenta e minacciosa.'

[4] It is the thesis of Demougeot's *De l'unité à la division* as a whole that the break

most unwise to use Claudian as evidence for any such hypothesis.

First, it should not be forgotten that Claudian was himself an
easterner, and had in all probability spent all his life before 394
in the eastern provinces of the Empire. Thus it is *a priori* not
a little unlikely that after his brief stay in Italy (of which only
a matter of months was spent in Rome itself) Claudian should
suddenly have turned from an easterner into a westerner hating
the East. Moreover, it has, I hope, been amply shown already in
the preceding pages that Claudian cannot be regarded as in any
sense a spokesman of the Roman senate. He was the spokesman of
Stilico alone: and Stilico was not only an easterner too himself,
as Claudian openly admits on more than one occasion (*Ruf.* ii.
95 f., *Eutr.* ii. 534 f.), but his one overriding political goal was to
control the East. Nor will it do to say that Claudian's hostility
to the East was a desperate attempt to cover up his provincial
origin by being more Roman than the Romans.[1] Claudian was
proud of being an Alexandrian, as well he might be (*c.m.*
xxii).

Second, and more important, it has not been noticed that Claudian's anti-eastern comments are confined to *Eutr.* ii and *Stil.* i–iii
—that is to say to the last quarter of 399. They are absent even
from *Eutr.* i. Nor are there any traces in *Ruf.*, like *Eutr.* a two-
book invective on an eastern minister, and thus offering ample
opportunity for a display of anti-eastern sentiment in general.
The answer is very simple.

As explained in Chapter VI, in *Eutr.* i Claudian's venom was
aimed at Eutropius alone: his purpose was to discredit Eutropius,
in the hope that after he had gone normal relations between
East and West might be resumed. It was not till it became apparent
that Eutropius' fall had made no difference to eastern hostility to
Stilico that the East as a whole came in for the same treatment.
Nor was this mere senseless spite, but (as usual) calculated policy.

between East and West became irrevocable precisely during the Stiliconian
period.
[1] As suggested in a different context by Levy, in *TAPhA* lxxix (1948), 91.

The idea was to represent the East as being in the hands of irresponsible criminals who would lead it to disaster—unless Stilico intervened to set things straight again. Hence the appeal to Stilico from the East personified, with which *Eutr.* ii closes.

This, then, is why Claudian does not attack the East in his earlier poems. Nor is this merely an argument from silence. At *Ruf.* ii. 54–5 Constantinople is referred to in perfectly neutral terms as

> urbs etiam, magnae quae dicitur aemula Romae
> et Calchedonias contra despectat harenas.

There is no suggestion here that Constantinople had no right to the title 'aemula Romae'.[1] Compare also *Gild.* 60 f., where Roma describes how after the foundation of Constantinople she was restricted to the African corn harvest, while Egyptian corn went to feed Constantinople. Claudian is at pains to paint Roma's plight in the most pitiful colours. Yet all he says is

> cum subiit par Roma mihi divisaque sumpsit
> aequales Aurora togas, Aegyptia rura
> in partem cessere novae [sc. Romae].

Here was a perfect opening for an attack on Constantinople, had Claudian wished it. Instead he does no more than state the bare facts, in a remarkably dispassionate manner under the circumstances. More generally, throughout the earlier poems Claudian insists on the unity and concord between East and West—even when relations were in fact strained almost to breaking point.

It has been argued that Claudian deliberately omitted from *IV Cons.* the statutory section on Honorius' natal city, Constantinople, because of his dislike of that city.[2] It is true that there is no formal section on the natal city inside the section on γένος, as prescribed by the rules of the rhetoricians.[3] Yet Claudian does

---

[1] Paschoud, *Roma Aeterna*, 147, mistakenly alleges that Claudian is writing here 'avec mépris'.

[2] L. B. Struthers, *Harvard Studies* xxx (1919), 61–2.

[3] On the 'rules' and Claudian's practice in other poems, cf. Struthers, op. cit. 60–7.

not avoid the topic altogether. He has merely postponed it to a little later in the poem. Cf. 127 f.:

> Hispania patrem [sc. Theodosium]
> auriferis eduxit aquis, te gaudet alumno
> Bosphorus. Hesperio de limine surgit origo,
> sed nutrix Aurora tibi; pro pignore tanto
> certatur, geminus civem te vindicat axis.

Not an extended panegyric, but Claudian may have felt that this would not be suitable in front of a western audience (this is no doubt why he plays up Honorius' ultimate Spanish derivation). Possibly also he felt that a positive eulogy would be out of place under the present political situation. But there is certainly no trace of hostility, nor is there in the reference to Honorius' 'propria nutritor Bosphorus arce' at *VI Cons.* 81. Hostility to the East is confined to *Eutr.* ii and *Stil.*, where it reflects neither Claudian's own attitude, nor even that of his western contemporaries. It was designed to foster or create such an attitude for a very precise contemporary purpose.

II

It has often been alleged that Claudian only had eyes for the glorious Roman past, that he was blind to the weaknesses and dangers which assailed the Empire in his own day. And it is true that whenever things take a turn for the better, Claudian has no hesitation in proclaiming the return of the Golden Age:

> en aurea nascitur aetas, | en proles antiqua redit (*Ruf.* i. 45–6).

But these are empty clichés. Claudian was deceiving no one— least of all himself.[1] The words with which Stilico is made to exhort his men before Pollentia make it clear that Claudian was well aware that he lived in an age of crisis and decline:

---

[1] And certainly not the social-revolutionary aspirations of the masses, as supposed by I. Hahn, 'Die soziale Utopie der Spätantike', *Wiss. Zeitschr. der Martin-Luther-Universität* xi (1962), 1358. Such passages are exaggerated too by V. Stegemann, *Astrologie und Universalgeschichte* (1930), 245–6.

Romanum *reparate* decus molemque labantis
imperii fulcite umeris (*Get.* 571–2).

Compare too *Stil.* ii. 204–5:

solo poterit Stilicone medente
crescere Romanum vulnus tectura cicatrix.

But let us take a specific danger. By far the most important problem which faced the Roman world in Claudian's day was barbarization. It has long been a commonplace that writers like Claudian, Symmachus, and Rutilius Namatianus betray no awareness of the profound change in the equilibrium of the Empire that the inflow of barbarians was bringing about. With Symmachus and Rutilius we are not concerned here: though it may be doubted whether the traditional view of at any rate Rutilius will stand up to close scrutiny.[1] It is certainly not true of Claudian.

In an important paper H. L. Levy has argued that Claudian deliberately worked an 'anti-barbarian ethos' into his panegyrics and invectives.[2] This is an oversimplification and a misleading half-truth.

It is true (though natural and predictable enough) that, like other writers of his day, Claudian regarded barbarians as inferior to Romans.[3] It would indeed be astonishing if he had not. Yet for one who has as much to say as Claudian about the glories of Rome, there are in fact remarkably few traces of anything that

---

[1] On Rutilius, see *JRS* lvii (1967), 38: Symmachus' sharpest critic yet is Paschoud, *Roma Aeterna*, 105 f. For a more sympathetic interpretation, see Peter Brown, *JTS* N.S. xix (1968), 96 f.

[2] *TAPhA* lxxxix (1958), 345. For a more sophisticated approach, see now Paschoud, op. cit. 138–44—though his conclusions do not follow from the evidence he collects. Since then P. G. Christiansen, *TAPhA* xcvii (1966), 52 f., has pointed out that barbarians are represented in a more fearsome light in *Get.* than in any other poem: but this is sufficiently explained by the greater proximity of the Gothic danger in 402. Christiansen's study interestingly illustrates the imagery Claudian used to describe the barbarians, but makes insufficient allowance for the influence of the panegyrical tradition and the differing political contexts of the various poems.

[3] For this attitude, common since the late third century, cf. Sherwin-White, *Roman Citizenship*, 282 f. On the whole issue, see now J. Vogt, *Kulturwelt und Barbaren — Zum Menschheitsbild der spätantiken Gesellschaft* (Abh. Mainz, 1967).

might fairly be described as an anti-barbarian ethos. There is nothing, for example, to compare with the anti-barbarian tirades of Ammian.[1] Most of the examples quoted by Levy are either unconvincing or trivial. For example, it is implausible to suggest that Claudian's sole motive for not naming Gainas in *Ruf.* was that he was a barbarian: much deeper and weightier factors than this were involved.[2] And the dismissal of the Gothic *optimates* as 'pellita Getarum | curia' (*Get.* 481–2) is not of any real significance. The important examples are few—and tendentious.

At *Gild.* 231–2 Arcadius is made to say, when addressing his father Theodosius, 'da tangere dextram | qua gentes cecidere ferae.' Now it is indeed possible to produce examples of barbarians falling to the sword of Theodosius. But beyond doubt his chief contribution to the settlement of the barbarian question lay, not in victories on the field, but in peaceful negotiations—entailing the transfer of much gold from the Imperial treasury to the pockets of Gothic *optimates*.[3] He promoted men of barbarian stock, like Bauto, Arbogast, and Stilico himself to high commands, and came to depend heavily on German auxiliaries in the ranks: a policy deeply resented by all classes of the citizen population alike.[4] Orosius writes of Theodosius' 'benignitas' to the barbarians,[5] and Jordanes calls him 'amator pacis generisque Gothorum'.[6] Naturally Claudian cannot praise Theodosius' 'benignitas' to the Arian Goths in front of the fanatically barbarophobe Catholic audiences of Milan. So instead he briefly evokes some vague victories over 'ferae gentes' without being too implausibly specific. At *IV Cons.* 623–36 Claudian attributes to Theodosius himself a victory over some Ostrogoths, which was in fact won by one of his generals, Promotus.[7] Theodosius' own contribution was to

---

[1] For an anthology of texts and modern views on Ammian's attitude to barbarians, see A. Demandt, *Zeitkritik . . . Ammians* (1965), 30 f., with my comments in *CR* N.S. xvii (1967), 61. Cf. also H. T. Rowell, *A.M., Soldier-Historian* (1964), 38 f.

[2] Levy, p. 344: see above, pp. 146 f.

[3] E. A. Thompson, *Historia* xii (1963), 107 f.

[4] See M. Pavan, *La politica gotica di Teodosio nella pubblicista del suo tempo* (1964), with the reservations of J. F. Matthews in *JRS* lvi (1966), 245–6.

[5] *Adv. pag.* vii. 34. 7.   [6] *Get.* 146.   [7] Cf. Zosimus iv. 35. 1.

settle the survivors peaceably in Phrygia[1]—with disastrous consequences, since it was they who rose in rebellion under Tribigild
in 399. Particularly instructive is the eloquent section on Theodosius at *IV Cons.* 48–62:

'he alone when asked to rule was worthy to do so. For when unrest at
home drove barbarian hordes over unhappy Rhodope and the now
deserted north had poured its tribes in wild confusion across our borders,
when all the banks of Danube poured forth battles and broad Mysia
rang beneath the chariots of the Getae, when flaxen-haired hordes
covered the plains of Thrace, and amid this universal ruin all was either
prostrate or tottering to its fall, one man alone withstood the tide of
disaster, quenched the flames, restored to the husbandmen their fields
and snatched the cities from the very jaws of destruction. No shadow of
Rome's name had survived had not thy sire borne up the tottering
mass, succoured the storm-tossed bark and with sure hand averted
universal shipwreck (Platnauer).'

A fine tribute to Theodosius' achievement. But anyone who takes
the trouble to re-read the passage will see that Claudian nowhere
actually says how these obviously satisfactory results were obtained. He neither invents nor suppresses: he simply remains conveniently vague.

The last example is the Bastarnae campaign, already discussed
in an earlier chapter (pp. 71 f.). It will be remembered that,
according to Claudian, Rufinus tricked Theodosius into making
a treaty with the Bastarnae instead of exterminating them in
battle. In reality Theodosius was probably well satisfied with his
treaty. And, naturally enough, Claudian loses no opportunity to
extol the numerous supposed victories, amid rivers of Gothic
blood, won by Stilico as regent. There can be no doubt that
Claudian was anxious to represent both Stilico and Theodosius
as hammers of the barbarians—and that he was prepared to twist
the recalcitrant facts a little to do so.

Yet there are just as many passages in which Claudian positively

---

[1] Seeck, *Gesch. d. Untergangs* v (1913), 316, 563, and cf. Stein, *Bas-Empire* i
(1959), 521, n. 17.

praises both Stilico and Theodosius for using barbarians in their armies. Cf. *IV Cons.* 484 f.:

> obvia quid mirum vinci, cum barbarus ultro
> iam cupiat servire tibi [sc. Honorio]? tua Sarmata discors
> sacramenta petit; proiecta pelle Gelonus
> militat; in Latios ritus transistis, Alani.

Eutr. i. 382–3:

> bellorum alios [sc. barbaros] transcribit [sc. Honorius] in usus,
> militet ut nostris detonsa Sygambria signis.

At *Gild.* 242 f. Theodosius is made to exclaim, referring to his military requirements for the war against Eugenius:

> quis procul Armenius, vel quis Maeotide ripa
> rex ignotus agit qui me non iuvit euntem
> auxilio? *fovere Getae*, venere Geloni.

Claudian writes for all the world as though the advantages of enrolling all these native tribesmen in the Roman armies were too self-evident to require mention, still less justification. Yet his confident manner should not blind us to the fact that this was the very policy which was striking fear into the hearts of so many of Claudian's contemporaries; and, it must frankly be admitted, not without some justification. The Goths who 'fovere' Theodosius against Eugenius rebelled almost at once after the campaign, seized the Balkans, eluded all Stilico's attempts to destroy them, and eventually forced Eutropius to legitimize their *de facto* rule of a large portion of the Empire. The Ostrogoths settled in Phrygia soon rebelled against the eastern government. In *IV Cons.* 223 f. Claudian remarks with satisfaction that the Alans had 'crossed over' to serve the Romans. Four years later (*Get.* 581 f.) he was forced to admit that their indiscipline ruined Stilico's plans at Verona:

> ipsum te caperet letoque, Alarice, dedisset
> ni calor incauti male festinatus Alani
> dispositum turbasset opus.

Claudian cannot have been unaware of the unpopularity of this policy:[1] indeed it can be shown that he was not. Nevertheless he writes as though it was the obvious—and certainly a praiseworthy—course of action.

In fact there is no inconsistency between these two seemingly contradictory themes. The answer is that in this as in so many other matters Claudian was not just expressing his own view. He was writing to a brief. He knew that in the eyes of most of his listeners the only good barbarian was a dead one. So naturally he makes the most of all barbarian defeats. On the other hand there was no getting away from the hard fact that, like Theodosius before him, Stilico did make extensive use of barbarians in his own armies. So Claudian had to make the best of it. Instead of admitting that Stilico had to pay his barbarians large sums of money in order to get them to fight for him, he pretends that they implore Honorius to allow them to fight for Rome ('cum barbarus ultro | iam cupiat servire tibi'). And he is most careful to avoid giving the impression that Stilico is a genuine barbarophile. He makes it clear that Stilico was merely employing the age-old Roman policy of setting one lot of barbarians against another to get rid of both. If the Roman legions are tiring, he alleges, Stilico cunningly throws his barbarian auxiliaries into the fray, quite unconcerned whether they kill the enemy or the enemy kills them: either way is gain to Rome!

> fesso si deficit agmine miles
> utitur auxiliis damni securus, et astu
> debilitat saevum cognatis viribus Histrum [i.e. the Goths]
> et duplici lucro committens proelia vertit
> in se barbariem nobis [to our benefit] utrimque cadentem.[2]

Now Stilico did not enlist barbarians because he preferred them to citizens. He was only forced to turn to barbarians, because he could not get enough citizens. There were, of course, the many thousands of tenants on the huge senatorial estates. But the senators

---

[1] The unpopularity of the Alans enrolled by Gratian was remarked on by Zosimus (Eunapius) iv. 35. [2] *VI Cons.* 218 f.

refused to release them. Stilico could perhaps have forced them, but instead he chose to make the attempt—vain as it happened—to win them over. And without either these or the resources of Illyricum at his disposal, barbarians were the only alternative. This dilemma of Stilico's is unmistakably (if perhaps unconsciously) reflected in Claudian. So far from being blind to the ills and dangers of the present, it is clear that Claudian was only too well aware of this particular danger.

We have seen already in Chapter VII that Claudian recurs again and again to the theme of disloyalty and indiscipline among Stilico's troops. Sometimes he laments it, sometimes he denies it, sometimes he praises Stilico for suppressing it. The very variety of his pronouncements only serves to underline his preoccupation with the problem. He recurs no less frequently—and no less significantly—to the theme of Stilico's recruiting difficulties.

He knows, for example, and deems it worthy of mention, that after the return of the eastern army to the East in 395, Stilico had to spend 396 building up his army with barbarians (*IV Cons.* 439 f., *Stil.* i. 188 f.) before daring to face Alaric again (naturally Claudian does not put it quite like this). During the Gildonic crisis he knew that one of Stilico's primary duties had been 'veteres firmare cohortes, | explorare novas'[1] (*Stil.* i. 306–7). Even at a time of comparative peace, January 399, he describes Honorius and Stilico enrolling Germans 'bellorum . . . in usus' (*Eutr.* i. 382). On the news of Alaric's invasion of Italy late in 401, Claudian recounts in detail how Stilico was forced to make for Raetia straight away to enlist federates before taking any steps to halt the Gothic advance. Indeed, he furnishes several further most interesting details about this particular trip.

On his arrival there Stilico found the barbarians he had been planning to use (presumably the Alans) on the point of going over to the Goths. He recalled them to their allegiance and enrolled them at their own entreaty (or so Claudian implausibly alleges)— being careful, however, to include no more than an 'appropriate'

---

[1] *Explorare* means here, as several times in Claudian (cf. *CQ* N.S. xviii (1968), 393), 'test', 'try out', not 'enroll' (Platnauer).

(*congruus*) number, neither a burden to Italy nor an object of
fear to their own general:

> hoc monitu [sc. Stilico] pariter nascentia bella repressit
> et bello quaesivit opes, legitque precantes
> auxilio, mensus numerum qui congruus esset
> nec gravis Italiae formidandusve regenti (*Get.* 400–3).

Why should Claudian have felt it necessary to stress that Stilico's
new barbarian recruits would *not* cause trouble in Italy, and
would *not* cause anxiety to their own general—unless he had
reason to believe that his audience was afraid that they would
(or did) do both? The implication is that both these things had
happened in the past and might be expected to happen again.
And it will be remembered that in the event the Alans did prove
unreliable at both Pollentia and Verona. Once more, as so often,
Claudian is defending Stilico against criticism: on this occasion
against the criticism that he had enlisted more barbarians than
either Italy could support or he personally could control.

Fargues' claim that Claudian was ignorant of 'les faits d'un
ordre social et économique qui expliciaient la faiblesse de l'empire'
may be an inaccurate as well as an inappropriate verdict. He was
certainly not ignorant of the military weakness of the western
Empire. In addition to the passages already quoted note also
Get. 105–6, where he writes, referring back to the good old days
of the Republic:

> cum . . . *proprio* florerent milite patres.

Claudian knew well enough that Rome could no longer rely on
the Romans for her salvation. Most striking of all from this point
of view is *Get.* 463 f. Stilico has just relieved Milan, and the inhabitants rush out to greet him and his army:

> portas secura per omnes
> turba salutatis effunditur obvia signis.
> non iam *dilectus miseri* nec falce per agros
> deposita iaculum vibrans ignobile messor
> nec temptat clipeum proiectis sumere rastris
> Bellona ridente Ceres . . .

Conscription (*dilectus*) is something wretched (*miser*). It can be represented as a self-evident benefit that the farmer no longer needs to exchange his sickle for the spear. What an acknowledgement that the yeoman-soldier of better times was no more! And not only this. Claudian goes on to describe the troops Stilico has brought with him as 'tot lumina pubis' (ib. 472). Now these troops, as we have seen already, were hastily levied barbarians, in all probability the untrustworthy Alans. Not only does Claudian reveal himself well aware of the unpopularity and inefficiency of conscription of citizens.[1] He cleverly trades on the hostility of the landowners among his audience to conscription (at least to conscription of their own tenants) in order to place Stilico's recruitment of barbarians in a favourable light. At least it put an end to conscription.

Whether or not Claudian himself really approved of filling the gap left by citizens with barbarians, especially with barbarians fighting, like the Goths at the Frigidus or the Alans at Pollentia, under their own chieftains, is impossible to say. As a cultivated easterner and traditionalist he may have deplored it. As an intelligent and realistic observer of the political scene he may have acknowledged its expediency. But as the propagandist of Stilico he was bound publicly to defend it.

III

Since Claudian spent much of his stay in Italy at court, and composed no fewer than three panegyrics on Honorius, naturally enough he has much to say about the position and role of the Emperor.

Here again extravagant claims have been made. According to Mazzarino,[2] Claudian advocated nothing less than a retreat from Diocletianic absolutism to constitutional monarchy. It would indeed be of no small interest and importance if a panegyrist of the later Empire had advanced such far-reaching views. In fact

---

[1] Cf. on this Jones, *LRE* ii. 618.   [2] pp. 232 f.

we shall see good reason to doubt it. But Claudian's portrait of Honorius contains much of interest nevertheless.

At *IV Cons.* 46 f. Claudian writes that Theodosius became Emperor 'non generis dono, non ambitione potitus'. On the contrary, 'ultro se purpura supplex | obtulit, et solus meruit regnare rogatus.' It has also been pointed out that Claudian approves of Emperors who were adopted, Trajan, Marcus, and Pius, while he clearly disapproved of the hereditary dynasty of the Julio-Claudians. Hence it has been inferred that Claudian approved of the adoptive and disapproved of the hereditary principle.[1] Yet it is now becoming generally agreed that the 'adoptive principle' never existed as a political doctrine,[2] and since Claudian nowhere says that it was because of the means whereby they ascended the throne that he approved or disapproved of these Emperors, there is no evidence here either for the existence of the doctrine or for Claudian's adherence thereto. As we have seen in an earlier chapter, Claudian used their names simply because they were the traditional good and bad Emperors. As for Claudian's glorification of Theodosius' accession, is it really surprising that the panegyrist of an Emperor who was elected should have praised the elective principle? When Claudian comes to the praises of Honorius, on the other hand, in the very same poem (122–7), he extols the fact that Honorius had succeeded to his father and never suffered the ignominy of being a mere private citizen!

> nasceris aequaeva cum maiestate creatus
> nullaque privatae passus *contagia* sortis.
> . . . patrio felix adolescis in ostro.

What better proof could there be that the panegyrists' 'opinions' on this subject were conditioned entirely by the way the reigning Emperor happened to have won his throne? Indeed, the very fact that Claudian can glorify both these very different principles with equal enthusiasm within less than eighty lines of the same poem

---

[1] H. Steinbeiss, *Geschichtsbild Claudians* (1936), 52 f.

[2] See H. Nesselhauf, *Hermes* lxxxiii (1955), 477 f.; R. Syme, *Tacitus* i (1958), 234, n. 4.

is of itself sufficient indication of the facile clichés that both had become.

We might next consider again the famous passage from *Stil.* iii. 113 f.:

> fallitur, egregio quisquis sub principe credit
> servitium. numquam libertas gratior extat
> quam sub rege pio. quos praeficit ipse regendis
> rebus, ad arbitrium plebis patrumque reducit
> conceditque libens, meritis seu praemia poscant
> seu punire velint. posito iam purpura fastu
> de se iudicium non indignatur haberi.

'He errs who thinks that submission to a noble prince is slavery; never does liberty show more fair than beneath a good king. Those he himself appoints to rule he in turn brings before the judgement-seat of people and senate, and gladly yields whether they claim reward for merit or seek for punishment. Now the purple lays aside its pride and disdains not to have judgement passed upon itself' (Platnauer).

Mazzarino, in company with many others, does precisely what Claudian had hoped his less alert readers would do, by giving the passage an entirely general reference.[1] He assumes that Claudian is proclaiming that the power of the Emperor was not absolute. That while the Emperor could make appointments, these appointments had to be ratified by the senate and people. In fact, as the lines immediately preceding make clear, Claudian is referring very precisely to the unique occasion when Stilico handed over to the senate and people the invidious task of punishing the lieutenants of Gildo.[2] A very limited restoration of liberty! As usual, Claudian is not (of course) expressing his own personal view. He is extracting the maximum possible capital for Stilico and his figurehead Honorius from this one occasion. And that, as always, it is Stilico who is uppermost in Claudian's thoughts is proved by the fact that the very next line after the passage just

---

[1] p. 235. That the passage was given a general reference (though a different one) in seventeenth-century political controversy (see pp. 434–7) is naturally irrelevant to Claudian's intentions.

[2] See p. 234.

quoted begins: 'sic docuit regnare *socer* . . . verior Augusti genitor' (120 f.).

Naturally, if anyone was naïve enough to draw this wider inference from Claudian's words, so much the better. The passage is skilfully constructed to suggest it, without actually asserting any more than the trifling, solitary, and not disinterested concession about the trial of the Gildonians.

These are isolated passages. But at *IV Cons.* 214–352 we have a regular περὶ βασιλείας, cast, for obvious artistic reasons, in the form of advice from Theodosius to Honorius, 'anxious for the world's just governance'. The young Emperor is told that he must be king of himself before he can be the king of men. He must remember that the eyes of all are always upon him. He must be philanthropical, he must not listen to rumours, he must be protected by love, not fear. He must submit to his own laws, remember that he governs Romans, not effeminate Orientals. He must train his soldiers carefully, establish camps in healthy spots, post guards, study battle formations, routes, siege-warfare; watch out for ambushes, keep good discipline, and share the hardships of his men.

All very fine. The man who did all this would indeed be an ideal Emperor. A lesson, wrote Gibbon, which might 'compose a fine institution for the future prince of a great and free nation. It was far above Honorius and his degenerate subjects.' Yet it would be a serious error[1] to suppose that Claudian either intended or expected his advice to be taken seriously.[2] Still less does he bid Honorius model himself on Trajan because he realized that only a determined military effort could save the Empire.[3] His purpose was to entertain, not instruct. Surprise has been expressed that he should have spoken so freely on such a subject before his

[1] Made (e.g.) by Paschoud, *Roma Aeterna*, 150.

[2] That it was so taken in medieval times (see pp. 431–3) is again, of course, irrelevant to Claudian's intentions.

[3] So Paschoud, loc. cit. Trajan is chosen, of course, because he was the 'good Emperor' par excellence—and a fellow Spaniard. At *IV Cons.* 315 f. Claudian actually says that Trajan's glory will last 'non tam quod Tigride victo . . . quam patriae quod mitis erat'.

Emperor.¹ The answer is, of course, that neither Honorius (if that lethargic youth was still awake after 300 of Claudian's remorselessly polished hexameters) nor his courtiers would have thought for a moment that Claudian was really attempting to give Honorius a lecture on his duties. Thus there was no risk of giving offence. All the points Claudian makes—though strung together into a remarkably coherent and successful whole—are none the less commonplaces of the περὶ βασιλείας. The conventional nature of what Claudian says is sufficiently illustrated by the striking parallelism between this part of *IV Cons.* and Synesius' *De Regno*. We have seen already that neither was imitating the other. It is just that both were writing within a common tradition.²

It follows that we should hardly be justified in dignifying Claudian's homily with the title 'political philosophy'. Nor should the nobility of the sentiments blind us to the obvious inappropriateness of many of them to the circumstances at hand. Thirty-two lines of detailed advice on military matters were likely to be wasted on a thirteen-year-old boy who had never led an army in his life and was destined never to do so. Nor if he had wanted military advice, is he likely to have consulted a Greek poet.

It is significant, too, that nowhere in this long section on the duties of the Emperor (where it might have seemed most appropriate) do we find any hint of this 'constitutional monarchy' of the 'optimus princeps' who collaborates with the senate. Not surprisingly, however, for it was not till after the Gildonic war that such pretexts (flimsy enough in all conscience) for proclaiming the restoration of senatorial power became available.³ All that Claudian has to say about Honorius' relations with the senate in *IV Cons.* is a very brief and general exclamation:

> quae *denique* [i.e. at the end of a long list] Romae
> cura tibi! quam fixa manet reverentia patrum (503–4).

---

¹ Glover, *Life and Letters* (1901), 226.
² Above, p. 321.
³ The consultation of the senate to which so much space is accorded in *Stil.* took place before Claudian had to write *IV Cons.*

And the thirteen lines which follow on Honorius' just administration of the law make it perfectly clear that it is Honorius, not Honorius jointly with the senate, who is at once supreme legislator and judge.

There is another illuminating difference of emphasis between the portrait of Honorius in *IV Cons.*, recited at court in Milan, and the portrait we find in the later poems recited in Rome. At Milan Honorius is the typical Byzantine Emperor, carried aloft (as was proper) in a golden throne on the shoulders of his courtiers, like a god. Indeed, Claudian goes on to draw the parallel quite explicitly, with his comparison to the infant Sun-god borne on the shoulders of his priests at Memphis (565–76). Very different is Honorius' entry into Rome in 404 (*VI Cons.* 543 f.). In Rome the divine Emperor yields place to the *popularis princeps*. He forbids the senators to walk in front of him. He addresses the people in the Forum,

> veterumque exempla secutus
> digerit imperii *sub iudice* facta *senatu* (*VI Cons.* 590–1).

When watching the games in the Circus, he returns the salutation of the people (ib. 612 f.). Earlier Emperors had behaved like despots (*domini*) in Rome, Honorius alone (old and young alike agreed) like a fellow citizen (*civis*: ib. 559).

The reason for this difference in emphasis is not far to seek. There was a long-established tradition, going back at least as far as Pliny's panegyric on Trajan (§§ 22 f.), that while he might be honoured as a god in the provinces, the Emperor must behave like a citizen in Rome.[1] The most elaborate account we have of an imperial visit to Rome is Constantius II's of 357 in the pages of Ammian. Even the reserved and dignified Constantius, after entering the city borne aloft impassive and godlike, 'qualis in provinciis suis visebatur', condescended later to play the popular *princeps* with senate and people alike. Theodosius was careful to

---

[1] See the excellent discussion in Straub, *Vom Herrscherideal in der Spätantike* (1939), 187 f., correcting and expanding on R. Laqueur, *Probleme der Spätantike* (1930), 33 f. (on which cf. also *JRS* liv (1964), 24–5).

do the same during his visit in 389, and his behaviour was carefully chronicled by Pacatus:

> quis in curia fueris, quis in rostris [both Constantius and later Honorius
> addressed the people from the Forum as well as the senate in the Curia]
> . . . ut te omnibus principem, singulis exhibueris senatorem; ut crebro
> civilique progressu non publica tantum opera lustraveris, sed privatas
> quoque aedes divinis vestigiis consecraris, remota custodia militari
> tutior publici amoris excubiis (*Pan. Theod.* xlvii. 3).

Compare now what Claudian has to say about this same visit of
Theodosius, at the beginning of the same poem (*VI Cons.* 58 f.):

> cum se melioribus addens
> exemplis [i.e. earlier Emperors] civem gereret terrore remoto,
> alternos cum plebe iocos dilectaque passus
> iurgia, patriciasque domos privataque passim
> visere deposito dignatus limina fastu.

It seems obvious enough (and has long been recognized) that here,
as elsewhere, Claudian is drawing directly on Pacatus.[1] And we
learn from Ammian (xvi. 10. 13) that Constantius too 'dicacitate
plebis oblectabatur'. It is not surprising that the panegyrist of
Honorius should have read a panegyric on Theodosius, but what
is interesting is that Claudian should have singled out this particular detail. Clearly he was well aware that, whatever might
happen elsewhere, at Rome the Emperor must joke with the
common people and visit private houses, or forfeit the popularity
that was so vital to him.

   This, then, is why Claudian is at such pains to represent
Honorius as *civis*, not *dominus*, in Rome. It mattered—and not
to Honorius alone—that he should do the correct thing. This was
Honorius' first visit to Rome since he had accompanied Theodosius in 389, aged only 5. A successful visit could do Stilico a lot
of good, a bad one much harm. Then, as now, a royal visit was
a powerful propaganda weapon.

   Unfortunately, there is a gap in Zosimus' narrative of western

---

[1] Cf. Kehding, *De panegyricis Latinis* (1899), 29 f. On Pacatus' 'Herrscherideal'
cf. now A. Lippold, *Historia* xvii (1968), 228–50.

events stretching from 398 to 405,[1] so Claudian is our only source for Honorius' visit. However, we do have some information about his next visit, in 407–8. It seems that he lost his temper with the people and retired to Ravenna in a huff.[2] He was not the first Emperor who could not take the familiarity of the Roman mob. Diocletian had been intending to celebrate his ninth consulate in Rome, but 'libertatem populi ferre non poterat', and so he left early to celebrate it elsewhere.[3] Zosimus alleges that Constantine could not stand τὰς παρὰ πάντων ὡς εἰπεῖν βλασφημίας in Rome.[4]

Could it be that, in 404 as well, the poor boy, accustomed since the cradle to the adulation of a Byzantine court, did not in fact behave himself in every respect as the popular prince was supposed to in Rome? Claudian, of course, represents the whole affair as a huge success, as indeed it may have been. The fact that Claudian is at such pains to represent Honorius in the tradition of the popular prince visiting Rome does not (necessarily) mean that he is not telling the truth. After all, if Claudian knew the tradition, so no doubt did Stilico and Honorius. Yet even Claudian does betray two hints that things did not go quite as planned.

At *VI Cons.* 604 f. he praises Honorius at surprising and suspicious length for *not* distributing largess to the people. They welcome him, we are told, with open arms although he does not try to buy their affections with gold. Honorius does not need to go a-whoring after venal applause. To him who deserves it, love is offered unpurchased from a pure heart: 'procul ambitus erret! non quaerit pretium, vitam qui debet amori.'

Now was it really so reprehensible, or indeed unusual, for an Emperor to distribute largess to his people? When Theodosius did it, Claudian praises him as 'largitor opum' (*IV Cons.* 118 f.).

---

[1] Possibly already present in Eunapius: cf. Appendix C, p. 477.

[2] Theophanes, p. 118. 21 Bonn; Malalas, p. 349. 12 Bonn. I infer that both, despite their own chronology (Malalas seems to place the event in 400) are referring to the visit of 407–8, because both connect Honorius' retreat from Rome directly with Alaric's sack. Zosimus says nothing about it (v. 30), but it seems impossible to deny that some kernel of fact lies beneath the stories of Malalas and Theophanes.

[3] Lactantius, *De mortibus persecutorum*, 17.   [4] iv. 30. 1.

More striking still, he devotes fourteen lines to the largess distributed by Stilico during his triumphal entry into Rome as consul four years earlier. Stilico's liberality, we read, outdid the waters of Hermus, the touch of Midas, the shower of Jupiter. If the silver he gave away like base metal had been melted down, it would have turned into whole lakes and rivers (*Stil.* iii. 223 f.). Indeed, we can go even further. The consul was *expected* to give out largess at his inauguration (ὑπατείαν ῥίπτειν was the technical term by the sixth century), and whereas a private citizen was supposed to limit himself to silver, the Emperor was expected to give gold.[1] The clearest illustration of this is the fine painting (copy at two removes of a fourth-century original) of Constantius II in full consular regalia, obviously an official portrait: a shower of gold coins is falling from his open right hand.[2] We may be sure that Honorius' Roman subjects were waiting eagerly, like Corippus 150 years later at the consular procession of Justin II, till

> divite dextra
> egrediens princeps sacra trabeatus ab aula
> divitias vulgo, solemni munere donans,
> more nivis sparsurus erat (*Laud. Just.* iv. 9 f.).

We know enough of Claudian's technique by now to be able to read between the lines with some confidence. For whatever reason (perhaps genuine fiscal difficulties) Honorius had omitted the customary largess—and been criticized for his omission. With characteristic ingenuity Claudian attempts, not altogether convincingly, to turn this fault into a positive virtue.

If Honorius appeared something less than the perfect prince to the people, in at least one respect he was not a complete success with the senate either. His speech in the senate house was a flop. So at any rate is the natural inference from the fact that Claudian,

---

[1] R. Delbrück, *Die Consulardiptychen* (1929), 73.

[2] H. Stern, *Le Calendrier de 354* (1953), pl. xiv, with pp. 156 f., 163–4. The consul's largess is represented on a number of sixth-century diptychs: cf. Delbrück, pl. 16 (513), 23–5 (copies of an original of 518), 32 (530), and 34 (540). For the Emperor's largesses in general, R. MacMullen, *Latomus* xxi (1962), 159 f.

again with transparent ingenuity, praises him for dispensing with the arts of rhetoric!

> nil cumulat verbis quae nil fiducia celat;
> fucati sermonis opem mens conscia laudis
> abnuit (*VI Cons.* 592–4).

For Claudian of all people, rhetorician to his fingertips, to have praised anyone for honest bluntness without a very good reason passes belief. The importance of this failure should not be under-rated. In the eyes of senatorial writers, Emperors were judged in large measure by their cultural attainments, above all by their eloquence.[1] One contemporary writer, Aurelius Victor, made the immortal remark that, while the ideal Emperor would, of course, be both eloquent and virtuous, he should at least try to be the former![2] Julian describes with admiration how Constantius II climbed up on the rostrum to address his army, alone, bareheaded, in his ordinary clothes, trusting only in his impressive speech.[3] The importance of the *allocutio*, address to troops, is confirmed by many passages of Ammian. We may perhaps doubt whether Honorius really did deliver the stirring *allocutio* Claudian assigns him at the end of *Gild.*, though from the contemporary *IV Cons.* (515 f.) we hear of the 'docta facultas | ingenii linguaeque modus' with which he greeted ambassadors. But then a thirteen-year-old boy can get away with things a twenty-year-old man, Emperor for ten years, cannot.

To return from the details of Honorius' visit to Rome to the more basic matter of Claudian's presentation of Honorius as Emperor of Rome, it is of fundamental importance to observe that there is no trace in Claudian's portrait, whether at Milan or Rome, of the idea of the divine sanction of his rule. This doctrine (which can, of course, be traced back to Homer) was first evolved at a political level to justify the rule of Hellenistic monarchs, an imitation (μίμησις) of the rule of God himself.

---

[1] Alföldi, *Conflict of Ideas in the Late Roman Empire* (1952), 112 f.
[2] *Caesares* viii. 8.
[3] Julian, *Or.* iii (ii) 76D (i. 1. 150 Bidez).

Naturally enough it was taken up by the panegyrists and philosophers of the principate, and by Claudian's day had been for three quarters of a century a basic element in the official attitude to the now Christian Emperor. For remarkable though it might seem, within twenty years of the Great Persecution, when the Emperor must have seemed the embodiment of Antichrist to the unhappy Christians, the first Christian Emperor was hailed by Eusebius as the vice-regent of God on earth, his rule the terrestrial counterpart of the rule of God in heaven.[1] Thereafter it was a doctrine common to pagans and Christians alike.[2] Indeed, so far had the adaptation of what used to be dubbed the 'oriental' trappings of divine monarchy progressed that we find St. Gregory of Nazianzus going further than the pagan Themistius, and justifying at length the practice of prostration (προσκύνησις)—and prostration not only before the Emperor's person, but before his portraits and statues as well.[3] Even Synesius, though critical of some aspects of court ceremonial, still has no hesitation in seeing the earthly *basileia* as an imitation of the kingship of God.

Now we have seen that many of Claudian's views on the nature and duties of kingship coincide almost verbally with Synesius'. It is thus the more striking that Claudian should differ from Synesius over so fundamental a point as this. Clearly both were brought up in the same tradition—indeed both educated in the same city during the same period. We cannot doubt that Claudian was familiar with this Hellenistic–Byzantine conception of kingship. Arguments from silence are always dangerous, but the divine origin of earthly kingship is too crucial an element in kingship theory for its absence in Claudian to be assigned to mere chance.

[1] See N. H. Baynes's famous paper, 'Eusebius and the Christian Empire', *Mél. Bidez* (1933), 13 f. (= *Byzantine Studies* (1955), 168 f.).

[2] See most recently F. Dvornik, *Early Christian and Byzantine Political Philosophy* ii (1966), especially chapter 10, *passim*, for extensive quotation of texts and earlier bibliography. But Dvornik unaccountably omits all mention of Claudian, who has much of close relevance to his theme: and his discussion of Synesius (as of many other writers) completely ignores the immediate political background against which he wrote.

[3] *Or.* xviii. 80 (*PG* xxxv. 605 f.): cf. Dvornik ii. 686.

And its absence is the more striking in that in both *IV Cons.* and *VI Cons.* Claudian does have so much to say about the position and duties of the Emperor. And not only of Honorius as the reigning Emperor, but of Honorius as the ideal king. Claudian was no original thinker, and it seems inconceivable that he should genuinely have come to reject the political philosophy he had been brought up on for moral or intellectual reasons. We can only conclude that he deliberately adapted it for his western audiences, where absolutism was still felt to require a Republican veil. We may legitimately wonder whether Claudian would have written his imperial panegyrics in quite the same way if chance had taken him (as well it might) to the court of Arcadius in 395, instead of to that of Honorius.

Nor is there any trace in contemporary panegyrics on eastern Emperors of the constant harping on Honorius' respect for the senate that we find in Claudian, more particularly in the later, 'Roman', poems, but even in brief asides in a poem like *IV Cons.*, recited in Milan (e.g. 488–90, 494, 504).[1] When Julian tried to pay similar respect to the eastern senate, people thought it a little odd. It was unnecessary, even undignified.[2] And when he gave a speech before the eastern senate, Socrates for one thought that he was the first Emperor to do so since Julius Caesar (*HE* iii. 1). At Rome, however, the Emperor *did* have to address the senate. Constantius did so, Theodosius did so, and even poor Honorius had to do his best. And Claudian too had to do his best to present Honorius (and Stilico, the regent) as paying not only this but every other mark of respect and deference to the senate. Less necessary (and therefore less prominent) in the poems recited in Milan, but forming a central theme of those designed for Rome.

It has been necessary on a number of occasions in the preceding pages to rebut the view that Claudian was a spokesman for the senate. It is indeed a serious error—but understandable perhaps

---

[1] Another small but significant matter in which he reflects senatorial preoccupations is their desire for long tenure of certain offices: cf. *IV Cons.* 488 f., and my remarks in *CR* N.s. xviii (1968), 19–20.

[2] Cf. Dvornik ii. 665.

(if not pardonable) in view of the clarity and skill with which he presents the outlook and ideals of that order. Whether or not he shared them is perhaps after all only of secondary importance to the fact, astonishing in a Greek of any age and especially Claudian's, that he understood them.

In Milan Honorius could be allowed to appear more of an autocrat than in Rome. But in neither could he be the earthly counterpart of God in Heaven—as his own brother was in Constantinople. This is perhaps the most striking illustration of Claudian's assimilation of Roman tradition—a fascinating fusion of the Roman and the Byzantine.

XIII

LAST DAYS

THUS far we have been dealing almost exclusively with the political poems and Claudian's official activity as propagandist. Fortunately it is possible, mostly with the aid of the *carmina minora*, to fill in some of the gaps in his private life.

From the inscription to his statue we learn that he became tribune and notary. It is sometimes assumed that he received the post at the same time as the erection of the statue (400). But there is nothing to support this assumption, and it seems more natural to suppose that he was appointed as soon as he entered Stilico's service in 395–6. *C.m.* xxii, which is almost certainly to be dated to 397 (below), explicitly mentions Claudian's *cingulum* and *militia*, and it is difficult to see what such technical terms can refer to except his post as tribune and notary, since he is unlikely to have held any other post before this.

Critics have often speculated on the nature of Claudian's duties as notary, how much active service he saw. In vain. By Claudian's day the post had become virtually a sinecure, and was often held by young aristocrats.[1] This is not to deny the possibility that Claudian did see active service. He may well have accompanied Stilico on one or more of his campaigns. But it is unlikely that he was required to go in his official capacity to perform the secretarial duties which the post had originally involved.

In January 395 Claudian was in Rome, but by the following January he was at court in Milan. From the preface to *Stil.* iii we learn that he did not set foot in Rome again till early in 400.[2]

---

[1] A. H. M. Jones, *LRE* i. 127–8, ii. 572–5, misinterpreting, however, *ILS* 809, which reveals Petronius Maximus not as tribune and notary 'at the age of 19' (Jones, p. 574), but before he was 19.

[2] *Pr. Stil.* iii. 21–4, with Fargues, p. 14, n. 3.

Naturally we need not suppose that he spent all this period in Milan.

One of the best known of the minor poems is xx, 'The old man of Verona'. It is a fair, if not necessary inference that the poem was based on a real old man Claudian had met or seen near Verona. If so, then the poem (and *a fortiori* Claudian's visit) should be placed before late 401, for the old man is said never to have been troubled 'vario . . . tumultu', which could hardly have been written after the Gothic invasion of 401–2, culminating in a battle fought actually at Verona.

Then there is the poem on the warm springs of Aponus (Abano) near Padua (*c.m.* xxvi).[1] Latin writers frequently allude to the springs, but there is no other full-scale *ecphrasis* such as Claudian's extant, and no one who has studied the poem could be in a moment's doubt that Claudian had visited Padua for himself, and that much of the poem is based on personal observation, aimed at a Paduan audience. It was the regular practice of the professional poets of the age to write poems on the antiquities or tourist attractions of the various cities they visited—usually, no doubt, for a suitable reward from the local council.[2]

C.m. xviii 'De mulabus Gallicis' seems firm evidence of a visit to Gaul. It describes with some admiration and astonishment how the farmers of Gaul control their oxen, often from some distance, just by verbal commands:

> absentis longinqua valent praecepta magistri,
> frenorumque vicem lingua virilis agit (9–10).

These commands are styled 'barbaricos . . . sonos' and 'Gallica verba' (lines 8 and 20), so Claudian clearly means words spoken in a non-Latin dialect (? Frankish), and the natural assumption is

---

[1] For a commentary on the poem, see E. Bolisani, *Accad. patavina di scienze, lettere e arti, memorie* N.S. lxxiii (1960/1), 21–42.

[2] For examples, see *Historia* xiv (1965), 489. It was to the βουλή of Ancyra that Libanius commended the poet Dorotheus (*Ep.* 1517). The ἐγκώμιον πόλεως was an established literary genre: cf. Menander, *Rhet. Graec.* iii. 346 f., and for a summary of the 'rules', the introduction to W. Gernentz's *Laudes Romae* (Diss. Rostock, 1918), or R. A. Pack, *TAPhA* lxxxiv (1953), 184–5.

that he is describing a scene he had himself witnessed on a visit to Gaul.[1] We have seen in Chapter I that poets of the day were constantly on the move. Having toured the great cities of Asia Minor and Italy, it was only natural that Claudian should push on to the metropolises of Gaul: Trier, Arles, and of course Bordeaux, where he was sure to find an appreciative audience. Claudian's friend Florentinus was a Gaul, and after laying down the prefecture of Rome in 397, he seems to have retired to his estates somewhere in the neighbourhood of Trier (p. 492). Since the books of *Rapt.* which were dedicated to Florentinus were not completed till *c.* 402 (see Appendix A), it may be that Claudian visited Florentinus there at about this time.

C.m. xvii describes the statue in Catina (Catania) of the two brothers who rescued their parents on their shoulders from a burning house. Once more, many earlier writers had treated the heroism of the brothers, but it is perfectly clear that Claudian had seen the statue for himself. Indeed his poem presupposes that his audience can see, or are at least familiar with, the statue itself. He begins, 'Aspice sudantes venerando pondere fratres', and describes how the aged father is pointing back at the flames while the mother prays 'trepido . . . ore'; how one of the youths raises his right hand, supporting his father with the left alone, while his brother needs both hands to clasp his mother; how the skill of the artist has succeeded in making one resemble the father, the other his mother; how one is made to appear older than the other.

There can surely be little doubt that Claudian had visited Catina. *Rapt.* is set in Sicily, and more than one critic has suggested that some of Claudian's descriptions—of Aetna, for example, and the Sicilian countryside—bear the imprint of personal experience.[2] Now if Claudian had been to Catina, why should he not have seen more of Sicily—and taken a closer look at Aetna, for example?

---

[1] Compare the poem on the same subject by the Gallic exile Ennodius (*c.* cccxxviii, p. 243 Vogel), an imitation of Claudian's, and see also p. 492.

[2] Cf. P. Fabbri, 'Claudiano in Sicilia e il ratto di Proserpina', *Raccolta . . . Ramorino* (Milan, 1921), 91 f., and 'Del vero Claudiano', in *Athenaeum* xvii (1939), 27 f. (though there is little else I should be prepared to accept in either article).

It may be this voyage which is reflected in his account of the progress of Mascezel's fleet from Pisa down the Tuscan coast and out past Corsica to winter in the harbour of Caralis in Sardinia. It will be suggested in Appendix A that *Rapt.* i was probably written in the period 396–7, and it might tentatively be suggested that Claudian's Sicilian trip took place during this period. From late 397 to 400 he would have been rather too busy at court (below, p. 464).

Not all these inferences are equally secure, but it is in itself highly probable that Claudian would have taken every opportunity of travelling as widely as he could in the western provinces between official engagements at court.

What now of the circles he moved in at court? With the exception of his first patrons in Rome (Probinus and Olybrius), most of those he addresses or mentions in his epigrams were officials in the Imperial administration.

C.m. iii is a reply to a certain Aeternalis who had asked Claudian to write him something. This must be the Aeternalis who was proconsul of Asia in 396 (the name is unique).[1] There is not much

---

[1] According to *Cod. Theod.* iv. 4. 3 and xi. 39. 12, Aeternalis was proconsul of Asia on 21 March 396. Seeck, however (*Regesten*, 27), followed by Mazzarino (p. 377), and now B. Malcus, *Die Proconsuln von Asien von Diocletian bis Theodosius II, Opusc. Athen.* vii (1967), 127, 'corrected' the date of both laws to 402 (same consuls) because the *fasti* seemed too crowded. Aurelian (not *the* Aurelian) was in office on 3 Sept. 395 (*Cod. Theod.* xvi. 5. 28), Simplicius on 25 Mar. 396 (*Cod. Theod.* i. 12. 5), only four days after the two laws addressed to Aeternalis, and Nebridius three months later, on 22 July 396 (*Cod. Theod.* xi. 30. 56). Admittedly there is not much room for both Aeternalis and Simplicius between 3 Sept. 395 and 22 July 396, but there is enough. Exceptionally short tenures are well attested in prestige posts like the proconsulate of Africa and the prefecture of Rome (cf. Jones, *LRE* i. 380–1, 385), and there is clear evidence that the proconsulate of Asia was such a post during the reign of Theodosius (cf. Malcus, p. 153). And if any date is to be changed, it should be Simplicius', not Aeternalis' (if it were changed to Mar. 402, this would still allow the identification with Simplicius, prefect of Constantinople in 403: so Mazzarino, p. 377, and Malcus, p. 124). Quite apart from the fact that with Aeternalis *two* laws would have to be altered, neither Seeck, Mazzarino, nor Malcus took any account of Claudian's epigram. Yet it proves beyond doubt (what the man's unique name suggests too) that Aeternalis was a westerner, residing in the West during the Stiliconian period. And in view

time for Claudian to have got to know him before his tenure of the proconsulate, so presumably the poem was written after then. *C.m.* xix replies (again in the negative) to another request, from a Gennadius whom we learn from the poem to have been an inhabitant of north-eastern Italy, proconsul of Achaea, and prefect of Egypt. He happens to be attested as prefect of Egypt in 396, and his proconsulate is placed by Groag shortly before 395.[1] The poem can hardly be placed before Gennadius' return from Egypt in March 396. It is generally (and probably rightly) assumed that he is the Torquatus Gennadius who prepared an 'edition' of Martial in Rome in 401. Claudian adds that he was the greatest orator of the day;[2] not just a civil servant, then, but a man of culture and literary interests.

C.m. xxi is a lampoon on Mallius Theodorus, whose distinguished career was crowned with the consulate for 399, and Hadrianus, *comes sacrarum largitionum* (*CSL*) from 395 to 396/7, *magister officiorum* from 397 to 399, and praetorian prefect (*PPO*) of Italy from 401 to 405 (and again from 413 to 414):[3]

> Manlius indulget somno noctesque diesque
>   insomnis Pharius [Hadrian was an Egyptian] sacra profana rapit.
> Omnibus hoc, Italae gentes, exposcite votis,
>   Manlius ut vigilet, dormiat ut Pharius.

According to Fargues[4] and Mazzarino,[5] the poem is com-

of the political situation (cf. too Malcus, p. 153), it is inconceivable that a westerner should have received an eastern appointment as late as 402. But for 395 we have the parallel of Gennadius, proconsul of Achaea in that year (Mazzarino, p. 372). This was the brief period of harmony between Stilico and Eutropius (above, p. 85).

[1] *Die Reichsbeamten von Achaia in spätrömischer Zeit, Diss. Pannonicae* 1. 14 (1946), 64 f., and cf. the preceding note, *ad fin.*

[2] Jerome, *Chron.* s.a. 353 (p. 239. 3 Helm[2]: a curiously neglected entry) records that 'Gennadius forensis orator Romae insignis habetur'. Hardly our Gennadius, but perhaps his father.

[3] Mazzarino, pp. 343, 363, 365; J. Sundwall, *Weström. Studien* (1915), 86, no. 216. Hitherto Hadrian has been generally identified with the Rufius Synesius Hadrianus of *CIL* vi. 32202. But A. Chastagnol has now decisively assigned this inscription to the period 476 to 483, *Le Sénat romain sous le règne d'Odoacre* (Bonn, 1966), 43. Perhaps a grandson of our Hadrian.

[4] p. 34.   [5] *Rend. Ist. Lombardo* (1938), 249 f.

prehensible only if both Theodorus and Hadrian were in office when it was written. The only period, it is supposed, when this was so is from July 397 to January 399, when Hadrian was *mag. off.* and Theodorus *PPO*. Mazzarino thinks the point of the lampoon to be that Theodorus, as *PPO* Hadrian's superior, should have kept Hadrian in check but in fact failed to do so: hence the allusion to Theodorus' *somnus*. However, while the *PPO* was indeed senior to the *mag. off.*, the *mag. off.* was in no obvious or direct way responsible to the *PPO*.

I should prefer to follow Romano[1] in placing the poem in the period when Hadrian was *CSL*. This, surely, is why Claudian says that Hadrian '*sacra* profana rapit'. As *CSL*, Hadrian might be entitled to 'sacra'—but not 'profana' as well! This is much neater than to interpret 'sacra', with Birt,[2] as an allusion to the sequestration of property from pagan temples.

Birt ingeniously suggests that the poem was written when, and precisely because, Theodorus was not in office. From 377 to 383 Theodorus held a succession of official posts, but from 383 till January 397 he lived in complete retirement.[3] Nor is this long gap in his career simply the result of a gap in our sources. Theodorus really did cut himself off from public life, and devoted himself to literature and philosophy, as Claudian makes perfectly clear in his panegyric on Theodorus' consulate (61 f.). He represents him as being persuaded to return to public life with an impassioned appeal from Justice personified: 'nobiscum, Theodore, redi' (173). If then we place the poem in the period shortly before he agreed to return, the period when Hadrian was *CSL*, it could be argued that it was written when (and because) people were grumbling that Theodorus, a man of tried and tested integrity, kept aloof from public life while Hadrian, a man of less exacting standards, was all too active therein. An attractive view, yet there is

---

[1] p. 69, n. 7.   [2] p. xiii.

[3] Mazzarino, pp. 338 f. I suspect that Mazzarino was wrong to suggest placing the composition of Theodorus' surviving *De metris* during this period of retirement. Claudian chronicles Theodorus' scholarly work at length in *Theod.*, and would surely, being a poet himself, not have omitted a work on metre, had Theodorus written it by then.

something a little artificial in such a contrast. And it presupposes that people in Claudian's circle really deplored Theodorus' retirement, which seems a little unlikely. Such *otium cum dignitate* was eminently respectable.[1]

I propose to place the poem in the early months of 397. Theodorus became *PPO* in January 397, and though Hadrian is not in fact attested as *CSL* after August 395, it is more than likely that he continued in office till his promotion to *mag. off.* in July[2] 397. Between January and July 397 then Theodorus was *PPO* and Hadrian *CSL*. Claudian's point is a contrast between Hadrian's excessive (not to say dishonest) zeal, and the indolence of Theodorus' administration. That Hadrian was rapacious is likely enough, for the lampoon would otherwise have fallen rather flat. Naturally the same applies for Theodorus' *somnus*. And concerning Theodorus' *somnus* it is instructive to compare what Claudian has to say about Theodorus' administration precisely as *PPO* in his panegyric of 399. He praises him because 'quin etiam sontes expulsa corrigis ira | et *placidus* delicta domas' (221–2), he compares him to the Nile which '*lene* fluit' but is more useful than noisy mountain torrents (232 f.), concluding that 'peragit *tranquilla* potestas | quod violenta nequit, mandataque fortius urguet | imperiosa *quies*' (239 f.). Is not Claudian rather overdoing the 'placid' quality of Theodorus' administration? We are tolerably well informed, from our abundant source material, about the virtues for which officials were celebrated in late Imperial panegyrics: *quies* (which is after all but a synonym for *somnus*) does not normally feature among them. Surely Claudian is in fact repeating here, this time disguised as a graceful compliment, the same reproach that he had made two years

---

[1] Cf. Jones's section 'otium senatoris' in *LRE* ii. 557 f., and on *otium* devoted to literature and philosophy, see particularly Brown, *Augustine of Hippo*, 115–16. Aristocrats would seldom devote more than three or four years to holding public office, many much less.

[2] All that we know of the tenure of Paternus, Hadrian's successor as *CSL*, is that he was in office at the same time that a certain Sperchius was *com. rer. priv.* (Seeck, *Symmachus*, clvii). Sperchius is not attested as *CRP* before May 397, and his predecessor was still in office in August 396 (Mazzarino, p. 367).

earlier in his lampoon. Readers familiar with the lampoon—and familiar too, no doubt, with Theodorus' lackadaisical administration—would easily have spotted the subtle *double entendre*.

In general, however, the panegyric made handsome (if qualified) amends to Theodorus for the lampoon. But what of the allegations made against Hadrian? *C.m.* xxii is clearly relevant here, a curious poem entitled 'Deprecatio ad Hadrianum', which has called forth more discussion than any other of Claudian's works. This is obviously the same Hadrian (in both poems he is explicitly said to have been an Egyptian). The 'Deprecatio' consists of a long (58 lines) and pitiful lament on the straits to which Hadrian's wrath has reduced Claudian:

> Usque adeone tuae producitur impetus irae? . . .
> gratia defluxit, sequitur feralis egestas,
> desolata domus, caris spoliamur amicis:
> hunc tormenta necant, hic undique truditur exul.
> quid superest damni? quae saeva pericula restant? . . .
> audiat haec commune solum longeque carinis
> nota Pharos, flentemque attollens gurgite vultum
> nostra gemat Nilus numerosis funera ripis.

'Must the violence of thine anger last so long? . . . Now that I have lost thy favour I am become a prey to grinding poverty, my house is desolate, my friends reft from me. Death with torture is the fate of one, exile of another. What further losses can I suffer? What more cruel plagues can befall me? . . . Be my fate told to our common fatherland and to Pharos, known of all who sail the distant seas, and let Father Nile raise his weeping head from out the flood and mourn my cruel case along the banks of all his seven mouths' (Platnauer).

On the face of things, it certainly looks as if Claudian was in a bad way when he wrote these lines. Most scholars have referred them either to the period before Claudian entered Stilico's service or to the period after Stilico's death in 408, on the assumption that Hadrian would never have dared to humiliate Claudian like this while he enjoyed Stilico's favour. It will be shown later in the chapter that there are serious objections to the view that

Claudian outlived Stilico at all. And if he had been alive at the time of Stilico's execution, then his enemies would hardly have subjected him to the humiliations detailed in *c.m.* xxii: they would simply have had him executed as a Stiliconian together with Stilico's other leading supporters. In any event, had this been the case, one might have expected the poem to justify Claudian's conduct under Stilico. Instead Claudian apologizes only for his rashness, and for some error which clearly affects Hadrian alone. Nor is it any more plausible to refer the poem to the period before Claudian entered Stilico's service (i.e. before late 395), for the *militia* to which line 52 alludes can only be his post as tribune and notary, and he certainly cannot have obtained this before his arrival at court. He entered Stilico's service immediately on his arrival at court.

Mazzarino ingeniously ties the poem in with his theory of Claudian's abandonment by Stilico, dating it to 404, soon after Claudian's (on his view) last and most extreme outburst of pagan propaganda in *VI Cons.* Hadrian was *PPO* at this period and, on Mazzarino's view, leader of the Catholic extremists who were clamouring for Claudian's blood.[1] Yet there is no evidence that Hadrian was a Catholic extremist, nor is there anything in the poem to support such a view. There is no suspicion of an apologia for paganism. Still less anything to support Seeck's even more far-fetched suggestion that Claudian had been caught making pagan sacrifices![2]

All such reconstructions are based on the curiously naïve assumption that the poem is to be taken seriously. Romano, indeed, insists that it is 'dettata da un sincero dolore'.[3] Some years ago, E. Griset[4] advanced the theory that the Hadrian addressed is not the Hadrian we have been discussing so far, but the Emperor Hadrian, and that the poem as a whole is a declamation written in the *persona* of Juvenal appealing from exile. This is obviously absurd—not least because both Hadrian and the author

---

[1] *Rend. Ist. Lombardo* (1938), 252; see also p. 227 above.
[2] *Gesch. d. Untergangs* v. 296, 559–60.
[3] p. 69.   [4] *Il mondo classico* iii (1933), 329 f.

of the poem are stated without any equivocation to be Egyptians!
Nevertheless, Griset's paper did at least have the merit of showing
that the poem was a set rhetorical declamation. Birt quoted
several close parallels from a similar set-piece in a speech of
Libanius. He was not justified, of course, in concluding that
Claudian was 'imitating' Libanius: but the parallels are significant
none the less, as pointing to a common rhetorical model. The
whole thing is nothing more than a rhetorical *tour de force*. But
what prompted Claudian to write it?

The key is provided by lines 6–8, lines that earlier commentators
have failed to do justice to:

> me dolor incautus, me lubrica duxerit aetas,
> me tumor impulerit, me devius egerit ardor.
> te tamen haud decuit *paribus* concurrere *telis*.

In what way has Hadrian replied with the 'same weapons' as
Claudian? Naturally we cannot answer this question till we know
what weapon Claudian had used. Yet what can it have been but
a poem—and what poem but the lampoon on Hadrian just discussed? Claudian is saying that he wrote it in a moment of
youthful folly, of 'dolor incautus', unwise indignation—indignation, that is to say, at Hadrian's rapacity. If then Hadrian repaid
Claudian *paribus telis*, clearly all that he did was to lampoon him
back. The 'Deprecatio' is Claudian's reply to Hadrian's lampoon.
Claudian pretends that Hadrian's poem was so devastating that
it alone brought about all the dire effects chronicled with such
gusto in the 'Deprecatio'. So in effect the 'Deprecatio' is really
a compliment to Hadrian, as well as an apology for Claudian's
original lampoon. Hadrian, a fellow Egyptian[1] as well as a fellow
poet, will have appreciated and no doubt thoroughly enjoyed
both the joke and the compliment.

The 'Deprecatio' must presumably have been written very
shortly after the original lampoon. This is likely enough on *a priori*
grounds, and Claudian explicitly remarks that Hadrian's reply

---

[1] On the fondness of Egyptians for invective cf. the passages collected in
Historia xiv (1965), 479, notably Seneca, *Dial.* xii. 19. 6, Herodian iv. 9. 2, and
the numerous lampoons of Palladas.

to his lampoon came very quickly[1] ('*subitisne* favorem | permutas odiis'). Claudian will have wasted no time in producing his reply to Hadrian. Like the lampoon, then, the 'Deprecatio' belongs in the early months of 397.

That this is the true explanation of the 'Deprecatio' is confirmed—if further confirmation were necessary—by the following poem, *c.m.* xxiii, entitled 'Deprecatio in Alethium quaestorem'. Unfortunately nothing further is known about Alethius, not even when he was quaestor,[2] so the poem cannot be dated more narrowly than some time between 396 and 404. It is a similar 'apology' in similarly exaggerated and rhetorical fashion. But this time Claudian affirms that

> nulla meos traxit petulans audacia sensus,
> liberior iusto nec mihi lingua fuit.
> versiculos, fateor, non cauta voce notavi,
> heu miser! ignorans quam grave crimen erat.

Much the same sort of language, but this time Claudian is just a little more explicit: there can be no doubt that his *crimen* had been a lampoon on Alethius' own poetry. This time, however, Claudian has the last laugh: after a list of other and more famous poets who have been attacked but did not complain about it, Claudian ends:

> en, moveo plausus! en pallidus omnia laudo!
> et clarum repeto terque quaterque 'sophos'.
> ignoscat placidus tandem [sc. Alethius] flatusque remittat,
> et tuto recitet quodlibet ore—placet.

Neither of the 'Deprecationes' is to be taken very seriously. Similarly, it is to take the original lampoon on Theodorus

---

[1] This of itself is enough to put the hypotheses of both Seeck and Mazzarino out of court.

[2] He is even omitted from Mazzarino's prosopography of the Stiliconian period (quaestors at p. 365: another such omission is Florentinus, quaestor in 395, cf. Symm., *Ep.* iv. 50). He *may* be the 'Alevius' (an unlikely name) of Symm., *Epp.* viii. 15 (? 400, cf. Seeck's preface, p. cxcv) and ix. 65 (? 390, cf. Seeck, p. ccvii).

and Hadrian altogether too seriously to believe, as many have, that Claudian wrote his panegyric on Theodorus solely to placate him. Claudian wrote it quite simply to commemorate Theodorus' consulate: if Theodorus had never become consul it would probably never have been written. In addition he may genuinely have admired Theodorus' achievements as a philosopher and man of letters—and as we have seen he did not altogether withdraw his strictures on Theodorus' achievements as an administrator. No doubt both Theodorus and Hadrian would rather that the original lampoon had never been written, but (if they were sensible) they probably affected to be as amused as the next man—just as modern politicians have to when they see the cartoons in the daily papers.

Claudian's quarrels with both Hadrian and Alethius were then purely literary. Indeed most of his epigrams addressed to contemporaries concern requests for or criticisms of poetry. He was prompted to write his bitter attack on the *magister equitum* Jacob, because of the latter's criticism of his verses ('ne laceres versus, dux Iacobe, meos'). Note also *c.m.* xiii, lampooning the unnamed critic who, despite the metrical shortcomings of his own verses, had the audacity to criticize Claudian's on this score (p. 287).

Florentinus, too, though a quaestor and prefect of Rome, is known also (like his two brothers) for his literary interests.[1] And though the unfortunate Curetius is attacked for his profligacy (*c.m.* xliii–xliv), Claudian's remark at *c.m.* xliv. 4 that Curetius was 'procul a Musis' suggests that he too at least professed to be a poet, and that it was in this capacity that Claudian had come into contact with him. Palladius was a tribune and notary like Claudian. The father of his bride Celerina was *primicerius* of the notaries. Thus it was to oblige a colleague and a superior that Claudian wrote the epithalamium for Palladius' wedding. But Palladius too was a literary man; Claudian refers in the preface to their 'studia communia'.[2]

---

[1] On the trio, cf. Seeck, *Symmachus*, pp. cxli f.

[2] Or does this perhaps refer to their common duties as notaries?

So far then as can be judged, the circles in which Claudian moved were predominantly literary. Yet most of these men were functionaries in the Imperial service rather than members of the landed aristocracy, the class which it is customary to associate with literary pursuits at this period. Indeed, as pointed out in an earlier chapter, there is little reason to suppose that Claudian had anything to do with the literary patrons of Rome after his arrival at court.

Another common feature of the group—and one of no small interest in view of the accepted belief that Claudian was a diehard pagan—is that not one of them is known to have been a pagan. Some are known to have been Christians: not to mention Stilico, Serena, and Honorius, there is Jacob; and there is no reason to doubt that Theodorus (for all his Neoplatonism) was also a Christian. It has often been asserted that Florentinus was a pagan, but on no evidence. It must be borne in mind that Florentinus was appointed quaestor almost at once after the Frigidus, and by the end of 395 had passed on to the prefecture of Rome. His brother Minervius too entered on a career at court at the same time, and a third brother, Protadius, encouraged by their success, arrived in Milan in 395 hoping for similar preferment for himself.[1] One of the factors in their rise so soon after the collapse of the last pagan revival was surely their Christianity. At the very least it is hardly likely that either Protadius or Florentinus was a 'fervent défenseur du paganisme':[2] a judgement based solely on the naïve but all too common assumption that all secular men of letters were pagans. Gennadius and Aeternalis also held office very soon after the Frigidus, thereby suggesting that they too were not at any rate militant pagans. Both may perfectly well have been Christians.

In how close a relationship Claudian stood to these men we cannot be sure. Palladius, a fellow easterner as well as his colleague, may well have been an intimate. But most were his superiors in

---

[1] Cf. Seeck, *Symmachus*, pp. cxlii–cxliii.

[2] A. Chastagnol, *Fastes de la préf. urbaine de Rome* (1962), 253 (on Protadius), 248 (Florentinus).

the administrative hierarchy. Hadrian was an Alexandrian, and possibly not much older than Claudian. At any rate he is not attested in office till 395, the year in which Claudian, too, emerged as a public figure: and he enjoyed a second tenure of the praetorian prefecture extending as late as 416. Claudian may have known him in Alexandria before either made good in the West under Stilico. It may even be that Hadrian played a part in the summoning of his fellow Alexandrian to court in 395. Though if this were so, we might have expected Claudian to exploit this fact in the 'Deprecatio ad Hadrianum', representing Hadrian, the author of his fortune, with becoming in turn the author of his ruin. This he does not do. But (once granted that they are not to be taken seriously) the tone of the 'Deprecationes' to both Hadrian and Alethius, as also of his epigrams to men like Jacob and Aeternalis, reveals that Claudian was no cringing *cliens*.

This is a point worth making, since Claudian is so often dismissed precisely as a cringing *cliens*, prepared to stoop to any flattery, however base, to secure the favour of his patrons. But it would be a serious error to confuse obedience to the contemporary canons of the rhetorical encomium with an obsequious nature. When commissioned to write a panegyric on Stilico, Honorius, or Theodorus, Claudian naturally complied with convention, and duly produced no more and no less than what was expected of an Imperial panegyrist—and something that any of his contemporaries, in however exalted a position, would be glad to have written. Words like 'sincerity' and 'flattery' are simply not appropriate in such a context. Everyone knew that panegyrics contained few facts, and proclaimed or implied a great many things which were actually at variance with the facts.[1] But that was not the point. When not composing formal panegyrics, secure in the favour of Stilico and Honorius, Claudian was as independent and outspoken as his fellow Alexandrian Palladas: witness his attacks on Jacob and Curetius. Hadrian and Alethius

---

[1] As explicitly remarked by Augustine, when referring to the panegyric he recited on Valentinian II as *rhetor* of Milan: 'cum pararem recitare imperatori laudes, quibus *plura mentirer et mentienti faveretur ab scientibus*' (*Conf.* vi. 6. 9).

might justifiably have expected a little more respect from a mere tribune and notary.

Indeed, perhaps we can go a little further. In his prefaces and epigrams Claudian very frequently indulges in double comparisons, involving both his patron and himself. Time and again Stilico or Honorius (or whoever) is Jupiter, Scipio, or Augustus: Claudian is Orpheus, Ennius, or Vergil. Flattering to the patron, of course—but not unflattering to Claudian either. When someone criticizes his poetry Claudian instantly recalls that Orpheus, Vergil, and Homer had had their critics. We remember too Claudian's bold claim already in the Greek *Gigantomachia* that he was δεινὸς ἀοιδός, his remark in *pr. III Cons.* that he was 'Pieriis temptatum saepius antris'. We miss in the prefaces the motif of the poet's modesty and inability to do justice to his subject, so common in the literature of the period.[1] It looks as if Claudian had no mean opinion of his talent. The claim made on his statue,

εἶν ἐνὶ Βιργιλίοιο νόον καὶ μοῦσαν Ὁμήρου,

may not perhaps have seemed to him the absurd hyperbole it is for modern scholars.

We have seen that Claudian probably obtained his post as early as 396–7. But by 400, as we learn from the inscription to his statue, he was still only tribune and notary, and we have no grounds for supposing that he had risen any higher by 404, when he wrote his last datable poem. Now by Claudian's day, his poetic attainments would of themselves have been more than ample qualification for much higher office than this. Literary culture was very highly valued, and there was no higher manifestation of literary culture than the writing of poetry. Moreover, these were not Claudian's only qualifications. It is clear that he was fully in the confidence of Stilico, the fount of all patronage and promotion in the western court—and that he rendered Stilico no mean services in return. On the face of it there is no reason why Claudian should not have equalled or even excelled the

[1] Curtius, *European Literature* (1953), 83 f.; cf. Struthers, *Harvard Studies* xxx (1919), 57.

career of his friend and fellow countryman Hadrian, *CSL, mag. off.*, and twice *PPO*. One thinks of the meteoric career of Ausonius under Gratian. Forty years after Claudian, Merobaudes, the panegyrist of Aetius, Stilico's successor as uncrowned ruler of the West, soon found himself *magister utriusque militiae* and patrician.[1] At the same period Cyrus of Panopolis, with no qualifications but his poetic skill, became *PPO* of the East and prefect of Constantinople, the first man to hold both posts concurrently, and finally consul in 441. Later in the century another Egyptian poet from the same town, Pamprepius, played Claudian to the Stilico of the Isaurian Illus, and was rewarded with a quaestorship, honorary consulate, and the patriciate.[2] Why did not Claudian enjoy such a career?

It is perhaps legitimate to infer that he did not want one. One might compare the case of Andronicus, yet another Egyptian poet of the day, a man who could number such influential persons as Libanius, Symmachus, and Themistius among his connections, yet refused offers of a post in the civil service, and devoted himself to philosophy instead.[3] That Claudian was thoroughly immersed in the politics and intrigues of the day needs no further illustration here. Yet it does not necessarily follow from this that he wanted to burden himself down with the responsibilities of an administrative post. Indeed he must have been kept so busy with his poetic commissions for Stilico (especially in the period 397–9) as to have little time left for administration. Almost all his friends were literary men, and no doubt he was quite content to proceed no further than the sinecure of tribune and notary (which conferred the desirable minimum of senatorial rank)[4] and devote his leisure,

---

[1] Cf. Bury, *LRE* i². 251.

[2] On the careers of Cyrus, Pamprepius, and other poets of the age, cf. *Historia* xiv (1965), 497 f.

[3] Cf. ib. 500.

[4] There are still reputable scholars (Straub, *Vom Herrscherideal in der Spätantike* (Stuttgart, 1939), 151) prepared to infer from *pr. Get.* 8 'oraque *patricius* nostra dicavit honos' that Claudian was created patrician. But 'patricius honos' here means only 'honour granted by the *patres*' (senate), just as 'Siculus honos' at *c.m.* xvii. 42 means 'honour granted by the Sicilians' (cf. Fargues, pp. 26–7). Claudian is referring to the *honos* of his bronze statue (cf. the preceding line: 'prior effigiem

such as it was, to his poetry. In particular, one might conjecture, to his non-political poetry, like *Rapt.*, begun probably soon after his arrival at court, soon laid aside for more pressing business, and never completed.

Not the least among Claudian's patrons, and perhaps his friends, was Serena. Apart from the unfinished *Laus Serenae*, she features in a number of the *carmina minora*, and in several of the *carmina maiora* as well. Birt pointed out that she is not mentioned in *Ruf.* i or ii, or in *III* or *IV Cons.*, but first in *Nupt.* (119, 307 f.), and often thereafter (*Gild.* 310, *Stil.* i. 73, *VI Cons.* 93). From this he deduced that it was not till she became the mother-in-law of Honorius that Claudian deemed her worthy of his Muse: accordingly he dated all the epigrams which mention Serena in or after 398. There may be something in this. The position of Serena was obviously much strengthened by the marriage of her daughter to Honorius. But as the daughter (if only adoptive) of Theodosius and wife of the regent she had been a person of no slight importance even before then. It is hardly necessary to suppose that Claudian waited for the marriage before even writing a couple of distychs on her washbasin (*c.m.* xlv.) This could surely have been written at any time between 395 and 404. The *Laus Ser.* and *Ep. ad Ser.*, which certainly belong after 398, will be discussed shortly. Of the remaining poems, three in number (of 15, 15, and 12 lines respectively), all concerning horses or equestrian trappings which Serena presented to Honorius, two allude to the marriage and do therefore belong in or after 398. Not so *c.m.*

tribuit successus aënam'). Moreover, the patriciate was very sparingly granted in the fourth century (only 6 in all are known: cf. Jones, *LRE* iii. 155, n. 28), and neither Stilico himself, nor any other westerner, held it during the Stiliconian period (in the East, there were Eutropius, and, later, Anthemius and Aurelian). It is therefore *a priori* most unlikely that Claudian should have done so. It was being granted much more freely by the time Merobaudes and Pamprepius were so honoured. R. Guilland's study of the fourth- and fifth-century patricians in Ἐπετ. Ἑταιρ. Βυζ. Σπουδ. (1965), 139–74, includes on the one hand many dubious names from late sources and on the other omits such important figures as Merobaudes and Pamprepius—and the late fifth-century patrician Ammonius of *Anth. Pal.* ix. 674. With Claudian's line cf., too, Jerome's loose use of the word *patricius* to mean, apparently, no more than 'senator' at *Ep.* 54. 6 (cf. A. Chastagnol, *Fastes*, p. 252).

xlviii, entitled 'De zona equi regii missa Honorio Augusto a Serena', which opens:

> accipe parva tuae, princeps venerande, *sororis* | munera

and closes:

> augescit brevitas doni pietate Serenae,
> quae volucres etiam *fratribus* ornat equos.

There are here two allusions to the relationship between Serena and Honorius: and in each case it is to her position as sister. Birt[1] attributes this to mere chance, but in both the other poems, in other respects closely parallel, there is a quite explicit allusion to her status as Honorius' mother-in-law. This relationship was evidently felt to supersede that of sister, to which there is no reference. Compare *c.m.* xlvii. 13 f. 'sic quippe laborat | [sc. Serena] *maternis* studiis . . . *genero* . . .', and xlvi. 11 f. 'diversis . . . certant | obsequiis *soceri*. Stilico . . . Serena . . .' In fact Claudian does not bother to refer to Serena as the sister of Honorius in a single poem written after the marriage. Indeed it is striking that already in the marriage hymn Claudian plays down the sister and up the mother relationship (p. 58). In a passage which refers to the period before the marriage, Honorius is represented as already calling Serena mother (*Nupt.* 38 f.). While technically still only his sister ('stirpe soror') she had always been a mother in her feeling for him ('pietate parens')—and apart from the small matter of actually bearing him ('partuque remoto'), a truer mother to him than Flaccilla herself ('tu potius Flaccilla mihi').

Among a group of, for the most part, certainly spurious epigrams there is one (*c.m. app.* iv) entitled 'De zona missa ab eadem Arcadio Augusto', a companion piece designed to accompany a similar gift from Serena to Arcadius. On the ground of its inferior textual tradition the poem has sometimes been dismissed as a forgery, composed on the model of the genuine poem for Honorius. But it is possible to explain its omission from the archetype of MSS. containing the genuine *c.m.* (few of which contain the whole collection anyway) by simple haplography: a scribe's eye might easily have slipped from one to the other of

[1] p. lxi.

two such very similar looking titles and omitted the second. Or, in view of the circumstances of publication of the *c.m.*, it may be (as suggested already, pp. 203–4) that the odd genuine poem was just overlooked. One argument in favour of its authenticity (noticed already by Birt) is that the one for Honorius ends '*fratribus ornat equos*', suggesting by the plural that Serena did give a similar present to Arcadius as well as to Honorius, and thus licensing the existence of just such an epigram as *c.m. app.* iv. Another argument is that *c.m. app.* iv too makes no mention of Serena's status as an Imperial mother-in-law. I would suggest, then, that both poems were written at the same time, and for the same occasion, some time before 398.

It has been alleged that no such present could have been sent to Arcadius during the period of cold war between East and West which extended from 395 to 400. But it is easy to exaggerate the degree of hostility between East and West. Relations were certainly strained, and what with all the propaganda put out by both sides, it must have been very difficult to discover what was going on. But there had been no formal declaration of war, and until Stilico's harbour embargo (p. 246) no restrictions, so far as is known, on freedom of travel between East and West. An illustration of this point which has so far been overlooked is provided by a *subscriptio* at the end of Book ix of Apuleius' *Metamorphoses* in *Cod. Laur.* 68, 2: 'Ego Sallustius legi et emendavi Romae felix Olybrio et Probino v.c. cos. [i.e. 395] . . . Rursus Constantinopoli recognovi Caesario et Attico cos. [i.e. 397].' After 'editing' Apuleius in Rome in 395, Sallustius was evidently quite free to go to Constantinople and collate another MS. there in 397.[1] Diplomatic relations between East and West continued during this difficult period, and there seems no sufficient reason to deny that Serena could have sent her own brother a present then. Moreover such a present would have been a symbol of goodwill between the two courts which Serena, as wife of Stilico and sister of Arcadius, was uniquely qualified to offer. And, politics aside, it may be that Serena was genuinely fond of her

---

[1] I hope to discuss Sallustius' 'edition' elsewhere before long.

brother. In any event, in the period immediately after the fall of Rufinus it was fondly believed that all enmity between East and West had come to an end (cf. especially *Eutr.* ii. 543 f.). The present could have been sent then (some time, say, in 396) without any ulterior motives.

If so, then Claudian came into contact with Serena soon after his arrival at court. But his relationship with her was rather more personal than his dealings with her husband; not political poems, or formal panegyrics recited in open court, but trifles to accompany presents, or a poem on her washbasin. But what probably most endeared Claudian to her was his treatment of her in the epithalamium for the wedding of Honorius and Maria.

Attention is usually so focused on the bride at a wedding that little thought is spared for the mother. Skilful and sensitive courtier that he was, Claudian took care that Serena should not feel left out. When Venus appears to address Maria, she is made to stand in wonderment, not at Maria's beauty alone, but at Serena's too. Maria she compares to the crescent, Serena to the full moon: 'haec modo crescenti, plenae par altera lunae' (243). Then to the young laurel growing beneath the shade of its parent tree; or like two roses on one stalk: the one steeped in the dews of spring and fully open, the other nestling in its bud, not daring yet to allow the sun's warmth on its tender petals. Seldom can any mother have received such a charming compliment on her daughter's wedding day. Small wonder that a year or two later Serena was prepared to put herself out to help Claudian win the bride of his choice.

We come now to the thorny question of Claudian's last years, marriage, and death, which turns in large measure on the relative dating of *c.m.* xxx and xxxi. xxxi is a verse epistle to Serena announcing Claudian's marriage, arranged by Serena, and lamenting that she will not be able to attend since Claudian is in Africa. xxx is a (clearly unfinished) panegyric on Serena, taking her life up to 392 in 236 lines.

Vollmer[1] placed xxxi in 404 and xxx c. 398. xxxi he takes to be

[1] *PW*, s.v. Claudianus, iii. 2. 2655. His argument that xxx must be earlier than

Claudian's last poem, and thinks that he died on his honeymoon, reasoning as follows. xxxi opens, like many of the prefaces to Claudian's poems (p. 278), with an elaborate comparison of Claudian's marriage, sponsored by Serena, to Orpheus' marriage, sponsored by Juno. At lines 25 f. he describes how fond Juno was of Orpheus,

> qui sibi [i.e. to Juno] carminibus totiens lustraverat aras
>   Iunonis blanda numina voce canens,
> proeliaque altisoni referens Phlegraea mariti,
>   Titanum fractas Enceladique minas.

Vollmer compares this to the preface (lines 17 f.) of *VI Cons.*, where Claudian refers in allusive fashion to his poem on the Gothic war recited eighteen months before:

> Enceladus mihi carmen erat victusque Typhoeus:
>   hic subit Inarimen, hunc gravis Aetna domat.
> quam laetum post bella Iovem susceperat aether
>   Phlegraeae referens praemia militiae.

Here there can be no doubt that by Jupiter Claudian means Honorius, and by the giants the Goths. Vollmer assumes that by Orpheus in *c.m.* xxxi Claudian really means himself, and that by the giants he is again referring to the Goths, and hence to one or other of his own poems about the Goths, *Get.* or *VI Cons.*: i.e. that he cannot have written xxxi before 402–4.

Now obviously there is a sense in which, for the purposes of his comparison, Claudian is Orpheus. Yet it is quite another matter to assume that the comparison was intended to correspond with reality at every point. There are in fact two important discrepancies: while Juno went to Orpheus' wedding, Serena did not go to Claudian's; and Claudian did not 'often' ('totiens', line

---

xxxi because it does not allude to Claudian's marriage is worthless, because (*a*) nowhere else in his panegyrics does Claudian ever allude to his personal life, and (*b*) xxx breaks off in 392, 3 years before Claudian met Serena, and nearly 10 years before his marriage. No more convincing is N. Martinelli's case (*Misc. Galbiati* ii (1950), 64) for the priority of xxx,

25) write panegyrics on Serena. Indeed, his one and only panegyric on her is unfinished, and opens, moreover, with an apology
for his delay in writing in her honour. It is implausible to date
it (with Vollmer) as early as 398, and explain the unfinished state
by postulating a defective archetype: the poem is not the last in
the book, and there are other reasons for supposing that Claudian
wrote no more than we possess.

So if Orpheus is not Claudian *tout court*, there is no reason to
suppose that the giants he sings of are the Goths, or that the song
is either *Get.* or *VI Cons.* Not to mention the two *Gigantomachiae*,
Claudian makes frequent use of imagery from the battle of the
giants in all his poetry,[1] never (except in *Get.* and *VI Cons.*)
with an allusion to the Goths.

C.m. xxxi closes with the promise that if Claudian returns
safely to Italy, the Muses and the fount of Aganippe will sing the
praises of Serena in gratitude—i.e. that Claudian will write her
a panegyric. This of itself strongly suggests that (unlike Orpheus)
Claudian had not yet written a panegyric for his Juno. *Laus
Serenae* (xxx), then, is later than xxxi. More important, *Laus
Serenae* opens precisely with an allusion to the Muses and to the
fount of Aganippe. The most natural and economical inference is
that *Laus Serenae* is the panegyric promised in *c.m.* xxxi—and
(in view of the apology for delay) that it was written some little
while after xxxi, after Claudian's return to Italy.

xxxi cannot have been written before February 398, for it
alludes to Honorius' marriage. Now from early 398 to early 400
was the busiest period in Claudian's life: he wrote *Gild.*, *Theod.*,
Eutr. i and ii, and *Stil.* i, ii, and iii—in all nearly three and a half
thousand lines. It would not be easy to fit a protracted African
honeymoon during this period.

On the face of it, then, *c.m.* xxxi, and with it Claudian's marriage
and African trip, can hardly be dated before spring 400. Now it so
happens that after spring 400 not a single poem can be dated to the
next two years and more, till *Get.* in early summer 402. Nor is this
merely an argument from silence. *Get.* opens with a preface

---

[1] See Appendix B, p. 468.

making it clear that Claudian's pen had indeed been silent all this time:

> post *resides annos longo* velut excita *somno*
> Romanis fruitur nostra Thalia choris.

And the preface to *Rapt.* ii–iii, probably recited at about the same time (p. 463), refers in similar terms to a similar break. Claudian himself, then, evidently felt that his Muse had taken a long holiday between 400 and 402. What more natural than to place his own African holiday during this period?

There is one other reason which might be advanced in favour of the supposition that Claudian was not in Italy in late 401 or early 402. Quite undeterred by the obvious difficulty of continually devising fresh variations on the same theme, Claudian wrote panegyrics on the third, fourth, and sixth consulates of Honorius. Yet his fifth, in 402, went unsung. Of course Claudian was not bound to celebrate every one of Honorius' consulates, but there is a very good reason why he might have been expected to celebrate the fifth. At the end of *IV Cons.* he had expressed the pious wish that before long the restoration of the unity between the two Emperors might be symbolized by Arcadius and Honorius holding the *fasces* together. Honorius' colleague in 402 was Arcadius. Concord had been restored at last after the discord of the Rufinian and Eutropian regimes. Not quite the sort of concord Stilico had desired, but the best he could now hope for. On the part of the East this concord was signalled by *solidi* proclaiming 'SALVS ORIENTIS FELICITAS OCCIDENTIS'.[1] An offering by Claudian might certainly have been expected. A satisfactory (if not the only possible) explanation for his silence would be his absence from Italy at the time.

I would suggest, then, as the most natural and economical

---

[1] Cf. Demougeot, p. 264. It might be objected that the apprehension at court following Alaric's invasion of Nov. 401 (Demougeot, pp. 270–2) was not conducive to recitations, and that Claudian deliberately waited for the victory at Pollentia. Yet *IV Cons.* was recited during a similar period of tension, at the height of the Gildonic crisis—and another poem followed after the victory over Gildo. A skilfully composed panegyric might have done much to allay fear and discredit the sort of idle rumours to which Claudian alludes in *Get.* 217–313.

reconstruction from such evidence as we have, that some time in 400–1 Claudian left Italy for Africa, and did not return till 402, when his services were immediately called upon once more to celebrate—and justify—Stilico's most recent success at Pollentia.

Claudian tells us nothing of his bride, merely that a letter from Serena won over her parents. He describes how, poor poet that he was, he could not offer 'sollemni more procorum' herds of cattle, vines, olive-groves, corn-fields, or a lofty palace. Serena's letter

> et pecus et segetes et domus ampla fuit (44).

Birt, a romantic despite his massive erudition,[1] saw in her a childhood sweetheart from Alexandria. But 'Libyca plaga' in line 56 must surely refer to Africa, not Egypt—and certainly not Alexandria.[2] And we have no reason to suppose that Claudian made his trip solely in order to pay court to some girl he knew already—or even a girl selected in advance for him by Serena, as often assumed. By 400 Claudian had spent a year in Rome, four in and about Milan, and had probably paid a call to Sicily and visited other cities in both Italy and Gaul as well. He was no doubt tiring of court life—and of continually finding something new to say about Stilico and Honorius. The obvious next port of call for an Egyptian who had already probably toured round Asia Minor and Greece on his way to Italy, was Africa, to complete the circle. There were still many wealthy landowners in Roman North Africa,[3] and Claudian would have been able to count on a warm—and lucrative—welcome in Carthage. Latin poetry still flourished in Africa,[4] and continued to do so even under the Vandal kingdom: Corippus in the 550s, if one of the latest, is certainly not the least of the names Africa contributed to the

---

[1] Like Mommsen, he composed light verse in his spare time: see the obituary in *Bursians Jahresb.* (biogr.) 262 (1938), 31 f.

[2] Cf. Fargues, p. 29.

[3] Courtois, *Les Vandales et l'Afrique* (1955), 132 f.

[4] 'Latinarum literarum artifices Roma *atque Carthago*', said Augustine in 410 (*Ep.* 118. ii. 9 *ad fin.*). Cf. in general, Raby, *Sec. Latin Poetry* i², 105 f. (fifth century), and 142 f. (sixth century).

literary history of Rome. It was probably the daughter of some literature-loving African *grand seigneur* to whom Claudian paid court, and won with the aid of Serena.

By summer 402 Claudian was back in Rome, where he recited *Get.* in the temple of Apollo on the Palatine. It is often deduced from his description of Alaric's siege of Milan at *Get.* 455 f. that Claudian himself was present in Milan at the time. And when he writes that 'pulveris ambiguam nubem *speculamur* ab altis | turribus, incerti socios adportet an hostes | ille globus', it certainly looks as if he is writing from experience. Yet in *VI Cons.* he gives a very different account of Stilico's relief of Milan—not least, he now says that it took place at night, instead of in broad daylight (443 f.). The second version is placed in the mouth of Honorius himself, and it is hardly likely that it is less accurate than the first. For once Claudian could have had no motive for altering these small details—unless his earlier account had been incorrect. I would suggest that Claudian was not in fact in Milan during the siege, and did not even have an opportunity to go there or question eyewitnesses before writing *Get.* (it was probably written only a month or at most two after Pollentia). But in order to make his account of the relief more vivid, he used his imagination, and adopted the first person device. The inhabitants waiting on tenterhooks to see whether the cloud of dust announced friend or foe was an obvious enough—perhaps too obvious—motif. Later, however, after making inquiries, Claudian discovered that unfortunately Milan had been relieved at night! So he corrected his error in *VI Cons.*

At about the same time as he wrote *Get.* Claudian wrote *c.m.* l, the lampoon against Jacobus, and it is probably to about this period that we should assign *Rapt.* ii–iii, performed (as I should like to think, though I cannot prove) at Florentinus' home in Trier. Eighteen months later he recited *VI Cons.*, again in Rome—though there is no reason to suppose that he spent all the intervening period there. Indeed, it is a very reasonable assumption that he spent a few months at court in Ravenna. Certainly his descriptions of the unusual harbour at Classis and of the journey from Ravenna to Rome (*VI Cons.* 494–519) bear the imprint of personal observation. If so, this cannot have been before late 402 or 403, since court did not move to Ravenna till late in 402.

After *VI Cons.*, silence. Numerous explanations of this silence have (of course) been proposed (some discussed already), but by far the most likely is quite simply that he died, probably in 404 itself.[1]

It has often been suggested or assumed that Claudian perished with Stilico and Stilico's other supporters in 408. Had he still been alive at the time, he probably would have. But quite apart from the difficulty of explaining his silence between 404 and 408 (see next paragraph), if Claudian had been executed at that time, it may be regarded as certain that his name would have been erased from the inscription to his statue, standing conspicuously in the forum of Trajan, as were the names of Stilico himself and of all his leading supporters (e.g. Longinianus) from their statues.[2] A mutilated monument to Stilico stands in the forum to this very day.

Had Claudian lived even till the end of 404, it is difficult to explain his failure to celebrate Stilico's second consulate in 405, and even more difficult to explain his failure to extol Stilico's great victory over the huge Ostrogothic horde of Radagaisus in 406 at Faesulae.[3] It was the first really decisive victory Stilico had ever won, and after the dubious outcome of even Pollentia and Verona, it was a victory Stilico needed very badly indeed.

Another view which has occasionally found favour is that Claudian simply left Italy in 404 (as, on my reconstruction, he did earlier for a spell). From at least one point of view this is a very reasonable hypothesis. Hostility to and suspicion of Stilico was mounting at Rome, Milan, and Ravenna, among pagans and Christians alike. It is only too obvious from his defence of Stilico's policies that Claudian was fully aware of this, and it is perfectly credible that he might have decided that it was high time for him to bow out of Stilico's service before it was too late.

---

[1] For a survey of views, see E. Merone, 'La morte di Claudiano', *Giorn. ital. di. Fil.* vii (1954), 309 f., and Demougeot, pp. 288–93.

[2] Cf. *CIL* vi. 1188, 1190. [3] Demougeot, p. 361.

It has indeed been suggested that he returned to the East, and that it is he, and not the shadowy later Claudian, whose *floruit* Evagrius placed correctly under Theodosius II together with Cyrus of Panopolis. It is no real objection to this view that none of the Greek poems he might reasonably be expected to have written on his return has survived. Nothing, or virtually nothing, survives of the voluminous output of Soterichus, Andronicus, Olympiodorus, Cyrus, Pamprepius, Christodorus, Colluthus, and the other Egyptian *Zeitdichter* of the age. In the East such contemporary poems were ten a penny. Succeeding generations seem to have taken little interest in the forgotten deeds of forgotten men, and they perished almost without trace. The mythological poetry of the age evidently continued to appeal to later generations, and much survives (Nonnus, Triphiodorus, Colluthus' *Rape of Helen*): it is thus no mere fluke that the only one of Claudian's Greek poems to survive (if only in fragments) is the *Gigantomachia*. It was only in the West, where contemporary poetry was less common, that the contemporary works of a Claudian, a Sidonius, or a Corippus could survive entire.[1]

But there are other objections to the theory of a return to the East. One is that he could hardly have expected a very warm welcome in Constantinople after the insults he had hurled against the effeminacy of the eastern court in *Eutr.* A much more telling objection against his survival beyond 404 is the unfinished state of so many of his poems. His two mythological poems, *Rapt.* and *Gigantomachia*, are plainly unfinished, and I have argued in Appendices A and B that it is implausible to explain this as a falling off in interest on Claudian's part, or as due to his abandonment of mythological poetry when he turned to contemporary themes. Both were poems Claudian was working on in the period 402–3. Moreover, there is the equally clearly unfinished panegyric on Serena. It is impossible to suppose that Claudian was tactless

---

[1] Cf. *Historia* xiv (1965), 483–4. Much the same applies to the Greek historical writing of the fourth and fifth centuries—almost entirely lost save for the epitome of Zosimus, fragments preserved by Photius, the excerptors of Constantine Porphyrogenitus (who sometimes found it difficult to obtain copies themselves), and (from them) by Suidas.

enough to have 'lost interest' in this, and implausible to fall back on the lifeline of a defective archetype. As pointed out above, there is another reason apart from its unfinished state for placing it among Claudian's last poems.

Furthermore, it is not merely that these poems were left unfinished. It is the circumstances under which they were published despite this fact. Claudian's poems circulated in Antiquity in four different collections, over and above the original separate editions of the individual poems: the panegyric on Probinus and Olybrius (which has nothing to do with Stilico, and was presumably kept in circulation by the Anicii), an omnibus edition of the political poems, evidently issued at the wishes of Stilico (and hence before August 408), *Rapt.*, and (lastly) the *carmina minora*: the epigrams, *ecphraseis*, *Laus Serenae*, Latin *Gigantomachia*, verse epistles, etc.

At the head of the *carmina minora* stands the third of Claudian's Fescennines, the one which so emphatically proclaims 'Quae iam rabies livoris erit, | vel quis dabitur color invidiae? | Stilico socer est, pater est Stilico.' It has long been realized that this poem would not have been placed there had the book been published after Stilico's death and *damnatio memoriae*. It has not been noticed, however, that it would surely not have been placed there either after the premature death of Maria. Maria's death cannot unfortunately be dated precisely, but 404 is the accepted guess. She had presumably been dead some while when Honorius married Thermantia, probably in 407.[2] Claudian himself would never have prefaced the collection with one of his Fescennines in this way. Ancient poets were very careful to introduce collections of their poems with a suitable and proper dedicatory poem or letter (see for example, the collections of Statius, Martial, or Ausonius). Had Claudian wished to dedicate his *carmina minora* to Stilico himself, he could so easily have written a new and appropriate

---

[1] See below, p. 421.

[2] Demougeot, p. 375. Zosimus vi. 28. 1, after mentioning the consular pair for 408, says that Maria had died οὐ πρὸ πολλοῦ, but his chronology is notoriously inaccurate.

dedication. The Fescennine is not a dedicatory poem at all, and was in any case already included with its fellows among the *carmina maiora*. The answer can only be that the edition of the *carmina minora* was not published by Claudian himself, but by someone else, working to the orders of Stilico. This editor, stuck for a short poem which mentioned Stilico to serve as an introduction, could do no better than repeat *Fesc.* iii, the only one of the four Fescennines which did: a clumsy device, but better than nothing.

The hypothesis that the editor was someone other than Claudian is only confirmed by consideration of the haphazard arrangement of the poems. Brief epigrams, epithalamia, half-finished epics and panegyrics all jumbled up together in no apparent order, with a number of hexameter poems of 50–100 lines. Moreover some of these pieces (e.g. v and vi) have the appearance of being mere jottings from Claudian's notebooks, fragments destined some day to be worked into a longer poem, but not to be published in their present form.[1]

I would suggest then that the *carmina minora* are a clumsily edited collection of everything that could be found in Claudian's notebooks (finished or unfinished), published in honour of Stilico in 404, or very soon after.

Now it is of course possible that in 404 Claudian left Italy in such a hurry that he even left his notebooks behind. But why should he have left so suddenly—unless he had fallen foul of Stilico? And if he had done this, why should Stilico have seen to the editing of his literary remains? Stilico's reasons for republishing the *carmina maiora*, all of which concerned himself very closely, are obvious enough: but he stood to gain nothing from the publication of Claudian's minor works, mostly addressed to other people and on trivial, or at least non-political subjects. Their publication can only be interpreted as an act of *pietas* to Claudian. And such an act of *pietas* presupposes that Claudian was dead. I suggest then that he died in the course of 404, little more than 35 years old, still at the height of his fame, mourned by no one more than Stilico.

[1] Cf. Platnauer, Loeb edn., i (1928), xviii, n. 2.

XIV

CONCLUSION

In the declining decades of the ancient world Claudian was at once accorded his rightful place alongside the classic poets of Rome. We have noted already the attention and respect paid to his verses even by contemporaries, Augustine and Orosius, Prudentius and Rutilius, to whose number we may add Paulinus of Nola and Jerome. In the period of disintegration and chaos which followed his death, perhaps the greatest tribute to his power to charm is the distant and disparate areas over which his poems were at once read and imitated on a par with the ancients, areas which were already fast slipping out of effective Roman control.

In Vandal Africa, for example, he was a favourite poet of Dracontius and Corippus. His influence can be traced on virtually all the numerous poets of fifth- and sixth-century Gaul: Rutilius, Paulinus of Pella, Orientius, Prosper of Aquitaine, Rusticius Elpidius, Alcimus Avitus, Venantius Fortunatus, Claudius Marius Victor, and (above all) Sidonius Apollinaris. Seldom has any poet inspired (if that is the word) such a follower. Sidonius' panegyrics are monstrous ghosts; every theme, every trick, every tendency in Claudian pushed to its furthest extreme.

The less abundant (and on the whole less talented) poets of late Imperial Italy knew him too, of course: Merobaudes, Sedulius, Arator, Maximian, and (especially) Ennodius. More surprisingly, he was still being read in sixth-century Constantinople, not merely by the *émigré* professor Priscian, but by that part-time poet and antiquary John of Lydia.[1]

In the dark ages which follow, like so many other classical writers he lay neglected for a while—but never entirely forgotten.

---

[1] The lists of borrowings assembled by Birt (pp. lxxvi–lxxx) could easily be extended, but suffice for our present purpose.

Columban[1] knew him, as perhaps did Aldhelm[2] a century later. But Isidore did not, nor Bede, it seems.

One might have expected courtly poetry such as Claudian's to be congenial to the poets of Charlemagne's court, but no Carolingian manuscript of the panegyrics is known, and a catalogue recently assigned to the court library at Aix *c.* 790 lists almost all Claudian's poems but the panegyrics. Thus it is perhaps an accident more of transmission than of taste that Carolingian panegyrical poetry looks to Venantius Fortunatus instead of to so obvious a model as Claudian (or even Sidonius).[3]

But Claudian was beginning to evoke interest again: one ninth-century codex contains the Latin *Gigantomachia* (anonymously), and another, previously assigned to the ninth, but now recognized as eighth-century (probably from Verona), contains 31 of the *carmina minora* and 2 spurious poems.[4] The first ten lines of the preface to *VI Cons.* are transmitted as an independent elegy together with some poems of Petronius on the same subject in a ninth-century manuscript of Ausonius—an interesting early example of the separation of the preface from its poem, since many later manuscripts of *Rapt.* have it as the preface to *Rapt.* iii (Claudian himself having provided prefaces for Bks. i and ii, but left iii without one).

One German library catalogue of the ninth century lists 'Claudianus de Proserpina i'.[5] The Aix catalogue[6] lists not only

---

[1] Cf. M. Manitius, *Philologus* xlix (1890), 555.

[2] The passages cited by J. D. A. Ogilvy, *Books known to the English 597 to 1066* (1967), are insufficient to prove direct knowledge of Claudian in Aldhelm, since one is from a spurious work, the other the abbreviated quotation from *III Cons.* derived from Augustine and Orosius. See rather the passages quoted by Birt, p. lxxx.

[3] F. Bittner, *Studien zum Herrscherlob in der mittellatein. Dichtung* (Diss. Würzburg, 1962). Birt, p. lxxxi, lists a few dubious echoes in Carolingian poets.

[4] E. A. Lowe, *Cod. Lat. Antiq.* iv (1947), no. 516, and cf. G. Billanovich, *Italia med. e umanistica* ii (1959), 130.

[5] Except for special studies cited below my information on library catalogues is derived from the convenient handlist in M. Manitius, *Handschriften antiker Autoren in mittelalterlichen Bibliothekskatalogen* (*Zentralblatt für Bibliothekswesen,* Beiheft 67), 221–4.

[6] B. Bischoff, *Karl der Grosse* ii (1965), 57 f.

Rapt. but *Ruf.*, *three* books of *Eutr.* (presumably counting the preface to Bk. ii as a separate book), *Get.*, and *Gild.*: a good selection, and of especial interest in that by the time manuscripts of Claudian become more frequent (twelfth century and later), *Rapt.* is usually transmitted separately under the title 'Claudianus minor' or 'parvus', as distinguished from 'Claudianus maior' or 'magnus' (the political and minor poems). Birt was convinced that the transmission of the two corpora had been distinct from the end of Antiquity right down to the twelfth century, and he argues that when *Rapt.* is found in the same manuscript as the other poems, it was added from another source.[1] In some cases he is certainly correct, in others it is a mere hypothesis. It would perhaps be rash to take up too firm a stand. No complete manuscript of the political poems and no manuscript at all of *Rapt.* earlier than the twelfth century survives to test the hypothesis, and the Aix catalogue contradicts it.

In the decades which followed Claudian's death there were a number of different collections of his various works in circulation. The panegyric on the Anicii (which has no fixed relation to the other works in manuscripts), the *carmina minora*, *Rapt.*, and the omnibus edition of the political poems issued by (or for) Stilico. Separate copies of the individual political poems published as Claudian wrote them must still have been circulating as well— just as there is some evidence that at least as late as the sixth century separate copies of individual poems by Prudentius were still circulating alongside the omnibus edition published in 404-5.[2] *Rapt.* seldom occupies as many as twenty minuscule leaves, and cannot have made a very large book even in capitals. Can one really believe with any confidence that no one before the twelfth century thought of adding some at least of his other favourites to fill out a codex? Not everyone would have wanted all the Stilico poems, especially after his fall: nor all the panegyrics on Honorius, especially after his unlamented death. Why should

---

[1] Cf. Birt, p. lxxvii, especially n. 3, and (more recently) V. Paladini, *Claudianus Minor (Il ratto di Proserpina)*, 1952, p. 5, n. 3.

[2] See below, pp. 470-1.

not a selection of the more interesting poems, such as the Aix list, have existed as early as the fifth or sixth centuries? Another ninth-century catalogue (not eleventh, as formerly supposed),[1] from Bobbio, lists 'libros quatuor' of Claudian: we should like to know which four books. Yet another, from St. Oyan in the eleventh century, records a manuscript containing only *Ruf.* (an especial medieval favourite), a manuscript as old if not older than our earliest manuscript containing the poem (eleventh-century, from Gemblours), which itself contains only *Ruf.*, *Eutr.*, *Get.*, and *Gild.* Richard of Furnival listed *c.* 1250 in his *Biblionomia*, now known to be based on an actual contemporary library, a one-volume Claudian containing the political poems minus *Get.*, *Gild.*, and *Nupt.*, but including *Rapt.* The numerous manuscripts of the twelfth century and later contain the political poems in a variety of combinations and orders, sometimes with, sometimes without the other three corpora. And the *carmina minora* too are found in such a variety of combinations and orders, sometimes interspersed among the larger poems, sometimes not, as to suggest that a number of different combinations of all four (supplemented from copies of individual poems) may have existed from an early date alongside 'Claudianus maior' and 'Claudianus minor'.

The miraculous memory and unflagging industry of Max Manitius have collected allusions to or quotations from Claudian in nearly sixty medieval writers, for the most part from the twelfth and thirteenth centuries, from the greatest names of their day down to the humblest monastic chroniclers, from Spain and Britain to Poland and Denmark.[2] Probably the most striking (if not really the most substantial) illustration of Claudian's influence is Alan of Lille's *Anticlaudianus de Antirufino*.[3] Not that Alan's poem is in any sense a refutation of *Ruf.*, or even especially dependent on it (Alan's major source is Martianus Capella).

---

[1] See M. Esposito, *JTS* xxxii (1930/1), 337 f.

[2] *Philologus* xlix (1890), 554–60, supplemented by his *Geschichte d. latein. Literatur in Mittelalter*, especially vol. iii (1931), index, s.v. Claudian.

[3] Curtius, *European Literature*, pp. 119 f.

The poem is an allegory. Rufinus was for Alan the model of wickedness, the type of sinful man, as an antithesis to whom he created Antirufinus, the model of the virtuous man. It was for this reason rather than because he had borrowed from Claudian details like the infernal council that Alan chose his challenging title. But what a tribute to Claudian's success in elevating Rufinus to the status of archetypal villain! 'Rufinus crimine, forma Thersites', wrote Eberhard the German round about the same time, paying a similar compliment to Claudian's achievement by the conjunction.[1]

Since there are a good many moralizing passages in Claudian's panegyrics, and not a few epigrams in the invectives, it is not surprising that as early as the ninth century snippets from Claudian were included in collections of excerpts and florilegia. Such collections became common in the thirteenth century and after. Two survive from the ninth, one from the tenth/eleventh; a ninth/tenth-century manuscript contains glosses on Claudian.[2] Often, no doubt, it was from such a source that isolated quotations in medieval writers were drawn. As, for example, when Pope Innocent III quoted from *Ruf.* i. 22–3, 'tolluntur in altum | ut lapsu graviore ruant'—a favourite in anthologies.[3] In a later age it was to serve as motto for Montesquieu's *Considérations* on the decline of Rome. Compare too the following words written by Héloïse to Abélard: 'quanto . . . sublimiorem obtinui gradum, tanto hinc prostrata *graviorem* in te et in me pariter perpessa sum *casum.*' The combination of the verbal and thematic echo suggests a perhaps unconscious reminiscence of Claudian's line. But one manuscript (or more probably an unscrupulous eighteenth-century editor) has removed all doubt by inserting after *casum* 'et cum Claudiano "tollor in altum | ut lapsu graviore ruam" '.[4]

---

[1] *Laborintus* ii. 103.

[2] Birt, pp. clxxiii–clxxx, admirable as far as it goes, and E. M. Sanford, 'Classical Latin Authors in the Libri Manuales', *TAPhA* lv (1924), 190–248, nos. 16 and 39, 58 and 120, for ninth- to tenth-century excerpts omitted by Birt. Cf. too B. L. Ullman, *Class. Phil.* xxvii (1932), 10.

[3] *De contemptu Mundi* ii. 29 (*PL* ccxvii. 728).

[4] R. Rawlinson, in his edition of 1718, allegedly based on a MS. lent him by

It would be more interesting, of course, if Héloïse herself really did quote Claudian (if only at second hand): but for the student of Claudian's *Fortleben* it is still interesting even as an interpolation.

But knowledge of Claudian was by no means confined to the Florilegia. In thirteenth-century Paris, where literary studies were being overshadowed by the growth of philosophy and theology, the two most vocal champions of the liberal studies, Henri d'Andeli and the English exile John of Garland, both name Claudian among the classical authors now wrongfully neglected.[1]

Yet despite their protests Claudian had never been more popular since Antiquity than in the thirteenth century. For it was then that he first became a school author. Absent from the curriculum lists of Conrad of Hirsau and Alexander Neckham (beginning and end respectively of the twelfth century), he first appears in the *Laborintus* of Eberhard the German (some time before 1280) and the *Registrum multorum auctorum* of Hugo of Trimberg (1280):[2]

> Claudianus floruit regnante Florentino
> librosque suos edidit stilo repentino.

The first line may betray ignorance of history, but the second is a sound enough literary judgement. We have seen already that Richard of Furnival included most of Claudian's major works in his *Biblionomia* (*c.* 1250).[3] That the absence of Claudian's name from the two earlier lists is not just a coincidence seems proved by a point which does not seem yet to have been drawn into this connection. It is precisely in the course of the thirteenth century that *Rapt.* was added to the so-called *Libri Catoniani*, a collection

---

a friend he refused to name: cf. the preface to V. Cousin's edition, pp. 1–2, and *Ep.* 4, p. 87 for the letter.

[1] Cf. Curtius, *European Literature*, p. 56.

[2] Curtius again, pp. 48 f. Cf. also the list published by E. K. Rand, *Speculum* iv (1929), 265.

[3] Eberhard too names both *Rapt.* and the contemporary poems, though separately. This is not because (as Manitius supposed) Eberhard (or others) thought there were *two* Claudians, distinguished as *maior* and *minor*: but because the first time he was listing the elementary textbooks from the *Libri Catoniani* (see above), the second time the other works by the same authors. This is why he similarly lists the *Achilleid* and *Thebaid* of Statius separately, as pointed out by M. Boas, *Mnemos.* xlii (1914), 23–4.

of textbooks added successively to the *Disticha Catonis* from the ninth century on: in its earliest form only 'Cato' and the *Fables of Avianus*, in its definitive form 'Cato', Theodulus, Avianus, Maximian, Claudian's *Rapt.*, and Statius' *Achilleid*. Claudian is found in no manuscript of the collection before the thirteenth century—but is present in no fewer than fourteen of the thirteenth and fourteenth centuries.[1]

The simplest and clearest way to document the growth of Claudian's popularity is by chronological tabulation of extant manuscripts. Those for 'Claudianus maior' have yet to be counted, let alone dated and assessed. But the work has now (at last) been done for *Rapt.*, in exemplary fashion:[2]

Century	Number of manuscripts
xii	5
xii/xiii	2
xiii	25
xiii/xiv	11
xiv	14
xiv/xv	3
xv	62
xv/xvi	4
xvi	6

Unequivocal confirmation of the sudden interest shown in the thirteenth century. More striking still is the illustration of Claudian's vogue at the Renaissance. Sabbadini's list of only thirteen humanists who show knowledge of Claudian[3] is a misleading index of his popularity. Muretus, one of the later humanists, went so far as to complain that 'patres et avi nostri' preferred Lucan and Claudian to Vergil.[4] Petrarch boldly claimed him as

---

[1] M. Boas, *Mnemos.* xlii (1914), 17–46; Hall (next note), p. 70.

[2] See the preface to J. B. Hall's edition (1969).

[3] R. Sabbadini, *Le Scoperte dei cod. lat. e greci ne' secoli xiv e xv* (1914), 215–16.

[4] *Orationes et epistulae* (1605), Or. 2. 12. E. L. Etter, *Tacitus in d. Geistesgeschichte d. 16. u. 17. Jhdts.*, 1966, 6, argues that Muretus is referring back to the Middle Ages, and that it is the humanists who 'den Stil von Autoren der augusteischen Zeit als deren Hauptvertreter Cicero galt, zum Vorbild genommen hätten'. But

a Florentine—on no firmer evidence, apparently, than the dedication of *Rapt.* ii to a 'Florentinus' (as can be inferred from the
annotation to his own manuscript of Claudian, now in Paris).[1]
Despite rival claims for the honour of his birthplace, Petrarch
was followed by Boccaccio, Coluccio Salutati, and many others.[2]
Filippo Villani included him in his *Liber de civitatis Florentiae
famosis civibus.* For Francesco da Fiano (*Contra detractatores et
oblocutores poetarum, c.* 1400) Claudian was a Christian, like Vergil
and Statius before him. Strada naturally included Claudian (while
omitting Valerius Flaccus and Silius) in the curious contest of the
epic poets in his *Prolusiones* (1627).[3] The champion assigned to
Claudian was, appropriately enough, Baldassarre Castiglione,
whose famous *Book of the Courtier* (published 1528) has a paper-
back reputation even today.

It would be both pleasant and instructive to pursue Claudian's
story through European literature in detail, but this is a task, alas,
beyond both the scope of this book and the competence of its
author. In its place, and as a contribution against the time when
the full story comes to be written, rather than offer a desultory
and imperfect sketch of the whole period, it seemed best to
single out instead just three chapters in the literary history of
England, and conclude with a brief epilogue. Since the bulk
of this book has been concerned (as is proper) with Claudian's
role as a political poet, it is proper that these three chapters in his
posthumous fame should concern his influence on political
literature.

I

Claudian was better known in late medieval England than has
sometimes been supposed.[4] A recent survey of books known in

surely he is referring to the more strictly classical aims of the later humanists
(cf. on this R. R. Bolgar, *The Classical Heritage* (1954), 266 f.).

[1] P. de Nolhac, *Pétrarque et l'humanisme*[2] (1907), 202–4.
[2] R. Weiss, *Un inedito petrarchesco* (1950), 59, nn. 68–9.
[3] Translated for English readers by Steele, in the *Guardian* for 1713.
[4] e.g. E. Flügel, *Anglia* xxviii (1905), 430.

England between 597 and 1066 has only one entry to show against Claudian's name: Aldhelm.[1] But from the twelfth century on a steady influence can be traced. Indeed he was widely read (and quoted) in the educated circles of late twelfth- and thirteenth-century England. Nor was this popularity confined by any means to *Rapt.*, the only poem we know to have been regularly read at school. A (necessarily dry) list[2] of now somewhat unfamiliar names together with the works they quote from will illustrate the point.

Herbert of Bosham (*fl.* 1162–86) quotes from *Theod.*, Henry of Saltrey (*fl.* 1150) from *Ruf.*, Roger of Hoveden (d. ?1201) from *Gild.* Walter Map (*c.* 1140–1209) found congenial material in *Eutr.* for his own satirical poems, and quotes *IV Cons.* as well. William of Malmesbury (d. *c.* 1143) quotes from *Ruf.*, Benedict of Peterborough (d. 1193) from *Gild.* and *Eutr.*, Radulf of Diceto, Dean of St. Paul's between 1180 and 1202, quotes from *IV Cons.* and *Ruf. Rapt.* is cited four times in the *Derivationes* of Osbern of Gloucester (mid twelfth century). John of Salisbury has six substantial quotations from *IV Cons.* and another from *Ruf.* Nigel Wireker (*c.* 1130–1200), a monk at Canterbury once associated with Thomas à Becket, quotes from *Ruf.* in an attack on the corruption of the priesthood. Matthew Paris (d. 1259) quotes six times from *IV Cons.* as well as from *Ruf.* and *Rapt.*, Girald of Wales (d. *c.* 1223) from *Eutr.* and *Stil.* and four more substantial citations from *IV Cons.* These last are basically the same as the quotations in John of Salisbury's *Policraticus*, a work with which Girald was beyond question very familiar, and whence he may well have taken them. Yet it would be wrong to suppose that Girald only knew Claudian at second hand. When accused before the Pope by Hubert, Archbishop of Canterbury, Girald himself wrote to the Pope, picking up from Hubert's accusation the words 'cum deceat virtute magis quam sanguine niti' with the counter-accusation that Hubert had cribbed them from Claudian: 'istud mutuatus est a Claudiano, dicente "virtute decet,

---

[1] Ogilvy's *Books known to the English* (1967): above p. 420, n. 2.
[2] Largely drawn from the material collected by Manitius.

non sanguine niti." '¹ How many modern students of Latin poetry would have spotted the quotation from *IV Cons.* 220?

It has been remarked already that Claudian is absent from the curriculum list of Alexander Neckam (1157–1217), in his latter years Abbot of Cirencester. But this does not mean that Alexander did not himself know Claudian. In his *De naturis rerum* (i. 35) he quotes 53 lines of the *Phoenix*: indeed the readings he offers are not found together in any extant manuscript, and so deserve to be accorded the authority of a manuscript themselves.² More general influence in matters of style and metrical technique as well as verbal echoes from a number of Claudian's poems is revealed in the epic poem *Bellum Troianum* by Joseph of Exeter (d. *c.* 1210).³

Chaucer knew *Rapt.* well, and echoes or quotes from it several times, placing Claudian on a pillar of sulphur in the House of Fame:

> on a piler stood
> Of soulfre, lyk as he were wood,
> Daun Claudian, the sothe to telle,
> That bar up al the fame of helle.

In the preface to the *Legende of Goode Women* the god of love asks 'what seith . . . Claudyan?' The only noteworthy list of 'good women' in Claudian is to be found in *Laus Serenae*—all the women whom Serena (naturally) surpassed. Several lines from the preface to *VI Cons.* are freely translated in stanza xv of the *Parlement of Foules*. But it will be remembered that the preface to *VI Cons.* is found in many manuscripts of *Rapt.* (especially in the *Libri Catoniani*) as the preface to *Rapt.* iii. Since

---

¹ *De Invect.* 1. ii, p. 18 ed. Brewer (*Rer. Brit. M.A. Scr.* 21. 8). Girald also quotes the abbreviated passage from *III Cons.* which derives ultimately from Augustine and Orosius—further illustration of the danger of assuming that those who quote a writer once at second hand do not know him at first hand. We all of us sometimes locate via secondary sources quotations from works we have at one time read carefully at first hand.

² Manitius, *Geschichte* (p. 422, n. 2) iii. 768, n. 1.

³ Cf. W. B. Sedgwick, 'The *Bellum Troianum* of Joseph of Exeter', *Speculum* v (1930), 50 f. and especially 66 f.

Chaucer certainly knew *Rapt.* it was perhaps here that he read it.[1] After Chaucer we find quotations from *Ruf.* in Thomas Walsingham (d. *c.* 1422) and from *Rapt.* in Osbern Bokenham (d. 1445).

This picture receives strong confirmation from the evidence of library catalogues, which list no fewer than 20 manuscripts of Claudian in English libraries between 1195 and 1478—from two at Durham in the twelfth century to five at Canterbury in the fifteenth.

But from our point of view at least the most interesting piece of evidence is a Middle English version of *Stil.* ii made at Clare in Suffolk in the year 1445.[2] Despite its early date this important translation (in verse, and on the whole remarkably accurate) has been wholly ignored by historians of the classical tradition.[3] It cannot, of course, be claimed as the earliest English translation of a classical writer: King Alfred's version of Boethius' *Consolatio* leads all challengers by a comfortable margin, not to mention subsequent versions by Chaucer (1380) and Walton (1410). Yet it is far and away the earliest after these—and the *Consolatio* is in any case from many points of view more medieval than classical. The earliest English translations quoted by Bolgar[4] are of Cicero, *De senectute* and *De amicitia*, both in 1481. He can quote no English version of Claudian before Leonard Digges's *Rapt.* in 1617, and no vernacular version in any language before L. Sannuto's *Rapt.* in 1551. It is thus striking to find so early a translation of one of the less known works of a poet who, however popular, had never rivalled Vergil and Horace, Ovid and Statius.

More interesting still is the political aspect of the translation.

[1] See R. A. Pratt's useful study 'Chaucer's Claudian', *Speculum* xxii (1947), 419–29.

[2] Published with commentary by E. Flügel, *Anglia* xxviii (1905), 255–97, 421–38.

[3] It is anonymous, but a likely candidate for authorship is Osbern Bokenham, who lived and wrote at Clare up to the 1440s, was a dependent of the House of York, and knew Claudian (cf. Flügel, p. 430, n. 3). On Osbern and his age see S. Moore, 'Patrons of Letters in Norfolk and Suffolk *c.* 1450', *Publ. of the Modern Language Association of America* xxviii (1913), 79 f.

[4] *The Classical Heritage* (1954), pp. 508–41 (Appendix II: 'Translations of Greek and Latin Authors into the Vernaculars before 1600').

Not merely is Claudian's picture of Stilico held up (in the translator's epilogue) as a lesson in conduct for the ideal ruler (a theme to which we shall return):

> Claudyan now hath tawght
> in wordys thyrk, in sentens cleer. In whom as in a merour
> Princys may se her owtward gestys & yf hem vyce have caught,
> They owyn to leve yt hastly. gret ellys dyshonour
> Wyll sprynge ther off . . .

More important, Richard Duke of York (then absent in France), to whom the translation is addressed (the manuscript is decorated with the badges of the House of York) is explicitly compared to the 'gode prince' Stilico. The feeble King Henry VI, on the other hand, is implicitly likened to Stilico's enemy 'Ruffyne'. Not only did our translator know 'his othir boke clepid Claudianus in Ruffinum': he knew it well enough to adapt its theme to the current political situation. It is fairly clear, moreover, that he chose this particular book of *Stil.* to translate (ii, rather than i or iii) in large measure at least because it suited his political purpose: all the provinces of the West join in appealing to Stilico to return to Rome and assume the consulate, just as (he implies) all Britain appeals to York to return from France and assume the throne of Henry. He omits Claudian's fanciful conclusion to the book—the Sun's visit to the cave of Time to select Stilico's consular year—so that he can close instead with the return of the nobles from across the sea to welcome the consulate of their peer and *avenger*:

> ad socii properant et *vindicis* annum,

ominously enough translated 'venger of worship'.

The translation has a genuine historical importance. There is no other evidence for a party in England this early supporting York's designs on the throne—designs which did not become manifest till a year or two after Jack Cade's rebellion in 1450. Just to underline the contemporary allusions for the slower-witted, against the words 'thi grettest worshippe groweth', referring to Stilico of course, there is a marginal note 'deo gracias *Ricarde*'!

II

It is hardly likely that Claudian ever presumed to think of himself as a political philosopher. He was merely putting into concise and elegant form what Greek and Roman political writers had been saying about the duties of their rulers for centuries.[1] But to the less educated generations which followed, unfamiliar with the traditions Claudian was epitomizing, the particular form into which he had cast them, beautiful, coherent, simple, seemed peculiarly impressive. Thus it is that the great kingship speech of Theodosius to Honorius from *IV Cons.* is the most quoted passage of all Claudian in medieval times. Above all (though not exclusively) in the *Specula Principum*, 'Mirrors for Princes' ('Fürstenspiegel' in the convenient German term), treatises on the virtues and duties of the ideal ruler.

The leading authority on this form of literature remarks that there is scarcely one of the more than forty extant *Specula Principum* written between 1159 and 1379 in which at least one quotation from *IV Cons.* does not stand, from the most famous, the *Policraticus* of John of Salisbury, down to some of the very latest, for example the *De cura Reipublicae* of Philip of Leyden (some time after 1355).[2] And since there are so few traces of Claudian in medieval Spain (Manitius was able to list only one echo of Claudian in a Spanish writer and one mention in a Spanish library catalogue), it is worth noting that there are several quotations from *IV Cons.* in late medieval *Specula Principum* from Spain, in both Latin and the vernaculars: for example in the *Castigos é documentos* of King Sancho IV of Castile for his son Ferdinand.[3] The five quotations in John of Salisbury total 35 lines:

[1] Above, pp. 387 f.

[2] W. Berges, *Die Fürstenspiegel des hohen und späten Mittelalters* (*MGH Schriften* ii), 1938, 41, n. 3. Note the contrast with the 'Fürstenspiegel' of Carolingian times (cf. p. 420, n. 3).

[3] § 62 = *Bibliot. aut. españ.* 51, p. 190.

Girald of Wales has 5 too, totalling 20 lines (with 7 more lines
from *Stil.* and 2 from *III Cons.* for good measure), in his *De
principis instructione*, and there are 21 lines (including one 14-line
quotation) in the five pages of fragments which are all that survive
from the influential *De bono regimine principis* of Helinand, Abbot
of Froidmont (d. *c.* 1229). The most commonly cited lines are
299–302, embodying the principle that as the king behaves, so do
his people—'celebre illud versificatoris egregii sensum et verba
magni Theodosii exprimentis', as John of Salisbury remarked:

> componitur orbis
> regis ad exemplum . . .
> mobile mutatur semper cum principe vulgus.

The last line is perhaps the most widely quoted in all Claudian.
Indirectly it has gained still wider currency over the last three
centuries. Some wag in the seventeenth century had the idea of
shortening 'mobile vulgus' to just 'mob', the sort of fad word
which will often dominate the fashionable small talk for a season
and then vanish without trace. Early in the next century it was
still held a vulgarism (by Swift, for example)—but in vain.[1]
As we all know, it had come to stay.

In 1929 a poetical *speculum* 'ad imperatorem romanum' ascribed
to Petrarch was published from a fifteenth-century Vatican
manuscript. It would almost certainly have been claimed as an
original piece of work, addressed no doubt to the Emperor
Charles IV, had not the editor (fortunately) been classical scholar
enough to spot that the lines are not merely (as one might have
expected) based on Claudian: they *are* Claudian (*IV Cons.* 257–
75), with one or two trifling omissions and corruptions. For
a variety of reasons it seems unlikely that the piece has anything
to do with either Petrarch or Charles IV, and since there is no

---

[1] Claudian probably took the phrase, whether consciously or unconsciously,
from Stat., *Silv.* ii. 2. 123 f. (of the Persian King), 'quem non ambigui fasces,
non mobile vulgus, | non leges, non castra terent' (both passages are cited in the
new *Oxford Dictionary of English Etymology* (1966), 583), but in view of the popularity (and quotability) not merely of this one line of Claudian, but also of the
whole passage in which it occurs, it seems to me that the lion's share of the credit
should probably go to Claudian. I owe this point to Gilbert Highet.

other indication of date, it is impossible to hazard a worthwhile guess at the identity of the 'imperator' for whom it was adapted.[1]

Against this background it is the less surprising that our translator of 1445 should see *Stil.* as a 'merour' for 'Princys'. More striking is the pre-eminent place accorded Claudian by Sir Thomas Elyot in his *Boke named the Gouernour* (1531). In the first chapter of part ii of his work, devoted to the virtues required by 'governors', he writes:

These articles well and substantially graven in a nobleman's memory, it shall also be necessary to cause them to bee delectably written and set in a table within his bedchamber, adding too the verses of Claudian, the noble poete, which he wrote to Theodosius and Honorius, emperors of Rome.

He then offers a somewhat condensed and rearranged translation of the whole passage from *IV Cons.*, the first printed translation of any part of Claudian. 'These verses of Claudian,' he continues,

full of excellent wisdome, as I have said, would be in a table, in such a place as a governour once in a day may behold them, specially as they bee expressed in Latine by the saide poete, unto whose eloquence no translation in Englyshe may be equivalent. But yet were it better to conne them by heart; yea, and if they were made in the fourme of a ditty to be songe to an instrument, O what a sweet song would it bee in the eares of wise men!

It would be interesting to know if the latter suggestion was ever taken up. Another English translation of the speech was published in 1671 by 'R. T. Esquire', *An Essay upon the Third Punique War, to which are added Theodosius' advice to his Son and the Phoenix out of Claudian*—an odd trio.

Claudian was not slow in making his way to the New World. Already by the close of the sixteenth century he was being put to good use by no less a person than the almost legendary Captain

---

[1] P. Piur, 'Ein unbekannter Fürstenspiegel Petrarcas an Kaiser Karl IV?', *Euphorion* xxx (1929), 93–111. Despite W. Berges, *Die Fürstenspiegel* (1938), 41, n. 3, it seems clear from Piur's arguments that the poem can have no connection with Petrarch. It might be added that the variants it offers do not correspond with those of Petrarch's own MS.

John Smith, who quoted a verse translation of *IV Cons.* 284–9 in a pamphlet *On Loving-Kindness*, 'in order to encourage harmonious partnership of all hands for purposes of exploration and colonization'. It hardly seems likely that the translation, in 'excellent though rough Elizabethan', is the work of Smith himself, but it is otherwise unknown.[1]

In the course of the seventeenth century the speech of Theodosius yielded the palm of popularity to a brief quotation from another poem, *Stil.* iii. 113–15:

> fallitur egregio quisquis sub principe credit
> servitium; numquam libertas gratior exstat
> quam sub rege pio.

The earliest example I have been able to find is the word-for-word translation Ben Jonson put into the mouth of C. Silius fawning on the Emperor Tiberius in his *Sejanus* (1603):[2]

> Men are deceiv'd, who think there can be thrall
> Beneath a vertuous prince. Wish'd liberty
> Ne're lovlier lookes, than under such a crowne.

More interesting from our point of view is the use Jonson made of the same passage on one of the arches he designed for that new divinely appointed monarch James I to pass under during his triumphal entry into London the following year, 1604. The arch was in the form of a temple of Janus, erected at Temple Bar, and Jonson himself describes the relevant scene as follows:[3]

On the other side the second hand-maide was ELEVTHERIA, or Libertie, her dressing white, and some-what antique, but loose and free: her haire flowing downe her backe, and shoulders: In her right hand shee bare a club, on her left a hat, the Characters of freedome, and power: At her feet a cat was placed, the creature most affecting, and expressing libertie. She trod on DOVLOSIS, or Servitude, a woman in old and worne garments, leane and meager, bearing fetters on her feet, and hands, about her necke a yoake to insinuate bondage, and the

---

[1] R. M. Gummere, 'The Classics in a Brave New World', *Harvard Studies* lxii (1957), 132.   [2] Act I, lines 407–9.

[3] *Part of the King's Entertainment in passing to his Coronation*, in *Works* (ed. Herford-Simpson) vii (1947), 98.

word NEC VMQUAM GRATIOR Alluding to that other of Claud.
Nunquam libertas gratior extat, Quam sub Rege pio (De laud. Stil. li. 3)
And intimated, that libertie could never appeare more gracefull, and
lovely, than now under so good a prince.

There is no trace of *nec umquam gratior* as a motto in C. Ripa's
Iconologia, from which Jonson drew much of his iconographic
symbolism, including the representation of Servitude and the
yoke,[1] or in any other emblem or motto book of the period, so
it may well be that Jonson invented it himself.

It will be observed that the motto itself omits the key words in
Claudian, and would thus be incomprehensible to anyone who
did not recognize the allusion. Yet this need not mean that the
passage was widely known, since such mottoes were often intended to test the ingenuity and reading of those who saw them
on the arch, to be explained later (as Jonson explains his motto in
the passage quoted) in the triumphal records.

Whether or not the lines were already famous by Jonson's
day, they were soon to become so. Not exploited (because less
relevant) in medieval times, they were now recognized as a
subtle and elegant reconciliation of the claims of individual
liberty with absolute monarchy—a text tailor-made for defenders
of the divine right of kings. A congenial motto, therefore, for
Sir Robert Filmer's *Anarchy of a limited or fixed Monarchy* of 1648,
if in a slightly garbled form,[2]

> neque enim libertas gratior ulla est
> quam Domino servire bono,

and then again (correctly this time) for his *Freeholders Grand
Inquest* of the same year—and for its three successive republica-
tions in 1679, 1680, and 1684. It appears too on the title page[3]
of his most famous work, *Patriarcha, or the Natural Power of Kings,*
written by about 1640, but not published till after Filmer's death,

[1] See Simpson's notes, in *Works* x (1950), 391.
[2] Together with Lucan iii. 145-6.
[3] Presumably added from his earlier works to the posthumous edition, since
it is absent from the autograph MS. (*Cambr. Add. MS.* 7078) now in Cambridge
University Library: cf. Oswyn Murray, *Notes and Queries* (1968), 210.

in 1680. After that it served in the same capacity (again slightly misquoted) for Dryden's translation of Maimbourg's *History of the League*, a work commissioned for political reasons by Charles II. A further corruption of Filmer's original corrupt version was applied to the same monarch in the same year (1684) by Edward Pettit, in *Visions of Government*, designed to refute the anti-monarchical principles of 'phanatical commonwealthsmen':

neque enim libertas *tutior* ulla est
quam Domino servire bono.

As late as 1776 Samuel Johnson (who must have known what he was doing) chose it as the motto for his *Political Tracts*, whence it has received the more permanent fame of enshrinement in Boswell's *Life of Johnson*.[1] While he will certainly have been familiar with Filmer's *Patriarcha*, it was probably the recent example of Johnson (whose *Tracts* aroused much ill will) that directly inspired Gibbon to write in an acid footnote to *Decline and Fall* of 'the famous sentence so familiar to the friends of despotism'—adding 'But the freedom which depends on royal piety scarcely deserves that appellation.'[2]

The 'famous sentence' had evoked an earlier and different reaction from Pope: a bogus Bentleian critical note exactly reversing its sense, appended to the passage in *Dunciad* IV concluding[3]

May you, may Cam and Isis, preach it long!
The RIGHT DIVINE of Kings to govern wrong.

First Scriblerus, who comments that 'the words Liberty and Monarchy have been frequently confounded and mistaken one for the other by the gravest authors', and then emends 'rege pio' to 'lege pia'. Then another note (it will be remembered that the *Dunciad* was a variorum) signed 'Bentl.', and indeed a very clever

[1] Ed. Birkbeck Hill–Powell ii (1934), 315.
[2] Ed. Bury, iii (1909), 250, n. 55: cf. Gibbon, *Memoirs*, ed. Birkbeck Hill (1909), 312.
[3] See J. Sutherland's commentary in the Twickenham edition, v[3] (1963), 359, and (for the political aspects) Oswyn Murray, 'Divine Right in "The Dunciad" (iv. 175–188)', *Notes and Queries* (1968), 208 f.

parody of the great man's style and technique, which rejects
Scriblerus' solution, and instead emends 'exstat' to 'exit', giving
the sense: 'that Liberty was never lost, or went away with so good
a grace, as under a good King: it being without doubt a tenfold
shame to lose it under a bad one.'

But the 'famous sentence' was not the only sentence to play
a part in the Divine Right controversy. Claudian was only too
obvious a quarry for handy political tags. Out of the innumerable
tracts which flooded seventeenth-century England, most now
deservedly forgotten, I shook the dust off just five which happened
to stand together on the same shelf in Columbia University
library. As it happened all five quoted Claudian. Two from the
familiar passage in *IV Cons.*: J. Ussher, *The Power communicated
by God to the Prince* (1661), and 'G. S.', *The Dignity of Kingship
asserted* (1660), an attack on Milton, where two half-lines (obviously quoted from memory) are combined into one: 'Regis
ad exemplum ⟨totus⟩ componitur orbis.' Edward Pettit has been
quoted above. Dudley Digges comes up with an original one
(*Theod.* 224, 'Qui poena fruitur malus est') in *The Unlawfulness of
Subjects taking up arms against their Soveraigne* (1647). John Nalson,
in *The common Interest of King and People* (1678), quotes from *Eutr.*
i. 181 to illustrate the dire results when commoners attempt to
take over:

> asperius nihil est humili cum surgit in altum.

III

Claudian's popularity was at its height in seventeenth- and
eighteenth-century England, though he had been enjoyed as a poet
as well as a political writer since at least Elizabethan times. He was
included, for example, among the chief Latin authors by Thomas
Lodge, *Defence of Poetry* (1571), William Webbe, *Discourse of
English Poetrie* (1586), and Francis Meres, in the section 'Poetrie'
of his *Palladis Tamia* (1598). But such citations prove little Both
information and judgements in at least the latter work are often

taken over wholesale from continental encyclopedias like the *Officina* of Ravisius Textor.[1] And when Henry Peacham writes in his *Compleat Gentleman* (1622) that 'Claudian is an excellent and sweete poet, only overborne by the meanness of his subject; but what wanted to his matter he supplied by his wit and happie invention', he is merely translating from the elder Scaliger: 'Maximus poeta Claudianus, solo argumento ignobiliore oppressus, addit de ingenio quantum deest materiae' (*Poetice* vi. 7, 1561). Even Leonard Digges dutifully echoes Scaliger in the preface to his translation of *Rapt.* (1617)—and his threefold allegorical interpretation of the poem (its historical, natural, and allegorical senses) is taken with little alteration and no acknowledgement from the Italian translation and notes by G. Bevilacqua and A. Cingale (1586).[2] A massive collection of these instant judgements on Claudian was compiled by Kaspar von Barth (Barthius) in the prefaces to his two monstrous editions (1612 and 1650). Barth was hurt by Scaliger's criticism of his hero: did not Scaliger realize that it was the *duty* of a poet to immortalize virtue and condemn vice? A more influential and marginally more critical collection was published by A. Baillet, in § 1184 of his *Jugemens des Savans* (1685–6).

Nevertheless there were many who did know and enjoy Claudian at first hand. Both Spenser and Milton knew *Rapt.*— as was first pointed out by an eighteenth-century critic, Thomas Warton, in his *Observations on the Faerie Queene* (1754 and 1762).[3]

---

[1] See the useful commentary on Mere's 'Poetrie' by D. C. Allen in *Illinois Studies in Language and Literature* xvi (1933), *passim*, remarking at p. 123 that 'the opinions that the critics of this era expressed about Claudian are chiefly of the catch-word type', *facundissimus* (Casaubon), *luculentus* (Beroldus), *celeberrimus* (Merula), *cultissimus* (Rhenanus), et sim.

[2] See Douglas Bush, *Mythology and the Renaissance Tradition in English Poetry* (1932), 317, and the few notes by H. H. Huxley to the reissue of Digges's translation in *English Reprints Series* 16 (1959).

[3] Cf. E. Greenlaw, *Publ. Mod. Lang. Assoc. of America* xv (1918), 111. In *Spectator* 333 (22 March 1712) Addison pointed out an echo of the Latin *Gigantomachia* in *Par. Lost* vi. 643–6, where Milton took over 'the imagination of Claudian, without its puerilities'. On Milton and Claudian cf. too M. Hammond, *Studies in Philology* xxx (1933), 1–16.

Ben Jonson closely imitates a large number of passages, and refers with particular admiration to the infernal council in *Ruf.*[1] Abraham Cowley was an admirer—though not an uncritical one[2]—and wrote a famous translation of the 'Old Man of Verona' (inferior to the original, in Gibbon's judgement). Dryden included some brief but penetrating remarks on the difference between the styles of Vergil and Claudian in his preface to the *Sylvae* (1685). Swift inscribed a motto from Claudian under his personal picture of the Earl of Oxford—as he remarked to the Earl in a letter, repeating the information for the benefit of the second Earl a few years later.[3]

We might recall too a few translations, now long forgotten. Less known than Cowley's version of the 'Old Man of Verona' are others by Sir John Beaumont (brother of Fletcher's collaborator), published in his posthumous *Bosworth Field* in 1629, Andrew Symson, at Edinburgh in 1708, and Elijah Fenton, collaborator in Pope's *Odyssey*. F. Fawkes, the 'best translator since Pope' produced another in 1761. Another of Pope's friends, William Warburton, translated the whole of *III Cons.* in his *Miscellaneous Translations* of 1724. Pope himself one of the epigrams on the drop of water in the crystal, Addison another.[4] Indeed Addison translated a number of excerpts from almost all Claudian's poems in the course of his second *Dialogue on Medals*, and even more in his *Remarks on Italy* (1705), not to mention some happy observations from time to time in the *Spectator*. Laurence Eusden, future poet laureate and victim of the *Dunciad*, translated portions of *Nupt.* ('The Court of Venus') and *Rapt.* in the pages of Steele's *Guardian* in 1713. William Pattison managed to produce another version of the 'Court of Venus' before an early death in 1727 (*Poetical Works*, 1728). Jabez Hughes (to whom we shall return) no fewer than four poems (including *Nupt.* again) between 1714 and 1731.

[1] *Masque of Queenes*, 116 note (ed. Herford-Simpson vii. 287).
[2] See his remark to Hobbes quoted above, p. 285.
[3] *Correspondence*, ed. H. Williams (1963), ii. 438 and iii. 86.
[4] *Pope's own Miscellany*, ed. N. Ault (1935), p. 82 (and cf. pp. xlviii–xlix for the ascription to Pope): Addison, *Remarks on Italy* (*Works*, ed. Greene, ii. 158).

In addition to a few trifling translations, Samuel Johnson at one time formed the surprising intention of editing Claudian, '*cum notis variorum*, in the manner of Burman'.[1] And it is to an essay on memory in the *Idler*[2] alone, it seems, that we owe the story that Barth claimed to have written the whole of his commentary on Claudian 'without consulting the text'—a claim which no one who has ever tried to read that work will find any reason to dispute. Gibbon, of course, used Claudian as a source for the Stiliconian period, but he also admired him greatly as a poet. The last pages of chapter xxx of *Decline and Fall* contain perhaps the most judicious as well as the most eloquent assessment of Claudian's achievement ever written.

We have already seen Rufinus serve as one modern tyrant, Henry VI. Why not another? The art in which Claudian had excelled, the writing of political invective, has never flourished in England as it did in the London of Queen Anne and Walpole. Pamphlet after pamphlet, satire after satire (mostly unsigned) was tossed into the fray, alternately for and against the chief ministers of the day—the opposition usually having the best of at least the literary battle.[3] Add to this Claudian's popularity in the literary circles of the day, and it is not surprising that contemporary satirists should have seen and exploited the possibility of redirecting against contemporary 'Favourite-ministers' the barbs Claudian had thrown at the minister of Arcadius. The only surprise is that no fewer than three such doctored versions of *Ruf.* appeared within less than 20 years—'Rufinus' in each case being a different victim.

All three pamphlets are anonymous, and so the only one which has been dignified with even a passing mention in the literary histories is *Rufinus: or an Historical Essay on the Favourite-Ministry under Theodosius the Great and his Son Arcadius, to which is added a Version of part of Claudian's Rufinus* (1712, in both Edinburgh and

---

[1] Boswell, *Life*, ed. Birkbeck Hill–Powell iv (1934), 381, n. 1.

[2] *Idler* 74 (15 Sept. 1759).

[3] See M. Percival, *Political Ballads illustrating the Administration of Sir Robert Walpole* (1916), with useful introduction and commentary, and W. T. Laprade, *Public Opinion and Politics in Eighteenth-Century England* (1936).

London). And the reason for this is that it was included by Joseph Browne in his edition of the posthumous works of the well-known poet, humorist, and Tory controversialist Dr. William King (who among other literary endeavours had been unwise enough to engage in the controversy between Bentley and Boyle over the letters of Phalaris, 'one of those', as Johnson put it in his *Life*, 'who tried what wit could perform in opposition to learning, on a question which learning alone could decide'). King died in 1713, the *Posthumous Works* appeared in 1739. Whether or not Browne had conclusive evidence for assigning *Rufinus* to King, regrettably he did not disclose it. J. Nichols, King's next editor in 1776, claimed to know (again without giving his evidence) that King wrote the work in 1711, but did not publish it till the very end of that year.

For our purposes, what matters more than the authorship is the fact that *Rufinus* is a sharp attack on the (of course unnamed) Duke of Marlborough. Marlborough was dismissed from office by Queen Anne on the last day of 1711. So if Nichols's information is reliable, *Rufinus* must have been written before Marlborough's fall, but did not appear till after.

The 'Historical Essay' is an account of Rufinus' career and crimes adapted so as to suit the Duke rather better than Rufinus. For example, the civilian Rufinus had never been a 'Captain of the Guards'—but Marlborough had been. The senate under Rufinus, 'that is the *majority* of it [i.e. the former Whig majority in Parliament overthrown in the election of 1710] was become little better than a collection of Pensioners, Preferment-hunters, Boy-politicians, Sham-patriots, Peti-orators and Court-slaves', whereas the opposition to Rufinus is described as 'A party, though hitherto smaller in numbers than his own, yet always more considerable in esteem, being composed of men of the first rank, the largest properties and the greatest abilities . . . who could not without horror reflect on the consequences of an endangered church, a subverted constitution, an exhausted treasury, and a perpetual war.' Of course there had been no such party and no such perpetual war in Rufinus' day: the resemblance to at least the pretensions of the new Tory peace party of 1711 is somewhat closer. Arcadius, notoriously and beyond any possibility of confutation a spineless booby, is (as in the last of these three tracts) styled 'a Prince adorned with every virtue'. Like Claudian (see p. 52), King knew better than to include the monarch in his attack on the minister.

Just to make sure readers *would* look for contemporary parallels in his rather loose translation (of *Ruf.* i. 1–272), King adds at the end of his preface that he has 'so industriously avoided all paraphrase' that he will not feel 'obliged to account for any applications or parallels other readers may make'. In fact there is very little actual tampering—largely because it was scarcely necessary. So much of what Claudian says would suit an overpowerful favourite minister of any age as originally written. But of course there are some insertions. The man whom Rufinus

> condemns to silence, and from truth restrains

(there is nothing in the Latin) must be the Rev. Dr. Sacheverell, impeached by the Whigs for a controversial sermon in 1710 and, though convicted, punished by no more than a three-year ban from his pulpit (hence the 'silence').[1] Hence too the historically unjustified attack on Rufinus' interference in church affairs in the *Essay*.

King inveighs with what might seem uncalled-for warmth against Rufinus' building activity (compared in its results with Wolsey's in the *Essay*), and somewhat overtranslates *Ruf.* i. 193–4, 'orbisque ruinas | accipit *una domus*'

> erects a Tow'r
> To lodge the plunder'd World's collected Store.

And 'haec mihi tecta | culminibus maiora tuis' (204–5) appears as

> Give me my solitary native Home.
> Take thou thy rising Tow'r, thy lofty Dome . . .
> Though each Apartment, every spacious Room . . .

---

[1] King had published a defence of Sacheverell in 1711—a year *after* Sacheverell's conviction. The fact that *Rufinus* similarly appeared a year after the fall of its subject might be considered an argument in favour of King's authorship!

To cap it all, on the title page stands a tag from Juvenal (x. 105–7, on Sejanus),

> numerosa parabat
> excelsae *Turris* tabulata, unde altior esset | casus.

The capital and italics are King's. King was writing in 1711. Marlborough House was completed in 1711. And work on that scandal in Tory eyes, Blenheim Palace, suspended by the new Tory administration in 1710, was finally allowed to continue —at public expense—in 1711. Hence '*rising* Tow'r'.

So much for William King. While *Rufinus* appeared in 1712, 1711 had seen a curiously similar, though briefer, effort: a four-page free rendering, entitled *The Stumbling Block*, of the first 23 lines of *Ruf.* i. This (it will be remembered) is the debate on the apparent prosperity of the wicked, resolved for Claudian by the fall of Rufinus. Like *Rufinus*, the poem has been ascribed to King. Though omitted by Browne and Nichols, it was added without comment in the next (and still latest) three editions of King's works, in 1781, 1795, and 1810. An attribution which does little credit to the intelligence of three successive editors: nor is it much to the credit of more recent scholarship that its absurdity remains to be exposed. King's *Rufinus*, as befits a Tory controversialist, is an attack on Marlborough and the Whigs. *The Stumbling Block* is a Whig attack on the Tories. *Ruf.* i. 15–18,

> causaeque viam non sponte sequebar
> alterius, vacuo quae currere semina motu
> affirmat, magnumque novas per inane figuras
> fortuna non arte regi,

is translated

> A Vacuum's another Maxim
> Where, he brags, Experience backs him:
> Denying that all Space is full
> From inside of a Tory's Skull.

A closer date is suggested by the penultimate stanza, where what clears divine providence and disproves Epicureanism is

> Anna's curb to lawless Louis,
> which as illustrious as true is.

Now, Queen Anne did *not* administer a curb to Louis XIV in 1711.[1] Nor did that year see the peace which the Tories who ruined Marlborough had promised. Surely these lines allude to the Queen's speech in the Lords of December 7 obliquely attacking Marlborough as a warmonger and announcing that 'both time and place are appointed for opening the treaty of a general Peace.' It soon became obvious that this, as politicians say, was over-optimistic. That (of course) is the point of the lines: the 'curb to lawless Louis' was *not* true—and so not illustrious either.

Those who are described as 'tyrants' and 'Pimps rais'd to Honour, Riches, Rule' are, not Marlborough of course, long in power, but the newly emergent Tories, especially St. John (soon Bolingbroke) and the recently created Earl of Oxford. They are 'vile sycophants' because of the arts by which they turned the Queen against Marlborough. The long and clever development of 'the Sceptic's hypothetic Cause' (Epicureanism), concluding scornfully

> As to his Deity, his Tenet
> Swears by it, there's nothing in it;
> Else 'tis too busy or too idle,
> With our poor bagatelles to meddle,

would have been especially appropriate in an attack on that notorious freethinker and deist Bolingbroke.

That the same poem of Claudian should have been twice independently used as a vehicle of political satire within a matter of months, once by a Whig, once by a Tory, might seem to stretch even the long arm of coincidence a little too far. The dates of publication would seem to suggest that King was inspired by *The Stumbling Block*. But if he did write *Rufinus* in 1711, and if *Stumbling Block* was written not before December 1711, it looks as if both must have been in the press at about the same time. One possible solution is to allow that news of King's project leaked out before publication (as happened with the *Dunciad*

---

[1] For a full account of the events of these years, see Winston Churchill's *Marlborough* iv (1938), *passim*.

a few years later), and that a Whig stole his idea and pipped him to the post.

The third pamphlet appeared in 1730, *Claudian's Rufinus: or the Court-Favourite's Overthrow. Being a curious and correct edition of one of the best satyrical poems, of one of the best poets, of one of the worst Statesmen that ever lived.* The title, the lay-out (introductory essay followed by a translation of *Ruf.* i—the whole book this time), and the treatment as a whole suggest direct imitation of King's *Rufinus.* Yet the translations appear independent of each other, and the translator claims that his version is the 'first published in English', a claim not perhaps altogether frankly made, since he continues, obviously tongue in cheek, to claim that he has 'compared with Authentick manuscripts', 'still to be seen by the curious in the Vatican and Bodleian libraries'. And his translation of *Ruf.* i. 22–3, 'tolluntur in altum | ut lapsu graviore ruant',

> Like meteors mount these monsters of the state,
> Then shoot to ruin with full force from fate,

is surely an inferior adaptation of the last couplet of *Stumbling Block*:

> Tyrants *mount* but like a *meteor*
> To make their headlong fall the greater.

The pamphlet has failed to attract even the fleeting attention accorded King's *Rufinus.* A pity, for it has more than one claim on our interest. First, it can be ascribed with certainty to a well-known writer and celebrity of the day. Second, it is a thinly disguised satire, not this time on Marlborough or Bolingbroke, but (unnamed, of course, but unmistakable) on Walpole.

The preface, where not depicting Rufinus' career at somewhat tedious length in Walpolian colours, is punctuated by playful appeals to Pope, assuring him that the poem is 'a finer satire than has ever been published in the English Language since the memory of man, by any bookseller or author within the limits of London and Westminster'. Mr. Pope will surely agree at once that it is far superior to the *Dunciad.* Claudian is second only to Vergil, better even than 'Mr. Pope's favourite Statius himself' (an allusion, surely, to the use made of a line of Statius in the preface to the *Dunciad*).[1] After a while it emerges that the translator had been one of Pope's dunces. A broad hint is provided by the closing sentence: '[the translator] will be content to subscribe himself what he is allow'd to be in the Dunciad, when he was last new christen'd and dipp'd in the muddy lake . . . NAMELESS NAME'!

Now in the 1729 edition of the *Dunciad* the names of almost (but not quite) all the dunces, represented by initials only in the 1728 edition, were spelled out in full. Obviously our translator, writing in 1730, was one of the few allowed to remain anonymous in the 1729 edition as well. Obviously too he must have been one of the dunces made to dive into the mud in Bk. ii. The final clue is provided by an appeal to Pope two pages earlier to raise a subscription for the new translation, so as to 'raise my name as the Dunciad depress'd it, it will be only saying

> That I but lightly skim'd the sable Streams
> Then soar'd afar among the Swans of Thames.'

No contemporary could have failed to recognize the allusion to *Dunciad* ii. 283–6:

> Then ** try'd, but hardly snatch'd from Sight,
> Instant buoys up, and rises into Light;
> He bears no Token of the sabler Streams,
> And mounts far off, among the Swans of Thames.

There can be no doubt that our translator was **. And **, as Pope himself half admitted, and as was indeed plain enough from the long and rather disingenuous note appended to the line, was the celebrated dramatist, projector, and bore, Aaron Hill.[2]

Hill's talents were many and varied, 'traveller, tutor, secretary, poet, translator, historian, dramatist, stage manager, opera

---

[1] Cf. Sutherland's edition (ed. 3, 1963), p. 205.

[2] See Sutherland again, pp. 136–7 and 444–5, and D. Brewster, *Aaron Hill* (1913), pp. 201–38 (a full and judicious account of the relations between Hill and Pope). For fuller discussion of *Claudian's Rufinus*, see my forthcoming paper 'An unrecognized work of Aaron Hill'.

librettist, and commercial projector' all by the time he was thirty.[1]
But it has been remarked that he seems not to have engaged in
political controversy. *Claudian's Rufinus* proves otherwise. Such
historical attacks on Walpole were monotonously frequent at the
time. In the period 1730–1 alone the citizens of London were
regaled, on the stage or in the weeklies, with accounts of the
fall of Buckingham, Essex, Gaveston, Mortimer, Sejanus, and
Wolsey—and probably other ill-fated favourite ministers too.
Why not Rufinus?

We will not linger longer on the prefatory essay. In the again
rather free (but sometimes effective) translation we find 'detrudat
avitis | finibus' (191–2) expanded into

> Begs titles from his Prince, *new Lords creates*,
> Gives them new names, and takes their old estates.

And 'sit licet ipse Numa gravior, sit denique Minos' (of Theodosius) becomes

> Than Numa the divine though graver he,
> Nay tho' a Minos (as he may) he be;
> He, by our *Craftsman*'s rules shall form his sway.

The *Craftsman*, of course, was the leading organ of the opposition
to Walpole.

In what purports to be an 'Afterthought' Hill promises that
he will bring out Bk. ii when he can afford it (if Mr. Pope will
help raise a subscription, that is): meanwhile he has decided to
'satisfy the reader's curiosity with some hints of the argument
upon which the second book is founded'—Rufinus' ambition
and greed leading directly and inescapably to his grisly end,
concluding 'how good a moral does it teach?' We may be sure
that he had no intention of bringing out Bk. ii: the hint (heavy
enough in all conscience) was sufficient.

In view of the difference of style between the suave Marlborough and the bluff Walpole, Hill might have done better
to use the *In Eutropium* instead. However, though less successful
than its predecessors, the piece is not contemptible, and evidently

[1] Brewster, *Aaron Hill*, 275.

found some favour with contemporaries, for it rapidly ran into a second edition.

At this point one might have thought that the market for translations of *Ruf.* into heroic couplets was nearing saturation point. Extraordinarily enough, however, while Hill's version was still being passed round the salons of London, another minor poet of the day, Jabez Hughes, was putting the finishing touches to yet another, this time of both books. But Hughes died suddenly in 1731, and his version did not see the light till 1737. It is a vigorous version, typical of the age, and remarkably independent of its predecessors. Unlike its predecessors too, it does *not* appear to be a satire on anybody. I have read both books with care, and can detect no contemporary allusions or pointed expansions of the original. To judge from the fact that Hughes had published a translation of *Rapt.* as far back as 1714 (running to two more editions by 1723), and also that versions of both Claudian's Epithalamia were found among his papers and published in the same posthumous volume of *Miscellanies* as his *Ruf.*, it looks as though he liked Claudian simply as a poet. But no doubt Walpole read it rather carefully just in case.

Claudian might justifiably have drawn some satisfaction from these successive tributes paid to the power of his creation after 1,300 years. Shrewd time-server that he was he would have been the first to excuse, perhaps even to admire, the successive 'adjustments' to his poem. Indeed, one feels that Claudian would have felt very much at home in early eighteenth-century London, winning the favour of some noble Lord, living in a comfortable house at Twickenham, vilifying Walpole unmercifully, and crossing swords from time to time with Mr. Pope.

IV

Gibbon could still assume that Claudian was 'read with pleasure in every country which has retained or acquired the knowledge of the Latin tongue'. But with the advent of the nineteenth century the circle of those on whose bookshelves Claudian could claim a place as by right began to diminish. Slowly at first, but surely—and probably for good. Coleridge's remark in *Table Talk* (1833) that 'Claudian deserves more attention than is generally paid him' suggests of itself that he was no longer widely read. Indeed, his judgement that Claudian was 'the transitional link between the Classic and Gothic mode of thought' suggests that he had not read very much himself. Byron, comparing the nineteenth-century poets to Pope, dismissed them as 'wretched Claudians'.[1] His partial retraction, 'I wrong Claudian, who *was* a poet, by naming him with such fellows', is probably to be viewed as an additional insult to contemporary poets rather than a significant modification of the implied verdict on Claudian. Oddly enough the same comparison between contemporary poets and Claudian—that is to say between the poets of two implied periods of literary decadence—was suggested to George Grote a few years later: Grote too affected to prefer Claudian.[2]

More typical was the violent attack by Sir C. A. Elton, in the third volume of his *Specimens of the Classic Poets* (1814). 'In all the work of Claudian', he remarked coldly, 'it would be difficult to point to a single natural, unaffected sentiment.' Even the passages which he allows to be readable 'have less the happiness of genius than the trick of art'. Claudian was doomed. Others might forgive the sin of artificiality; but they could not take the adulation of the panegyrics.

No more political translations of the invectives. A sedate version of *Rapt.* by a retired clergyman at Lichfield in the intervals of gout was more characteristic of the age.[3] *Rapt.* (perhaps predictably) was the most popular of Claudian's poems now. Richard Polwhele translated it in 1792, J. G. Strutt, otherwise known for his etchings of 'grand and romantic forest scenery', did the job again in 1814. And a few years later, some time between the ages of 11 and 14, Tennyson put the first 93 lines into Popian couplets—

---

[1] *Ep.* 325, 25 Jan. 1819 (*Letters and Journals of Byron*, ed. Moore, 1829).

[2] M. L. Clarke, *George Grote* (1961), 175.

[3] H. E. J. Howard, 1854, together with *Phoenix* and *Nilus*. He deserves the credit of pointing out that *Nilus* (like so many other of the *c.m.*, cf. p. 418) is unfinished.

returning to the subject (and to Claudian) nearly seventy years later in *Demeter and Persephone*.[1]

The nearest Claudian came to politics in the nineteenth century was to be quoted by Disraeli in his obituary of the Duke of Wellington, in the House of Commons on 15 November 1852:

emicuit Stiliconis apex et cognita fulsit | canities

applied to the grizzled summit of the victor of Waterloo. This was one of Disraeli's less happy efforts. Three days after a warm reception in the House, the *Globe* printed in parallel columns a portion of Disraeli's speech and a portion of an obituary of Marshall St. Cyr by Thiers in the *Revue Trimestre* for 1829 (which had been republished in English in the *Morning Chronicle* in 1848).[2] The resemblances were striking. But whatever the rights and wrongs of what was a very embarrassing week for Disraeli, the quotation from Claudian did not (as sometimes implied)[3] occur in the 'borrowed' portion. And since it does not feature in the standard quotation books of the age, we may perhaps give Disraeli the benefit of the doubt and pass it as the fruit of his own reading.

But Claudian did take on one strange and unexpected new role in the nineteenth century—one of which he would certainly *not* have approved. At the conclusion to a remarkable demolition of Christianity in one of his own notes to *Queen Mab* (1813), Shelley quoted six lines from *c.m.* xxxii, *De Salvatore*.[4] Seldom can the paradoxes inherent in the idea of the Incarnation have been thrown into sharper relief than in these lines. Whether or not Claudian's heart really lay with the old gods, we may be reasonably sure where his tongue was when he wrote of the unmarried mother giving birth to her own father, and similar verbal gymnastics. What a curious irony that Shelley should have seen the last great pagan poet of Rome not as an ally, but, judged by this one *tour de force*, as the epitome of all that was worst in Christianity. 'Does not', he wrote after quoting the lines, 'so

[1] Douglas Bush, *Mythology and the Romantic Tradition in English Poetry* (1937), 199, 220–1, and the notes to C. Ricks' new edition of Tennyson (1969).

[2] Monypenny and Buckle, *Life of Disraeli* iii (1914), Appendix C.

[3] e.g. C. A. Vince, 'Latin Poets in the British Parliament', *CR* xlvi (1932), 104.

[4] *Poems* iv (ed. H. B. Forman), 517.

monstrous and disgusting an absurdity carry its own infamy and refutation with itself?'

In the present century Claudian is hardly read even by classical scholars. There has been no complete edition since those of Birt and Koch in the 1890s, and subsequent editions of individual poems have generally been assigned to doctoral candidates, as a suitably obscure and simple task to cut their teeth on. After nearly eighty years Birt's edition remains the most substantial contribution to the understanding of Claudian ever published. Fargues' *Claudien* (1933) received only three competent reviews, Romano's *Claudiano* (1958) but one.

R. M. Pope's verse translation of *Rapt.* in 1933 was one welcome sign of a revival of interest in wider circles, and more recently (1966) there has appeared a novel on Claudian, in Dutch (*Een nieuwer Testament*, by Hella S. Haasse)—a complement to Hermann Sudermann's play *Die Lobgesänge des Claudian* (1914), where one of the main characters is Claudian's wife Eudora, a disciple of St. Augustine who refuses Claudian conjugal rights because of his paganism![1]

The truth is, in fact, that since the late nineteenth century few but the historians have really bothered with Claudian. From the 1850s on a rash of dissertations issued forth from Germany, earnestly if often wrong-headedly inquiring *Quid ad historiam conferat Claudianus, De fide historica Claudiani, De fontibus. . . .* Claudian was simply a source. The problem was straightforward: was he a better or worse source than Zosimus? And despite some more sophisticated recent work (again by historians), the old simple-minded approach is still all too prevalent. How Claudian would smile to think that what he wrote to entertain and deceive his contemporaries is treated by modern scholars as history.

---

[1] Claudian appears in one other play—as a councillor of the Emperor Tiberius (*sic*) in a strange drama on the life and miracles of Christ by Jehan Michel (d. 1447): Claudian's fellow councillors are Horace, Terence, Porphyry, Maximian, and Juvenal (cf. Highet, *Juvenal the Satirist* (1954), 199–200). Claudian is given nothing of interest to say. Unfortunately he does not appear in Thomas Corneille's *Stilichon* (1691), or in the opera *Onorio* adapted therefrom and performed at the Haymarket in 1734.

APPENDIX A

The date of the De Raptu Proserpinae

It is the purpose of this appendix to expose the fragility of the arguments for all datings of *Rapt.* so far proposed, and to offer another, more solidly based hypothesis in their place.

Not much space need be wasted on the arguments for placing it either before or after all Claudian's other datable poems (i.e. before 395 or after 404), since they are based principally on the anachronistic view stigmatized above (p. 24) that Claudian's poetic development passed through different phases in which he wrote different sorts of poetry. Romano, for example, argues (*Claudiano*, pp. 31 f.) that it must have been written before Claudian had turned to contemporary poetry, Fabbri (*Athenaeum* xvii (1939), 39) that it 'dev'essere nato nel ritiro e nella meditazione', i.e. after he had abandoned contemporary poetry. There is no reason at all to doubt that it was written during the period in which all his other Latin poems were written—indeed I believe that it was. Equally unconvincing are arguments based on the (highly questionable) claims that there are more grecisms or less imitations of Latin poets in *Rapt.*, or that it is 'less mature' than Claudian's other Latin poems. For the first two points see V. Cremona, *Aevum* xxii (1948), 248, n. 1; criteria for maturity are notoriously hard to devise—especially with a poet all of whose surviving Latin works were written during his youth within a period of only eight years.[1] The parallels with Licentius prove nothing either way, but the probability is that Claudian is the imitator (see above, p. 219). The following arguments require more serious discussion:

(*a*) The preface to Bk. i describes how the man who first made a

---

[1] Similarly I have no confidence in Romano's view (pp. 18 f., and cf. his *Appendix Claudianea: questioni d'autenticità*, 1958) that most of Claudian's epigrams were early compositions. His only reason is that many of them are rather feeble. But is it really a safe assumption that Claudian only wrote feeble epigrams when he was very young? The weakness of the assumption is only accentuated when Romano is constrained to push back some of the *c.m. app.* (which are even feebler) even further, to his 'Alexandrian' period, in order to believe them genuine. Did Ausonius 'progress' from his epigrams to his *Mosella*? And Naucellius, author of some of the still feebler *Epigrammata Bobiensia*, wrote them when he was over 90 (*Ep. Bob.* 9).

ship started off by hugging the coast, then when bolder crossed broad
bays, and only gradually built up the confidence to venture forth into
the open sea. The theme is developed at some length, but its relevance
is not made explicit (a regular feature in Claudian's prefaces). There can
be little doubt however that it was intended as a simile, heralding
Rapt. as the most ambitious poem Claudian had written so far. Birt
argues (p. xv) that Claudian could not have written thus 'post magnae
molis carmina quae sunt de Rufino, de bello Gildonis, de Eutropio
vel post amplam laudem Stiliconis'. He thinks *Rapt.* was begun in 395,
after *Prob.* alone of Claudian's Latin poems had appeared ('angustioris
pectoris temptamina'). This does not seem to me the only or even the
most natural way to interpret the simile. Surely it implies rather that
Claudian had already written a certain number of poems, though less
ambitious poems than *Rapt.*: less ambitious, that is, not so much in
bulk as in scope and conception. Every poet of the day wrote panegyrics
and epics for victorious generals by the score, especially where Claudian
came from (cf. *Historia* xiv (1965), 481 f.). But not so many tried their
hand at a full-scale mythological epic in several books—and even
fewer succeeded. Claudian might well have thought that he was
moving on to higher things (or to use his own simile venturing forth
into open sea) when he progressed from panegyrics to a mythological
epic with all the trappings. From this point of view *Rapt.* is more ambitious than anything else Claudian wrote. To anticipate my conclusions, I believe that Bk. i was written soon after *Ruf.* ii (see p. 463).
The progression from *Prob.*, *III Cons.*, *Ruf.* i and ii to *Rapt.*, planned
in several books, fits Claudian's simile admirably from the point of
view of both sheer bulk and loftiness of scope and subject-matter.

  (b) At the end of the preface to Bk. ii, after describing at some
length how Orpheus sang of the deeds of Hercules, Claudian concludes:

> Thracius haec vates. sed tu Tirynthius alter,
>   *Florentine*, mihi: tu mea plectra moves,
> antraque Musarum longo torpentia somno
>   excutis, et *placidos* ducis in orbe choros (49 f.).

Who is Florentinus? Many scholars, especially in recent years, have
been seduced by the curious theory of Wedekind that Florentinus was
a cognomen awarded to Stilico after his victory over Radagaisus
and his Ostrogoths at Fiesole, near Florence, in 406. At least four
decisive objections may be raised to this suggestion, quite apart from

the fact that there is not a scrap of evidence that Stilico ever bore such a cognomen. (1) It is true enough that Roman generals and emperors were frequently awarded cognomina in recognition of victories they had won, but the cognomen such victors took was always formed from the name of the defeated people (e.g. Creticus, Parthicus, Alamannicus, etc.), not the place where they were defeated. There does not seem to be any ancient parallel to titles such as 'Montgomery of Alamein'. (2) One of the most compelling reasons for placing Claudian's death in 404 or early 405 is precisely that he does *not* celebrate Stilico's victory over Radagaisus in 406. It would be most remarkable if after 8 years of defending Stilico from accusations of philobarbarism and even treachery, Claudian had refrained from singing of the first real victory Stilico had ever won over a barbarian army, had he still been alive at the time. (3) It is impossible to believe that Claudian would have alluded to this great victory so obliquely. Nowhere else in all his corpus of poems does he display such reticence in praising Stilico's victories, real or imaginary. Nor could such an event be said without absurdity to call forth '*placidi* chori' of Muses. (4) The strongest single objection is perhaps that Stilico himself apparently did not think that *Rapt.* was dedicated to him. All Claudian's poems which celebrate Stilico were, as we have seen, published in an omnibus edition by or at the orders of Stilico soon after Claudian's death (cf. Birt, p. lxxviii). *Rapt.* was not included in this edition: it has a different textual tradition.

(*c*) The obvious candidate for Florentinus is the Florentinus who was city prefect of Rome between 395 and 397. Birt argued that *Rapt.* was dedicated to this Florentinus actually during his city prefecture, and his argument has been widely, if not universally accepted. Nevertheless it is very far from cogent. He suggests that Claudian wrote the poem to celebrate Florentinus' efficient discharge of his duties in administering the corn supply of Rome during the Gildonic crisis. This is why, according to Birt, Claudian says his purpose is to relate 'unde datae populis *fruges*' (i. 30). And why in the preface to Bk. ii, still addressing Hercules, he says

> te Libyci stupuere sinus, te maxima Tethys
> horruit imposito cum premerere polo (45–6).

Birt thinks these lines apply to Florentinus as well as Hercules, and that the coast of Africa is astonished because, though Rome normally depended on Africa for her corn, Florentinus was managing to obtain it from elsewhere while the African harvest was being withheld. Birt can even explain why *Rapt.* is unfinished. Florentinus was dismissed from office at the end of December 397 (see Chastagnol, *Fastes*, pp. 248–9) for refusing to accede to Stilico's demands for conscription of retainers from senatorial estates for the war against Gildo. Naturally therefore Claudian was unable to continue a poem begun in honour of a man now very much *persona non grata* with Stilico. Indeed in later poems (*Eutr.* i. 402 f., *Stil.* i. 307 f., ii. 392 f., iii. 92 f.) Claudian expressly assigns the credit of provisioning Rome during the Gildonic crisis to Stilico.

Admiration of Birt's brilliance and ingenuity must unfortunately yield to overdue recognition of how utterly far-fetched it all is. These two lines, read in context, simply continue the list of Hercules' labours: line 45 refers to his visit to the pillars named after him, 46 to the occasion when he temporarily relieved Atlas—not, as Birt claims, to the burden of provisioning Rome. None of the other labours listed in the preface can be pressed into a contemporary allusion (see (*d*) below), so why should these two? And though the bringing of corn to mankind is indeed the theme of the myth which forms the subject of *Rapt.*, are we really to suppose that Claudian selected the subject of his most ambitious poem so far solely so that he could indulge in a subtle and very oblique allusion to one of Florentinus' duties as city prefect in the preface to the *second* book? Claudian must have realized that a poem projected on this scale—especially with his other commitments as Stilico's official poet—would not be completed till years after Florentinus had laid down office: the normal tenure of the prefecture of Rome was 'little over one year' (Jones, *LRE* i. 380), and Florentinus had held it since September 395, already two years by the time of the Gildonic crisis. The very obliqueness of this supposed allusion in a poet not normally reticent in such matters is almost enough of itself to discredit Birt's hypothesis. Had Claudian wanted to praise Florentinus he would have written a panegyric on him. Birt (very weakly) argues that Florentinus' deeds were not worthy of a whole panegyric; *a fortiori* then they were not worthy of *Rapt.* That this is the right Florentinus is very probable (no other is known at this period, and his two brothers, Minervius and Protadius, were both literary men, and all three received numerous letters from Symmachus: cf. Seeck, *Symmachus*, pp. cxli f.). But there is no reason whatever to suppose that *Rapt.* was dedicated to him during his urban prefecture.

(*d*) Again in the preface to Bk. ii, we read

> Caci flamma perit; rubuit Busiride Nilus;
> prostratis maduit nubigenis *Pholoe* (43–4).

According to Fargues (p. 17, n. 6) line 44 is an allusion to Stilico's 'victory' over Alaric at Mt. Pholoe in Arcadia in 397 (see above, p. 175), a suggestion regarded as certain by Fabbri (*Athen*. xvii (1939), 29). But the line in question is firmly embedded in a passage of 16 lines devoted exclusively to listing labours of Hercules, including several not in the canonical 12. All his usual victims are there—the Cretan bull, Cerberus, Nemaean lion, Amazons, Stymphalian birds, Geryon, Antaeus, Hydra, Diana's hind, Cacus, Busiris—and it is difficult to entertain the possibility of any contemporary allusion in the mention of any of these. Hercules' clash with the Centaurs is well attested among his exploits, and would merit inclusion in any list. And it is equally well attested that the engagement did take place on Mt. Pholoe, the legendary home of the Centaurs (whether Mt. Pholoe in Arcadia or Thessaly was uncertain at an early date). To quote only a selection of references from authors with whom Claudian was beyond doubt familiar, cf. Lucan iii. 198, Statius *Theb*. iii. 604, x. 228, *Ach*. 168: both the Centaurs and Mt. Pholoe are particularly often mentioned, together with most of Hercules' other labours, by Statius, one of Claudian's favourite poets (cf. the index to Kohlmann's Teubner ed., s.v. Centaurus, Pholoe, Lapithae, Hercules). It seems natural to assume that Claudian's line is of purely literary inspiration and refers solely to Hercules' mythical battle with the Centaurs. Had Claudian intended an allusion to Stilico's 'victory', he would surely not have camouflaged it in such a way that any educated reader familiar with the habitat of the Centaurs would have been almost certain to miss it.

Equally implausible is Fabbri's contention (*Athen*. xvii (1939), 30) that line 45 is an allusion to the Gildonic war. For Fabbri the coast of Libya is astonished at Gildo's sudden and unexpected defeat. What possible significance or relevance such an allusion could have in the context he does not explain. Moreover it requires that Florentinus should be Stilico—a possibility which cannot even be entertained.

(*e*) Romano (p. 30, n. 52 *ad fin.*) returns to a view which is at least as old as a thirteenth-century gloss in Bodl. Auct. J. 2. 16 *ad loc.* (cf. Haverfield, *Journ. Phil.* xvii (1899), 272 and Birt, ad loc.) that the preface to Bk. ii in fact belongs to some other poem, now lost, which Claudian wrote in Florentinus' honour, but got wrongly placed at an early date in front of *Rapt.* ii.[1] The idea is not wholly absurd. There are two apparent parallels. Several MSS. place *pr. VI Cons.* before *Rapt.* iii, thus giving all three books a preface. And the preface to *Ruf.* ii is found in some MSS. in front of *Gild.* This error presumably arose from another error, the false reading *Gildonis* for *et Geticam* in line 14 (unless this error followed the transposition of the preface before *Gild.*). In any case, since *Ruf.* has two prefaces, and *Gild.*, which immediately follows *Ruf.* in most MSS., has none, it was not wholly stupid of a scribe to transpose the preface of *Ruf.* ii to *Gild.* But both these prefaces are misplaced in only a minority of MSS.; their true position can be established with certainty from others. It seems probable that we have Claudian's entire literary output in Latin, even down to two or three unfinished poems. Why should the panegyric on Florentinus have disappeared without trace while its preface survived? Moreover there are two good reasons for accepting that the preface to *Rapt.* ii belongs where all MSS. place it. First the '*placidos . . .* choros' of line 52 suits Claudian's one and only mythological poem (excluding the unfinished, or rather barely started *Gigantomachia*) much better than a political poem—even a panegyric. Second, as E. Bernert pointed out (*Philologus* xciii (1939), 376), a preface in which the theme of Hercules and Orpheus is expounded at such length is eminently appropriate for a poem such as *Rapt.* which is based in part at least on Orphic sources and tells the myth with one or two Orphic details (see above, p. 311).

(*f*) I record merely for the sake of completeness the most recent original attempt to secure a *terminus ante quem.* Cremona (*Aevum* xxii (1948), 245–6) points out that while in *pr. Rapt.* ii Claudian compares Florentinus to Hercules, at *Ruf.* i. 283–4 he says that Stilico's deeds are so outstanding that not even Hercules' labours can now be compared with them. 'Orbene mi pare palese', writes Cremona, 'qui un' intenzione polemica, di far notare cioè come Stilicone, il nuovo protettore, paragonato ora a Ercole, ha superata la gloria di Fiorentino, pure paragonato ad Ercole.' Therefore, he claims, *Rapt.* must have been written before *Ruf.* I give Cremona's own words so as to avoid any possibility of misrepresenting his view which, if I understand it aright, seems to me wholly arbitrary, and not worthy of further discussion.

(*g*) There is one secure *terminus post quem* for the publication (i.e. formal recitation) of any part of *Rapt.* Claudian states quite clearly

---

[1] Cf. Koenig's similar view of the preface to *Ruf.* ii (above, p. 78, n. 2).

in his letter to Probinus (*c.m.* xli. 12 f.) that his panegyric on Probinus and Olybrius was his very first Latin poem:

> Romanos bibimus primum te consule fontes
> et Latiae cessit[1] Graia Thalia togae.

Naturally Claudian is not saying that this was the very first time he had ever written anything in Latin (though Romano seems to think that all his predecessors had assumed this: p. 20, n. 39). He must have written scores of progymnasmata on a variety of topics to have attained the mastery of Latin revealed in *Prob.*: but there is no reason to doubt that *Prob.* was the first Latin poem he had formally recited. After all if all his life before 395 had been spent in Egypt and Asia Minor, he will not have had much call for writing in Latin. Nor, back home in Egypt, is he likely to have set the scene for the rape in Sicily (there were alternative locations, at least among Greek writers). The view of Romano (l.c.) and Cremona (*Aevum* xxii (1948), 247) that *Graia Thalia* means poetry of Hellenistic and therefore mythological inspiration, *Latiae . . . togae* poetry of Roman and therefore contemporary inspiration, is inadmissible for the reason already stated (above, p. 452). In any case, so far as can be judged most contemporary poetry in Claudian's day was written in *Greek*, not Latin (cf. *Historia* xiv (1965), 477 f.). Birt's view that all Claudian meant was that he had moved his domicile from Greece to Rome is adequately refuted by Fargues, p. 12, n. 4, and cf. C. Brakman, *Mnemosyne* lviii (1930), 378 and L. Alfonsi, *Latomus* xix (1960), 131 f.

Compare the close parallel of the preface to Corippus' *Johannis*, to which no one has yet called attention. In the course of a lengthy apology for the shortcomings of his Latin style, Corippus writes (*pr.* 37) 'rustica *Romanis* dum certat Musa *Camenis*'. Could the 'rustica Musa' be Corippus' native Punic, or even 'Libyan'? On the existence and strength of Punic in North Africa, where Corippus lived (*pr.* 25 f.), see now F. Millar, *JRS* lviii (1968), 130–4—though contrast P. Brown, ib., pp. 85–95. The remarkable number of Libyan proper names crammed into the *Johannis* certainly suggests familiarity with some language other than Latin. If so, then 'Romanis . . . Camenis' would have to mean Latin language, an exact parallel to Claudian's 'Latiae . . . togae'.

---

[1] We must accept the *cessit* of almost all MSS., not (with Birt) the *accessit* of only VA: see the arguments of Fargues, p. 12, n. 4; Romano, p. 20, n. 39; and L. Alfonsi, *Latomus* xix (1960), 131–2.

Now if Claudian had already embarked on a poem as ambitious in conception as *Rapt.*, he could hardly have claimed that his conventional little panegyric of less than 300 lines on Probinus and Olybrius was his very first Latin poem. Thus whenever Claudian may have first conceived the idea of writing *Rapt.*, he cannot have completed Bk. i and equipped it with a preface for formal recitation until after January 395. Such a conclusion is confirmed by the tone of the preface to Bk. i (see (*a*) above).

Now to my own positive suggestions:

(*h*) There are a number of notable parallels between *Rapt.* and *Ruf.*, most of which have not so far been pointed out, much less exploited. We have seen that Claudian plagiarizes himself as much as anyone (pp. 265, 276): it is my belief that he repeated in *Rapt.* ideas he had already utilized in *Ruf.* That is to say, that *Rapt.* was written after *Ruf.*

(i) Both poems open with a council of the Furies in Hades. The section in *Ruf.* (i. 28–117) is long and very detailed: the corresponding section in *Rapt.* is very much shorter (i. 39–67) and gives almost no details (e.g. about the personal appearance of the Furies, etc.). For example Claudian describes in colourful detail Megaera and Allecto in *Ruf.* i: in *Rapt.* i he described Tisiphone, the only one of the three he does not mention in *Ruf.* (for a possible explanation of her absence in *Ruf.*, see Levy, *AJPh* lxviii (1947), 68 f.). And contrast the full description of Allecto at *Ruf.* i. 42 f. and 66 f., with the mere mention of her name in *Rapt.* (i. 280). I would suggest that while re-using the motif of the council of Furies, Claudian preferred not to go over again in the later poem individual points he had adequately covered in the earlier poem. Moreover, the execution of the idea is far more successful in *Ruf.*, where it has often and justly been admired. On the other hand critics are unanimous that Claudian was singularly ill advised to make Pluto plot his revolt against Jupiter with the Furies because Jupiter had not given him a wife—and then abandon the plan at once when someone suggested that he simply *ask*! The motivation of this episode is indeed, as Fargues observes (p. 283), 'vraiment futile, et même quelque peu risible' ('ludicrous', is the word chosen by T. R. Glover, *Life and Letters*, p. 244). Another hint that Claudian was in *Rapt.* trying to adapt to an unsuitable setting an idea originally conceived for another context (cf. above, pp. 265, 303).

(ii) At *Rapt.* iii. 386–8 Claudian describes in a simile:

> qualis pestiferas animare ad crimina taxos
> torva Megaera ruit, Cadmi seu moenia poscat
> sive Thyesteis properet saevire Mycenis.

All three of these details about Megaera are also given—and in greater detail—in *Ruf.* For the first, cf. *Ruf.* i. 119–21, where Megaera seizes a pine tree from the scorched bank of Phlegethon and kindles it in the pitchy whirlpool. As for the other two, Claudian does not say in *Rapt.* what Megaera was going to do in either Thebes or Mycenae. Of course there was ample opportunity for a Fury to exercise her talents in both cities, the families of Laius and Atreus not being strangers to deeds of unnatural violence. Yet we can see from *Ruf.* i. 83 f. that oddly enough Claudian was not thinking of the numerous killings which took place in these two houses, but of the comparatively obscure incestuous unions which sparked off all the trouble. In the context of a series of unnatural crimes for which Megaera was *responsible* (not, as usual, crimes which she avenges), Claudian writes that 'hac [i.e. Megaera] auspice taedae | Oedipoden matri, natae iunxere Thyesten' (on Claudian's source for this last detail, cf. Levy, *TAPhA* lxxii (1941), 237 f.). Again, the allusion in *Rapt.* is less explicit.

Another point. Whereas in *Ruf.* all three details are integral elements in Claudian's representation of Megaera as a spirit of evil, in *Rapt.* they are all contained in one simile. Ceres lights herself an outsize torch (to light her search for the lost Proserpina) '*qualis ... torva Megaera ...*'. It is not even a very appropriate simile, apart from the outsize torch both wield. Ceres does not resemble Megaera in any other respect, nor is *her* torch designed, like Megaera's, to illuminate *crimina*. No earlier poet we know of uses this motif of Megaera lighting her torch in Phlegethon, and surely it only occurred to Claudian to use it in his simile in *Rapt.* because when describing the lighting of Ceres' torch he recalled his own earlier description of Megaera's.

(iii) There is a similar repetition of verbal details between the passages on the return of the golden age in *Ruf.* i. 380 f., and those in *Rapt.* i. 196 f. and iii. 20 f. Unfortunately there is no such pointer to priority here, but it should at least be noted that the motif is integral to the whole conception of *Ruf.* i. The poem opens with Megaera shattering the golden age of Theodosius by unleashing Rufinus on the world, and closes with Justitia prophesying his destruction by Honorius and the return of the golden age. In the *Rapt.* i passage it is merely an embellishment in a speech by Ceres (*Rapt.* iii, where it is more integral to the story, was written much later than *Rapt.* i; see below, p. 463).

(iv) At *Ruf.* ii. 481–93 Claudian gives a most interesting account of metempsychosis. He describes with examples how the human soul passes after death from one animal to another for 3,000 years, till it finally returns to human form after being purged in Lethe (above, p. 209). At *Rapt.* i. 61–2, after saying that Pluto is the sole arbiter of life and death, Claudian merely adds that 'certisque ambagibus aevi | rursus corporeos animae mittuntur in artus'. No details, no examples, no specification even of the length of time (though the *certis* shows that he did have a definite figure in mind). Surely again Claudian refrained from treating in detail what he had already said at length in *Ruf.*

(v) *Ruf.* i opens with a long and brilliant development of the theme of divine justice (above, p. 329). Do or do not the gods concern themselves with human affairs? Is there a divine law for the alternation of light and dark, for the movements of the stars and moon, for the seasons and crops? Why is it that evil seems to prosper? At *Rapt.* iii. 272–4 Claudian touches again on these weighty questions, in the very briefest of terms. Ceres rather weakly exclaims: 'quo iura deorum [because Proserpina has been stolen away from her]? | quo leges cecidere poli? quid vivere recte | proderit?' Precisely the topics treated at length in *Ruf.*: divine justice, the physical laws of the universe, and the point in living righteously. Of course, he was not *bound* to treat them at length in *Rapt.* even if he had not already written the section in *Ruf.* at the time. But the temptation to develop such a congenial *topos* is seldom resisted by Claudian, even at the cost of irrelevance and disproportion.

(vi) In support of this line of reasoning, I will cite two parallel examples from poems which can be exactly dated.

First, *Ruf.* i. 363 f. and *Theod.* 119–20. In the second, and later, passage Claudian describes how Justitia leaves her place in heaven to pay a call on Theodorus:

> deserit autumni portas, qua vergit in Austrum
> signifer, et noctis reparant dispendia Chelae.

What particular part of heaven is it that she is leaving? It is worth inquiring, since there is usually some sort of rationale behind Claudian's astronomical allusions (above, p. 343). In view of the explicit allusion to Libra (Chelae always stands for Libra: cf. *JRS* lvii (1967), 35) and the autumnal equinox, on the evidence of this passage alone one might have been forgiven for supposing that Justitia lived actually in Libra. After all, the connection between scales and justice might seem obvious and appropriate enough. Yet this would be wrong. Compare the passage from *Ruf.*, where Megaera tells Justitia to return to heaven:

> linque homines sortemque meam; pete sidera; notis
> *Autumni* te redde plagis, *qua vergit in Austrum*
> *signifer*; aestivo sedes vicina Leoni
> iampridem gelidaeque vacant confinia Librae.

It is clear that in *Theod.* Claudian is simply recapitulating in abbreviated form what he had said more fully two years earlier in *Ruf.* As so often, Claudian is plagiarizing himself. Now from this earlier passage it is clear that Claudian envisaged Justitia as living, not in Libra, but in the sign between Libra and Leo: namely Virgo. Less appropriate, it might have seemed, than Libra itself. But not really. Justitia is the Virgin Astraea, last of the deities to leave earth; cf. Ovid, *Metam.* i. 149–50: '*Virgo* caede madentes | ultima caelestum terras Astraea reliquit.' And sometimes the constellation Virgo is actually called Astraea (cf. Lucan ix. 535, with Housman's appendix, p. 333). The last link in the equation is provided by *Theod.* 132, where Claudian refers to Justitia simply as 'virgo'. All this might have been clear enough to the man who had already read *Ruf.* i. 363 f., but without this passage even readers equipped with the necessary astronomical and mythological background were likely to go wrong. In this case, of course, we *know* that *Ruf.* is the earlier of the two poems, but even without this knowledge, the way *Theod.* seems to presuppose *Ruf.* here would have been a strong pointer to the priority of *Ruf.*

Next *III Cons.* 162–72, where Claudian describes how the soul of Theodosius flew up through all seven of the planetary spheres to the abode of the blessed in the celestial sphere. Eager as always to show off his 'scientific' knowledge, Claudian devotes 10 lines to the journey, with a brief account of every sphere. In *Gild.*, recited just over two years later, Theodosius makes the return journey—obviously by the same route—as a ghost. But Claudian does not repeat every stage of the journey; he mentions only the last of the spheres this time. Indeed, his brevity has misled scholars: Platnauer translated 'circulus ut patuit Lunae' (223) 'at the rise of the full moon'. A possible interpretation of the words taken by themselves, but the parallel passage in *III Cons.*

shows beyond all doubt that *circulus* means the 'orbit' of the moon, the last of the seven spheres through which the ghosts must pass (cf. W. H. Semple, *CQ* xxxi (1937), 162).

Here then we have two clear examples of Claudian referring briefly and allusively to a subject he had treated at length in an earlier poem— precisely what I have been suggesting happened with *Rapt.* and *Ruf.* It is interesting, moreover, to notice that Claudian touches—very briefly—on the latter topic in *Rapt.* At ii. 298, having had occasion to mention the lunar sphere, Claudian adds 'qui septimus auras | ambit et aeternis mortalia separat astris'. A most suitable peg on which he could have hung a colourful account of all seven spheres—had he not already done so in *III Cons.* Indeed a 'serious' mythological epic might have seemed a much more suitable vehicle for the development of this as of the other topics discussed in this section (metempsychosis, cosmology) than works by their very nature so ephemeral as panegyrics and invectives. Yet in every one of the cases here quoted it is the panegyric or invective which contains the detailed treatment, and *Rapt.* the brief allusion. Is this just a coincidence? The cumulative effect perhaps increases the weight of the arguments adduced in the individual examples.

I suggest then that the *terminus post quem* for the publication of *Rapt.* i is Summer 397, on my chronology (cf. p. 78) the date of *Ruf.* ii (*Rapt.* i. 61 f. ~ *Ruf.* ii. 481 f., cf. (iv)).

(*i*) I was careful to say that Bk. i cannot have been written before Summer 397, since it seems clear from the preface to *Rapt.* ii that Bks. ii and presumably iii as well were not published till some while after i. This point has not, so far as I am aware, been made before, but Claudian states quite plainly at the end of the preface to Bk. ii that Florentinus

> antraque Musarum *longo torpentia somno*
> excutis, et placidos ducis in orbe choros (51–2).

We have seen already that when Claudian prefixes a new preface to a later book of a poem, this means that this book was written and recited later than the first book or books (cf. *Eutr.* ii, *Stil.* iii, and *Ruf.* ii, as explained above, pp. 77–8). Here Claudian actually draws attention to the interval which separated the appearance of i and ii by referring to the 'long sleep' of his Muse. It is quite illegitimate to use the preface to ii as evidence for the publication of *Rapt.* as a whole, as all who have studied the problem so far have. This vitiates the view of Birt (the only scholar, to give him his due, who attempted to explain this reference to a 'long sleep') that what Claudian meant was that a long time had elapsed since *anyone* had attempted a mythological epic on such a scale[1] (p. xviii). Why should Claudian have waited till after he had already recited the first book before making this claim? Nor is it the most natural way to have made such a claim. That *antra Musarum* refers to Claudian's Muse, and means that more time than usual has passed since he recited his last poem, is surely put beyond doubt by an exactly parallel couplet in the preface to *Get.*, recited in about May 402, nearly two and a half years since Claudian had recited his last poem, *Stil.* i–iii in January–February 400.

> Post resides annos *longo velut excita somno*
> Romanis fruitur nostra Thalia choris (1–2).

For a rapid and prolific writer like Claudian two and a half years was a long gap. In fact it is the only such gap in the brief period of his literary activity: not more than a year (and in some cases much less) separates any of his poems written between January 395 and January 400 (cf. *Chronologia Claudianea*). It seems natural therefore to assume that the *longus somnus* of the two prefaces refers to the *same* gap, and that *Rapt.* ii appeared in 402 as well, at about the same time as *Get.* Book iii presumably appeared at the same time as ii, since it does not have a new preface of its own.

If Bks. ii–iii did not appear till after this gap, then Bk. i must presumably have come out before it, that is to say before 400. Now fast worker though he was, even Claudian must have been kept very busy by pressing commissions for Stilico between late 397 and early 400. Between January 398 and January 400 he turned out in quick succession *IV Cons.* (656 lines), *Nupt.* and *Fesc.* (477), *Gild.* (526), *Eutr.* i (513) and ii plus preface (678), and *Stil.* i–iii plus preface (1,254)—in all well over 4,000 lines. Now while we cannot of course rule out the possibility that Claudian embarked on *Rapt.* as well during this period, it seems more natural to place *Rapt.* i during the (for Claudian) comparatively slack preceding two years: between January 396 and January 398 he wrote only *Ruf.* i–ii, well under 1,000 lines or less than a quarter of his output for the next two years. Thus it would seem that the appearance of *Rapt.* i should be placed in late Summer or early Autumn 397, after he had recited *Ruf.* ii and before he settled down to work on *IV Cons.* for January 398, and the series of poems which followed.

---

[1] This is not even true, if we include (as Claudian would have) Greek epic: e.g. Peisander, Quintus, Dionysius.

I would suggest then that while writing his *In Rufinum* Claudian conceived the idea of *Rapt.* and completed one book before more urgent contemporary themes claimed all his energies for the next two years. Indeed it may not be over-fanciful to suggest that it was while writing the brilliant underworld scenes of *Ruf.* that he first realized both the attractions and the possibilities of the underworld as a theme. In the course of 400, as we have seen (p. 413), Claudian married and left Italy altogether for a while, to go to 'Libya'. During this time he perhaps wrote more of *Rapt.* but did not publish it. Soon after his return to Rome in 402 he was called on to write *Get.* Shortly afterwards *Rapt.* ii and iii appeared. This I deduce from the emphatic allusion to '*placidos*[1] . . . choros' at the end of the preface to ii. This seems to me to imply that Claudian's last poem had been anything but *placidus*: and what can this be but his martial epic, *De bello Getico*. *Rapt.* probably appeared very shortly after *Get.*, for otherwise Claudian would hardly have written in such similar terms in the preface to *Rapt.* ii of the 'long sleep', now broken by *Get.* Since *Get.* will have been written hastily to commemorate Stilico's victory at Pollentia, it may well be that *Rapt.* ii–iii were nearly complete before he broke off to write *Get.*, and finished soon after. This would explain why he alludes to the gap since his earlier series of recitations in exactly the same terms in both prefaces. He dedicated this continuation to his friend Florentinus. Since *Rapt.* was a purely literary affair, there was no reason why this should have caused any offence to Stilico: it was several years now since Stilico had dismissed Florentinus from the urban prefecture, and by 402 he was trying hard to conciliate (with Claudian's aid) the landowning aristocracy.

Once again, however, *Rapt.* had to be postponed. *VI Cons.* was ordered for January 404, and then there was that panegyric he had promised Serena (above, p. 411), and the *Gigantomachia* he had been wanting to write for so long (see Appendix B). All these plans were cut short by death.

(*j*) Thus my explanation of the fact that *Rapt.* is unfinished is quite simply that Claudian did not live to finish it. This is at once more straightforward and more satisfactory than the explanations devised by those who believe *Rapt.* an early work. Even granted their chronology their reasons are inadequate. Romano (p. 30) thinks that once

---

[1] For the reading *placidos*, certainly correct, cf. the note in J. B. Hall's edition (1969), ad loc.

Claudian had turned his mind to contemporary poetry he could not return to mythology: this is of course based on his false view of Claudian's poetic development. Birt's explanation, though most ingenious, has been dismissed above (p. 455). Fargues's view that 'les longueurs' that may be found in Bk. iii 'attestent la lassitude de Claudien et permettent de penser qu'il n'a pas continué son poème au delà de ce chant' is a subjective impression not adequately borne out by my own reading of the poem. W. Barr (*The panegyrics of Claudian on the third and fourth consulates of Honorius*, unpublished thesis, London, 1954, p. 95) points out that there are proportionately more elisions in *Rapt*. iii than either of the other books or any of his other poems, claiming that 'the unusually high number of elisions in this book is eloquent of the falling away in interest which caused the poet to abandon the *De Raptu* in the end'. This strikes me as a hypothesis which could only be advanced by one who had not himself written Latin verses. It is my experience that one does not write out a whole copy of verses in rough and then go through eliminating the elisions. One either likes and uses elisions, or one does not. A writer trained, as both Claudian and the modern schoolboy composer (the parallel is really very close, since both write in a foreign language), on the Ovidian model learns not to form verses even in rough with the aid of elisions: I suspect that Claudian's drafts were as free from elisions as his fair copies. It is perhaps no more than coincidental that *Rapt*. iii should have so many elisions (44 in 448 lines, or 1 in 10). On the other hand it is interesting to note that Claudian's last major poem, *VI Cons.*, has the same number of elisions, though since it has 660 lines the proportion is only 1 in 15. And *Get.*, which for no stated reason Barr omitted from his table, has 53, or 1 in 12. These figures are both well over the average for all Claudian's other poems: on my chronology *Rapt*. iii belongs in the same period as *Get.* and *VI Cons.* Could it be that in some of his later poems Claudian made a conscious attempt to cultivate elision, having noticed perhaps how monotonously smooth his own verses were by comparison with Vergil and even the post-Augustans (see p. 289)? Be this as it may, I do not believe that the number of elisions in *Rapt*. iii (which by classical standards is still extremely low) can be used to explain why Claudian left the poem unfinished. If anything it might even be used to support the view that *Rapt*. ii and iii were among Claudian's last works, and that the poem was simply interrupted by his death.

APPENDIX B

The Date of the Latin Gigantomachia

I

A SIMILAR controversy has grown up around the question of the date of the Latin *Gigantomachia* (hereafter *Gig.*). The facts (*a*) that the poem is plainly unfinished (rather than merely fragmentary like the Greek *Gigantomachia*), and (*b*) that it was nevertheless published despite its unfinished state in the posthumous *c.m.* (p. 416) together with other unfinished work, strongly suggest that Claudian left it unfinished at his death. If so, then since he was evidently a rapid and facile composer, the natural inference is that it was only shortly before his death that he began it.

Most modern critics, however, believe that it was a youthful poem, which Claudian left unfinished because he had tired of it, or because (an argument we have met before, gaining nothing by repetition) he 'grew out of' mythological poetry (in the middle of a poem, after only 127½ lines!). Fargues (p. 18, n. 1) finds in it 'les mêmes hyperboles juvéniles, les mêmes fautes de goût, les mêmes procédés de composition' as in the Greek *Gigantomachia* (which we may allow to have been an early work: p. 25, n. 3). The alleged 'juvenility' we need not waste many words on: it has been suggested already (p. 14) that it is the impossible subject-matter which inspires these hyperboles. And are there not just as colossal (by our standards) 'fautes de goût' in Claudian's latest writings? The shortcomings of *Gig.* are, in fact, as Addison remarked in an essay in the *Spectator* (22 March 1712), entirely characteristic of Claudian's work as a whole. For Romano (p. 28, n. 50) it is the 'elementi retorici' which betray 'inesperienza giovanile'. As though there was no 'rhetoric' in the later poems!

Less subjective (though not less false) is the argument of Fargues (loc. cit.), Fabbri (*Athen.* xvii (1939), 29), and Martinelli (*Misc. Galbiati* ii (1951), 59)[1] that Claudian's use in *Rapt.* of motifs from the

---

[1] Martinelli also resurrects the old view that *pr. VI Cons.* 11–20 alludes to *Gig.* (p. 60). In fact, of course, the reference is to *Get.* Other considerations aside (Fargues, p. 18, n. 1), Claudian could hardly have referred to the recitation of a poem he left unfinished at his death.

Gigantomachy theme presupposes the priority of *Gig*. The use of these motifs is interesting, to be sure, but it is far from obvious why they point to the priority of *Gig*.

It will prove instructive to compare the allusions to the Gigantomachy theme in Claudian's other poems. At *III Cons.* 159–61 Claudian claims that even if the Giants were to burst out of their prisons, they would fall before Stilico. At *c.m.* xxxi. 27–8 Orpheus is described singing to Juno of Jupiter's victory over the Giants (see p. 410). At *Rapt.* i. 44 f. the notion of releasing the Giants is briefly entertained in connection with Pluto's original plan to overrun the world: and at i. 154 f. Enceladus' tomb is mentioned in the course of a description of Aetna. Now the Gigantomachy theme was extremely popular in the art and literature of the Roman Empire, and there is nothing especially noteworthy in any of these allusions.

Yet in the works written in Claudian's last two years (402–4), *Get.*, *VI Cons.*, and *Rapt.* ii–iii, such allusions are both more frequent and more detailed: 9 in all the poems from just this short period. To enumerate, *Rapt.* ii. 157–61, 255–7, iii. 182–8, 196–7, 337–56, *Get.* 63–76, 342–3, *pr. VI Cons.* 17–20, *VI Cons.* 185. The increased preoccupation with the theme is evident. In *Get.* and *VI Cons.* the explanation is simple: in view of his fascination with the theme in general, not unnaturally it was the imagery of the gods and Giants that he chose to represent the struggle between Roman and barbarian. And the rape of Proserpina was set at a point in mythology not far removed from the Gigantomachy itself—and, moreover, close by the very spot where the actual battle had taken place. Aetna is the tomb of Enceladus, 'Giganteos numquam tacitura triumphos'; Ceres visits the grove where hang the trophies of Phlegra. But the use of the theme is not restricted to topography. Note *Rapt.* ii. 255 f. where Proserpina reminds Jupiter as she is being carried off that she had supported him against the Giants; and iii. 182 f. where Ceres wonders (for several lines) whether it is the Giants who have taken Proserpina. At *Get.* 342 when describing the Goths dying of cold, Claudian's mind turned at once to the Giants 'frozen' by Athena's aegis: not a very natural comparison, except for one with the Giants running around in his head.

I would venture to suggest that it was precisely because his enthusiasm for a theme which had always fascinated him was kindled afresh by its special relevance to the subject-matter of both the political and the mythological poems he was working on in the period 402–4, that Claudian decided to write a full-scale *Gigantomachia* in Latin, as he had earlier in Greek.

It has been claimed that *Rapt.* draws on *Gig.* in other matters too. For example, *Gig.* 42 f. (summoning of a council of gods on Olympus) has been compared with the longer and more elaborate development of the same theme in *Rapt.* (iii. 1 f.). But the criteria for re-use of themes established in Appendix A would point to the priority of *Rapt.* here, not *Gig.* Moreover, while in *Rapt.* a large number of those present are named, in *Gig.* the only two named are, oddly enough, Pluto and Proserpina. Now why, before writing *Rapt.* and becoming preoccupied with the gods of the underworld, should Claudian have thought to single out from all the gods and goddesses two who play no part whatever in conventional accounts of the conflict?

The other parallel is the description of Pluto's chariot bursting into the light of day (*Gig.* 45–8), described twice in *Rapt.* (ii. 191 f., iii. 235 f.). Obviously Claudian thought the topic promising: hence the two treatments in *Rapt.* (once when it happens, and again when Ceres is told about it)—perhaps two drafts he was unable to decide between. Is not the *Gig.* version a third draft? Why otherwise should Claudian have devoted so much space to the journey to heaven of two such strangers to the myth (and to heaven) as Pluto and Proserpina, when he says not a word of the journey made by any of the real protagonists in the battle?

Naturally such considerations cannot be held decisive. But if any inference as to priority is licensed by these parallels between the two poems, it is hardly that *Gig.* is the earlier.

II

Claudian and Prudentius

Lastly, and more tentatively, I should like to put forward for consideration the possibility that *Gig.* 106–7 echo lines 111–12 of Prudentius' *Apotheosis.* If accepted, this would certainly place *Gig.* among Claudian's last works. Even if not accepted, it is hoped that the preliminary discussion of the relationship between Claudian and Prudentius will have a value independent of its immediate conclusion.

Claudian and Prudentius were contemporaries, and both were

prolific poets. That Prudentius knew and imitated Claudian can be shown by a number of verbal parallels: for the fullest collection see O. Hoefer, *De Prudentii ... carminum chronologia* (Diss. Marburg, 1895), 17 f., drastically (and properly) reduced by C. Weyman, *Berl. Phil. Woch.* xvii (1897), 977–86 (= *Beitr. der christl. latein. Poesie* (1926), 64–71). For an echo of *Eutr.* in *C. Symm.* see too *CQ* N.S. xviii (1968), 406. Yet despite the fact that Prudentius was much the older of the two men, no one has ever suggested that he might have been imitated in turn by Claudian.

The explanation is simple enough: it has generally been assumed that none of Prudentius' poems was published before 405. And since none of Claudian's poems can be dated after 404, it would seem that Claudian could not have imitated Prudentius. Yet the date 405 is less certain than usually supposed. Prudentius announces in the preface to the *Cathemeron* that he has completed his fifty-sixth year. But as Lana has recently pointed out (*Due Capitoli Prudenziani* (1962), 1, n. 2), since we do not know when in the year his birthday fell, the year in which he was writing could as easily be 404 as 405 (cf. too M. P. Cunningham's remark in *TAPhA* lxxxix (1958), 33, that 'the problem is simply one of Roman arithmetic and inclusive counting').

More important, the conventional view rests on the assumption that the preface to *Cath.* is the preface to an omnibus edition of all Prudentius' poems, none of which had been published previously. This assumption is arbitrary and implausible. Even granted that the preface to *Cath.* is the preface to an omnibus edition (it could as easily be a *reprise* of the themes of Prudentius' earlier poems prefixed to the latest), it certainly does not follow that none of the poems included had been published before. Indeed, it would be without parallel in ancient times for such a substantial corpus of long and disparate poems to have been held back after being written one by one over a period of years and then finally released together. Compare the case of Claudian's political poems: an omnibus edition was published after Claudian's death—but all the poems included had been published separately before, even the multi-book works. So too with the *c.m.*: the verse epistles must all have been sent off to their several recipients separately before the collected edition.

To return to Prudentius, there are indications in the constitution of the sixth-century *Puteanus* that it was compiled, not from a complete omnibus edition, but from separate copies of individual poems still circulating at that date (for example, it does not contain, and never did, the vexatious preface to *Cath.*: see Cunningham, *TAPhA* lxxxix (1958), 32–7, *Class. Phil.* lx (1965), 146, and for the question of a double edition, K. Thraede, *Studien zu Sprache u. Stil. d. Prudentius* (*Hypomnemata* xiii), 1965, 76–8, with full bibliography). And *C. Symm.* refers with such exultation to the victory of Pollentia that it must surely have been written very shortly after it: after Claudian's *Get.* (of which it has a number of certain echoes), but probably before July/August 402, because Prudentius' enthusiasm is limited to Pollentia, with not even a hint of the second victory at Verona two or three months later. Roma's appeal to Honorius to come to Rome in triumph (*C. Symm.* ii. 731 f.) must in any case antedate Honorius' decision to do just that in January 404 as consul. If then *C. Symm.* was published when it was written, when it was relevant, why not the other poems? Some of them are considerably longer than poems of Claudian which we know to have been published separately.

It seems certain that none were published before 392 (or else Jerome would have included Prudentius in his catalogue of Christian writers to that date), and even those who deny that all Prudentius' works are named in the preface to *Cath.* (Hoefer, Lana), admit (as they must) that *Apoth.* is there—and first on the list. If this, and its usual place in MSS., and certain internal indications have any validity, *Apoth.* is earlier than both *Hamartigenia* and *Psychomachia*. I. Rodriguez-Herrera, *Poeta Christianus; Prudentius' Auffassung vom Wesen und von der Aufgabe des christlichen Dichters* (Diss. München, 1936), 16–18, places the composition of *Apoth.* in the period 398–400. There is little that really amounts to evidence for such precision, but it is probably not far from the truth.

If (as Lana supposes) the preface to *Cath.* does date from 404 rather than 405, then *Apoth.* would certainly be pushed back into the last period of Claudian's poetical activity, since (as we have seen) the preface plainly names *Apoth.* And if (as seems highly probable on a variety of grounds) *Apoth.* was both written and published by 403 (if not earlier), then obviously Claudian would have been able to read it, delighting, no doubt, in the reminiscences of his own poems in the work of a Christian poet.

Here then, at last, is the parallel between *Apoth.* and *Gig.*:
Apoth. 111–12, of God the father,

> pater est, quem cernere nulli | est licitum.

Gig. 106–7, of Athene and her aegis which turns to stone,

    Te, dea, respexit, solam quam cernere nulli / *bis* licuit.

The parallelism is very striking: not merely the identical $2\frac{1}{2}$ closing feet, but also the corresponsion of *licitum* and *licuit* in the same *sedes* in the following line. In view of the proven borrowing of Prudentius from Claudian, one's first reaction is naturally to suspect that here too it is Prudentius who is the borrower. Yet *Gig.* (whenever begun) was indisputably left unfinished: the story is unfinished, and the last line incomplete. A famous poet does not *publish* a draft $127\frac{1}{2}$ lines of an unfinished epic. Indeed, it is virtually certain that it was published posthumously with Claudian's other literary remains.

Now Claudian was still alive in January 404, and though he may not have seen the next January and Stilico's second consulate, we have no grounds for supposing that he died immediately after the recitation of *VI Cons.*, or that his posthumous works were collected and issued by the time Prudentius wrote *Apoth.*, certainly by 405, almost certainly by 404, and very probably two or three years earlier still.

So if the parallel is judged sufficiently close to warrant the assumption of direct imitation of one poet by the other (and it certainly seems so to me), then it must be Claudian who imitated Prudentius. This would be of obvious importance as support for the view maintained earlier in this Appendix that *Gig.* was one of the last poems Claudian was working on when he died. It would also have an altogether different significance if Claudian was (as it might seem) deliberately (and humorously) transferring the notion of *never* being able to gaze on the person of God the father into being able to gaze on Athene—but only once. It would be the only anti-Christian barb in all Claudian's *œuvre*—and even so hardly more than playful.

The relationship between Claudian and Prudentius would probably repay further close critical study. No serious attention has been paid to the problem since Hoefer and Weyman (for more recent bibliography see *CQ* N.S. xviii (1968), 406). It might, for example, be possible to narrow down the *termini* for *Rapt.* if an imitation could be found in a datable poem of Prudentius like *C. Symm.* Conversely, an imitation of *VI Cons.* by Prudentius would serve to date one at least of his poems after 404. So far, I must confess, both attempts have proved vain. The last poem of Claudian Prudentius shows any knowledge of is *Get.*—an *argumentum* (however slight) *e silentio* for the posteriority of *VI Cons.*

to all Prudentius' œuvre (thus favouring, however faintly, a date of 404 rather than 405 for the preface to *Cath.*).

In any event it may be helpful to list the few cases where it seems to me that parallels are sufficiently striking to warrant conclusions as to priority (in each case of Claudian) and *termini post quem* for poems of Prudentius:

Cath. iii. 11: 'te sine dulce nihil'	*Ruf.* ii (summer 397) 268: 'te sine dulce nihil'
Cath. xii. 126: 'lucis ipso in limine'	*Stil.* ii (January 400) 63: 'lucis in ipso | limine' (closer than Sil. It. xiii. 548, 'in limine lucis')
Psych. 736: 'conscendunt . . . sublime tribunal . . . aggere conspicuae' (738)	*Eutr.* i (early 399) 311: 'scandit sublime tribunal'
	Gild. (mid 398) 425: 'aggere conspicuus'
Perist. xi. 225: 'sublime tribunal'	*Ruf.* ii (mid 397) 382: 'scandat sublime tribunal'
Perist. xi. 115: 'per silvas, per saxa ruunt, non ripa retardat | fluminis aut torrens oppositus cohibet'	*Gild.* 472: 'per saxa citati | torrentesque ruunt; nec mons aut[1] silva retardat'

Largely, no doubt, because of the subject-matter, there are many more echoes of the more positive variety in *C. Symm.* To save space I have merely added the Claudian parallels in brackets: *C. Symm.* i. 14 (*Stil.* ii. 204, *Eutr.* ii. 15), i. 153 (*Theod.* 334), ii. 26 (*III Cons.* 144, *Stil.* i. 31), ii. 75 (*Get.* 103), ii. 435 (*IV Cons.* 118), ii. 475 (*Theod.* 228), ii. 697 (*Get.* 81), ii. 715 (*Get.* 633), ii. 719 (*Get.* 423), ii. 750 (*Gild.* 52), ii. 763 (*Get.* 88). For the rejuvenated Roma taken over from *Gild.*, see p. 248. The numerous echoes of *Get.* would thus have assured a *terminus* of 402 even without the allusion to Pollentia. It is irritating that there should be such an abundance of firm Claudianic echoes in the only poem which can be dated on other grounds already.

[1] *nec mons aut silva* is the reading of VPC, preferred to the *non mons non silva* of ΠBA by Jeep, Koch, and (in a last minute δευτέρα φροντίς at p. 611) by Birt. Not one of them quotes the Prudentian imitation, which guarantees the *aut*. For *aut* after negatives see Leumann–Hofmann–Szantyr, *Lat. Gramm.* ii. 499, 4 (§ 269, c, α), and, for a fourth-century example, add *HA Prob.* 12. 2.

APPENDIX C

Zosimus, John of Antioch, and Eunapius on Stilico's two expeditions to the Balkans

THAT Stilico made two expeditions to the Balkans, the first to Thessaly in 395, the second to the Peloponnese in 397, is certain (for the date of the second see especially J. Koch in *Rhein. Mus.* xliv (1889) 572 f., accepted by all later authorities (cf. Demougeot, p. 170, n. 272) except J. H. E. Crees (*Claudian* (1908), pp. 79–80), who offers no adequate reasons for returning to the older view which placed it in 396 or even late in 395). Zosimus and John of Antioch both conflate the two. It is the purpose of this appendix to sift out which details in their accounts refer to which of the two expeditions, and to show that both writers derive their confusion from Eunapius. For Zosimus I have used Mendelssohn's edition (Leipzig, 1887): the relevant fragment of John is 190 in Müller (*Frag. Hist. Graec.* iv (1885), 610a).

Details John and Zosimus have in common:

(a) John describes (omitting inessentials) how Rufinus, eager for the purple, invited Alaric and his barbarians to devastate πᾶσαν ὁμοῦ τὴν Ἑλλάδα καὶ τὰ περὶ τὴν Ἰλλυρίδα. The reference to Hellas shows that John is writing here of 397, not 395. He concludes this section ὡς καὶ δῆλος ἅπασι γενέσθαι [sc. Rufinus] τῇ τῆς τυραννίδος ἐπιβουλῇ. Zosimus too relates how Rufinus invited Alaric and his barbarians to invade Greece (v. 5. 1–7. 1: his much fuller narrative devotes three pages to an account of the devastation), and then how, hearing of τοῦ περὶ τὴν Ἑλλάδα πάθους, ἐπίδοσιν ἐλάμβανεν ἧς εἶχε περὶ τὴν βασιλείαν ἐπιθυμίας (v. 7. 1). The same events in the same *mistaken* order. Both place the devastation of Greece, which did not begin till *after* the expedition of 395, *before* the only one they know of. And both take it as proof of Rufinus' designs on the purple.

(b) Then, according to John, Stilico sailed to Greece (διέπλευσε μὲν αὐτὸς ἐς τὴν Ἑλλάδα), pitying the sufferings of the inhabitants. According to Zosimus too Stilico ναυσὶ στρατιώτας ἐμβιβάσας, τοῖς κατὰ τὴν Ἀχαΐαν δυστυχήμασιν ὥρμητο βοηθεῖν (v. 7. 1). Again the same detail in the same place. Zosimus, who regularly tones down Eunapius' notoriously exuberant style, writes simply that Stilico was 'eager to assist': John, perhaps reproducing the rhetorical trimmings of his source more faithfully here, has him 'pitying their sufferings'. What matters however is that both unmistakably refer to a sea-crossing to the Peloponnese. This can only be the 397 expedition, for in 395 Stilico marched *overland* to Thessaly. Cf. especially *IV Cons.* 172–4, where Claudian neatly distinguishes the two as follows: 'Illyricum peteres: campi montesque patebant. | vexillum navale dares: sub puppibus ibat | Ionium.'

(*c*) According to John, when there, Stilico τοὺς βαρβάρους σπάνει τῶν ἀναγκαίων διαφθείρας, ἔπαυσε τῆς [κατὰ] τῶν ἐπιχωρίων ὁρμῆς. Zosimus continues, καὶ ῥᾷστα διέφθειρεν ἂν αὐτοὺς σπάνει τῶν ἐπιτηδείων, if Stilico had not let his army get out of control, with the result that Alaric was able to escape to Epirus. Again both are clearly writing of 397: Claudian confirms the blockade, the starvation, and even the escape to Epirus (see p. 170). But there is an obvious prima facie contradiction between the two: John implies that the campaign was a success, Zosimus makes it clear that it was not. However, there is no direct contradiction. For by driving Alaric out of the Peloponnese to Epirus, Stilico *did* save the ἐπιχώριοι from his ravages—a point of which Claudian made much (pp. 175–6). It may be (assuming that John has not just completely misunderstood his source) that in compressing it he omitted the details about the blockade and Alaric's escape, and therefore distorted the original emphasis.

(*d*) According to John, Stilico next summoned Gainas and ἀρτύει τὴν κατὰ 'Ρουφίνου σκευήν. Zosimus too continues with Stilico's plan to remove Rufinus, but does not introduce Gainas till the next sentence. With John's use of the word σκευή compare Zosimus' θάνατον ἔγνω 'Ρουφίνῳ κατασκευάσαι (v. 7. 3). But what really matters is that both have now switched back from 397 to 395.

(*e*) Next both John and Zosimus describe the return of the eastern army. As underlined above (pp. 165 f.), unlike Claudian neither connects this with the conclusion of Stilico's expedition. It may be added that Socrates too (*HE* vi. 1), who conscientiously consulted all available sources, pagan and Christian (cf. the preface to W. Bryce's edition, 1893, pp. xviii–xix), and will obviously therefore have referred to Eunapius (the only available work) for secular events, lends no support whatever to Claudian's version in his reference to the return of the eastern army.

(*f*) Both then describe how Arcadius, accompanied by Rufinus in his capacity as praetorian prefect, came to meet Gainas and the army outside Constantinople, both explaining that this was an old custom. Here too it seems legitimate to see traces of the Eunapian version in Socrates who writes (loc. cit.) that Arcadius κατὰ τὸ εἰωθὸς πρὸ τῶν πυλῶν ἀπήντησε τῷ στρατῷ.

(*g*) Lastly, both describe the acclamation of Arcadius, followed by the dissection of Rufinus, adding that his wife and daughter took refuge in a church and were spared.

The similarity between the two accounts, above all in their common errors, is obvious. The possibility that John was drawing on Zosimus himself can be ruled out at once, since he records at least two details he could not have obtained from Zosimus.

Details John did not derive from Zosimus:

(*a*) According to John, Stilico sailed to Greece although it was μηδὲν προσήκουσαν τοῖς τῆς ἑσπερίας τέρμασιν. There is nothing in the relevant chapter of Zosimus to suggest that Greece was not part of Honorius' share of the Empire, nor that Stilico had no business to be there. At the end of Bk. iv Zosimus says that Theodosius entrusted to Honorius Italy, Spain, Gaul, and Africa, whence it would presumably have been possible to infer that Greece did not belong to him: but this is not the procedure of a compiler like John—and why should he have bothered to add such an inference at this point?

(*b*) Zosimus says only that Stilico persuaded Honorius to return to Arcadius τέλη τινὰ στρατιωτικά. John specifies the army which had fought Eugenius and chased the barbarians in Illyricum—and in this again he is certainly correct, confirmed by Claudian. But there is nothing in Zosimus that could have suggested this to John. It is interesting to note that Philostorgius, who certainly used Eunapius for this period (see L. Jeep, *Quellenuntersuchungen zu den griechischen Kirchenhistorikern* (*Jhb. f. cl. phil.*, Suppbd. xiv), 1884, 56–73), writes (xi. 3) of ὁ ἀπὸ ῾Ρώμης ἀνακομισθεὶς στρατός, οἳ τῷ Θεοδοσίῳ κατὰ τοῦ τυράννου συνεστρατεύσαντο. The similarity of Socrates' phraseology (vi. 1) confirms that he was indeed drawing on Eunapius too: ὁ [sc. στρατός] ἅμα τῷ βασιλεῖ Θεοδοσίῳ κατὰ τοῦ τυράννου στρατεύσας.

Socrates cannot have been drawing direct on Philostorgius here for Philostorgius omits the detail common to John, Zosimus, and Socrates that the greeting of the army outside the city was an old custom.

So John cannot be drawing direct from Zosimus. Yet both share so many details, true and false alike, and in the same mistaken order, that a common source must obviously be postulated. It is certain that Zosimus' source was Eunapius, and it is difficult to see who else John could be using: so far as is known no one else wrote a history of this period. If not Eunapius direct, then it would have to be some inter-mediary (other than Zosimus) who did use Eunapius, in which case the argument is hardly affected. Elsewhere for this period, indeed for this very same year 395, John can be shown to depend on Eunapius (if only indirectly): cf. John, frag. 188 with Eun., frag. 63 (*FHG* iv. 610 with Müller's note ad loc.). Thus it may be confidently assumed that both John and Zosimus represent the Eunapian version. And if so, then it follows that the telescoping of the two campaigns was already present in Eunapius, and not a later confusion by Zosimus, as hitherto supposed. Zosimus has been much vilified. 'It will not be denied, I think,' wrote E. A. Thompson not long ago, 'that Zosimus is one of the most incompetent of the Greek Historians' (*Antiquity* xxx (1956), 163). Perhaps so. But it may be that one of his greatest faults (or virtues, depending on one's point of view) was that he copied his sources too faithfully on occasions. Perhaps much else that is criticized in Zosimus (e.g. his complete omission of the Pollentia campaign) should really be laid at Eunapius' door.

APPENDIX D

Triphiodorus and Nonnus

PENDING the publication of the new Triphiodorus papyrus, and in
view of the shortcomings of L. Ferrari's recent monograph *Sulla presa
di Ilio di Trifiodoro* (Palermo, 1962) in metrical and stylistic matters,
it seems worth while summarizing here a number of features in the
'Ιλίου ἅλωσις which make the new pre-Nonnian date of the poem less
surprising than it might appear. This appendix lays no claim to originality (I am particularly indebted to the preface to Keydell's *Nonnus*,
Maas's *Greek Metre*, Wifstrand's *Von Kallimachos*, and Weinberger's
'Studien zu Tryphiodor und Kolluth' in *Wien. Studien* xviii (1896),
161–79), but to the best of my knowledge no such comprehensive
conspectus of the relationship (or lack of it) between Nonnus and
Triphiodorus exists.

(*a*) Of the 32 possible combinations of dactyl and spondee in the
first five feet of the hexameter, Nonnus uses only 9. His followers
similarly restrict themselves to the most dactylic forms, ranging from
Paul the Silentiary, with only 6, to Christodorus with 11 and Colluthus
with 15. Triphiodorus has 17.

(*b*) As was demonstrated at length by Ludwich in his *Beiträge zur
Kritik des Nonnos* (1873), 16–36, Nonnus greatly restricted the use of
elision (for example, he never elides the final syllable of nouns, adjectives,
verbs, or even pronouns: for a summary, Keydell's *Nonnus*, 1959,
pp. 41–2*, § 19). There are more un-Nonnian elisions in Triphiodorus
(e.g. ἔρρ', μ', ἐνθάδ', ἔτ', μάλ', τάχ', and ἅτ') than in any of the indisputable imitators of Nonnus, Christodorus, Colluthus, Musaeus,
John of Gaza, Paul (for the statistics, Ludwich, p. 30, and Weinberger,
p. 173).

(*c*) Nonnus never has spondees in both of the first two feet, nor do
Christodorus, Colluthus, Musaeus, etc. Triphiodorus does so frequently
(Ferrari, pp. 124–9).

(*d*) As Wifstrand has illustrated, from Callimachus onwards poets
became increasingly reluctant to place a spondaic word before the

strong caesura (pp. 37–53). Triphiodorus has more than any of the Nonnians, and proportionately more than Quintus.

(*e*) Triphiodorus completely ignores the restrictions on the placing of monosyllables which had again been developing since Callimachus, but were further refined by Nonnus (Wifstrand, pp. 56–64, p. 62 for Triphiodorus).

(*f*) As remarked above (p. 16), Triphiodorus is relatively unaffected by the Nonnian developments in the use of the definite article. A. Svensson concludes his section on Triphiodorus (*Gebrauch d. best. Artikels in d. nachklass. griech. Epik* (Lund, 1937), 127) with the remark that he 'überhaupt nicht als Nonnianer gerechnet werden kann'.

(*g*) It is well known that Nonnus contrived to avoid ending even one of his 20,000 odd hexameters with a proparoxytone word. Paul, John, and Pamprepius have no exceptions. Christodorus, oddly enough, has just one (*Anth. Pal.* ii. 386), and Musaeus one dubious example (146: Gelzer, *Mus. Helv.* (1968), 39). Colluthus, for once, has several but (accepting Ludwich's θαλάσσης at 207) never a proparoxytone trisyllable, more damaging perhaps to the cadence than a proparoxytone quadrisyllable. So it may be that Colluthus did regulate his final accent, though on a less rigid basis than Nonnus. Triphiodorus, with over 100 proparoxytona, 39 of them trisyllables, plainly has no system (Ludwich, p. 80, Weinberger, p. 177, Wifstrand, pp. 75–6). Indeed, as §§ *h–j* will show, he paid no attention to accent whatever.

(*h*) With very few exceptions, Nonnus always has a paroxytone word before the strong caesura (Keydell, p. 38*, § 13). Colluthus, again, is laxer, admitting a few oxytones and perispomena, but no proparoxytones. Triphiodorus admits even proparoxytones quite freely (Wifstrand, pp. 76–7).

(*i*) Triphiodorus, unlike the Nonnians, completely ignores Wifstrand's 'first law' (formulated p. 4, cf. pp. 3–20, p. 19 for Triphiodorus): an oxytone word can only stand before the feminine caesura when there is also a trihemimeral caesura.

(*j*) Triphiodorus alone completely ignores Wifstrand's second 'Nonnian law' too (pp. 21–5): a proparoxytone word can only stand before the hephthemimeral caesura if there is also bucolic diaeresis. Colluthus, so often classed by editors and commentators as Triphiodorus' inseparable twin, observes all three 'rules'—(*i*) more strictly than even Nonnus. Unlike Triphiodorus, then, Colluthus did pay attention to accent regulation.

(*k*) Nonnus has no violation of 'Hillberg's bridge' (no word-end after a second-foot spondee—monosyllabic fourth element in Maas's terminology). Discounting cases where the fourth element is a conjunction, preposition, etc., there is one clear violation in Triphiodorus: 99, αὐτὰρ ἐπειδὴ | πάντα . . .

(*l*) Triphiodorus also has six clear violations of 'Naeke's law' (no word end after a fourth-foot spondee—monosyllabic eighth element), respected without exception by Nonnus: 5, 52, 148, 408, 461, 640 (cf. Ferrari, p. 130—missing 408).

(*m*) As pointed out in Chapter X, Triphiodorus' low proportion of direct speech, 20 per cent, belongs with Quintus (24 per cent) and the Orphic *Argonautica* (12 per cent), in the period before its revival in Nonnus and his successors (Nonnus, 36 per cent; Musaeus, 34 per cent; Colluthus, 37 per cent: for figures, not including Musaeus, see G. W. Elderkin, *Aspects of the Speech of the Later Greek Epic*, Diss. Baltimore, 1906).

There are other 'pre-Nonnian' features which lend themselves less easily to measurement and tabulation, such as Triphiodorus' use of epithets (see above, p. 15, and Wifstrand, pp. 129, 137). But let us turn now to the features which have led previous scholars to assume regardless that Triphiodorus was a true (if irregular) disciple of the master—apart, that is, from the merely historical association with Colluthus (for all his 'loyalty' to Nonnus an immeasurably inferior poet, let it be said, even to Triphiodorus).

On the basis of only six of the factors tabulated above (*d, e, g, h, i, j*), Wifstrand remarked that it was merely confusing to call Triphiodorus a 'Nonnianer': 'wären nicht die zahlreichen Phrasen und Versteile, die er offenbar aus der Dionysiaka geholt hat, würde man geneigt sein, ihn sogar vor Nonnos zu setzen' (p. 75). What then of these 'countless' phrases and tags 'obviously' borrowed from Nonnus that decided the question of Nonnus' priority for Wifstrand despite the trend of his own investigations?

Certainly there are a great many verbal parallels. The fullest collection is still that embodied in F. A. Wernicke's massive commentary (Τρυφιοδώρου Ἰλίου ἅλωσις, Lips. 1819), indispensable for study of Triphiodorus, yet (together with Wifstrand) unknown to Ferrari.

So numerous indeed are the parallels that on p. 434 Wernicke could say that in diction and style 'laus . . . in Nonnum recidit, ex quo ceu fonte perenni Tryphiodorus hausit'. At p. 64 (on line 20) he gives a good selection of 'Nonnian' clausulae used by Triphiodorus: e.g. πατρώϊος Αἴθηρ (Tr. 28~N. xxxvi. 90), πεπεδημένον ὕπνῳ (Tr. 29 ~N. xvii. 1). Much further material is scattered throughout the commentary, but see especially pp. 81–7, and for the repetition of words that is so characteristic of Nonnus, p. 375. For some additions to Wernicke's material, again taking Nonnian priority for granted, see G. Giangrande, *CR* N.S. xv (1965), 283.

But so great an authority as Professor Keydell has added to earlier kindnesses (and to his services to the field he has illuminated for half a century) by re-reading Triphiodorus for me in the light of the new discovery, as though the question of priority were still open. To his surprise he found 'daß die Stellen, wo unbedingt einer vom andern abhängig sein muß, garnicht so zahlreich sind' (a letter dated 22 July 1967). In fact he could find (and I agree with him) only four: Tr. 14~N. xxv. 306; Tr. 26~N. vii. 357; Tr. 48~N. xxv. 362; Tr. 326~N. vi. 230. Of these only one, the first, licenses an inference as to priority—and it is to the priority of Triphiodorus. In both passages the situation is the same: war has dragged on inconclusively for some time. In Tr. the horses of the heroes stand disconsolate ἀεργηλῆς ἐπὶ φάτνης, that is to say (transferring the epithet), 'idly by the manger'. In Nonnus it is Dionysus' team of lions that stand ἀεργηλῆ παρὰ φάτνη. Obviously Triphiodorus is describing a much more natural stable scene, and prima facie it might seem that the more natural is the original. It was Nonnus who adapted Triphiodorus' phrase to his own unusual context.

All the other words, tags, and tricks Triphiodorus uses which have hitherto been classified as 'Nonnisms' may derive, not from Nonnus at all, but from a common source—or rather a common style. To quote just one example, with the characteristic Nonnism ἴαχε φωνήν ('he spoke'), compare Tr. 264, ἴαχε μῦθον. But here too there is a pointer to priority. Why should Tr. have altered the Nonnian φωνήν to μῦθον? Nonnus, on the other hand, who always ends the line wherever possible with a naturally long syllable (Keydell, p. 37*, § 12), would certainly have felt it desirable to alter μῦθον to φωνήν.

This will mean, of course, a re-evaluation of Nonnus' position in the development of Greek epic. He will emerge as less wholly original (though hardly less remarkable) than commonly supposed. His contribution was, perhaps, rather to have welded stylistic tendencies already developing (no doubt among his prolific and talented Egyptian predecessors[1]) together with his own further (and especially metrical) refinements into the fantastic unity that is the style of the *Dionysiaca*—the style which influenced Greek epic more fundamentally than any other since Homer himself.

[1] There are traces among the fourth-century papyrus fragments: cf. M. L. West, *CR* N.S. xiv (1964), 214.

BIBLIOGRAPHY

This list does not purport to be either a full bibliography of the subject or an inventory of all works cited. In particular, it omits encyclopedia articles and literary histories, works singled out for special mention on p. xi, and several works cited for points of marginal relevance to the themes of the book as a whole. I have sacrificed some of the older and less accessible dissertations for more recent works, with bibliographies of their own (there is a particularly full and useful one in F. Paschoud's *Roma Aeterna* (1967)—an interesting though unsympathetic study of many western writers of the period). A few works of special interest or importance (apart from those listed on p. xi) are marked with an asterisk.

ALFÖLDI, A. *A conflict of ideas in the late Roman Empire* (Oxford, 1952).

ARENS, E. *Quaestiones Claudianeae* (Diss. Münster, 1894).

BARBU, N. I. 'Observaţii asupra poeziei lui Claudian', *Studii clasice* v (1963), 259–68.

*BAYNES, N. H. *Byzantine studies and other essays* (London, 1955).

BERNERT, E. 'Die Quellen Claudians in "De Raptu Proserpinae" ', *Philologus* xciii (1939), 352–76.

BIRT, T. *De fide Christiana quantum Stilichonis aetate in aula imperatoria occidentali valuerit* (Programm Marburg, 1885).

—— *Zwei politische Satiren des alten Rom* (Marburg, 1888).

BOAS, M. 'De librorum Catonianorum historia atque compositione', *Mnemosyne* N.S. xlii (1914), 17–46.

BOISSIER, G. *Fin du paganisme* ii (Paris, 1891).

BOLISANI, E. 'Il carme su Abano di Claudiano', *Accademia patavina di scienze, lettere e arti, memorie* N.S. lxxiii (1960/1), 21–42.

BORN, L. K. 'The perfect prince according to the Latin panegyrists', *AJPh* lv (1934), 20 f.

BRAUNE, J. 'Claudian und Nonnus', *Maia* i (1948), 176 f.

*BROWN, PETER. 'Aspects of the Christianization of the Roman aristocracy', *JRS* li (1961), 1–11.

—— *Augustine of Hippo: a biography* (London, 1967).

—— 'Pelagius and his supporters', *JTS* N.S. xix (1968), 93 f.

BRUÈRE, R. T. 'Lucan and Claudian: the invectives', *Class. Phil.* lix (1964), 223–56.

BURY, J. B. *History of the later Roman Empire* i² (London, 1923). [*LRE*]

CALATAYUD, LUCRECIA BRACELIS. 'La influencia literaria de Virgilio sobre

Claudio Claudiano', *Revista de estudios clásicos* x (1966), 37–100, ibid. xi (1967), 65–105.

CAMERON, ALAN. 'Literary allusions in the Historia Augusta', *Hermes* xcii (1964), 363–77.

—— 'The Roman friends of Ammianus', *JRS* liv (1964), 15–28.

—— 'Palladas and the fate of Gessius', *Byz. Zeitschrift* lvii (1964), 279–92.

*—— 'Wandering poets: a literary movement in Byzantine Egypt', *Historia* xiv (1965), 470–509.

—— 'St. Jerome and Claudian', *Vigiliae Christianae* xix (1965), 111–13.

—— Review of J. Straub, *Heidnische Geschichtsapologetik in der christlichen Spätantike* (1963) *JRS* lv (1965), 240–9.

—— 'Palladas and Christian polemic', *JRS* lv (1965), 17–30.

—— 'The date and identity of Macrobius', *JRS* lvi (1966), 25–38.

—— 'A biographical note on Claudian', *Athenaeum* xliv (1966), 32–40.

—— 'Rutilius Namatianus, St. Augustine, and the date of the *De Reditu*', *JRS* lvii (1967), 31–9.

—— Review of A. Demandt, *Zeitkritik und Geschichtsbild im Werk Ammians*, *CR* N.S. xvii (1967), 60–3.

—— 'Iamblichus at Athens', *Athenaeum* xlv (1967), 143–53.

—— 'Three notes on the *Historia Augusta*', *CR* N.S. xviii (1968), 17–20.

—— 'Celestial consulates: a note on the Pelagian letter *Humanae referunt*', *JTS* N.S. xix (1968), 213–15.

—— 'Theodosius the Great and the regency of Stilico', *Harvard Studies* lxxiii (1968), 247–80.

—— 'Notes on Claudian's invectives', *CQ* N.S. xviii (1968), 387–411.

—— 'The date of Zosimus' *New History*', *Philologus* cxiii (1969).

—— 'Pap. Ant. iii. 15 and the iambic preface in late Greek poetry', *CQ* N.S. xx (1970).

—— 'An unrecognized work of Aaron Hill', forthcoming.

CAMUS, P.-M. *Ammien Marcellin: témoin des courants culturels et religieux à la fin du IVᵉ siècle* (Paris, 1967).

CAVENAILE, R. 'Un pastiche de Virgile: le P.S.I. ii. 142', *Les Ét. Class.* xviii (1950), 285f.

—— *Corpus Papyrorum Latinarum* (Wiesbaden, 1958).

CERRATO, L. 'De Claudii Claudiani fontibus in poemate De Raptu Proserpinae', *Riv. di Fil.* ix (1881), 273–395.

CHASTAGNOL, A. *Les Fastes de la préfecture de Rome au Bas-Empire* (Paris, 1962).

CHRIST, F. *Römische Weltherrschaft in der antiken Dichtung* (*Tüb. Beitr. z. Altertumswissenschaft* xxxi), 1938.

CHRISTIANSEN, PEDER G. 'Claudian versus the opposition', *TAPhA* xcvii (1966), 45–54.

—— *The use of images by Claudius Claudianus* (The Hague, 1969).

CLARKE, A. K. 'Claudian's De Raptu Proserpinae', *Proc. Class. Assoc.* xxvii (1930), 38–41.

—— 'Claudian's methods of borrowing in "De Raptu Proserpinae" ', *Proc. Camb. Phil. Soc.* 181 (N.S. 1) 1950/1, 4–7.

—— 'Claudian and the Augustinian circle of Milan', *Augustinus* xiii (1968), 125–33.

COLLART, P. 'Les papyrus latins littéraires', *Rev. de phil.* xv³ (1941), 112 f.

*COURCELLE, P. *Les Lettres grecques en occident de Macrobe à Cassiodore*² (Paris, 1948).

COURTOIS, C. *Les Vandales et l'Afrique* (Paris, 1955).

CREES, J. H. E. *Claudian as an historical authority* (*Cambridge Historical Essays* xvii), Cambridge, 1908.

CREMONA, V. 'Originalità e sentimento letterario nella poesia di Claudiano', *Studi italiani pubblicati dall'Istituto di Filologia classica di Bologna*, 1948, 37–70.

—— 'La composizione del De Raptu Proserpinae di Claudiano', *Aevum*, 1948, 23 f.

CURTIUS, E. R. *European literature and the Latin Middle Ages* (English translation by W. R. Trask, New York), 1953.

DELBRÜCK, R. *Die Consulardiptychen* (Berlin–Leipzig, 1929).

DEMANDT, A. *Zeitkritik und Geschichtsbild im Werk Ammians* (Diss. Marburg: Bonn, 1965).

DEMOUGEOT, É. 'Le préfet Rufin et les barbares', *Mélanges Grégoire* ii (1950), 185 f.

—— 'Saint Jérôme, les oracles sibyllins et Stilicon', *RÉA* liv (1952), 83–92.

DILKE, O. A. W. 'Patterns of borrowing in Claudian's "De Raptu Proserpinae" ', *Revue belge de phil. et d'histoire* xliii (1965), 60–1.

D'IPPOLITO, G. *Studi Nonniani* (Palermo, 1964).

DOSTÁLOVÁ-JENIŠTOVÁ, R. 'Tyros a Bejrut v Dionysiakách Nonna z Panopole', *Listy Filologické* v (1957), 36–54.

—— 'Alte vorderasiatische Lokaltraditionen in Nonnos Dionysiaka', *Klio* xlix (1967), 39–45.

DUCKWORTH, G. E. 'Five centuries of Latin hexameter poetry: Silver Age and Late Empire', *TAPhA* xcviii (1967), 77–150.

DUDDEN, F. HOMES. *The life and times of St. Ambrose*, i–ii (Oxford, 1935).

DVORNIK, F. *Early Christian and Byzantine political philosophy* ii (Washington, 1967).

EATON, A. H. *The influence of Ovid on Claudian* (Diss. Washington, 1943).

FABBRI, P. 'Claudiano in Sicilia e il Ratto di Proserpina', *Raccolta di scritti in onore di Felice Ramorino* (Milan, 1927), 91–100.

—— 'Del vero Claudiano', *Athenaeum* xvii (1939), 27–40.

FLETCHER, G. B. A. 'Imitationes vel loci similes in poetis latinis: Claudianus', *Mnemosyne* i³ (1933), 196–201.

FLÜGEL, E. 'Eine mittelenglische Claudian-Übersetzung (1445)', *Anglia* xxviii (1905), 255–97 and 421–38.

FRIEDLAENDER, P. 'Die Chronologie des Nonnos von Panopolis', *Hermes* xlvii (1912), 43–59.

GENNARO, S. 'Lucrezio e l'apologetica latina in Claudiano', *Miscellanea di studi di letteratura cristiana antica* vii (1957), 5–60 (also published separately, Catania, 1958).

—— 'Da Claudiano a Merobaude: aspetti della poesia cristiana di Merobaude', *Miscellanea di studi di letteratura cristiana antica* viii (1958), 7–71 (also published separately, Catania, 1959).

*GLOVER, T. R. *Life and letters in the fourth century* (Cambridge, 1901).

GRISET, E. *Contributi a Claudiano Alessandrino poeta greco* (Pinerolo, 1930).

—— 'Di un carme declamatorio di Claudiano e l'esilio di Giovenale', *Il mondo classico* iii (1933), 329–35.

*GRUMEL, V. 'L'Illyricum de la mort de Valentinien Ier (375) à la mort de Stilicon (408)', *Rev. ét. byz.* ix (1951), 5–46.

HAGENDAHL, H. *Studia Ammianea* (Diss. Uppsala, 1921).

—— *Latin Fathers and the Classics* (*Studia graeca et latina Gothoburgensia* vi) (Göteborg, 1958).

HELM, R. 'Heidnisches und Christliches bei spätlateinischen Dichtern', *Natalicium Johannes Geffcken* (Heidelberg, 1931), 1–46.

HERZOG, R. *Die allegorische Dichtkunst des Prudentius* (*Zetemata* xli), 1966.

HODGKIN, T. *Claudian: the last of the Roman poets* (Newcastle, 1875).

HOPKINS, M. K. 'Eunuchs in politics in the later Roman Empire', *Proc. Camb. Phil. Soc.* clxxxix (N.S. ix), 1963, 62–80.

JONES, A. H. M. *Later Roman Empire*, i–iii (Blackwell, Oxford, 1964). [*LRE*]

KEHDING, O. *De panegyricis Latinis capita quattuor* (Diss. Marburg, 1899).

KEYDELL, R. 'Zur Komposition der Bücher 13–40 der Dionysiaka des Nonnos', *Hermes* lxii (1927), 393 f.

—— 'Die griech. Poesie der Kaiserzeit', *Bursians Jahresbericht über die Fortschritte der Altertumswissenschaft* ccxxx (1931), 41–161 and cclxxii (1941), 1–71.

—— 'Die Dichter mit Namen Peisandros', *Hermes* lxx (1935), 301–11.

—— Πάτρια Ἑρμουπόλεως', *Hermes* lxxi (1936), 465–7.

—— 'Mythendeutung in den Dionysiaca des Nonnus', *Gedenkschrift für Georg Rohde* (ΑΠΑΡΧΑΙ, Band 4) (Tübingen), 1961, 105–14.

*KNOCHE, U. 'Ein Sinnbild römischer Selbstauffassung', *Symbola Coloniensia J. Kroll* (Cologne, 1949), 143–62.

*KOCH, J. 'Claudian und die Ereignisse der Jahre 395–398', *Rhein. Mus.* xliv (1889), 572–612.

LACOMBRADE, C. 'Notes sur deux panégyriques', *Pallas* (*Annales publiées par la faculté des lettres de Toulouse*) v (1956), 15–26.

LAQUEUR, R. 'Das Kaisertum und die Gesellschaft des Reiches', in R. Laqueur/ H. Koch/W. Weber, *Probleme der Spätantike* (Stuttgart, 1930), 1–38.

LAVAGNINI, B. 'Claudiana Graeca', *Aegyptus* xxxii (1952), 452 f.

LEVY, H. L. 'Claudian's *In Rufinum* i. 83–4 and a Vatican Vase-Painting', *TAPhA* lxxii (1941), 237–44.

—— 'Claudian's *In Rufinum* and the rhetorical ψόγος', *TAPhA* lxxvii (1946), 57–65.

—— 'Two notes on Claudian's *In Rufinum*', *AJPh* lxviii (1947), 64–73.

—— 'Claudian's *In Rufinum* and an epistle of St. Jerome', *AJPh* lxix (1948), 62–8.

—— 'Claudian's neglect of magic as a motif', *TAPhA* lxxix (1948), 87–91.

*—— 'Themes of encomium and invective in Claudian', *TAPhA* lxxxix (1958), 336–47.

LIND, L. R. 'The date of Nonnus of Panopolis', *Class. Phil.* xxix (1934), 69–73.

LIPSCOMB, H. C. *Aspects of the speech in the later Roman epic* (Diss. Baltimore, 1909).

LITCHFIELD, H. W. 'National *exempla virtutis* in Roman literature', *Harvard Studies* xxv (1914), 1–71.

LOYEN, A. 'L'Albis chez Claudien et Sidoine Apollinaire', *REL* xi (1933), 203 f., 321 f.

—— *Sidoine Apollinaire et l'esprit précieux en Gaule aux derniers jours de l'Empire* (Paris, 1943).

LUDWICH, A. 'Zur griechischen Gigantomachia Klaudians', *Rhein. Mus.* xxxvi (1881), 304 f.

MCGEACHY, J. A., JR. *Quintus Aurelius Symmachus and the senatorial aristocracy of the West* (Diss. Chicago, 1942).

*MACMULLEN, RAMSAY. 'Some pictures in Ammianus Marcellinus', *Art Bulletin* xlvi (1964), 435–55.

MAENCHEN-HELFEN, O. J. 'The date of Ammianus Marcellinus' last books', *AJPh* lxxvi (1955), 384 f.

MANITIUS, M. 'Beiträge zur Geschichte römischer Dichter im Mittelalter. 2. Claudianus', *Philologus* xlix (N.F. iii) 1890, 554–60.

*MARROU, H.-I. *S. Augustin et la fin de la culture antique*[4] (Paris, 1958).

MARSILI, A. 'Roma nella poesia di Claudiano. Romanità occidentale contrapposta a quella orientale', *Antiquitas* i (1946), 3–24.

—— 'Personificazioni e quadri allegorici in Claudiano', *Antiquitas* i (1946), 49–55.

MARTIN, GLADYS. 'Claudian and the *Pervigilium Veneris*', *Classical Journal* xxx (1935), 531–43.

—— 'Claudian, an intellectual pagan of the fourth century', *Studies in honor of Ullman* (Missouri, 1960), 69–80.

MARTINELLI, N. 'Saggio sui carmi greci di Claudiano', *Miscellanea G. Galbiati* ii (1951), 47–76.

*MAZZARINO, S. 'La politica religiosa di Stilicone', *Rendiconti dell'Istituto Lombardo* (Cl. di Lettere) lxxi (1938), 235 f.

MEHMEL, F. 'Die Illustrationen des älteren vatikanischen Virgil und der spätrömische Stil um 400', in *Virgil und Apollonius Rhodius* (*Hamburger Arbeiten z. Altertumsw.* i, Hamburg, 1940), 99–132.

MERONE, E. 'La morte di Claudiano', *Giorn. ital. di fil.* vii (1954), 309 f.

MOMIGLIANO, A. (editor). *The conflict between paganism and Christianity in the fourth century* (Oxford, 1963).

MOMMSEN, T. 'Stilicho und Alarich', *Hermes* xxxviii (1903), 101–15 (= *Gesammelte Schriften* iv, 516 f.).

MOORE, C. H. 'Rome's heroic past in the poems of Claudian', *Classical Journal* v (1910), 108–15.

—— 'Latin exercises from a Greek schoolroom', *Class. Phil.* xix (1924), 317–26.

MUELLER, A. 'Studentenleben im IV. Jahrhundert', *Philologus* lxix (1910), 292 f.

MUNARI, F. 'Die spätlateinische Epigrammatik', *Philologus* cii (1958), 127–39.

MURRAY, O. 'Divine right in "The Dunciad" (IV. 175–188)', *Notes and Queries* (June 1968), 208–11.

—— 'Panegyric and advice to rulers in late antiquity and the early middle ages', *Journal of the Warburg Institute* xxxiii (1970).

NISCHER-FALKENHOF, E. *Stilicho* (1947).

*NISSEN, T. 'Historisches Epos und Panegyrikus in der Spätantike', *Hermes* lxxv (1940), 298–325.

NOCK, A. D. 'A vision of Mandulis Aion', *Harv. Theol. Rev.* xxvii (1934), 53–104.

NORMAN, A. F. 'Libanius' library', *Rhein. Mus.* cvii (1964), 158–75.

OOST, S. I. 'Count Gildo and Theodosius the Great', *Class. Phil.* lvii (1962), 27–30.

PARRAVICINI, A. *Studi di retorica sulle opere di Claudio Claudiano* (Milan, 1905).

—— 'Le prefazioni di Claudio Claudiano', *Athenaeum* ii (1914), 183–94.

*PASCHOUD, F. *Roma Aeterna: études sur le patriotisme romain dans l'occident latin à l'époque des grandes invasions* (*Bibliotheca Helvetica Romana* vii), 1967.

PAVLOVSKIS, Z. 'Statius and the late Latin epithalamia', *Class. Phil.* lx (1965), 164–77.

PERTUSI, A. *Giorgio di Pisidia: I, panegirici epici* (Studia patristica et byzantina 7), Ettal, 1960.

PIUR, P. 'Ein unbekannter Fürstenspiegel Petrarcas an Kaiser Karl IV?', *Euphorion* xxx (1929), 93–111.

PRATT, R. A. 'Chaucer's Claudian', *Speculum* xxii (1947), 419–29.

RABY, F. J. E. *Secular Latin poetry* i² (Oxford, 1957).

REITZENSTEIN, R. *Das iranische Erlösungsmysterium* (Bonn, 1921).

RIST, J. M. 'Hypatia', *Phoenix* xix (1965), 216 f.

ROBERTS, C. H. 'The Antinoe fragment of Juvenal', *JEA* xxi (1935), 199–207.

ROLFE, J. C. 'Claudian', *TAPhA* l (1919), 135–49.

SCHMID, W. 'Ein verschollender Kodex des Cuias und seine Bedeutung für die Claudiankritik', *Studi italiani* (1956), 498–518.

—— 'Claudianus' I and II in *RAC* iii (1957), 152–69.

SEECK, O. *Geschichte des Untergangs der antiken Welt* v (Berlin, 1913).

SEMPLE, W. H. 'Notes on some astronomical passages of Claudian', *CQ* xxxi (1937), 161–9 and xxxiii (1939), 1–8.

SOLMSEN, F. 'The conclusion of Theodosius' oration in Prudentius' *Contra Symmachum*', *Philologus* cix (1965), 310–13.

STEIN, E. *Histoire du Bas-Empire* i, French editon by J.-R. Palanque (Bruges, 1959).

STEINBEISS, H. *Das Geschichtsbild Claudians* (Diss. Halle, 1936).

STOECKER, E. *De Claudiani poetae veterum rerum Romanarum scientia quae sit et unde fluxerit* (Diss. Marburg, 1889).

*STRAUB, J. *Vom Herrscherideal in der Spätantike* (Stuttgart, 1939).

—— 'Parens Principum', *La Nouvelle Clio* iv (1952), 94 f.

STRUTHERS, L. B. 'The rhetorical structure of the encomia of Claudius Claudian', *Harvard Studies* xxx (1919), 49–87.

SVENSSON, A. *Der Gebrauch des bestimmten Artikels in der nachklassischen griechischen Epik* (Lund, 1937).

SYME, R. *Ammianus and the Historia Augusta* (Oxford, 1968).

THOMPSON, E. A. 'Olympiodorus of Thebes', *CQ* xxxviii (1944), 43 f.

—— 'The Visigoths from Fritigern to Euric', *Historia* xii (1963), 105–26.

TOYNBEE, J. M. C. 'Roma and Constantinopolis in late antique art', *JRS* xxxvii (1947), 135–44, and *Studies . . . D. M. Robinson* ii (1953), 261–77.

TURCEVIČ, J. 'Cl. Claudianus und Johannes Lydos: zur Frage der Herkunft Claudians', *Byz. Zeit.* xxxiv (1934), 1–9.

VIAN, F. 'La guerre des géants devant les penseurs de l'antiquité', *RÉG* lxv (1952), 1 f.

—— *Recherches sur les Posthomerica de Quintus de Smyrne* (Paris, 1959).

VOGT, J. *Kulturwelt und Barbaren—zum Menschheitsbild der spätantiken Gesellschaft* (*Abh. Mainz*), 1967.

WARREN BONFANTE, LARISSA. 'Emperor, God and Man in the fourth century: Julian the Apostate and Ammianus Marcellinus', *Parola del passato* xx (1964), 401–27.

WES, M. A. *Das Ende des Kaisertums im Westen des Römischen Reichs* (*Archeologische studiën van het Nederlands Historisch Instituut te Rome*, deel II), 's-Gravenhage, 1967.

WESTON, A. H. *Latin satirical writing subsequent to Juvenal* (Diss. Yale, 1915).

*WIFSTRAND, A. *Von Kallimachos zu Nonnos: metrisch-stilistische Untersuchungen zur späteren griechischen Epik und zu verwandten Gedichtgattungen* (Lund, 1933).

ZAKRZEWSKI, C. *Le Parti théodosien et son antithèse* (*Eos* Supplementa 18, 1931).

ADDENDA

p. 1, *n.* 2. For a new publication of the inscription to Claudian's statue, based on a fresh examination of the stone (now in Naples) and illustrated with a photograph, see L. Moretti, *Inscriptiones Graecae Urbis Romae* i (1968), no. 63, pp. 56–8.

p. 5. On the contemporary poetry of the period see now T. Viljamaa, *Studies in Greek Encomiastic Poetry of the Early Byzantine Period* (Comm. Hum. Litt. Societas Scientiarum Fennica 42. 14), 1968—a solid and useful piece of work, but perhaps lacking the insight and background to exploit the subject in a truly illuminating fashion (contrast L. Robert's *Épigrammes du Bas-Empire* (*Hellenica* iv, 1948), unknown to Viljamaa).

p. 82, *n.* 1. As John Matthews points out to me, Fl. Eutolmius Arsenius, *praeses Thebaidos* in 388 (*P. Lips.* i. 63. 6) looks very like a relative of Tatian (Fl. Eutolmius Tatianus). If so, another illustration of Tatian's nepotism, another Lycian whose career came to an abrupt end in 392.

p. 103, *n.* 1. Gildo's position was more delicate than has generally been appreciated. Technically, there can be no question but that his allegiance was to Arcadius. Till 394 Theodosius had administered Africa for the Western Augustus Valentinian II, like Honorius a mere boy, direct from Constantinople (Grumel, *Rev. ét. byz.* ix (1951), 24, with *Harvard Studies* lxxiii (1968), 271–2). If the new senior Augustus informed Gildo that he wished to restore this state of affairs, what could Gildo do but obey—or else be dubbed a rebel by Arcadius as he was in the event by Honorius? Both Claudian's versions—Gildo the straightforward *tyrannus* and Gildo the tool of eastern treachery—are understandable Western attitudes, but hardly do justice to the true complexity of the situation.

p. 248. G. Manganaro's argument (*Giorn. ital. di filol.* xiii (1960), 210 f.) that the so-called *carmen adversus Flavianum* (usually dated *c.* 395 but to 409 or later by Manganaro) was influenced by Claudian is unconvincing: see now John Matthews in *Historia* xix (1970).

p. 255. In the East, where panegyrists still learned their craft from a

living rhetorical tradition now inaccessible to the West, verse panegyrics continued to be written according to the Menandrean pattern,
whether in Greek (Pamprepius) or Latin (Priscian). Abstract personifications, however, are almost wholly absent—which tends to support
my suggestion that they are an infusion from Latin epic, idio-
syncratic among Easterners to Claudian and taken over from him and
exaggerated by his Western successors.

p. 279. On imitations and descriptions in Claudian see now A. Gualan-
dri, *Aspetti della tecnica compositiva in Claudiano* (Milan, 1969). I wish I
had been able to use U. Keudel, *Poetische Vorläufer und Vorbilder in
Claudians De consulatu Stilichonis*, to appear in the *Hypomnemata* series at
Göttingen in 1970.

p. 293, *line* 22. Cf., however, Menander, *Rh. Gr*. iii. 402, on the rules
for the epithalamium: περὶ δὲ δένδρων ἐρεῖς ὅτι κἀκεῖνα οὐκ ἄμοιρα
γάμων.

p. 304, *n*. 2. Discussing recently the relation of the *Scriptores Historiae
Augustae* to late antique art, R. Syme points to 'examples of the same
person on *sarcophagi* repeated with different clothing; and three
statues are known of one individual, viz. one as *togatus*, and two in the
dress of a hunter' (*Tardo antico e alto medioevo* (Acc. Naz. dei Lincei
1968), p. 27, with references). The *SHA* offer a fivefold representation
of the Emperor Tacitus, 'semel togatus, semel chlamydatus, semel
armatus, semel palliatus, semel venatorio habitu' (*Tac*. 16. 2). Compare
now Claudian's description of the statues of Eutropius that adorned
Constantinople: 'haec iudicis, illa togati, / haec nitet armati species;
numerosus ubique / fulget eques' (*Eutr*. ii. 72–4). Claudian's account of
Theodorus' consular games at *Theod*. 320 f. is also neatly paralleled by
an *HA* passage, *Car*. 19 f. (cf. Syme, op. cit., p. 26). For a different sort
of parallel between Claudian and the *HA*, see *CR* N.S. xviii (1968), 20.

p. 321, *line* 7. I should perhaps have added that Claudian's attitude was
by no means unique in his day. As the ideal of the perfect prose style
became more difficult of attainment—and diverged more widely
from common speech—the more stable medium of verse began to
invade fields formerly dominated (like the panegyric, cf. p. 254) by
prose. The honorific inscription is another good example: cf.
L. Robert, *Hellenica* iv (1948), 108 f.

p. 326, *n.* 4. On neoplatonic interpretations of Vergil's Underworld I should perhaps have referred to Courcelle's classic study 'Les pères de l'église devant les Enfers Virgiliens', *Archives d'histoire doctr. et littér. du Moyen Âge* xxx (1955), 5–74.

p. 345. We have seen that it was from late Greek epic that Claudian derived the supposed Germanic custom of throwing babies into the Rhine (*Ruf.* ii. 212, cf. p. 314). Could it be from some specific poem dealing in whole or part with the antiquities of Germany that he obtained both this and another curious piece of otherwise unattested Germanic lore: that it was in NE. Gaul (Boulogne, according to Norden, *Germanische Urgeschichte in Tacitus Germania* (1920), 187) that Ulysses descended into the underworld (*Ruf.* i. 123 f.)? *Anth. Pal.* ix. 125 (cf. p. 314, n. 5) might be a fragment of this very poem.

p. 370, *n.* 2. See too now Christiansen's monograph, *The Use of Images by Claudius Claudianus* (Mouton, The Hague, 1969).

p. 391, *line* 24. 'In post-Roman times a driver, especially if in charge of a team of four oxen yoked abreast on a long yoke, walked backwards in front of his team, a "caller", as his Welsh name (hywel) signifies' (C. Singer, E. J. Holmyard, A. R. Hall, T. I. Williams, *A History of Technology* ii (1956), 92, with figs. 52 and 503). Is this the sort of practice Claudian had in mind?

p. 392. The Treviran origin of Florentinus and his brothers is less certain than generally assumed. The only evidence is Symmachus' remark to Protadius, 'non iisdem sedibus immoraris, dum aut Treviros civica religione aut Quinque provincias otii voluntate commutas' (*Ep.* iv. 30. 1). John Matthews points out that 'civica religio' could refer, not to Protadius' 'civic' connection with Trier, but to his work as a court official there. And his 'otium' would presumably have been spent at home in the 'Quinque provinciae' (S. Gaul).

p. 436. Before actually quoting *Stil.* iii. 114–15, Pettit paraphrases it in reference to Charles II, 'the best of Monarchs whose service (like HIS, whose minister he is) is PERFECT FREEDOM' (*Visions of Government*, 1684, 89). Plainly Pettit was thinking, not just of Claudian, but of the second collect for peace, from the Book of Common Prayer, 'O God, who art the author of peace and lover of concord . . . whose service is perfect freedom'. This prompts the question (as Oswyn Murray remarked to me), if Pettit could be reminded of the collect by Claudian, was Cranmer perhaps thinking of Claudian when he framed the collect?

The collect is basically an adaptation of Gelasian Sacramentary 1476 Mohlberg (= ii. 56, p. 272 Wilson), 'Deus auctor pacis et amator ... cui servire regnare est'. Yet as Henry Chadwick pointed out when discussing the point most helpfully with me, 'Cranmer's adaption is interesting precisely because it abandons its Latin model at the crucial point'. We could not trace any other ancient or patristic tag to the effect that service is perfect freedom (greatly though the paradox would have appealed to the panegyrists and rhetoricians of the Empire). The closest (with a rather different emphasis) would appear to be Epicurus (fr. 199 Usener) ap. Seneca, *Epp.* 8. 9, '*philosophiae* servias oportet, ut tibi contingat vera libertas.'

Claudian was well known in England at this time, and by the next century *Stil.* iii. 114–15 was the best-known passage in Claudian. It could easily have been quoted as early as Cranmer's day (the so-called commonplace-book of Cranmer in the British Museum (MS. Reg. 7 B xi–xii) unfortunately contains only theological extracts). Cranmer's colleague Elyot certainly knew Claudian well (p. 433). It is by no means impossible that the last pagan poet of Rome inspired one of the most famous phrases in the Book of Common Prayer.

p. 439. Note too the *Lectures on Poetry* (1742) of Joseph Trapp, first professor of poetry at Oxford: '*Claudian*, though his Style is frequently too swelling, and borders upon the Bombast, yet often hits upon the true Sublime' (p. 85). And at the conclusion of his last lecture, on 'Epic, or Heroic Poetry', 'the best, and most perfect kind', Trapp adds two writers of 'an heroical Genius, though they never wrote an Heroic Poem' (p. 353). One is Dryden—the other Claudian, 'most eminent among the Latins'.

p. 448. The British Museum and Bodley have a second edition of Hughes's *Rapt.* dated 1723, but Roger Lonsdale informs me that he has an earlier 'second edition', dated 1716.

INDEX

This is a virtually complete index of people and places, and seeks to include all important subjects as well. The entry for Claudian himself is naturally selective and makes no attempt (for example) to index his changing treatment of political issues; nor in general does it duplicate the *Chronologia Claudianea* or individual entries for people and subjects discussed by Claudian. And though it does list passages where his major poems and epigrams are discussed, dated or characterized as a whole, again a complete index locorum would have been too long to be of any practical service.

Abano, warm springs of, 295, 391.
Abélard, 423.
abstract personifications, 254–5, 276–9, 282, 364.
Abundantius, cos. 393, 85, 128, 147.
Achilles, 118, 357.
Addison, Joseph, 273–4, 284, 295 n. 3, 296, 438 n. 3, 439, 467.
Addua, river, 350.
Adrasteia, 311.
Adrianople, battle of, 156, 160, 165, 351, 362.
Aeneas, 357.
Aeneas of Gaza, 319.
Aeolus, 191.
Aeternalis, proconsul of Asia, 320, 393–4, 402, 403.
Aetius, 405.
Aetna, 264, 392.
Africa, 192, 233, 247–8, 413–14, 419, 458; Roman campaigns in, 94, 117; personified, 105, 124, 142, 263, 265, 273–4, 364.
Agamemnon, 357.
Aganippe, 411.
Agathias Scholasticus, 319.
Agave, 284.
Agesilaus, 342.
Aion, 11; cave of, 205 f., 311; at Alexandria, 205–7; identified with Osiris and Adonis, 206.
Aix, court library of Charlemagne at, 420.
Alan of Lille, 301, 422–3.
Alans, 181, 268, 374 n. 1, 375–6, 377.
Alaric, Visigothic king, 37, 60, 73, 85–6, 87, 97, 129, 134, 139, 156 f., 165,

168 f., 242, 250, 259, 268, 282, 300, 375, 474; at Frigidus, 156; Arian, 195; and Theodosius, 156, 179; *mag. militum* in Illyricum, 172, 176, 178–9; crosses Alps, 180 f.; after Pollentia, 183 f., 363; alleged pacts with Stilico, 157 f. See, too, Stilico, Eutropius, and Ch. VII, *passim*.
Aldhelm, 420, 427.
Alethius, quaestor, 308, 400–1, 402, 403.
Alexander the Great, 3, 118, 358; Claudian's knowledge of, 342–3.
Alexandria, 5, 7, 14, 22, 25, 29, 189, 190, 206, 239, 322, 327, 343–4, 360, 403, 413; Claudian's native city, 3; source of poets, 4; third city of Empire, 6; Latin schools of, 20, 316; and pagan syncretism, 199 f.
Alexandrian poets, 25.
Allecto, 459.
allegory, 15, 277–9.
Alps, 179, 180, 226.
Ambrose, St., 164, 209, 219, 237, 240; and Stilico, 39; death, 116; lends posthumous aid to Mascezel, 116, 198; use of mythology, 199: Claudian's knowledge of, 219.
Ammianus Marcellinus, 20, 30–1, 33, 70, 264 n. 3, 272–3, 284, 331–2, 333, 347–8, 351, 371, 383–6; and Claudian, 316 f.; and Rome, 358–61; style of, 317–20; 'camp' Latin of, 318; polytheist or monotheist, 196–7.
Ammonius of Alexandria, 4 n. 3, 22, 23, 29, 192 n. 2, 245 n. 1.
Ammonius, patrician, 405 n. 4 (on p. 406).

Ammonius Saccas, 327.
Anacreon, read in fourth century, 307.
Anastasius, Emperor, 12 n. 1, 25, 342.
Anazarbus, 7, 9, 10, 26, 355.
Andronicus of Hermupolis, poet, 4, 23, 31, 192 n. 2, 307, 316, 405, 416.
Anicii, 30, 31 f., 190, 276, 417, 420.
Anthemius, Emperor, 193, 195.
— minister of Arcadius, 51, 135.
Antinoupolis, 4, 5.
Antioch, 22, 64, 316.
Antiochus, 119, 377.
Antipater of Thessalonica, poet, 24, 31.
Antoninus Pius, 341, 378.
Aphrodisias, 10.
Aphroditopolis, 5, 23.
Apis, 201–2.
Apollonius of Rhodes, 15–16, 267, 292, 306.
Aponus, *see* Abano.
Appian, 359.
Apuleius, 408.
Aquitanians, promoted by Gratian, 81.
Arabia, 345.
Arator, 419.
Aratus, 306.
Arbogast, 38, 156, 371.
Arcadia, 169.
Arcadius, Emperor, 38, 39, 47, 50, 51, 59, 62, 64–5, 66, 86, 87, 90, 92, 97, 107, 109–10, 112, 121–2, 149, 152, 154, 159, 161–3, 166–8, 172, 174, 203, 243, 248–9, 260, 263, 388, 407–8, 412, 476; marriage, 53–4, 75, 80; and Rufinus, 64–5, 88; and Eutropius, 52–3, 128, 144, 146; dissociated from actions of his ministers by Claudian, 52, 121–2, 152; death, 114, 155.
Archelas, Egyptian governor, 5.
Archimedes, sphere of, 344.
Arinthaeus, cos. 372, 133.
Aristides, Aelius, 321, 354–5, 358.
— the just, 342.
aristocracy of Rome, 30, 32, 129, 189, 360, 365; pagans, 221, 228; not all pagans, 230; propaganda of, 221.
Aristophanes, 3.
Arles, 392.
Armenia, 131.
Armenians, 162.
army, Stilico's, 113.
Arnobius, 329.

Arnuphis, magician, 223.
Arsenius, Fl. Eutolmius, 490.
Astraios, 11.
astrology, 208 f.
astronomy, 343, 461–3.
Athens, 22, 23, 342, 356, 360.
Athos, 262.
Audacia, 282.
Augustine, St., 219, 283, 305, 323–5, 328; on Claudian, 1, 191–2, 214–15, 217.
Augustus, 336, 358, 404.
Aurelian, minister of Arcadius, 51, 135, 147, 148, 152, 155, 245–6.
— proconsul of Asia, 393.
Aurora, the East personified, 136, 141–3, 364.
Ausonius, 197, 292, 307 n. 3, 309, 315, 316, 405, 417, 420; *gratiarum actio*, 195; 'pagan' character of poetry, 195 f.
Avemus, 193.
Avianus, 425.
Avitus, Alcimus, 318.
Avitus, Emperor, 193, 195, 286.

Babylon, 347.
Bacchus, 297.
Baldassarre Castiglione, 426.
Balkans, seized by Alaric, 85–6, 262, 373.
barbarians, invasions, 65; blamed on individual treachery, 74; Rufinus and, 71 f.; in Roman armies, 164 f., 370 f.; inferiority to Roman armies, 187–8; attitude of Claudian to, 370–7.
Barthius (Barth, Kaspar von), 438, 440.
Bartholomew, St., 218.
Basil, St., 22.
βασιλικὸς λόγος, 245–6, 322.
Basilius, cos. 480, 275.
Bastarnae, 55, 71, 72–3, 81, 96, 149–50, 159, 372.
Bauto, 156, 371.
Beaumont, Sir John, 439.
Becket, Thomas à, 427.
Bede, venerable, 420.
Bellona, 139, 177 n. 1.
Bemarchius, rhetor, 216 n. 2.
Benedict of Peterborough, 427.
Berytus, 7, 9, 10, 11, 26, 355, 357–8; Nonnus on, 9.
Bethlehem, 244.

Bithynia, 130.
Blemmyes, 5, 26.
Bobbio, ninth-century manuscript from, 422.
Boccaccio, 426.
Bordeaux, 392.
Brennus, 105, 337.
Britain, 143; Britannia, 207, 277, 364.
Bructeri, 96.
Brunhilda, 194.
Brutus, L. Junius, 224, 351.
Busiris, 338.
Byron, Lord, 449.

Caesar, 298, 388.
Caesarius, 135, 152.
Cagliari, 115.
Callimachus, 4, 25, 292, 306, 307, 319, 478, 479.
Camillus, 33, 268, 337, 350.
Cannae, 72, 351.
Cappadocia, 131-2.
Capraria, 116.
Caralis, 393.
Carinus, 341.
Carthage, 413.
Catina, 392.
Cato, 268, 314.
Catoniani libri, 424-5.
Catullus, 315.
Caucasus, 345.
Celerina, 341.
Celsinus of Castabala, 323 f.
Centaurs, not the Goths, 456.
ceremonial, 37, 253, 276, 304, 385.
Ceres, 265, 269 n. 3, 460, 468.
Chaucer, Geoffrey, 428-9.
Chelae, always stands for Libra, 461.
Cherusci, 96, 346.
China, 345-6.
Christian apologetic, 330-1.
Christian epitaphs, 209.
Christianity, 209, 212, 214, 222, 224, 225, 365-6.
Christodorus of Coptus, 4, 10, 23, 25, 192 n. 2, 207 n. 2, 416, 478-9.
Christodorus of Thebes, poet, 5.
Cicero, 20, 68, 211, 258, 318, 324.
Cimbri, 9, 187, 346.
circus games, 221.
Classis, harbour of, 414.
Claudian, poems: prefaces, in general,

76-8, 136-8; *Prob.*, 32 f., 417; *Ruf.*, date of, 82; difference between two books, 76 f., 83-4, 256, 259; contrast with *Eutr.*, 256-7; and *Rapt.*, 459-63; i *pr.*, 278; ii *pr.*, 87, 457; i, 79, 83; i, 440 f.; *Gild.*, 78, 95, 102 f., 115-16, 133, 258, 262 f., 271; *Eutr.*, i, 78, 79, 127, 133-4, 145; ii, 78, 79, 130, 134, 136-8, 143, 145, 152, 259; ii *pr.*, 77, 136-8, 149; contrast with *Ruf.*, 256-7; *Fesc.*, 98-9, 418; *Nupt.*, 95, 99-102, 271; *III Cons.*, 40 f.; *IV Cons.*, 95, 96, 245, 253-4, 322, 381, 431 f.; *Theod.*, 126 f., 323 f.; *Stil.*, 149 f., 230; i, 118 f., 145, 230; ii, 429 f.; iii *pr.*, 77; iii, 149, 230, 234, 434 f.; *VI Cons.*, *pr.*, 420, 457; 154, 180, 185, 230, 253-4, 259; *Get.*, 102, 134, 180, 184-5, 230; *Rapt.*, 264-6, 302-3, 310, 393, 452-66; i *pr.*, 278; ii *pr.*, 77, 453 f.; and *Ruf.*, 459-463; *c.m.*, publication of, 203-4, 417; *c.m.*, ii, 27; iii, 321, 393-4; xiii, 287-8, 401; xv-xvi, 13 n. 1; xvii, 392; xviii, 391-2; xix, 2, 394; xx (*De sene Ver.*), 294-5, 391, 439; xxi, 394 f.; xxii (*Depr. ad Hadr.*), 390, 397 f.; xxiii, 400; xxvi (*Aponus*), 391; xxvii (*Phoinix*), 284-5; xxx (*Laus Ser.*) and xxxi (*Ep. ad Ser.*), 406-11; xxxii (*De Salv.*), 214 f., 450; xxxiii ff. (*De crystallo*), 12-14; xl (*Ep. ad Ol.*) and xli (*Ep. ad Prob.*), 7, 458; xliii, 401; xlviii, 407; l (*in Iac.*), 218, 224 f., 401; li, 14; lii (*Gig. Lat.*), 14, 467-72; *Gig. Graeca*, 7-8, 14 f., 25, 308; *c.m. app.*, iv, 407 f.; ix, x, xi, 203 f.; *Anth. Lat.* 723 (Riese) (*In Lunam*), 202 f.; manuscript tradition and transmission of Claudian's poems in general, 115, 202, 215, 227, 252, 407-8, 417-18, 425, 429; Greek epigrams, *AP* i. 19 (*spurious*), 7; *AP* ix. 140, 27; ix. 753, 14; ix. 754, 13; *see too* s.v. *Patria*;
  date and place of birth, 2-3; names, 1, 202; marriage and death, 409 f.; position in imperial service, 330, 398; ambition limited, 404; statue, 1, 361, 415; not a modest man, 404; a professional poet, 22 f.; travels, 26 f., 391-3; friends and patrons, *see* Chs. II

Claudian (*cont.*):
and XII *passim*; not a member of the so-called circle of Symmachus, 402; alludes to Symmachus, 233; never mentioned by Symmachus, 249; not a senatorial spokesman, 235; or pagan propagandist, 220 f.; on astrology, 208 f.; on Christian writings, 217 f.; on omens and portents, 221; and Victoria, 237 f.; polytheistic references, 197 f.; perhaps a nominal Christian, 216; view of deity as beneficent, 212 f.; not a fatalist, 208, 212; on wrath of gods, 211 f.; not stuff of martyrs, 189–90;

not a historian, 66–7; to be regarded as official propagandist of Stilico, Ch. III *passim*; for his propagandist activity, *see* Chs. IV–VII *passim*, and s.vv. Arcadius, barbarians, Eutropius, Gainas, Rufinus, Stilico, Theodosius I, etc.;

culture, Ch. XI *passim*; knowledge of Greek literature, 306 f.; *see too* s.v. panegyrics, rhetorical theory; knowledge of Roman history, 331 f.; of natural science and medicine, 344; of geography, 345 f.; and natural phenomena, 292 f.; allegory, 277 f.; style, Ch. X *passim*; narrative technique, 259 f.; speeches, 262 f., 266 f.; descriptions, 263 f.; characterization, 268; and contemporary art, 270 f., 304; similes, 296 f.; numerical composition, 295 n. 1; self-plagiarism, 276, 459–63; influence of political considerations on style, 258 f.; borrowings from earlier poets, 279–84; fondness for the dramatic, 273; prosody, 287–8; metric generally, 287–92, 12 and 16–17 for his Greek poetry; caesurae, 320; elision, 289, 466; golden line, 290, 292;

did not live in past, 369 f.; aware of barbarian menace, 369 f., and problem of recruitment, 376 f.; attitude towards Rome, Ch. XII *passim*; towards the Emperor, 377 f.;

reaction of contemporaries, 241 f. (*and see* s.vv. Augustine, Orosius, Prudentius, Rutilius); influence on later centuries, Ch. XIV.

Claudian, Greek poet of late fifth century, 7–12, 27 n. 2, 416.
Claudian's Rufinus, 445.
Claudius (= Claudian?), 202 f.
Clementia, 207, 213.
Cleobulus, Egyptian poet, 5, 24 n. 3.
Cleopatra, 358.
clibanarii, 273.
coins, and Claudian, 273–4.
Coleridge, S. T., 284, 449.
Colluthus of Lycopolis, 4, 16, 25, 267, 357, 416, 478–80.
Columban, 420.
Concordia, 100.
Concordia motif, in Claudian, 51–2, 97–8, 102, 110–11, 368.
Conrad of Hirsau, 424.
— of Mure, 252.
Constantine I, 130, 384, 387.
Constantine III, 156.
Constantinople, 10, 22, 23, 26, 27, 31, 44, 65, 67, 88–9, 93, 107, 121, 134, 151, 155, 160, 163, 179, 192, 198, 236, 242, 243–4, 356, 366–9, 389, 408, 416.
Constantius II, 130, 303, 361, 383, 385, 386, 388.
consular diptychs, 32, 275.
consular robes, 47–8, 303–4.
consulship, 31–2, 63, 133; Eutropius', 125 f.
contorniates, 221.
Coptus, 4.
Corippus, Flavius Cresconius, 197, 261, 385, 413, 416, 419, 458.
corn supply of Rome, 93–4, 119, 231, 365, 368.
Corsica, 393.
cosmogony, of Claudian, 344.
cosmological poem, 5, 261.
Cowley, Abraham, 285, 439.
Craftsman, The, 447.
Cranmer, Thomas, 493.
Crinagoras of Mytilene, 24, 31.
crystal ball, Claudian's poems on, 12–14, 344.
Ctesiphon, 347.
Cupid, 100, 194.
Curae, 277, 282.
Curetius, profligate poet, 208 n. 3, 401.
Curtius, Quintus, 342.
Cyrus of Panopolis, 4, 7, 8, 11, 23, 356, 405, 416; alleged paganism, 192.

— of Antinoupolis, 4, 23.
— Persian king, 342.

Dacia, 65.
Damascius, 200, 206.
Damasus, pope, 215.
Danube, 345.
Decius, Decii, 33, 182, 337, 350.
definite article, 16, 479.
Demeter, 210; *see also* Ceres.
Dentatus, Curius, 182, 351.
Dexippus, 359.
Diana, 281, 298, 304.
Dido, 283.
Digges, Dudley, 437.
— Leonard, 271, 429, 438.
Dio Cassius, 359.
Dio of Prusa, 323.
Diocletian, Emperor, 5, 19, 25, 131, 261, 377, 384.
Diodorus of Sicily, 319.
Dionysius (author of *Gigantias*), 307, 311.
— of Halicarnassus, 358.
— Periegetes, poet, 307, 311, 312.
Dionysus, in Nonnus, 9, 481; in Orphic writings, 210.
Dioscorus of Aphroditopolis, poet, 5, 23.
Diphilus, poet, 23.
Disraeli, Benjamin, 449–50.
divine machinery of epic, 193 f., 196 f.
Donatism, 248; Gildo and, 106, 117, 196, 198.
Dracontius, Blossius Aemilius, 194, 419.
Drusus, 97.
Dryden, John, 290, 436, 439.
Dunciad, 446.

Eberhard the German, 423–4.
ecphrastic poetry, 272, 294 f.
education, 21–2, 24, 305–6.
Egypt, especially Upper Egypt, as source of poets, 4 f., 20, 22–4.
Egyptians, 6, 24, 27, 201, 316, 416, 482; Egyptian poets usually pagans, 192.
Elbe, 346–7.
Elpidius, Rusticius, 419.
Elton, Sir C. A., 449.
Elyot, Thomas, 433.

encomium, *see* panegyrics.
England, influence of Claudian in, 426 f.
Ennius, 283, 315, 404.
Ennodius, Magnus Felix, 318, 419; epithalamia, 194.
epic fragments, 12, 314.
— poetry, 260 f.
— poetry, late Greek, 15–18, 291–2, 312–15, 344, 482, 492.
Epicureanism, 327–30.
Epicurus, 329.
Epirus, 169–70, 174, 475.
epithalamium, 22, 98 f.; pagan character of, 194 f.
epithets, treatment of, 15–16, 290, 292, 480.
Erebus, 193.
Eucherius, great-uncle of Arcadius, 64, 154.
— son of Stilico, rumours about, 46–9, 192; proposed marriage with Galla Placidia, 47–8, 54, 154, 272.
Eudaemon of Pelusium, 4, 23, 192 n. 2.
Eudora, Claudian's wife, 451.
Eudoxia, Empress, wife of Arcadius; marriage, 53–4, 64, 75; and Eutropius, 53–4, 91, 135, 148.
Eugenius, usurper, 32, 35, 103, 113, 164, 217, 373, 476.
Eunapius of Sardis, 1, 4, 135, 146, 159, 165–7, 169, 180, 246, 359, 474–7.
eunuchs, 41, 304; and consulate, 127 f.
Euphrates, 347.
Eurotas, river, 34.
Eusden, Laurence, 439.
Eusebius, church historian, 223, 387.
— author of *Gainea*, 245.
Eutropius, chamberlain, 6, 51–2, 120, 122, 152, 175, 235, 242–4, 246–7, 259, 267, 285–6, 332, 341, 344, 364; rise to power, 128; relations with Arcadius, 128; and Arcadius' marriage (*see also* Eudoxia), 53–4, 64–5; victory over Huns, 125; consulate, 125 f., 146, 363; piety, 128, 229; alleged cruelty, greed, etc., 128–31; legislation, 130; division of provinces, 131, 136; sale of offices, 130; reliance on new men, 140; works against Rufinus, 91–2; succeeds to Rufinus, 85, 111; relations with

Eutropius (*cont.*):
Stilico, 124 and Chs. V and VI *passim*;
declares Stilico *hostis publicus*, 58,
86, 124, 149, 151, 176–7, 230; intrigues
against Western army, 113, 120,
151, 171; and Tribigild, 129, 134 f.;
and Gainas, 134, 146–8; and Alaric,
86, 172, 174, 176, 179, 373; period
of harmony with Stilico, 168;
alleged appeal to Stilico, 141 f.; disgrace, 118, 120, 122, 175; fall, 143 f.;
exile, 136 n. 1;
Claudian's portrait of, 256–7, 300–
2, 367; in *Eutr.* i, 127 f., 133; in
Eutr. ii, 139 f.; not mentioned in
early poems, 92, 95.
— historian, 331, 332.
Eutychian, 135, 245 n. 2.
Evagrius, ecclesiastical historian, 7, 11–
12, 311 n. 4, 416.
exempla virtutis, 182, 337 f., 350–2, 361.

Fabius Maximus, Q., 182, 352, 363.
Fabricius, C., 182.
Faesulae, battle of, 56, 415, 453–4.
Faleria, 205.
Fawkes, F., 439.
federates, 72, 187, 377.
Fenton, Elijah, 439.
Filmer, Sir Robert, 435–6.
Firmus, 94, 96, 107–9, 117.
Flaccilla, Empress, 44, 407.
Florentinus, prefect of Rome in 395–7
and dedicatee of *Rapt.*, 211, 392,
400 n. 2, 401, 402, 414, 454–5, 456,
457, 463, 465, 492; not a title of
Stilico, 454 f.
florilegia, 423.
Florus, 316, 331, 332, 333–4, 335, 340.
Fortunatus, Venantius, 318, 420; epi-
thalamia, 194.
Fortune, wheel of, in Claudian, 202–3.
Francesco da Fiano, 426.
Franks, 96.
Fravittas, 135, 147.
Frigidus, battle of, 32–3, 35, 156, 158,
164, 169, 190, 217, 275, 377, 402.
Furies, in Claudian, 67, 256, 265, 459 f.

Gainas, 59, 66, 72, 134–5, 142, 143, 144,
146–9, 245; and fall of Rufinus, 146,
475; and fall of Eutropius, 134–5,

146; Stilico's rival, not creature,
146–8, 371; coup of, 135, 147; never
mentioned by Claudian, 146, 371.
Gaiseric, 196.
Galatia, 130.
Galla Placidia, daughter of Theo-
dosius I, 47, 54, 154, 272.
Gallia, 207, 277, 364.
Gallus, Caesar, 304.
games, 32, 241.
Gaul, 143, 186, 233, 392–3.
Gauls, 113, 162.
Gaza, sophists of, 24, 78 n. 1.
Geloni, 71, 347.
Gennadius (? Torquatus), orator and
proconsul, 2, 249, 394, 402.
geographical knowledge, 345–7.
George of Pisidia, 261–2, 314, 315, 344.
German babies, thrown in Rhine, 314–
15, 492.
Germanus, general, 5.
Gessius, rhetor, 208 n. 3.
Gibbon, Edward, 21, 100, 380, 436,
440, 448.
gigantomachy theme, 11, 211, 468 f.
Gildo, 52, 58, 122, 124, 127, 132, 145,
150–1, 173, 193, 231, 233, 235, 247–8,
260, 263, 286, 347, 364, 365, 379;
appointment as count of Africa,
104–5; alleged agrarian reform, 106–
7; and Firmus, 108; and Theodosius,
103–5; cruelty, 106, 116; cuts off corn
supply, 94; defeat, 95; and Donatism,
106, 117, 196; relations with Constantinople, 103, 120, 151, 490.
Gildonic war, 230 f., 233, 362 f., 381,
456.
Girald of Wales, 427, 432.
gladiatorial games, 222, 240.
gods, jealousy and anger of, 211–12.
— justice and beneficence of, 212–14.
golden age, in Claudian, 369, 460–1.
Gospels, 217.
Goths, 72, 135, 156 f., 164 f., 170 f.,
226, 251, 352, 362, 360–7, 411. *See
too* barbarians *and* Alaric.
grammatici, 306 f., 320; often also
poets, 24 n. 3.
Gratia, 100.
Gratian, Emperor, 195, 365, 405.
Greece, 168, 170–1, 175.
Greek Anthology, 7, 8, 27 n. 1, 31.

Gregory Nazianzen, 314, 387.
Grote, George, 449.

Haasse, Hella S., 451.
Hades, 69, 218, 281–2, 304, 326, 459 f., 491.
Hadrianus, CSL, *mag. off.*, PPO, 2, 343; relations with Claudian, 394–401, 402, 403, 405.
— Rufius Synesius, not the foregoing, 394 n. 3.
Haemus, 262.
Hannibal, 182, 337, 351.
Hardouin, 274.
Harmonia, 11, 344.
Harpocration, Egyptian poet, 5, 23, 31.
Hector, 283.
Helladius of Alexandria, 4 n. 3, 22, 24, 29, 192 n. 2.
— of Antinoupolis, 4.
Héloïse, 423–4.
Helpidius Rusticius, 215.
Henna, 264.
Henri d'Andeli, 424.
Henry VI, king, 430.
Hephaestion of Thebes, 208.
Heraclianus, friend of Libanius, 23.
Heraclius, Emperor, 261.
— general of Zeno, 5.
Herbert of Bosham, 427.
Hercules, 297, 453, 457.
Hermetic corpus, 206.
Hermias, 327.
Hermupolis, 4, 5, 261.
Herodian, 359.
Herodotus, 319, 347.
Hesychius of Miletus, on Claudian, 3.
Hill, Aaron, 446–8.
Himerius, 307 n. 2., 319.
Historia Augusta, 78 n. 3, 491.
History, Claudian's knowledge of, 331 f.
Hobbes, Thomas, 285.
Homer, 15, 25, 267, 292, 296, 298, 306, 307, 386, 404, 482.
Honorius, Emperor, 35–6, 38–9, 40 f., 62, 90, 94–5, 97, 109, 112, 113, 121, 125, 152, 154–5, 166, 168, 177–8, 180–1, 191, 195, 201, 209, 216, 222–3, 231–2, 239–41, 249, 263, 268, 271–2, 297, 304, 349, 362, 363, 365, 369, 375, 377–80, 381–8, 402–3, 410–12, 471,

476; marriage to Maria, 76, 95, 98 f., 114; and marriage of Arcadius, 53–4; visits Rome in 404, 181, 382–9; piety, 190, 194; independence, alleged signs of, 113–14; had there been any real signs, this entry might have been more informative.
Horace, 315, 346.
Horapollon of Phenebith, 4, 5 n. 6, 22, 24, 192 n. 2, 307 n. 2.
Horatius Cocles, 133, 350.
Hosius, 140, 259.
Howard, H. E. J., 449 n. 3.
Hubert, archbishop of Canterbury, 427.
Hughes, Jabez, 439, 448, 493.
Hugo of Trimberg, 424.
Huns, 38, 125, 129, 132, 150, 257, 333, 347.
Hymen, 100.
Hypatia, daughter of Theon, 306.

Iamblichus, 210.
Illus, minister of Zeno, 23, 405.
Illyricum, 59–62, 85–6, 172–3, 178, 187; as recruiting-ground, 158, 375.
India, 345–6.
Innocent III, pope, 423.
invective, 22, 68 f., 83–4, 255, 258–9, 399 n. 1.
Isidore of Alexandria, 200.
— of Seville, 420.
Isis, 200, 203–5, 227.
Italy, 233, 235; personified, 364 (*see too* Oenotria).
iudicia populi, 234.
Ixion, 210.

Jacob, *dux*, 225–6, 401, 402, 403, 414.
Jerome, St., 105, 224, 244, 305, 327, 419.
John, alleged lover of Eudoxia, 135, 152.
— of Antioch, 159, 166, 180, 244, 474–7.
— Chrysostom, St., 98 n. 2, 243.
— Egyptian hermit, 6.
— of Garland, 424.
— of Gaza, 207 n. 2, 478.
— the Lydian, 311 n. 4, 419; on Claudian, 3, 244–5.
— Philoponus, 311 n. 4.
— of Salisbury, 427, 431.

Johnson, Samuel, 436, 440.
Jonson, Ben, 434–5, 439.
Jordanes, 371.
Joseph of Exeter, 428.
Jugurtha, 94, 119.
Julian, Chaldaean theurgist, 223.
— Emperor, 170, 212, 272–3, 296, 356, 388; and Apis bull, 202; culture, 307 n. 2, 314; attitude to Latin, 358.
Juno, 410, 468.
Jupiter, 105, 107, 193, 212, 248, 263, 265, 276, 293, 297, 365, 404, 410, 459, 468; temple of in Rome, 220.
Justin II, Emperor, 261, 385.
Justinian, 243, 314, 319.
Justitia, 207, 256, 276, 277, 395, 461–2.
Juvenal, 281, 284, 291, 303, 315, 316, 328, 332, 337, 340, 351, 361, 398; studied in late Roman Egypt, 20.
Juvencus, 218.

King, Dr. William, 441 f.
kingship, Claudian's views on, 96, 377 f.
Κρόνιον πέλαγος, 312–13.
κτίσεις, hellenistic foundation literature, 25.

Lachesis, 265.
Lactantius, 212, 218, 220, 329, 331.
landowners, 129, 189, 377.
Lares, 198.
largess, of consuls, 385.
Latin, knowledge of by Greeks, 19–21, 244, 245, 321; utility of for law and civil service, 19; in Constantinople, 242.
Laudes Romae, 341, 354 f.
Laurence, St., 275.
lemmata to Anthology, 8, 9.
Leo, 140, 143, 259.
Leto, 297.
Libanius, sophist, 23, 24, 31, 399, 405; attitude to Latin, 19, 21, 358; culture of, 305, 307 n. 2, 314.
library of Constantinople, 27.
Libya, 345.
Licentius, 219, 452.
Livian epitomators, 332, 334.
Livy, 331–2, 334, 339.
Lodge, Thomas, 437.

Longinianus, Fl. Macrobius, 216 n. 1, 415.
loyalty, of Stilico's troops, 162 f., 171 f., 181.
Lucan, 3, 266, 279–81, 284, 286, 289, 290, 292, 297, 298, 315, 316, 328, 332, 337, 339, 340, 343, 361, 425, 456.
Lucian, *comes Orientis*, 64, 71, 75, 80.
Lucilius, 315.
Lucretius, 315, 328–31.
Luctus, 277, 282.
Luna, hymn to, 202 f.
Lycia, 81–2.
Lycians, banned from imperial service by Rufinus, 81–2.
Lycurgus, 342.
Lydia, 130.

Macedonia, 65, 156.
Macrobius, 14, 30 n. 1, 201–2, 287, 305, 328 n. 2.
Maeotis, 71, 345.
Maggiore, Santa Maria, 366.
Magna mater, 190.
Magnus, doctor, 306.
Majorian, 193, 195, 286.
Manilius, 299, 315.
Manitius, Max, 422.
Manlius Torquatus, 224.
Map, Walter, 427.
maps, cosmic, in Claudian and Nonnus, 11.
Marcellinus, *comes*, 243, 244.
Marcellus, M. Claudius, 182, 352.
Marcomanni, 38.
Marcus Aurelius, 212, 223–4, 341, 378.
Maria, wife of Honorius and daughter of Stilico, 47, 153 n. 1, 194, 219, 270–1, 417; marriage, 57–8, 95, 98–9, 109, 409; rumoured pregnancy, 153.
Marius, 152, 187, 335, 338.
Marlborough, Duke of, 441.
Mars, 139, 193, 196, 198, 229, 297.
Martial, 394, 417.
Mascezel, brother of Gildo, 94, 112, 114–19, 123, 151, 198, 260; piety of, 229; expedition against Gildo, 95; supporter of Firmus, 108–9.
Massagetae, 71, 347.
Maurice, *dux*, 23.
Maximian, 419, 425.
Maximus, Petronius, 390 n. 1.

Maximus, usurper, 103–6, 113, 158.
medicine, 306, 344–5.
Megaera, 67, 69, 70, 256, 277, 459 f.
Melania the elder, St., 220.
Memnon, 118.
Memphis, 4, 201, 382.
Menander, read in fourth century, 307.
Menander Rhetor, 23, 84, 253–5, 294, 491.
Mercury, 265.
Meres, Francis, 437.
Merobaudes, Flavius, 215, 255, 405, 419.
Meroe, 345.
Messalina, 351.
Metelli, 33, 350.
metempsychosis, 209–10, 326, 461.
Michel, Jehan, 451.
Milan, 6, 35–6, 41, 44, 66, 70, 94, 107, 116, 127, 151, 180, 190, 192, 199, 218, 219–20, 222, 228, 229–30, 232, 241, 246–7, 249, 251, 268, 303, 350, 362, 371, 376, 382, 386, 388–9, 390–1, 402, 413, 415; siege of by Alaric, 414.
Miletus, 10.
Miltiades, 342.
Milton, John, 438.
Minervius, brother of Florentinus, 402, 455.
Minos, 69.
Minucius Felix, 218, 331.
'Mirrors for Princes', 431 f.
Mithradates, 119.
mobility of poets, 23 f.
Moesia, 72, 156, 158.
monotheism, 196 f.
Montesquieu, 423.
Monza, cathedral treasure, 48.
Moschus, 306.
Moses, 212.
Muretus, 425.
Musaeus, 5, 267, 311 n. 5, 357, 478–80.
mythological poetry, 14, 24, 25, 453 f.
mythology, pagan, 199, 205; in Claudian, 277, 416.

Nacle, 10.
Nalson, John, 437.
Narcissus, 341.
narrative technique, 260 f.
Narses, 132.
natural science, 344.

Nature personified, 205–7, 277.
Naucellius, 452 n. 1.
Neckham, Alexander, 424, 428.
neoplatonism, 209 f., 325–7.
Nereids, 194, 270.
Nero, Emperor, 341.
Nestor, 357.
Nestor of Laranda, poet, 12 n. 3, 24, 31, 307.
Nicaea, 7, 9, 10, 26, 355; Nonnus on, 9.
Nicomachi Flaviani, 35.
Nicomachus Flavianus, 340.
Night, 311.
Nile, 2, 6, 308, 344, 345, 396, 449 n. 3.
Nonnus, of Panopolis, 4, 7–11, 14–15, 16, 20, 25, 192 n. 2, 207, 263 n. 1, 264 n. 2, 267, 286, 291–2, 293, 296, 310–12, 343, 357–8, 416, 478 f.; date, 7, 11–12; and Claudian, 9 f.; and Panopolis, 4–5; and Triphiodorus, 478–82.
Notitia Dignitatum, 364.

Oasis, 4.
obelisk of Theodosius in Constantinople, 27–8, 47.
Odysseus, 357.
Oenotria, 277.
Olybrius, Anicius Hermogenianus, cos. 395, 31, 32 n. 4, 36, 198, 393, 458.
Olympiodorus of Thebes, 1, 4, 6, 23, 59, 192 n. 2, 311, 355, 360, 416; and Rome, 355–6, 361; knowledge of Latin, 20.
Olympiodorus, philosopher, 307 n. 3, 311 n. 4.
Olympius, pagan philosopher, 29.
Olympus, 193, 229, 304.
Oppian, 6 n. 1, 16, 292, 299, 300, 306, 307.
Oriental religions, 200.
Orientius, 419.
Orosius, 215, 217, 223, 248, 371; on Claudian, 1, 28, 191–2, 214, 419; on Stilico, 157, 169, 181.
Orpheus, 210, 309, 313, 404, 410, 453, 468.
Orphic *Argonautica*, 309, 312–13.
Orphic poems, 210, 277, 309–11, 344, 457.
Orphism, 209–10, 310–11.

Osbern Bokenham, 429.
Osbern of Gloucester, 427.
Osiris, festival of Heuresis, 205.
ostrich, 300.
Ostrogoths, 139, 371, 415.
otium, 396.
Ovid, 20, 25, 286, 289, 293, 310, 315, 316, 320, 328, 344.

Pacatus, 106, 254, 383.
Padua, 391.
pagan propaganda, alleged, 220 f., 230 f., 398.
paganism, 1, 22, 187–227 *passim*.
Palladas of Alexandria, 3, 4, 22, 29, 192 n. 2, 207, 208 n. 3, 306 n. 2, 307, 308–9, 328 n. 2, 399 n. 1, 403; and Claudian, 308–9; paganism, 200 f.; and Serapis, 200.
Palladius, author of *Lausiac History*, 220.
— notary, 341, 401, 402.
Pamprepius of Panopolis, 4, 23, 192 n. 2, 293, 314, 342, 356, 360, 405, 416.
Pancratius, 4 n. 3.
panegyrics, rules of, 22–3, 32 f., 40, 41–2, 96, 253–5, 257, 259, 260 f., 297, 321, 368, 388, 453; topoi of, 83, 315; of Emperors, 36–7, 40 f.; of cities, 354 f.; verse panegyrics, 254–5; fusion with epic, 254, 261 f.; link with contemporary art, 275; *see also* rhetorical theory.
panegyrists, prose, 195.
Pannonians, promoted by Valentinian, 81.
Panopolis, prolific source of poets, 4, 5, 356.
Παφλαγών, nickname, 3, 245.
papyri, Latin, from Egypt, 20, 320; papyri of Greek contemporary poetry, 5, 260.
Paris, Matthew, 427.
Pater, Walter, 303.
Paternus, CSL, 396 n. 2.
Patria, foundation poems, 7, 8, 9, 10, 25, 28, 261, 355.
patriciate, 405.
Pattison, William, 439.
Paul of Alexandria, 208.
— the Silentiary, 16, 478.
— St., 209; Pauline epistles, 217–18.

Paulinus, biographer of Augustine, 192.
— of Nola, 344, 419; and Christian epithalamium, 194.
— of Pella, 419.
Paullus, Aemilius, 337.
Paulus Diaconus, 215.
Peisander of Laranda, poet, 307, 310–11, 313.
Peisistratus, 342.
Pelusium, 4.
Περὶ βασιλείας, 254, 322, 327, 380–1.
Persephone, *see* Proserpina.
Perseus, king, 119.
Persia, 140, 261, 347, 356.
Pervigilium Veneris, 293–4.
Peter, St., 218.
Petrarch, 425, 432–3.
Petronius, 420.
Pettit, Edward, 436, 437, 492–3.
Phalaris, 68, 338.
Philip of Leyden, 431.
Philip II of Macedon, 342.
Philip V of Macedon, 119, 333.
Philip of Thessalonica, 24.
Philodemus of Gadara, poet and philosopher, 24, 31.
philosophy, Claudian's knowledge of, 323.
Philostorgius, 91, 476.
Phoebus, 205, 211.
Phoibammon, *comes*, 23.
Phrygia, 130, 372, 373.
Phrygian, synonym for coward, 3.
Physis, 11, 205, 207 n. 3; *see also* Nature.
Pindar, read in fourth century, 307.
Pisa, 115.
planetary spheres, 107, 209, 463.
Planudes, 206 n. 5.
Plato, 327, 342.
plebs of Rome, 231, 383–4.
Pliny the elder, 312.
— the younger, 254, 382.
Plotinus, 210, 326, 327.
Plutarch, 358.
Pluto, 265, 459, 461, 468–9.
poetic contests, 26.
political theory, Greek, 322–3, 377 f.
Pollentia, battle of, 160, 171, 173, 178, 179, 180, 181–6, 188, 221, 248, 363, 369, 376, 377, 413, 465, 471, 477.
Polwhele, Richard, 449.

Polybius, 319.
polytheism, 196.
Pompey, 152.
Pontus, 130.
Pope, Alexander, 436, 439, 445–6.
Pope, R. M., 451.
Porphyry, 210, 327.
Porsenna, 350.
Porus, 118, 342.
Praetextatus, Vettius Agorius, 237.
Priscian, 244, 419.
Priscus, Helvidius, 341.
Proba, 199, 297.
Probinus, Anicius, cos. 395, 7, 31, 36,
   32 n. 4, 36, 198, 309, 393, 458.
Probus, Sex. Petronius, 33–4.
Proclus, neoplatonist, 15, 20, 327.
Procopius of Gaza, 319, 342, 358.
— historian, 3.
Proculus, son of Tatian, prefect of
   Constantinople in 392, 63, 71, 80, 81.
profession, poetry as a, 22 f.
Promotus, 63, 71, 75, 371.
Propertius, 315.
prose style, 318–21.
Proserpina, 264, 270, 293, 297, 304,
   344, 468–9; rape of, by Zeus, 210; by
   Pluto, 311; *De Raptu*, Appendix A
   passim.
Prosper of Aquitaine, 419.
Protadius, brother of Florentinus, 402,
   455.
Prudentius, 184, 222, 230, 237, 239,
   240, 241, 271 n. 2, 275, 287, 344,
   419, 421; on Pollentia, 181, 248, 471;
   and Roma, 248, 364–5; and Claudian,
   218, 248, 278–9, 469–73; publication
   of poems, 470–1.
Ptolemaeus, *comes stabuli*, 285.
Pulcheria, 130.
Punic, language, 458.
puns, in Claudian, 259.
Pyrrhus, 119, 182.
Python, 278.

Quadi, 223.
Quintus of Smyrna, 6 n. 1, 15, 16,
   20 n. 7, 292, 293, 300, 307, 311 n. 4,
   357, 479, 480.

Radagaisus, 156, 187, 415.
Radulf of Diceto, 427.

Raetia, 179, 186, 262, 375.
Ravenna, 218, 252, 355, 362, 384, 414–15.
Ravisius Textor, 438.
recitations, 77–8.
recruitment, difficulties of, 158, 374–7.
Rhapsodic Theogony, so-called, 311.
rhetoric, 21–2, 305–6, 317, 321–3, 337–
   9; influence of on Claudian, 253–5,
   321–3. *See also* invective, panegyrics.
rhetorical handbooks, 337–9, 343, 350,
   368.
rhetorical theory, Greek, 321 f., 354 f.
Rhine, 150, 168, 173, 314, 346.
Rhodope, 262.
Richard, duke of York, 427.
Richard of Furnival, 422, 424.
Roger of Hoveden, 427.
Roma, personification, 33, 35, 105, 125,
   145, 182, 193, 232, 248, 263, 265, 270,
   274–6, 277, 286, 471; growth of,
   363 f.; rejuvenated, 107, 365; Christianization of, 365 f.
Roman state religion, 193 f.
Rome, city, 6, 24, 30–1, 219, 222, 223,
   228–30, 232–3, 236–7, 241, 245–6,
   251, 390, 415; sack of, 157, 184, 188,
   250; eulogized, 236, 352 f.; *see*
   Ch. XII *passim*.
Romulus, 355.
Romus, 355.
Rufinus, praetorian prefect, 44, 51–2,
   60, 63 f., 76, 106, 111, 129, 134, 159,
   160–1, 163, 167–8, 210, 212, 267, 277,
   278, 283, 330; trusted by Theodosius but not Arcadius, 64; consulate, 70; plan to marry daughter
   to Arcadius, 64–5; relations with
   Arcadius, 128; alleged coercion of
   Arcadius, 88–9; piety, 229; bars Lycians from civil service, 81–2; alleged
   treachery, of, 71 f., 87, 244, 247, 372;
   alleged cruelty and greed, 70–1;
   alleged designs on purple, 89–90,
   474; enemies other than Stilico, 64–5,
   91–2; death, 66, 90 f.; Claudian's
   portrait of, 133, 258, 301.
Rufinus, or an Historical Essay . . ., 440 f.
Rufinus, Tyrannius 200.
Rutilius Namatianus, 157, 169, 349,
   364, 370, 419; on Stilico, 250–1;
   paganism, 196 f.; and Claudian,
   250–1.

Sacheverell, Revd. Dr., 442.
Sallust, 317, 331, 334–5, 347.
Sallustius, 'editor' of Apuleius, 408.
Salutati, Coluccio, 426.
Sannuto, L., 429.
Sappho, in late Empire, 307 n. 2.
Scaevola, Q. Mucius, 133.
Scaliger, Julius Caesar, 438.
Scipio, 182, 352, 404.
Scipiones, 33, 268, 337.
Sciron, 68, 338.
Scythia, 72, 345.
sea, allusion to in Claudian, 26.
secret pacts, 157 f.
Sedulius, 215, 318–19, 419.
Sejanus, 351.
senate, of Constantinople, 230, 366, 388.
— of Rome, 35, 230, 231, 232, 234, 238, 247–8, 251, 366: and Gildonic war, 233 f., 362–3; consulted by Stilico, 231 f., 381 f.; declares war on Gildo, 235–6; did not have monopoly on literary culture, 402; *see also* aristocracy.
— house, 237.
senatorial courts, 234.
Seneca, 333, 337.
Serapeum, destruction of, 200.
Serapis, 200, 214.
Serena, wife of Stilico, 38, 48, 153 n. 1, 195, 203, 271, 402, 406–11, 414; marriage to Stilico, 56–7; adoption by Theodosius, 57; mother-in-law of Honorius, 58, 407; bigotry, 190, 198.
Serenus, Egyptian poet, 5.
serpent, symbolizing time, 206 f.
Serranus, 337.
Servius, 287.
Severus, patriarch of Antioch, 20, 200.
Shelley, 214, 450.
Sicily, 392–3.
Sidonius Apollinaris, 197, 242, 249 n. 1, 286, 288, 318, 323 n. 2, 336, 343 n. 2, 416; on Claudian, 3; influenced by Claudian, 8, 255, 420; epithalamia, 194 f.; and astrology, 208; 'pagan' character of panegyrics, 193 f.
Silius, 267, 304, 315–16, 339–40, 426.
Simplicius, proconsul of Asia, 393.
Sinis, 68, 338.
Sisyphus, 210.

Smith, Captain John, 433–4.
Smyrna, 26–7.
Socrates, 388, 475, 476–7.
Solon, 342.
Soterichus of Oasis, poet, 4, 5, 25, 262, 307, 416.
Spain, 233, 364.
Spaniards, promoted by Theodosius, 81.
Spartacus, 338.
Spenser, Edmund, 438.
Sperchius, CRP, 396 n. 2.
Statius, 255, 263 n. 1, 267, 272, 280, 282, 284, 286, 288, 291, 293, 294, 295, 297, 301, 311, 315, 316, 417, 425, 426, 446, 456; influence on epithalamium tradition, 195, 271.
Stephanus of Byzantium, 311 n. 4.
Stilico, 1, 35, 75–6, 85, 195, 198, 199, 203, 216, 228, 229–30, 236, 239, 241, 243–4, 246–8, 250–2, 259–60, 262, 267–8, 271–2, 277, 300, 304, 349–50, 362–4, 367, 383–5, 390, 397–8, 402–6, 415–18;
  marriage to Serena, 56, 115; continuity of policy with Theodosius, 58, 115, 243; dynastic pretensions, 47–9, 54, 153–4; 'regency', 38–40, 42–4, 49–51, 87, 152, 154; and Arcadius, 52, 121–2, 147; loyalty of, 88, 157;
  military prowess, 55–6; control of troops, 161 f.; *consilium* of, 114–15; alleged designs on Illyricum, 59–62; true aims, 62, 157–8, 188; relations with East, 124, 135, 138, 143, 149 f., 155; plots against, 120; marries Maria to Honorius, 98–101;
  and Rufinus' fall, 90–2, 145; Rhine campaign of 396, 96–7; and Gainas, 146–8; and Bastarnae, 72 f., 150; rivalry with Eutropius, 93 f., and Chs. V–VII *passim*;
  danger during Gildonic crisis, 94; defeat of Gildo, 124–5, 145, 150; and Gildonians after Gildo's fall, 234 f.; actions during war, 114, 119, 132–3; declared *hostis publicus*, 94, 101, 114, 124–5, 149, 151, 242; does not recognize Eutropius' consulate, 235; ultimata to Eutropius, 122; and Tribigild, 152; and Eutropius' fall, 144 f.;

and Alaric in 395, 88 f., 159 f.; in 397, 97 f., 168 f.; *see too* 474–7 and Ch. VII *passim*; and barbarians in general, 371 f.; consulate, 70, 118, 124–5; consular robe as described by Claudian, 47–8, 154, 271–2, 303–4; triumphal entry into Rome, 149, 385; relations with senate, 231 f., 241, 379, 380; toleration of pagans, 199, 227; and Sibylline books, 220 f.; and heretics, 116; achievement, 188;
and Claudian, *see passim*, but especially 268; republished omnibus edition of Claudian, 227, 252.

Strada, 426.
Strutt, J. G., 449.
Stumbling Block, The, 443.
Sudermann, H., 451.
Suidas, 261.
Sulla, 68, 338.
Susanna, St., 218.
Sygambri, 96.
Symmachus, Q. Aurelius, 30–1, 36, 126, 231–3, 237–8, 240, 247, 249–50, 317, 370, 405; and Stilico, 250; paganism, 197, 200, 365; alleged circle of, 249.
Synesius of Cyrene, 245–6, 387; culture, 307 n. 2; and Claudian, 321: *De Regno*, 321, 327, 381; *De Providentia*, 245.
Syria, 130.
Syrianus, philosopher, 309–10.

Tacfarinas, 94.
Tacitus, 97, 328, 331, 334–6, 341, 346–7, 359.
Tantalus, 69, 210, 282.
Tarquins, the, 105.
Tarsus, 7, 9, 10, 26, 355.
Tartarus, 193.
Tatian, cos. 391, 63, 69, 71, 80, 81.
Tennyson, 449.
Teucer, 357.
Teutones, 187.
Theagenes, 342.
Thebaid, source of poets, 4 f.
Thebes, Egyptian, 1, 4, 5.
Thecla, St., 218.
Themistius, 5, 31, 328 n. 2, 387, 405.
Themistocles, 342, 356.

Theocritus, 306.
Theodorus, Mallius, cos. 399, 61, 209, 222, 229, 241, 276, 296, 300, 323, 394–7, 401, 402, 403; consulate, 125–7, as a philosopher, 323–7. Mallius is the form attested by inscriptions, chronicles, and the like, but MSS. suggest that Claudian wrote Manlius (see Birt, p. xl).
Theodosius, *comes*, 57, 94, 107, 263; African campaign of, 96.
Theodosius I, the Great, 6, 27, 28, 33–4, 35, 37 f., 42, 47, 51, 58, 63, 70, 72, 80, 95, 103, 107, 109–11, 112, 129, 169, 239, 243, 260, 263, 272, 275, 365–6, 378, 380, 383–4, 388, 406, 460, 476; and Stilico, 55 f.; preferred Rufinus, 70; and Honorius' marriage to Maria, 99; and sale of offices, 130; and division of provinces, 131; and games, 222; and paganism, 230, 234; anti-pagan laws, 189; persecutor, 199; victory over Eugenius, 191, 217; and Gothic problem, 72 f., 156, 164, 371 f.; and Alaric, 156, 158; and Gildo, 103–5; as represented by Claudian, 92, 103, 111, 162, 224, 268, 283.
Theodosius II, Emperor, 8, 11, 46–7, 155, 192, 356.
Theon, mathematician, 206–7, 306, 308, 309.
Theophilus, patriarch of Alexandria, 28–9, 189, 200 n. 3.
Thermantia, daughter of Stilico, second wife of Honorius, 48, 153 n. 1, 272; marriage prospects, 54.
Thessalonica, 10.
Thessaly, 66, 170, 355, 475.
Thomas, St., 218.
Thrasea Paetus, 341.
Thucydides, 319.
Tiber, 34, 269, 350.
Tiberianus, 293.
Tiberius, Emperor, 341.
Tibullus, 315.
Tigranes, 119.
Tigris, 347.
Timarus, river, 180.
Timasius, general of Theodosius, 85.
Time, deified, 205 f., 277.
Tisiphone, 459.

Titans, 69, 210, 265.
Titus, Emperor, 341.
Tityos, 69, 210, 282.
Tomarian Jupiter, 313.
Trajan, Emperor, 341, 347, 356, 378, 380, 382; forum of, 248, 361, 415.
Tralles, 10.
translation of Greek epigrams into Latin, 13 n. 1.
Trapp, Joseph, 493.
Tribigild, 129, 131, 139, 140, 143, 144, 152, 161 n. 1, 177 n. 1, 259.
tribune and notary, post of, 390, 401, 404, 405.
Trier, 362, 392, 414.
Triphiodorus, 4, 292, 307, 357, 416, 478–82; date, 18; metric, style, etc., 478–81; knowledge of Latin, 20.
Triton, 100, 270.
tyrannus, usurper, 103.

Underworld, *see* Hades.
Ussher, J., 437.

Valens of Pettau, 74.
Valentinian II, Emperor, 38, 81, 107, 237.
Valerius Flaccus, 267, 288–9, 291, 304, 315, 316, 426.
— Maximus, 294, 337–9.
Venus, 100, 193–4, 270–1, 293.
Vergil, 21, 107, 193, 266, 269, 276, 280–3, 288–91, 297, 315–16, 320, 328,

332, 340, 346, 361, 404, 425, 426, 466; studied in late Roman Egypt, 20.
Verona, 294–5, 391; battle of, 180, 183–6, 373, 376, 471.
— eighth-century manuscript from, 420.
Vibius Sequester, 345.
Victor, Aurelius, 331, 386.
Victoria, 227, 237, 239, 241; altar of, 237–41; statue of, 239; temple of, 238.
Villani, Filippo, 426.
Virgin, the, 219.
Visigoths, 65; *see* barbarians, Goths, *and* Alaric.

Walpole, Sir Robert, 440 f.
Walsingham, Thomas, 429.
Warton, Thomas, 438.
Webbe, William, 437.
Wellington, Duke of, 449–50.
whale, 299.
William of Malmesbury, 427.
Wireker, Nigel, 427.

Zacharias of Mytilene, 200.
Zeno, Emperor, 5, 12 n. 1, 130 n. 3.
Zephyrus, 294.
Zosimus, 1, 64–5, 75, 80, 130, 147, 159, 161, 164, 166, 169–70, 175, 180, 220, 244, 383–4; and Eunapius, 1 n. 3, 474–7.

ISBN 0–19–	Author	Title
8264011	ALEXANDER Paul J.	The Patriarch Nicephorus of Constantinople
8143567	ALFÖLDI A.	The Conversion of Constantine and Pagan Rome
9241775	ALLEN T.W	Homeri Ilias (3 volumes)
6286409	ANDERSON George K.	The Literature of the Anglo-Saxons
8219601	ARNOLD Benjamin	German Knighthood
8208618	ARNOLD T.W.	The Caliphate
8142579	ASTIN A.E.	Scipio Aemilianus
8144059	BAILEY Cyril	Lucretius: De Rerum Natura (3 volumes)
814167X	BARRETT W.S.	Euripides: Hippolytos
8228813	BARTLETT & MacKAY	Medieval Frontier Societies
8219733	BARTLETT Robert	Trial by Fire and Water
8118856	BENTLEY G.E.	William Blake's Writings (2 volumes)
8111010	BETHURUM Dorothy	Homilies of Wulfstan
8142765	BOLLING G. M.	External Evidence for Interpolation in Homer
814332X	BOLTON J.D.P.	Aristeas of Proconnesus
9240132	BOYLAN Patrick	Thoth, the Hermes of Egypt
8114222	BROOKS Kenneth R.	Andreas and the Fates of the Apostles
8214715	BUCKLER Georgina	Anna Comnena
8203543	BULL Marcus	Knightly Piety & Lay Response to the First Crusade
8216785	BUTLER Alfred J.	Arab Conquest of Egypt
8148046	CAMERON Alan	Circus Factions
8143516	CAMERON Alan	Claudian
8148054	CAMERON Alan	Porphyrius the Charioteer
8148348	CAMPBELL J.B.	The Emperor and the Roman Army 31 BC to 235
826643X	CHADWICK Henry	Priscillian of Avila
826447X	CHADWICK Henry	Boethius
8222025	COLGRAVE B. & MYNORS R.A.B.	Bede's Ecclesiastical History of the English People
8131658	COOK J.M.	The Troad
8219393	COWDREY H.E.J.	The Age of Abbot Desiderius
8241895	CROMBIE A.C.	Robert Grosseteste and the Origins of Experimental Science 1100–1700
8644043	CRUM W.E.	Coptic Dictionary
8148992	DAVIES M.	Sophocles: Trachiniae
814153X	DODDS E.R.	Plato: Gorgias
825301X	DOWNER L.	Leges Henrici Primi
814346X	DRONKE Peter	Medieval Latin and the Rise of European Love-Lyric
8142749	DUNBABIN T.J.	The Western Greeks
8154372	FAULKNER R.O.	The Ancient Egyptian Pyramid Texts
8221541	FLANAGAN Marie Therese	Irish Society, Anglo-Norman Settlers, Angevin Kingship
8143109	FRAENKEL Edward	Horace
8142781	FRASER P.M.	Ptolemaic Alexandria (3 volumes)
8201540	GOLDBERG P.J.P.	Women, Work and Life Cycle in a Medieval Economy
8140215	GOTTSCHALK H.B.	Heraclides of Pontus
8266162	HANSON R.P.C.	Saint Patrick
8581351	HARRIS C.R.S	The Heart and Vascular System in Ancient Greek Medicine
8224354	HARRISS G.L.	King, Parliament and Public Finance in Medieval England to 1369
8581114	HEATH Sir Thomas	Aristarchus of Samos
8140444	HOLLIS A.S.	Callimachus: Hecale
8212968	HOLLISTER C. Warren	Anglo-Saxon Military Institutions
9244944	HOPKIN-JAMES L.J.	The Celtic Gospels
8226470	HOULDING J.A.	Fit for Service
2115480	HENRY Blanche	British Botanical and Horticultural Literature before 1800
8219523	HOUSLEY Norman	The Italian Crusades
8223129	HURNARD Naomi	The King's Pardon for Homicide – before AD 1307
9241783	HURRY Jamieson B.	Imhotep
8140401	HUTCHINSON G.O.	Hellenistic Poetry
9240140	JOACHIM H.H.	Aristotle: On Coming-to-be and Passing-away
9240094	JONES A.H.M.	Cities of the Eastern Roman Provinces
8142560	JONES A.H.M.	The Greek City
8218354	JONES Michael	Ducal Brittany 1364–1399
8271484	KNOX & PELCZYNSKI	Hegel's Political Writings
8212755	LAWRENCE C.H.	St Edmund of Abingdon
8225253	LE PATOUREL John	The Norman Empire
8212720	LENNARD Reginald	Rural England 1086–1135
8212321	LEVISON W.	England and the Continent in the 8th century
8148224	LIEBESCHUETZ J.H.W.G.	Continuity and Change in Roman Religion
8143486	LINDSAY W.M.	Early Latin Verse
8141378	LOBEL Edgar & PAGE Sir Denys	Poetarum Lesbiorum Fragmenta
9240159	LOEW E.A.	The Beneventan Script
8115881	LOOMIS Roger Sherman	Arthurian Literature in the Middle Ages
8241445	LUKASIEWICZ, Jan	Aristotle's Syllogistic
8152442	MAAS P. & TRYPANIS C.A .	Sancti Romani Melodi Cantica

8113692	MANDEVILLE Bernard	The Fable of the Bees (2 volumes)
8142684	MARSDEN E.W.	Greek and Roman Artillery—Historical
8142692	MARSDEN E.W.	Greek and Roman Artillery—Technical
8148178	MATTHEWS John	Western Aristocracies and Imperial Court AD 364–425
9240205	MAVROGORDATO John	Digenes Akrites
8223447	McFARLANE K.B.	Lancastrian Kings and Lollard Knights
8226578	McFARLANE K.B.	The Nobility of Later Medieval England
814296X	MEIGGS Russell	The Athenian Empire
8148100	MEIGGS Russell	Roman Ostia
8148402	MEIGGS Russell	Trees and Timber in the Ancient Mediterranean World
8141781	MERKELBACH R. & WEST M.L.	Fragmenta Hesiodea
8143362	MILLAR F.G.B.	Cassius Dio
8142641	MILLER J. Innes	The Spice Trade of the Roman Empire
8147813	MOORHEAD John	Theoderic in Italy
8264259	MOORMAN John	A History of the Franciscan Order
8181469	MORISON Stanley	Politics and Script
8142218	MORITZ L.A.	Grain-Mills and Flour in Classical Antiquity
8274017	MURRAY H.J.R.	History of Board Games
8274033	MURRAY H.J.R.	History of Chess
9240582	MUSURILLO H.	Acts of the Pagan Martyrs & Christian Martyrs (2 volumes)
9240213	MYRES J.L.	Herodotus The Father of History
9241791	NEWMAN W.L.	The Politics of Aristotle (4 volumes)
8219512	OBOLENSKY Dimitri	Six Byzantine Portraits
8270259	O'DONNELL J.J.	Augustine: Confessions (3 volumes)
8144385	OGILVIE R.M. & RICHMOND I.A.	Tacitus: Agricola
263268X	OSLER Sir William	Bibliotheca Osleriana
8116020	OWEN A.L.	The Famous Druids
8131445	PALMER, L.R.	The Interpretation of Mycenaean Greek Texts
8143427	PFEIFFER R.	History of Classical Scholarship (volume 1)
8143648	PFEIFFER Rudolf	History of Classical Scholarship 1300–1850
8111649	PHEIFER J.D.	Old English Glosses in the Epinal-Erfurt Glossary
8142277	PICKARD–CAMBRIDGE A.W.	Dithyramb Tragedy and Comedy
8269765	PLATER & WHITE	Grammar of the Vulgate
9256497	PLATNER S.B. & ASHBY T.	A Topographical Dictionary of Ancient Rome
8213891	PLUMMER Charles	Lives of Irish Saints (2 volumes)
820695X	POWICKE Michael	Military Obligation in Medieval England
8269684	POWICKE Sir Maurice	Stephen Langton
821460X	POWICKE Sir Maurice	The Christian Life in the Middle Ages
8225369	PRAWER Joshua	Crusader Institutions
8225571	PRAWER Joshua	The History of The Jews in the Latin Kingdom of Jerusalem
8143249	RABY F.J.E.	A History of Christian Latin Poetry
8143257	RABY F.J.E.	A History of Secular Latin Poetry in the Middle Ages (2 volumes)
8214316	RASHDALL & POWICKE	The Universities of Europe in the Middle Ages (3 volumes)
8154488	REYMOND E.A.E & BARNS J.W.B.	Four Martyrdoms from the Pierpont Morgan Coptic Codices
8148380	RICKMAN Geoffrey	The Corn Supply of Ancient Rome
8141556	ROSS Sir David	Aristotle: De Anima
8141076	ROSS Sir David	Aristotle: Metaphysics (2 volumes)
8141084	ROSS Sir David	Aristotle: Parva Naturalia
8141092	ROSS Sir David	Aristotle: Physics
9244952	ROSS Sir David	Aristotle: Prior and Posterior Analytics
8142307	ROSTOVTZEFF M.	Social and Economic History of the Hellenistic World (3 volumes)
8142315	ROSTOVTZEFF M.	Social and Economic History of the Roman Empire (2 volumes)
8264178	RUNCIMAN Sir Steven	The Eastern Schism
814833X	SALMON J.B.	Wealthy Corinth
8171587	SALZMAN L.F.	Building in England Down to 1540
8218362	SAYERS Jane E.	Papal Judges Delegate in the Province of Canterbury 1198–1254
8221657	SCHEIN Sylvia	Fideles Crucis
8148135	SHERWIN WHITE A.N.	The Roman Citizenship
825153X	SHERWIN WHITE A.N.	Roman Society and Roman Law in the New Testament
9240167	SINGER Charles	Galen: On Anatomical Procedures
8113927	SISAM, Kenneth	Studies in the History of Old English Literature
8113668	SKEAT Walter	Langland: The Vision of William Concerning Piers the Plowman (2 volumes)
8642040	SOUTER Alexander	A Glossary of Later Latin to 600 AD
8270011	SOUTER Alexander	Earliest Latin Commentaries on the Epistles of St Paul
8222254	SOUTHERN R.W.	Eadmer: Life of St. Anselm
8251408	SQUIBB G.	The High Court of Chivalry
8212011	STEVENSON & WHITELOCK	Asser's Life of King Alfred
8212011	SWEET Henry	A Second Anglo-Saxon Reader—Archaic and Dialectical
8143443	SYME Sir Ronald	Ammianus and the Historia Augusta
8148259	SYME Sir Ronald	History in Ovid
8143273	SYME Sir Ronald	Tacitus (2 volumes)
8142714	THOMPSON E.A.	The Goths in Spain
9256500	THOMPSON Sir E.Maunde	Introduction to Greek and Latin Palaeography
8200951	THOMPSON Sally	Women Religious
924023X	WALBANK F.W.	Historical Commentary on Polybius (3 volumes)
8201745	WALKER Simon	The Lancastrian Affinity 1361–1399
8161115	WELLESZ Egon	A History of Byzantine Music and Hymnography
8140185	WEST M.L.	Greek Metre

8141696	WEST M.L.	Hesiod: Theogony
8148542	WEST M.L.	The Orphic Poems
8140053	WEST M.L.	Hesiod: Works & Days
8152663	WEST M.L.	Iambi et Elegi Graeci
9240221	WHEELWRIGHT Philip	Heraclitus
822799X	WHITBY M. & M.	The History of Theophylact Simocatta
8206186	WILLIAMSON, E.W.	Letters of Osbert of Clare
8208103	WILSON F.P.	Plague in Shakespeare's London
8247672	WOODHOUSE C.M.	Gemistos Plethon
8114877	WOOLF Rosemary	The English Religious Lyric in the Middle Ages
8119224	WRIGHT Joseph	Grammar of the Gothic Language